OXFORD STUDIES ON THE ROMAN ECONOMY

General Editors

ALAN BOWMAN   ANDREW WILSON

OXFORD STUDIES ON THE ROMAN ECONOMY

This innovative monograph series reflects a vigorous revival of interest in the ancient economy, focusing on the Mediterranean world under Roman rule (*c*.100 BC to AD 350). Carefully quantified archaeological and documentary data is integrated to help ancient historians, economic historians, and archaeologists think about economic behaviour collectively rather than from separate perspectives. The volumes include a substantial comparative element and thus will be of interest to historians of other periods and places.

This volume was edited by **Andrew Wilson**, Professor of the Archaeology of the Roman Empire, University of Oxford, and **Miko Flohr**, Postdoctoral Researcher at the Institute for History, Leiden University.

Contributors

Ilias Arnaoutoglou, Wim Broekaert, Jean-Pierre Brun,
Alessandro Christofori, Kerstin Dross-Krüpe, Miko Flohr,
Christel Freu, Penelope Goodman, Orsolya Láng,
Lena Larsson Lovén, Nicolas Monteix, Jeroen Poblome,
Candace Rice, Kai Ruffing, Carla Salvaterra,
Nicolas Tran, Carol Van Driel-Murray, Andrew Wilson

Urban Craftsmen and Traders in the Roman World

Edited by
ANDREW WILSON
and
MIKO FLOHR

OXFORD
UNIVERSITY PRESS

OXFORD
UNIVERSITY PRESS

Great Clarendon Street, Oxford, OX2 6DP,
United Kingdom

Oxford University Press is a department of the University of Oxford.
It furthers the University's objective of excellence in research, scholarship,
and education by publishing worldwide. Oxford is a registered trade mark of
Oxford University Press in the UK and in certain other countries

© Oxford University Press 2016

The moral rights of the authors have been asserted

First published 2016
First published in paperback 2020

Impression: 4

Published in the United States of America by Oxford University Press
198 Madison Avenue, New York, NY 10016, United States of America

British Library Cataloguing in Publication Data
Data available

Library of Congress Cataloging in Publication Data
Data available

ISBN 978–0–19–874848–9 (Hbk.)
ISBN 978–0–19–885290–2 (Pbk.)

Printed and bound by
CPI Group (UK) Ltd, Croydon, CR0 4YY

Preface

The chapters in this volume have their origin in a workshop organized by the Oxford Roman Economy Project and held at Wolfson College, Oxford, United Kingdom, 21–23 July 2011. The workshop, entitled *Beyond Marginality: Craftsmen, Traders and the Socio-Economic History of Roman Urban Communities*, was funded by the European Science Foundation as an ESF exploratory workshop, and brought together researchers from nine different countries with the aim of exploring the topic of Roman urban crafts and trades and to build bridges between different national scholarly traditions and disciplines (ancient history, archaeology, epigraphy, papyrology). Like the workshop from which it originates, this volume focuses on four key themes: the history of research, economic strategies of craftsmen and traders, the position of crafts and trade in urban space, and craftsmen and traders in their social environment.

We thank the ESF for the exploratory workshop grant that made the workshop possible, all the speakers who took part and subsequently contributed papers, and also Prof. Kristin Kuutma (Helsinki), who acted as the ESF observer and rapporteur. We are grateful to the staff of Wolfson College for their practical assistance during the workshop, and also to All Souls College for the provision of accommodation for some speakers. As ever, we are extremely grateful to Baron Lorne Thyssen for his continued support of the Oxford Roman Economy Project.

Andrew Wilson
Miko Flohr

August 2015

Contents

List of Contributors

Ilias N. Arnaoutoglou graduated at the Faculty of Law, Aristotelian University of Thessaloniki. He holds a Ph.D. in ancient Greek history from the University of Glasgow (1993). He was assistant editor for the *Lexicon of Greek Personal Names*, Oxford, from 1994 to 1999. Currently, he is senior researcher in the Research Centre for the History of Greek Law, Academy of Athens. He has written extensively on Hellenistic and Greco-Roman associations, ancient Greek legal history and institutions, and institutions in pre-nineteenth-century Turkish-occupied Greece.

Wim Broekaert is a postdoctoral researcher in Ancient History at Ghent University. He has published widely on many aspects of Roman trade. His first monograph, *Navicularii et negotiantes: A Prosopographical Study of Roman Merchants and Shippers*, was published in 2013.

Jean-Pierre Brun is a professor at the Collège de France in Paris, and, until 2012, director of the Centre Jean Bérard at Naples. He is a renowned specialist in the archaeology of Roman agriculture and crafts, and has published widely on olive-oil and wine production in the Greco-Roman world, and on urban crafts in Roman Italy.

Alessandro Cristofori is Professor of Ancient History at the University of Bologna, formerly Professor of Roman History at the University of Calabria. His research has focused both on the epigraphy of crafts in Roman Italy and on the historiography of craftsmen and traders in twentieth-century Italy. In 2004, he published a monograph on the epigraphy of crafts in Picenum (*Non Arma Virumque: le occupazioni nell'epigrafia del Piceno*).

Carol van Driel-Murray (Leiden University) is Assistant Professor of Provincial Roman Archaeology at the University of Leiden. Her research focuses on Roman and medieval leathercraft, Roman military equipment, and gender issues in relation to the Roman army. She has published extensively on Roman leatherwork and footwear from archaeological excavations, skin-processing technologies, and the role of footwear in ritual complexes. Reconstruction and experiment figure prominently in her research into the structure and use of military equipment such as tents and saddles.

Kerstin Droß-Krüpe studied classical archaeology, ancient history, and business administration at Philipps-University of Marburg, Germany. Her thesis, supervised by Kai Ruffing and Hans-Joachim Drexhage at Marburg, focused on textile production in Roman Egypt. It was published as *Wolle–Weber–Wirtschaft* (2011). During her research she participated actively in the EU research project 'DressID', where she presented several invited papers. During recent years she has published several essays about the use of Geographic Information Systems (GIS) in historical context. Currently, she is working as scientific assistant at Kassel University.

Miko Flohr is lecturer in Ancient History at the Institute for History of Leiden University, formerly assistant director of the Oxford Roman Economy Project. His main research focus lies with urban history in the Roman world, with a particular emphasis on economic life in Roman Italy, and on textile economies. His first monograph, *The World of the Fullo*, was published in 2013; he has since published on the textile economy of Pompeii, and on public investment in commercial space.

Christel Freu is Professor of Roman History in the University Laval in Quebec and member of *Année épigraphique*. After publishing a monograph on representations of the poor in late antique texts (*Les Figures du pauvre chez les auteurs italiens de l'antiquité tardive* (2007)), she is currently studying labour relationships in the Roman Empire on the basis of papyri, and literary and epigraphic texts.

Penelope Goodman is a lecturer in Roman history at the University of Leeds with a particular interest in the spatial characteristics of Roman urbanism. Her first monograph, *The Roman City and its Periphery: From Rome to Gaul* (2007), explored the demarcation of Roman urban centres and the uses of space just beyond their boundaries. She has also published articles on the locations of temples in Roman Gaul and Britain, the peripheries of Italian cities, the boundaries of Rome, and the spatial distribution of *terra sigillata* workshops. Her current research is concerned with receptions of the emperor Augustus.

Orsolya Láng is deputy head of the department of Roman Archaeology at the Aquincum Museum in Budapest, Hungary. She has worked extensively on the civilian settlement of Aquincum, both in the field, and in the archives. Her thesis and her published work focus on the history and use of urban space in Aquincum, particularly in the north-eastern quarter of the town.

Lena Larsson Lovén is lecturer in Classical Archaeology and Ancient History at the Department of Historical Studies, University of Gothenburg. Her main research focus lies with gender studies, iconography, and socio-economic history in the Roman world, with a particular emphasis on the Roman west. She has edited several volumes and has published on aspects of Roman textile production, dress studies, family iconography and economy, and women's work identities.

Nicolas Monteix holds a position as associate professor in Roman history and archeology at the University of Rouen. He wrote a dissertation on shops and workshops in Herculaneum (published in 2010) and was then awarded a postdoctoral fellowship at the *École française de Rome* (2007–10). He led the *Pistrina* project that studied of thirty-nine bakeries in Pompeii (2008–14); his current interest lies with the archaeology of technology in the long term.

Jeroen Poblome holds a chair in Archaeology at the University of Leuven, Belgium. As Francqui Research Professor he coordinates research projects on aspects of the ancient economy related to the production, distribution, and consumption of artisanal goods, the associated study of ancient society, focusing on the development, sustainability, and resilience of communities and regions, in the period between 1,000 BC and AD 1,000, as well as innovative research on digital archaeological information systems. He is involved in fieldwork in Boeotia, Kinet Höyük, and at ancient Sagalassos. He co-founded and co-edits *HEROM: Journal on Hellenistic and Roman Material Culture.*

Candace Rice is Lecturer in Classical Archaeology at the University of Edinburgh. She completed a D.Phil. at the University of Oxford (2013) and was a Senior Fellow at the Research Center for Anatolian Civilizations in Istanbul. Her research focuses on regional economic development in the Roman world and the impact of maritime connectivity as evidenced by the archaeological record. She is currently preparing a monograph on the economic landscape of the southern coast of Turkey in the Roman period; additional forthcoming and published work includes articles on Roman trade, connectivity, and maritime infrastructure.

Kai Ruffing holds the chair of Ancient History at Kassel University. He has published extensively on many aspects of Roman economic history, particularly crafts and trade. His first monograph (1999) focused on viticulture in Roman Egypt. His second monograph (2008) analysed specialization in crafts and trade in the Roman east, mainly based on epigraphic and papyrological evidence.

Carla Salvaterra is senior researcher and Vice-Rector at the University of Bologna. She initially specialized in Egypt, and wrote a dissertation on the city of Alexandria in the Flavian Period, but has also published on the history of the study of labour in the Roman world.

Nicolas Tran is Professor of Roman History at the University of Poitiers and at the Institut Universitaire de France. His research focuses on craftsmen and traders in the western part of the Roman empire. He has published monographs on Roman professional associations (2006) and on the professional lives of craftsmen and traders in the Roman west (2013), besides co-editing a volume on Roman *collegia* (with Monique Dondin-Payre, 2012) and on the professional knowledge of Roman artisans (with Nicolas Monteix, 2011).

Andrew Wilson is Professor of the Archaeology of the Roman Empire, at the University of Oxford. His research interests include the economy of the Roman Empire, ancient technology, ancient water supply and usage, Roman North Africa, and archaeological field survey. Recent publications include: *Settlement, Urbanization and Population* (ed. with Alan Bowman, 2011); *Alexandria and the North-Western Delta* (ed. with Damian Robinson, 2010), *Maritime Archaeology and Ancient Trade in the Mediterranean* (ed. with Damian Robinson, 2011), *The Roman Agricultural Economy* (ed. with Alan Bowman), and articles on Saharan trade (*Azania*, 2012) and Capitolia (*JRS*, 2013, with Jo Quinn).

List of Figures

List of Tables

List of Abbreviations

Journal abbreviations follow the style of *L'Année philologique*. Other abbreviations used in this volume are:

AAST   *Atti della Reale Accademia delle Scienze di Torino* (Turin, 1865-)

AE   *L'Année épigraphique* (Paris, 1888–)

ANRW   H. Temporini and W. Haase (eds), *Aufstieg und Niedergang der römischen Welt* (Berlin and New York, 1972–)

BE   J. and L. Robert et al., *Bulletin Épigraphique* (in *REG* 1938–)

CIL   *Corpus Inscriptionum Latinarum, consilio et auctoritate Academiae litterarumregiae Borussicae editum* (1863–)

FXanthos *Fouilles de Xanthos* (Paris, 1968–)

IG   *Inscriptiones Graecae* (Berlin, 1902–)

IG²   *Inscriptiones Graecae: Editio Minor* (Berlin, 1913–)

IGR   R. Cagnat et al., *Inscriptiones Graecae ad res Romanas pertinentes* (Paris, 1906–27)

IJO II   W. Ameling, *Inscriptiones Judaicae Orientis*, ii. *Kleinasien* (Tübingen, 2004)

IK   *Inschriften griechischer Städte aus Kleinasien* (Bonn, 1972–)

ILAfr   R. Cagnat and A. Merlin, *Inscriptions latines d'Afrique (Tripolitaine, Tunisie, Maroc)* (Paris, 1923)

ILGN   É. Espérandieu, *Inscriptions latines de Gaule (Narbonnaise)* (Paris, 1929)

ILLRP   A. Degrassi, *Inscriptiones Latinae liberae rei publicae* (Florence, 1957–63)

ILS   H. Dessau, *Inscriptiones latinae selectee* (1892–1916)

ILTG   P. Wuilleumier, *Inscriptions latines des Trois Gaules* (Paris, 1963)

IMilet   P. Herrmann, *Inschriften von Milet*, ii. *Inschriften n. 407–1019* (Vienna, 1998)

IMM   O. Kern, *Die Inschriften von Magnesia am Maeander* (Berlin, 1990)

IPerinthos M. H. Sayar, *Perinthos-Herakleia (Marmara Ereglisi) und Umgebung: Geschichte, Testimonien, griechische und lateinische Inschriften* (Vienna, 1998)

IPriene   I. Hiller von Gaertringen, *Inschriften von Priene* (Berlin, 1906)

LGPN   P. M. Fraser and E. Matthews (eds), *Lexicon of Greek Personal Names* (Oxford, 1987–)

LTUR   E. M. Steinby (ed.), *Lexicon topographicum Urbis Romae* (Rome, 1993–2000)

MAMA   *Monumenta Asiae Minoris Antiqua* (London, 1928–)

SEG   *Supplementum epigraphicum graecum* (Amsterdam, 1923–71, 1979–)

TAM   *Tituli Asiae Minoris* (Vienna, 1901–)

Introduction

Miko Flohr and Andrew Wilson

Roman cities bustled with commercial activity. Streets were lined with long rows of *tabernae*, and people involved in manufacturing, retail, and trade occupied a defining and prominent place in urban space and urban society. Craftsmen, shopkeepers, and traders made up a significant proportion (if not the majority) of the population in many urban communities. In most cities, manufacturing and retail were never far away—neither physically, nor socially: even for elite families that based their wealth primarily on their property on the countryside, there were often craftsmen and retailers operating the *tabernae* in the street frontage of their town house.[1] Indeed, in many ways, it was the people who spent their days in shops and workshops who made up the social core of Roman urban neighbourhoods, while elites played out their role rather more in the background—in the peristyles and courtyards, away from the street. In everyday life in urban space, it was much easier to avoid the elite than it was to avoid urban commerce.

If the Roman world was characterized by unusual or even unprecedented degrees of urbanization, as seems to have been the case, and if cities were to such a large extent defined by commerce and manufacturing, then it is hard fully to understand Roman history without having a clear idea of the social, economic, and cultural history of urban trade, manufacturing, and retail.[2] Fortunately, since the early 1990s, the fundamental centrality of economic life to our understanding of the Roman world has become widely acknowledged, with a corresponding upsurge in scholarly interest in the subject. The study of crafts and trade has been moving steadily towards the centre of the scholarly field, as is reflected by the space devoted to it in key journals, in monographs

---

[1] Wallace-Hadrill (1991).
[2] On urbanization in the Roman World, see Bowman and Wilson (2011). For Italy, see also De Ligt (2012: 193–246).

written by generalists, and, recently, in handbooks and companions.[3] Crucially, evidence for urban manufacturing and commerce is no longer the exclusive domain of specialists working in relative isolation: an increasingly interdisciplinary and international scholarly field is emerging, and it is a field that is quickly moving away from the models that characterized the study of everyday work in the ancient world for most of the twentieth century.

Things were, of course, different in the past. For quite some time, the shadow of elite disgust loomed over the study of Roman crafts and trade. In particular, the famous passage in the first book of Cicero's *De officiis* has been quoted time and again to illustrate the disdain of the Roman elite for crafts and trade, and to illustrate the marginal or even controversial position of these activities in Roman society: the workshop was no place for a free-born person, working for wages was little better than slavery, and trade was problematic as well.[4] Forty years ago, Moses Finley argued at length that Cicero's statement represented 'not a bad guide to prevailing values', explicitly refuting those who dismissed it as 'elite snobbery'.[5] Finley was not alone. Many twentieth-century scholars made similar comments based on Cicero and other authors. Craftsmen and traders were not generally or automatically seen as 'normal' Romans, and there has been a strong emphasis on the servile or freed status of many craftsmen and traders, which not only meant that they suffered from the stigma of slavery, but also quietly implied that they did not have true 'Roman' roots.[6] Essentially, mainstream scholarly thinking on crafts and trade long adopted, implicitly or explicitly, the perspective of the Roman elite, and marginalized both the activities and the people involved in them—either by simply neglecting them as irrelevant, or by emphasizing how they differed from 'normal' Romans, and how controversial their status was. Since the mid-1990s, this way of thinking has lost ground, and scholars have more and more abandoned the perspective of elite authors.

The present volume reflects this development towards the 'normalization' of crafts and trade, and aims to add to it. The sixteen chapters that follow this introduction discuss a wide variety of data sets—both textual and archaeological—and focus on a wide variety of research questions, but they share some common features. In the first place, the emphasis lies, throughout the book, on analysing processes and decisions rather than on measuring performance. The macroeconomic issues that were prominent in past decades, such as the economic impact of certain crafts and trades for the income portfolio of specific cities, or the nature of urban economies in general, play only a marginal role here.[7] This is emphatically

---

[3] Journal articles: Bradley (2002); Wilson (2002b); Ellis (2004); Tran (2007); Flohr (2013b). Monograph chapters: e.g. Clarke (2003: 95–129); Petersen (2006); Cuomo (2007: 77–102). Handbooks: Kehoe (2007); Morley (2007); Hawkins (2012); Broekaert and Zuiderhoek (2013); Liu (2013).

[4] Cic. *De off.* 1.150–1.   [5] Finley (1973: 57).

[6] On the role of slaves and freedmen in the Roman economy, see, e.g. Joshel (1992) and Mouritsen (2011: 206–47).

[7] On this issue, see also Flohr and Wilson, Chapter 1, this volume.

not because we think that these are unimportant questions, but because we feel that, before we can properly address them in the light of the evidence now available, there needs to be a prior stage of research in building up a new picture from the ground up. Hence, the emphasis here is on the micro-scale: the direct social and physical environment in which people lived and worked, and the smaller and larger decisions that these people made to realize their social and economic ambitions. Indeed, a second feature that connects most of the chapters in this volume is that the focus is not only on crafts and trade, but also, and perhaps more, on craftsmen and traders, and the economic strategies these people embraced in their everyday working lives.

There are several developments in the wider field of Roman social and economic history that have informed the approaches in this volume. It seems relevant briefly to highlight three of these at this point. In the first place, recent years have seen the emerging use of social network perspectives to look at aspects of Roman social history. Groundbreaking in this respect was the 2008 monograph by Giovanni Ruffini on *Social Networks in Byzantine Egypt*, but scholars working on issues more closely related to this volume have also embraced social network theory, including, prominently, Shawn Graham in his work on the brick industry in the Tiber Valley.[8] One of the present authors has applied a social-networks approach to the material remains of fulling workshops to understand the social dynamics of the world in which fullers spent their days.[9] In a 2011 article on Roman merchants, Wim Broekaert emphasized the role of social networks in trading processes.[10] A social-network perspective is essential to the study of crafts and trade, both for understanding the dynamics of everyday economic processes and for making sense of the social position of craftsmen and traders. In particular, it forces us to think harder about the economic impact of the nature and strength of the social ties between economic actors, and about the communicative contexts in which work-related statuses were negotiated and maintained. A social network approach also makes the traditional discourse about the 'low' and 'dependent' statuses of craftsmen and traders increasingly hard to defend: if the social statuses of these people were for a large part constructed within networks in which many agents had comparable backgrounds, as seems to have been the case, they can scarcely be characterized as 'low' or 'dependent'—even if many craftsmen and traders had social superiors to deal with.

A second point that is less often explicitly stated but seems to have become widely accepted in recent years concerns the nature of the relation between society and economy. In the second half of the twentieth century, several classical scholars, most prominently Finley, championed Karl Polanyi's idea that pre-modern economies were 'embedded' in society—meaning, essentially, that societal and cultural norms dictated the terms of everyday economic life.[11]

---

[8] Ruffini (2008); Graham (2006). [9] Flohr (2009; 2013a: esp. 242–87).
[10] Broekaert (2011). [11] Polanyi (1944: 45–58); Block (2001: pp. xxiii–xxv).

While few scholars have rejected the idea that social patterns and cultural preferences could have significant impact on economic processes, many scholars now seem to think of the relation between society and economy in a more reciprocal way: economic processes could also have an impact on social and cultural patterns. This, of course, comes naturally if one approaches urban economies from a spatial perspective: the almost total dominance of commercial space in Roman streetscapes makes it hard to maintain that urban social and cultural processes were *not* somehow affected by economic life. Yet it also follows from the proliferation of evidence for social networks that were primarily economically defined—such as the many professional associations (*collegia*) that bought burial grounds for their members, or the many trading diasporas that can be found throughout the Roman world.[12] Religious feasts, such as the *Quinquatrus*, could also to a large extent be organized along divisions that were based on urban economic life.[13] This prominent role of (everyday) economic life in shaping social and cultural practice obviously further enhances the need to understand the historical dynamics of urban crafts and trade in the Roman world.

A final issue to be highlighted here concerns the impact on recent approaches to urban crafts and trade of a loosely defined set of ideas commonly known as the 'New Institutional Economics'. This analytical perspective was catapulted into the centre of debate on the Roman economy in 2007 by the editors of the *Cambridge Economic History of the Greco-Roman World*.[14] Approaches inspired by New Institutional Economics focus heavily on understanding the relation between cultural, societal, and legal institutions, and economic processes, and, particularly, on the role played by such institutions in overcoming information deficits and lowering transaction costs.[15] This focus has had a mixed effect on the study of urban crafts and trade. On the one hand, scholars are encouraged to invest heavily in understanding the everyday processes of trade and manufacturing, and the social environment in which these took place, and this has clearly enriched our understanding of trade and manufacturing. On the other hand, however, the common emphasis on the meaning of individual institutions has sometimes tempted scholars towards a level of abstraction that lacks historical specificity—essentially leading to theoretical modelling rather than historical analysis.[16] Moreover, approaches based on New Institutional Economics have sometimes put a lot of emphasis on the dominant role of institutions in guiding economic behaviour, and in doing so they have tended to privilege structure and underplay the role

---

[12] On professional associations, see Van Nijf (1997); on trading communities, see Verboven (2011); Terpstra (2013).

[13] See, e.g. Ovid, *Fasti* 809–48.

[14] Morris, Saller, and Scheidel (2007). See also Frier and Kehoe (2007).

[15] See, e.g. Frier and Kehoe (2007); Verboven (2012).

[16] Cf. Verboven (2012: 913). For a spirited (and sometimes overstated) critique of New Institutional Economics as applied to ancient history, see Boldizzoni (2011).

of agency in economic processes.[17] In writing the history of urban crafts and trade, it is not only the institutions that matter, but also their specific role in particular places and moments in the Roman world, and the way they were acted upon by specific economic agents: in everyday discourse, institutions must be seen as starting points for economic strategies rather than end points—they may be embraced in some situations, but might be circumvented or neglected in others, and they may be long-lasting or short-lived. Nevertheless, the emerging trend among classical scholars to study urban crafts and trade on the level of the everyday social and economic processes may, in some way, be related to the emergence of New Institutional Economics as an analytical perspective, and this broader trend is clearly reflected in the contributions to this volume, even if the way in which authors in this volume relate to the New Institutional Economics varies considerably.

The present volume is divided into four parts. It starts with three chapters focusing on the intellectual history of the study of Roman crafts and trade—an aspect of the field that does not often receive the attention it deserves. After this exercise in scholarly history, the history of craftsmen and traders in the Roman world is approached from three different angles. The second part of the book consists of four chapters all focusing on the economic aspects of crafts and trade, and on the core economic strategies embraced by craftsmen and traders to secure their position in the market. Subsequently, there are five chapters concentrating on the social contexts and social networks surrounding the daily work of craftsmen and traders, and the degree to which these shaped everyday economic life. The final four chapters discuss the position of crafts in their spatial environment, addressing questions related to the genesis of urban commercial landscapes. Obviously, the separation between the three parts is not rigid: if social, economic, and spatial issues sometimes overlap in everyday practice, the same is true in this volume. Moreover, an effort has been made to provide a mix of archaeological and textual approaches for each of the three themes discussed, and to maintain a reasonable geographical balance between the eastern and western part of the empire, and Mediterranean and non-Mediterranean regions.

HISTORY OF RESEARCH

While scholarly priorities, for understandable reasons, often lie more with discussing past realities than with discussing modern discourse about them, it is arguably essential also to understand the factors and actors that have shaped

---

[17] See, e.g. Scheidel (2012: 9–10): 'overriding significance of historically specific "rules of the game", the incentives and constraints that were instrumental in determining Roman economic development.'

our ideas about Roman craftsmen and traders over the last few centuries. The three chapters that follow this Introduction serve to sketch the development of this discourse. The first chapter, by the present authors, discusses the development of the debate in general terms, focusing specifically on the German and Anglo-Saxon scholarly traditions. It assesses the relative impact of new evidence and new ideas on discourse about Roman urban craftsmen and traders in the nineteenth and twentieth centuries, but it also highlights the key role played by certain individual scholars and their networks. Subsequently, Carla Salvaterra and Alessandro Cristofori sketch the development of Italian scholarship on the theme in, specifically, the twentieth century. This chapter emphasizes how political developments on a national level, both in the fascist era and in the post-war decades, had a decisive influence on the way in which Italian scholars discussed Roman crafts and trade. At the same time, Salvaterra and Cristofori argue that Italian scholarship has, since the mid-1990s, increasingly integrated itself into international debates. The chapter by Jean-Pierre Brun focuses on French scholarship, and shows how recent approaches to the archaeology of urban workshops in Roman Italy have been shaped by a long French tradition of scholarship on urban crafts that goes back to the early twentieth century. Brun puts particular emphasis on the gradual integration of the material remains into the debate, arguing that the major breakthrough in this respect came only in the late 1980s.

Together, these three chapters, though different in their approach and scope, give a good impression of the dynamics of the debate, and of the impact of ideological and political developments in the outside world on discourse within classical studies: one may think of the devastating impact of the First World War on German *Altertumswissenschaft*, and of the corporatism promoted by the Fascist regime on Italian approaches to craftsmen and traders. At the same time, all three highlight the crucial role of scholarly networks and institutions in fostering debate—the networks around Mommsen and Meyer in that respect do not differ fundamentally from the classical seminar of the *Istituto Gramsci*, or, indeed, of the French collaborative effort to the archaeology of urban workshops in southern Italy.

While it may at first sight seem strange to treat the three traditions separately—after all, should not any scholar working on the Roman economy be expected to cope with the relevant scholarship in all the major western European languages?—it is in fact clear from these chapters that the different traditions have had rather different concerns and focuses, and that the effect of language barriers has been significant—the impact of many works has been limited outside the scholarly tradition in the same language. On a general level, the three chapters suggest that the combined German/Anglo-Saxon discourse acted as the dominant tradition from the nineteenth century right up to the present day. Debates in the English and German languages always interacted closely, and there is a more-or-less direct sequence of debate from Rodbertus through Meyer and Rostovtzeff to Finley and beyond, especially in the so-called consumer city debate. Because of linguistic and logistical barriers, francophone and italophone discourses for a long time developed more independently, and, more often than not, they were on the receiving end of influence—not only from Rostovtzeff or Finley, but also, as Salvaterra and Cristofori suggest, from scholars like Joshel.[18] In contrast to anglophone scholarship, French and Italian scholarship has been less fixated on the 'consumer city debate', and Finley's views gained less traction in France and Italy. French research has focused instead to a considerable extent on advancing our knowledge of the detail and infrastructure of workshops, to enhance the evidence base for interpretation.[19] Italian scholarship has paid much attention to the role and concept of the workshop. Nevertheless, there is, of course, a close parallel between the emergence of social history in the Anglo-Saxon world in the late 1960s and the appearance of a generation of Marxist scholars in Italy (and France) around the same period. Here, it is zeitgeist rather than anything else that is at stake. Similarly, the emergence of provincial archaeology after the Second World War was a European development that, especially in Germany and France, as Brun suggests, may have its roots in the post-war (re)construction boom. The same is true, obviously, for the emergence of rescue archaeology, which Brun correctly sees as a watershed in the archaeology of urban crafts. Scholarly traditions thus in many ways developed parallel to each other throughout the twentieth century. Arguably, however, future scholars might mark the digital revolution of the late 1990s and onwards as another watershed, as it has fostered a sharp increase in interaction across national and linguistic boundaries. The time is now ripe to integrate these various traditions and, with a new understanding of the archaeology of urban manufacturing processes, to reassess what the mass of evidence we now have means in terms of the wider urban economy.

ECONOMIC STRATEGIES

The second set of chapters looks at the core issue of professional crafts and trade: the strategies embraced by craftsmen and traders to make sure that their everyday work actually resulted in profit. While it may be true that economic agents in the Roman world were not seeking to 'maximize profit' in the modern sense of the word, they had a clear interest in running their businesses efficiently, in order to minimize risks, or reduce costs, especially if it is true

[18] Rostovtzeff (1926); Finley (1973); Joshel (1992).
[19] e.g. Borgard (2002); Borgard et al. (2002, 2003); Borgard and Puybaret (2004); Leguilloux (2002, 2004); Monteix (2010); Brun, Chapter 3, this volume; Monteix, Chapter 7, this volume.

that those who earned their living in urban economies had to deal with substantial economic insecurity on an everyday basis, as Cameron Hawkins has recently argued.[20] Moreover, those craftsmen and traders who were not struggling at subsistence level but were slightly better off may have had socio-economic ambitions that were best furthered with a well-functioning business. In other words, there were reasons for all to think hard about how to approach their everyday work.

For craftsmen and traders alike, the two key strategic decisions to be made were, first, what to do, and, second, how to do this? Such decisions were profoundly influenced by an array of factors, including the specific (local) economic circumstances in which people operated. The chapter by Candace Rice discusses the economic strategies of maritime traders. It starts from the observation that the epigraphic evidence for *negotiatores* suggests that specialization among traders was widespread, and that, by focusing on a particular niche, traders could become successful entrepreneurs. Rice sketches an array of strategies for maritime trade and transport, and shows how each of these strategies can also be traced back in our evidence, which suggests that trade practice in the Roman Mediterranean was flexible and adapted to specific economic circumstances. To enhance their chances for economic success, some traders also formed permanent trading communities in key port cities. The subsequent chapter by Kai Ruffing also emphasizes the issue of specialization, but on a more local level. Focusing particularly on epigraphic and documentary evidence from Egypt and Asia Minor, Ruffing investigates three incentives for specialization: first, the intense competition on the market, which drove craftsmen to explore economic niches that would give them a decent customer base; second, the possibility to increase the quality and quantity of their output by focusing on a smaller subset of services or products, and, third, location factors—the specific local circumstances, such as the availability of certain resources, that caused certain places to have a high concentration of particular crafts. Ruffing argues that the market—and particularly consumer demand—was the main driving force for specialization, and that the evidence illustrates Adam Smith's observation that the extent to which specialization took place depended on the size of the market.

While the chapters by Rice and Ruffing focus on strategies at a general level, the other two chapters offer case studies each looking at strategies in the manufacturing of a specific product category. One discusses the manufacturing of footwear, the other the production of bread. In her chapter on the footwear economy, Carol van Driel-Murray uses consumer theory to sketch the economic landscape in which manufacturers operated in, particularly, Roman Europe. Starting from the observation that there were empire-wide

---

[20] Hawkins (2012, 2013).

trends in footwear design, van Driel-Murray argues that shop-bought shoes were widely accessible for men, women, and children alike, and that the footwear economy of Roman Europe should be seen as a consumer economy, with craftsmen adapting their strategies to diversified and changing consumer demand, sometimes customizing their designs to specific needs of individual consumers, but more often following standardized decorative patterns that allowed for a reasonably high productivity. Interestingly, however, the leather economy seems to have remained an economy of outsiders: after the collapse of Roman rule, leatherworking technology seems to have disappeared. The bread economy worked rather differently from the footwear economy: demand was much more predictable, and much less diversified—bread is, basically, bread. The commercialization of bread production that is well attested for Roman Italy led to the emergence of combined mills–bakeries that produced standardized bread loaves on a large scale.[21] The bakeries of Pompeii are the focus of the chapter by Nicolas Monteix, who discusses the ways in which the technology used for milling, kneading, and baking, and the spatial organization of the operational sequence could improve the functionality of the workshop. Emphasizing that all workshops, essentially, were a compromise between available space and economic ambition—all the bakeries in Pompeii had to be integrated into pre-existing buildings—Monteix argues that the rationalization of workshop designs increased with their size, and shows how the analysis of the design of these workshops can help to understand the economic history of Roman urban crafts. One might remark that the correlation between workshop size and rational design that Monteix observes at Pompeii is also found elsewhere: at Ostia, a bigger town with a larger market, and one that unlike Pompeii, continued in existence beyond the late first century AD, even larger, highly rationalized mill-bakeries are found, some of which are purpose-built as new constructions.[22] This chapter complements, from an archaeological point of view, Ruffing's text-based discussion of specialization: Monteix shows how entrepreneurs who had found a niche could use technology and the organization of the production process to enhance efficiency and increase profit.

Taken together, these four chapters place a lot of emphasis on limiting the range of products produced or offered, and on reducing the costs involved in producing or offering them. As might be expected, all stress the central role of the market in strategic decision-making: economic actors—whether or not one prefers to call them 'rational'—responded to market circumstances in very strategic ways and adapted their business strategies according to the challenges and opportunities they encountered. What these chapters also quietly suggest is

---

[21] For Ostia, see, e.g. Bakker (1999); for Rome, and the use of water power for milling grain, cf. Wilson (2000; 2002a: 12–15).

[22] Wilson (2008).

that, with the increased complexity and urbanization of the Roman world, and with the increased integration of economic networks, the array of economic strategies embraced became considerably wider than it had been before, even if traditional ways of working did not start to disappear (or even lose prominence). The point of Roman economic history is *not* that traditional, small-scale, low-investment models of manufacturing and distribution were widespread. The point is that, alongside these, new models developed that owed their appearance to the unique economic circumstances in the Roman world.

SOCIAL ENVIRONMENT

Roman craftsmen and traders were, of course, not living and working in isolation from the outside world. As households were the basis of the large majority of urban workshops in the Roman world, economic life and family life overlapped to a considerable degree, and took place in the same physical environment—as is well exemplified in almost all urban excavations where workshops have been found.[23] As many urban craftsmen were also involved in retail, they enjoyed interaction with customers, and, as they often spent their days in shops visible to all passers-by, they were publicly known for their professional skills, which enabled them to develop a public occupational identity. This, in turn, fostered the emergence of informal and formal group-ings of people working in the same (or similar) craft, which eventually would lead to the system of professional associations that is so well attested in the epigraphic record. At the same time, many people involved in crafts and trade had long-lasting ties with social superiors who had legal or practical authority over parts of their social or economic lives. Craftsmen and traders were thus part of several, sometimes overlapping, social networks, and understanding these networks is essential for understanding both the social and the economic history of Roman urban crafts and trade.

The chapter on apprenticeship by Christel Freu highlights the role of formal (and informal) education in the construction of such networks. Her chapter shows how apprenticeship provided pupils with much more than just the skills needed to perform a certain craft in a decent manner: it also gave them the possibility to profit from the good name of their master, and it introduced them to relevant social and professional networks. Freu argues that formal apprenticeship was common practice, which suggests that it played a central role in the reproduction of the professional networks, albeit alongside the more informal system in which knowledge and networks were transferred

---

[23] For Pompeii, see Flohr (2007, 2012).

within households from father to son. The subsequent chapter by Lena Larsson Lovén discusses the position of women in urban professional networks. While female work tends often to remain much less visible in our textual and iconographic sources, there is sufficient evidence to make it clear that women played a crucial role in many sectors of urban economies. Often, however, they did so within a family business that, publicly, was mostly associated with their husbands. Thus, while men were often commemorated with reference to their occupational identity, their wives were not. Indeed, Larsson Lovén suggests that many epigraphically attested working women were actually working in rather exceptional contexts, which means that occupations with which these women were commonly associated give a false impression of what women's work was like. Wim Broekaert analyses the role of freedmen in the economic network of their former owner. The specific social and legal position of freedmen brought both the freedman and his patron certain economic opportunities. Using the freedman as an agent reduced risk for the patron, and provided the freedman with ready access to capital and to the business network of his patron. There were various models along which freedman agency could take shape, with varying degrees of independence, but the bottom line is that working in close collaboration with the former owner provided more chances of success, resulting in 'dependent' freedmen being more visible in our sources than 'independent' freedmen, who worked without their patrons. Arguably, the close ties between patrons and social dependants were fundamental to many networks of crafts and trade throughout the Roman world.

Whereas the first three chapters of this section stayed close to the household and the networks of friends and dependants surrounding it, the last two chapters present two case studies on professional associations—one in the Latin-speaking West, the other in the graecophone East. Nicolas Tran discusses the professional associations in the harbour economy of Arles, showing that there was a clear hierarchy of professional associations, with the *navicularii* at the top, but with key occupations, particularly *negotiatores* and *mercatores*, almost completely lacking from the record. Tran argues that the specific context of Arles meant that these people played a central role in the local community as, for example, *seviri augustales*, and preferred to refer to their political, rather than to their occupational, identity. At Arles, these people constituted a 'plebeian' elite, whose existence emphasizes the integration of crafts and trade into the urban community. This connects well with the argument of Ilias Arnaoutoglou, who discusses the evidence of professional associations from Hierapolis, arguing that they were particularly involved in 'memory management': epigraphic evidence reveals how individuals, not necessarily themselves members of professional associations, endowed associations with sums of money to maintain their tomb, or perform certain rituals related to their post-mortem well-being—to the social benefit of both the commemorated individual and the professional association. Craftsmen and traders thus were not at all marginal people—neither in Arles, nor in Hierapolis: they were well integrated into the urban community and, through their associations, maintained close ties with the urban elite.

What unites these five chapters, besides their focus on social networks, is the emphasis on the role of agency—by individuals or by groups: craftsmen and traders were no passive victims of a subordinate social position, but contributed, actively, to building up and maintaining their social and economic status—men and women alike. This is not to say, of course, that craftsmen and traders were completely autonomous. More often than not, there were social superiors in the background who could have considerable influence, and there were always the social and cultural expectations that limited people's radii of action and coloured the way in which their decisions were perceived: any autonomy was always bounded.[24] Yet, however low the socio-economic status of some of these people may have been in the eyes of the literary elite, almost all were, for most of the time, primarily surrounded by others who were in similar positions, and with whom relational ties could be established on a more-or-less equal basis. It is those everyday social ties that coloured the world of craftsmen and traders—to a much larger extent than any judgement by outsiders.

ECONOMIC LIFE AND THE URBAN LANDSCAPE

The position of crafts, trade, and retail in urban space is an issue that has enjoyed some popularity in recent years—for understandable reasons, given the dominance of commercial activities in the streets of many Roman cities.[25] There are two sides to this.[26] First, there is the physical interaction of crafts and trade with the direct environment, including the sensory impact of crafts, and eventual measures taken to minimize nuisance caused. Second, there is the spread of economic activities over the urban area, and the degree to which certain activities were, in some way or another, spatially concentrated. A key question in the debate so far has been to which extent there were moral or legal codes dictating the location of certain activities, but it has increasingly been questioned whether this actually was the case, and whether other factors should not play a more prominent role in the debate.[27] It is increasingly

[24] On the 'bounded autonomy' of *fullones* in Roman Italy, see Flohr (2013a: 307–9).

[25] See, e.g. Esposito and Sanidas (2012). See also Flohr and Wilson, Chapter 1, this volume; Goodman, Chapter 13, this volume.

[26] Cf. Flohr (2013a: 189–239), also distinguishing between 'public' and 'private' environments.

[27] Goodman, Chapter 13, this volume.

recognized that there is plentiful evidence for polluting and smelly industries inside the walls of cities—the fish-salting industry, for example, is now seen to be far more urban than we used to think, and where it is extra-mural this is more a result of the need for space for large-scale workshops than because of a desire to keep smells out of the city.[28] The four chapters of this section reflect the development of the debate over the location of urban industries.

The first two chapters focus on the issue of economic clustering in Roman cities—an issue that has not (yet) received a lot of explicit scholarly attention, but is fundamental to our understanding of urban economic geographies in the Roman world. Penelope Goodman approaches the issue from a predominantly archaeological perspective. She starts from two modern (British) examples of economic clusters, and then goes on to analyse three cases of clustering that are identifiable in the archaeological record, discussing evidence from Pompeii, Timgad, and Silchester, before assessing the evidence for clustering in texts. Goodman argues that clustering was a common phenomenon in Roman cities, and that this was essentially due to landlords—the elite—allowing the market to do its work, as this was in their social and economic interests. The subsequent chapter by Kerstin Droß-Krüpe focuses on a specific subset of crafts—textile crafts—and starts from the papyrological evidence from Roman Egypt. Tax and property registers show how, in Roman Egypt, textile crafts such as dyeing and fulling were not clustered, but appear to have been more or less equally distributed over the urban quarters. Using modern cluster theory, Droß-Krüpe argues that this also makes sense, as most textiles are convenience goods, rather than shopping goods, which means that clustering would actually be disadvantageous for entrepreneurs. This leads then to a rethinking of the craft-related toponyms known from textual sources, which need to be approached with caution, and to a comparison with Medieval Europe, where local governments and guilds, much more than in Roman cities, played an active role in establishing craft clusters. At first sight, Droß-Krüpe appears more cautious when it comes to clustering than Goodman, but the two arguments complement rather than exclude each other: while Goodman shows that clustering could emerge in Roman cities, and was not an exceptional phenomenon, Droß-Krüpe shows that circumstances in the Roman world were still much less advantageous for clustering than in the guild-dominated cities of Medieval Europe.

The final two chapters present two case studies that discuss the development of economic landscapes of a specific city over a longer period. These focus on Aquincum and Sagalassos respectively. The chapter by Orsolya Lang gives a thorough analysis of the archaeology of manufacturing and retail in the Roman city of Aquincum. While most of this site was excavated in the late nineteenth century, recent fieldwork has reshaped our view of the commercial history of this town. As the civilian settlement—situated some 3 kilometres

---

[28] Wilson (1999; 2002b; 2007: 178–80); Ellis (2011).

north of the legionary camp—developed from a *vicus* into a *municipium* and, later, into a *colonia*, its commercial landscape became more varied, and spread out over a larger area. Yet the original main street of the *vicus* always kept a strongly commercial character, illustrating how existing situations impacted on subsequent developments. A similar point emerges from the contribution by Jeroen Poblome, who discusses the urban history of the potters' quarter at Sagalassos. Production of red-glazed fine-ware pottery started here in the Augustan period, probably as a result of a concerted effort of the community to move a pre-existing Hellenistic potters' quarter from the place where the Roman odeon now stands. Production continued until the sixth century AD. Poblome outlines how the area gradually became more densely built up, and became dominated by small-scale pottery workshops: local economic circumstances left little room for investment on a larger scale. The analysis shows the impact that a locally important craft could have on the urban landscape—even if the Roman potters' quarter was not directly in the city centre.

Readers will notice that these four chapters in several respects move in similar directions. Two issues deserve to be highlighted here. First, in the end, all chapters move away from the 'moral' approach to the position of economic life in urban space: no argument is made in favour of the idea that cultural (negative) attitudes of the Roman elite towards manufacturing dictated the economic topography of cities, or restricted location choices for certain trades. Rather, the location of shops and workshops has become a matter of economic strategy, being determined by customer base, supply lines, and land prices. Perhaps, this may even lead us to reconsider slightly our ideas on the spatial position of trades like prostitution: prostitution, at Pompeii, was not concentrated in back streets in the city centre because nobody wanted to know it existed, but because customers did not want to be seen—economically, these locations were more viable than highly visible hot spots along the main streets. A second issue that emerges from these chapters is the role of path dependence in the history of urban economic topographies: whatever is already there has a big impact on what subsequently develops. This is true both for clusters and for commercial landscapes in general. As Goodman argues, economic clusters, once established, reinforce themselves—and this is precisely what can be seen at Sagalassos; similarly, in Aquincum, the cluster of commercial activities in the original *vicus* had a significant impact on the commercial landscape of the later city—even though the geographic emphasis shifts away from the original main road of the settlement.

CRAFTSMEN, TRADERS, AND THE WIDER DEBATE

Methodologically, the volume highlights the significance of space: understanding the spatial context in which the work took place is seminal to all aspects of urban crafts and trade—social, cultural, and economic. This obviously points to the important role archaeology can play in the debate (and to the problematic accessibility of much of the archaeological evidence), but, as exemplified by Droß-Krüpe's chapter, texts, too, contain spatial information. Rather, therefore, the argument is that the analysis of crafts and trade needs to be spatially aware: whether discussing the organization of the production process, social interaction among professionals, or the social position of craftsmen and traders, space is a crucial concept that cannot be overlooked.

At the same time, the volume shows the relevance of approaches integrating textual and archaeological evidence: textual and material evidence each provides only a partial picture of the historical realities of crafts and manufacturing in the Roman world, and the different data sets are extremely badly connected to each other—direct links between the textual and archaeological record, such as on the tomb of Eurysaces in Rome, through the combination of iconography and epigraphy, or in Pompeii, through election notices written on the walls of workshops that have left identifiable remains, are rare.[29] Building more bridges between text and archaeology is essential for our understanding of urban manufacturing, trade, and retail: any approach privileging one over the other risks ending up seriously flawed.

As to the everyday world of craftsmen and traders, there is a shared emphasis on the role of both consumers and elites. The users of products made and sold were prominent figures in the lives of many craftsmen and traders. While their role in shaping production and retail strategies and economic topographies seems straightforward, it should be emphasized that they also played a role in the social positioning of craftsmen and traders: direct interaction with customers was a key element in the occupational identity of craftsmen and traders alike. Indeed, it may be suggested that occupations with more direct interaction with customers had a higher chance of developing a strong occupational identity— and, particularly if one catered for an elite audience, this also enhanced the chances for epigraphic commemoration.[30] The impact of the elite was shaped through their landowning and patronage—though it may be pointed out that the chapters in this volume almost unanimously refer to local elites rather than to the senatorial and equestrian elites whose cultural ideas pervade literary discourse. These elites invested in trade and manufacturing because they wanted to get something out of it—socially or economically. Crucially, however, their impact on everyday decision-making processes seems in many cases to have been limited: they operated in the background, and left the business to those who had most experience of conducting it, giving craftsmen and traders a considerable amount of de facto autonomy.

---

[29] The tomb of Eurysaces, of course, combines iconographic depictions of the bread-baking process with an inscription describing the man as a *pistor*. See also Ruffing, Chapter 5, this volume.

[30] See the discussion of inscriptions commemorating craftsmen in Flohr (2013a: 328–32).

However, ultimately, the picture that emerges from this volume is very much one of variation. While it is patently obvious that certain strategies, institutions, and practices were known and embraced throughout the Roman world—one can think of specialization, clustering, professional networks, and client agency—the contributions to this volume, collectively, also suggest that the ways in which these took shape, and the extent to which they were popular in certain places and at certain moments, could be profoundly influenced by specific local circumstances. Rather than being an impediment to understanding the history of craftsmen and traders in the Roman world, this variation must be seen as a key historical fact. Practically, it points to two issues. In the first place, it suggests flexibility: when we are looking at urban crafts and trade in the Roman world, we are looking at people who were able to adapt their ways of working according to the problems (or opportunities) they encountered. Flexibility and adaptation were key properties of Roman craftsmen and traders. The implication is that the world of manufacturing, trade, and retail was also open to innovation, especially under exceptional circumstances—as can be found, for example, in the Roman metropolis and the other major cities of the Roman Mediterranean: extreme urbanization caused problems and brought opportunities for which traditional strategies and practices sometimes were less adequate. Similarly, the romanization, and urbanization, of Europe and Britain created a new socio-economic landscape that fostered new strategies and practices, or caused existing practices and institutions to take on new forms or meanings. The second issue follows directly from the first: if variation and flexibility are central to the history of urban crafts and trade in the Roman world, a task high on the scholarly agenda should be making sense of it. Thus, without denying the need also to explore institutions, practices, and strategies on a conceptual or empire-wide level, and without contesting the usefulness of exploring theoretical models for thinking through possible historical scenarios, 'time' and 'place' also need to be central concepts in the historiography of urban crafts and trade in the Roman world: it is only through the thorough analysis of situations in specific localities and at specific moments, and through comparing these, that it becomes possible to understand how this flexible system worked, and developed—in other words, the debate needs to take place in the tension between model-building and close reading. The chapters in this volume offer some suggestions about ways in which this might be done.

REFERENCES

Bakker, J.-Th. (1999). *The Mills-Bakeries of Ostia: Description and Interpretation.* Amsterdam.

Block, F. (2001). 'Introduction', in K. Polanyi, *The Great Transformation: The Political and Economic Origins of Our Time.* Boston, pp. xviii–xxxviii.

Boldizzoni, F. (2011). *The Poverty of Clio: Resurrecting Economic History*. Princeton.

Borgard, P. (2002). 'A propos des teinturies de Pompei: L'Exemple de l'officina infectoria V 1, 4', in J. C. Béal and J. C. Goyon (eds), *Les Artisans dans la ville antique* (Collection Archéologie et Histoire de l'Antiquité). Lyons, 55–67.

Borgard, P., and Puybaret, M. P. (2004). 'Le Travail de la laine au début de l'empire; l'apport du modèle pompeien. Quels artisans? Quels équipements? Quelles techniques?', in C. Alfaro, J. P. Wild, and B. Costa (eds), *Purpureae Vestes: Textiles y tintes del Mediterráneo en época romana*. Valencia, 47–59.

Borgard, P., Forest, V., Bioul-Pelletier, C., and Pelletier, L. (2002). ' "Passer les peaux en blanc": Une pratique gallo-romaine? L'Apport du site de Sainte-Anne à Dijon (Côte-d'Or)', in F. Audoin-Rouzeau and S. Beyries (eds), *Le Travail du cuir de la préhistoire à nos jours*. Antibes, 231–49.

Borgard, P., Brun, J-P., Leguilloux, M., and Tuffreau-Libre, M. (2003). 'Le produzioni artigianali a Pompei: Ricerche condotte dal Centre Jean Berard', *Rivista di studi pompeiani* 14: 9–29.

Bowman, A. K., and Wilson, A. I. (2011). *Settlement, Urbanization, and Population* (Oxford Studies on the Roman Economy). Oxford.

Bradley, M. (2002). ' "It all comes out in the wash": Looking Harder at the Roman Fullonica', *JRA* 15/1: 21–44.

Broekaert, W. (2011). 'Partners in Business: Roman Merchants and the Potential Advantages of being a Collegiatus', *Ancient Society* 41: 221–56.

Broekaert, W., and Zuiderhoek, A. (2013). 'Industries and Services,' in P. Erdkamp (ed.), *The Cambridge Companion to Ancient Rome*. Cambridge, 317–35.

Clarke, J. (2003). *Art in the Lives of Ordinary Romans*. Berkeley.

Cuomo, S. (2007). *Technology and Culture in Greek and Roman Antiquity*. Cambridge.

De Ligt, L. (2012). *Peasants, Citizens and Soldiers: Studies in the Demographic History of Roman Italy 225 BC–AD 100*. Cambridge.

Ellis, S. J. R. (2004). 'The Distribution of Bars at Pompeii: Archaeological, Spatial and Viewshed Analyses', *JRA* 17/1: 371–84.

Ellis, S. J. R. (2011). 'The Rise and Reorganization of the Pompeian Salted Fish Industry', in S. Ellis (ed.), *The Making of Pompeii: Studies in the History and Urban Development of an Ancient Town* (JRA Supplement 85). Portsmouth, RI, 59–88.

Esposito, A., and Sanidas, G. (eds) (2012). *Quartiers artisanaux en Grèce ancienne: Une perspective méditerranéenne*. Villeneuve d'Ascq.

Finley, M. I. (1973). *The Ancient Economy*. London.

Flohr, M. (2007). 'Nec quicquam ingenuum habere potest officina? Spatial Contexts of Urban Production at Pompeii, AD 79,' *BABesch* 82/1: 129–48.

Flohr, M. (2009). 'The Social World of Roman Fullonicae', in M. Driessen, S. Heeren, J. Hendriks, F. Kemmers, and R. Visser (eds), *TRAC 2008: Proceedings of the Eighteenth Annual Theoretical Roman Archaeology Conference*. Oxford, 173–86.

Flohr, M. (2012). 'Working and Living under One Roof: Workshops in Pompeian Atrium Houses', in A. Anguissola (ed.), *Privata Luxuria: Towards an Archaeology of Intimacy: Pompeii and Beyond*. Munich, 51–72.

Flohr, M. (2013a). *The World of the Fullo: Work, Economy, and Society in Roman Italy* (Oxford Studies on the Roman Economy). Oxford.

Flohr, M. (2013b). 'The Textile Economy of Pompeii', *JRA* 26/1: 53–78.

Frier, B. W., and Kehoe, D. (2007). 'Law and Economic Institutions', in Scheidel, Morris, and Saller (2007), 113–42.

Graham, S. (2006). *Ex Figlinis: The Network Dynamics of the Tiber Valley Brick Industry in the Hinterland of Rome* (BAR International Series 1468). Oxford.

Hawkins, C. (2012). 'Manufacturing', in W. Scheidel (ed.), *The Cambridge Companion to the Roman Economy*. Cambridge, 175–94.

Hawkins, C. (2013). 'Labour and Employment', in P. Erdkamp (ed.), *The Cambridge Companion to Ancient Rome*. Cambridge, 336–51.

Joshel, S. R. (1992). *Work, Identity and Legal Status at Rome*. London.

Kehoe, D. (2007). 'The Early Roman Empire: Production', in Scheidel, Morris, and Saller (2007), 543–69.

Leguilloux, M. (2002). 'Techniques et équipements de la tannerie romaine: L'Exemple de l'officina *coriaria* de Pompéi', in F. Audoin-Rouzeau and S. Beyries (eds), *Le Travail du cuir de la préhistoire à nos jours*. Antibes, 267–82.

Leguilloux, M. (2004). *Le Cuir et la pelleterie à l'époque romaine* (Collection des Hespérides). Paris.

Liu, J. (2013). 'Professional Associations', in P. Erdkamp (ed.), *The Cambridge Companion to Ancient Rome*. Cambridge, 352–68.

Monteix, N. (2010). *Les lieux de métier: Boutiques et ateliers d'Herculaneum*. Rome.

Morley, N. (2007). 'The Early Roman Empire: Distribution,' in Scheidel, Morris, and Saller (2007), 570–91.

Morris, I., Saller, R., and Scheidel, W. (2007). 'Introduction', in Scheidel, Morris, and Saller (2007), 1–12.

Mouritsen, H. (2011). *The Freedman in the Roman World*. Cambridge.

Petersen, L. (2006). *The Freedman in Roman Art and Art History*. New York.

Polanyi, K. (1944). *The Great Transformation: The Political and Economic Origins of our Time*. Boston.

Rostovtzeff, M. (1926). *The Social and Economic History of the Roman Empire*. Oxford.

Ruffini, G. (2008). *Social Networks in Byzantine Egypt*. Cambridge.

Scheidel, W. (2012). 'Approaching the Roman Economy,' in W. Scheidel (ed.), *The Cambridge Companion to the Roman Economy*. Cambridge, 1–21.

Scheidel, W., Morris, I., and Saller, R. (eds) (2007). *The Cambridge Economic History of the Greco-Roman World*. Cambridge.

Terpstra, T. (2013). *Trading Communities in the Roman World: A Micro-Economic and Institutional Perspective*. New York.

Tran, N. (2007). 'Le "Procès des foulons": L'Occupation litigieuse d'un espace vicinal par des artisans romains,,' *MEFRA* 119/2: 597–611.

Van Nijf, O. M. (1997). *The Civic World of Professional Associations in the Roman East*. Amsterdam.

Verboven, K. (2011). 'Resident Aliens and Translocal Merchant Collegia in the Roman Empire', in O. Hekster and T. Kaizer (eds), *Frontiers in the Roman World: Proceedings of the Ninth Workshop of the International Network Impact of Empire (Durham, 16–19 April 2009)*. Leiden, 335–48.

Verboven, K. (2012). 'Cité et réciprocité: Le Rôle des croyances culturelles dans l'économie romaine', *Annales. Histoire, Sciences Sociales* 67: 913–42.

Wallace-Hadrill, A. (1991). 'Elites and Trade in the Roman Town,' in J. Rich and A. Wallace-Hadrill (eds), *City and Country in the Ancient World.* London, 241–72.

Wilson, A. I. (1999). 'Commerce and Industry in Roman Sabratha', *Libyan Studies* 30: 29–52.

Wilson, A. (2000). 'The Water-Mills on the Janiculum', *Memoirs of the American Academy at Rome*, 45: 219–46.

Wilson, A. (2002a). 'Machines, Power and the Ancient Economy', *JRS* 92: 1–32.

Wilson, A. I. (2002b). 'Urban Production in the Roman World: The View from North Africa', *PBSR* 70: 231–73.

Wilson, A. I. (2007). 'Fish-Salting Workshops in Sabratha', in L. Lagóstena, D. Bernal, and A. Aréval (eds), *Cetariae 2005: Salsas y Salazones de Pescado en Occidente durante la Antigüedad. Actas del Congreso Internacional (Cádiz, 7–9 de noviembre de 2005)* (BAR International Series 1686). Oxford, 173–81.

Wilson, A. I. (2008). 'Large-Scale Manufacturing, Standardization, and Trade', in J. P. Oleson (ed.), *Handbook of Engineering and Technology in the Classical World.* Oxford, 393–417.

I

Approaches

1

Roman Craftsmen and Traders: Towards an Intellectual History

Miko Flohr and Andrew Wilson

Although the study of everyday socio-economic processes, such as crafts and trade, and of the people involved in them has occupied a marginal position within classical studies from its beginnings until fairly recently, there is a long history of scholarly research that has had a decisive, though often implicit, impact on the way in which craftsmen and traders are approached by scholars nowadays. It is self-evident that an understanding of this scholarly history is essential in making sense of the way in which scholars have come to think about Roman craftsmen and traders in the way they do. Yet, thus far, the intellectual past of scholarly discourse on this topic has received relatively little attention. The present chapter therefore intends to sketch, in rough strokes, how scholarly approaches to craftsmen and traders have developed since the early nineteenth century. It does so by focusing on the contributions from Germany, Britain, and the United States of America. These are three dominant classical traditions that have played a key role in shaping and reshaping debates and approaches. They have, however, done so in rather different ways, and at different moments. In this chapter these three traditions are discussed together, and contrasted where they diverge, and thus a core historical framework emerges that is also of use in discussions of other research traditions, such as those from Italy and France—both of which are treated in subsequent chapters.[1]

The question at stake is obviously one of intellectual history, and concerns analysing the modern historical background against which ideas about Roman craftsmen and traders emerged. The last decades of the twentieth century saw a gradual increase of interest in the modern reception of the Greco-Roman world among classical scholars, and, while most of this concerns those debates and issues that were traditionally most central to classical studies, there is also

---

[1] Salvaterra and Cristofori, Chapter 2, this volume; Brun, Chapter 3, this volume.

a growing amount of published work on the lives and careers of the scholars who played a role in discourse on crafts and trade in the Roman world. There is a substantial, and growing, bibliography on key figures such as Theodor Mommsen, Eduard Meyer, Mikhail Rostovtzeff, and Moses Finley.[2] The twentieth-century history of the debate about the ancient economy has also been discussed by a variety of scholars, especially in recent years.[3] The 2006 monograph by Jonathan Perry on the modern history of the Roman *collegia* sheds light on the role of some key scholars in nineteenth- and twentieth-century thinking on professional associations; for Germany, Dissen has recently published a similar analysis, which focuses more on the later twentieth century.[4] However, besides the work of Perry, there has been little reflection specifically focusing on the historiography of Roman craftsmen and traders.

By definition, debates in classical studies evolve around the tension between evidence and ideas, which means that the discovery of large quantities of new data, the increased accessibility of data sets, or the emergence of new ways of looking at the world, including political ideologies, tend to have a direct impact on the way certain themes are discussed. As will become clear, both the changing nature of the evidence available, and changing modern political and ideological discourses, have played key roles in approaches to Roman craftsmen and traders. Yet people matter as well: scholarly networks and scholarly competition may foster, or curb, debate, and may privilege certain approaches over others. In what follows, the development of discourse on Roman craftsmen and traders will be analysed with a special emphasis both on the broader developments in evidence and ideology, and on the role played by specific people or specific networks of people in fostering the debate. The focus will be on five subsequent developments that shaped discourse on the subject between the mid-nineteenth and the early twenty-first centuries. These developments should not be seen as 'phases': to some extent they overlap chronologically and developments that emerge in one period tend to continue subsequently at varying levels of intensity.

BEFORE THE MOMMSEN ERA

There is no doubt that the second half of the nineteenth century marks a major watershed in the study of Roman craftsmen and traders. The publication of the large epigraphic corpora in the late nineteenth century, the

---

[2] Mommsen: Christ (1972: 84–118); Rebenich (2002); A. Overbeek (2005); Perry (2006: 23–60); Meyer: Christ (1972: 286–333); Calder and Demandt (1990); Rostovtzeff: Christ (1972: 334–49); Wes (1990); Finley: Morris (1999); Harris (2013).

[3] e.g. Morley (2004: 33–50); Schneider (2009); Wagner-Hasel (2009).

[4] Perry (2006); Dissen (2009). For French discourse on the topic, see also Tran (2001).

increasing amounts of archaeological evidence for crafts and trade in the Roman world, and the encyclopaedia frenzy completely changed the scholarly playing field, as well as the rules of the analytical game. Before, roughly, 1850, very few well-excavated shops and workshops from the Roman world were known to a wide audience, and inscriptions were not easy to find, even if they had been published. This largely restricted scholars to literary sources and legal texts. Moreover, as scholars focusing on the history of antiquity were, until well into the nineteenth century, mainly occupying themselves with the works of Latin and Greek historians, there were few incentives for them to focus on craftsmen and traders.[5] In consequence, publications focusing directly on craftsmen and traders in a more than passing manner were rare, and stood on their own rather than being part of a debate. Such accounts were often also not primarily interested in questions of social or economic history. For example, one of the very few works from before 1850 that were occasionally referred to by later scholars is Johann August Ernesti's *De Negotiatoribus Romanis* (1737), which is essentially a lexicographical exercise focusing on what, actually, was understood under the term *negotiator* by the Roman authors (especially Cicero), and only sporadically alludes to the socio-economic roles of *negotiatores*.[6] In a rather similar way, Johann Christian Schöttgen discussed the history of fulling in the ancient world in his *Antiquitates Triturae et Fulloniae* (1727).[7]

The paradox is that, while classical scholars of the eighteenth century were not interested in detailed study of ancient economies, scholars in other fields were already developing ideas that would have a huge impact on later debates. Highly relevant were the eighteenth-century developments in political economy, and particularly the thinking of people such as Hume, Steuart, and Smith.[8] Whereas the classical political economists of this period, unlike the social theorists of the nineteenth century, did not see antiquity as fundamentally different from their own world, they did observe that trade and industry were less fully developed in antiquity than they were in their own time, and debated why this was the case, blaming low demand and, to a lesser degree, underdeveloped technology.[9] For instance, Hume claimed that commerce was mainly based on exchange of commodities that were tied to certain types of soil and climate, and emphasized that no ancient author ascribed the growth of a city to the establishment of industries.[10] Steuart believed that the

---

[5] Cf. Momigliano (1950: 291–2).

[6] Ernesti (1737). Cf., e.g. Hatzfeld (1919: 1), who erroneously dates Ernesti's work to 1802.

[7] Schöttgen (1727). Cf., e.g. W. Smith (1848: s.v. *fullo*).

[8] e.g. Hume (1752); Steuart (1767); A. Smith (1776) and *Lectures on Jurisprudence*. See Meek et al. (1978).

[9] Morley (1998: 109–11). Morley notes that the classical political economists stayed away from the issue of economic mentality.

[10] Hume (1752: 207). Cf. Morley (1998: 109). See also Finley (1985: 137).

widespread use of slave labour, and the corresponding lack of economic opportunities for the free population, kept demand low.[11]

A crucial development in this debate came when, in the nineteenth century, scholars started to distinguish more sharply between 'pre-industrial' and 'industrial' societies.[12] This had a profound effect on the perception of the Roman world. Adam Smith had seen the development of mankind as consisting of four stages, progressing from hunting, to pastoralism, to agriculture, and, finally, to commerce.[13] In this model, the classical world was interpreted as developing from the agricultural to the commercial stage, though, with the fall of Rome, the commercial system collapsed, only to emerge again in the medieval period.[14] Yet, by the late 1840s, Karl Marx had developed an adapted, and more teleological, version of the four-stages theory, sketching, for the West, a historical progress from primitive communism (tribalism) through the slave society to feudalism and capitalism.[15] In this model, the ancient world fitted neatly into the second stage. Contrary to Smith, Marx thus put the Roman world in a structurally different category from the early modern world. To some extent, it might be argued that the twentieth-century debates about the Roman economy developed in the tension between the views of Smith and Marx.

BUILDING A CANON

These grand theories did not have a very deep impact on the actual study of Roman crafts and trade before the 1890s. Nevertheless, the period between the mid-nineteenth century and the start of the First World War in 1914 did see some crucial developments in classical scholarship that would fundamentally change the dynamics of the discourse: for the first time, classical scholars engaged with the evidence for everyday economic life in a systematic way. Three developments deserve to be highlighted.

In the first place, there was a revolution in the archaeology of crafts and trade. An exemplary role in this was undoubtedly played by Pompeii, where,

---

[11] Steuart (1767: ii. 35–40). Cf. Morley (1998: 110).   [12] Morley (1998: 110).

[13] See Brewer (2008); cf. Finley (1977: 313).

[14] Brewer (2008: 15–17). Smith discusses antiquity only in passing in the *Wealth of Nations*, but notes taken at his *Lectures on Jurisprudence* give a good idea of his thoughts, esp. 24 February 1763. Cf. Meek et al. (1978: 223–8).

[15] Cf. Hobsbawm (1964: 19). Marx sketches the road from primitive communism to feudalism in *Die Deutsche Ideologie*, which was written in 1845 but not published until after his death. Cf. Marx and Engels (1932: 11–15). On the fundamental differences between ancient and medieval economic life, see also *Pre-Capitalist Economic Formations* (1857); see the edition by Hobsbawm (1964: 72–8).

from 1860 onwards, the speed of excavation increased dramatically, and numerous workshops, of several kinds, were excavated.[16] Well-documented and regularly updated guides in both the English and the German language began to circulate, such as Gell's *Pompeiana* and Dyer's *Pompeii: Its History, Buildings and Antiquities*.[17] Johann Overbeck's *Pompeji in seinen Gebäuden, Alterthümern und Kunstwerken* was revised and expanded three times between its first appearance in 1856 and 1884, including new discoveries every time.[18] Its final edition would be the basis for August Mau's *Pompeii in Leben und Kunst*, which also appeared in English and would be the leading handbook on Pompeii for most of the twentieth century.[19] These guides discussed the discovered remains of workshops in considerable detail, so that their existence became known to a wide scholarly audience. Moreover, the establishment of the *Notizie degli Scavi di antichità* in Italy in 1876, and the *Jahrbuch des Deutschen Instituts* in the same year, ensured that knowledge of new discoveries in Pompeii and elsewhere spread quickly through the scholarly community. What happened at Pompeii also happened at other sites, such as Delos, Timgad, and Ostia, although slightly later and with less direct impact on the overall debate.[20] Moreover, with an increasing proportion of archaeological activity focused on more everyday (urban) environments, archaeologists also began to develop a more explicit interest in the archaeology of crafts and manufacturing, as is attested by, for example, the groundbreaking work on centres of pottery production by Dragendorff, and by the work on a number of production sites, such as Arezzo, Rheinzabern, Lezoux, and La Graufesenque.[21]

Second, there was the appearance of large corpora of evidence. An increased frustration caused by the poor accessibility of Latin epigraphy led in the late 1840s and early 1850s to the establishment of the *Corpus Inscriptionum Latinarum* (*CIL*), which under the leadership of Theodor Mommsen published, in a few decades, and in a systematic manner, an enormous quantity of inscriptions from all over the Roman world.[22] More than the archaeological discoveries at Pompeii, the *CIL*, quickly, completely, and definitively, changed the scholarly field: while Ernesti, in his work on the *negotiatores*, had to make do with a few literary references, the *CIL* published no fewer than 175 texts

---

[16] For a discussion of the history of excavations at Pompeii, see Pesando and Guidobaldi (2006: 25–8). Between 1860 and 1914, about 50% of the area currently excavated was unearthed.

[17] Gell (1834); Dyer (1867, 1868, 1871).

[18] J. Overbeck (1856, 1866, 1875); Overbeck and Mau (1884).

[19] Mau (1900; English edn 1899).

[20] Delos was excavated from 1873 onwards; cf. Chamonard (1922); Bruneau and Ducat (1966: 25). The excavations of Timgad ('la Pompéi africaine') began in 1880; cf. Ballu (1897: 3). At Ostia, true excavations began in 1907, under Vaglieri; cf. Olivanti (2001).

[21] Dragendorff (1895); Rheinzabern: Reubel (1912). See also Dechelette (1904).

[22] The first thirteen volumes had appeared, at least partially, before the end of the nineteenth century. For an overview, see <cil.bbaw.de> (accessed 3 October 2013).

featuring the occupation.[23] The relevance of the *CIL* became clear from the upsurge of interest in the study of professional associations that emerged in the late nineteenth century. Scholars such as Liebenam, Maué, and, particularly, Waltzing noted the (potential) impact of the *corpus* on the debate.[24] Waltzing's classic multi-volume *Étude historique des corporations professionels* can perhaps even be seen as a direct result of the publication of the first volumes of the *CIL*.[25] The *CIL* was by far the largest, but it was not the only relevant data set made accessible through systematic publication, and some efforts were specifically devoted to crafts and trade. Otto Jahn, who worked closely with Mommsen in parts of his career, collected and published depictions of crafts and trade on reliefs and wall paintings.[26] After the turn of the century, there was Espérandieu's *Receuil générale des bas reliefs de la Gaule romaine*, including many reliefs with scenes of everyday economic life.[27]

Finally, and perhaps most importantly for the scholarly understanding of crafts and trade in the late nineteenth century, there were the handbooks, dictionaries, and encyclopaedias focusing on the ancient world. The lemmas and entries in these works quickly became standard points of reference in discussions of specific crafts and trades and remained so throughout the twentieth century. Obviously, the late nineteenth century saw Georg Wissowa initiating the extended version of Pauly's *Realencyclopädie der classischen Altertumswissenschaft*, but, as many relevant entries in this encyclopaedia appeared only in the course of the twentieth century, other works were more influential on topics related to crafts and manufacturing. These include general works such as Smith's *Dictionary*, Daremberg and Saglio's *Dictionnaire des antiquités grecs et romaines*, and De Ruggiero's *Dizionario epigrafico di antichità romane*.[28] More specifically focusing on aspects of economic life was Hugo Blümner's *Technologie und Terminologie der Gewerbe*, which gave detailed descriptions of all kinds of production processes and linked these to the material and textual evidence available.[29] The second volume of *Das Privatleben der Römer* by Joachim Marquardt contained comparable encyclopaedic information on crafts and trade.[30] It may be noted that both these two works were produced in the circles around Theodor Mommsen: Blümner, whose dissertation was a monograph on crafts and trade, was a student of Otto Jahn, while Marquardt edited together with Mommsen the *Handbuch der Römischen Alterthümer*, of which the volumes on private life were part.[31] Generally, the dictionaries and encyclopaedias of this period used almost identical sets of

[23] See <db.edcs.edu>, search on *negotiator* in *CIL* (accessed 1 March 2015).
[24] Liebenam (1890: v); Maué (1886); Waltzing (1892: 5). Indeed, Mommsen's work on the *collegia*, which was published before the *CIL* project had begun, seems to have confirmed his determination for it. Mommsen (1843). Cf. Perry (2006: 29).
[25] Waltzing (1895, 1896, 1900). Cf. Perry (2006: 64).   [26] Jahn (1861, 1868).
[27] Espérandieu (1907–).
[28] W. Smith (1848); Daremberg and Saglio (1873–); De Ruggiero (1895–).
[29] Blümner (1875–84).   [30] Marquardt (1882).   [31] Blümner (1869).

evidence, referring to the same passages in the literary authors, and to the same legal texts, using (if any) the same subset of inscriptions, and the same examples from the archaeological record, most of which came from Pompeii. This resulted in a rather sharply defined canon of evidence for crafts and trade, from which it would be hard to escape for much of the twentieth century: scholars often approached the encyclopaedias and handbooks as received knowledge rather than as the artificial constructs they often were.[32]

FROM RODBERTUS TO ROSTOVTZEFF

While classical scholars in Germany were busy cataloguing the evidence, debates among economic theorists continued, and increasingly followed Marx in emphasizing the fundamental difference between antiquity and the modern world. The (socialist) economist Johann Karl Rodbertus, discussing the tax system of the Roman Empire, depicted the Roman economy as an *Oikenwirtschaft*—a system organized around households that were, in principle, autarkic, and in which trade and commercial manufacturing played no meaningful role.[33] The model of Rodbertus would be picked up and elaborated by Karl Bücher, who used it in his version of the *Wirtschaftsstufentheorie*, in which he envisaged a linear progress from the ancient *Oikenwirtschaft* through a *Stadtwirtschaft*—the medieval period—to the modern *Volkswirtschaft*.[34] It was Bücher's model that would, finally, provoke a response from the German community of classical scholars: in a famous paper given at the 1895 meeting of Geman historians, Eduard Meyer argued that Rodbertus and Bücher had completely misunderstood the structure of the Greek and Roman economies, and that trade and industry played a defining role throughout antiquity.[35] As has recently been emphasized by Helmut Schneider, Meyer's response cannot be seen apart from contemporary scholarly politics: in a field that felt threatened in its relevance to the modern world, Meyer wanted to show the continued significance of studying the ancient world and its economy for the present day.[36] Meyer was not alone: Julius Beloch also responded with an argument that highlighted the widespread existence of large-scale industry from archaic Greece onwards.[37] Studying the economic history of Rome, Karl Hoffmeister attempted to reconcile Bücher's three stages with Meyer's optimism, leading to the argument that Rome started as an *Oikenwirtschaft*, quickly developed into a *Stadtwirtschaft* and reached, already in the late Republic, the level of a *Volkswirtschaft*.[38]

---

[32] See, e.g. Bradley's critique (2002: 21–2) of 'dictionary fulling'.
[33] Rodbertus (1865: 345–6). [34] Bücher (1893). [35] Meyer (1895).
[36] Schneider (2009: 349–53). Cf. Meyer (1895: 1). [37] Beloch (1899).
[38] Hoffmeister (1899: 93).

Thus, in the German debate about Rodbertus's model of the *Oikenwirtschaft* (often slightly misleadingly reduced to a 'Bücher–Meyer controversy'), the classical scholars were consistently and significantly more optimistic about the structure and performance of the ancient economy than the economic theorists.[39] Generally, leading German classical scholars of the late nineteenth and early twentieth centuries thus tended to believe that trade and manufacturing, through-out antiquity, both socially and economically played an important role. Meyer indeed refers to the existence of centres of trade and industry 'everywhere' in the archaic Aegean.[40] For the Roman Empire he envisaged busy transport and widespread commercial exchange.[41] Beloch, though arguing that small-scale manufacturing was the norm in Italy, claimed that large-scale factories were common in the eastern provinces.[42] Hoffmeister described second-century BC Rome as a *Weltverkehrsstadt* that had 'thousands of shops' where people could buy products from all known regions.[43] However, none of these works made use of the archaeological and epigraphic evidence that was being published in the late nineteenth century, and Meyer and Beloch dealt mostly with the Greek rather than the Roman world. As Schneider has observed, the responses to Bücher by Meyer and Beloch did not contain a lot of new research—rather, they put interpretations that had long been known into a new ideological framework.[44] It would be well into the twentieth century before the possibilities of the newly available evidence began to be seriously explored.

Nevertheless, there is no doubt that the determined responses of influential *Altertumswissenschaftler* such as Meyer and Beloch to the ideas of Bücher and Rodbertus had an enormous impact on the way in which classical scholars came to think about Greek and Roman economies. Moreover, Meyer in particular seems to have encouraged people to engage with the archaeological and epigraphic evidence for crafts and trade. One of the most productive scholars of the first decades of the twentieth century was Herman Gummerus, who did a doctorate with Meyer on Roman agriculture and subsequently wrote a series of articles on Roman crafts and trade, including the long discussion of industry and trade in the *Realenzyklopädie*.[45] Moreover, Meyer also seems to have had a direct impact on the thought and careers of two leading figures in Roman economic history of the first half of the twentieth century: Tenney Frank and Mikhail Rostovtzeff. Frank, educated as a philologist more than an ancient historian, met Meyer when he was in the USA in 1909, and subse-quently spent parts of a sabbatical in Berlin with Meyer in 1910–11.[46] Shortly

---

[39] Cf. Schneider (2009: 354). On the Bücher–Meyer controversy, see also Reibig (2001).
[40] Meyer (1910: 113).   [41] Meyer (1910: 144).   [42] Beloch (1899: 25–6).
[43] Hoffmeister (1899: 39).   [44] Schneider (2009: 353).
[45] Gummerus (1906, 1913, 1915, 1916). Wissowa, the editor of the *Realenzyklopädie*, be-longed to Meyer's inner academic circle; cf. Audring (2000). His student Georg Kuhn wrote a dissertation (1910) on Roman craftsmen that would be frequently cited by Gummerus (1916).
[46] Chambers (1990: 115).

afterwards, he began publishing his first articles on aspects of the Roman economy, research that would culminate in his *An Economic History of Rome* (1920).[47] It was also Meyer who, together with Wilamowitz, asked Rostovtzeff to write his social and economic histories of the Hellenistic and Roman worlds.[48]

Both Frank and Rostovtzeff made extensive use of the archaeological and epigraphic evidence that had been published in the preceding decades, and they would integrate a whole paradigm of observations into an attractive and coherent narrative, which would emphasize the social and economic import- ance of urban crafts and trade, though Frank at least seems to have regarded Meyer's views as exaggerated.[49] Frank, in his chapters on industry under the early empire, makes a case for the existence of monopolistic production concentrated in large factories or specialized centres of mass production in the manufacturing of everyday consumer goods such as red-glazed pottery, glass, bricks, iron, and bronzes.[50] Luxury products, on the other hand, such as gold and gems, were produced by specialist craftsmen on a small scale.[51] A lengthy case study of Pompeii highlights the role of commerce and industry in the town, and argues that Pompeii specialized in the production of *garum* and textiles, importing iron and bronze ware from the nearby production centres of Puteoli and Capua.[52] Rostovtzeff put more emphasis on commerce, and made the important link between economic basis and urban growth, arguing that, in the second century AD, the many flourishing urban centres throughout the empire derived their wealth from their role in 'inter-provincial commerce' in 'articles of prime necessity', not luxuries.[53] In manufacturing, Rostovtzeff sees in this period an empire-wide emergence of specialized, regional centres of production, which catered for local and regional markets, and deprived Italy of its export industries.[54] In larger centres, Rostovtzeff even envisaged a 'development towards capitalistic mass-production'.[55]

While Rostovtzeff's book would eventually end up as the key reference for the so-called modernist school of thought, the role of Frank in shaping the debate from the 1910s onwards should not be underestimated, and their two main works do not completely overlap: Frank's focus was primarily on the Republic and the first century of our era, while Rostovtzeff, in his monograph, was more interested in the second and third centuries. Moreover, Frank

---

[47] Frank (1910, 1914, 1918, 1920).

[48] Christ (1972: 340). Rostovtzeff (1926) does not refer to this request in the preface to his book.

[49] Frank (1927: 219), referring to the debate between Rodbertus, Bücher, and Meyer: 'the advocates of both views have gone to untenable extremes.'

[50] Frank (1927: 220–38).   [51] Frank (1927: 241–4).

[52] Frank (1927: 245–67). The Pompeian case study was reproduced almost verbatim from Frank (1918).

[53] Rostovtzeff (1926: 148).   [54] Rostovtzeff (1926: 161–9).

[55] Rostovtzeff (1926: 165).

continued his study of crafts and trade well after the 1920s, when Rostovtzeff had long moved on to studying the Hellenistic world. Still used nowadays is the *Economic Survey of Ancient Rome* (1933–40), which was initiated, edited, and partially written by Frank. The five volumes contain detailed descriptions that outlined the evidence of trade and production for the individual parts of the empire. Of particular relevance was the volume by Allan Chester Johnson on the economy of Roman Egypt, which included a long section on commerce and industry in the papyri—it was one of the first discussions of its kind in this emerging field.[56] The final volume, written by Frank, was completed after his death in 1939 by his students Evelyn Holst Clift and Helen Jefferson Loane; the latter also wrote a monograph on commerce and industry in the city of Rome, which was not included in the series but written in the same period, and shows clear influence of Frank's thinking.[57]

The circle around Frank and Rostovtzeff dominated the debate from the 1910s to the 1930s, which seems to have been a rather American debate: most other scholars who published on these topics between the wars were also operating from the east coast regions of the United States, and, in general, they subscribed to the optimistic views that dominated the field. Ethel Hampson Brewster wrote a thesis on the depiction of craftsmen and traders in Roman satiric verse.[58] Louis C. West published extensively on trade.[59] There seems to have been less interest in studying Roman crafts and trade in Germany or Britain; exceptions included the monograph of Martin Percival Charlesworth on Roman trade routes and Eric Herbert Warmington's book on the Indo-Roman trade.[60] At least for Germany, the lack of debate can be partially explained by the consequences of the First World War, and this is not exemplified better than by Rostovtzeff himself, who was predominantly oriented towards Germany until the war—in 1905 he was even considered for a position in Halle—but spent his post-war life in exile in America, apparently without maintaining active ties with many German scholars.[61]

THE SUBSTANTIVIST DECADES

Frank's death in 1939, and the completion of his *Economic Survey* a year later, symbolized the end of an era. While the optimistic reading of Rome's

---

[56] Johnson (1936: 331–88). Rostovtzeff, of course, also made use of papyrological evidence, but mentioned crafts and trade in Egypt only in passing.

[57] Frank (1940); Loane (1938).

[58] Brewster (1917). See the rather negative review by Wright (1918). See also Brewster (1927, 1931); Wright (1917).

[59] West (1917, 1924, 1932, 1939).   [60] Charlesworth (1924); Warmington (1928).

[61] On Rostovtzeff and Halle, see Audring (2000: 195–9): letter from Wissowa to Meyer, dated 29 December 1905, and Meyer's immediate response dated 30 December 1905.

economic history would remain dominant among classical scholars in the decades immediately following the Second World War, and would pervade publications of newly discovered or studied data sets, a competing school of thought was already starting to emerge in the late 1930s, and it was considerably more sceptical about the economic history of the Roman world than Frank and Rostovtzeff had been. This school of thought would eventually become associated primarily with Moses Finley, and his *The Ancient Economy* would become the standard reference.[62] However, it is important not to underestimate the key role of Arnold Hugh Martin Jones, an Oxford-trained scholar who took up the chair of Ancient History at London (1946) and Cambridge (1951).[63]

Indeed, as early as 1940, Jones discussed the economy of Greco-Roman cities in terms not fundamentally different from what Finley would write more than thirty years later.[64] He sketched how cities performed a role as market place for the surrounding countryside, emphasizing that the low purchasing power of the rural community meant that the role of industry was 'neglegible'. Long-distance trade was restricted to luxury goods, and large-scale export-oriented industry did not play an important role in the ancient world. Crucially, Jones states: 'Both trade and industry were in fact dependent upon a rich urban class, which cannot itself have derived any large proportion of its total wealth from these activities.'[65]

Instead, urban elites derived their wealth from the ownership of land. Throughout antiquity, cities were, Jones argued, 'economically parasitic on the countryside'.[66] Fifteen years later, in 1955, Jones published a more detailed study focusing on the economic life of Roman towns, which conveyed a similar message. In this article, Jones emphasized that trade and industry contributed very little to urban tax incomes, that traders and manufacturers were poor, and that city governments were not interested in fostering their activities; he emphasizes that *collegia* were primarily social organizations that were not involved in urban government or engaged in economic activities.[67] As a source of wealth, Jones concluded that 'commerce could not compete with land'.[68] Unfortunately, Jones tended to avoid direct debate with others: while he was obviously familiar with the work of Rostovtzeff and Frank, he did not explicitly engage with it.[69] Similarly, while he may have known the ideas of Bücher and Weber about the economic basis of ancient cities, he does not refer to them.

---

[62] Finley (1973).   [63] On Jones, see Meiggs (1970).   [64] Jones (1940: 259–69).
[65] Jones (1940: 263).   [66] Jones (1940: 268).
[67] Jones (1955: 163, 173–5). The *collatio lustralis*, a tax paid by traders, and its role in understanding the socio-economic position of craftsmen had already been discussed by Jones in his inaugural address in London: Jones (1948: 11–12).
[68] Jones (1955: 192).
[69] Both Frank and Rostovtzeff feature in the bibliography of Jones (1940). On Jones's style of referencing, see Brunt (2004).

The ideas of Moses Finley about the ancient economy are so well known that they do not need to be introduced at great length, but it may be useful to emphasize once again that Finley never specifically focused on the *Roman* economy, and had a background in Greek history.[70] Moreover, while *The Ancient Economy* was published only in 1973, Finley seems already to have developed some of his core ideas in the late 1940s and the early 1950s, before leaving the USA, under the influence of Polanyi.[71] However, Jones was also a great influence: Finley's 1965 article on technical innovation and economic progress in the ancient world clearly echoes Jones's work on ancient cities, arguing: 'Even in the Roman Empire, the quantitative contribution of trade and manufacture was tiny, their social position low, their future without interest.'[72]

This, according to Finley, made it unattractive to take risks in investment in manufacturing, and thus is one of the reasons why there was not an awful lot of technical development in the ancient world. Contrary to Jones, Finley did also engage directly, and often combatively, with his opponents. Discussing the *terra sigillata* industry, and Rostovtzeff's idea that a decentralization of manufacturing prevented emerging industrial capitalism in Italy from continuing, Finley made no secret of his feelings, and called the theory an 'anachronistic burlesque of the affluent society': according to Finley, the decline of Arezzo and the related emergence of production centres in Gaul and Germany was a meaningless event in a minor trade, without wider economic implications.[73] As far as urban craftsmen and traders are concerned, the core of Finleyan thought already seems to have been present in his 1965 article, and *The Ancient Economy* did not dramatically alter the picture.[74] However, what Finley did add in the book was a link to the German debate of the late nineteenth century through the work of Max Weber and his idea that the ancient city was a centre of consumption, an idea that Weber had taken from Bücher and Rodbertus.[75] This link would be further elaborated in a 1977 article on the historiography of the ancient city, where Finley first explicitly coins the term 'consumer city', and in the 'Further Thoughts' added to the second edition of the *Ancient Economy*.[76]

While a lot has been written in recent years about the debate between 'modernists' and 'primitivists' that followed the publication of Finley's monograph, it may be useful to reiterate the point made by Saller in 2002 that the debate has tended to overemphasize the differences between Rostovtzeff and Frank, on the one side, and Finley and Jones, on the other.[77] Both 'camps' seem diametrically opposed when it came to the general importance of supra-

---

[70] Finley (1973).   [71] See esp. Morris (1999).
[72] Finley (1965: 40). The accompanying footnote refers to Jones (1955).
[73] Finley (1965: 42).   [74] Finley (1973: 125; cf. 138). Cf. Wagner-Hasel (2009: 178–80).
[75] Finley (1973: 125).   [76] Finley (1977; 1985: esp. 191–6).
[77] Saller (2002: esp. 252–6).

regional trade and (export-oriented) manufacturing in the urban economy as a whole. However, Rostovtzeff and Frank appear to have had more nuanced views about the *average* Roman city than their enthusiasm in highlighting trading centres suggest.[78] Finley, in turn, may have had a more nuanced idea about, especially, port cities than *The Ancient Economy* reveals.[79] A second point of apparent difference concerns the role of commerce as a vehicle of social mobility: Frank and Rostovtzeff were much more open to the idea of people gaining socio-economic prominence through their involvement in crafts and trade than Jones and Finley, who saw any scenario other than landowning elites as highly exceptional.[80] Again, however, Frank and Rostovtzeff *did* acknowledge the central role of landed property in the socio-economic status of elites, and Finley did acknowledge that people got wealthy from commerce—just not very many.[81] Moreover, both camps believed that the social position of craftsmen and traders was influenced negatively by the low status of their occupations.[82] Thus, while there were fundamental points of disagreement, it is, on the issue of urban craftsmen and traders, crucial not to overstate the differences between the two camps: part of it comes down to a matter of style and emphasis.

AFTER JONES AND FINLEY

The ideas of Jones and Finley received a mixed response among classical scholars. Despite Hopkins's repeated claim that Finley's model of the ancient economy presented a 'new orthodoxy', this was the case only to a very limited extent.[83] As has been observed by one of us, material specialists who worked with the evidence of ancient economic life on an everyday basis have often been unable to connect their data to the model outlined in *The Ancient Economy*.[84] Partially, this was due to the fact that Finley assigned little, if any, interpretative value to documentary and material evidence; in doing so, he failed to provide archaeologists, epigraphists, and papyrologists with an

---

[78] See, e.g. Rostovtzeff's discussion of the economic basis of cities, culminating in the statement that 'to move large masses of foodstuffs by the land-roads was . . . beyond the resources of smaller and poorer cities', which essentially means that a large majority of cities had to live off their hinterland. Rostovtzeff (1926: 133–8). Cf. Saller (2002: 255).

[79] Finley (1973: 130–1).

[80] Rostovtzeff (1926: 161): 'commerce provided the main sources of wealth in the Roman empire.' Finley (1973: 89): 'the land was the chief source of wealth.' Cf. Saller (2002: 256).

[81] Rostovtzeff (1926: 142–5): many senators were still primarily landowners; wealth aquired by commerce was invested in land; Finley (1973: 59): 'of course there were exceptions'.

[82] Frank (1927: 274); Finley (1973: 41–61).   [83] Hopkins (1978: 47; 1983: pp. xi–xii).

[84] Wilson (2002: 231).

interpretative framework they could use to make sense of their observations.[85] This was in sharp contrast with Rostovtzeff and Frank, who had highlighted the value of epigraphy, archaeology, and papyrology throughout their work. Essentially, substantivist thinking along the lines of Finley and Jones found most fertile ground among generalists, and even there it was not accepted without qualification.[86] Thus, rather than establishing an orthodoxy, the ideas of Jones and Finley sparked debate, especially after the appearance of *The Ancient Economy*, and, for the first time, the epicentre of that debate was in Britain, where scholars until after the Second World War had remained mostly indifferent to the study of economic life in the Roman world.[87] Evidence for urban crafts and traders eventually came to play a key role in debates between 'modernists' and 'primitivists' of the 1980s and 1990s, particularly after Finley's defiant defence of his ideas in the second edition of *The Ancient Economy*.[88] The issue in the debate that is most relevant in the present context is related to the model of the consumer city.

Much more than research in other parts of the world, anglophone scholarship on urban craft production has been dominated by the consumer city debate, which ran from the late 1970s until the early 2000s. It started with Finley's 1977 article on the ancient city, and the response, a year later, by Keith Hopkins, who mostly embraced the model, though assigning a larger role to trade and urban manufacturing than Finley had done.[89] Finley's view that urban manufacturing was essentially petty was a plank of his model of the ancient city as consumer city (or, perhaps, his faith in that model required him to believe that urban craft production had to be insignificant). This involved the assumptions that urban workshops were small and numerically insignificant, that the status of craftsmen was low, that demand for their products was low or, even if it was not, came principally from elite consumption, and that revenue from urban production played no real role in elite portfolios. His views provoked reactions from archaeologists in particular, and, in the debate over the consumer city that raged in the 1980s and 1990s, the scale, nature, and status of urban crafts were a recurrent feature. Initially, archaeologists tended to point to a variety of workshops in different towns to emphasize the vitality of urban production, while ancient historians pointed out that the numbers of identifiable workshops for particular crafts in any one town were few, and minimized the scale of the phenomenon. The textile industry at Pompeii was at the centre of such debate—but, in focusing on the textile industry, the argument

---

[85] Cf., e.g. Finley (1965: 41): 'We are too often victims of that great curse of archaeology, the indestructibility of pots.'

[86] See esp. Hopkins (1978, 1980).

[87] With some obvious exceptions: e.g. Charlesworth (1924) and Warmington (1928).

[88] Finley (1985: esp. 191–6).   [89] Finley (1977); Hopkins (1978: esp. 75).

largely ignored other crafts attested at Pompeii and so failed to assess the scale of the urban productive economy *in toto*.[90]

The most intense stage of the debate took place from the late 1980s onwards, and was decisively shaped through a series of edited volumes that were produced in the United Kingdom in the 1990s and focused specifically on the relation between city and country.[91] More than any other debate discussed in this chapter, the consumer-city debate was predominantly a British affair: while Philippe Leveau had fostered some debate on the issue in France in the 1980s, scholars from Germany and the United States only incidentally got involved.[92] Critics came up with a variety of responses to Finley. In the 1980s there were scholars who rejected the consumer city model, but proposed an alternative model instead, such as Leveau's *cité organisatrice* and Donald Engels's service city.[93] During the 1990s archaeologists were publishing more urban workshops, but usually individually or in small groups, still without really convincing the historians that what they had added up to anything of structural significance in urban economies as a whole. Champions of the consumer city model tried to counter its critics by rephrasing the model, or by adding elements to it. C. R. Whittaker, for example, published in the *Journal of Roman Archaeology* an article entitled 'The Consumer City Revisited: The *vicus* and the City', in which he argued that craft production was confined to small towns, or *vici*, which he saw as essentially rural. This now seems misguided, and may be due to the extensive publication of several small towns in Britain—for example, Water Newton or *Durobrivae*—where the ancient remains were not covered by modern habitation and the evidence for craft production was well recognized in careful excavation. By contrast, many more important ancient cities have remained inhabited, limiting the picture available, and it is only since the early 1990s that the growth of urban rescue archaeology outside Britain, in France, Italy, and Spain, has accumulated a critical mass of information to change the picture.

By the early 2000s, studies of sites such as Sabratha and Timgad had begun to show that there were cities with large numbers of workshops and to point out the difficulties in the survival and recovery of evidence, and the problems of sampling urban areas to assess the distribution and number of workshops, and their overall contribution to the urban economy.[94] The phenomenon of urban production now began to look more significant, even if we might still be wary of replacing the 'consumer city' model with the equally simplistic

---

[90] Moeller (1976); Jongman (1988). See now also Flohr (2013).

[91] Rich and Wallace-Hadrill (1991); Parkins (1997); Parkins and Smith (1998); Mattingly and Salmon (2000). To a lesser extent also Cornell and Lomas (1995).

[92] See esp. Leveau (1985). Obviously, scholars were aware of the model, and several individuals ventured their opinions, but there were no debates going on.

[93] Leveau (1984, 1985); Engels (1990).   [94] Wilson (1999, 2000, 2002).

'producer city'. In the face of this newly assembled evidence, some scholars, like Paul Erdkamp, conceded that cities could easily make substantial money from export-oriented manufacturing, as long as, in the end, all urban consumption was based on revenues from landed property.[95] More generally, a combination of studies that did manage to synthesize evidence for zones of urban production across broad areas of several cities—a new focus on the long-distance Mediterranean connectivity advocated in Horden and Purcell's *The Corrupting Sea*—and general boredom with the consumer city debate led to an adjustment of perspectives. It was increasingly recognized that the terms of the consumer city debate had focused excessively on the idea that a city and its territory formed a cellular self-sufficient unit; instead, a new appreciation of the numbers, sizes, and populations of Roman cities emphasizes that cities must be seen as part of broader economic networks; few Roman cities could be supplied exclusively from their own hinterland, and archaeology suggests that almost none was isolated in this way. More and more scholars came to reject the use of all one-size-fits-all models for explaining the economic role of cities in the Roman world, arguing that the variation between cities was simply too big for such models to be meaningful.[96]

The primary relevance of the consumer city debate for the study of urban crafts and trade is that it encouraged scholars to think harder about urban economies, and to confront evidence with models and vice versa.[97] Both champions and sceptics of the model engaged actively with the material remains of urban workshops and, to a lesser extent, with the epigraphic and papyrological evidence. For example, Michael Fulford used the excavated remains of cities in Roman Britain to argue that these cities indeed were 'parasitical' on the countryside.[98] Andrew Wallace-Hadrill used the evidence of Pompeii to show that Finley's claim that elites were not involved in commerce and manufacturing was problematic.[99] David Mattingly used survey data from Leptiminus to sketch how the economy of this town was much more complex than the consumer city model would allow for.[100] One of the present authors used material remains from Sabratha and Timgad, and a number of other sites, to argue against the idea that these towns depended solely or primarily on agriculture for their income.[101] Such approaches fostered the scholarly emancipation of material evidence for urban crafts, and encouraged a greater focus on understanding the strengths and limitations of both archaeological and textual evidence and how they might affect our ability to construct a picture of ancient craft economies and to draw comparisons with other periods. The assumed contrast between the supposedly productive

---

[95] Erdkamp (2001).   [96] Mattingly (2000); Wilson (2002).
[97] Cf. Wilson (2002: 232).   [98] Fulford (1982); Whittaker (1991: 113).
[99] Wallace-Hadrill (1991).   [100] Mattingly (2000).
[101] Wilson (1999, 2000, 2002).

medieval city and the unproductive classical city was at least in part a product of not comparing like for like: classical written sources tend to treat economic issues only anecdotally, and for the ancient world we lack the bulk of economic documents—letters, accounts, and so on—that medieval historians are used to working with: if one were to compare only the archaeological evidence, one might get the impression of *more* craft production in Roman towns, and sometimes on a larger scale, than in medieval European towns.[102]

The years after the publication of *The Ancient Economy* also saw increased attention paid to craftsmen and traders beyond the issue of the consumer city. John D'Arms responded to Finley's ideas about the social standing of traders with a monograph in which he made a case for the socio-economic independence of traders, and for the respectability of Roman *negotiatores*.[103] In Germany, a special role in the post-Finley discourse was played by the *Münstersche Beiträge zur Antiken Handelsgeschichte* (*MBAH*), a journal founded in the early 1980s by Hans-Joachim Drexhage and Wolfgang Habermann. The *MBAH* was an explicit response to the emerging debate about the Ancient Economy, and was meant to provide a platform for the study of evidence related to ancient economic life.[104] While there is a clear emphasis on epigraphic and papyrological evidence, the journal also published archaeological papers, particularly from provincial Roman archaeologists working on *terra sigillata*.[105] The journal addressed a wide variety of themes. Drexhage himself published extensively on papyrological and epigraphic evidence for individual trades and occupations—with a particular emphasis on the food sector, including papers on cheese, beer, meat, pulses, and *garum*.[106] Other scholars published on other trades, and there are also papers focusing on occupational terminology on a more general level.[107] Another recurring theme concerns transport and its infrastructure, including roads and ports, but also ships, seafaring routes, and tolls.[108] Trade itself is, of course, also a central theme, and it is approached from a variety of directions—including case studies of trade cities or trade routes as well as the study of the geographical spread of certain objects, particularly pottery.[109] The broad focus of the journal and its evidence-oriented emphasis ensured that large amounts of material and textual evidence for craftsmen and traders were integrated into the debate, and its tables of contents give a good impression of the (changing) priorities within the

---

[102] Wilson (2002).   [103] D'Arms (1981).   [104] *MBAH* 1 (1982), 1.

[105] e.g. Raepsaet (1987); Strobel (1987); Berke (1988); Mees (1994); Stuppner (1994); Zaniers (1994); Poblome et al. (1998); Fülle (2000).

[106] H.-J. Drexhage (1993, 1996, 1997a, b, 2002a).

[107] Wine: e.g. Ruffing (2001); brokers: Kudlien (1997); occupational terminology: e.g. Kneissl (1983); Ruffing (2002); H.-J. Drexhage (2002b, 2004).

[108] Roads: Schneider (1982); ports: Habermann (1982); Sidebotham (1986); Matei (1989); Fellmeth (1991); tolls: H.-J. Drexhage (1982); Habermann (1990); H.-J. Drexhage (1994); ships: Konen (2001); seafaring: Holtheide (1982); Bounegru (1984).

[109] Trade, e.g. R. Drexhage (1982); H.-J. Drexhage (1983); Schleich (1983, 1984); Monfort (1999); Henning (2001). On *terra sigillata*, see n. 105.

field. Originating from the late 1970s Finley debate, the *MBAH* quickly came to play a key role in German discourse on Roman urban crafts and trade—as its successor, the *Marburger Beiträge*, still does.

The question remains, however, why it was precisely Finley's *The Ancient Economy* in 1973 that unleashed such a vibrant debate—after all, especially as far as craftsmen and traders are concerned, the core arguments were already on the table in the 1950s and 1960s. Jones and Finley did not publish their earlier ideas in places that were widely read by classical scholars, but this can hardly have been the only reason. Arguably, other developments in the field of classical studies (in the widest sense of the word) played a much more fundamental role in the impact of *The Ancient Economy*. In the first place, as will be discussed below, classical studies had not remained completely indifferent to the upsurge of interest in social history that characterized the later 1960s and the 1970s in the humanities.[110] Second, but equally importantly, the 1960s and 1970s saw a remarkable increase in archaeological activity in Europe and Britain: many urban sites from the Roman north-western provinces were thoroughly investigated for the first time, while other sites were reinvestigated.[111] While most projects did not have a primarily economic focus, the nature of these cities, and the absence of large urban monuments, meant that a lot of the evidence that was dug up was better able to tell stories about manufacturing and trade than about monumental architecture, and this evidence was increasingly being analysed.[112] In a way, one should thus see *The Ancient Economy*, not as *causing* the debate, but rather as providing the ideal occasion for a debate that was waiting to happen anyway, though it obviously helped that Finley went in a radically opposite direction from many of his contemporary scholars.

FROM ECONOMY TO SOCIETY AND CULTURE

Besides fuelling the vibrant debate on the ancient economy, the turn towards social history in the last decades of the twentieth century also fostered a significant scholarly engagement with the social and cultural aspects of urban crafts and trade—raising many issues that had been almost completely unexplored from the early twentieth century until the late 1960s.[113]

---

[110] See esp. Treggiari (1975b); key example of this trend is Alföldy (1975).

[111] Cf. Burnham and Wacher (1990: 3). In Germany, excavations at, e.g. Xanten were intensified in the 1970s. Similar developments took place elsewhere in Europe. Examples include the excavations at Alésia, Autun, and Kaiseraugst. See, e.g. Mangin (1981); Chardron-Picault and Pernot (1999); *Forschungen in Augst* 1– (1977–).

[112] See, e.g. Strong and Brown (1978).

[113] Giving an overview of scholarship on Roman social history, Treggiari (1975b) lists only the works by Loane (1938) and Maxey (1938) on occupations, and the work of Waltzing

An important strand of research that emerges in this period focuses on the epigraphic and iconographic representation of craftsmen and traders in, especially, the city of Rome. A key role in this debate was played by the work of Susan Treggiari, who, in the late 1970s, published a series of articles on occupations in Rome, focusing on domestic jobs in the household of Livia, on female labour in the Roman urban economy, and on urban labour in Rome.[114] Treggiari's work, with its strong focus on gender and (legal) status, would set a model for several later approaches, and particularly for Sandra Joshel's important monograph on work, identity, and legal status in Rome, which uses the epigraphic evidence from Rome to discuss the role of work and legal status in constructing social identity.[115] Treggiari also stood at the start of a tradition that uses epigraphic and iconographic evidence to study the role of women in urban crafts and trade; important here is also the work on textile crafts done by Suzanne Dixon and Lena Larsson Lovén.[116] Further, in her important book on working women in Ostia, Natalie Kampen integrated the work of Treggiari on female labour with iconographic representations of women at work.[117]

The works of Kampen and Larsson Lovén, however, are also related to a second development of the 1970s and 1980s: the rediscovery of the iconography of crafts and trade. This development was part of a broader trend in Roman art history to invest in understanding forms of art produced by or for people from the strata below the imperial elite—a trend exemplified by, among others, the work of Paul Zanker on freedman reliefs.[118] The iconography of crafts and trade had been largely neglected since Jahn and Gummerus, but achieved new prominence through the work of Kampen and, particularly, through that of Gerhard Zimmer, a student of Paul Zanker at Munich who catalogued and (re)studied depictions of everyday work from Italy and Gaul.[119] Zimmer's *Römische Berufsdarstellungen* laid an indispensable foundation for the more interpretative work on the iconographic representation of crafts that emerged from the late 1980s onwards. Interestingly, the study of the iconography of crafts and trade also attracted the attention of scholars specializing in Roman art. Relying heavily on the work of both Zimmer and Kampen, Eve d'Ambra made a detailed study of two tombs at Ostia that had been found with reliefs depicting craftsmen at work.[120] Lauren Hackworth Petersen made a

---

(1895–6) and De Robertis (1938) on *collegia* as dealing specifically with craftsmen and traders. Though Treggiari omits several publications, this gives a good idea of the state of the field at that point.

[114] Treggiari (1975a, 1976, 1979, 1980).
[115] Joshel (1992; on Treggiari, see esp. pp. 20–3).
[116] Dixon (2001); Larsson Lovén (2002). See also Larsson Lovén, Chapter 9, this volume.
[117] Kampen (1981, 1985). On Treggiari, see esp. Kampen (1981: 108 n. 5).
[118] Zanker (1975). Fundamental was Bianchi Bandinelli (1967).
[119] Zimmer (1982, 1985).   [120] D'Ambra (1988).

detailed study of the tomb of Eurysaces as part of her work on 'freedman art'.[121] John Clarke devoted a chapter in his book on Roman popular art to the social and cultural meaning of iconographic representations of everyday work.[122] Arguably, this development contributed significantly to the integration of the study of craftsmen and traders into mainstream classical scholarship.

A development of the 1980s and 1990s was a renewed interest in the study of Roman professional associations, especially focusing on Roman Italy and Asia Minor. For Italy, it all started with the prosopographical work of Royden on magistrates of the professional *collegia*, and the work of John Patterson on the social roles of *collegia*.[123] Important, too, was the work of Beate Bollmann on the *scholae* used by professional associations—it provided an essential link between the epigraphic debate on *collegia* and the emerging archaeological debate about the dynamics of urban space.[124] After the turn of the millennium, the debate was enriched by some studies on specific *collegia*, such as DeLaine's work on the *Fabri Tignarii* at Ostia, and the monograph of Jinyu Liu on the *collegia centonariorum*.[125] Ground-breaking for the Roman east was the monograph by Onno van Nijf on the role of professional associations in civic life, but it was quickly followed by two other monographs.[126] Imogen Dittmann-Schöne published a monograph on the evidence from Asia Minor, while Carola Zimmermann made a comparative effort, studying the associations for the entire Greek-speaking east, including Egypt.[127] While these works focus on a variety of directions, they all have in common that the primary emphasis is on the *social* role of professional associations—which is also the issue about which the evidence is most explicit. The (disputed) economic role of *collegia* has come to the fore only towards the end of the first decade of the new millennium.[128]

A final development of the late twentieth century that deserves to be highlighted here concerns what is sometimes referred to as the 'spatial turn' that, from the early 1990s onwards, began to transform approaches to urban space in the Roman world, and fostered scholars to think about the spatial context of crafts and trade, and their interaction with the urban environment. A leading role in this was played by Ray Laurence and his book on the relation between space and society in Roman Pompeii.[129] Laurence argued that various uses of space, including retail and manufacturing, in pre-modern cities were intermingled, and showed how this worked out in practice for several sectors

---

[121] Petersen (2003; 2006: 84–120).   [122] Clarke (2003).

[123] Royden (1988, 1989); Patterson (1993, 1994; cf. 2006: 252–63).

[124] Bollmann (1998). The link between urban space and collegiate life was further elaborated for Ostia by Stöger (2011).

[125] DeLaine (2003); Liu (2009); see also Liu (2008).   [126] Van Nijf (1997).

[127] Dittmann-Schöne (2001); Zimmermann (2002).   [128] See, e.g. Venticinque (2009).

[129] Laurence (1994). Raper (1977) and La Torre (1988) had also discussed the economic geography of Pompeii but without an explicit spatial interest.

of the Pompeian economy: shops and workshops were to be found directly next to or even associated with residential complexes, and not spatially restricted to certain quarters of the city. This picture was subsequently elaborated and refined by several others, including Wallace Hadrill, Damian Robinson, and one of the present authors.[130] Outside Pompeii, Penelope Goodman has analysed the position of crafts in the urban periphery in Italy and Gaul.[131] Related to this is a more text-oriented discourse on the sensory impact of certain potentially 'dirty' crafts on their urban environment.[132]

DISCUSSION

This has, of course, been only a limited survey, which has tried to sketch, very roughly, some broad developments in the study of Roman craftsmen and traders; there is a broad variety of debates about specific crafts and trades that could not be addressed here, and there are important issues related to the history of crafts and trade that have barely been touched upon, including the debates about (slave) labour and technology. Important European research traditions have been mentioned only in passing, and only a couple of these will be dealt with elsewhere in this volume. Nevertheless, some general points deserve to be made.

First, modern discussions of the debate about the ancient economy have put a lot of emphasis on Rostovtzeff and Finley, who are commonly seen as the almost proverbial representatives of the two 'camps' in the debate about the ancient economy. This is obviously a gross oversimplification. The merit of either of those two scholars is obvious and need not be doubted, but, in terms of moving the debate forward, other scholars seem to have been equally or more important—both Rostovtzeff and Finley stand at the end, rather than at the start, of a development. As far as the twentieth century is concerned, three scholars must be mentioned. In the first place, one should not underestimate the influence of Eduard Meyer on the thinking and the career of both Frank and Rostovtzeff. Meyer was a key figure who, through his network, had a profound impact on the debate, even if he did not himself publish a lot that has stood the test of time. Second, it may be suggested that the key figure in the decades between 1910 and 1940 was very much Frank, and not Rostovtzeff. Not only did Frank, through his publications in the 1910s, lay down a solid basis on which Rostovtzeff could build, but he also continued feeding the discourse on the Roman economy long after Rostovtzeff had moved on to greener pastures. Third, it is A. H. M. Jones who, much more than Finley,

---

[130] Robinson (2005); Flohr (2007, 2012).   [131] Goodman (2007: 105–18).
[132] Esp. fulling. Cf. Bradley (2002); Kudlien (2002). See also Papi (2002); Béal (2002).

must be seen as the protagonist of the primitivist reaction—not so much because he hired Finley in Cambridge, but because, especially regarding urban crafts and trade, he was the first to write down many of the ideas that, later on, would be primarily associated with Finley. Finley, at least partially, reaped what Jones had sown, and the legacy of his work profited immensely from the fact that he published at a time when there was a substantial upsurge of interest in the social and economic history of the ancient world.

A second point concerns the historical development of the debate. There seem to be three key phases. First, there is the late nineteenth century, which saw the emergence of a large canon of easily accessible and well-known evidence for urban crafts and trade, and, independently of that, the development of several models for the history of urban societies. From the 1890s onwards, the German debate about Rodbertus's idea of the *Oikenwirtschaft* fostered classical scholars to analyse the economic background of the evidence for crafts and trade, which in the 1920s and 1930s would culminate in the works of Frank and Rostovtzeff. Intellectually, this period saw a shift from cataloguing the evidence for manufacturing and trade to actually using it for discussing aspects of economic history. It may be argued that this second phase was quite decisively influenced by the First World War, the outcome of which completely changed the social dynamics of the debate: essentially, it ended a flourishing German scholarly tradition, and caused the geographic focus of the debate to shift from Europe to North America, where it stayed until well after the Second World War. The third phase began in the late 1960s, when classical scholars started to develop an interest in the more mundane aspects of everyday life. Both the debate about *The Ancient Economy* and the other developments in the field are essentially a product of this trend. What sets this phase apart from the preceding phase is the increased prominence of questions pertaining to the realm of social and cultural history. This has made scholarly discourse about craftsmen and traders considerably more complex and multifaceted, and it has put new questions on the agenda. Most of the old questions, however, have not completely disappeared.

Finally, there is the question as to what moved the debate forward. In this respect one cannot help but noticing the similarity between the 'German' debate of the 1890s and 1900s, and the 'British' debate of the 1980s and 1990s. In both cases, the debate was preceded by a long build-up in which new sets of evidence were added to the field: the upsurge in Roman provincial archaeology of the 1960s and 1970s mirrors the systematic publication of the first epigraphic corpora in the 1870s and 1880s. Moreover, in both cases, the developments in evidence were paralleled by theoretical debates taking place among generalists outside or in the margins of classical studies, which, at some point, gained prominence and provoked a (dismissive) response by specialists, who then began to explore the possibilities of the new evidence to prove the theoretical models wrong. Rodbertus and Bücher played a role that is to some extent similar to that played by Jones and Finley eighty years later, though the latter two of course were operating from within the field of classical studies. In both cases, there also seems to have been a clear political element that motivated the response by specialists: if Meyer felt that it was essential for the future of classical studies to prove the relevance of ancient economies to the modern world, many of the epigraphists, papyrologists, and archaeologists who took on Finley also implicitly or, occasionally, explicitly opposed the way in which his approach to the ancient economy marginalized epigraphic, documentary, and material evidence in favour of the literary canon. On this level, it is also obvious that the specialists, in both cases, got their way: in the 1890s as well as in the 1980s, the most easily observable outcome of the debate was a markedly increased integration of new data sets into the debate about Roman urban craftsmen and traders.

REFERENCES

Alföldy, G. (1975). *Römische Sozialgeschichte.* Wiesbaden.

Audring, G. (2000). *Gelehrtenalltag: Der Briefwechsel zwischen Eduard Meyer und Georg Wissowa (1890–1927).* Hildesheim.

Ballu, A. (1897). *Les ruines de Timgad (antique Thamugadi).* Paris.

Béal, J.-C. (2002). 'L'artisanat et la ville: Relecture de quelques textes', in J. C. Béal and J. C. Goyon (eds), *Les artisans dans la ville antique.* Paris, 5–14.

Beloch, J. (1899). 'Die Grossindustrie im Altertum', *Zeitschrift für Sozialwissenschaft* 2: 18–26.

Berke, S. (1988). 'Zum Export mittelgallischer und früher Rheinzaberner Terra Sigillata in das Barbaricum nördlich der mittleren Donau', *MBAH* 7/1: 46–61.

Bianchi Bandinelli, R. (1967). 'Arte Plebea', *Dialoghi di Archeologia* 1: 7–19.

Blümner, H. (1869). *Die gewerbliche Thätigkeit der Völker des klassischen Alterthums.* Leipzig.

Blümner, H. (1875–84). *Technologie und Terminologie der Gewerbe und Künste bei Griechen und Römern.* Leipzig.

Bollmann, B. (1998). *Römische Vereinshäuser. Untersuchungen zu den Scholae der römischen Berufs-, Kult- und Augustalen-Kollegien in Italien.* Mainz.

Bounegru, O. (1984). 'Beiträge zur Handelsschiffart im westlichen Schwarzen Meer in hellenistischer und römischer Zeit', *MBAH* 3/2: 1–17.

Bradley, M. (2002). '"It all comes out in the wash": Looking harder at the Roman *fullonica*', *JRA* 15: 21–44.

Brewer, A. (2008). 'Adam Smith's Stages of History', Bristol University Department of Economics Discussion Papers 08/601.

Brewster, E. (1917). *Roman Craftsmen and Tradesmen of the Early Empire.* Menasha, WI.

Brewster, E. (1927). 'A Weaver of Oxyrhynchus: Sketch of a Humble Life in Roman Egypt', *Transactions and Proceedings of the American Philological Association* 58: 132–54.

Brewster, E. (1931). 'A Weaver's Life in Oxyrhynchus: His Status in the Community', in G. D. Hadzsits (ed.), *Classical Studies in Honor of John C. Rolfe*. Philadelphia, 19–45.

Bruneau, P., and Ducat, J. (1966). *Guide de Délos*. 2nd edn. Paris.

Brunt, P. A. (2004). 'Jones, Arnold Hugh Martin', in C. Matthew, B. Harrison, and L. Goldman (eds), *Oxford Dictionary of National Biography*. Oxford.

Bücher, K. (1893). *Die Entstehung der Volkswirtschaft*. Tübingen.

Burnham, B., and Wacher, J. (1990). *The 'Small Towns' of Roman Britain*. London.

Calder, W. M., and Demandt, A. (1990) (eds). *Eduard Meyer: Leben und Leistung eines Universalhistorikers*. Leiden.

Chambers, M. (1990). 'The "Most Eminent Living Historian: The One Final Authority": Meyer in America', in Calder and Demandt (1990), 97–131.

Chamonard, J. (1922). *Exploration archéologique de Délos—Le Quartier du théatre*. Paris.

Chardron-Picault, P., and Pernot, M. (1999). *Un quartier antique d'artisanat métal lurgique à Autun: Le Site du Lycée militaire*. Paris.

Charlesworth, M. P. (1924). *Trade Routes and Commerce of the Roman Empire*. Cambridge.

Christ, K. (1972). *Von Gibbon zu Rostovtzeff: Leben und Werk führender Althistoriker der Neuzeit*. Darmstadt.

Clarke, J. (2003). *Art in the Lives of Ordinary Romans*. Berkeley.

Cornell, T., and Lomas, K. (1995) (eds). *Urban Society in Roman Italy*. London.

D'Ambra, E. (1988). 'A Myth for a Smith: A Meleager Sarcophagus from a Tomb in Ostia', *American Journal of Archaeology* 92/1: 85–99.

Daremberg, C., and Saglio, E. (1873) (eds). *Dictionnaire des antiquités grecques et romaines*. Paris.

D'Arms, J. (1981). *Commerce and Social Standing in Ancient Rome*. Cambridge, MA.

Dechelette, J. (1904). *Les Vases céramiques ornés de la Gaule romaine (Narbonnaise, Aquitaine, Lyonnaise)*. Paris.

DeLaine, J. (2003). *The Builders of Roman Ostia: Organisation, Status and Society*. Madrid.

De Robertis, F. M. (1938). *Il diritto associativo romano dai collegi della repubblica alle corporazioni del basso impero*. Bari.

De Ruggiero, E. (1895–). *Dizionario epigrafico di antichità romane*. Rome.

Dissen, M. (2009). *Römische Kollegien und deutsche Geschichtswissenschaft im 19. und 20. Jahrhundert* (Historia: Einzelschriften 209). Stuttgart.

Dittmann-Schöne, I. (2001). *Die Berufsvereine in den Städten des kaiserzeitlichen Kleinasiens*. Regensburg.

Dixon, S. (2001). 'How do you Count them if they're not there? New Perspectives on Roman Cloth Production', *Opuscula Romana* 25–6: 7–17.

Dragendorff, H. (1895). 'Terra sigillata: Ein Beitrag zur Geschichte der griechischen und römischen Keramik', *BJ* 96: 18–155.

Drexhage, H.-J. (1982). 'Beitrag zum Binnenhandel im römischen Ägypten aufgrund der Torzolquittungen und Zollhausabrechnungen des Faijum', *MBAH* 1/1: 61–84.

Drexhage, H.-J. (1983). 'Die Expositio totius mundi et gentium: Eine Handelsgeographie aus dem 4. Jahrhundert n. Chr.', *MBAH* 2/1: 3–41.

Drexhage, H.-J. (1993). 'Garum und Garumhandel im Römischen und spätantiken Ägypten', *MBAH* 12/1: 27–54.

Drexhage, H.-J. (1994). 'Einflüsse des Zollwesens auf den Warenverkehr im römischen Reich - handelshemmend oder handelsförderend', *MBAH* 13/2: 1–15.

Drexhage, H.-J. (1996). 'Der Handel, die Produktion und der Verzehr von Käse nach den griechischen Papyri und Ostraka', *MBAH* 15/2: 33–41.

Drexhage, H.-J. (1997a). 'Bierproduzenten und Bierhändler in der papyrologischen Überlieferung', *MBAH* 16/2: 32–9.

Drexhage, H.-J. (1997b). 'Einige Bemerkungen zu Fleischverarbeitung und Fleischvertrieb nach den griechischen Papyri und Ostraka vom 3. Jh. v. bis zum 7. Jh. n. Chr.', *MBAH* 16/2: 97–111.

Drexhage, H.-J. (2002a). 'Der erebinthas namens Kosmas und sein Produkt: Zum Anbau und Vertrib von Kichererbsen nach dem papyrologischen Befund', *MBAH* 21/2: 10–23.

Drexhage, H.-J. (2002b). 'Zum letzten Mal zu den Komposita mit -poles?! Einige Bemerkungen zur literarischen Überlieferung', *MBAH* 21/2: 74–89.

Drexhage, H.-J. (2004). 'Zu den Berufsbezeichnungen mit dem Suffix -âs in der literarischen, papyrologischen und epigraphischen Überlieferung', *MBAH* 23/1: 18–40.

Drexhage, R. (1982). 'Der Handel Palmyras in römischer Zeit', *MBAH* 1/1: 17–34.

Dyer, T. H. (1867). *Pompeii: Its History, Buildings, and Antiquities*. London: Bell and Daldy.

Dyer, T. H. (1868). *Pompeii: Its History, Buildings, and Antiquities*. 2nd edn. London.

Dyer, T. H. (1871). *Pompeii: Its History, Buildings, and Antiquities*. 3rd edn. London.

Engels, D. (1990). *Roman Corinth: An Alternative Model for the Classical City*. Chicago.

Erdkamp, P. P. M. (2001). 'Beyond the Limits of the Consumer City', *Historia: Zeitschrift für Alte Geschichte* 50: 332–56.

Ernesti, J. A. (1737). *De negotiatoribus Romanis diputatiuncula*. Leipzig.

Espérandieu, E. (1907–). *Recueil général des bas-reliefs de la Gaule romaine*. Paris.

Fellmeth, U. (1991). 'Die Häfen von Ostia und ihre wirtschaftliche Bedeutung für die Stadt Rom', *MBAH* 10/1: 1–32.

Finley, M. I. (1965). 'Technical Innovation and Economic Progress in the Ancient World', *Economic History Review* 18/1: 29–45.

Finley, M. I. (1973). *The Ancient Economy*. Berkeley.

Finley, M. I. (1977). 'The Ancient City: From Fustel de Coulanges to Max Weber and Beyond', *Comparative Studies in Society and History* 19: 305–27.

Finley, M. I. (1985). *The Ancient Economy*. 2nd edn. London.

Flohr, M. (2007). 'Nec quicquam ingenuum habere potest officina? Spatial Contexts of Urban Production at Pompeii, AD 79', *BABesch* 82/1: 129–48.

Flohr, M. (2012). 'Working and Living under One Roof: Workshops in Pompeian Atrium Houses', in A. Anguissola (ed.), *Privata Luxuria: Towards an Archaeology of Intimacy: Pompeii and Beyond*. Munich, 51–72.

Flohr, M. (2013). 'The Textile Economy of Pompeii', *JRA* 26/1: 53–78.

Frank, T. (1910). 'Commercialism and Roman Territorial Expansion', *Classical Journal* 5/3: 99–110.

Frank, T. (1914). *Roman Imperialism*. New York.

Frank, T. (1918). 'The Economic Life of an Ancient City', *Classical Philology* 13/3: 225–40.

Frank, T. (1920). *An Economic History of Rome to the End of the Republic*. Baltimore.

Frank, T. (1927). *An Economic History of Rome*. New York.

Frank, T. (1933). *An Economic Survey of Ancient Rome*, i. *Rome and Italy of the Republic*. Baltimore.

Frank, T. (ed.) (1937). *An Economic Survey of Ancient Rome*, iii. *Britain, Spain, Sicily, Gaul*. New Jersey.

Frank, T. (ed.) (1938). *An Economic Survey of Ancient Rome*, iv. *Roman Africa; Roman Syria; Roman Greece; Roman Asia*. Baltimore.

Frank, T. (1940). *An Economic Survey of Ancient Rome*, v. *Rome and Italy of the Empire*. Baltimore.

Fülle, G. (2000). 'Die Organisation der Terra sigillata-Herstellung in La Graufesenque: Die Töpfergraffiti', *MBAH* 19/2: 62–98.

Fulford, M. (1982). 'Town and Country in Roman Britain—a Parasitical Relationship', in D. Miles (ed.), *The Romano-British Countryside: Studies in Rural Settlement and Economy*, part 2 (BAR British Series 103). Oxford, 403–19.

Gell, W. (1834). *Pompeiana: The Topography, Edifices and Ornaments of Pompeii: The Result of Excavations since 1819*. London.

Goodman, P. (2007). *The Roman City and its Periphery: From Rome to Gaul*. London.

Gummerus, H. (1906). *Der römische Gutsbetrieb als wirtschaftlicher Organismus nach den Werken des Cato, Varro und Columella*. Leipzig.

Gummerus, H. (1913). 'Darstellungen aus dem Handwerk auf römischen Grab- und Votivsteinen in Italien', *Jahrbuch des Deutschen Archäologischen Instituts* 28: 63–126.

Gummerus, H. (1915). 'Die römische Industrie: Wirtschaftliche Untersuchungen. Bd I. Das Goldschmied- und Juweliersgewerbe', *Klio: Beiträge zur alten Geschichte* 14: 129–89.

Gummerus, H. (1916). 'Industrie und Handel bei den Römern', in G. Wissowa and W. Kroll (eds), *Paulys Real-Encyclopädie der Classischen Altertumswissenschaft: Neue Bearbeitung*. Stuttgart, 1439–535.

Habermann, W. (1982). 'Ostia, Getreidehandelshafen Roms', *MBAH* 1/1: 35–60.

Habermann, W. (1990). 'Statistische Datenanalyse an den Zolldokumenten des Arsinoites aus römischer Zeit', *MBAH* 9/1: 50–85.

Harris, W. V. (2013). *Moses Finley and Politics*. Brill.

Hatzfeld, J. (1919). *Les Trafiquants italiens dans l'Orient hellenique*. Paris.

Henning, D. (2001). 'Die antike Seehandelsroute um Kap Malea', *MBAH* 20/1: 23–37.

Hobsbawm, E. (ed.) (1964). *Karl Marx, Pre-Capitalist Economic Formations*. London.

Hoffmeister, K. (1899). *Die Wirtschaftliche Entwicklung Roms: Eine sozialpolitische Studie*. Vienna.

Holtheide, B. (1982). 'Zum privaten Seenhandel im östlichen Mittelmeer, 1.–3. Jh. n. Chr.', *MBAH* 1/2: 3–12.

Hopkins, K. (1978). 'Economic Growth and Towns in Classical Antiquity', in P. Abrams and E. Wrigley (eds), *Towns in Societies: Essays in Economic History and Historical Sociology*. Cambridge, 35–78.

Hopkins, K. (1980). 'Taxes and Trade in the Roman Empire', *JRS* 70: 101–25.

Hopkins, K. (1983). 'Introduction', in P. Garnsey, K. Hopkins, and C. R. Whittaker (eds), *Trade in the Ancient Economy*. London.

Hume, D. (ed.) (1752). *Political Discourses*. Edinburgh.

Jahn, O. (1861). 'Darstellungen antiker Reliefs, welche sich auf Handwerk und Handelsverkehr beziehen', *Berichte über die Verhandlungen der Königlich Sächsischen Gesellschaft der Wissenschaften zu Leipzig. Philologisch-Historische Classe* 13: 291–374.

Jahn, O. (1868). 'Ueber Darstellungen des Handwerks und Handelsverkehrs auf Antiken Wandgemälde', *Abhandlungen der Philologisch-Historischen Klasse der Königlich-Sächsischen Gesellschaft der Wissenschaften* 5/4: 266–318.

Johnson, A. C. (1936). *Roman Egypt to the Reign of Diocletian* (= T. Frank (ed.), *An Economic Survey of Ancient Rome*, ii). Baltimore.

Jones, A. H. M. (1940). *The Greek City from Alexander to Justinian*. Oxford.

Jones, A. H. M. (1948). *Ancient Economic History*. London.

Jones, A. H. M. (1955). 'The Economic Life of the Towns of the Roman Empire', *Recueils de la Société Jean Bodin pour l'Histoire Comparative des Institutions* 7: 161–92.

Jongman, W. (1988). *The Economy and Society of Pompeii*. Amsterdam: Gieben.

Joshel, S. R. (1992). *Work, Identity and Legal Status at Rome*. Norman, OK, and London.

Kampen, N. (1981). *Image and Status: Roman Working Women in Ostia*. Berlin.

Kampen, N. (1985). 'Römische Straßenhändlerinnen: Geschlecht und Sozialstatus', *Antike Welt* 16/4: 23–42.

Kneissl, P. (1983). 'Mercator–negotiator: Römische Geschäftsleute und die Terminologie ihrer Berufe', *MBAH* 2/1: 73–90.

Konen, H. (2001). 'Die Schiffsbauer und Werften in den antiken Häfen von Ostia und Portus', *MBAH* 20/2: 1–36.

Kudlien, F. (1997). 'Der antike Makler—ein verleugneter Beruf', *MBAH* 16/1: 67–84.

Kudlien, F. (2002). 'P. Patulcius L.f., Walker und Probulos um späthellenistischen Magnesia', *Laverna: Beiträge zur Wirtschafts- und Sozialgeschichte der alten Welt* 13: 56–68.

Kuhn, G. B. (1910). *De opificum Romanorum condicione privata quaestiones*. Halle.

La Torre, G. (1988). 'Gli impianti commerciali ed artigiani nel tessuto urbano di Pompei', in L. Dell'Orto (ed.), *Pompei, l'informatica al servizio di una città antica*. Rome, 73–102.

Larsson Lovén, L. (2002). *The Imagery of Textile Making: Gender and Status in the Funerary Iconography of Textile Manufacture in Roman Italy and Gaul*. Göteborg.

Laurence, R. (1994). *Roman Pompeii—Space and Society*. London.

Leveau, P. (1984). *Caesarea de Maurétanie: Une ville romaine et ses campagnes*. Rome.

Leveau, P. (ed.) (1985). *L'Origine des richesses dépensées dans la ville antique*. Aix-en-Provence.

Liebenam, W. (1890). *Zur Geschichte und Organisation des römischen Vereinswesens: 3 Untersuchungen*. Leipzig.

Liu, J. (2008). 'Pompeii and Collegia: A New Appraisal of the Evidence', *Ancient History Bulletin* 22: 53–70.

Liu, J. (2009). *Collegia Centonariorum: The Guilds of Textile Dealers in the Roman West*. Leiden and Boston.

Loane, H. J. (1938). *Industry and Commerce of the City of Rome*. Baltimore.

Mangin, M. (1981). *Un quartier de commerçants et d'artisans d'Alésia: Contribution à l'histoire de l'habitat urbain en Gaule*. Paris.

Marquardt, J. (1882). *Das Privatleben der Römer*. II: *Erwerb und Unterhaltung*. Leipzig.

Marx, K., and Engels, F. (1932). *Die Deutsche Ideologie*. Berlin.

Matei, C. (1989). 'Notes on the Activity in the Port of Ancient Tomis', *MBAH* 8/1: 39–55.

Mattingly, D. J. (2000). 'Leptiminus (Tunisia). A "Producer" City?', in Mattingly and Salmon (2000), 66–89.

Mattingly, D. J., and Salmon, J. (eds) (2000). *Economies beyond Agriculture in the Classical World*. London.

Mau, A. (1900). *Pompeji in Leben und Kunst*. Leipzig.

Mau, A., and Kelsey, F. W. (1899). *Pompeii: Its Life and Art*. London.

Maué, H. (1886). *Die Vereine der fabri, centonarii und dendrophori im römischen Reich: Die Natur ihres Handwerks und ihre sacralen Beziehungen*. Frankfurt am Main.

Maxey, M. (1938). *Occupations of the Lower Classes in Roman Society as Seen in Justinian's Digest*. Chicago.

Meek, R. L. et al. (eds) (1978). *Adam Smith: Lectures on Jurisprudence*. Oxford.

Mees, A. W. (1994). 'Datierung und Vertrieb von reliefverzierten Sigillaten aus Banassac', *MBAH* 13/2: 60–9.

Meiggs, R. (1970). 'Obituary: Arnold Hugh Martin Jones', *JRS* 60: 186–7.

Meyer, E. (1895). 'Die wirtschaftliche Entwicklung des Altertums', *Jahrbücher für Nationalökonomie und Statistik*.

Meyer, E. (ed.) (1910). *Kleine Schriften zur geschichtstheorie und zur Wirtschaftlichen und politischen Geschichte des Altertums*. Halle.

Moeller, W. O. (1976). *The Wool Trade of Ancient Pompeii*. Leiden.

Momigliano, A. (1950). 'Ancient History and the Antiquarian', *Journal of the Warburg and Courtauld Institutes* 13/3–4: 285–315.

Mommsen, T. (1843). *De collegiis et sodaliciis Romanorum*. Kiel.

Monfort, C. C. (1999). 'The Nature of the Roman Trade: An Archaeological Perspective', *MBAH* 18/2: 87–114.

Morley, N. (1998). 'Political Economy and Classical Antiquity', *Journal of the History of Ideas* 26: 95–114.

Morley, N. (2004). *Theories, Models and Concepts in Ancient History*. London.

Morris, I. (1999). 'Foreword to the Updated Edition', in M. I. Finley, *The Ancient Economy*, 3rd edn. Los Angeles, pp. ix–xxxvi.

Olivanti, P. (2001). 'Les Fouilles d'Ostie de Vaglieri à nos jours', in J. P. Descoeudres (ed.), *Ostia: Port et porte de la Rome antique*. Geneva, 56–65.

Overbeek, A. (2005). 'Realistische Geschiedschrijving. Theodor Mommsen's "Römische Geschichte"'. Unpublished Dissertation. Groningen.

Overbeck, J. (1856). *Pompeji in seinen Gebäuden, Alterthümern und Kunstwerken: Für Kunst- und Alterthumsfreunde*. Leipzig.

Overbeck, J. (1866). *Pompeji in seinen Gebäuden, Alterthümern und Kunstwerken: Für Kunst- und Alterthumsfreunde*. 2nd edn. Leipzig.

Overbeck, J. (1875). *Pompeji in seinen Gebäuden, Alterthümern und Kunstwerken: Für Kunst- und Alterthumsfreunde.* 3rd edn. Leipzig.

Overbeck, J., and Mau, A. (1884). *Pompeji in seinen Gebäuden, Alterthümern und Kunstwerken.* 4th edn. Leipzig.

Papi, E. (2002). 'La Turba inpia: Artigiani e commecianti del Foro Romano e dintorni (I sec. a.C.-64 d.C.)', *JRA* 15/1: 45–62.

Parkins, H. M. (ed.) (1997). *Roman Urbanism: Beyond the Consumer City.* London.

Parkins, H. M., and Smith, C. (eds) (1998). *Trade, Traders and the Ancient City.* London.

Patterson, J. (1993). 'Patronage, Collegia and Burial in Imperial Rome', in S. Bassett (ed.), *Death in Towns. 100–1600.* Leicester, 15–27.

Patterson, J. (1994). 'The Collegia and the Transformation of the Towns of Italy in the Second Century AD', in *L'Italie d'Auguste à Dioclétien: Actes du colloque international organisé par l'École française de Rome.* Rome, 227–38.

Patterson, J. (2006). *Landscapes and Cities: Rural Settlement and Civic Transformation in Early Imperial Italy.* Oxford.

Perry, J. (2006). *The Roman Collegia: The Modern Evolution of an Ancient Concept.* Leiden.

Pesando, F., and Guidobaldi, M.-P. (2006). *Pompei Oplontis Ercolano Stabiae.* Rome.

Petersen, L. H. (2003). 'The Baker, his Tomb, his Wife, and her Breadbasket: The Monument of Eurysaces in Rome', *Art Bulletin* 85/2: 230–57.

Petersen, L. H. (2006). *The Freedman in Roman Art and Art History.* New York.

Poblome, J., Degryse, P., Librecht, I., and Waelkens, M. (1998). 'Sagalassos Red Slip Ware: The Organization of a Manufactory', *MBAH* 17/2: 52–64.

Raepsaet, G. (1987). 'Aspects de l'organisation du commerce de la céramique sigillée dans le Nord de la Gaule au IIe siècle de notre ère, 1. Les données matérielles', *MBAH* 6/2: 1–29.

Raper, R. (1977). 'The Analysis of the Urban Structure of Pompeii: A Sociological Examination of Land Use (Semi-Micro)', in D. Clarke (ed.), *Spatial Archaeology.* London, 189–221.

Rebenich, S. (2002). *Theodor Mommsen: Eine Biographie.* Munich.

Reibig, A. (2001). 'The Bücher–Meyer Controversy: The Nature of the Ancient Economy in Modern Ideology'. Unpublished Dissertation. Glasgow.

Reubel, G. (1912). *Römische Töpfer in Rheinzabern: Ein Beitrag zur Geschichte der verzierten Terra sigillata.* Speier am Rhein.

Rich, J., and Wallace-Hadrill, A. (1991). *City and Country in the Ancient World.* London.

Robinson, D. (2005). 'Re-Thinking the Social Organisation of Trade and Industry in First Century AD Pompeii', in A. MacMahon and J. Price (eds), *Roman Working Lives and Urban Living.* Oxford, 88–105.

Rodbertus, J. K. (1865). 'Untersuchungen auf dem Gebiete der Nationalökonomie des Klassischen Altertums. II. Zur Geschichte der römischen Tributsteuern seit Augustus', *Jahrbücher für Nationalökonomie und Statistik* 4: 341–427.

Rostovtzeff, M. (1926). *The Social and Economic History of the Roman Empire.* Oxford.

Royden, H. L. (1988). *The Magistrates of the Roman Professional Collegia in Italy from the First to the Third Century AD.* Pisa.

Royden, H. L. (1989). 'The Tenure of Office of the Quinquennales in the Roman Professional Collegia', *American Journal of Philology* 110/2: 303–15.

Ruffing, K. (2001). 'Einige Überlegungen zum Weinhandel im römischen Ägypten (1.–3. Jh. n. Chr.)', *MBAH* 20/1: 55–80.

Ruffing, K. (2002). 'Die Berufsbezeichnungen auf -poles und -prates in der epigraphischen Überlieferung', *MBAH* 21/1: 16–58.

Saller, R. (2002). 'Framing the Debate over Growth in the Ancient Economy', in W. Scheidel and S. Von Reden (eds), *The Ancient Economy*. Edinburgh, 251–69.

Schleich, T. (1983). 'Überlegungen zum Problem senatorischer Handelsaktivitäten (1)', *MBAH* 2/2: 65–90.

Schleich, T. (1984). 'Überlegungen zum Problem senatorischer Handelsaktivitäten (2)', *MBAH* 3/1: 37–72.

Schneider, H. (1982). 'Die Bedeutung der römischen Strassen für den Handel', *MBAH* 1/1: 85–95.

Schneider, H. (2009). 'Die Erforschung der antiken Wirtschaft vom Ende des 18. Jahrhunderts bis zum Zweiten Weltkrieg: Von A. H. L. Heeren zu M. I. Rostovtzeff', in V. Losemann (ed.), *Alte Geschichte zwischen Wissenschaft und Politik: Gedenkschrift Karl Christ*. Wiesbaden, 337–85.

Schöttgen, C. (1727). *Antiquitates triturae et fulloniae, ex antiquorum temporum reliquiis congestae*. Utrecht.

Sidebotham, S. E. (1986). 'Ports of the Red Sea and the Arabia–India trade', *MBAH* 5/2: 16–36.

Smith, A. (1776). *An Inquiry into the Nature and Causes of the Wealth of Nations*. London.

Smith, W. (1848). *A Dictionary of Greek and Roman Antiquities*. London.

Stöger, H. (2011). 'The Spatial Organization of the Movement Economy: The Analysis of Ostia's Scholae', in R. Laurence and D. Newsome (eds), *Rome, Ostia, Pompeii: Movement and Space*. Oxford, 215–42.

Strobel, K. (1987). 'Einige Bemerkungen zu den historisch-archäologischen Grundlagen einer Neuformulierung der Sigillatenchronologie für Germanien und Rätien und zu wirtschaftsgeschichtlichen Aspekten der römischen Keramikindustrie', *MBAH* 6/2: 75–115.

Strong, D., and Brown, D. (eds) (1976). *Roman Crafts*. London.

Steuart, J. (1767). *An Inquiry into the Principles of Political Economy*. London.

Stuppner, A. (1994). 'Terra Sigillata im Nördlichen Niederösterreich', *MBAH* 13/2: 70–94.

Tran, N. (2001). 'Le Collège, la communauté et le politique sous le Haut-Empire romain: Remarques sur l'histoire du droit à la fin du XIXe siècle', *Cahiers Centre Glotz* 12: 181–98.

Treggiari, S. (1975a). 'Jobs in the Household of Livia', *PBSR* 43: 48–77.

Treggiari, S. (1975b). 'Roman Social History: Recent Interpretations', *Social History/Histoire Sociale* 8: 149–64.

Treggiari, S. (1976). 'Jobs for Women', *American Journal of Ancient History* 1: 76–104.

Treggiari, S. (1979). 'Lower-Class Women in the Roman Economy', *Florilegium: Carleton University Annual Papers on Classical Antiquity and the Middle Ages* 1: 65–86.

Treggiari, S. (1980). 'Urban Labour in Rome: Mercennarii and Tabernarii', in P. Garnsey (ed.), *Non-Slave Labour in the Roman World*. Cambridge, 48–64.

Van Nijf, O. M. (1997). *The Civic World of Professional Associations in the Roman East*. Amsterdam.

Venticinque, P. (2009). 'Common Causes: Guilds, Craftsmen and Merchants in the Economy and Society of Roman and Late Roman Egypt'. Unpublished dissertation. University of Chicago.

Wagner-Hasel, B. (2009). 'Hundert Jahre Gelehrtenstreit über den Charakter der antiken Wirtschaft', *Historische Anthropologie* 17: 178–201.

Wallace-Hadrill, A. (1991). 'Elites and Trade in the Roman Town', in J. Rich and A. Wallace-Hadrill (eds), *City and Country in the Ancient World*. London, 241–72.

Waltzing, J.-P. (1892). *L'Épigraphie latine et les corporations professionnelles de l'empire Romain*. Gand.

Waltzing, J.-P. (1895). *Étude historique sur les corporations professionelles chez les Romains, I: Le Droit d'association à Rome. Les Collèges professionelles considérés comme associations privées*. Louvain.

Waltzing, J.-P. (1896). *Étude historique sur les corporations professionnelles chez les Romains, II: Les Collèges professionels considérés comme institutions officielles*. Louvain.

Waltzing, J.-P. (1900). *Étude historique sur les corporations professionnelles chez les Romains. Indices. Liste des collèges connus, leur organisation intérieure, leur caractère religieux, funéraire et public, leurs finances*. Louvain.

Warmington, E. H. (1928). *The Commerce between the Roman Empire and India*. Cambridge.

Wes, M. A. (1990). *Michael Rostovtzeff, Historian in Exile: Russian Roots in an American Context* (Historia: Einzelschriften 65). Stuttgart, Steiner.

West, L. C. (1917). 'Phases of Commercial Life in Roman Egypt', *JRS* 7: 45–58.

West, L. C. (1924). 'Commercial Syria under the Roman Empire', *Transactions and Proceedings of the American Philological Association* 55: 159–89.

West, L. C. (1932). 'The Economic Collapse of the Roman Empire', *Classical Journal* 28/2: 96–106.

West, L. C. (1939). 'Notes on Diocletian's Edict', *Classical Philology* 34/3: 239–45.

Whittaker, C. R. (1991). 'The Consumer City Revisited: The Vicus and the City', *JRA* 3: 110–18.

Wilson, A. (1999). 'Commerce and Industry in Roman Sabratha', *Libyan Studies* 30: 29–52.

Wilson, A. (2000). 'Timgad and Textile Production', in Mattingly and Salmon (2000), 271–96.

Wilson, A. (2002). 'Urban Production in the Roman World: The View from North Africa', *PBSR* 70: 231–74.

Wright, F. W. (1917). 'Roman Factories', *Classical Weekly* 11/3: 17–19.

Wright, F. W. (1918). 'Review of Brewster, Roman Craftsmen and Traders', *Classical Weekly* 12/5: 38–9.

Zaniers, W. (1994). 'Handelsfragen der Rheinzaberner Sigillata', *MBAH* 13/2: 60–9.

Zanker, P. (1975). 'Grabreliefs römischer Freigelassener', *Jahrbuch des Deutschen Archäologischen Instituts* 90: 267–315.

Zimmer, G. (1982). *Römische Berufsdarstellungen*. Berlin.

Zimmer, G. (1985). 'Römische Handwerker', *Aufstieg und Niedergang der Römischen Welt* 12/2: 205–28.

Zimmermann, C. (2002). *Handwerkervereine im griechischen Osten des Imperium Romanum*. Mainz.

2

Twentieth-Century Italian Scholarship on Roman Craftsmen, Traders, and their Professional Organizations

Carla Salvaterra and Alessandro Cristofori

Italian scholarship of the twentieth century has contributed significantly to the questions discussed in this volume. This is explained partly by the traditional strength of classical studies in Italy, and by the concentration there of a considerable proportion of the relevant ancient evidence—the archaeological and epigraphic sources in particular. Yet an additional, and more interesting, reason is to be found in the centrality of the concept of 'labour' in shaping the social, political, and constitutional structures of Italy in various periods during the twentieth century.

The first two decades of the twentieth century saw the growth of workers' organizations and trade unions.[1] The subsequent period under the Fascist regime saw the top-down development of a corporate system, with the creation of organizations, the *corporazioni*, uniting either the employers or the workers of one sector. The idea was to solve the class struggle that, according to the champions of *corporativismo*, had resulted in the bankruptcy of both the liberal and the socialist model: the system was aimed at fostering the greater interests of the nation.[2] After the Second World War, labour played an essential role in the founding ideology of the new Italian republic, as attested by the first article of the Italian constitution.[3] This political and cultural climate inevitably also

---

[1] On the origins and development of labour unions in Italy until the first decades of the twentieth century, see, most recently, Varni (1992), Antonioli (1997), Ciampani and Pellegrini (2005), Napoli (2007), and Vallauri (2008). Still useful is Horowitz (1963). On the revolutionary syndicalism as a left-wing stream within the *Partito Socialista Italiano*, see, above all, Laghi (1990).

[2] Among the most recent contributions to the debate on the corporative system of the Fascist era, see Gagliardi (2010).

[3] On this topic, see particularly Turone (1992) and Musso (2002).

influenced the priorities of classical scholars, and caused a particular interest in issues related to the world of labour in the Roman era.

Despite all this, from an international perspective it is clear that, in the footnotes of publications dedicated to the role of craftsmen and traders in the Roman economy, publications written in Italian appear as references only very rarely in this debate. Among the reasons for this state of affairs is the prevalence in Italy, at least until some decades ago, of 'empirical' approaches to the theme, with sectorial studies focusing particularly on a single subset of sources, which strongly reflected traditional disciplinary subdivisions. This tendency is accompanied by a certain disconnection between Italian classical studies and the methodological reflection taking place beyond the national borders, and the joint results of investigations focusing on other historical periods. In part, this situation may also be due to an imperfect knowledge of Italian scholarly discourse in the international field, as a result of linguistic factors or the difficulty of finding contributions that may have an extremely limited circulation.

Our modest aim in this chapter is to contribute to overcome some of these difficulties, and to highlight the most influential approaches to craftsmen and traders in the Roman world in twentieth-century Italy. The discussion is structured thematically—although a chronologically ordered arrangement, emphasizing the parallels between the developments in research and the changes in the political and cultural realm, would also have been interesting.[4]

GENERAL APPROACHES

As already noted, there have not been many works of a methodological nature on the theme of commercial and artisanal labour in the Roman world; in the first part of the twentieth century, such works were produced in the context of general reconstructions of the ancient economy by scholars influenced, in varying ways, by Marxist and socialist thinking.[5] The first contributions in this vein include a speech given at the opening of the academic year 1905/6 at the University of Macerata by the jurist Siro Solazzi on the topic of free work in the Roman world, and a monograph by Giuseppe Salvioli, who also had been educated as a jurist.[6] The difficult socio-economic conditions in Sicily at the

---

[4] The present chapter develops further some of the points already presented in Salvaterra (2006).

[5] Still important for the influence of the thinking of Marx and of socialist streams on ancient historiography in Italy is Mazza (1976), who rightly insisted on the necessity of distinguishing the personal lives of classical scholars such as Corrado Barbagallo, Ettore Ciccotti, Guglielmo Ferrero, and Giuseppe Salvioli, often erroneously ranked under one Marxist front within Italian classical scholarship.

[6] Solazzi (1906). The text of the speech can also be read in Solazzi (1955: 141–60).

end of the nineteenth century—Salvioli had been appointed to the chair of history of Italian law at the University of Palermo in 1884—led him to investigate the economic history of antiquity and the Middle Ages. His work, *Il capitalism antico: Storia dell'economia romana*, appeared posthumously in Italian in 1929, but which had already been published in French in 1906.[7] Salvioli insisted particularly on the prominence, in real terms, of free labour in urban crafts in the Roman world, and on the failure of the organization of production to develop from the small-scale workshop to the large factory in the modern sense of the word.[8] He sketched a nuanced picture of the role of merchants in the Roman economy.[9] Besides the work of Salvioli, there is the œuvre of Ettore Ciccotti, a follower of Mazzini, who served the socialist party in the late nineteenth and early twentieth centuries, and became attached to Fascism in the last phase of his life—though he was highly critical of Mussolini's dictatorship.[10] Ciccotti wrote *Il tramonto della schiavitù nel mondo antico*, on the decline of slavery in the ancient world, and *Commercio e civiltà nel mondo antico*, which, though mostly dedicated to the nature of commercial relations from prehistory to the Roman era, has some relevant sections on the profile of traders in the Greco-Roman world.[11] Both works have had an influence lasting until recent times through re-editions and reprints.

Francesco Maria de Robertis

However, the fundamental name to remember when it comes to general approaches to craftsmen and traders is that of Francesco Maria de Robertis, a scholar educated in the 1930s at the Scuola di Perfezionamento in Studi Corporativi, at the University of Bari, a school heavily promoted by the Fascist regime.[12] De Robertis was nonetheless able to demonstrate in his early works

---

[7] Salvioli (1929). The book can also be found in the edition prepared by Andrea Giardina: Salvioli (1985). French version: Salvioli (1906). The book also was translated into German, before it appeared in Italian: Salvioli (1912).

[8] Salvioli (1985: 61–84).

[9] Salvioli (1985: 115–32).

[10] On Ciccotti as a historian of the ancient economy, see, briefly, Giardina in the preface of Salvioli (1985: pp. xlviii–liii).

[11] On slavery, see Ciccotti (1899), 2nd edn Ciccotti (1940), repr. as Ciccotti (1977). On commerce, see Ciccotti (1929); for merchants in the Greek world, see esp. pp. lxxix–lxxxi; for traders in the Roman world, see particularly pp. cxxvii, cxxxvi–cxxxix.

[12] An excellent account of the education of De Robertis and the development of his thinking, against the background of the ever-changing political realities during his long scholarly career, is to be found in Perry (2006: esp. 93–102, 114–18, 165–6, 193–200). Now one can also refer to the contributions focusing on De Robertis in the proceedings of a 2004 conference dedicated to the great scholar, who had died the previous year: Musca (2007), esp. the chapter by Filippo Gallo on De Robertis and the labour relations in Roman law. For a brief account of the conference, see Quadrato (2004).

an admirable independence from the propagandistic positions of Fascism, and after the war he had a deep influence on Italian scholarship, regarding both the concept of 'labour' in the Roman world, and the *fenomeno associativo*, the professional *collegia*. In both these themes, he appears to have been influenced by the social doctrines of the left wing of the *Democrazia Cristiana*, the party that, until the early 1990s, was the pivot of every Italian government, and of which the leader, Aldo Moro, was a personal friend of De Robertis, and lecturer at the juridical faculty in Bari where De Robertis spent his entire academic life.

Regardless of how one wishes to judge the value of his ideas, De Robertis had the unequivocal merit of recognizing the importance of documentary sources in discussing the social position of labour in Rome: before him, in Italy, such discussions were almost completely dominated by literary sources. De Robertis distinguished, in a series of works published between the 1940s and the 1960s, a 'noble' realm, which belonged to the ruling class of Rome, and of which the literary sources were an expression.[13] In this realm, there was substantial contempt for most occupations. Opposite these ideas stood those championed in the 'vulgar' realm of the lower classes and the provincials, illustrated principally by the epigraphic, papyrological, and iconographical records. In this realm, representing the large majority of the empire's population, work was a source of personal pride and social prestige, as was demonstrated by the explicit mention of the occupation of the deceased in commemorative inscriptions, and the numerous reliefs with occupational scenes from various parts of the Roman world.

The interpretative model of De Robertis evoked and still evokes some perplexity.[14] Much can be said, for example, about his characterization of the two realms, and about the boundary between 'noble' and 'vulgar', definitions that De Robertis basically borrowed from the leading name in Italian art history of his time, Ranuccio Bianchi Bandinelli.[15] One could also note that De Robertis's model risks undue inflexibility, as it rigidly contrasts a supposedly coherent ideology of the upper classes with another supposedly coherent ideology of the lower classes.[16] This led him to consider the

---

[13] Particularly De Robertis (1945), a monograph, and De Robertis (1959, 1962), articles that subsequently also appeared in De Robertis (1963: 21–47, 49–95).

[14] Cristofori (2004: 79–80) aims to explore the inherent contradictions, showing how, on the one hand, it is impossible to speak of a unique and coherent labour ideology among the Roman ruling class—instead there was a plurality of ideas, that had some points in common, but were not congruent and indeed sometimes divergent, sometimes even within the thinking of one and the same author, like Cicero (pp. 81–90); on the other hand, an attempt is made to demonstrate, based on the scanty evidence, that there was not always an opposition between 'noble' and 'vulgar' ideas, and that in some cases ideas expressed by the ruling class penetrated into the realm of the occupational class (pp. 90–6).

[15] De Robertis (1959: 55–6, n. 7).

[16] Nörr (1965: 70–73) had already warned against the rigidity of the interpretative model of De Robertis. In the same years in which De Robertis developed his model, the great historian of

ideas expressed by literary authors as abstract speculations of some aristocrats, completely disconnected from the problems and values of real life, and thus, in the end, not representative of historical reality.[17] Nevertheless, he had the undeniable merit of launching, in Italy, a discussion about these issues.

The Classical Seminar of the Istituto Gramsci

After De Robertis, the debate continued especially through the contributions of a collective of scholars from various disciplines within the field of *Altertumswissenschaft*, including historians, but also philologists, archaeologists, and jurists. This group convened in 1974 at the Instituto Gramsci, the cultural institute connected to the Italian Communist Party—a party whose cultural weight at Italian universities in the 1960s, 1970s, and 1980s was without any doubt more relevant than one would think on the basis of its marginal political role of the period.[18] The basis for this collaboration was laid at the *Colloques sur l'esclavage*, the first of which was held in 1971 at Besançon. Here, Italian scholars who later became part of the group of the Istituto Gramsci met their French colleagues.[19]

Against this background appeared the collection of methodological essays, in 1978, in *Analisi marxista e società antiche*, which published, in more elaborate form, the papers presented in this study group during the first two years of its existence, and, in 1979, *L'anatomia della scimmia*, in which the archaeologist Andrea Carandini reinterpreted the evolution of the entire precapitalist economy in the light of the fundamental chapter of Karl Marx's *Grundrisse der Kritik der Politischen Ökonomie* dedicated to the systems that preceded the capitalist system.[20] The strictly theoretical character of these two publications means that they are of only limited relevance in debates

---

ancient philosophy Rodolfo Mondolfo proposed a reading contrasting with that of De Robertis, showing, particularly among the thinkers of the Greek and Roman worlds, the recognition of a positive value of labour, especially as a tool for experiencing reality. See esp. Mondolfo (1965). The very possibility of an analysis like that of Mondolfo (though it may be criticized, cf. Pasoli (1980: 75–9, particularly 77, n. 28)) should warn us against the risks of an interpretation assuming the univocal and completely coherent nature of thinking among the nobility.

[17] As objected by Galeno (1960: 143–4). The response by De Robertis (1962: 3, n. 1) does not seem to have picked up the fundamental nature of the criticism that had been aimed at him.

[18] Lussana (2000) recalls, briefly, the cultural activities of the Istituto Gramsci (now Fondazione Istituto Gramsci) in the second half of the twentieth century. The communist party was restricted to opposing the governments led by Christian democrats.

[19] Cf. Brutti (1978: 10).

[20] Capogrossi Colognesi, Giardina, and Schiavone (1978); Carandini (1979). The first work was received with great interest by the Italian scholarly community, as attested by some of the contributions to the *Quaderni di Storia*: Bretone et al. (1978); Di Benedetto (1978); Narducci (1978); but also internationally. Cf. Clavel-Lévêque and Favory (1980); Kreissig (1982).

about the themes discussed in this volume.[21] Highly relevant, however, remains the monumental collaborative effort edited by Andrea Giardina and Aldo Schiavone, *Società romana e produzione schiavistica*, published in 1981, as the result of several years of work of the classical seminar at the Istituto Gramsci.[22] Even though the volume has a strong focus on agricultural activities, ample space is also devoted to manufacturing and trade, especially in the second volume, which focuses on goods, markets, and exchange in the Mediterranean. The broad approach of the 1981 publication, compared to the two earlier works mentioned, and its more careful consideration of the insights offered by the ancient evidence, as opposed to theoretical models, explain the outstanding resonance of the volume also among scholars adhering to non-Marxist schools of thought.[23] The activities of the classical seminar of the Istituto Gramsci subsequently also led to the publication, in 1986, of a second volume of economic studies, devoted to late antiquity—*Società romana e impero tardoantico*.[24] This book aimed to highlight the moment at which the slave mode of production, whose origins and consolidation in the late Republic and under the High Empire the earlier volume had explored, broke up; it also significantly broadened the scope of the analysis by including the provinces of the empire, whereas in *Società romana e produzione schiavistica* most of the attention was focused on south-central Italy.

One of the most fertile and durable results of the activities of the classical seminar of the Istituto Gramsci, besides the reflections on applying the interpretative framework of Marxist thought to the ancient world, was that it underlined the importance of collaboration between historians, philologists, jurists, and archaeologists. In this sense, the continuity between the Istituto Gramsci seminar and *Opus*, an international journal focusing on the economic and social history of antiquity, was evident—also because some of the scholars involved in the seminar played a key role in its foundation. The journal, edited by the Greek philologist Carmine Ampolo and by the archaeologist Giuseppe Pucci, was the first Italian periodical dedicated to the economy and society of

---

[21] The theoretical merit of the volume was noted by Narducci (1978: 50), who, concluding his thoughts on Capogrossi Colognesi, Giardina, and Schiavone (1978) and on the contemporaneous collection of essays by Vegetti (1977), wrote 'one can only applaud that the realm of the sacred texts is definitively being abandoned in favour of more practical investigation, of an empiricism that is not always "vulgar"'.

[22] Giardina and Schiavone (1981).

[23] Cf., for the discussion in Italy, the debate published in *Opus*, a report of a conference held at Pavia, 21 January 1982, on *Società romana & produzione schiavistica*. Cf. Gabba (1982); Lo Cascio (1982); Luraschi (1982), and the subsequent and shorter contributions by Bona et al. (1982); for the reception of the book abroad, see the synthesis of the contributions to a conference at the Collège de France on 27 November 1981, published in *Quaderni di Storia*: Nicolet et al. (1982), and reviews by Thébert (1982), Gros (1983), and Rathbone (1983), appearing in some of the most widespread journals in classical studies.

[24] Giardina (1986). See the reviews of this book by Silvestrini (1989) and Andreau and Leveau (1992).

the ancient world, and first appeared in 1982. It was an explicit aim of the journal to overcome the disciplinary boundaries that separated scholars based on the different properties of the evidence they worked with—literary and material—and to open a broad international collaboration.[25] Significant in this respect is the fact that the first volume of the journal published the proceedings of a conference on Moses Finley's *Ancient Slavery and Modern Ideology*, which had been translated into Italian by Elio Lo Cascio shortly beforehand.[26] This volume also included a contribution by Finley himself.[27] It may also be pointed out that *Opus* also readily accepted the contributions of Italian scholars coming from cultural traditions other than Marxism, such as Guido Clemente and Emilio Gabba. In the last years of the twentieth century, the activities discussed here gradually vanished: shortly after the publication of *Società romana e impero tardoantico*, the classical seminar of the Istituto Gramsci ceased its activities. In 1992, the publication of *Opus* also was suspended.

After this period, as far as the theme of this volume is concerned, one can point to some interesting syntheses, particularly by Guido Clemente and Giusto Traina, or to arguments inserted in volumes of broader scope, like the classic *Economia e società nell'Italia annonaria* of Lellia Cracco Ruggini, published for the first time in 1961, but with a second, updated, edition appearing in 1995, or the 2011 handbook on the Roman economy published by Filippo Carlà and Arnaldo Marcone.[28]

EVIDENCE-BASED APPROACHES

Besides the works mentioned so far, some publications dedicated to certain literary texts that play a key role in discourse about labour in Rome succeeded in reaching a rather wide audience.[29] In particular, the well-known passage

---

[25] For the programmatic aims of the journal, see the presentation of the journal by Ampolo and Pucci (1982). Indeed, some of the most famous names of the ancient economy debate published in *Opus*, including Jean Andreau, Jean-Michel Carrié, Yvon Garlan, Peter Garnsey, Jerzy Kolendo, Jean-Paul Morel, Claude Mossé, Dominic Rathbone, André Tchernia, Pierre Vidal-Naquet, and C. R. Whittaker.

[26] Finley (1981).

[27] Finley (1982). Among the other contributions to this first volume of *Opus* relevant to the issues discussed here is the article of Giardina (1982), which explores, in a very broad manner, the role of labour in antiquity from an economic, social, political, and also ideological point of view, with a particular emphasis on late antiquity.

[28] Clemente (1991); Traina (2000); Cracco Ruggini (1961, 1995); of special interest for the present purpose are the very solid chapters dedicated to the *negotiatores frumentarii* and their organizations in the era of Ambrosius (pp. 56–146); Carla and Marcone (2011: 33–58 (production) and 167–211 (trade)).

[29] Among the publications with a general reach, making a necessary but in a certain sense arbitrary selection, one can list Tozzi (1961), Storchi Marino (1979), Gabba (1980), and several of

in Cicero, *De Officiis* I.150–1, in which the author, taking inspiration from a pre-existing cultural tradition, and particularly from Panaetius of Rhodes, lists the *artes* that should be considered *sordidae* and those that, on the contrary, can be considered *honestae*, concluding, in the end, with the usual praise of agriculture; the passage, because of its abstract thinking, disconnected from contingencies, systematic and general, has become an almost obligatory point of departure for any discussion of the issue, in Italy as elsewhere.[30] Much interest has also been evoked by a passage in a letter to Lucilius in which Seneca discusses Posidonius' four categories of *artes*, and by a brief text from Livy dedicated to the famous *plebiscitum Claudianum* of 219 or 218 BC, championed by Caius Flaminius, which in fact prohibited senators from engaging in maritime trade on a large scale.[31] Other detailed studies have been dedicated to the attestations of occupations in the comedies of Plautus and Terence, and to a passage of the *Bellum Catilinae*, in which, surprisingly, agriculture itself is ranked among the *servilia officia*.[32] Elena Giannarelli, on the other hand, has focused her attention on Christian texts from Late Antiquity.[33] There also has been a lot of interest in juridical texts, especially because of the traditional strength of the study of Roman law in Italy. This interest was initially directed chiefly at analysing to what extent the Roman state intervened in the economy to regulate it, but later on it has more often been sociological in character, analysing mostly how Roman legislation reflects the socio-economic developments of the time.[34]

A lot of attention has also been devoted to the epigraphic record, initially mainly to inscriptions. Besides the short but interesting discussion by Danilo Mazzoleni about the meaning of references to occupations in Christian commemorative epigraphy, research initially focused largely on the reconstruction of processes of production and trade from occupational inscriptions, but, in more recent years, more attention has been paid to the social roles of craftsmen and traders, particularly since the publication of Sandra Joshel's fundamental book on occupation and identity in Rome.[35]

In the fertile field of epigraphic studies, three main lines of research can be distinguished. The first consists of scholars studying the epigraphic record

---

the essays collected in Gabba (1988); Clemente (1984), Lana (1984), De Salvo (1987), and Giardina (1994).

[30] Particularly on this text, which obviously is also discussed in many of the publications listed in the preceding note, see Gabba (1979); Lotito (1981); and Narducci (1985).

[31] For a comment on the passage in Seneca, see, above all, Pani (1985); for the *plebiscitum Claudianum*, see, among others, Guarino (1982) and Clemente (1983).

[32] On Plautus and Terence, see particularly Gabba (1985) and Lentano (1996). On the passage by Sallustius, see Bianco (1985).

[33] Giannarelli (1986, 1991).

[34] See, e.g. Di Porto (1984), Giacchero (1987); Merola Reduzzi (1990); Polichetti (2001); and Mantello (2008).

[35] Mazzoleni (1986); Joshel (1992).

of individual occupations, or closely related professions over a wide area of the entire Roman world—exemplary is the monograph by Ida Calabi Limentani on artists and artisans in the Roman world, based principally on the evidence from inscriptions on stone.[36] Closely related, because of the emphasis on the work itself, are general investigations dedicated to a single occupation, using all kinds of evidence available, as, for example, reflected by the work of Fabio Vicari on the textile sector, and that of Francesca Diosono on professions related to wood-working and trade.[37] A second line of research consists of projects that aim to investigate, in a general way, production and trade in a certain part of the Roman world, especially in order to reconstruct its economic structure. This line of research has a long history that goes back at least to an early twentieth-century article by Aristide Calderini on crafts and occupations in the epigraphy of *Gallia Transpadana*.[38] Recently, there has been an upsurge in such approaches.[39] The last and perhaps most productive line of research concerns investigations on individual epigraphic documents, which often provide the opportunity to make more general points about our knowledge of a particular occupation, or to reconstruct a microhistory of the person involved, which then can be used as an example for the social roles of people involved in that specific craft.[40]

An evolution similar to that detectable in the study of inscriptions on stone—from an emphasis on production and trade to an increasing emphasis on the people involved in the processes of manufacturing and trade—can be found in the studies of the epigraphy on *instrumentum domesticum*, the study of which has strongly developed in Italy from the 1960s and 1970s onwards, with pioneering studies of the epigraphy of amphorae from Ostia by Fausto Zevi, and, for northern Italy, by Paolo Baldacci.[41] In recent decades the study of texts, stamped or painted, on amphorae, tableware, lamps, glass bottles, bricks, and other moveable objects, has seen a remarkable development, mostly through studies dedicated to specific sets of evidence from a limited

---

[36] Calabi Limentani (1958). See also, e.g. Panciera (1980) on the *olearii*, Chioffi (1999) on professions related to the production and sale of meat, Mennella (2001) on marble merchants active in the region of present-day Piemonte, and De Salvo (2004) on the *navicularii*.

[37] Vicari (2001); Diosono (2008).

[38] Calderini (1907). Among the older studies, to mention some of the more representative examples, are Panciera (1957) on Aquileia, and Bivona (1984) on Sicily.

[39] See, e.g. Rizzo (1993) on Sicily; Buonopane (2003a) on textile professions in *Altinum*; Cristofori (2004) on Picenum.

[40] Among other publications of this type, one may note Granino Cecere (1994) on the *diffusor olearius D. Caecilius Abascantus*; Mennella (2001) on a *negotiator vestiarius*; Tisé (2001) on the inscription of a *mercator* from Brundisium; Buonopane (2003b) on a *vestiarius centonarius* from Aquileia; Boscolo (2005) on the *piscatrix Aurelia Nais*; and Gasperini (2005) on a *materiarius* from *Sena Gallica*.

[41] Zevi (1966); Baldacci (1967–8).

part of Roman Italy, though there have also been some contributions of a more general character.[42]

Still in the realm of documentary evidence, one should remember also the work on labour contracts found on Egyptian papyri, which were discussed in the works of Orsolina Montevecchi and Aristide Calderini in the 1950s, even though perhaps the most interesting contribution in this field of research is the monograph by Montevecchi and Mariadele Manca Masciandri on wet-nursing contracts.[43]

As far as the field of archaeology is concerned, the separation from the traditional approach, with its emphasis on objects and their aesthetic value, and in particular on objects that had artistic qualities, was particularly slow in Italy. A decisive turn was brought about when *Dialoghi di Archeologia* began to appear in 1967. This journal was promoted by Ranuccio Bianchi Bandinelli, assisted by his many pupils, and in particular by Andrea Carandini, Filippo Coarelli, Mario Torelli, and Fausto Zevi. The separation of Bianchi Bandinelli from the more traditional settings of Italian archaeology was also motivated by his adherence to Marxist ideology and was manifest in his important research on 'popular' art in Italy and the provinces, in which the artistic object was approached as a product of the world in which it was created.[44]

This change of direction was also upheld after the *Dialoghi di Archeologia* ceased to be published in 1992: it was immediately succeeded by the new journal *Ostraka*, a direct and explicit continuation, starting under the leadership of Mario Torelli, one of the principal pupils of Bianchi Bandinelli, and of the jurist Vincenzo Scarano Ussani, to guarantee the multidisciplinary character of the journal, which was explicitly emphasized by Torelli in an editorial in the first volume.[45] As a result, sociological approaches to artistic and artisanal production became widespread in Italy as well.

---

[42] For detailed studies, see, e.g. Buchi (1979) on ceramic production in the territory of Aquileia; Marengo (1981) on the production in *Picenum* from Q. Clodius Ambrosius; Zaccaria (1985) on the commercial relations between Aquileia and Illyricum; Palazzo and Silvestrini (2001) on the Brindisian amphorae from Apani, Cipriano and Mazzochin (2002) on some series of Dressel 6B; Geremia Nucci (2006) on the stamps of the *plumbarii* of Ostia; and Malfitana (2006) on the possible falsification of the 'brand' *Arretinum*. More general studies include Taborelli (1982) on glass; Carandini (1989) on wine amphorae; Manacorda (1989) on the social and economic aspects of amphorae production in the Republican period; Pucci (1993) on stamped *terra sigillata*; Nonnis (2001) on the production and commercialization of Adriatic amphorae and (2003) on the social implications of the production and commercialization of ceramics in the republican era. Fundamental, too, are the proceedings of the conference *Epigrafia* 1994.

[43] Montevecchi (1950); Calderini (1954); Montevecchi and Manca Masciandri (1984); see also Pintaudi (2001).

[44] Fundamental in this respect was the new introduction prepared for the second edition of *Storicità dell'arte classica*: Bianchi Bandinelli (1950), first edition Bianchi Bandinelli (1943). The ideas of Bianchi Bandinelli are most fully developed in *Roma: L'arte romana nel centro del potere* (1969) and *Roma: La fine dell'arte antica* (1970). Fundamental studies on Bianchi Bandinelli are Barbanera (2000, 2003); see also Barbanera (1998) for a useful synthesis of archaeological studies in Italy.

[45] Torelli (1992).

Moreover, attention paid to the remains of products that were mass consumed or had significant economic impact has also increased, even though such
evidence helps us mostly to reconstruct production processes and flows of
commerce rather than the social roles of craftsmen and traders; in this field of
studies, there is one more general discussion, by Tiziano Mannoni and Enrico
Giannicheda, and a quantity of publications dedicated to individual goods,
among which should be remembered the work of Patrizio Pensabene on the
production and circulation of marbles.[46] In very recent years, one observes a
progressive shift of interest from products towards producers.[47] This is also true
for approaches to workshops, which are now being studied as social and
economic spaces in which the craftsmen and traders operated.[48] Limited attention, on the other hand, compared to what happens on the other side of the
Alps, has been devoted to the iconographic record, though one could mention
the work of Fabrizio Bisconti on labour scenes in early Christian art and, more
recently, the investigation of Sebastiana Mele on Roman Spain.[49]

PROFESSIONAL ASSOCIATIONS

The theme of professional associations deserves separate treatment. Research in
this area flourished in Italy in the 1930s, in connection with the system of
professional associations established by the Fascist regime.[50] Research in this
period focused mainly on the juridical nature of the relation between the state
and the associations, aiming to reconstruct how the Roman state promoted and
controlled the *fenomeno associativo*, in a way that cannot always be discarded as
apologetic for the Fascist regime: among the enormous amount of studies
published in these years are the first monograph on this theme by De Robertis,
whose nuanced position, free of propagandistic tendencies, was also recognized
by foreign reviewers.[51] There was also the publication of a short but rather
explicit lecture by Aristide Calderini, *Le associazioni professionali in Roma
antica*, in which, with a certain polemical vigour, he insisted on the fundamental

---

[46] Mannoni and Giannichedda (1996); Pensabene (1983, 1990, 1995) are among his most
significant contributions to this theme.

[47] See, e.g. Sampaolo (1995) and the essays collected in Santoro (2004).

[48] For some publications of the last two decades on this line of research, see n. 61. Specifically
on workshops, see, e.g. Manacorda (1990) on brick/tile kilns, and Taborelli (1998) on glass kilns.

[49] Bisconti (2000) and Mele (2008). See also Giuliani (2003), and Marcone (2000), on the
iconography of the Igel column. Cf. Mele (2010).

[50] See the bibliography of Frangioni (1998), starting from the index under 'Roma (antica)'
(p. 515), which helps to find relevant items in this work, in which books are simply ordered by
the surname of their author.

[51] De Robertis (1938); cf. De Visscher (1939) and Duff (1942), with the remarks by Perry
(2006: 94–95).

differences between the *collegia* of the Roman world and the labour organizations of subsequent periods, including the Fascist corporations.[52]

This 'juridical' line of research continued, at a much lower level of intensity,
after the Second World War, when perspectives naturally changed because of
the return of the free labour union and because of the influence of progressive
developments in Catholic thinking. This continuity is represented above all in
the works of De Robertis, which were essentially further developments of his
impressive monograph of 1938.[53]

From the 1970s onwards, after a rather long period of stagnation, probably
owing to the dangerous association of the Fascist past evoked by the theme—
the silence was only interrupted by the works of De Robertis and by a
contribution from Mario Attilio Levi—a new line of research emerged focusing
more on the nature of the professional associations themselves and on their
socio-economic environment.[54] The protagonist of the renaissance of *collegia*
studies was undoubtedly Lellia Cracco Ruggini, through a series of long articles
that put significant emphasis on Late Antiquity and on the eastern part of the
Roman world, where the documentation allowed for in-depth analysis of
sociological issues that had earlier remained mostly unexplored.[55] It was the
merit of Guido Clemente, to have undertaken, for the first time since Waltzing's synthesis, and following the line of research of Cracco Ruggini, the study
of the patrons of professional *collegia*.[56] Though starting from another historiographical setting, Mario Mazza investigated, in the same years, the political value of the professional associations in Roman Asia Minor.[57]

After the turn brought about by Mazza and by Cracco Ruggini and her
school, the socio-historical approach has remained vital, as expressed by contributions from Giovanni Mennella, Marcella Chelotti, and Filippo Boscolo
(among others) on the evidence from Roman Italy, by the impressive monograph by Lietta de Salvo on the associations of *navicularii*, by the reinterpret-
ation, in social terms, of the famous inscription of the bakers of Sardis by Marco
di Branco, and, finally, by the useful synthesis of Francesca Diosono.[58] This
direction of the debate has, to some extent, also 'contaminated' the most recent
work on *collegia* by scholars specializing in Roman law, as is, for example, clear
from a recent discussion by Giovanna Merola of a possible reference to a *lex
collegii* related to maritime transporters preserved in the *Digesta*.[59]

---

[52] Calderini (n.d.), with the remarks of Perry (2006: 113–14), which do not completely do
justice to the value of what Calderini wrote. Among the other studies of significance from this
period, one can include Monti (1934); Bandini (1937); and Accame (1942).
[53] De Robertis (1955, 1971).   [54] Levi (1963).
[55] Cracco Ruggini (1971, 1973, 1976a, b).   [56] Clemente (1972).
[57] Mazza (1974).
[58] Mennella and Apicella (2000) provided an epigraphic update of the anthology of Waltzing
for Roman Italy. See further Boscolo (2002, 2004–5); Chelotti (2007); Mennella (2010); De Salvo
(1992); Di Branco (2000); Diosono (2007).
[59] Merola (2007).

RECENT YEARS

In the most recent research, the general tendency in Italy now seems to be to put research on craftsmen and traders in the Roman world into closer relation with the research being conducted in international contexts, and to debates on periods other than antiquity. Significant in this sense are the contributions dedicated in the 2000s to the position of artisanal and commercial activities in their topographical context—a theme already anticipated by Emilio Gabba and Filippo Coarelli in the 1970s and 1980s.[60] Exemplary of this tendency, also because of *where* it was published—in the *Journal of Roman Archaeology*—is the work of Emanuele Papi on craftsmen and traders around the Forum of Rome.[61]

Another fruitful line of research, the development of which has to be seen in conjunction with the positive reception in Italy as elsewhere of the seminal monograph by Joshel, focuses on the role that the occupation of craftsman or trader plays in relation to the juridical and social status of the person who exercises it. In this respect one can mention the interesting work of Ulrico Agnati and David Nonnis on the entrepreneurial activities of the ruling classes of late republican Italy.[62]

A third area in which Italian scholarship is quickly recovering ground is that of the meaning of professional activities in the negotiation of gender roles, which has seen an interesting upsurge of interest since the late 1990s, although one should not forget the ideas offered by the monographs of Vito Antonio Sirago and Franca Comucci Biscardi from the 1980s, which focused more generally on the role of women in the Roman world.[63] This culminated in the conference on women and work in the epigraphic record organized by Francesca Cenerini and Alfredo Buonopane, and the useful lexicographical work by Elena Malaspina.[64]

In the span of over a century of studies on craftsmen and traders in the Roman world, one can thus confirm that Italian scholarship has, progressively, integrated itself into international discourse on the theme, and provided a not insignificant contribution: the hope is that it will be possible to continue in this direction in the coming years, at the same time preserving the particular approaches that have characterized Italian classical studies.

---

[60] Gabba (1975); Coarelli (1982).

[61] Papi (2002). Along the same line of research, see, e.g. Ortalli (1993); Lo Cascio (2000); Baratto (2003–4); Proto (2006); and Zevi (2008).

[62] Agnati (1996, 1997) and Nonnis (1999). See also Manacorda (1985) and Torelli (1996).

[63] Recent approaches include that of a prominent scholar of women's studies in antiquity, Cantarella (1999), specifically on the professional activities of women at Pompeii; see also Morretta (1999) on the role of women in the production and trade of Baetican olive oil. For earlier approaches on women in general, see Sirago (1983) and Comucci Biscardi (1987).

[64] Buonopane and Cenerini (2003); Malaspina (2003).

REFERENCES

Accame, S. (1942). 'La legislazione romana intorno ai collegi nel I secolo a.C.', *Bulletino del museo dell'impero romano* 13: 13–48.

Agnati, U. (1996). 'Alcune correlazioni tra mestiere e *status libertatis* nella Roma tardo-repubblicana e imperiale', *RAL* 7: 601–24.

Agnati, U. (1997). *Epigrafia, diritto e società: Studio quantitativo dell'epigrafia latina di zona insubre.* Como.

Ampolo, C., and Pucci, G., *Opus*, 1/1.

Andreau, J., and Leveau, Ph. (1992). 'Recensione', *Annales (ESC)* 47: 402–8.

Antonioli, M. (1997). *Il sindacalismo italiano: Dalle origini al fascismo. Studi e ricerche.* Pisa.

Baldacci, P. (1967–8). 'Alcuni aspetti dei commerci nei territori cisalpini', *Atti CeSDIR* 1: 5–50.

Bandini, V. (1937). *Appunti sulle corporazioni romane.* Milan.

Baratto, C. (2003–4). 'Le *tabernae* nei *fora* delle città romane tra l'età repubblicana e il periodo imperiale', *RdA* 27: 67–87; 28: 45–65.

Barbanera, M. (1998). *L'archeologia degli italiani: Storia, metodi e orientamenti dell'archeologia classica in Italia.* Rome.

Barbanera, M. (2000). *Ranuccio Bianchi Bandinelli e il suo mondo.* Bari.

Barbanera, M. (2003). *Ranuccio Bianchi Bandinelli: Biografia ed epistolario di un grande archeologo.* Milan.

Bianchi Bandinelli, R. (1943). *Storicità dell'arte classica,* Florence.

Bianchi Bandinelli, R. (1950). *Storicità dell'arte classica.* 2nd edn. Florence.

Bianchi Bandinelli, R. (1969). *Roma: L'arte romana nel centro del potere.* Milan.

Bianchi Bandinelli, R. (1970). *Roma: La fine dell'arte antica.* Milan.

Bianco, O. (1985). '*Servilia officia* (Sall. *Cat.* 4, 1)', *Index* 13: 127–33.

Bisconti, F. (2000). *Mestieri nelle catacombe romane: Appunti sul declino dell'iconografia del reale nei cimiteri cristiani di Roma.* Città del Vaticano.

Bivona, L. (1984). 'Il contributo dell'epigrafia latina allo studio dei mestieri nella Sicilia antica', in *Atti del II Congresso internazionale di studi antropologici siciliani.* Palermo, 25–33.

Bona, F., Canfora, L., Capogrossi Colognesi, L., Carandini, A., Foraboschi, D., Lepore, E., Panella, C., and Torelli, M. (1982). 'Discussione', *Opus* 1/2: 413–36.

Boscolo, F. (2002). 'Due iscrizioni di tradizione manoscritta e il *collegium centonariorum Comensium*', *Patavium* 20: 91–105.

Boscolo, F. (2004–5). 'I battellieri del lago di Como in età romana', *AAPat* 117: 221–40.

Boscolo, F. (2005). '*Aurelia Nais, piscatrix de horreis Galbae* e i *piscatores* di Roma', *RSA* 35: 181–8.

Bretone, M., Canfora, L., Clemente, G., Pani, M., and Silvestrini, M. (1978). 'Dibattito su "Analisi marxista e società antiche"', *QS* 4/8: 5–38.

Brutti, M. (1978). 'Introduzione', in L. Capogrossi Colognesi, A. Giardina, and A. Schiavone (eds), *Analisi marxista e società antiche.* Rome, 9–41.

Buchi, E. (1979). 'Impianti produttivi del territorio aquileiese in età romana', *AAAd* 15: 439–59.

Buonopane, A. (2003a). 'La produzione tessile ad Altino: Le fonti epigrafiche', in G. Cresci Marrone and M. Torelli (eds), *Produzioni, merci e commerci in Altino preromana e romana.* Rome, 285–97.

Buonopane, A. (2003b). 'Un *vestiarius centonarius* ad Aquileia: Sulla genuinità di CIL, V, 50', *AN* 74: 301–14.

Buonopane, A., and Cenerini F. (eds) (2003). *Donna e lavoro nella documentazione epigrafica: Atti del I Seminario sulla condizione femminile nella documentazione epigrafica.* Faenza.

Calabi Limentani, I. (1958). *Studi sulla società romana: Il lavoro artistico.* Milan and Varese.

Calderini, A. (n.d.). *Le associazioni professionali di Roma antica.* Milan.

Calderini, A. (1907). 'Arti e mestieri nelle epigrafi della Gallia Transpadana (specialmente nelle raccolte milanesi)', *RIL* 40: 523–44.

Calderini, A. (1954). 'Contratti di lavoro di XX secoli fa', *Studi Romani* 2: 649–62.

Cantarella, E. (1999). 'Qualche considerazione sul lavoro femminile a Pompei', *Saitabi*, 49: 259–72.

Capogrossi Colognesi, L., Giardina, A., and Schiavone, A. (eds) (1978). *Analisi marxista e società antiche.* Rome.

Carandini, A. (1979). *L'anatomia della scimmia: La formazione economica della società prima del capitale. Con un commento alle "Forme che precedono la produzione capitalistica" dai "Grundrisse" di Marx.* Turin.

Carandini, A. (1989). 'L'economia italica tra tarda repubblica e medio impero considerata dal punto di vista di una merce: Il vino', in *Amphores romaines et histoire économique: Dix ans de recherche.* Rome, 505–21.

Carlà, F., and Marcone, A. (2011). *Economia e finanza a Roma.* Bologna.

Chelotti, M. (2007). 'Le associazioni di artigiani, commercianti e artisti nella *regio* seconda augustea', in E. Lo Cascio and G. D. Merola (eds), *Forme di aggregazione nel mondo romano.* Bari, 243–58.

Chioffi, L. (1999). *Caro: il mercato della carne nell'Occidente romano. Riflessi epigrafici e iconografici.* Rome.

Ciampani, A., and Pellegrini, G. (eds) (2005), *La storia del movimento sindacale nella società italiana: Vent'anni di dibattiti e di storiografia.* Soveria Mannelli.

Ciccotti, E. (1899). *Il tramonto della schiavitù nel mondo antico.* Turin.

Ciccotti, E. (1929). *Commercio e civiltà nel mondo antico.* Milan; repr. Bologna, 1977.

Ciccotti, E. (1940). *Il tramonto della schiavitù nel mondo antico.* 2nd edn. Udine.

Ciccotti, E. (1977). *Il tramonto della schiavitù nel mondo antico*, ed. M. Mazza. Bari.

Cipriano, S., and Mazzocchin, S. (2002). 'Analisi di alcune serie bollate di anfore Dressel 6B (*Ap. Pulchri, Flav. Fontan e Fontani, L. Iuni. Paetini, L. Tre. Optati)*', *AN* 73: 305–40.

Clavel-Lévêque, M., and Favory, F. (1980). 'Recensione', *Labeo* 26: 390–401.

Clemente, G. (1972). 'Il patronato nei *collegia* dell'Impero Romano', *SCO* 21: 142–229.

Clemente, G. (1983). 'Il plebiscito Claudio e le classi dirigenti romane nell'età dell'imperialismo', *Ktèma* 8: 253–59.

Clemente, G. (1984). 'Lo sviluppo degli atteggiamenti economici della classe dirigente fra il III e il II sec. a.C.', in W. V. Harris (ed.), *The Imperialism of Mid-Republican Rome.* Rome, 165–83.

Clemente, G. (1991). 'Arti, mestieri, vita associativa, *collegia*', in S. Settis (ed.), *Civiltà dei Romani: Il potere e l'"esercito.* Milan, 83–91.

Coarelli, F. (1982). 'L' "Agora des Italiens" a Delo: Il mercato degli schiavi?', in F. Coarelli, D. Musti, and H. Solin (eds), *Delo e l'Italia*, = *Opuscula Instituti Romani Finlandiae*, 2: 119–45.

Comucci Biscardi, F. (1987). *Donne di rango e donne di popolo nell'età dei Severi.* Florence.

Cracco Ruggini, L. (1961). *Economia e società nell'"Italia annonaria": rapporti fra agricoltura e commercio dal IV al VI secolo d.C.* Milan.

Cracco Ruggini, L. (1971). 'Le associazioni professionali nel mondo romano-bizantino', in *Settimane di studio del Centro italiano di studi sull'alto medioevo. XVIII. Artigianato e tecnica nella società dell'alto medioevo occidentale. 2–8 aprile 1970*, vol. i. Spoleto, 59–193.

Cracco Ruggini, L. (1973). 'Stato e associazioni professionali nell'età imperiale romana', in *Akten des VI. Internationalen Kongresses für Griechische und Lateinische Epigraphik München 1972.* Munich, 271–311.

Cracco Ruggini, L. (1976a). '*Collegium* e *corpus*: La politica economica nella legislazione e nella prassi', in G. G. Archi (ed.), *Istituzioni giuridiche e realtà politiche nel tardo impero (III–V sec. d.C.): Atti di un incontro tra storici e giuristi. Firenze, 2–4 maggio 1974.* Milan, 63–94.

Cracco Ruggini, L. (1976b). 'La vita associativa nelle città dell'Oriente greco: Tradizioni locali e influenze romane', in D. M. Pippidi (ed.), *Assimilation et résistance à la culture gréco-romaine dans le monde ancien: Travaux du VIe Congrès International d'Études Classiques (Madrid, Septembre 1974).* Bucharest and Paris, 463–91.

Cracco Ruggini, L. (1995). *Economia e società nell' "Italia annonaria": Rapporti fra agricoltura e commercio dal IV al VI secolo d.C.* 2nd edn. Bari.

Cristofori, A. (2004). Non arma virumque. *Le occupazioni nell'epigrafia del Piceno.* Bologna.

De Robertis, F. M. (1938). *Il diritto associativo romano dai collegi della Repubblica alle corporazioni del Basso Impero.* Bari.

De Robertis, F. M. (1945). *Storia sociale di Roma: Le classi inferiori.* Bari; repr. Rome, 1981.

De Robertis, F. M. (1955). *Il fenomeno associativo nel mondo romano: Dai collegi della Repubblica alle corporazioni del Basso Impero.* Naples.

De Robertis, F. M. (1959). 'Sulla considerazione sociale del lavoro nel mondo romano', in *Problemi economici dall'antichità ad oggi: Studi in onore del prof. Vittorio Franchini nel 75° compleanno.* Milan, 54–70.

De Robertis, F. M. (1962). *Ancora sulla considerazione sociale del lavoro nel mondo romano (II: l'ambiente aulico),* in *Studi in onore di Amintore Fanfani*, i. Milan, 3–37.

De Robertis, F. M. (1963). *Lavoro e lavoratori nel mondo romano.* Bari.

De Robertis, F. M. (1971). *Storia delle corporazioni e del regime associativo nel mondo romano.* Bari.

De Salvo, L. (1987). 'Il giudizio sulla mercatura nel mondo romano', *AFLM* 20: 9–32.

De Salvo, L. (1992). *Economia privata e pubblici servizi nell'Impero romano: I corpora naviculariorum.* Messina.

De Salvo, L. (2004). 'Nuove testimonianze (e riletture) di testi epigrafici relativi a *navicularii* e battellieri', in L. Ruscu (ed.), *Orbis antiquus: Studia in honorem Ioannis Pisonis.* Cluj-Napoca, 120–4.

De Visscher, F. (1939). 'Recensione', *RHE* 35: 78–82.

Di Benedetto, V. (1978). 'Appunti su marxismo e mondo antico', *QS* 4/8: 53–97.

Di Branco, M. (2000). 'Lavoro e conflittualità sociale in una città tardoantica: Una rilettura dell'epigrafe di Sardi CIG 3467 (= Le Bas – Waddington 628 = Sardis VII, 1, n. 18)', *Antiquité tardive* 8: 181–208.

Di Porto, A. (1984). *Impresa collettiva e schiavo manager in Roma antica (II sec. a. C –II sec. d. C.)*. Milan.

Diosono, F. (2007). Collegia: *Le associazioni professionali nel mondo romano*. Rome.

Diosono, F. (2008). *Il legno: Produzione e commercio*. Rome.

Duff, P. W. (1942). 'Review of F. M. De Robertis, *Il diritto associativo romano dai collegi della Repubblica alle corporazioni del basso impero*', *JRS* 32: 129–31.

Epigrafia (1994). *Epigrafia della produzione e della distribuzione: Actes de la VIIe rencontre franco-italienne sur l'épigraphie du monde romain organisée par l'Université de Rome—La Sapienza et l'École française de Rome, Rome 5–6 juin 1992*. Rome.

Finley, M. I. (1981). *Schiavitù antica e ideologie moderne*. Rome and Bari.

Finley, M. I. (1982). 'Problems of Slave Society: Some Reflections on the Debate', *Opus* 1/1: 201–7.

Frangioni, L. (1998). *Corporazioni & dintorni: Saggio bibliografico sulle corporazioni e i gruppi professionali dall'età romana alla fascista (e oltre)*. Florence.

Gabba, E. (1975). 'Mercati e fiere nell'Italia romana', *SCO* 24: 141–63; repr. in Gabba (1988), 143–61.

Gabba, E. (1979). 'Per un'interpretazione politica del "de officiis" di Cicerone', *RAL* 34: 117–41.

Gabba, E. (1980). 'Riflessioni antiche e moderne sulle attività commerciali a Roma nei secoli II e I a.C.', in J. H. D'Arms and E. C. Kopff (eds), *The Seaborne Commerce of Ancient Rome: Studies in Archaeology and History (MAAR 36)*. Rome, 91–102; repr. in Gabba (1988), 89–105.

Gabba, E. (1982). 'Per la storia della società romana tardo-repubblicana', *Opus* 1/2: 373.

Gabba, E. (1985). 'Arricchimento e ascesa sociale in Plauto e Terenzio', *Index* 13: 5–15; repr. in Gabba (1988), 69–82.

Gabba, E. (1988). *Del buon uso della ricchezza: Saggi di storia economica e sociale del mondo antico*. Milan.

Gagliardi, A. (2010). *Il corporativismo fascista*. Rome and Bari.

Galeno, G. (1960). 'Letture', *Labeo* 6: 143–4.

Gasperini, L. (2005). 'Sul *materiarius* di Sena Gallica (CIL XI, 6212)', *Picus* 25: 129–38.

Geremia Nucci, R. (2006). 'I *plumbarii* ostiensi: Una sintesi delle nuove evidenze', *ArchClass* ns 7: 448–67.

Giacchero, M. (1987). 'Il mondo della produzione e del lavoro nell'*Edictum de pretiis*', in *Studi in onore di Arnaldo Biscardi*, vi. Milan, 121–32.

Giannarelli, E. (1986). 'Il tema del lavoro nella letteratura cristiana antica: Fra costruzione ideologica e prassi letteraria', in S. Felici (ed.), *Spiritualità del lavoro nella catechesi dei Padri del III–IV secolo*. Rome, 213–24.

Giannarelli, E. (1991). 'Il concetto di lavoro nel monachesimo antico: Temi e problemi', *Codex Aquilarensis* 5: 31–53.

Giardina, A. (1982). 'Lavoro e storia sociale: antagonismi e alleanze dall'ellenismo al tardoantico', *Opus* 1: 115–46.

Giardina, A. (ed.) (1986). *Società romana e impero tardoantico*. Bari.

Giardina, A. (1994). *Il mercante nel mondo romano*, in A. Giardina and A.J. Gurevic, *Il mercante dall'antichità al Medioevo*, Rome and Bari, 5–59.

Giardina, A., and Schiavone, A. (eds) (1981). *Società romana e produzione schiavistica*. Rome and Bari.

Giuliani, R. (2003). 'Scene di mestiere nelle catacombe: Il restauro del cubicolo dei Bottai nel cimitero di Priscilla', *MiChA* 9: 9–18.

Granino Cecere, M. G. (1994). '*D. Caecilius Abascantus, diffusor olearius ex provincia Baetica* (CIL VI 1885)', *Epigrafia* 705–19.

Gros, P. (1983). 'Recensione', *Gnomon* 55: 609–20.

Guarino, A. (1982). '*Quaestus omnis patribus indecorus*', *Labeo*, 28: 7–16.

Horowitz, D. L. (1963). *The Italian Labour Movement*. Cambridge, MA.

Horowitz, D. L. (1972). *Storia del movimento sindacale in Italia*. Bologna.

Joshel, S. (1992). *Work, Identity and Legal Status at Rome: A Study of the Occupational Inscriptions*. Norman, OK, and London.

Kreissig, H. (1982). 'Zu einer Diskussion am Gramsci-Institut über sozialökonomische Probleme des Altertums', *JWG* 23/2: 169–76.

Laghi, I. (1990). *La rivoluzione sociale del primo sindacalismo: Antologia del sindacalismo rivoluzionario*. Rome.

Lana, I. (1984). *L'idea del lavoro a Roma*. Turin.

Lentano, M. (1996). 'Acquisire, conservare, consumare: Spunti per una lettura in chiave economica degli *Adelphoe* di Terenzio', *Aufidus* 29: 77–100.

Levi, M. A. (1963). 'Iscrizioni relative a *collegia* dell'età imperiale', *Athenaeum* 41: 384–405.

Lo Cascio, E. (1982). '"Modo di produzione schiavistico" ed esportazioni italiche', *Opus* 1/2: 389–97.

Lo Cascio, E. (ed.) (2000). *Mercati permanenti e mercati periodici nel mondo romano: Atti degli incontri capresi di storia dell'economia antica (Capri 13–15 ottobre 1997)*. Bari.

Lotito, G. (1981). 'Modelli etici e base economica nelle opere filosofiche di Cicerone', in Giardina and Schiavone (1981), iii, 80–126.

Luraschi, G. (1982). 'Per una valutazione della società romana e dell'economia schiavistica', *Opus* 1/2: 399–412.

Lussana F. (ed.) (2000). *La Fondazione Istituto Gramsci: Cinquant'anni di cultura, politica e storia. Un catalogo e una guida*. Florence.

Malaspina, E. (2003). 'La terminologia latina delle professioni femminili nel mondo antico', *Mediterraneo antico* 6/1: 347–91.

Malfitana, D. (2006). 'Appropriazione di copyright, falsificazione o ingannevole messaggio pubblicitario nel marchio ARRETINVM?: Nota sui rapporti fra archeologia e storia del diritto romano', *MBAH* 25/2: 149–68.

Manacorda, D. (1985). 'Schiavo manager e anfore romane: A proposito dei rapporti tra archeologia e storia del diritto', *Opus* 4: 141–51.

Manacorda, D. (1989). 'Le anfore dell'Italia repubblicana: Aspetti economici e sociali', in *Amphores romaines et histoire économique: Dix ans de recherche*. Rome, 443–67.

Manacorda, D. (1990). 'Le fornaci di Visellio a Brindisi: Primi risultati dello scavo', *Vetera christianorum* 27/2: 375–415.

Mannoni, T., and Giannichedda, E. (1996). *Archeologia della produzione*. Turin.

Mantello, A. (2008). 'Etica e mercato tra filosofia e giurisprudenza', *SDHI* 78: 3–78.

Marcone, A. (2000). 'Tra archeologia e storia economica: Il mausoleo dei Secundini a Igel', *Athenaeum* 88/2: 485–97.

Marcone, A. (2005). 'Riflessioni sugli as petti giuridici dell'artigianato romana', in M. Polfer (ed.), *Artisanat et économie romaine*. Montagnác, 7–16.

Marengo, S. M. (1981). 'I bolli laterizi di Quinto Clodio Ambrosio nel Piceno', *Picus* 1: 105–13.

Mazza, M. (1974). 'Sul proletariato urbano in epoca imperiale: Problemi del lavoro in Asia minore', *Syculorum Gymnasium* 27: 237–78; repr. in Mazza (1986), 75–117.

Mazza, M. (1976). 'Marxismo e storia antica: Note sulla storiografia marxista in Italia', *Studi storici* 17/2: 95–124.

Mazza, M. (1986). *La fatica dell'uomo: Schiavi e liberi nel mondo romano*. Catania.

Mazzoleni, D. (1986). 'Il lavoro nell'epigrafia cristiana', in S. Felici (ed.), *Spiritualità del lavoro nella catechesi dei Padri del III–IV secolo*. Rome, 263–71; repr. in Mazzoleni (2002), 39–48.

Mazzoleni, D. (2002). *Epigrafi del Mondo Cristiano antico*. Rome.

Mennella, G. (2000). 'Un *negotiator vestiarius cisalpinus et transalpinus* a Fara Novarese', *Epigraphica* 62: 125–35.

Mennella, G. (2001). 'Evidenze epigrafiche sul commercio del marmo nel Piemonte romano', in M. G. Angeli Bertinelli and A. Donati (eds), *Varia epigraphica: Atti del colloquio internazionale di epigrafia. Bertinoro, 8–10 giugno 2000*. Faenza, 329–37.

Mennella, G. (2010). 'Il *collegium nautarum* e l'integrazione delle risorse forestali nell'economia di *Luna*', in F. Javier Navarro (ed.), *Pluralidad e integración en el mundo romano: Actas del II coloquio internacional Italia Iberia–Iberia Italia, Pamplona-Olite del 15 al 17 de octubre de 2008*. Pamplona, 279–85.

Mennella, G., and Apicella, G. (2000). *Le corporazioni professionali nell'Italia romana: Un aggiornamento al Waltzing*. Naples.

Merola, G. D. (2007). 'Una *lex collegii* marittima? A proposito di *D.* 14, 2, 9', in E. Lo Cascio and G. D. Merola (eds), *Forme di aggregazione nel mondo romano*. Bari, 259–72.

Merola Reduzzi, F. (1990). *'Servo parere': Studi sulla condizione giuridica degli schiavi vicari e dei sottoposti a schiavi nelle esperienze greca e romana*. Naples.

Mondolfo, R. (1965). 'Tecnica e scienza nel pensiero antico', *Athenaeum* 43: 279–94.

Montevecchi, O. (1950). *I contratti di lavoro e di servizio nell'Egitto greco-romano e bizantino*. Milan.

Montevecchi, O., and Manca Masciandri, M. (1984). *I contratti di baliatico*. Milan.

Monti, G. M. (1934). *Le corporazioni nell'evo antico e nell'alto medioevo*. Bari.

Morelli, F. (2011). 'Dal Mar Rosso ad Alessandria: il verso (ma anche il recto), del "papiro di Muzirus" (SB XVIII 13167)', *Tyche* 26: 149–233.

Morretta, S. (1999). 'Donne imprenditrici nella produzione e nel commercio dell'olio betico (I–III sec. d.C.)', *Saitabi* 49: 229–45.

Musca, D. A. (ed.) (2007). *Francesco Maria De Robertis: L'uomo, il docente, lo studioso: Atti di un Incontro di studio. Bari, 20 novembre 2004*. Bari.

Musso, S. (2002). *Storia del lavoro in Italia: Dall'Unità a oggi*. Venice.

Napoli, M. (ed.) (2007). *Alle radici del sindacalismo italiano*. Milan.

Narducci, E. (1978). 'Note in margine a due libri recenti', *QS* 4/8: 39–50.

Narducci, E. (1985). 'Valori aristocratici e mentalità acquisitiva nel pensiero di Cicerone', *Index* 13: 93–125.

Nicolet, C., Andreau, J., Vallet, G., Mossé, C., and Morel, J.-P. (1982). 'Interventi su *Società romana e produzione schioavistica*, a cura di A. Giardina e A. Schiavone', *QS* 8/16: 287–323.

Nonnis, D. (1999). 'Attività imprenditoriali e classi dirigenti nell'età repubblicana: Tre città campione', *CCG* 10: 71–109.

Nonnis, D. (2001). 'Appunti sulle anfore adriatiche di età repubblicana: Aree di produzione e di commercializzazione', *AAAd* 46: 467–500.

Nonnis, D. (2003). 'Le implicazioni socio-politiche della produzione e della distribuzione nell'Italia repubblicana: Per un repertorio prosopografico', in C. Zaccagnini (ed.), *Mercanti e politica e nel mondo antico*. Rome, 245–74.

Nörr, D. (1965). 'Zur sozialen und rechtlichen Bewertung der freien Arbeit in Rom', *ZRG* 82: 67–105.

Ortalli., J. (1993). *Mestieri, merci, mercati: Luoghi e memorie per l'economia di Bologna romana*, in R. Scannavini (ed.), *Piazze e Mercati nel centro antico di Bologna: Storia e Urbanistica dall'età romana al medioevo, dal Rinascimento ai giorni nostri*. Bologna, 251–81.

Palazzo, P., and Silvestrini, M. (2001). 'Apani: Anfore brindisine di produzione "aniniana"', *Daidalos* 3: 57–107.

Panciera, S. (1957). *Vita economica di Aquileia in età romana*. Aquileia.

Panciera, S. (1980). 'Olearii', in J. H. D'Arms and E. C. Kopff (eds), *The Seaborne Commerce of Ancient Rome: Studies in Archaeology and History (MAAR* 36). Rome, 235–50.

Pani, M. (1985). 'La polemica di Seneca contro le *artes* (*Ep.* 90): Un caso di sconcerto', in *Xenia: Scritti in onore di Piero Treves*. Rome, 141–50; repr. in Pani (1992), 99–112.

Pani, M. (1992). *Potere e valori a Roma fra Augusto e Traiano*. Bari.

Papi, E. (2002). 'La *turba inpia*: Artigiani e commercianti del foro Romano e dintorni (I sec. a.C.–64 d.C.)', *JRA* 15/1: 45–62.

Pasoli E. (1980). 'Scienza e tecnica nella considerazione prevalente del mondo antico: Vitruvio e l'architettura', in *Scienza e tecnica nelle letterature classiche*. Sassari, 63–80.

Pensabene, P. (1983). 'Osservazioni sulla diffusione dei marmi e sul loro prezzo nella Roma imperiale', *DArch* 1/1: 55–63.

Pensabene, P. (1990). 'Trasporto, diffusione e commercio dei marmi: Aggiornamenti e nuove interpretazioni', *Journal of the European Study Group on Physical, Chemical, Biological & Mathematical Techniques Applied to Archaeology* 27: 231–64.

Pensabene, P. (1995). *Le vie del marmo: I blocchi di cava di Roma e di Ostia. Il fenomeno del marmo nella Roma antica*. Rome.

Perry, J. (2006). *The Roman* collegia: *The Modern Evolution of an Ancient Concept*. Leiden.

Pintaudi, R. (2001). 'Quattro contratti di trasporto verso Panopolis', in T. Gagos and R. S. Bagnall (eds), *Essays and Texts in Honor of J. David Thomas*. Oakville, CT, 211–15.

Polichetti, F. (2001). *Figure sociali, merci e scambi nell'*Edictum Diocletiani et collegarum de pretiis rerum venalium. Naples.

Proto, F. (2006). '*Tabernae, officinae* ed altri impianti a carattere commerciale della *Regio I* di Pompei: Un campione d'indagine socio-economica', *Rivista di studi pompeiani* 17: 15–28.

Pucci, G. (1993). 'I bolli sulla terra sigillata: Fra epigrafia e storia economica', in W. V. Harris (ed.), *The Inscribed Economy: Production and Distribution in the Roman Empire in the Light of instrumentum domesticum: The Proceedings of a Conference Held at the American Academy in Rome on 10–11 January, 1992* (JRA Supplementary Series, 6). Ann Arbor, 73–9.

Quadrato, E. (2004). 'Francesco Maria De Robertis: Appunti di un incontro di studio', *Rivista di Diritto Romano* 4: 1–8 <http://www.ledonline.it/rivistadirittoromano/allegati/dirittoromano04quadrato.pdf> (accessed 21 July 2015).

Rathbone, D. W. (1983). 'The Slave Mode of Production in Italy', *JRS* 73: 160–8.

Rizzo, F. P. (1993). *La menzione del lavoro nelle epigrafi della Sicilia antica (Per una storia della mentalità)*. Palermo.

Salvaterra, C. (2006). 'Labour and Identity in the Roman World: Italian Historiography during the Last Two Decades', in B. Waldijk (ed.), *Professions and Social Identity: New European Historical Research on Work, Gender and Society*. Pisa, 15–38.

Salvioli, G. (1906). *Le Capitalisme dans le monde antique: Études sur l'histoire de l'économie romaine*. Paris.

Salvioli, G. (1912). *Der Kapitalismus im Altertum: Studien über die römische Wirtschaftsgeschichte*. Stuttgart.

Salvioli, G. (1929). *Il capitalismo antico: Storia dell'economia romana*. Bari.

Salvioli, G. (1985). *Il capitalismo antico: Storia dell'economia romana*, ed. A. Giardina. Rome and Bari.

Sampaolo, V. (1995). 'I decoratori del Tempio di Iside a Pompei', *MNIR* 54: 200–13.

Santoro, S. (ed.) (2004). *Artigianato e produzione nella Cisalpina*, i. *Proposte di metodo e prime applicazioni*. Florence.

Silvestrini, M. (1989). 'Recensione', *QS* 15/30: 199–208.

Sirago, V. A. (1983). *Femminismo a Roma nel Primo Impero*. Soveria Mannelli.

Solazzi, S. (1906). *Il lavoro libero nel mondo romano*. Macerata.

Solazzi, S. (1955). *Scritti di diritto romano*, i. Naples.

Storchi Marino, A. (1979). 'Artigiani e rituali religiosi nella Roma arcaica', *RAAN* 54: 333–57.

Taborelli, L. (1982). 'Vasi di vetro con bollo monetale (Note sulla produzione, la tassazione e il commercio degli unguenti aromatici nella prima età imperiale)', *Opus* 1/2: 315–40.

Taborelli, L. (1998). 'Un antico forno vetrario ad Ancona', *Picus* 18: 219–24.

Thébert, Y. (1982). 'Recensione', *Annales ESC* 37: 788–91.

Tisé, B. (2001). 'Osservazioni su CIL IX, 60', in S. Alessandrì and F. Grelle (eds), *Dai Gracchi alla fine della Repubblica: Atti del V convegno di studi sulla Puglia romana. Mesagne, 9–10 aprile 1999*. Galatina, 155–70.

Torelli, M. (1992). 'Editoriale', *Ostraka* 1/1: 3–5.

Torelli, M. (1996). 'Industria laterizia e aristocrazie locali in Italia: appunti prosopografici', *CCG* 7: 291–6.

Tozzi, G. (1961). *Economisti greci e romani: Le singolari intuizioni di una scienza moderna nel mondo classico*. Milan.

Traina, G. (2000). 'I mestieri', in A. Giardina (ed.), *Storia di Roma dall'antichità a oggi. Roma antica.* Rome, 113–31.

Turone, S. (1992). *Storia del sindacato in Italia: Dal 1943 al crollo del comunismo.* Rome and Bari.

Varni, A. (1992). *Il sindacato nella società italiana fra '800 e '900.* Florence.

Vallauri, C. (2008). *Storia dei sindacati nella società italiana.* Rome.

Vegetti, M. (1977). *Marxismo e società antica.* Milan.

Vicari, F. (2001). *Produzione e commercio dei tessuti nell'Occidente romano* (BAR International Series, 910). Oxford.

Zaccaria, C. (1985). 'Testimonianze epigrafiche dei rapporti tra Aquileia e l'Illirico in età imperiale romana', *AAAd* 26/1: 85–127.

Zevi, F. (1966). 'Appunti sulle anfore romane', *ArchClass* 18.2: 208–47.

Zevi, F. (2008). 'I collegi di Ostia e le loro sedi associative tra Antonini e Severi', in C. Berrendonner, M. Cébeillac-Gervasoni, and L. Lamoine (eds), *Le Quotidien municipal dans l'Occident romain.* Clermont-Ferrand, 477–505.

3

The Archaeology of Roman Urban Workshops: A French Approach?

Jean-Pierre Brun

Since 2000, the Centre Jean Bérard, the Naples-based research centre of the Centre National de la Recherche Scientifique and the École Française de Rome, has been developing a research programme on ancient urban workshops in southern Italy, focusing principally on Pompeii and Herculaneum, but also including other excavations such as those at Saepinum, Paestum, and Levanzo in Sicily.[1] The aim of the programme is to advance our understanding of certain artisanal activities that can be particularly difficult to identify in places where the evidence is less well preserved, in order to propose criteria for interpreting those poorly preserved remains.

The programme comes from a tradition of study that has been evolving in France since the beginning of the twentieth century and that has been renewed by the development of rescue archaeology since 1990.

ROMAN URBAN CRAFTS IN FRENCH STUDIES

Even though the history of technology in antiquity has long been limited by the scarce availability of written sources that deal mainly with agriculture and, in France, by the non-participation of scholars in the theoretical debate on the nature of the ancient economy that occurred in Germany at the beginning of the twentieth century, the French did develop a specific interest in the artisanal

[1] This programme involves colleagues from the Centre Jean Bérard, the Centre Camille Jullian of CNRS (Philippe Borgard), the CNRS (with Magali Cullin-Mingaud, Marie T. Libre), the École française de Rome (Nicolas Monteix, Emmanuel Botte), the Centre Archéologique du Var (Martine Leguilloux). It is supported by a grant from the Ministère des Affaires Étrangères and by a financial support from the Agence Nationale de la Recherche (programme Artifex).

world using literary, epigraphic, and archaeological sources. These studies started at the turn of the twentieth century with some excellent articles published in Daremberg and Saglio's *Dictionnaire des antiquités* and some syntheses about the history of Greek economic activities.[2] After the First World War, they were followed by the grand syntheses on Africa by Stéphane Gsell and by Camille Jullian's work on Gaul that explored economic issues and the state of the question at that time.[3]

In the 1930s, the study of the history of technology became particularly fashionable. Historians of this period, fascinated by the take-off of modern innovations, wanted to study technological development and its relationship with historical and social development. This was one of the main projects of the Annales School, clearly defined by Lucien Febvre in a manifesto published in 1935.[4] The historians from this school made some important contributions, but these mainly concerned the medieval period, and they greatly underestimated the role of ancient technology. As far as antiquity was concerned, they followed the opinions of one specialist, Commandant Lefebvre des Noëttes, a cavalry officer who argued, in a series of books published between 1924 and 1932, that ancient technology was deeply deficient, and explained the development of slavery as a result of these shortcomings. The title of one of his books—*L'Attelage et le cheval de selle à travers les âges: Contribution à l'histoire de l'esclavage*—is highly significant.[5]

From the beginning of the twentieth century, archaeological excavations started to return increasing amounts of evidence, which Albert Grenier summarized for Gaul in his 1934 *Manuel d'archéologie gallo-romaine*. In this book, he compared the small-scale artisanal activities located in towns and villages to large-scale industries, quarries, ceramic productions, mines, and metallurgical workshops located in the countryside close to the natural resources they exploited.

Three years later, the same author published a synthesis in the series of the *Economic Survey of Ancient Rome* edited by Tenney Frank.[6] In his introduction on the working methods he intends to follow there is no allusion to the ongoing debate about the nature of the ancient economy: he exposed a careful and empirical process based mainly on texts, considering that 'in economic matters, the archaeological evidence needs, as well as inscriptions, a certain degree of generalization, but this is often arbitrary'; thus he planned to use archaeology only when the interpretation of the remains was well established. Significantly, he insisted on the use of evidence from pottery production, and

---

[2] Daremberg, Saglio, and Pottier (1877–91); Guiraud (1900); Francotte (1900–1).
[3] Gsell (1913–28); Jullian (1920–6).   [4] Febvre (1935: 531–5).
[5] Lefebvre des Noëttes (1924, 1931, 1935). It is well known that these theories have been abandoned—see, e.g. Amouretti (1991) and Rapsaet (2002).
[6] Grenier (1937: esp. 382 (for the method) and 586–7).

he mentions textile production, but only through written sources.[7] Thus, the scarcity of texts and archaeological remains, with the notable exceptions of pottery and metalworking, have meant that artisanal research was almost absent in French studies of the ancient economy until the mid-1980s.

From the 1950s to the 1970s, a period that witnessed the destruction of many archaeological sites during post-war reconstruction, there was however a slow accumulation of data, and several large syntheses were published, including *L'Histoire générale du travail*, *L'Histoire générale des techniques*, *Le Dictionnaire archéologique des techniques*, and *Histoire des techniques*.[8] They followed the pre-war theories that postulated a stagnation of technological development during antiquity and they integrated archaeological documentation into the discourse but only through iconographic representations and artefacts, mainly in stone, metal, or terracotta. The artisan himself was presented through the filter of the aristocratic mentality reflected by the surviving literature, and the workshops were not discussed. Scholars stood on the threshold of studying the productive installations, but they did not enter the subject.

Changes came with the 1980s. In the *Histoire de la France urbaine*, whose first volume was published in 1980, the economic role of towns was scrutinized. Venceslas Kruta's presentation of Iron Age *oppida* insisted on their role as artisanal centres, while Christian Goudineau argued that towns in Roman Gaul were parasitic on the countryside.[9] The latter picture, which used all the archaeological data available at the time, is still impressive. According to Goudineau, the role played by towns as production centres was limited to local needs and the overall urban output was low, even if he recognizes that it is impossible to determine the proportion of urban to rural production. As the commercial role of cities was limited mainly to local trade between town and country—with the exception of towns located along the main trade routes: Mediterranean and Rhône–Rhine axes—his conclusion is clear: the town in antiquity was definitely a 'consumer city'.

Soon after, Philippe Leveau expounded another interpretation published in several articles.[10] He argued that towns and their elites organized the countryside and improved agricultural production through their estates through a new type of management, introducing new crops and farming methods. In this sense, ancient cities were not parasitic: they paid for their provisions through services. But the role played by urban production was not considered as important. In Leveau's doctoral thesis on Caesarea of Mauretania, which provides a wide range of new data, especially on the countryside, the city is

---

[7] Grenier (1937) devoted twenty-two pages to pottery, four to metallurgy, and two to textile production, and does not even mention leather production.

[8] Rémondon (1959); Duval (1962); various authors (1963–4); Gilles (1978).

[9] Février et al. (1980: 206–10, 365–81).   [10] Leveau (1983); Février and Leveau (1982).

reckoned to be a political town whose purpose was to organize and administer the territory.[11]

Another approach emerged at the end of the 1970s, with scholars such as Marie-Claire Amouretti for the Greek period, Jean-Paul Morel for the Roman Republic, and Jean-Pierre Sodini for late antiquity. They paid attention to technical processes, to social and cultural environments, and to the artisans themselves as men, trying to re-create their technical movements within the *chaîne opératoire* and to understand their daily lives.[12] They all insisted on the interdependence between agriculture and craftsmanship. The craftsmen provided the necessary tools and devices to peasants and landowners, from iron tools to jars and amphorae for storing and trading the crops. The agricultural development of antiquity is inconceivable without the parallel development of artefacts produced in workshops located in cities or villages. Jean-Paul Morel recently argued that artisanal products are indispensable for farming, especially for advanced and highly productive farming techniques, and, further, that in some regions these products were made principally in towns, where in some cases these activities were undertaken at manufactories.[13]

Research into artisanal establishments really took off only from the end of the 1980s, following the development of rescue archaeology. These excavations shed new light on artisanal activities that encouraged the development of research programmes on themes such as urban and rural metallurgy or on well-preserved sites such as those destroyed by Vesuvius.[14] New data were presented at several conferences: at Lyons in 1996 and 2002, at *Erpeldange* in 1999, 2001, and 2004, at Autun in 2007, at Aix-en-Provence in 2007, at Rome in 2009, at Naples in 2009.[15] Several workshop monographs were also published.[16] Partial syntheses are now available—for example, on the professional associations by Nicolas Tran, published in 2006, on the fish-salting industry in Italy by Emmanuel Botte in 2009, and on the workshops of Herculaneum and Pompeii by Nicolas Monteix in 2011.[17]

DEFINING THE 'ARTISAN'

A key question to ask is what type of activities we intend to study when we are looking at artisanal activities. Several French scholars have attempted to define

---

[11] Leveau (1984).   [12] Amouretti et al. (1977); Morel (1976, 1992); Sodini (1979).
[13] Morel (1985, 1996, 2009).   [14] Mangin (1981, 1985).
[15] Various authors (1996); Béal and Goyon (2002); Polfer (1999, 2001, 2005); Brun (2009); Chardron-Picault (2010); Fontaine, Satre, and Tekki (2011); Monteix and Tran (2011).
[16] Many publications of rescue excavations present workshops of various types: e.g. Rivet (1992) and Chardron-Picault and Pernot (1999).
[17] Tran (2006); Botte (2009); Monteix (2011).

this area of research, but within very different boundaries. For Jean-Pierre Sodini, writing in 1979, the word 'artisan' included all professional activities except agriculture, food preparation, and intellectual professions. In his essay on 'the artisan' published in 1992, Jean-Paul Morel did not give a precise definition, mentioning only the disdain of aristocratic circles for craftsmen recorded by Cicero and Seneca. In 2005, Alain Ferdière, independently of Sara Santoro,[18] proposed to limit the field of artisanal activities to craftsmanship, excluding artisans who prepared food and those involved in construction (especially builders).[19] In two pieces published in 2011, Nicolas Monteix and Jean-Paul Morel revisited the argument. Monteix sees Ferdière's and Santoro's definitions as too restrictive and decides not to use the term *artisanat* because of its ambiguity and anachronism, preferring instead the broader term *métier*.[20] Jean-Paul Morel recognized the problem: 'définir strictement [l'artisanat] est devenu un exercice sinon nécessaire, du moins obligé: exercice redoutable pour l'Antiquité, et pas seulement pour elle.' He proposed the following definition: 'the artisan is a man who, apart from agricultural work, makes something, using mainly his hands and working alone, or with the help of a small team.'[21] Such a definition includes workers making products, such as potters, producing food, such as bakers, or providing services, such as barbers, but also those undertaking domestic activities such as weaving for one's own family.

Personally, I think that we should consider as 'artisanal' any type of productive activity that is carried out in a non-domestic context and paid for by a customer or a patron in money or kind. Using such a broad definition enables a wider investigation of the entire range of urban economic activities, including the preparation of food, building activities—from the extraction of stone in the quarries to construction work—and obviously all craftsmanship. It may also include workshops in *villae* that were actually enterprises.

The archaeology of these activities should be studied with the same attention as that previously paid to aristocratic houses, sanctuaries, or necropoleis, because these remains are often the only key to the infrastructure of ancient civilization. Ancient literature written by aristocrats presents the upper-class vision of the working world, and there are very few inscriptions mentioning craftsmen compared to the thousands of inscriptions dealing with the careers of the aristocrats or with the worship of gods. Archaeological remains are the only evidence left by the lower classes, who had neither the power nor the intellectual means to transmit the memory of their activities and their way of life. These remains are also poorly preserved, and thus difficult to identify. Furthermore, their location, often outside city centres, means that they are sometimes ignored: there is thus a need to study them more carefully than has previously been done.

[18] Santoro (2004: 24–6).   [19] Ferdière (2005).   [20] Monteix (2011: 8–9).
[21] Morel (2011).

THE 'ARTIFEX' PROGRAMME

Consequently, the aim of our research at Pompeii, and in southern Italy, was first and foremost archaeological and practical, rather than historical. Generally speaking, ancient written sources paid little attention to artisanal activities and to their contribution to economic life, if we exclude the producers of luxurious items. Archaeology is barely able to compensate for this lack because many activities used perishable materials, and thus their importance remains underestimated. In any book about the archaeology of artisanal productions pottery, metalworking, and glassmaking take the main stage because they leave durable remains such as kilns, pottery sherds, slag, and fused glass.[22] On the other hand, weavers and dyers, tanners and cobblers, wood-workers and carpenters, basket-makers and perfumers, are almost absent. Their installations are difficult to characterize, and they used materials that are no longer present. If we want to present a more balanced view of artisanal production within the ancient economy in the future, archaeologists must learn how to recognize the remains of these activities.

Workshops at Pompeii and Herculaneum

The excavated remains of the towns buried in the AD 79 eruption of Vesuvius give us a unique opportunity to study these remains. Obviously the necessary observations and analyses were not done during the initial excavations, but the state of preservation is still much better than anywhere else. The catastrophe fixed as many as 270 workshops in time, which contained tools, rubbish, and sometimes artefacts or graffiti. In many cases they can be clearly identified and interpreted.

Dyeing Plants

Four wool-washing and dyeing plants that were in use in AD 79 were cleaned and excavated.[23] The first ones, probably belonging to the same complex, were installed after the earthquake of 62 or 63, in two shops V 1, 4 and V 1, 5 opening onto the Via di Nola. At the entrance, both of them present a large boiler lined with lead that was used for degreasing wool with alum, together with several other boilers used for dyeing either in heating solutions or in fermenting ones. Reconstruction of the boilers and dyeing experiments in

---

[22] e.g. Fontaine, Sartre, and Tekki (2011).
[23] Borgard (2002); Borgard and Puybaret (2004).

2008 and 2009 helped further understanding of the various features.[24] The Casa della Regina d'Inghilterra (VII 14, 5.17–19) facing onto the Via dell'-Abbondanza was studied in 2001–2: in the garden of the house, after the earthquake of 62 or 63, two working complexes were built (see Fig. 3.1). The first one is composed of a boiler and two benches in limestone used to clean the wool. The second part is equipped with nine boilers for dyeing the fibres. A similar association is visible in workshop I 8, 19, which was studied between 2003 and 2006: a semi-underground room was used to prepare the wool, which was dyed in an adjacent ground-floor space following the processes already mentioned. Further investigations were undertaken in workshop VII 12, 23, which is unique for its probable wool-cleaning installation, with its two types of boilers (high and low). In parallel, the textile remains that survived through carbonization were studied.[25]

Perfumeries

Perfumeries are usually difficult to identify, because their remains are not at all characteristic except when a workshop located near the centre of a town is

Fig. 3.1. The dye plant situated in house VII 14, 5 at Pompeii studied by Ph. Borgard. The photo shows nine heaters for dyeing in several colours, two basins, and a workshop for cleaning the textile fibres. Photo: Jean-Pierre Brun.

---

[24] Alfaro et al. (2011).   [25] Study by Fabienne Médard, not yet published.

Fig. 3.2. Perfume shop in the Via degli Augustali at Pompeii excavated in 2002. The vats belong to oil presses destroyed by the AD 62/63 earthquake. Photo: Jean-Pierre Brun.

equipped with a press-bed. Wilhelmina Jashemski, in her book about the gardens of Pompeii, and later David Mattingly, in an article published in 1990, suggested that an oil press found in a shop opening off the Via degli Augustali (VII 4, 24) belonged to a perfume workshop.[26] Excavating this shop in 2001, I found two large tanks underneath the floor laid after AD 65, which residue analysis proved to have contained vegetal oils, and also a boiler nearby, probably used for the preparation of the perfumes (see Fig. 3.2).[27] In May 2011, in collaboration with the Spanish team of Valencia, we excavated three other shops along the street, and were able to identify more perfume shops.[28]

Tanneries

A large tannery, occupying the main part of the fifth block of Regio I, was excavated in the years 1873 and 1874; an architectural and stratigraphic study was carried out between 2001 and 2010. During the second quarter of the first century AD, two tanneries were installed in existing houses. Then, the great earthquake of AD 62 or 63, having severely damaged the houses, offered the opportunity for someone to buy the entire block and to create a single large

[26] Jashemski (1979: 276); Mattingly (1990). [27] Brun and Monteix (2009).
[28] Brun et al. (2012).

Fig. 3.3. Balloon photograph of the tannery I 5 at Pompeii, showing the work area in the peristyle, and the tanning room in the lower right corner of the building. Photo: Jean-Pierre Brun.

tannery equipped for washing the skins and tanning them in a set of fifteen cylindrical pits (see Fig. 3.3).[29]

Basket-making

A study of ancient basket-making recently published presents the excavations conducted in the house I 14, 2 where bunches of carbonized flexible shoots and a long tank used to soak them were discovered (see Fig. 3.4). The results of the excavations have been integrated in a full synthesis on what we know about this rarely detectable craft.[30]

We have thus progressed in our understanding of some branches of ancient technology not limited to these four examples. The programme also studied plumbers' workshops (Nicolas Monteix), blacksmiths' establishments (Marie-Pierre Amarger), painters' workshops (Marie Tuffreau-Libre), colour workshops and pottery workshops (Laëtitia Cavassa), and bakeries (Monteix).[31]

---

[29] Leguilloux (2004).   [30] Cullin-Mingaud (2010).
[31] Borgard et al. (2005); Amarger and Brun (2007). Pompeian bakeries are discussed in Monteix, Chapter 7, this volume.

Fig. 3.4. The tank used for basket-making in house I 14, 2 at Pompeii studied by M. Cullin-Mingaud. Photo: Jean-Pierre Brun.

Results

As a result of the programme, it is now possible to describe artisanal activities, such as, the entire wool- or skin-making cycle, and illustrate them with photos and plans. Taking into account observations made on the well-identified workshops from Pompeii and Herculaneum, we extended our enquiries to other areas of southern Italy. For example, the excavations of the tannery of Pompeii helped us to interpret other less well-preserved tanning installations known in Italy, such as at Pompeii itself,[32] at Saepinum (see Fig. 3.5), and under the church of Santa Cecilia at Rome.[33] It is obvious that tanneries were common, with several workshops of this type existing in each town, but our knowledge does not yet allow the presentation of a chronological synthesis of this industry.

The aim is to understand what traces would remain if the walls, instead of being 1 or 2 metres high, were preserved at only ground level or, worse, at the level of the foundations. To give some examples, archaeologists can identify a perfume factory thanks to press-beds, tanks, boilers, and broken perfume

---

[32] Excavations directed by Steven Ellis and Gary Devore: Devore and Ellis (2008: 9 and fig. 21).

[33] Parmigiani and Pronti (2004) reject the interpretation of the cylindrical tanks as tanning pits and propose identifying them as silos, which is not possible as the silos are bottle-shaped for chemical reasons. But the traditional interpretation has strong support: see Coarelli (1974: 309, 316); Breccia Fratadocchi (1976: 217–22). A full description of the tannery of Saepinum is provided by Brun and Leguilloux (2014).

Fig. 3.5. Balloon photograph of the water-mill, used to produce tannin by crushing bark at Saepinum, Molise. Photo: Jean-Pierre Brun.

flagons. A tannery might leave tools, cylindrical tanks, alum amphorae from Lipari, and specific bone assemblages. A dye plant could be equipped with tanks and various types of boilers lined with lead; because of the work done by the programme, it was possible easily to identify such an installation in a recent excavation at Frejus.[34] A wool-cleaning installation is equipped at Pompeii with a concrete or stone bench and with at least one heater where the wool fibres were washed in hot water containing roots of soapwart (*saponaria officinalis*). These remains are characteristic enough to be identified everywhere.[35] For example, in a rescue excavation I directed in 1997 in the Roman village of Pignans (Var), I found benches, hearths, and channels that were the remains of a wool-washing workshop.

THE PLACE OF ARTISANAL ACTIVITIES IN ECONOMIC LIFE

Excavating various workshops even from a strictly archaeological point of view cannot be disconnected from research into the evolution of economic life at Pompeii and its place within the economy of Italy at the beginning of the empire, assuming that Pompeii was representative of a wealthy medium-sized

---

[34] Pasqualini et al. (2005–6).

[35] I will not enter here into the debate on the identification of these installations. Moeller (1976: 30–5) thought these were used for washing wool; Jongman (1991: 168–9) contested this interpretation, thinking that they were perhaps linked with some food preparation installations, and Flohr (2013a) has recently defended this idea; Borgard and Puybaret (2004) are convinced that they are installations for cleaning and washing wool, two of them being associated with dye plants. Monteix (2011: 170–2; 2013) also follows Moeller's interpretation.

town. As a result of our work, we have now a less dramatized vision than Amedeo Maiuri's theories would lead us to believe.[36] Most of the known workshops were actually built after the earthquake, but these economic activities often succeeded previous activities of the same nature. Recent research shows a complex and versatile situation: some workshops were repaired and adapted after the earthquake, others, such as the tannery, were totally transformed, and yet further workshops were built inside aristocratic houses, which were sold or rented by their previous owners.

Having changed the perception of the chronology, we have to assess the place of artisanal activities within economic life. Did the artisans of Pompeii serve only the needs of the inhabitants of the town and its territory or was part of the production exported towards larger cities such as Rome? The question is pointless for builders, plumbers, painters, or bakers, but worth asking for products such as perfumes, fish sauce, leather, or textiles.

The latter activity was the focus of a polemic between the supporters of relatively large-scale production for export and the supporters of production limited to the needs of the inhabitants of the towns and the countryside. The first option is supported by Moeller, who thought that this industry was controlled by the fullers and involved the local elites.[37] Willem Jongman and recently Miko Flohr have rightly refuted this hypothesis.[38] Jongman concluded that the wool washed and dyed at Pompeii was not exported. Philippe Borgard, on the contrary, has argued that the wool could have brought a significant income to some artisans and traders. Does the dispersion and the size of washing and dyeing plants and the absence of large factories indicate locally focused activity? We must recall that medieval towns with an export textile industry did not, in fact, have larger or more concentrated workshops and, using archaeology without the help of the archives, it would have been impossible to estimate their nature and productive output.

We face the same questions with leather production. The large tannery of Pompeii is clearly a manufactory employing at least twenty more or less specialized workers to crush the bark, carry out the beamhouse work, manipulate the hides in the pits, lift the water, dry, cut, and grease the leather. With its fifteen large tanning pits, its size can be compared with eighteenth-century tanneries from Europe: for example, the model of the tannery proposed by the *Encyclopédie* of D'Alembert and Diderot is equipped with twelve pits.[39] Most of the twenty-four tanneries recorded at Aniane (Languedoc) in 1859 were about the same size as the one at Pompeii.[40] For example, the tannery owned by Antoine Jouillé was equipped with eight cylindrical tanning pits and twelve rectangular tanks. Does the similarity of size imply that

---

[36] Maiuri (1942: 217–20).   [37] Moeller (1976).
[38] Jongman (1991); Flohr (2013b).
[39] Diderot and Le Rond d'Alembert (1765: xiv. 889–92).   [40] David (2002).

production was, at least, proto-industrial? This depends mainly on the number of tanneries operating at the same time in the town. At Aniane, in 1745, the town included at least twenty-nine tanneries with a total of fifty-one tanning pits. At Pompeii, the presence of several plants would be a strong suggestion for an export industry, but we know only one plant of this type, which is, however, close to a non-excavated part of the town, where similar plants could be hidden.

Knowing the number and size of the tanning pits, can we quantify output? We would like to attempt to estimate the maximum level of production, but the modern example of Aniane shows that the production of leather could be intense for some years, drop dramatically, and then restart. Our figures, based on the material remains of workshops, will never be able to take into account these unpredictable variations.

In any case, tanning was certainly profitable, and the very size of the installation seems to respond to a booming demand for this essential product. On the other hand, we must recognize that funerary monuments erected by tanners are rare. But it is not surprising: this job was considered by society as an *ars sordida*, which would not be mentioned by wealthy tanners who became integrated into local aristocracy and became landowners. Epigraphy is thus a misleading clue, giving a slightly false insight into the social facade of wealth but not into the origin of that wealth.

Even in the well-known case of Pompeii, because of the lack of archives, it is difficult either to support or to reject hypotheses about export industries. Systematically studying a single town has its limits: to go further we would need to extend excavations over the surrounding territory. Although Pompeii has been largely excavated and gives a picture of a city in the late first century AD, that picture is still partial and distorted. Excavations have tended to focus on the centre of the town, and we know very little about the suburbs, which were certainly crucial in term of economic activities. North of the Porta Vesuvio, a metallurgical complex was excavated in 1901. The size of the workshop is much larger than the metallurgical workshops inside the city walls.[41] More recently, in June 2011, the Soprintendenza partially excavated a suburb located between Pompeii and Torre Annunziata, where there was at least one big kiln perhaps used to fire bricks and tiles.[42] There are indications that larger plants of any type could lie outside Pompeii and indeed outside every other city, like Bordeaux, where on the site Jean Fleuret, a tannery has recently been excavated.[43]

---

[41] The excavations in Fondo Barbatelli are mentioned in the *Notizie degli Scavi* (1897: 534; 1900: 501; 1901: 599; 1902: 399).

[42] Unpublished excavations mentioned by the Soprintendenza.

[43] Unpublished excavations directed by Christophe Sireix; the leather, fully preserved under the water table, is currently being studied by Martine Leguilloux, who identified several inscriptions and recognized that the tanning process mixed vegetal tanning and alum treatment.

CONCLUSION

Were the ancient towns only consumer cities? Was there a division of labour, a standardization, a rationalization of the work processes and to what extent? We have been looking at these questions for more than a century without reaching any clear and uncontested answers, essentially because of the scarcity of written sources and their nature. The surviving texts are almost exclusively interpretations that allow us to see how the ruling class perceived their economic and social world, but they do not reveal the realities of the work and their evolution, nor do they provide quantified data. Using these sources, we are unable to break out of this vicious circle.

Our programme proposed to leave theoretical considerations to one side for now and look instead at the archaeological documentation, asking precise questions such as: what are the technical and environmental conditions in which various artisanal processes were developed? When did the fundamental mechanical innovations appear, such as the screw, camshaft, and connecting rod? How, when, why, and to what extent did these innovations spread around the Mediterranean area and across the Empire?

Archaeological clues are often ambiguous, but they constitute the only form of documentation that is in fact increasing and that can be quantified and serialized. Thus, scholars should focus on gathering new data from archaeological excavations until we reach a statistically representative picture of the ancient situation, before elaborating new models in order to explain these observations: theorization may be useful for opening new research perspectives, and often it pushes us to ask the right questions of the field research, but ultimately it never answers them.

REFERENCES

Alfaro, C., Brun, J.-P., Borgard, Ph., and Pierobon, R. (eds) (2011). *Purpurae vestes III: Textiles y tintes en la ciutad Antigua* (Archéologie de l'artisanat antique, 4). Valencia.

Amarger, M.-P., and Brun, J.-P. (2007). 'La forge de l'insula I 6,1 de Pompéi', *Quaderni di Studi Pompeiani* 1: 147–68.

Amouretti, M.-C. (1991). 'L'attelage dans l'Antiquité: Le Prestige d'une erreur scientifique', *Annales: Économies, Sociétés, Civilisations* 46/1: 219–32.

Amouretti, M.-C., Comet, G., Pomponi, F., Durbiano, C., et al. (1977). *Campagnes méditerranéennes, permanences et mutations*. Aix–Marseilles.

Béal, J.-C., and Goyon, J.-C. (eds) (2002). *Les artisans dans la ville antique* (Archéologie et Histoire de l'Antiquité, 6). Lyons and Paris.

Borgard, Ph. (2002). 'À propos des teintureries de Pompéi: L'Exemple de l'*officina infectoria* V, 1, 4', in J.-C. Béal and J.-C. Goyon (eds), *Les Artisans dans la ville antique*. Lyons, 55–67.

Borgard, Ph., and Puybaret, M.-P. (2004). 'Le Travail de la laine au début de l'Empire: L'Apport du modèle pompéien. Quels artisans? Quels équipements? Quelles techniques?' in C. Alfaro, J. P. Wild, and B. Costa (eds), *Purpureae vestes: Textiles y tintes del Mediterráneo en epoca romana. International Symposium on Textiles and Dyes in the Mediterranean Roman World, Eivissa 8–10. novembre 2002.* Valencia, 47–59.

Borgard, Ph., Brun, J.-P., Leguilloux, M., Monteix, N., Cullin-Mingaud, M., and Libre, M. T. (2005). 'Recherches sur les productions artisanales à Pompéi et à Herculanum', in P. Guzzo and M.-P. Guidobaldi (eds), *Nuove ricerche archeologiche a Pompei ed Ercolano* (Studi della Soprintendenza Archeologica di Pompei, 10). Naples, 295–317.

Botte, E. (2009). *Salaisons et sauces de poissons en Italie du Sud et en Sicile durant l'Antiquité.* Naples.

Breccia Fratadocchi, M. M., Ricci, S., and Sarlo, B. M. (1976). 'Considerazioni su un nuovo ambiente sottostante la basilica di Santa Cecilia in Trastevere', *BdA* 61/3–4: 217–28.

Brun, J.-P. (ed.) (2009). *L'Artisanat antique en Italie méridionale et en Gaule, Mélanges offerts à Maria-Francesca Buonaiuto* (Collection du Centre Jean Bérard, 32; Archéologie de l'artisanat antique, 2). Naples.

Brun, J.-P., and Monteix, N. (2009). 'Les parfumeries en Campanie antique', in Brun (2009), 115–33.

Brun, J.-P., Bustamente, M., Chapelin, G., and Ribera, A. (2012). 'Parfumeries de la via degli Augustali', *Chronique des activités archéologiques de l'École française de Rome* <http://cefr.revues.org/540>. (accessed 21 July 2015).

Brun, J.-P., and Leguilloux, M. (2014). *Les installations artisanales romaines de Saepinum. Tannerie et moulin hydraulique.* Naples.

Chardron-Picault, P. (ed.) (2010). *Aspects de l'artisanat en milieu urbain: Gaule et Occident romain, Actes du colloque international d'Autun, 20–22 sept. 2007* (Suppléments de la RAE, 28). Dijon.

Chardron-Picault, P., and Pernot, M. (1999). *Un quartier antique d'artisanat métallurgique à Autun, Saône-et-Loire—Le Site du Lycée militaire* (Documents d'Archéologie française, 76). Paris.

Coarelli, F. (1974). *Roma* (Guide archeologiche Laterza). Rome and Bari.

Cullin-Mingaud, M. (2010). *La Vannerie dans l'Antiquité romaine: Les Ateliers de vanniers et les vanneries de Pompéi, Herculanum et Oplontis.* Naples.

Daremberg, Ch., Saglio, E., and Pottier, S. (1877–91). *Dictionnaire des antiquités grecques et romaines.* Paris.

David, P. (2002). *Le Travail du cuir à Aniane et en Languedoc* (Cahiers d'arts et traditions rurales, 15). Montpellier.

Devore, G., and Ellis, S. J. R. (2008). 'The Third Season of Excavations at VIII.7.1–15 and the Porta Stabia at Pompeii: Preliminary Report', *Fasti Online Documents & Research* <www.fastionline.org/docs/FOLDER-it-2008-112.pdf> (accessed 7 July 2015).

Diderot, D., and Le Rond d'Alembert, J. (1765). *Encyclopédie ou dictionnaire raisonné des sciences, des arts et des métiers, tome neuvième.* Neuchâtel.

Duval, P.-M. (1962). 'L'Apport technique des Romains', in M. Dumas (ed.), *Histoire générale des techniques.* Paris, 218–54.

Febvre, L. (1935). 'Réflexions sur l'histoire des techniques', *Annales d'histoire économique et sociale* 7: 531–5.

Ferdière, A. (2005). 'L'Artisanat en Gaule romaine', in L. Rivet (ed.), *Société française d'étude de la céramique antique en Gaule: Actes du congrès de Blois, 5–8 mai 2005.* Marseilles, 7–14.

Février, P.-A., and Leveau, Ph. (eds) (1982). *Villes et campagnes dans l'Empire romain. Actes du colloque d'Aix, mai 1980.* Aix-en-Provence.

Février, P. A., Fixot, M., Goudineau, Chr., and Kruta, V. (1980). 'La Ville antique', in G. Duby (ed). *Histoire de la France urbaine* i. Paris.

Flohr, M. (2013a). 'The Textile Economy of Pompeii', *JRA* 26/1: 53–78.

Flohr, M. (2013b). *The World of the fullo: Work, Economy and Society in Roman Italy* (Oxford Studies on the Roman Economy). Oxford.

Fontaine, S., Satre, S., and Tekki, A. (eds) (2011). *La Ville au quotidien: Regards croisés sur l'habitat et l'artisanat, Afrique du Nord, Gaule et Italie.* Aix-en-Provence.

Francotte, H. (1900–1). *L'Industrie dans la Grèce ancienne.* Bruxelles.

Gilles, B. (1978). *Histoire des techniques.* Paris.

Grenier, A. (1937). 'La Gaule romaine', in T. Frank (ed.), *An Economic Survey of Ancient Rome.* Baltimore, 379–644.

Gsell, St (1913–28). *Histoire ancienne de l'Afrique du Nord.* Paris.

Guiraud, P. (1900). *La main-d'œuvre industrielle dans l'ancienne Grèce.* Paris.

Jashemski, W. F. (1979). *The Gardens of Pompeii, Herculaneum and Villas Destroyed by Vesuvius.* New Rochelle.

Jongman, W. (1991). *The Economy and Society of Pompeii.* Amsterdam.

Jullian, C. (1920–6). *Histoire de la Gaule.* Paris.

Lefebvre des Noëttes, R. (1924). *La Force animale à travers les âges.* 2nd edn. Paris.

Lefebvre des Noëttes, R. (1931). *L'Attelage et le cheval de selle à travers les âges. Contribution à l'histoire de l'esclavage.* Paris.

Lefebvre des Noëttes, R. (1935). *De la marine antique à la marine moderne: La Révolution du gouvernail—Contribution à l'étude de l'esclavage.* Paris.

Leguilloux, M. (2004). 'Identification des tanneries romaines par le mobilier archéologique et l'archéozoologie', in E. De Sena and H. Dessales (eds), *Metodi e approci archeologici: L'industria e il commercio nell'Italia antica. Colloque de l'American Academy in Rome et de l'École Française de Rome. Avril 2002* (BAR International Series, 1262). Oxford, 38–48.

Leveau, Ph. (1983). 'La ville antique et l'organisation de l'espace rural, villa, ville, village', *Annales ESC* (July–August), 920–42.

Leveau, Ph. (1984). *Caesarea de Maurétanie, une ville romaine et ses campagnes.* Rome.

Maiuri, A. (1942). *L'ultima fase edilizia di Pompei.* Rome.

Mangin, M. (1981). *Un quartier de commerçants et d'artisans d'Alésia: Contribution à l'histoire de l'artisanat urbain en Gaule.* Paris.

Mangin, M. (1985). 'Artisanat et commerce dans les agglomérations secondaires du Centre-Est des Gaules sous l'Empire', in Ph. Leveau (ed.), *L'Origine des richesses dépensées dans la ville antique.* Marseilles, 113–31.

Mattingly, D. J. (1990). 'Painting, Presses, and Perfume Production at Pompei', *Oxford Journal of Archaeology* 9/1: 71–90.

Moeller, W. O. (1976). *The Wool Trade of Ancient Pompeii* (Studies of the Dutch Archaeological and Historical Society, 3). Leiden.

Monteix, N. (2011). *Les lieux de métier: Boutiques et ateliers d'Herculanum* (Collection du Centre Jean Bérard, 34). Rome.

Monteix, N. (2011). 'De l'artisanat aux métiers: Quelque réflexions sur le savoir-faire du monde romain à partir de l'exemple pompéien', in Monteix and Tran (2011), 7–26.

Monteix, N. (2013). 'The Apple of Discord: Fleece-Washing in Pompeii's Textile Economy. A Response to Miko Flohr', *Journal of Roman Archaeology* 26/1: 79–88.

Monteix, N., and Tran, N. (eds) (2011). *Les Savoirs professionnels des gens de métier: Études sur le monde du travail dans les sociétés urbaines de l'empire romain* (Archéologie de l'artisanat antique, 5). Naples.

Morel, J.-P. (1976). 'Aspects de l'artisanat dans la Grande-Grèce romaine', in *La magna Grecia nell'età romana: Atti del XV° convegno di studi sulla Magna Grecia, Taranto, 5–10 Ottobre 1975*. Naples, 263–323.

Morel, J.-P. (1985). 'La manufacture, moyen d'enrichissement dans l'Italie romaine?', in Ph. Leveau (ed.), *L'Origine des richesses depensees dans la ville antique: Actes du colloque 1984*. Aix-en-Provence, 87–111.

Morel, J.-P. (1992). 'L'artisan', in A. Giardina (ed.), *L'Homme romain*. Paris, 267–302.

Morel, J.-P. (1996). 'Élites municipales et manufacture en Italie', in M. Cebeillac-Gervasoni (ed.), *Les Élites municipales de l'Italie péninsulaire des Gracques a Néron: Actes de la table ronde de Clermont-Ferrand, 28–30 novembre 1991*. Naples and Rome, 181–98.

Morel, J.-P. (2009). 'Entre agriculture et artisanat: Regards croisés sur l'économie de l'Italie tardo-républicaine', in J. Carlsen and E. Lo Cascio (eds), *Agricoltura e scambi nell'Italia tardo-repubblicana*. Bari, 63–90.

Morel, J.-P. (2011). 'Habitat et artisanat: Quelques impressions finales', in Fontaine, Satre, and Tekki (2011), 233–41.

Parmigiani, N., and Pronti, A. (2004). *Santa Cecilia in Tevere: Nuovi scavi e ricerche* (Monumenti di antichità cristiana XVI). Vatican City.

Pasqualini, M., Excoffon, P., Michel, J.-M., and Botte, E. (2005–6). 'Fréjus, Forum Iulii. Fouilles de l'Espace Mangin', *Revue archéologique de Narbonnaise*, 38–9: 283–341.

Polfer, M. (ed.) (1999). *Artisanat et productions artisanales en milieu rural dans les provinces du nord-ouest de l'empire romain: Actes du colloque, Erpeldange, Luxembourg les 4 et 5 mars 1999* (Monographies Instrumentum, 9). Montagnac.

Polfer, M. (ed.) (2001). *L'artisanat romain: Évolutions, continuités et ruptures, Italie et provinces occidentales: Actes du 2ᵉ colloque d'Erpeldange, 26–28 octobre 2001* (Monographies Instrumentum, 20). Montagnac.

Polfer, M. (ed.) (2005). *Artisanat et économie romaine, Italie et provinces occidentales: Actes du 3ᵉ colloque d'Erpeldange, 14–16 octobre 2004* (Monographies Instrumentum, 32). Montagnac.

Rapsaet, G. (2002). *Attelages et techniques de transport dans le monde gréco-romain*. Brussels.

Rémondon, R. (1959). 'Le monde du travail', in L.-H. Parias (ed.), *Histoire générale du travail*. Paris, 257–369.

Rivet, L. (1992). 'Un quartier artisanal d'époque romaine à Aix-en-Provence, Bilan de la fouille de sauvetage du "parking Signoret" en 1991', *Revue archéologique de Narbonnaise* 25: 325–96.

Santoro, S. (2004). 'Artigianato e produzione nella Cisalpina romana: Proposte di metodo e prime applicazioni', in S. Santoro (ed.), *Artigianato e produzione nella Cisalpina, 1. Proposte di metodo e prime applicazioni*. 2nd edn (Flos Italiae. *Documenti di archeologia della Cisalpina Romana*, 3). Florence, 19–69.

Sodini, J.-P. (1979). 'L'artisanat urbain à l'époque paléochrétienne', *Ktèma* 4: 71–119.

Tran, N. (2006). *Les membres des associations romaines: Le Rang social des collegiati en Italie et en Gaules sous le Haut-Empire* (Collection de l'École française de Rome, 367). Rome.

Various authors (eds) (1963–4). *Le dictionnaire archéologique des techniques*. 2 vols. Paris.

Various authors (1996). *Aspects de l'artisanat du textile dans le monde méditerranéen, Égypte, Grèce, monde romain*. Lyons.

II

Strategies

4

Mercantile Specialization and Trading Communities: Economic Strategies in Roman Maritime Trade

Candace Rice

Archaeological material leaves little doubt as to the significance of maritime transport in the Roman Mediterranean; thousands of shipwrecks, tens of thousands of ceramic sherds, glass products, and imported building products from bricks to coloured marbles clearly illustrate that transport over longer distances was a constant feature of the Roman world. Yet despite the archaeological visibility of many of the transported commodities (or their containers), identifying the mechanisms through which they moved is difficult. What do the main modes of long-distance commerce suggest about market conditions and the organization of trade? What types of people were involved and what types of decisions were made? There is little direct archaeological or textual evidence for the ways in which Roman producers, merchants, shippers, and buyers coordinated their transactions. We may forget that every producer needed a buyer and a shipper, or that every shipowner needed a cargo, and that every consumer needed all of these. In the face of prolific material evidence, it is often too easy to exclude the human element.

This chapter seeks to explore the mechanisms and transactions through which maritime transport was conducted and the social networks and physical infrastructure in port cities that made it possible. In doing so, the argument moves through the processes of maritime trade to establish the pre-eminent characteristics of Roman maritime trade and highlight the major mechanisms involved, bringing the role of the individuals involved to the fore. This chapter briefly introduces the merchants who played a major role in maritime trade, not just in terms of buying and selling, but also in the decision-making process, and then examines the trading process from product acquisition, to shipment, to purchase, finally tying these elements together in a discussion of the phenomenon of 'trading communities'.

THE MERCHANTS

The primary Latin terms for those involved in maritime trade are *negotiator, mercator, navicularius,* and occasionally *nauta.* In Greek, the terms are ἔμπορος, ναύκληρος, and ναύτης (hereafter transliterated).[1] The distinction between the terms *negotiator* and *mercator* is not entirely apparent; interpretations are complex, as one could be both a *negotiator* and a *mercator,* and furthermore the definition of a *negotiator* changes between the republic and the empire.[2] In general, it would seem that the term *negotiator* signifies trade on a larger scale, while *mercator* is often used to describe someone working on a fairly small scale.[3] One indication of this is that *mercator* frequently appears in inscriptions without any indication of further specialization, while the application of the term *negotiator* is frequently further clarified by some sort of specialization.

A detailed look at the Latin inscriptions related to *negotiatores* is revealing. A total of 311 inscriptions from the *Epigraphik-Datenbank Clauss - Slaby (EDCS)*

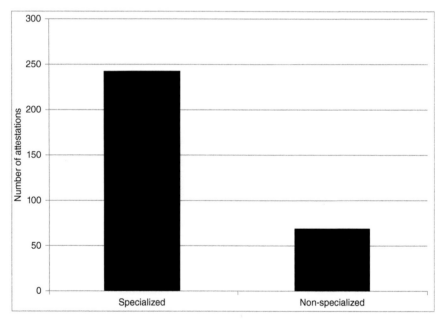

Fig. 4.1. Specialized versus non-specialized *negotiatores* (*N* = 311). Image: Candace Rice.

---

[1] *Negotiatores, mercatores,* and *emporoi* were, of course, not limited to the maritime trading sphere.

[2] Andreau (2000).

[3] Numerous studies have examined the role of *negotiatores* in the Roman world. See most recently Tran (2014); as well as Feuvrier-Prevotat (1981); Kneissl (1983); Andreau (2000); Verboven (2007a); and Arnaud (2011: 73–5); and Verboven (2007a) analyses the inscriptions related to *negotiatores,* sorting them according to geographical location.

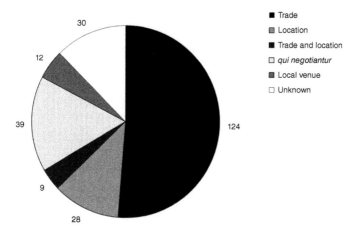

Fig. 4.2. Subdivision of *negotiator*-inscriptions indicating some form of specialization (*N* = 242). Image: Candace Rice.

refer to *negotiatores*; these have been grouped according to specialization.[4] As can be seen in Fig. 4.1, 242 of the inscriptions (78 per cent) provide some degree of amplification of the title *negotiator*. The most common indicator of specialization is the trade in which the *negotiator* was engaged (Fig. 4.2). There are 124 such inscriptions—which is 40 per cent of all inscriptions referring to *negotiatores*. *Negotiatores vinarii*, or wine traders, are the most common with twenty-nine attestations. Geographically, most of these inscriptions come from Rome (eleven), and eleven more are from Italy (three at Ostia), but there are also several in Gaul (three in Narbonensis and five in Lugdunensis), as well as Germany and Dalmatia. Numerous other trades are also recorded, including *negotiatores artis cretariae* (pottery dealers), *negotiatores frumentarii* (grain merchants), *negotiatores ferrarii* (iron merchants), *negotiatores eborarii* (ivory merchants), and several cloth and clothes merchants (*negotiatores lanarii, sagarii, vestiarii*).

Inscriptions also record those *negotiatores* who specialized in trade with a certain region rather than a certain commodity—for example, the *negotiatores Cisalpini et Transalpini*. Such inscriptions account for 9 per cent of all *negotiator* inscriptions. A further group of inscriptions (12 per cent) that deal with location are the very specific *qui negotiantur* inscriptions, discussed in more detail below. An additional 3 per cent of inscriptions record *negotiatores* who specialized in a particular product from a particular region. At Rome, for example, an inscription records a certain Tiberius Claudius Docimus who traded in wine and *salsamenta* from Mauretania.[5] Twelve of the inscriptions (4 per cent) refer to *negotiatores* who sold products in a specific part of their own city—for example, the *negotiatores ex area Saturni* from Ostia.[6]

---

[4] *EDCS* <db.edcs.eu> (accessed 3 December 2013).   [5] *CIL* 6.9676.   [6] *CIL* 14.397.

The terminology was not consistent. Olive-oil dealers, for example, only rarely referred to themselves as *negotiatores olearii*, but more commonly identify themselves as simply *olearii*; there are twenty-nine Latin inscriptions mentioning *olearii*, only four of which refer to *negotiatores olearii*. Rome has the highest concentration (nine), but, as expected, there are several from Spain (five from Baetica and two from Hispania Citerior), and four of those from Rome are traders in Baetican oil. There are also three inscriptions from North Africa and others from Gaul and Dalmatia.

THE TRADING PROCESS

The specialization of merchants is an important indicator of the developed nature of Roman maritime trade: specialization comes with higher risk and is typically unsustainable in underdeveloped economies,[7] yet specialized traders were not uncommon in the Roman period.[8] The fact that merchants also chose to highlight their specialization indicates that they were successful in their chosen ventures. The rest of this chapter briefly focuses on the practicalities of the trading process in order to discuss the ways in which merchants managed their business affairs so as to secure profits.

The initial stage of product movement typically involved short transport, overland, by river or by sea, or by a combination thereof, in order to move products from their production site to a harbour for export. The evidence suggests that the products of multiple estates and productive centres were commonly combined for maritime shipment. It was often the case that from the time the products were loaded onto a ship, and potentially from the time they were transported from their production site, the goods were no longer linked directly to their producers. While there is ample evidence to cite in support of this mode of organization, this chapter is intended as a brief sketch of the evidence and I therefore focus on three examples.

The first example comes from Baetulo, where, in 2004, excavations revealed two large dumps of Roman amphorae, as well as three dolia.[9] The deposits

---

[7] Cf. Doerflinger (1983).

[8] Erdkamp (2005: 177–8) asserts that specialized grain (p. 108) and wine merchants (pp. 128–9) must be related to the vast demand of the city of Rome, and that only 'populous and wealthy cities' had specialized merchants and large-scale trade. Rome was surely the largest consumer base of the Roman world, and significant maritime infrastructure was developed to facilitate its supply, both in Italy and further abroad. The integration of markets and subsequent specialization of production and trade are, however, visible in much greater quantities across the Roman world than Erdkamp allows. If we consider only the epigraphic evidence related to *negotiatores*, Verboven (2007b) has clearly shown that areas such as Gaul, Germany, and Britain contained a significant proportion (nearly 32%) of the epigraphic references to *negotiatores*.

[9] Comas and Padrós (2008).

were located near previously identified docking facilities and have been interpreted as the results of harbour loading activities.[10] Both deposits span the late first century BC through the first century AD and contain primarily Tarraconensian amphorae. The first deposit (over 3,000 sherds) contained 72 per cent Tarraconensian amphorae (54 per cent Pascual 1 and 18 per cent Dressel 2–4).[11] Eight per cent of the amphorae were Gauloise 4, which may or may not have been imported; they could be local imitations. There were also Dressel 7–11 amphorae from both Baetica and Tarraconensis and Dressel 20s from Baetica. The second deposit (over 10,000 sherds) contained 74 per cent Tarraconensian Dressel 2–4 and only 15 per cent Pascual 1 amphorae. The remaining 11 per cent were primarily Baetican (Dressel 20 and Dressel 7–11). What is particularly interesting about this second deposit is that six amphorae stamps and six graffiti were recovered. While not all were readable, three of the amphorae stamps indicated the production sites of the amphorae. Two stamps (AC and M) are associated with the production site of Can Tintorer and one (NI or IN) with the site of Can Pedrerol, both of which were located in the Llobregat river valley. These deposits are significant, as they provide terrestrial evidence that the products of different sites were assembled near the harbour before being loaded onto ships.

The second example is the Madrague de Giens wreck. This well-known Republican wreck (70–50 BC) carried approximately 350–450 tons of cargo, including some 6,000–7,000 amphorae, the majority of which are Dressel 1B wine amphorae.[12] Recent reappraisal of the stowage arrangements of the cargo of the Madrague de Giens wreck clearly shows that not only did the wine amphorae come from multiple production sites (identified through stamps on the amphorae) but that no effort was made to keep the products separated by their origin, thus implying that their production location was no longer important. Indeed, the amphorae were not even arranged by the merchants' stamps, which were seemingly applied by merchants after they had purchased the wine from the producers.[13] This strongly suggests that, by the time the cargo was loaded onto the ship itself, it was under the ownership of a single merchant and intended for a single destination.[14]

Evidence such as the Baetulo deposits and the cargo of the Madrague de Giens wreck suggests that, while the number of producers represented by a

---

[10] Comas and Padrós (2008: 83).   [11] Comas and Padrós (2008).
[12] For the most complete publication, see Tchernia et al. (1978).   [13] Hesnard (2012).
[14] Similar cargoes composed of collections of amphorae-borne products from a variety of local producers are found on the Cap del Vol, La Giraglia, Grand Ribaud D (wine cargoes), and the Plemmirio B and Chiessi wrecks (olive oil and salted-fish products). It is important to note that the composition of the cargoes from these wrecks suggests that these ships were primarily carrying cargoes on the first stage of their maritime export. This type of interpretation is obviously not possible for the more heterogenous wrecks, where cargoes have potentially been bought and sold multiple times.

single shipload may be substantial, the control of the product, and often the ownership of the product, had been drastically consolidated by the time the product was placed on the ship.[15] Indeed in some cases, the *naukleros* of the ship and the owner of the goods were one and the same, which leads us to the third example.[16]

The final example is that of the second-century AD *P. Bingen* 77, which provides strong evidence that cargoes were owned by a limited number of merchants and *naukleroi*.[17] This papyrus records eleven ships entering the port of what is probably Alexandria. All of the ships originated at a single place, and most have either one or two types of cargo. The names of the *naukleroi* are preserved for all eleven ships (though in one case only the latter part of the name is preserved), and the names of the owner of the cargo are preserved for nine of the ships. No cargo has more than two owners, and six of the ships have only one owner attested for the cargo. For example, the final ship recorded on the register originated from Anemurium and was carrying 2,500 jars of wine owned by Ninos, son of Tounis, also the *naukleros*.

This evidence suggests a separation between producer and maritime exporter, a phenomenon that is also supported by several textual sources.[18] Merchant middlemen often provided the link between the producers and the maritime traders. A system in which maritime traders bought their wares from middlemen would perhaps have created a simplified network of communication and exchange where the locally or regionally based merchant coordinated transactions through fostered local contacts, while the merchant specializing in long-distance trade established and maintained a different set of contacts.

Our understanding of the maritime phases of transport depends largely on shipwrecks, which preserve cargoes as they were *en route*. *Negotiatores* dealt broadly with three main cargo types: export cargoes, re-export cargoes assembled at emporia, and return cargoes. It is, however, important to realize that these are not mutually exclusive categories. Export cargoes are often regarded as homogeneous shiploads that were exported from an assembly port in their production region to an emporion or a centre of mass consumption.[19] Cargoes originating from a localized production zone, such as the previously discussed Madrague de Giens, are often indicative of products in their initial stage of maritime export. The term homogeneous is, however, misleading, particularly as it obscures the relationships between a multiplicity of producers and merchants; while it is often the case that cargoes are homogeneous in terms

---

[15] For discussion of the potential processes involved in the movement of goods from the farm to the market as interpreted from the literary sources, see Erdkamp (2005: 118–30).

[16] A striking exception appears to be the Port-Vendres II wreck, which contained the products of at least nine merchants (Colls et al. 1977).

[17] Heilporn (2000).

[18] e.g. Cato, *On Agriculture* 144–8, Pliny, *Letters* 8.2.1 and the *Digest* 18.6.1, 18.6.6, 18.6.15.

[19] e.g. Boetto (2012: 156).

of the type of product (for example, wine or salted-fish products), they are rarely homogenous in terms of the estate or farm where the product was produced (stone cargoes are an important exception).[20] We can imagine that the *negotiatores* who specialized in the trade of a particular product (for example, *negotiatores vinarii*) were particularly associated with export cargoes.

The second main cargo type consisted of shiploads of products that had been assembled at emporia and were being re-exported. Emporia acted as both regional and inter-regional collection points of products, and cargoes assembled in these places frequently included a mix of products from various places of origin. Cargoes loaded at emporia might contain products on their original stage of maritime export, products that had previously arrived at an emporium and were being re-exported, or a combination of the two.

A third regular cargo type is the return cargo.[21] Return cargoes are closely related to trade between emporia: after a merchant has moved a cargo from emporium A to emporium B, he ideally returns to emporium A with a new cargo. Economically speaking, return cargoes ensured that both ends of a journey were potentially profitable: given the choice between sailing with only ballast or sailing with a cargo, it often made financial sense to take on a cargo. Return cargoes are thought to have been responsible for the widespread distribution of many low-value products across the Roman world: Italian bricks were used in the construction of bath complexes and cisterns in numerous North African port sites, and Cilician roof tiles were used in Syria and Phoenicia. [22] The argument behind this idea is that the profits from high-value products in effect subsidize the shipment of low-value products, and, while this is certainly true, we should not automatically equate return cargoes with low-value or afterthought cargoes. After all, it is often the return cargoes that are responsible for the import products that are locally needed at the home port and its environs; this could be bricks for a specific building project or a selection of foreign wines. As a result, it is extremely difficult, if not impossible, to identify return cargoes among shipwrecks, despite the ample evidence of return cargoes visible through terrestrial archaeology.

---

[20] When amphorae were produced on location with the oil, wine, etc., as was often the case, the association between the actual product and its container is clear. Amphorae were, however, also produced at kiln sites that are unattached to a particular farm or estate. These manufacturing sites served as bottling centres for producers or merchants who did not have kilns themselves. In these cases, apparent homogeneity can be deceptive. Given that these kiln sites were independent from production, however, it is probable that they were used to bottle the products of many agricultural production units. The San Anastasia amphorae kiln, which produced two-thirds of the Dressel 1B amphorae aboard the Madrague de Giens wreck, was just such a kiln. Many of the amphorae from the San Anastasia kiln, however, had stoppers with merchants' marks, indicating that they were meant to be distinguishable from each other during the period between the bottling and the point at which they were loaded onto the ship.

[21] On return cargoes, see Tchernia (2011: 124, 344–5).

[22] For the use of Italian bricks in North African port sites, see Wilson (2001); Wilson, Schörle, and Rice (2012). On Cilician roof tiles in Syria and Phoenicia, see Mills (2005).

Significantly, the trading process as described above presupposes a stable system in which there was relatively reliable information available about the market situation in remote ports; at least, the process was based on the expectation that one can sell particular cargoes in places with which one maintains regular trading connections. By establishing themselves as merchants of known routes, cities, or products, these *negotiatores* and merchants improved the efficiency of the trading process. Actual selling strategies may have varied: a merchant who specialized in long-distance trade might regularly sell his products to a local merchant in a destination city—the counterpart to the merchant middleman on the production end. As with the merchant middleman on the production end, this would allow a simplification of the communication network. However, merchants could also sell their products on the local market themselves, setting up shop in the forum, *macellum*, or agora, or making use of more transient fairs and markets.[23]

COORDINATING TRADE

Roman maritime trade thus operated within a complex and sophisticated system where several groups of actors played several specific roles in different places; the modalities of trade suggest reliance on some degree of information about distant markets, rather than casual opportunistic tramping from one port to another.[24] This did, however, complicate the coordination of various stages of the trading process. Pre-industrial maritime trade was limited by a number of factors, the two most important being a dependence on wind for sailing and the difficulties of long-distance communication. As early modern parallels suggest, these factors were not wholly prohibitive; the Venetians, the Portuguese, and the Dutch all had successful maritime trading empires; while none of these empires overcame the dependence on the sail, they all found ways around the problem of communication, whose resolution did not really begin until the invention of deep-sea cables in the 1860s.[25]

The primary way in which the Romans dealt with communication issues in the context of trade was the establishment of diaspora communities in major trading centres across the Roman world.[26] The term 'trading diasporas' was coined in 1971 by anthropologist Abner Cohen to describe 'dispersed, but highly interrelated communities'. In his view, a trading diaspora is established to 'co-ordinate the co-operation of its members in the common cause and establish channels of communication and mutual support with members from

---

[23] On markets and fairs, see De Ligt (1993).
[24] Arnaud (2011); Wilson (2011), *contra* Bang (2008: 141).   [25] Stopford (2009: 27).
[26] For an overview of Roman trading communities, see now Terpstra (2013).

communities of the same ethnic group in neighbouring localities who are engaged in the trading network'.[27] Historical diaspora communities include the Venetians in Constantinople and the Dutch in Venice.[28] Excellent evidence for the workings of medieval merchant communities comes from the documents of the Cairo Geniza.[29]

One category of Latin inscriptions mentions specific ethnic groups of people who trade in specific locations. The construction used in these inscriptions is typically very formulaic: 'ethnic group-*qui* location-*negotiantur*'. In contrast with other inscriptions referring to traders, these inscriptions are also largely concentrated in the eastern Mediterranean and are occasionally bilingual. Thirty-nine inscriptions belonging to this category are known (Fig. 4.3),[30] twenty-seven of which (73 per cent) are from the eastern Mediterranean, primarily from the provinces of Asia and Achaia. Some of the earliest inscriptions come from Delos, where four inscriptions from the first century BC have been found that refer to the 'Italians and Greeks who trade at Delos'.[31]

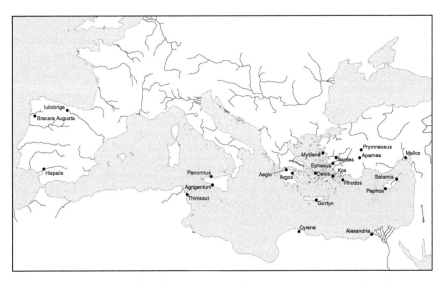

Fig. 4.3. Places where '*qui negotiantur*' inscriptions have been found.
Map: Miko Flohr.

---

[27] Cohen (1971: 267).

[28] Constantinople: Dursteler (2008); Venice: Van Gelder (2007).   [29] Goitein (1967).

[30] *EDCS* <db.edcs.eu> (accessed 3 December 2013): *CIL* 1.746, 830, 831, 836, 2955, 2958, 2970; *CIL* 2.242, 1168, 1169, 2423; *CIL* 3.532, 5230, 6051, 7043, 7237, 7240, 12101, 12266, 13542, 13617, 14195.39; *CIL* 6.40903; *CIL* 10.1797; *CIL* 11.7288; *CIL* 13.11825; *AE* 1912, 51; *AE* 1924, 69, 72; *AE* 1968, 480; *AE* 1974, 671; *AE* 1975, 803; *AE* 1990, 938; *AE* 1996, 1453; *InscCret-4*, Gortyn 290, 291; *IK* 12. 409.

[31] e.g. *CIL* 3.7240.

Many of the inscriptions mention *cives Romani*, who traded with various locations across the Mediterranean.[32] At Ephesos, numerous inscriptions show the presence of associations of Italian traders. Around 60 BC, the *Italicei quei Ephesi negotiantur* dedicated a statue of a certain L. Agrius Publeianus, and in 37 BC they dedicated an honorary inscription placed in the western hall of the agora to the consul M. Cocceius Nerva.[33] In 36 BC, the *conventus civum Romanorum quei Ephesi negotiantur* dedicated another inscription to M. Cocceius Nerva.[34] In the AD 40s, the *conventus civum Romanorum qui in Asia negotiantur* made two dedications to Claudius, one of which was an equestrian statue.[35]

Groups of *cives Romani* also appear on Crete. Several inscriptions attest groups of Roman traders at Gortyn—the *cives Romani qui Gortynae negotiantur*.[36] In the first century BC, these people set up an honorific inscription to Doia Procilla, probably a member of a duumviral family from Knossos.[37] In the second century AD, the *cives Romani*—who instead of being identified as *negotiatores* are now described as those who settled in Gortyn (*qui consistunt*)—along with two priests of the imperial cult dedicate an honorary inscription to Septimius Severus.[38]

Groups of merchants (probably Italian) doing business in Alexandria, Asia, and Syria are also identified in an inscription dedicated to L. Calpurnius Capitolinus:

Calpurnio L(uci) f(ilio) | Capitolino || C(aio) Calpurnio L(uci) f(ilio) | [[6]] || mercatores qui Alexandr[iai] Asiai Syriai negotiantu[r].[39]

Aside from the above inscriptions, some of our best examples of trading diasporas come from Ostia and Puteoli. So-called *stationes* are attested in several harbour cities and were probably present in many others. The best attested are those in the Piazzale delle Corporazioni at Ostia. The Piazzale consists of sixty-one individual *stationes*, many of which preserve mosaics reflecting various economic activities. Surviving inscriptions attest *navicularii* and *negotiatores* from fourteen different cities: ten are in North Africa, two in Gaul, and two in Sardinia (Fig. 4.4).[40] Offices are also indicated for traders of

---

[32] There are twelve overall that refer to the *cives Romani*. They come from Ephesos (3), Kos (1), Mytilene (1), Prymnessus (1), Gortyn (1), Limnia (2), Bracara (1), Terracina (1), Thinissut, Africa Proconsularis (1).

[33] *IvE* 6, 2058.   [34] *IvE* 3, 658.   [35] *IvE* 2, 409; *IvE* 7.1, 3019.

[36] *I.Cret.* 4, 291.   [37] *I.Cret.* 4, 290; Baldwin Bowsky (1999: 310).

[38] *I.Cret.* 4, 278, *CIL* 3.4.   [39] *CIL* 10.1797.

[40] North Africa: Misua (*CIL* 14.4549.10), Musluvium (*CIL* 14.4549.11), Hippo Diarrytus (*CIL* 14.4549.12), Sabratha (*CIL* 14.4549.14), Gummi (*CIL* 14.4549.17), Carthage (*CIL* 14.4549.18), Sullecthum (*CIL* 14.4549.23), Colonia Iulia Curubis (Kurba, Tunisia) (*CIL* 14.4549.34), Alexandria (*CIL* 14.4549.40), and Mauretania Caesariensis (*CIL* 14.4549.48). Gaul: Arelate (Statio 27), Narbo Martius (*CIL* 14.4549.32). Sardinia: Turris Libisonis (Porto Torres) (*CIL* 14.4549.19) and Carales (Cagliari) (*CIL* 14.4549.21).

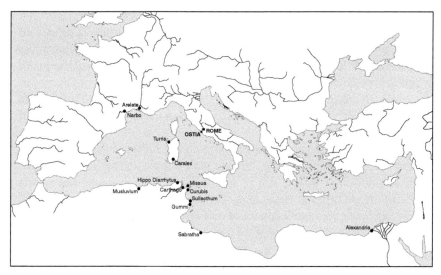

Fig. 4.4. Cities with a *statio* in the *Piazzale delle Corporazioni* at Ostia.
Map: Miko Flohr.

flax and rope, leather traders, and wood traders. The individual offices in the building are relatively small; they were certainly not for the storage of any goods and were most likely offices where one could coordinate trading agreements with members of various represented areas of the empire. The building thus facilitated commercial transactions at Ostia by creating a centrally defined location where one could readily find representatives from key emporia.

A well-known inscription from Puteoli dated to AD 174 records the request of an association of Tyrians resident in Puteoli for assistance from Tyre in paying the annual rent for their *statio*.[41] Other foreign groups were also active at Puteoli, though none is attested as explicitly as the Tyrians.[42] The presence of residents from Berytus is indicated by an inscription set up by the Berytian worshippers of Jupiter Heliopolitanus dedicated to Trajan.[43] Another inscription mentioning Jupiter Heliopolitanus was set up by a *corpus* of worshippers from Berytus or Heliopolis that apparently owned a seven-*iugera* necropolis with a cistern and *tabernae*.[44]

It is likely, on the basis of several cultic inscriptions to the principal god of the Nabataeans, Dusares, that there was also a community of Nabateans at Puteoli.[45] The evidence suggests there was a temple to this deity, possibly

[41] Editions: Mommsen (1843: 57–62); *CIG* 3.5853; *IG* 14.830. Discussed by D'Arms (1974: 105); Duncan-Jones (1974: 210, 236); Sosin (1999).

[42] On foreign communities in Puteoli, see particularly D'Arms (1970, 1974) and Terpstra (2013: 51–94).

[43] *CIL* 10.1634.   [44] *CIL* 10.1579.

[45] *AE* 1971, 86; *AE* 1994, 422–3; *AE* 2001, 843; *CIL* 10.1556.

located in the vicus Lartidianus, an area of Puteoli believed to have been inhabited largely by foreigners, on the basis of an inscription dedicated to Hadrian by the *inquilini* of the *vicus Lartidianus*.[46] The numerous references to this cult, and the probable location of the temple in an area associated with foreign groups coupled with the general scarcity of the worship of Dusares in Italy, certainly point to a resident community of Nabateans in Puteoli. The existence of foreign cults in harbour cities can be a useful marker of groups of foreign residents.[47]

The presence of long-standing diaspora communities and particularly of resident foreign merchants links directly with a sophisticated and organized model of trade; that is, the idea of premeditated harbour-to-harbour trade linked with trade through emporia. It was the recurring trade among specific parties that made the establishment of diaspora communities of merchants a desirable strategy. The amounts of money invested in maintaining such communities, whether for the maintenance of a *statio* or the installation of a new cult, suggests regular and sustained contact between regions.

THE SOCIAL STATUS OF BUSINESSMEN

The key role of trading communities makes it relevant briefly to consider the social situation of the people discussed. The social status of merchants and traders, and indeed of businessmen in general, has generated much debate among scholars. This is unsurprising given not only the general debate over the nature of the Roman economy, but also because it seems to have been a somewhat controversial topic among authors of the Roman period. In the trading scenarios outlined, it is quite possible for the elites to avoid the actual marketing processes altogether—at least visibly. The elites often owned the estates on which agricultural products were grown, yet, as seen in passages from Cato and Pliny, as well as the *Digest*, they did not market the products personally, but sold them to merchants.[48] D'Arms and Tchernia have argued that the separation of the producers from the traders allowed a way for the landed elites to maintain at least a symbolic separation from trade.[49]

---

[46] *AE* 1977, 200.   [47] See Wilson, Schörle, and Rice (2012).

[48] e.g. Cato, *On Agriculture* 144–8, Pliny, *Letters* 8.2.1 and the *Digest* 18.6.1, 18.6.6, 18.6.15. See Erdkamp (2005: 118–34) for a thorough discussion of the advance sale of agricultural products.

[49] D'Arms (1981); Tchernia (2011). There were, of course, exceptions. The senatorial Sestius family at Cosa, well known for the production and trade of wine during the latter half of the second century through the first century BC, is a prime example. They owned vineyards, produced amphorae, owned ships, and seemingly expanded into the fish-salting industry. Cf. McCann (2002). Numerous amphora sherds discovered around Cosa stamped with Sestii family

The most obvious way in which elites could maintain a discreet role in the world of commerce was through the agency of freedmen.[50] There are numerous ways in which freedmen, or even slaves, could have been involved in commercial partnerships with their patron, from selling the products of their patron (as already discussed) to handling specific stages of transactions or coordinating supply.[51] This idea has been most prominently put forward by Frier and Kehoe, who discuss the idea of freedman agency within the framework of New Institutional Economics. They conclude as follows:

> This method of managing businesses through friends or social dependants had significant implications for the organization of the Roman economy. For one, it tended to reinforce the strict social hierarchy that helped to preserve the economic and social privileges of the landowning elite: there was little capacity for developing a class of artisans let alone entrepreneurs who were fully independent of elite patronage or control. Successful freedmen who gained wealth as artisans or business managers were ultimately dependent on a master or patron for an initial investment in skills and capital, and they often remained socially bound at least to some degree to their patron.[52]

Frier and Kehoe do, however, argue that slaves 'could operate with a great deal of independence' despite being socially bound to their patrons.[53]

The ideas presented by Frier and Kehoe are largely credible—there is abundant evidence that freedmen and even slaves often acted as agents for their elite owner or former owner's business. Wim Broekaert, who analyses the issue much more closely elsewhere in this volume, concludes that tracing the relationship between patron and freedmen is extremely difficult with the evidence at hand, and he agrees with Frier and Kehoe, largely because of the significant advantages that a freedmen with start-up capital from a patron would have over an independent freedman.[54] But is this really to say that behind every freedman *negotiator* there was an elite patron in control?

It is important not to underestimate the independence of freedmen businessmen, particularly within certain environments.[55] This is not to say that they did not get their beginnings in trade through their patrons, or that many of them did not continue to work with the same families following manumission. What must be kept in mind, however, are the environments in which merchants and traders were working. Within a busy port where merchants,

---

stamps indicate the production of amphorae, which were exported on a significant scale, with distribution extending primarily to Gaul and Spain, but also to Athens and Delos. Cf. Manacorda (1978). Cicero refers to the *navigia luculenta* that Sestius contributed to Brutus' forces during the civil wars (Cic. *Att.* 16.4.4).

[50] For the most recent work on freedmen, see Mouritsen (2011).
[51] Broekaert (2012). Broekaert (Chapter 10, this volume) identifies six basic levels of agency.
[52] Frier and Kehoe (2007: 133–4).   [53] Frier and Kehoe (2007: 134).
[54] Broekaert, Chapter 10, this volume.   [55] See also Tran (2014).

traders, and shippers interacted, it cannot always have been the familial connections that dictated social and economic interactions. Instead, the evidence presented above seems to suggest that merchants—freedmen or not—had a considerable say in the ways in which products moved after they had been purchased from estates. It is also evident from epigraphy that self-identifying as a merchant was acceptable and, in fact, quite common in some locales. This strongly suggests that there was a recognizable group of entrepreneurs in the Roman world who were responsible for negotiating their own reputation and were not relying on the reputation of their patrons.

In a controversial book published in 2012, Mayer argues for the existence of a Roman middle class with not just shared economic standing, but also 'a class-specific set of values'.[56] His methodology, and in particular his assertions regarding shared cultural norms between the supposed ancient and modern middle class, have been justifiably questioned.[57] While Mayer's arguments for the existence of a 'middle class' stretch the evidence to overreaching conclusions, Verboven has argued in several articles that there was in fact a Roman 'business class'.[58] His approach is more circumspect than that of Mayer and he makes a very strong argument for the emergence of a business class of merchants, producers, and traders in the north-west provinces. He argues that the strong military presence in these provinces provided a large emerging market unlike anything previously in the region and that this created an environment for a business class to prosper.[59] While the disproportionately large amount of epigraphy related to merchants and traders in Gaul and Germany must depend on factors other than the military—otherwise the same pattern would occur in every militarized frontier zone—the point that regions with large markets create extended opportunities for businessmen is valid.[60]

Port cities create a similar type of environment; commerce was their *raison d'être*, and the people involved in this commerce formed the largest and in some respects most important social class present within them.[61] Without imposing modern ideas of class and value on the commercial actors of the Roman world, the fact remains that in some environments, such as port cities and other large market zones, people involved in commerce, particularly at its upper levels, would have had a substantial income and elevated status. Whether or not they should be termed a 'class' is debatable, but, as the complexity of the Roman economy continues to be explored, it is certainly worth pursuing further the societal place of the commercial agents of the Roman world.

---

[56] Mayer (2012: 6).

[57] On the reception of the book, see, e.g. reviews by Flohr (2013), Noreña (2013), and Wallace-Hadrill (2013).

[58] Verboven (2007b, 2009, 2011a, b). See also Broekaert (2012).   [59] Verboven (2007b).

[60] I would like to thank Tyler Franconi for his discussion of this phenomenon.

[61] Cf. Mouritsen (2001); Heinzelmann (2010: 7).

CONCLUSION

It has been suggested by Whittaker that the widespread distribution of wine amphorae around the Mediterranean was due not to market trade, but to elites transporting their own products among their familial estates.[62] While I would not deny that this practice sometimes occurred, the evidence presented here illustrates a scale and sophistication across all aspects of the trading process that would not have been necessary outside a market system. Facilitated by physical, infrastructural, and social networks, Roman maritime trade involved advanced commercial processes that operated within a market economy. The discussion of ports, shipwrecks, merchants, traders, and producers in this chapter has outlined the broad mechanisms of maritime trade. By thinking of trade as a composite process in which production, transport, and marketing processes are intrinsically linked, the level of organization and development that were required to succeed in commerce becomes readily apparent. Each category demonstrates a specific part of the processes of maritime trade; when considered together, they produce a detailed picture of how maritime trade was carried out during the Roman period. The evidence of the people involved in maritime trade further brings to light the complexity of managing success-ful trading ventures: trading diasporas reveal a high level of sophistication in dealing with problems of communication inherent in pre-industrial trade; the obvious level of specialization among merchants and traders further speaks to the advanced structure and scale of maritime trade. It also indicates that trade could make a profitable career.

REFERENCES

Andreau, J. (2000). 'Negotiator', *Brill's Neue Pauly*, Brill Online.

Arnaud, P. (2011). 'Ancient Sailing-Routes and Trade Patterns: The Impact of Human Factors', in Robinson and Wilson (2011), 61–80.

Baldwin Bowsky, M. W. (1999). 'The Business of Being Roman', in A. Chaniotis (ed.), *From Minoan Farmers to Roman Traders*. Stuttgart, 305–47.

Bang, P. F. (2008). *The Roman Bazaar: A Comparative Study of Trade and Markets in a Tributary Empire*. Cambridge.

Boetto, G. (2012). 'Les Épaves comme sources pour l'étude de la navigations et des routes commerciales: Une approche methodologique', in S. Keay (ed.), *Rome, Portus and the Mediterranean*. Rome, 153–73.

Broekaert, W. (2012). 'Joining forces. Commercial partnerships or societates in the early Roman Empire', *Historia* 61: 221–53.

---

[62] Whittaker (1985, 1989).

Cohen, A. (1971). 'Cultural Strategies in the Organization of Trading Diasporas', in C. Meillassoux (ed.), *The Development of Indigenous Trade and Markets in West Africa*. Oxford, 266–78.

Colls, D., Etienne, R. Lequément, R., Liou, B. and Mayet, F. (1977). *L'épave Port-Vendres II et le commerce de la Bétique à l'époque de Claude* (Archaeonautica, 1). Paris.

Comas, M., and Padrós, P. (2008). 'Deux grands dépotoirs d'amphores Léétaniennes, Bétiques et Gauloises, hors les murs de la ville de Baetulo (Badalona)', *SFECAG, Actes du Congrès de L'Escala-Empúries*. Marseilles, 75–86.

D'Arms, J. H. (1970). *Romans on the Bay of Naples: A Social and Cultural Study of the Villas and their Owners from 150 BC to AD 400*. Cambridge, MA.

D'Arms, J. H. (1974). 'Puteoli in the Second Century of the Roman Empire: A Social and Economic Study', *JRS* 64: 104–24.

D'Arms, J. H. (1981). *Commerce and Social Standing in Ancient Rome*. Cambridge, MA.

De Ligt, L. (1993). *Fairs and Markets in the Roman Empire: Economic and Social Aspects of Periodic Trade in a Pre-Industrial Society* (Dutch Monographs on Ancient History and Archaeology). Amsterdam.

Doerflinger, T. M. (1983). 'Commercial Specialization in Philadelphia's Merchant Community, 1750–1791', *Business History Review* 57: 20–49.

Duncan-Jones, R. P. (1974). *The Economy of the Roman Empire*. Cambridge.

Dursteler, E. (2008). *Venetians in Constantinople: Nation, Identity, and Coexistence in the Early Modern Mediterranean* (The Johns Hopkins University Studies in Historical and Political Science). Baltimore.

Erdkamp, P. (2005). *The Grain Market of the Roman Empire: A Social, Political and Economic Study*. Cambridge.

Feuvrier-Prevotat, C. (1981). '*Negotiator* et *mercator* dans le discours cicéronien: Essai de définition', *Dialogues d'histoire ancienne* 7: 367–405.

Flohr, M. (2013). Review of E. Mayer, 'The Ancient Middle Classes: Roman Life and Aesthetics in the Roman Empire', *JRS* 103: 308–9.

Frier, B., and Kehoe, D. P. (2007). 'Law and Economic Institutions', in W. Scheidel, I. Morris, and R. P. Saller (eds), *The Cambridge Economic History of the Greco-Roman World*. Cambridge, 113–43.

Goitein, S. D. (1967). *A Mediterranean Society: The Jewish Communities of the Arab World as Portrayed in the Documents of the Cairo Geniza*, i. *Economic Foundations*. Berkeley (repr. 1999).

Heilporn, P. (2000). 'Registre de navires marchands', in H. Melaerts (ed.), *Papyri in honorem Johannis Bingen Octogenarii (P. Bingen)*. Leuven, 339–59.

Heinzelmann, M. (2010). 'Supplier of Rome or Mediterranean marketplace? The Changing Economic Role of Ostia after the Construction of Portus in the Light of New Archaeological Evidence', *Bollettino di Archeologia Online*, Volume Speciale: 5–10 <http://www.bollettinodiarcheologiaonline.beniculturali.it/documenti/generale/2_Heinzelmann_paper.pdf> (accessed 14 July 2015).

Hesnard, A. (2012). 'L'épave La Madrague de Giens (Var) et la plaine de Fondi (Latium)', *Archaeonautica* 17: 71–93.

Kneissl (1983). '*Mercator-negotiator*. Römischer Geschäftsleute und die Terminologie ihrer Berufe', *Münstersche Beiträge zur Antiken Handelsgeschichte* 2.1: 73–90.

McCann, A. M. (2002). *The Roman Port and Fishery of Cosa: A Short Guide = Il porto romano e la peschiera di Cosa: Guida breve.* Rome.

Manacorda, D. (1978). 'The Ager Cosanus and the Production of the Amphorae of Sestius: New Evidence and a Reassessment', *JRS* 68: 122–31.

Mayer, E. (2012). *The Ancient Middle Classes : Urban Life and Aesthetics in the Roman Empire, 100 BCE–250 CE.* Cambridge, MA, and London.

Mommsen, T. (1843). *De collegiis et sodaliciis Romanorum.* Kiel.

Mouritsen, H. (2001). 'Roman Freedmen and the Urban Economy: Pompeii in the First Century AD', in F. Senatore (ed.), *Pompeii tra Sorrento e Sarno.* Roma, 1–28.

Mouritsen, H. (2011). *The Freedman in the Roman World.* Cambridge.

Noreña, C. F. (2013). 'Emanuel Mayer: The Ancient Middle Classes: Urban Life and Aesthetics in the Roman Empire, 100 BCE–250 CE', *American Historical Review* 118/5: 1576–7.

Robinson, D. and Wilson, A. (eds) (2011). *Maritime Archaeology and Ancient Trade in the Mediterranean* (Oxford Centre for Maritime Archaeology, Monograph 6). Oxford.

Russell, B. (2011). 'Lapis Transmarinus: Stone Carrying Ships and the Maritime Distribution of Stone in the Roman Empire', in Robinson and Wilson (2011), 139–55.

Russell, B. (2013). *The Economics of the Roman Stone Trade.* Oxford.

Sosin, J. D. (1999). 'Tyrian stationarii at Puteoli', *Tyche* 14: 275–84.

Stopford, M. (2009). *Maritime Economics.* Abingdon.

Tchernia, A. (2011). *Les Romains et le commerce.* Naples.

Tchernia, A., Pomey, P., Hesnard, A., Girard, M., Hamon, E., Laubenheimer, F., Lecaille, F., Carrier-Guillomnet, A., Chene, A., Gassend, J.-M., Reveillac, G., and Rival, M. (1978). *L'Épave Romaine de la Madrague de Giens (Var) (Campagnes 1972-1975): Fouilles de l'Institut d'archéologie méditerranéenne.* Paris.

Terpstra, T. (2013). *Trading Communities in the Roman World: A Micro-Economic and Institutional Perspective* (Columbia Studies in the Classical Tradition, 37). Leiden and Boston.

Tran, N. (2014). 'Les Hommes d'affaires romains et l'expansion de l'Empire (70 av. J.-C.–73 apr. J.-C.)', *Pallas* 96: 111–26.

Van Gelder, M. (2007). 'Trading Places: The Netherlandish Merchant Community in Venice, 1590-1650'. Ph.D. thesis, University of Amsterdam.

Verboven, K. (2007a). 'Ce que negotiari et ses dérivés veulent dire', in J. Andreau, J. France, and V. Chankowski (eds), *Vocabulaire et expression de l'économie dans le monde antique*, Bordeaux, 89–118.

Verboven, K. (2007b). 'Good for Business: The Roman Army and the Emergence of a "Business Class" in the Northwestern Provinces of the Roman Empire (1st Century BCE–3rd Century CE)', in L. De Blois, E. Lo Cascio, O. Hekster, and G. de Kleijn (eds), *The Impact of the Roman Army (200 BC–AD 476): Economic, Social, Political, Religious and Cultural Aspects: Proceedings of the Sixth Workshop of the International Network Impact of Empire (Roman Empire, 200 BC–AD 476), Capri, March 29–April 2, 2005.* Leiden and Boston, 295–314.

Verboven, K. (2009). 'Magistrates, Patrons and Benefactors of *Collegia*: Status Building and Romanisation in the Spanish, Gallic and German Provinces', in B. Antela

Bernárdez and T. Ñaco Del Hoyo (eds), *Transforming Historical Landscapes in the Ancient Empires: Proceedings of the First Workshop, December 16–19th 2007*. Oxford, 59–167.

Verboven, K. (2011a). 'Resident Aliens and Translocal Merchant Collegia in the Roman Empire', in O. Hekster and T. Kaizer (eds), *Frontiers in the Roman World: Proceedings of the Ninth Workshop of the International Network Impact of Empire (Durham, 16–19 April 2009)*. Leiden and Boston, 335–48.

Verboven, K. (2011b). 'Professional Collegia: Guilds or Social Clubs?', *Ancient Society* 41: 187–95.

Wallace-Hadrill, A. (2013). 'Trying to Define and Identify the Roman "Middle Class"', *JRS* 26: 605–9.

Whittaker, C. R. (1985). 'Trade and the Aristocracy in the Roman Empire', *Opus* 4: 49–75.

Whittaker, C. R. (1989). 'Amphorae and Trade', in D. Lenoir, D. Manacorda, and C. Panella (eds), *Amphores romaines et histoire économique: Dix ans de recherche. Actes du colloque de Sienne, 22–24 mai 1986*. Rome, 537–9.

Wilson, A. (2001). 'Ti. Cl. Felix and the Date of the Second Phase of the East Baths', in L. M. Stirling, D. J. Mattingly, and N. Ben Lazreg (eds), *Leptiminus (Lamta): The East Baths, Cemeteries, Kilns, Venus Mosaic, Site Museum and Other Studies. Report No. 2* (JRA Supplementary Series, 41). Portsmouth, RI, 25–8.

Wilson, A. I. (2011). 'Developments in Mediterranean Shipping and Maritime Trade', in Robinson and Wilson (2011), 33–59.

Wilson, A., Schörle, K., and Rice, C. (2012). 'Mediterranean Connectivity and Roman Ports', in S. J. Keay (ed.), *Rome, Portus and the Mediterranean*. Rome, 367–91.

5

Driving Forces for Specialization: Market, Location Factors, Productivity Improvements

Kai Ruffing

The high degree of specialization of crafts and trades in the Greco-Roman world has long been considered in modern research as a negative sign of the respective underlying economies.[1] This was especially true for the study of the economy of the Roman Empire in the time of the 'primitivist orthodoxy', which prevailed in modern historiography on the ancient economy from the 1970s until the 1990s.[2] In the primitivist view and in research influenced by primitivist or substantivist positions, the city of Rome of the early and high empire was seen as an example of an absurd fragmentation of occupations in crafts and trades. Taking the evidence of literary and epigraphic sources together, some 160 terms for crafts are attested in the city of Rome alone, whereas one can find 225 designations for occupations in the whole western part of the empire. These figures were thought to reflect an extravagant division of labour, which was caused by the absence of specialized, skilled craftsmen. The presence of large masses of slaves caused a strong segmentation in production: in this way, unskilled labourers were able to produce at a relative high level of quality. This, in turn, led to an increase in medium-sized and large workshops, where the connection between master and apprentice was lost. To support this interpretation, comparisons were made with early modern metropoleis, such as eighteenth-century Paris or fifteenth-century Florence, where only about a hundred crafts are attested. In his masterpiece on the history of the Roman Empire, Karl Christ expressed a similarly negative view: he believed that the Roman Empire was characterized by an archaic mode of production. This was caused by extensive specialization, which led to small-

---

[1] See, e.g. Morel (1991: 256–8). See also De Robertis (1946: 53–4), who had already taken such positions.

[2] Named in this way by Hopkins (1983: p. ix). But see Flohr and Wilson, Chapter 1, this volume.

Kai Ruffing

scale workshops combining manufacturing with retail. Owing to specialization, competition, and a lack of capital, only an atomized mode of production was possible—one that was based on the family as workforce.[3]

Harry Pleket, who compared the economic history of the Roman Empire with that of modern Europe, developed a more positive interpretation of the specialization of crafts in Rome. He identified some 500 Latin terms for crafts or associations of craftsmen in the Roman Empire and some 200 for Rome itself. He compared this evidence with mid-eighteenth-century London, where some 350 occupations are to be found. This led him to the conclusion that, in terms of craft specialization, the Roman Empire was not very different from early modern Europe.[4] A more negative view on specialization was again formulated by Hans Kloft, who saw the extensive craft specialization as a consequence of the humble social status of craftsmen, though he also acknowledged that economic demand and location factors were incentives for it.[5] In general, most modern research is now inclined to see economic conditions rather than social structures or a dependence on slave labour as causes for extensive specialization. Increasingly, this is also now judged as a positive indicator for the underlying economy.[6]

Thus, modern research has discussed specialization in the light of the presumed character of the economy of the Roman Empire in general, using occupational terms for crafts and trades in Latin literary texts and inscriptions as evidence.[7] This is not without methodological problems. First of all, in the Latin epigraphic record, the city of Rome is heavily over-represented: only a minority of texts comes from elsewhere in Italy or from the provinces.[8] Secondly, modern research often focused on crafts, but to apply the modern terminological differentiation between 'craft' and 'trade' to Latin (and Greek) texts involves imposing a modern distinction on ancient evidence that is not entirely unproblematic. To address these issues, some years ago I used the evidence of Greek inscriptions and documentary papyri in an attempt to trace chronological developments in the use of Greek occupational terms and to analyse the development of specialization itself, especially in the Roman Empire. In this context, causes for labour specialization were analysed, such as location factors, apprenticeship, and competition.[9] A key aim of this research

---

[3] Christ (1995: 495–6).

[4] Pleket (1990: 121).   [5] Kloft (1992: 214).

[6] See, e.g. Kolb (1995: 464–9) regarding the city of Rome; Landmesser (2002: 76–8) regarding classical Athens. In his innovative study of the ancient economy, which was based on the theoretical framework of the German national economy, Heichelheim had already taken the number of attested occupational terms as an indicator for the level of development of an economy: Heichelheim (1938: 335–6, 373–4, 735, 819–21).

[7] For the Latin occupational terms, see Petrikovits (1981a, b); Wissemann (1984). For modern research on Latin occupational terms, see the excellent discussion in Cristofori (2004: 18–23).

[8] See Petrikovits (1981a: 79); for the chronological and spatial distribution of Latin inscriptions, see Eck (1997: 98–100).

[9] See Ruffing (2008).

was to show that specialization cannot be taken as an argument in favour of a primitivist interpretation of the economy of the Roman Empire. The approach made it possible to observe terminological changes during antiquity, which meant that the sheer existence of designations for crafts and trades in itself cannot be taken as evidence for an extravagant specialization. Moreover, it became clear that even seemingly odd specializations were caused by the market and its structural framework and that there was no linear development of specialization in antiquity. Starting from the results of this project, this chapter will discuss three conditions and incentives for the development of different occupations in the Roman Empire: the demands of the market, the desire to increase productivity, and location factors.

SPECIALIZATION

Before a discussion of driving forces for specialization, it is necessary to make some remarks on the term itself and on the concept of 'profession' used to identify specialized trades and crafts in the documentary Greek sources. The concepts used in economic theory and in sociology in describing specialization are discussed by Edward Harris in his groundbreaking paper regarding the economy of classical Athens and the occupations attested there.[10] Thus, in the present context a few words may suffice.

Economic theory distinguishes between 'horizontal' and 'vertical' specialization. Horizontal specialization describes the diversity of goods and services produced in a society by using different professional formations or work roles. Thus, for example, the demand for skills for the production of amphorae is different from that for the production of shoes or textiles, and so on. The number of goods and services produced in an economy in this way is proportional to the number of specializations. Vertical specialization, on the other hand, describes the number of separate work roles and skills used in manufacturing a single product. A good example is the building of an ancient ship, which requires a set of different skills: carpentry, ironwork (for nails), rope-making, as well as textile production (for the sails). Moreover, both the building process itself and the supply of building materials and finished products need to be coordinated. Sociologists use the concepts of Max Weber, who differentiated between 'specification of function' and 'specialization of function'.[11] In the first case, one worker performs all steps in the production process for finishing a product; in the second case, the product is made in different steps by different specialized workers.[12]

---

[10] Harris (2001).
[11] Weber (1947: 225); but see Tran (2011: 8-10) with a different approach focusing on technologies used for the production of different goods and negating the usefulness of the concept of 'crafts'.
[12] Harris (2001: 70-1).

Using Greek and Latin inscriptions and documentary papyri as a source for analysing specialization in crafts and trades creates a certain problem regarding the status of occupational or professional terms in these types of sources. First of all, in many cases it is impossible to decide whether a specific term designates a craft or a trade. This is, for example, true for all Greek and Latin substantives ending with the suffixes -άριος or -arius, and for Greek substantives ending in -ᾶς. For example, a κιναρᾶς may be a producer or seller of artichokes, or both. At the same time, some terms that at first sight seem to be associated with trade are used to designate crafts: thus, a ζυτοπώλης is a brewer, not a trader of beer, although he also distributed his product.[13] As a necessary consequence, crafts and trades must be treated together; drawing a sharp distinction between them is often impossible.[14] Yet such a distinction is also unnecessary, given the fact that presumably most artisanal products reached the consumer through direct retail, rather than through networks of trade: as a rule, craftsmen themselves sold their products in their shops, and producers of agricultural goods sold these at markets themselves. Both practices are well attested for—for example, the Sarapeion market of Oxyrhynchos.[15]

Finally, some words need to be devoted to the use of terms such as 'occupation' and 'profession'. In using documentary sources we deal with a variety of contexts for naming crafts and trades in a written document. It is sometimes very difficult to judge whether a term used to refer to a trade or craft in a document is really an occupational term in Max Weber's sense. For Weber, a 'profession' is characterized through specification and through a typical combination of the different capacities of an individual, which is the basis of the ability to gain a livelihood continuously.[16]

THE MARKET

Since the days of Adam Smith, it has generally been assumed that there is a direct relation between specialization or division of labour and the market.[17] For Smith, the size of the market was the factor determining the degree of specialization. As the size of a market is defined by the number of persons who interact by means of it, the size of the population of settlements and the degree

---

[13] Drexhage (1997).

[14] This is not only a problem for antiquity; it also exists in analysing occupations and specialization in the nineteenth and twentieth centuries: see Leeuwen, Maas, and Miles (2002: 26–9).

[15] *SB* 16.12695. On this document, see Parsons (2007: 103–4). For Rome itself, however, the system of the retail trade is much more sophisticated: see Holleran (2012: 62–98, 194–231).

[16] Hofbauer and Stooß (1977: 468).   [17] e.g. for the Roman world, Wilson (2008).

of specialization are directly proportional.[18] This basic assumption is also used in the New Institutional Economics, at least by Douglass North.[19] Applying it to ancient economies in general and to the economy of the Roman Empire in particular is legitimate and useful for two reasons: first, the Roman economy without any doubt is to be characterized as a market economy; secondly, specialization is a necessary consequence of economies beyond autarky.[20] The correlation between the size of the population and the number of professions can be demonstrated, for example, for Rome. Certainly, it is due to the epigraphic habit and certain social conditions that about three-quarters of the occupational terms attested in Latin inscriptions come from Rome. On the other hand, Rome with its population of about a million people was also the largest market of the Roman Empire and depended heavily on commerce and importation of goods of every kind from all over the empire and beyond. What becomes visible here is a close connection between the size of population, commerce, and importation, and the degree of specialization, which fits well with the hypotheses of Adam Smith and Douglass North already mentioned. While Rome is without parallels, a similar picture emerges if we compare the evidence for Ephesos and other cities of Asia Minor.[21] It is very interesting to see that these principles, to a certain degree, were already observed by Plato, as has been convincingly demonstrated by Edward Harris.[22]

If we take the proportionality between size of market and degree of specialization as a given, we must ask: what are the driving forces that cause this interdependence? For Adam Smith the predisposition of human beings for the exchange of goods was caused either by nature or by the human capacity to speak and to think, which, in consequence, is the main driving force for specialization. In his view, the discovery of individuals that they have certain skills by which they can gain their livelihood with the exchange of goods and services on the market causes specialization and consequently the division of labour in a society.[23] For Plato, on the other hand, specialization was caused by a desire for greater efficiency and higher quality. In this way he believed a general increase of wealth was possible.[24] These explanations are certainly all but satisfying. A more convincing explanation for the way in which the market fostered specialization is the existence of competition between craftsmen, retailers, and traders.

Competition as a phenomenon of ancient business life has not attracted a lot of attention in modern research, although presumably it is of great importance for specialization as well as for other aspects of the economic

---

[18] Smith (1789: 16–22).   [19] North (1992: 141) with a focus on commerce.
[20] See Temin (2001). The same is true for the Greek economies: see Loomis (1998: 251–4); Bresson (2008).
[21] Ruffing (2008: 230–69).   [22] Harris (2001: 72–7).   [23] Smith (1789: 16–18).
[24] Plat,. *Rep.* 369–71; Harris (2001: 72).

history of antiquity.[25] The question of how competition influenced specialization in crafts and trades is connected with two other issues. First, the problem
of living standards, here understood as the possible extent of costs over
earnings in relation to purchasing power, and, secondly—as a result of
probably low living standards—the presumably high economic pressure on
individuals.[26] Unfortunately we cannot go much beyond impressions, but it
seems that for the majority of craftsmen and retailers the earning of a
livelihood was not without difficulties.[27] This means that there was strong
economic pressure on most individuals acting on the market to guarantee
their subsistence.[28] At the same time, actors on the market also wanted to
make a profit. Two mosaics from Pompeii demonstrate this clearly—one is a
salute to profit, the other one to the pleasure caused by it.[29] In a similar way,
the self-representation of merchants and craftsmen, which shows their pride
in their abilities and a presumed superiority over other individuals in the same
business, also must be seen as an indicator of competition.[30]

Thus, most craftsmen and retailers for one reason or another are likely to
have been exposed to intense competition on the market. There are also some
direct hints for this in our sources. A very interesting group of texts in this
respect are the curse tablets in which rivals in business life are bound or
cursed.[31] Most of those tablets date to the Hellenistic period, but a couple of
texts date to the High Empire.[32] For example, there is the binding of the profit
of a competitor in a curse tablet from Nomentum: 'in these tablets I bind [his]
business profits and health [*sc.* of a certain Malcius, son or servant of
Nicona].'[33]

Other, and to modern eyes more efficient, strategies for avoiding competition on the market are attested in the literary sources. In the *Metamorphoses* of
Apuleius, a certain Aristodemus, a seller of honey, cheese, and other such
things, attempts to buy up all the cheese in a certain region, but fails to do so

---

[25] See Wacke (1982); Kudlien (1994).

[26] On living standards, see Rathbone (2009: 299); also Allen (2009: 327–8), with a discussion
of how 'living standards' can be assessed. The assumption of 'living standards' that can be
defined by an objective set of data is not without problems, since 'living standards' are defined
also by cultural practice and the subjective behaviour of individuals: see Drexhage, Konen, and
Ruffing (2002: 161).

[27] See Drexhage, Konen, and Ruffing (2002: 181–3); see also Rathbone (2009: 322); Droß-
Krüpe (2011: 41–102).

[28] But see Rathbone (2006: 108), who maintains that poverty in Roman Egypt was relatively
absent. I am grateful to Alan Bowman, who called my attention to this article. Against the view
formulated by Rathbone, see Harris (2011: 36, 54), who argues 'that most parts of the Roman
Empire harboured a population of fluctuating size that was constrained to struggle for life below
the level of subsistence'.

[29] *CIL* 10.874: *salve lucru(m)*; *CIL* 10.875: *lucrum gaudium*.

[30] On self-representation, see Drexhage (1990: 27–32); Ruffing (2004).

[31] Gager (1992: 151–4); Kudlien (1994: 28–9).   [32] Gager (1992), nos 79, 82.

[33] Gager (1992), no. 80 (undated). The English version is Gager (1992: 172).

because another trader was faster than him and had already bought it up.[34] A similar case is documented in a letter from Roman Egypt: a certain Ammonios, his brother Apion, and a relative called Dionysius the Deaf intended to buy all the peaches on the market to have a private monopoly, so that they could sell peaches on the market without competition from others.[35] A further sign of competition on the market is the advertising of products by the craftsmen themselves by means of *tituli picti* on amphorae or through the use of shop signs.[36]

Without any doubt, competition on the market was further aggravated by the concentration of crafts and trades in specific areas of towns, which is hinted at by the existence of toponyms related to certain crafts and trade.[37] In the city of Rome toponyms such as the Street of the Sickle-Makers or the Street of the Glassmakers are known.[38] Other examples can be found in the east of the Empire—a διῶρυξ γναφικός (fullers' channel) at Antioch and a Cobblers' Street (Σκυτικὴ Πλατεῖα) at Apamea in Phrygia.[39] Other examples are documented in Roman Egypt, like the Great Street of the Goldsmiths (ῥύμη μεγάλη χρυσοχόων) in Ptolemais Euergetis.[40] Spatial concentration of crafts also shows in the name of some professional associations, such as the purple dyers 'of the eighteenth street' at Thessalonike (ἡ συνήθεια τῶ|ν πορφυροβάφ|ων τῆς ὀκτω|καιδεκάτης [sc. πλατείας] κτλ).[41] Further evidence for the concentration of crafts in local areas can be found in the archaeological record.[42] On the one hand, these local concentrations of crafts and trades lowered transaction costs, because consumers knew where they could buy certain products. Yet, on the other hand, one can certainly assume that as a result competition among craftsmen and traders became even fiercer.

Under these circumstances, further specialization could provide an 'economic niche' for individuals. The concept of the 'niche' has its origins in ecology, but has for a long time been used in economics too. Although it is not clearly defined by economists, the term can be applied to ancient economic history using a broad definition.[43] In modern economic theory, an 'economic niche' is a subsection of the market; focusing on a niche improves the level of need satisfaction, lowers the intensity of competition, or protects against it

---

[34] Apul. *Met.* 1.5.3–5   [35] *P. Ross. Georg* III 3 (third century AD).

[36] Curtis (1984–6); Gassner (1986: 43–5); Kruschwitz (1999); Berdowski (2003).

[37] More elaborately on this issue, see Goodman, Chapter 13, this volume; ß-Krüpe, Chapter 14, this volume.

[38] Sickle-makers: *inter falcarios*, Cic. *Cat.* 1.8; glassmakers: *vicus vitrarius*, Curios. *Urb. Rom.* 73.12 (ed. Nordh); von Petrikovits (1981a: 70–1); Morel (1987); Kolb (1995: 496–507); Holleran (2012: 51-60).

[39] Antioch: *SEG* 35.1483 = *AE* 1986, 694 (AD 73–4); Apamea: *IGR* 4.790.

[40] *P. Berl. Leihg.* II 42 A 12 (AD 176–9).

[41] *IG* 10.2,1 291. On this inscription, see Robert (1937: 535 n. 3).

[42] See Goodman, Chapter 13, this volume, on the spatial concentration of crafts and trades.

[43] Trachsel (2007: 6–9, esp. 8).

altogether, and it may foster a willingness to pay on the side of the customer. Concentrating on a subsection of the market means that a producer or a trader sells his products to a narrower group of consumers—for example, by consciously choosing to focus on certain products and/or regions. Because of this concentration on a market segment, a better satisfaction of consumer needs becomes possible. This leads to a protection against competition or to a lower intensity of competition, as competitors offering a wider spectrum of products on the market may be less able to satisfy more specific needs. The 'willingness to pay' is a consequence of this in the sense that consumers are willing to pay more to have their needs satisfied more specifically or closely.[44]

While this is not the place to discuss these criteria and their application at length, the use of applying the concept of the 'economic niche' to ancient economic history becomes clear in the following example. Since clothes are a basic need of human beings, their production and distribution were a sector of major importance in the economy of the Roman Empire. Thus, many occupational terms dealing with the production and distribution of clothing are documented in the literary and documentary sources, suggesting that many entrepreneurs sought and found economic niches.[45] One telling example of an economic niche in this sector is the commerce in silk. From a dedicatory inscription from Gabii we know a silk-trader called Aulus Plutius Epaphroditus, who evidently had great economic success in this town near Rome. He was able to make generous donations to the temple of *Venus Vera Felix Gabina*. On the occasion of the dedication of these offerings he gave five *denarii* to each *decurio*, three *denarii* to each *sevir Augustalis*, and one *denarius* to each *tabernarius* inside the walls of Gabii. Furthermore he made another donation of HS 10,000 to the city of Gabii in order to provide a public dinner for the local elite each year on the occasion of his daughter's birthday.[46] Apparently, Aulus Plutius chose to limit himself to selling only one product to his clientele, which consisted of a group of consumers willing to buy silk for—presumably—a high price. The high price and the nature of the product lowered the intensity of competition, and partially protected Aulus Plutius, since he sold a product that was available only through long-distance commerce via the harbours of the Levant or Egypt.[47]

Thus, we may conclude that the high economic pressure on individuals acting on the market—either to gain enough for supplying basic needs or to make more substantial profit—together with fierce competition could stimulate them to look

---

[44] Trachsel (2007: 41–7).

[45] Von Petrikovits (1981a: 123–4); Wissemann (1984); Labarre and Le Dinahet (1996); Vicari (2001: 37–69, 94–115); Droß-Krüpe (2011: 47–102).

[46] *CIL* 14.2793.

[47] The import of silk via Palmyra is documented through silk draperies found in Palmyra: Stauffer (1996: 426–7) and Falkenhausen (2000). The import of silk via Egypt is documented in the *Periplus Maris Erythraei*: see *Periplus Maris Erythraei*, 49.56. Other evidence for the import of silk is provided by Dig. 39.4.16.7.

for an economic niche. In practice, limiting oneself to a segment of the market of course is nothing other than specialization. Indeed, there are some hints in the sources of people in search of such a niche. A good example is a certain Onesimus, whose activities in various years are documented by five papyri. Onesimus was acting as a trader of young pigs ($\chi o\iota\rho\iota\delta\acute{\epsilon}\mu\pi o\rho o\varsigma$), as a butcher ($\mu\acute{\alpha}\gamma\epsilon\iota\rho o\varsigma$), and as a seller of meat ($\kappa\rho\epsilon o\pi\acute{\omega}\lambda\eta\varsigma$ $\kappa\alpha\grave{\iota}$ $\tau\alpha\rho\iota\chi\epsilon\upsilon\tau\acute{\eta}\varsigma$).[48] Another possible example is provided by a graffito from Pompeii, with a long list of occupations that had allegedly been exercised by one man:

> [cum] de[d]uxisti octies tibi superest ut (h)abeas sedecies coponium fecisti cretaria fecisti salsamentaria fecisti pistorium fexisti agricola fuisti aere minutaria fecisti propola fuisti languncularia nunc facis si cunnu(m) linx<s>e<e>ris, consummaris omnia.

> Since you've held eight jobs all that's left for you now is to have sixteen. You worked as an innkeeper, you worked as a clay man, you worked as a pickler, you worked as a baker, you were a farmer, you worked as a maker of bronze trinkets, you were a retailer, now you work as a jug man. If you perform cunnilingus you'll have done everything.[49]

To sum up: specialization in one economic niche was a response to economic pressure and competition on the market enabling people to earn a livelihood or even to be very successful on the market and make substantial profit. The consequence of this is that the market is to be seen as one of the main driving forces for professional specialization.

INCREASE OF PRODUCTIVITY

Specializing in one product had further advantages for craftsmen: it made it possible to increase both the quality and the quantity of their output. The quantity of goods produced per day rises notably through specialization, because, as has already been noticed by Adam Smith, it allows workers to focus completely on one specific production process.[50] A good example of that is the nailsmith. The occupational term ($\acute{\eta}\lambda o\kappa\acute{o}\pi o\varsigma$) emerges in the Greek documentary sources in the second century AD.[51] In Latin inscriptions, too, there is evidence for the profession of the nailsmith (*clavarius*) from the imperial period onwards.[52] Nails were also produced by normal smiths, but, if one looks at evidence from the medieval and early modern period, one gets

---

[48] Drexhage (1991: 34–6).
[49] *CIL* 4.10150. Translation: after Peña and McCallum (2009: 63), corrected.
[50] Smith (1789: 12).   [51] Drexhage (2008: 169–72).
[52] Petrikovits (1981a: 91) with the relevant inscriptions. As far as I see there is no further evidence.

the impression that the productivity of someone specialized in producing nails was considerably higher than that of a 'normal' smith. Similarly, Adam Smith in the chapter in his *Wealth of Nations* on the division of labour took the example of the production of nails when he discussed the increase of productivity and quality by specialization. According to him, a smith not accustomed to making nails can produce only 200 or 300 pieces a day, whereas a smith frequently making nails can produce between 800 and 1,000 pieces a day. A specialized nail-smith, on the contrary, was able to make more than 2,300 nails a day.[53] In today's research one finds that in the later Middle Ages and in the modern era production of between 800 and 4,000 pieces per day by nailsmiths was possible.[54] Since the method of producing nails did not change between antiquity and the early modern era, we have every reason to believe that a similar increase of productivity was possible for nailsmiths in the Roman Empire.[55] If this is true, the emerging profession of the nailsmith is at least a hint at the possibility of increasing productivity by specialization.[56]

While the case of the nailsmith can be used as an example to show increasing productivity by means of horizontal specialization, it is also possible to do this by means of vertical specialization.[57] Although evidence for vertical specialization in antiquity is rare, some examples can be mentioned. A good starting point, although seemingly rather unimpressive at first sight, is a dedicatory inscription from third-century Side by a certain Aurelius Kendeas, commemorating the harmony (ὁμόνοια) between the 'sifters of flour' (ἀλευροκαθάρται) and the 'formers of bread' (ἀβακῖται).[58] The importance of this inscription, which has been dated between AD 220 and 250, becomes clear if we read it in the light of a famous funerary monument in Rome: that of Marcus Vergileius Eurysaces, a baking contractor, as he is styled in his inscription.[59] On the monument, which dates from the first decade of the Augustan period, there is a frieze illustrating the individual steps of labour in the mass production of bread.[60] The sifters of flour can be found on the northern part of the frieze, while the formers of bread are displayed on the southern side. In this light, and together with other evidence for the existence of huge bakeries in Side, the inscription of Aurelius Kendeas becomes a clear indication for the production of bread in third-century Side, with a division of

---

[53] Smith (1789: 12).   [54] Stahlschmidt (1991: 179).

[55] On the production method, see Hug (1935: 1581–2). For lower estimates, see Drexhage (2008: 178).

[56] Wilson (2008).

[57] On this topic, see also Silver (2009); Broekaert (2012).

[58] *SEG* 33.1165; *IK* 43.30, pp. 296–7. See the rich commentary to this inscription by Nollé (1983). See also Zimmermann (2002: 167–8).

[59] *ILS* 7460 a–d: *hoc est monimentum Marcei Vergileius Eurysacis pistoris redemptoris apparet*. See also discussion by Wilson (2008).

[60] On the date of the grave monument, see Ciancio Rossetto (1973: 66–7); Zimmer (1982: 108).

labour in the production process apparently similar to that in Rome in the time of Eurysaces.[61] In the case of Eurysaces, the division of labour meant an increase of productivity, because every step in the production process was reduced to a simple operation. This allowed Eurysaces to mass-produce bread. The whole production process is vertically specialized, which can be interpreted as an indication that Eurysaces made the most of the opportunities provided by the emerging new market of his era.[62] A similar practice seems to have developed in Roman imperial Side.

In a certain way, specialization aimed at increasing productivity is also fostered by the market. For example, there are several indications that there was a high demand for nails in the Roman Empire. In the Roman legionary fortress of Inchtuthil in Scotland over 875,000 nails were found, buried unused when the unfinished fort was abandoned.[63] Papyrological evidence from Roman Egypt also points in this direction.[64] Further, that there was already a very huge market in Rome for bread in Augustan times is beyond doubt, in view of the number of inhabitants (about a million people).[65] The fact that even the medium-sized town of Pompeii had at least thirty-seven specialized workshops dedicated to the production of bread is all the more illuminating in this respect.[66] Thus we may conclude that high demand fostered an increase of productivity, which was made possible through horizontal as well as vertical specialization.

LOCATION FACTORS

All aspects of the production, distribution, and consumption of goods are closely linked to the realities of economic geography. In modern economic geography, this connection is described using the theory of location factors. These location factors are, on the one hand, determined by the geomorphology of a given region and the available natural resources and, on the other hand, by anthropogenic factors. Anthropogenic factors include, among others, the specific roles of a location on the economic, political, and religious level, the changes to its natural environment caused by human activity, and its place in the geographies of transport.[67] All factors are interlinked, which results in a very complex framework for the economy of individual localities, where changes in one factor influence all others. Discussing this in great detail is clearly beyond the scope of this chapter, but some observations may serve to

---

[61] Nollé (1983: 135–9). [62] Silver (2009: 177–8). [63] Wright (1961: 160).
[64] Drexhage (2008: 173–8). [65] Kolb (1995: 457).
[66] Mayeske (1972: 167). See Monteix, Chapter 10, this volume.
[67] For a catalogue of location factors, see Fellmeth (2002: 7–9).

illustrate how location factors could be a major driving force for professional specialization.

A good example is Hierapolis in Phrygia with its hot springs. These springs were the *raison d'être* of the town, because, together with the *Ploutonion*, they were the centre of the sanctuary of Apollo. The *Ploutonion* was believed to be an entrance to Hades, because every creature entering this cave died quickly. Strabo tells the story that he himself visited the *Ploutonion* and threw sparrows into the cave, which died as soon as they breathed its air.[68] The deadliness of the *Ploutonion*, which is prominent in ancient literature, was the result of the chemical composition of the water of the hot springs: it contained a high percentage of carbonic acid gas.[69] Furthermore, the water contained a high concentration of lime, which was responsible for the other natural spectacle of Hierapolis: the lime deposits.[70] Thanks to the water and its natural wonders, Hierapolis and its sanctuary were an attractive destination for travellers in Roman times.[71]

Yet the water of Hierapolis also had another important feature. According to Strabo, it was very useful for dyeing wool. Using a plant not clearly named by the geographer, the craftsmen of the town were able to produce red clothes of high quality.[72] As a consequence, textile production was of great importance for the economy of the city. This also shows in the city's epigraphic record, in which craftsmen related to the production of clothes are rather prominent, suggesting that producers and traders of textiles had an elevated social position, which must have been the result of their economic success.[73] The inscriptions also reveal a strong horizontal specialization in textile production. Inscriptions refer to wool-cleaners (ἐριοπλύται), dyers (βαφεῖς), who honoured the *boule* with a statue, and red-dyers. Furthermore there are sellers of red clothes.[74]

The following scenario may help to clarify the situation at Hierapolis. The natural location factors—especially the hot springs and their chemical properties—are fundamental features for the sanctuary as well as for the production of clothes. The sanctuary of Apollo and the *Ploutonion* were a reason for the

---

[68] Strabo, 13.4.14.   [69] Ritti (1985: 7–15).   [70] Humann (1898: 2–4).

[71] Casson (1974: 232); Kreitzer (1998: 382).

[72] On red dyeing in Hierapolis, see Herz (1985: 98).

[73] See also Arnaoutoglou, Chapter 12, this volume.

[74] Wool-cleaners: Labarre and Le Dinahet (1996: no. 64; cf. *IGR* 4.821), dated to the third century AD. Dyers: *SEG* 41.1201; cf. Labarre and Le Dinahet (1996: no. 56); *IK* 36.1/6*; cf. Labarre and Le Dinahet (1996: no. 67); Labarre and Le Dinahet (1996: no. 68). Red-dyers: Labarre and Le Dinahet (1996: no. 66; cf. *IGR* 4.816); Labarre and Le Dinahet (1996: no. 59), second century AD; Labarre and Le Dinahet (1996: no. 57), second/third century AD; Labarre and Le Dinahet (1996: no. 62; see also *SEG* 46.1656; *AE* 1994, 1660; Miranda (1999: 131, 23)), second/third century AD; Labarre and Le Dinahet (1996: no. 65), AD 206/208–9, see also Ritti (1985: 108, b); Labarre and Le Dinahet (1996: no. 63; cf. *IGR* 4.822), third century AD. Sellers of red clothes: Labarre and Le Dinahet (1996: no. 58); Labarre and Le Dinahet (1996: no. 69; cf. *BE* (1971: 650–37).

supra-regional importance of the cult place: the cult evidently attracted visitors from at least Asia Minor and maybe from the entire eastern part of the empire.[75] In this way, the special red clothes of Hierapolis came to the attention of people in Asia Minor, which increased demand for this product. As a consequence, production increased, which fostered horizontal specialization in crafts and trade. This appears to have generated wealth for the Hierapolitan producers and traders of clothes: they become visible in the epigraphic record as an important social group. For this reason, Pleket considered Hierapolis a Weberian 'producer city'.[76] The case of Hierapolis demonstrates the importance of interlinked location factors such as natural resources, religious centrality, and transport geography for the specialization in crafts and trades.

CONCLUSION

The market was the main driving force for specialization in crafts and trades, and the degree of specialization was proportional to the extent of the market—that is, the number of individuals who were involved in the market as buyers and sellers. The sheer number of people acting on the market created competition among producers and sellers of goods. Evidently such competition in the Roman Empire was very fierce, and it was often further aggravated by the concentration of certain crafts in specific areas of towns. This competition also meant that there was a high economic pressure on most individuals to make ends meet. One response to this pressure was to seek an economic niche, which allowed people to avoid or minimize competition. Operating within an economic niche meant specialization, and this specialization—in its horizontal as well as in its vertical form—in certain sectors also brought with it an increase in productivity. This increase in productivity, in turn, made it easier for people to avoid competition. Yet, throughout the Roman world, the market and its niches were influenced to a considerable extent by location factors, which in this way provided the framework for the economic performance of a given location or region in general and for specialization in crafts and trades in particular.

REFERENCES

Allen, R. C. (2009). 'How Prosperous were the Romans?: Evidence from Diocletian's Price Edict (AD 301)', in A. K. Bowman and A. I. Wilson (eds), *Quantifying the*

---

[75] On the supra-regional importance of the cult of Hierapolis and its consequences for the economy, see Ruffing (2009). See also Ruffing (2008: 256–65).

[76] Pleket (1984: 22–6; 1988: 33–5). See also Ritti (1995).

Roman Economy: Methods and Problems (Oxford Studies on the Roman Economy). Oxford, 327–45.

Berdowski P. (2003). 'Tituli picti und die antike Werbesprache für Fischprodukte', *MBAH* 22/2: 18–55.

Bresson, A. (2008). *L'Économie de la Grèce des cités (fin VIe–Ier siècle a.C.)*, ii. *Les Espaces de l'échange*. Paris.

Broekaert, W. (2012). 'Vertical Integration in the Roman Economy: A Response to Morris Silver', *AncSoc* 42: 109–25.

Casson, L. (1974). *Travel in the Ancient World*. London.

Christ, K. (1995). *Geschichte der römischen Kaiserzeit: Von Augustus bis zu Konstantin*, 3rd edn. Munich.

Ciancio Rossetto, P. (1973). *Il sepolcro del fornaio Marco Virgilio Eurisace a Porta Maggiore*. Rome.

Cristofori, A. (2004). *Non arma virumque: Le occupazioni nell'epigrafia del Piceno*, 2nd edn (Tarsie, 2). Bologna.

Curtis, R. I. (1984–6). 'Product Identification and Advertising on Roman Commercial Amphorae', *AncSoc* 15–17: 209–10.

de Robertis, F. M. (1946). *La organizzazione e la tecnica produttiva: Le forze di lavoro e i salari nel mondo romano*. Naples and Bari.

Drexhage, H.-J. (1990). 'Zum Selbstverständnis arbeitender Menschen im Imperium Romanum', *Humanistische Bildung* 14: 7–40.

Drexhage, H.-J. (1991). 'Einige Bemerkungen zu den ἔμποροι und κάπηλοι im römischen Ägypten (1.–3. Jh. n.)', *MBAH* 10/2: 28–46.

Drexhage, H.-J. (1997). 'Bierproduzenten und Bierhändler in der papyrologischen Überlieferung', *MBAH* 16/2: 32–9.

Drexhage, H.-J. (2008). 'Einige Bemerkungen zu den Nagelschmieden (ἡλοκόποι) nach dem papyrologischen und epigraphischen Befund', *MBAH* 25/2: 169–82.

Drexhage, H.-J., Konen, H., and Ruffing, K. (2002). *Die Wirtschaft des Römischen Reiches (1.–3. Jahrhundert): Eine Einführung*. Berlin.

Droß-Krüpe, K. (2011). *Wolle—Weber—Wirtschaft: Die Textilproduktion der römischen Kaiserzeit im Spiegel der papyrologischen Überlieferung* (Philippika, 46). Wiesbaden.

Eck, W. (1997). 'Lateinische Epigraphik', in F. Graf (ed.), *Einleitung in die lateinische Philologie*. Stuttgart and Leipzig. 92–111.

Falkenhausen, L. von (2000). 'Die Seiden mit chinesischen Inschriften', in A. Schmidt-Colinet and A. Stauffer (eds), *Die Textilien aus Palmyra*. Mainz, 58–81.

Fellmeth, U. (2002). *'Eine wohlhabende Stadt sei nahe . . .': Die Standortfaktoren in der römischen Agrarökonomie im Zusammenhang mit den Verkehrs- und Raumordnungsstrukturen im römischen Italien*. St Katharinen.

Gager, J. G. (1992). *Curse Tablets and Binding Spells from the Ancient World*. Oxford.

Gassner, V. (1986). *Die Kaufläden in Pompeji*. Vienna.

Harris, E. M. (2001). 'Workshop, Marketplace and Household: The Nature of Technical Specialization in Classical Athens and its Influence on Economy and Society', in P. Cartledge, E. E. Cohen, and L. Foxhall (eds), *Money, Labour and Land: Approaches to the Economy of Ancient Greece*. London and New York, 67–99.

Harris, W. V. (2011). 'Poverty and Destitution in the Empire', in W. V. Harris (ed.), *Rome's Imperial Economy: Twelve Essays*. Oxford, 27–54.

Heichelheim, F. M. (1938). *Wirtschaftsgeschichte des Altertums vom Paläolithikum bis zur Völkerwanderung der Germanen, Slaven und Araber*, vols 1–3. Leiden (repr. Leiden, 1969).

Herz, P. (1985). 'Parthicarius und Babyloniarius: Produktion und Handel feiner orientalischer Lederwaren', *MBAH* 4/2: 89–106.

Hofbauer, H., and Stooß, F. (1977). 'Beruf und Berufsbildung', in W. Albers, K. E. Born, E. Dürr, H. Hesse, A. Kraft, H. Lampert, K. Rose, H. H. Rupp, H. Scherf, K. Schmidt, and W. Wittmann (eds), *Handwörterbuch der Wirtschaftswissenschaft*, i. 468–78.

Holleran, C. (2012). *Shopping in Ancient Rome: The Retail Trade in the Late Republic and the Principate*, Oxford.

Hopkins, K. (1983). 'Introduction', in P. Garnsey, K. Hopkins, and C. R. Whittaker (eds), *Trade in the Ancient Economy*. London, pp. ix–xxv.

Hug, A. (1935). *s.v.* Nagel, *RE* XVI.2: 1576–82.

Humann, C. (1898). 'Topographie und Bauten', in C. Humann, C. Cichorius, W. Judeich, and F. Winter (eds), *Altertümer von Hierapolis* (Jahrbuch des Kaiserlich Deutschen Archäologischen Instituts Ergänzungsheft, 4). Berlin, 1–17.

Kloft, H. (1992). *Die Wirtschaft der griechisch-römischen Welt: Eine Einführung*. Darmstadt.

Kolb, F. (1995). *Rom: Die Geschichte der Stadt in der Antike*. Munich.

Kreitzer, L. J. (1998). 'The Ploutonion of Hierapolis and the Descent of Christ into the "Lowermost Parts of the Earth" (Ephesians 4,9)', *Biblica* 79: 381–93.

Kruschwitz, P. (1999). 'Römische Werbeinschriften', *Gymnasium* 106: 231–53.

Kudlien, F. (1994). 'Die Rolle der Konkurrenz im antiken Geschäftsleben', *MBAH* 13/1: 1–39.

Labarre, G., and Le Dinahet, M.-Th. (1996). 'Les Métiers du textile en Asie Mineure de l'époque hellénistique à l'époque imperiale', in *Aspects de l'artisanat du textile dans le monde mediterranéen (Égypte, Grece, monde Romain)* (Collection de l'Institut d'archéologie et d'histoire de l'Antiquité, 2). Paris, 49–115.

Landmesser, D. (2002). *Wirtschaftsstil und wirtschaftliche Entwicklung im klassischen Athen*. Munich.

Leeuwen, M. H. D. van, Maas, I., and Miles, A. (2002). *HISCO: Historical International Standard Classification of Occupations*. Löwen.

Loomis, W. T. (1998). *Wages, Welfare Costs and Inflation in Classical Athens*. Ann Arbor.

Luik, M. (2002). 'Handwerk in den Vici des Rhein-Maas-Gebietes', in K. Strobel (ed.), *Die Ökonomie des Imperium Romanum: Strukturen, Modelle und Wertungen im Spannungsfeld von Modernismus und Neoprimitivismus. Akten des 3. Trierer Symposiums zur Antiken Wirtschaftsgeschichte* (Pharos, 17). St Katharinen, 169–209.

Mayeske, B. J. B. (1972). 'Bakeries, Bakers, and Bread at Pompeii: A Study in Social and Economic History'. Ph.D. dissertation, Ann Arbor.

Miranda, E. (1999). 'La comunità giudaica di Hierapolis di Frigia', *EA* 31: 109–55.

Morel, J.-P. (1987). 'La Topographie de l'artisanat et du commerce dans la Rome antique', in *L'Urbs: Espace urbain et histoire (Ier siècle av. J.-C.-IIIe siècle ap. J.-C.): Actes du colloque international organisé par le Centre national de la recherche scientifique et l'École française de Rome (Rome, 8–12 mai 1985)* (Collection de l'École française de Rome, 98). Rome, 127–55.

Morel, J.-P. (1991). 'Der Handwerker', in A. Giardina (ed.), *Der Mensch in der römischen Antike*. Frankfurt–New York–Paris: 243–75.

Nollé, J. (1983). 'Die Eintracht der Mehlsieber und Brotformer in Side', *EA* 1: 131–40.

North, D. (1992). *Institutionen, institutioneller Wandel und Wirtschaftsleistung* (Die Einheit der Gesellschaftswissenschaften, 76). Tübingen.

Parsons, P. (2007). *City of the Sharp-Nosed Fish: Greek Lives in Roman Egypt*. London.

Peña, J. T., and McCallum, M. (2009). 'The Production and Distribution of Pottery at Pompeii: A Review of the Evidence; Part 1, Production', *American Journal of Archaeology* 113/1: 57–79.

Petrikovits, H. von (1981a). 'Die Spezialisierung des römischen Handwerks', in H. Jankuhn, W. Janssen, R. Schmidt-Wiegand, and H. Tiefenbach (eds), *Das Handwerk in vor- und frühgeschichtlicher Zeit*, Teil I: *Historische und rechtshistorische Beiträge und Untersuchungen zur Frühgeschichte der Gilde: Bericht über die Kolloquien der Kommission für die Altertumskunde Mittel- und Nordeuropas in den Jahren 1977 bis 1980* (Abhandlungen der Akademie der Wissenschaften zu Göttingen, Philologisch-Historische Klasse III 122). Göttingen, 63–132.

Petrikovits, H. Von (1981b). 'Die Spezialisierung des römischen Handwerks II (Spätantike)', *ZPE* 43: 285–306.

Pleket, H. W. (1984). 'Urban Elites and the Economy in the Greek Cities of the Roman Empire', *MBAH* 3/1: 3–36.

Pleket, H. W. (1988). 'Greek Epigraphy and Comparative Ancient History: Two Case Studies', *EA* 12: 25–37.

Pleket, H. W. (1990). 'Wirtschaft', in W. Fischer, J. A. van Houtte, H. Kellenbenz, I. Mieck, and F. Vittinghoff (eds), *Handbuch der europäischen Wirtschafts- und Sozialgeschichte*, i. Stuttgart, 25–160.

Rathbone, D. (2006). 'Poverty and Population in Roman Egypt', in M. Atkins and R. Osborne (eds), *Poverty in the Roman World*. Cambridge, 100–14.

Rathbone, D. (2009). 'Earnings and Costs: Living Standards and the Roman Economy (First to Third Centuries AD)', in A. K. Bowman and A. I. Wilson (eds), *Quantifying the Roman Economy: Methods and Problems* (Oxford Studies on the Roman Economy). Oxford, 299–326.

Ritti, T. (1985). *Fonti letterarie ed epigrafiche* (Hierapolis. Scavi e Ricerche, 1). Roma.

Ritti, T. (1995). 'Associazioni di mestiere à Hierapolis di Frigia', in B. M. Giannattasio (ed.), *Atti. VII Giornata Archeologica: Viaggi e commerci nell'antchità*. Genova, 65–84.

Robert, L. (1937). *Études anatoliennes: Recherches sur les inscriptions grecques de l'Asie Mineure*. Paris (repr. Amsterdam, 1970).

Ruffing, K. (2004). 'Die Selbstdarstellung von Händlern und Handwerkern in den griechischen Inschriften', *MBAH* 23.2: 85–101.

Ruffing, K. (2008). *Die berufliche Spezialisierung in Handel und Handwerk: Untersuchungen zu ihrer Entwicklung und zu ihren Bedingungen in der römischen Kaiserzeit im östlichen Mittelmeerraum auf der Grundlage der griechischen Inschriften und Papyri* (Pharos, 24). Rahden/Westfalen.

Ruffing, K. (2009). 'Thermalquellen und Kult: Das Beispiel Hierapolis', in E. Olshausen and V. Sauer (eds), *Die Landschaft und die Religion: Stuttgarter Kolloquium zur Historischen Geographie des Altertums 9, 2005* (Geographica Historica, 26). Stuttgart: 287–300.

Silver, M. (2009). 'Glimpses of Vertical Integration/Disintegration in Ancient Rome', *AncSoc* 39: 171–84.

Smith, A. (1789). *The Wealth of Nations: An Enquiry into their Nature and Origins*. 5th edn. London (German translation: *Der Wohlstand der Nationen: Eine Untersuchung seiner Natur und seiner Ursachen*. Munich, 1974).

Stahlschmidt, R. (1991). 'Nagelschmied', in R. Reith (ed.), *Lexikon des alten Handwerks. Vom Spätmittelalter bis in das 20. Jahrhundert*. Munich, 176–81.

Stauffer, A. (1996). 'Textiles from Palmyra: Local Production and the Import and Imitation of Chinese Silk Weavings', *AAAS* 42: 425–30.

Temin, P. (2001). 'A Market Economy in the Early Roman Empire', *JRS* 91: 169–81.

Trachsel, M. (2007). *Nischenstrategien und ihre Bedeutung für den Unternehmenserfolg*. Wiesbaden.

Tran, N. (2011). 'De "l'artisanat" aux métiers: Quelques réflexions sur les savoir-faire du monde romain à partir de l'exemple pompéien', in N. Monteix and N. Tran (eds), *Les Savoirs professionnels des gens de métier: Études sur le monde du travail dans les sociétés urbaines de l'empire romain* (Collection du Centre Jean Bérard, 37. Archéologie de l'artisanat antique, 5). Naples, 7–26.

Vicari, F. (2001). *Produzione e commercio dei tessuti nell'Occidente romano* (BAR International Series, 916). Oxford.

Wacke, A. (1982). 'Wettbewerbsfreiheit und Konkurrenzverbotsklauseln im antiken und modernen Recht', *ZRG* 99: 188–215.

Weber, M. (1947). *The Theory of Social and Economic Organization*. New York.

Wilson, A. I. (2008). 'Large-Scale Manufacturing, Standardization, and Trade', in J. P. Oleson (ed.), *Handbook of Engineering and Technology in the Classical World*. Oxford, 393–417.

Wissemann, M. (1984). 'Die Spezialisierung des römischen Handels', *MBAH* 3/1: 116–24.

Wright, R. P. (1961). 'Roman Britain in 1960'. *JRS* 51: 157–98.

Zimmer, G. (1982). *Römische Berufsdarstellungen* (Archäologische Forschungen, 12). Berlin.

Zimmermann, C. (2002). *Handwerkervereine im griechischen Osten des Imperium Romanum* (Römisch-Germanisches Zentralmuseum, Forschungsinstitut für Vor- und Frühgeschichte, 57). Mainz.

6

Fashionable Footwear: Craftsmen and Consumers in the North-West Provinces of the Roman Empire

Carol van Driel-Murray

In the Roman world, leather was used for a multitude of purposes, and it specifically played a key role in footwear. This chapter will focus on the economy of footwear and will analyse the remarkable similarities, throughout the empire, in both the final products and the technologies used in making them. Globalization is too fraught a concept, but there does seem to be integration to the extent that travellers would be familiar with most of the footwear displayed on market stalls wherever they went (Figs 6.1 and 6.7).[1] Regional differences may have persisted to a degree—certain forms of sandals in Egypt, for instance, or a preference for single-piece shoes (so-called *carbatinae*) in Germany—but craftsmen everywhere seem to have been able to participate in an empire-wide dialogue that comes close to our concept of 'fashion', in the sense of the contemporaneous stylistic development of clothing accessories across a wide geographical area and available to almost all social classes.[2]

The archaeological record is somewhat uneven in that finds tend to be concentrated at military settlements and in the frontier regions, while comparative material from the civilian hinterland is distressingly scarce. Nevertheless, in addition to a number of huge complexes, there are sufficient scattered finds to

---

[1] Woolf (1998: 169 ff.) also emphasizes the role of common 'goods' in the development of provincial culture.

[2] For dating and development, see van Driel-Murray (2001b). The term *carbatinae* is one of convenience used by archaeologists to identify footwear made of a single piece of leather, seamed at the back, of type without modern equivalents (Fig. 6.1, nos 10, 20, 25). For details of manufacture and shoe styles, see van Driel-Murray (2001a) and Volken (2014). See also Goldman (1994) and Leguilloux (2004), which includes Egyptian material,

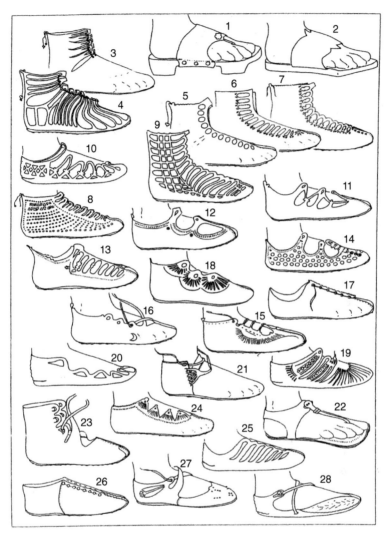

Fig. 6.1. Selection of Roman footwear, from first century AD (top left) to fourth century (bottom right). Image: Carol van Driel-Murray.

confirm that footwear was easily available, widely used, and readily discarded by both urban and rural populations (see Table 6.1). It was not a scarce and luxurious good, available only to the rich: indeed, footwear gave people of modest means a way of exhibiting individuality, taste, and style. As such it is not only the craftsmen but also the consumers who need to be taken into account when attempting to explain the remarkable similarities in the surviving material.

INTEGRATION

Images on coinage may have introduced the provincial population to elite hairstyles, but how did shoemakers acquire the knowledge of the latest models and the special technologies used to make them? That the *caligae* worn by Roman soldiers in Augustan Mainz are similar to those left by legionaries at Qasr Ibrim or Didymoi in Egypt is perhaps explicable in terms of military manufacturing conventions (Fig. 6.1, no. 4), but other parallels are more intriguing.[3] With remarkable perspicacity, Martine Leguilloux recognized that a small fragment from Didymoi resembles a child's sandal from a barrack room in Vindolanda (Fig. 6.2).[4] Identical shoes, of an infrequent and complicated pattern, appearing at the extreme north and the extreme south of the empire might suggest the movement of an individual, but this instance is by no means unique. Also recorded from Didymoi are front-laced shoes with frilled edges (style designation: Irthing, Fig. 6.3), well known in north Britain in the Antonine period, as well as the slightly later shoes with integral laces of style Geltsdale (Fig. 6.1, no. 16).[5] Many more examples from Egypt or the Near East that happen to find their way into the published record can be paralleled in northern Europe, suggesting a considerable degree of uniformity in footwear

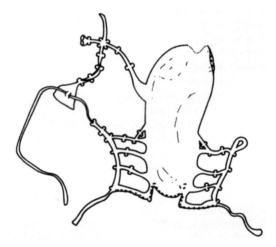

Fig. 6.2. Child's sandal from Vindolanda period IV (scale 1:3). Image: Carol van Driel-Murray.

---

[3] Van Driel-Murray (1985; 1999a; 2001a: 362–4).

[4] Leguilloux (2006: 31, fig. 9); van Driel-Murray (1998: fig. 5).

[5] For ease of identification, common shoe styles are named after a settlement site or a location near a characteristic find spot: van Driel-Murray (2001b); Volken (2014: 78-9). Irthing: Leguilloux (2006: pl. 26, no. 135), cf. Charlesworth and Thornton (1973: no. 5). Geltsdale: Leguilloux (2006: pl. 26, no. 134) (laces snapped); cf. van Driel-Murray (2001a: 366–7). In all these cases, as with the *caligae*, there are sufficient differences for local manufacture to be certain.

design and technology throughout the Roman period. Connections over vast regions are even more pronounced in the case of sandals. Not only do the shapes, decorative motifs, and quite complex details of manufacturing technology appear in every province, but the entire trajectory of stylistic development also runs parallel throughout the empire. Thus the exaggerated shape of sandals after the second quarter of the third century can be paralleled at numerous sites all over the empire, from remote villas in the Yorkshire Wolds to North Africa (see Fig. 6.8).[6]

Remarkable expressions of what might be called Zeitgeist are the patterns in which shoe nails are arranged. Basically, the nails serve to hold the shoe construction together and to reinforce the sole, but shoemakers regularly embellished their work with elaborate, non-essential decorative patterns (Fig. 6.5). Some, like tridents and swastikas, occur fairly regularly, but others are quite restricted in their popularity. Thus diamonds tend to occur after AD 150, elaborate tendrils appear after AD 170, S's after *c.*190, big asymmetrical

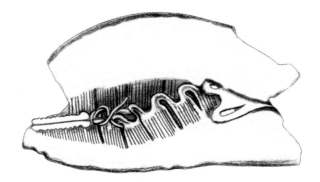

Fig. 6.3. Shoe style Irthing from Didymoi, Egypt. Image: Carol van Driel-Murray after Leguilloux (2006: pl. 26).

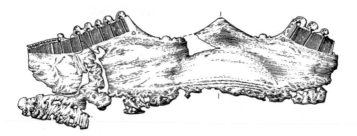

Fig. 6.4. Shoe style Irthing from Hardknott UK. Image: Charlesworth and Thornton (1973: fig. 5). Not to scale.

---

[6] Dunbabin (1990); Mould (1990), van Driel-Murray (2001b: fig. 3).

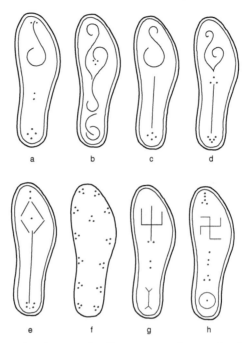

Fig. 6.5. Diagrammatic selection of nailing patterns. Image: Carol van Driel-Murray.

S-shapes *c.* AD 220–30, while groups of triple nails are characteristic of the second half of the third and early fourth centuries.[7] These are not random momentary inspirations: people evidently drew on common experiences that could be expressed in a tangible form. Whatever the actual meaning of the symbolism, or the methods by which this knowledge was communicated, the choices made clearly involve the mechanisms of production as well as the desires of consumers.

LEATHER PRODUCTION AS AN ALIEN TECHNOLOGY

In the northern provinces, the Roman Conquest marked a distinct change in leatherworking practices. Not only was the method of vegetable-tanning introduced as a new procedure, but an entire package of novel products appeared, together with the specific technologies associated with their manufacture.[8] There was a considerable increase in the scale of leather production, and procedures

[7] Van Driel-Murray (1999b: fig. 1).
[8] Groenman-van Waateringe (1967); van Driel-Murray (2001a: 345–8; 2008); Winterbottom (2009).

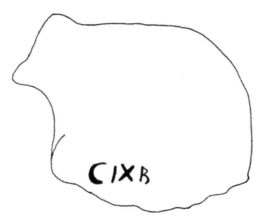

Fig. 6.6. Vindolanda: off-cut stamped with *C(oh). IX Bat(avorum)* (scale 1:3). Image: Carol van Driel-Murray.

became more complex and time-consuming. Newly introduced, alien technologies often remain divorced from the pre-existing economic structures, and retain their separate organization primarily on account of capital investment and the restriction of technical knowledge.[9] In the case of tanning, we may also be seeing a shift from female-controlled skin-processing to male-dominated large-scale manufacturing, which would further dislocate native practices.

Although tannery structures have been identified in the cities of Roman Italy, north of the Alps tanning was not an urban industry: as a newly introduced technology, operations could be freely sited in the most appropriate location, and the economic rationale for organization may well differ from what we would expect on the basis of medieval and early modern practice.[10] For instance, separating operations such as flaying and initial cleansing from the actual tanning process may have made economic sense, in order to maximize the extraction of what we would now deem 'waste products'. Recuperating horn, sinew, hair, and glue in addition to the hides would affect not only the location of the industry but also the nature of the waste left over. This is perhaps why it is so very difficult to identify tannery locations in the archaeological record.[11]

The military demand for leather goods—footwear, tents, covers of all kinds, horse gear—was vast, and the introduction of tanning was initially geared exclusively to military supply.[12] The imposition of taxes in kind, such as the cowhide tax levied on the Frisians, drew raw materials from underdeveloped regions for processing in the more stable hinterland, and, though soldiers may have been

[9] Bennett (1996: 82–4).
[10] On tannery structures in Roman Italy, see Leguilloux (2002).
[11] Vanderhoeven and Ervynck (2007); van Driel-Murray (2011).
[12] Groenman-van Waateringe (1967); van Driel-Murray (1993); Winterbottom (2009).

involved in preparing the hides for transport, tanning (in contrast to shoemaking) was not carried out at the forts themselves.[13] Tanning seems always to have remained in the hands of large operators—it is a capital-intensive industry, where investments are tied up for several years, and it also requires a well-organized infrastructure with secure and continuous supplies of hides and other raw materials. The organization of the process and the installations involved also imply an increase in the scale of production and the availability of leather, thus further stimulating its use. Presumably only major entrepreneurs would have the managerial skills and financial resources to do this, but details of tannery organization are obscure. It may be significant that the so-called tanners' stamps on hides are generally in the *tria nomina* form, but examples are relatively infrequent, and there is so little duplication that extreme consolidation is unlikely.[14] Indeed, it is strange that such a major industry has left so little epigraphic or iconographic evidence, and I sometimes wonder whether major estate-owners controlled the entire chain of activities, from slaughter to glue making, using their own personnel, but perhaps putting certain activities, like tanning itself, out to specialists. Likewise, the Cohors IX Batavorum, stationed at Vindolanda, seems to have retained administrative control of hides taken from its own food animals, putting them out to be tanned by non-military entrepreneurs (Fig. 6.6).[15] Exactly how a new industry is established, and how the transition from military to civilian control occurs, are difficult to track archaeologically. However, here an analogy with the introduction of vegetable tanning in sub-Saharan Africa may be instructive. In this region, the spread of leather technology was closely associated with that of Islam, and the first tanners were brought to Niger in the 1850s as slaves of the sultan. As freed men, they later worked in the households of the great pre-colonial merchants; as a result, leatherworkers and tanners still continue to be regarded as outsiders.[16] The restriction of knowledge to select groups might account for the loss of tanning technology in the northern provinces, as Roman influence waned in the fourth century.

CRAFTSMEN AND PRODUCERS

Archaeologically, shoemakers' workplaces are practically invisible: the tools are simple, and the products are sold and dispersed—all that is left is the characteristic refuse, small snippets of leather that reveal the presence of shoemakers at settlements of all kinds: urban, military, and roadside settlements (*vici*), and even some rural locations. The mass market in Rome may have encouraged considerable specialization, but modern re-enactors have

---

[13] Van Driel-Murray (1985, 2008).   [14] Van Driel-Murray (1977).
[15] Van Driel-Murray (1993: 64–5, figs 26–7).   [16] Arnould (1984: 137).

convincingly demonstrated that a competent craftsman is quite capable of producing the full range of footwear, from cork-soled slippers to nailed boots, using the same basic toolkit.[17] Shoemakers in the mining community at Vipasca were expected to supply varied footwear styles as well as their own hobnails as part of their concession, and failure to do so meant clients were free to take their custom elsewhere.[18] The small provincial town at Nijmegen (*Ulpia Noviomagus*) was able to support a professional association of shoemakers, which suggests the presence of a number of independent craftsmen, while rather enigmatic, official-looking stamps on late-second-century AD sandals and slippers in the Rhineland also hint at craftsmen working in some sort of corporate organization (see Fig. 6.10, right).[19] Details of organizational structures are elusive, and it is here that one could perhaps expect the differences between the northern provinces and the Mediterranean areas to be most marked.

This all tends to suggest a lack of product specialization, but whether these individuals worked alone or were collected into larger workplaces must remain open. Perhaps too much conditioned by medieval analogies and literary conventions, we frequently envisage the shoemaker as a humble, poverty-stricken, yet independent and argumentative figure.[20] Nevertheless, the apparent personal links recorded between wealthy families and freedmen involved in shoemaking in Pizzone and Ostia are a salutary reminder that, in a society with slaves, freedmen, and—in the northern provinces—tribal dependants, larger-scale organizations are certainly conceivable, particularly when the technology had been introduced to new regions in the wake of military conquest.[21] In many cases, tombstones with depictions of craftsmen in all probability commemorate entrepreneurs controlling the activity rather than the workers themselves, with symbolic vignettes illustrating the trade concerned.[22] Bringing craftsmen together could lead to specialization and economies of scale, but individual shoemakers would have the advantage of flexibility, and, perhaps, innovation. Nevertheless, the contrast between the ubiquity of shoemakers' off-cuts, the scarcity of shoemakers' tombstones, and the remarkable lack of memorials to tanners suggests considerable caution in the interpretation of this sort of evidence.

Without documentation, degrees of dependency cannot be reconstructed from finds alone. Moreover, shoemaking and cobbling are mobile trades relying more on the skill of the craftsman than a complex toolkit or fixed installations, and are therefore easily taken up by individuals seeking means of support. On the

---

[17] As Ivor Lawton demonstrated vividly in 2007 in the archaeological park at Xanten. See also Volken (2008, 2014). On specialization in Rome, see Leguilloux (2004: tableau IIA).

[18] Domergue (1983).   [19] Van Driel-Murray (1977; 2001a: 33, 38–9, figs 2–3 and 26c).

[20] Lau (1967).   [21] De' Spagnolis (2000: 71–3).

[22] Such as the well-dressed Septimia Stratonice, who flourishes what seems to be a last or a shoemaker's anvil as a trade symbol (*CIL* 14, suppl. 4698), while the sarcophagus dedicated to T. Flavius Trophimus by friends with links to Pizzone depicts both shoemaking and the twining of flax or tendons. Zimmer (1982: nos 47–52); van Driel-Murray (2008: 491).

other hand, dependent craftsmen answering to a distant master, and the personal networks of slaves and freedmen acting as agents abroad, would enable the rapid dissemination of new ideas and technological information.[23] Furthermore, the widespread use of papyrus patterns in the Egyptian textile industry raises the intriguing possibility of the more general existence of craftsmen's workbooks with details of manufacturing technology.[24] Parallel modes of transmission, applicable to both free and dependent labour, may be found in apprenticeships.[25] Apprenticeships outside the family, coupled to the mobility of trained craftsmen in order to reduce competition in their home town, provide a dynamic context for transmission of ideas. There is likely to be considerable diversity in actual practice, with operators acting at different levels of complexity. Regional markets also provide an environment for communication and competition, with craftsmen from different areas coming together to offer their wares for sale, interacting with each other as well as with clients.

CONSUMERISM

All military camps on the frontiers—legionary as well as auxiliary—were self-sufficient in footwear manufacture, and it is a small step to seeing ex-servicemen as the initiators of this craft in the new provinces. The role of military shoemakers may also explain the overwhelming preference for nailed footwear in the northern provinces (Table 6.1). Though evidence is not particularly abundant, in the Mediterranean and Egypt civilian footwear is

Table 6.1. Shoe types per site

Site	Carbatina (%)	Sewn (%)	Sandal (%)	Nailed (%)	Slipper (%)	Total no.
Vindolanda VI	5	5	5	83	2	333
Vindolanda 7/8	8	5	12	72	3	365
London NFW	2	11	26	59	2	129
Voorburg	6	4	15	75	0	111
Valkenburg Marktveld	1.5	1.5	13	83	1	304
Welzheim	24	6	8	57	5	177
Saalburg	18	12	10	60	?	262

Sources: Vindolanda: van Driel-Murray (2001b: 187); Saalburg: Busch (1965); Welzheim: van Driel-Murray (1999c); London: MacConnoran (1986); Valkenburg: Hoevenberg (1993); Voorburg: van Driel-Murray, Pollmann, and Richter (2014). The sites are not all quantified in the same way, though it may be assumed that each author is consistent. The totals for the Saalburg have been corrected to account for fragmentation.

[23] Broekaert, Chapter 10, this volume.   [24] Stauffer (2008).
[25] Freu, Chapter 8, this volume.

generally soft soled, and only certain forms of heavy-duty footwear—as worn by soldiers or labourers—had the additional hobnails. But north of the Alps, shoes and sandals with nailed soles are the norm, even for very young children, and remain so until the fourth century.

Civilian settlements founded in Britain soon after conquest already reveal a rapid uptake of new footwear types, all radically different in style and technology from the footwear of the Iron Age communities and by the mid-second century even quite remote areas were obtaining Roman-style shoes and boots. On the continent the process is completed rather earlier, and it seems as though it takes about three generations from the earliest introduction in towns and military settlements to general availability in rural areas.

The population at large was being offered an unprecedented choice of desirable novelties, a situation not repeated till the 'consumer revolution' of the seventeenth and eighteenth centuries (Fig. 6.7). Kevin Greene has shown the potential of applying the concept of 'consumerism' to Roman material culture, drawing the wishes of the consumer into explanations for techno-logical innovation in craft production.[26]

Roman footwear of the first three centuries AD answers all the consumerist criteria. In the northern provinces, for the first time, a simple desire for novelties becomes visible in the basic apparel of a wide segment of the population. The adoption is not just a matter of improved quality: shoes are indeed better made and longer lasting than previously, but they are above all extremely attractive and varied (Figs 6.1 and 6.7). Hallmarks of consumerism

Fig. 6.7. A choice of fourth-century shoes from Cuijk (reproductions made by Olaf Goubitz 2004). Image: Carol van Driel-Murray.

[26] Greene (2007, 2008).

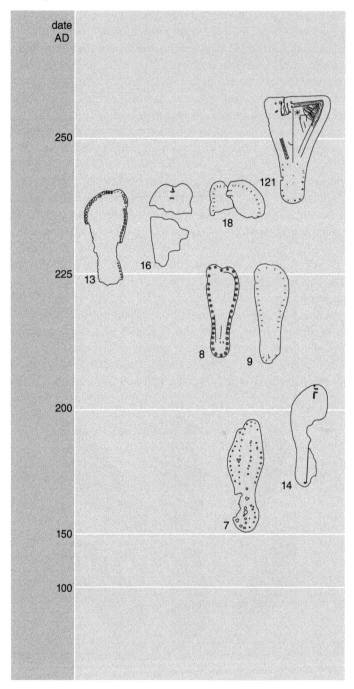

Fig. 6.8. Dated sequence of changing sandal shapes from Voorburg (The Netherlands). Image: Carol van Driel-Murray.

are rapidity of change and inbuilt redundancy: and this is exactly what we see in footwear. Change is often radical, following classic fashion cycles—high to low, narrow to broad, rounded toes to pointed—the extremes often being followed by the disappearance of the style and the emergence of something completely new. Within the general trend there is also ample room for personal expression. At Voorburg (*Forum Hadriani*), a small and not very successful town in the territory of the *Canannefates* in *Germania Inferior*, most men wore fashionable wide sandals in the 220s and 230s, but a few trend-setters went for really exaggerated forms—forms that also appear elsewhere across the empire, as though defining a particular lifestyle (Figs. 6.5 and 6.9). These exaggerated soles are more simply made than earlier sandals: perhaps they were meant to be worn only briefly during the summer, but a simple construction also allows for more experimentation and a quicker turnover. Renewal of clothing in the spring (as is suggested by the appearance of springtime astrological symbolism on third-century sandal soles) may also lie behind the rather abrupt changes in shape in this period.[27]

Among the issues emerging in the debate surrounding pre-industrial consumerist behaviour is functional differentiation in material culture. In contrast to both earlier and later periods, the provincial Roman population had access

Fig. 6.9. Sandal soles from Voorburg (mid-second century—*c.* AD 230). Image: A. Dekker, Amsterdam Archaeological Centre, University of Amsterdam.

[27] Van Driel-Murray (1999b: 134, figs 2–3); van Driel-Murray, Pollmann, and Richter (2014: 723–5, fig. II-10.20)

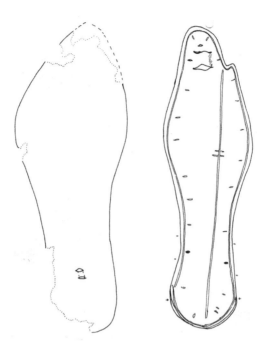

Fig. 6.10. De Meern: the boatman's shoes. One of each pair: left, insole of the nailed shoe; right, sandal (scale 1:3). Image: Carol van Driel-Murray.

to footwear made for different purposes, and individuals evidently possessed more than one set of shoes.[28] Unsurprisingly, the family of the commander at Vindolanda possessed a wide range of footwear, but even the boatmen on two capsized barges in the Rhine aspired to sandals for best wear in addition to their closed, work shoes (Figs. 6.10–6.11).[29] Simply differentiating footwear from a number of late second- and early third-century sites on the basis of construction method reveals the extent of consumer choice (Table 6.1). Within each technological group further variation in style, fastening method, and decoration was available, allowing the consumer to vary apparel according to the occasion. The high proportion of single-piece shoes in *Germania Superior* contrasts markedly with the scarcity of the form elsewhere at this time, while sandals increase sharply in popularity in the third century, especially in urban centres like London. Military sites are characterized by very high (<70 per

---

[28] Closed shoes, low-cut shoes, boots, sandals, shoes with soft soles or with hobnails, slippers, wooden pattens, single-piece shoes (*carbatinae*): for the range available at a particular point in time at a single site, see Van Driel-Murray (1999c) (Welzheim).

[29] Vindolanda: Van Driel-Murray (1993: 45–7, fig. 16); Woerden: Van Driel-Murray (1996: fig 11–12).

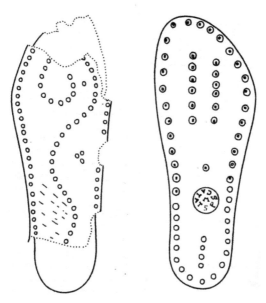

Fig. 6.11. Woerden: the boatman's shoes. One of each pair: left, nailed shoe; right, sandal (scale 1:3). Image: Carol van Driel-Murray.

cent) percentages of closed, nailed footwear, but the extent of the accompanying civilian population at some forts, like the Saalburg, is revealed by the more even distribution across the different types.

The importance of being correctly dressed resonates with studies stressing the role of gentility, style, and good manners in the consumer revolution of the eighteenth century. Leaving aside the ongoing discussion around 'Romanization', such factors evidently affect any assessment of the depth of Roman influence on daily life as experienced by the provincial population. At present the provincial Roman debate is dominated by the idea of 'elites' stimulating the uptake of Roman goods, with acquisition being seen in terms of competition and political status. But imitation is not necessarily emulation, and the varying proportions illustrate rather a sense of community, within which personal display was negotiable.[30] In its recognition of the cumulative power of small inexpensive purchases, consumer theory is particularly relevant for items like footwear. As Spufford shows for the immediately pre-industrial period, such novelties gave people of modest means the opportunity of expressing both taste and individuality within their own circles. Even the workers at a remote upland cattle yard at Pontefract (Yorkshire) aspired to fashionably pointed hobnailed boots, contrasting with a distinct lack of interest in Roman pottery.[31] The appearance of Roman-style footwear on rural sites

---

[30] Woolf (1998: 170–1).   [31] Van Driel-Murray (2001d: pl. 9).

especially reveals a very real diversion of resources towards items of readily discarded apparel, something hardly seen at all either in the Iron Age or for much of the Middle Ages.

While it is widely recognized that clothing and accessories are culturally constructed commodities, with complex symbolic properties, there is little research into exactly why people purchase some items but not others. Was choice dependent on availability (that is, production driven) or does the consumer actually activate the producer?

CONSUMERS

In some circumstances the makers were certainly free to respond to specific client demand. At both the Saalburg (late second or early third century) and Cuijk (Netherlands, fourth century) a substantial proportion of the footwear collection is composed of distinctive styles with parallels in north Germany and Denmark, which were made for the Germanic mercenaries (and their families) serving at the fort (Fig. 6.1, no. 19; Fig. 6.7, top right).[32] Style and design are foreign, but the materials and technology follow the established traditions of provincial Roman footwear manufacture. Here, the desire of clients to maintain their tribal identity stimulated local craftsmen to add to their repertoire.[33]

The shoe sizes themselves can tell us something about who was making the purchases. The size distribution of footwear in most Roman settlements reveals fairly equal proportions of men, women, and children, a pattern comparable to that seen in Late Medieval towns such as Lübeck or London.[34] Here, the increasing prominence of children's shoes throughout the Middle Ages is an indicator of prosperity levels and contrasts strongly with prehistoric and early medieval footwear, which is largely confined to male sizes. Footwear is not actually an essential item of clothing: until quite recent times, women and children went barefoot in rural Ireland and Scotland, while men were shod.[35] Even though the very poorest remain invisible to us, in the Roman provinces shoes seem to have been accessible to much of the population: men, women, and children alike. This seems to me to be a fairly obvious measure of increasing standards of living and attention to the comfort of the entire family. Indeed, the obviously Mediterranean fashion of wearing sandals seems to have been seized upon by women already in the first century AD, while men begin to wear sandals regularly only from the later second century AD onwards. In

[32] Busch (1965); van Driel-Murray (2007).   [33] Van Driel-Murray (2009: 815–6).
[34] Vons-Comis (1982: fig. 90); Grew and Neergard (1988: 104); van Driel-Murray (2001a: 360–1).
[35] Lucas (1956: 353).

footwear, we can to some extent see gendered responses to Roman consumer goods. The feminization of consumption is a significant factor in the development of seventeenth- and eighteenth-century production and retail distribution, and it would certainly be worth investigating other Roman consumption patterns from this perspective.

MARKETING

Did people simply buy what was on offer? Studies of early modern consumerism emphasize the importance of developing communication networks and retail outlets in making novelties accessible to a wide clientele. Margaret Spufford, in her study *The Great Reclothing of Rural England*, emphasized the role of chapmen and peddlers in the quite rapid diffusion of novelties in apparel from urban centres to rural areas and the mechanisms she describes for the seventeenth century would certainly be applicable to the Roman world. The interesting thing here is that the whole system of suppliers, distributors, and retailers mediated between producers and consumers. Knowledge of the most recent developments in fashion and accessories was passed via personal networks to the country towns and into the rural hinterlands. But, ultimately, it was the consumer who actually made the choices, thereby affecting the selection of goods on offer on the chapman's next journey out.

For the Mediterranean area De Ligt has discussed the networks of local and regional markets and annual festivals that brought consumers and producers together.[36] This model of periodic gatherings for commercial exchange has never been fully exploited to explain the spread of low-value consumer goods in the northern provinces, though it would reinforce the significance of rural cult centres and roadside settlements in the social and economic structures of poorly urbanized regions. In conjunction with travelling peddlers, even quite remote areas could connect with international trends. Markets also form the arena for negotiation between consumer and producer: leatherworkers from different ethnic groups congregating at weekly markets in West Africa exchange ideas, and, though distinct ethnic traditions are maintained, Frank observed that craftsmen are prepared to make anything according to the wishes of the customer.[37] The Germanic-style shoes and *fibulae* manufactured on the Saalburg are products of similar processes of negotiation, where customer demand prevailed. Shoes may have been made in series and hawked around, but sandals at any rate seem to have been made individually, and the regular finds of small

---

[36] De Ligt (1993).   [37] Frank (1998: 148–9).

amounts of offcuts in rural sites from the mid-second century onwards may even suggest itinerant shoemakers making to order.

However, the interpretation of rural consumer economies is not so straight-forward. Indeed, it may be questioned whether people had free access to consumer goods at all. Many possibly lived in various forms of dependency and may have been constrained, receiving goods only on special occasions or directly through their patron, and landowners may have controlled not only travel to fairs and markets, but also the goods offered there, if these were on their land—as was the case on Russian and Polish serf estates.[38] This makes some find contexts hard to interpret. Large numbers of worn-out shoes dumped in wells in, for example, Welzheim or Tollgate Farm (Staffordshire) may represent the welcome visit of an itinerant shoemaker, but could just as well be the result of a great re-clothing of estate (or military) personnel.[39] Complicating the interpretation of such unusual complexes still further is the widespread use of footwear in ritual activities, which makes finds from wells and water sources somewhat suspect for simple economic explanations.[40]

MOBILITY

The mobility of the customers themselves is an issue hardly raised in connection with consumption patterns, despite the evidence for regular private travel.[41] Indeed, the worn-out boots left by travellers could well have served as models for local craftsmen. Occasionally individual travellers may be suspected, and the Germanic-style footwear on military sites such as the Saalburg and Cuijk (Netherlands) has already been mentioned. Familiarity with Roman footwear, and some actual imports, seem to have influenced shoes outside the frontier, in Scotland and northern Germany.[42] Especially in the frontier provinces, the influence of the highly mobile military population— soldiers as well as their families—should not be underestimated in the spread of new ideas. Fashion change in the sixteenth century is strongly related to military movements, and, though the army cannot be the only instigator, the general impression of the appearance of new stimuli at times of high military mobility does remain. The elaborate nailing and the spread of sandal-wearing among males at the time of the Marcomannic wars may not be coincidence, while the profusion of new forms in the first half of the third century is

[38] Domanial markets, cf. de Ligt (1993: 156–8).

[39] Van Driel-Murray (1999c); Tollgate Farm: Hollis (2011); Thomas and Thomas (2012).

[40] Van Driel-Murray (1999b).   [41] Handley (2011: 11).

[42] Hald (1972: 56–7) was the first to draw attention to this, and work in progress on finds in various northern museums confirms the extent of influence on native footwear, particularly in decorative details.

suggestive of social as well as political insecurity. But such renewal in fashions can also signal times of social change and increasing competition, and the lack of comparative evidence from the Mediterranean regions makes me wary of such simplistic explanations. Nevertheless, personal mobility, both military and civilian, must be a factor in the homogenization of fashion consciousness and the development of a communal aesthetic sense.

CONCLUSION

Many scholars dispute whether it is possible to reach the mass of the population of the Roman Empire, and, indeed, the poorest will no doubt remain ever invisible. But consumer theory, developed in relation to the material legacy of the period immediately before the Industrial Revolution, does offer the possibility of understanding the motivation of the non-elite and the influence their individual choices brought to bear on the manufacturing process. Items of dress such as shoes (but also *fibulae*, hairpins, and buckles), widely distributed and easily discarded, offer an insight into the way quite ordinary people (the 'middling sort' of consumer studies) accessed new idioms and developed a taste for goods that made them recognizably part of the wider world. They were prepared to divert resources from basic subsistence needs to obtain ephemeral goods that added to the comfort of themselves and their family as well as enhancing their feelings of self-worth. That international styles of footwear are so widespread and are found in such large quantities reveals, I believe, that the Roman impact on technology, craft production, and personal bearing went far deeper than is often allowed.

REFERENCES

Arnould, E. J. (1984). 'Marketing and Social Reproduction in Zinder, Niger Republic', in R. M. Netting, R. R. Wilk, and E .J. Arnould (eds), *Households. Comparative and Historical Studies of the Domestic Group*. Berkeley, 130–62.

Bennett, J. M. (1996). *Ale, Beer, and Brewsters in England: Women's Work in a Changing World 1300–1600*. Oxford.

Busch, A. L. (1965). 'Die römerzeitlichen Schuh- und Lederfunde der Kastelle Saalburg, Zugmantel und Kleiner Feldberg', *Saalburg-Jahrbuch* 22: 158–210.

Charlesworth, D., and Thornton, J. H. (1973). 'Leather Found in Mediobogdum, the Roman fort of Hardknott', *Britannia* 4: 141–52.

De' Spagnolis, M. (2000). *La Tomba del Calzolaio: Dalla necropolis monumentale romana di Nocera Superiore*. Rome.

Domergue, C. (1983). *La Mine antique d'Aljustrel (Portugal) et les tables de bronze de Vipasca*. Paris.

Driel-Murray, C. van (1977). 'Stamped Leatherwork from Zwammerdam', in B. L. van Beek, R. W. Brandt, and W. Groenman-van Waateringe (eds), *Ex Horreo, IPP 1951–1976*. Amsterdam, 151–64.

Driel-Murray, C. van (1985). 'The Production and Supply of Military Leatherwork in the First and Second Centuries AD: A Review of the Archaeological Evidence', in M. C. Bishop (ed.), *The Production and Distribution of Roman Military Equipment* (BAR International Series, 275). Oxford, 43–81.

Driel-Murray, C. van (1993). 'The Leatherwork', in R. Birley (ed.), *Vindolanda Research Reports*, iii. *The Early Wooden Forts*. Hexham, 1–75.

Driel-Murray, C. van (1996). 'Die Schuhe aus Schiff I und ein lederner Schildüberzug', in J. K. Haalebos, 'Ein römisches Getreideschiff in Woerden', *Jahrbuch des Römisch-Germanischen Zentralmuseums Mainz* 43: 493–8.

Driel-Murray, C. van (1998). 'Women in Forts?', *Gesellschaft Pro Vindonissa. Jahresbericht 1997*: 55–61.

Driel-Murray, C. van (1999a). 'Dead Men's Shoes', in W. Schlüter and R. Wiegels (eds), *Rom, Germanien und die Ausgrabungen von Kalkriese*. Osnabrück, 169–89.

Driel-Murray, C. van (1999b). 'And did those feet in ancient time . . . Feet and Shoes as a Material Projection of the Self', in P. Baker, C. Forcey, S. Jundi, and R. Witcher (eds), *TRAC 98: Proceedings of the Eighth Annual Theoretical Roman Archaeology Conference, Leicester 1998*. Oxford, 131–40.

Driel-Murray, C. van (1999c). *Das Ostkastell von Welzheim, Rems-Murr-Kreis: Die römischen Lederfunde* (Forschungen und Berichte zur Vor- und Frühgeschichte in Baden-Württemberg, 42). Stuttgart.

Driel-Murray, C. van (2001a). 'Footwear in the North-Western Provinces of the Roman Empire', in O. Goubitz, W. Groenman van Waateringe, and C. van Driel-Murray, *Stepping through Time: Archaeological Footwear from Prehistoric Times until 1800*. Zwolle, 337–75.

Driel-Murray, C. van (2001b). 'Vindolanda and the Dating of Roman Footwear', *Britannia* 32: 185–97.

Driel-Murray, C. van (2001c). 'Technology Transfer: The Introduction and Loss of Tanning Technology during the Roman Period', in M. Polfer (ed.), *L'Artisanat romain: Évolutions, continuités et ruptures (Italie et provinces occidentales)*. Montagnac, 55–68.

Driel-Murray, C. van (2001d). 'Hobnails', in S. Wrathmell, *Romano-British Enclosures at Apple Tree Close, Pontefract, West Yorkshire*. Wakefield, 20–23.

Driel-Murray, C. van (2007). 'Mode in de nadagen van het Keizerrijk: De schoenen van Cuijk', *Westerheem* 56: 133–41.

Driel-Murray, C. van (2008). 'Tanning and Leather', in J. P. Oleson (ed.), *Oxford Handbook of Engineering and Technology in the Classical World*. Oxford, 483–95.

Driel-Murray, C. van (2009). 'Ethnic Recruitment and Military Mobility', in A. Morillo, N. Hanel, and E. Martín (eds), *Limes XX: Roman Frontier Studies*. Madrid, 813–23.

Driel-Murray, C. van (2011). 'Are we Missing Something? The Elusive Tanneries of the Roman Period,' in R. Thomson and Q. Mould (eds), *Leather Tanneries: The Archaeological Evidence*. London, 69–83.

Driel-Murray, C. van, Pollmann, K., and Richter, E. (2014). 'De leervondsten van Voorburg-Arentsburg', in M. Driessen and E. Besselsen (eds), *Voorburg-Arentsburg. Een Romeinse havenstad tussen Rijn en Maas* (University of Amsterdam, Themata 7). Amsterdam, 717–39.

Dunbabin, K. M. D. (1990). '*Ipsa deae vestigia* . . . Footprints Divine and Human on Graeco-Roman Monuments', *JRA* 3: 85–109.

Frank, B. E. (1998). *Mande Potters and Leatherworkers: Art and Heritage in West Africa.* Washington.

Goldman, N. (1994). 'Roman Footwear', in J. L. Sebesta and L. Bonfante (eds), *The World of Roman Costume.* Madison, 101–29.

Greene, K. (2007). 'Late Hellenistic and Early Roman Invention and Innovation: The Case of Lead-Glazed Pottery', *AJA* 111: 653–71.

Greene, K. (2008). 'Learning to Consume: Consumption and Consumerism in the Roman Empire', *JRA* 21: 64–82.

Grew, F., and Neergard, M. de (1988). *Shoes and Pattens: Medieval Finds from Excavations in London 2.* London.

Groenman-van Waateringe, W. (1967). *Romeins lederwerk uit Valkenburg Z.H.* Groningen.

Hald, M. (1972). *Primitive Shoes: An Archaeological–Ethnological Study Based upon Shoe Finds from the Jutland Peninsula.* Copenhagen.

Handley, M. (2011). *Dying on Foreign Shores: Travel and Mobility in the Late-Antique West* (JRA, Supplementary Series, 86). Portsmouth, RI.

Himmler, F. (2008). 'Testing the 'Ramshaw' Boot—Experimental Calceology on the March', *Journal of Roman Military Equipment Studies* 16: 347–57.

Hoevenberg, J. (1993). 'Leather Artefacts', in R. M. Dierendonck, D. P. Hallewas, and K. E. Waugh (eds), *The Valkenburg Excavations 1985–1988.* Amersfoort, 217–340.

Hollis, W. (2011). 'Rubbish or Ritual? Roman Well Yields its Booty', *Current Archaeology* 253: 36–41.

Lau, O. (1967). *Schuster und Schusterhandwerk in de griechisch-römischen Literatur und Kunst.* Inaugural-Dissertation Rheinischen Friedrich-Wilhems-Universität, Bonn.

Leguilloux, M. (2002). 'Techniques et équipements de la tannerie romaine: L'Example de l'*officina coriaria* de Pompéi', in F. Audoin-Rouzeau and S. Beyries (eds), *Le Travail du cuir de la préhistoire à nos jours (XXIIe rencontres internationales d'archéologie et d'histoire d'Antibes Octobre 2001).* Antibes, 267–81.

Leguilloux, M. (2004). *Le Cuir et la pelleterie à l'époque romaine.* Paris.

Leguilloux, M. (2006). *Les Objects en cuir de Didymoi, praesidium de la route caravanière Coptos-Bérénice.* Le Caire.

Ligt, L. de (1993). *Fairs and Markets in the Roman Empire.* Amsterdam.

Lucas, A. T. (1956). 'Footwear in Ireland', *County Louth Archaeological Journal* 13: 309–94.

MacConnoran, P. (1986). 'Footwear', in L. Millar, J. Schofield, and M. Rhodes (eds), *The Roman Quay at St Magnus House, London: Excavations at New Fresh Wharf, Lower Thames Street, London 1974–78* (London & Middlesex Archaeological Society, Special Paper, no. 8). London, 218–26.

Mould, Q. (1990). 'The Leather Objects', in S. Wrathmell and A. Nicholson (eds), *Dalton Parlours: Iron Age Settlement and Roman Villa* (Yorkshire Archaeology, 3). Wakefield, 231–5.

Overton, H., Whittle, J., Dean, D., and Hann, A. (2004). *Production and Consumption in English Households 1600–1750*. London.

Spufford, M. (1984). *The Great Reclothing of Rural England: Petty Chapmen and their Wares in the Seventeenth Century*. London.

Stauffer, A. (2008). *Antike Musterblätter: Wirkkartons aus dem spätantiken und frühbyzantinschen Ägypten*. Wiesbaden.

Thomas, D., and Thomas, M. (2012). 'Roman Shoes Report', Stoke-on-Trent Museum, Archaeological Society <http://www.stokearchaeologysociety.org.uk/html/tgfm_shoes.htm>.

Vanderhoeven, A., and Ervynck A. (2007). 'Not in my Backyard? The Industry of Secondary Animal Products within the Roman Civitas Capital of Tongeren, Belgium', in R. Hingley and S. Willis (eds), *Roman Finds: Context and Theory: Proceedings of a Conference Held at the University of Durham 2002*. Oxford, 156–75.

Volken, M. (2008). 'Making the Ramshaw Boot, an Exercise in Experimental Archaeology', *Journal of Roman Military Equipment Studies* 16: 359–66.

Volken, M. (2014). *Archaeological Footwear: Development of Shoe Patterns and Styles from Prehistory till the 1600s*. Zwolle.

Vons-Comis, S. Y. (1982). 'Das Leder von Lübeck, Grabung Heiligen-Geist-Hospital, Koberg 9–11', *Lübecker Schriften zur Archäologie und Kulturgeschichte* 6: 239–50.

Weatherill, L. (1996). *Consumer Behaviour and Material Culture in Britain 1660–1760*. 2nd edn. London.

Winterbottom, S. (2009). 'The Leather and Other Organic Artefacts', in C. Howard-Davis (ed.), *The Carlisle Millennium Project: Excavations in Carlisle 1998–2001*. Lancaster, 817–41.

Woolf, G. (1998). *Becoming Roman: The Origins of Provincial Civilization in Gaul*. Cambridge.

Zimmer, G. (1982). *Römische Berufsdarstellungen*. Berlin.

7

Contextualizing the Operational Sequence: Pompeian Bakeries as a Case Study

Nicolas Monteix

One way of approaching the material remains of Roman workshops is to investigate how they were designed specifically to accommodate the activity that took place within them. Such an approach may be based on the analysis, from a technological point of view, of a specific kind of workshop whose elements are all considered in their spatial context. In terms of theoretical background, such an approach relies on the notion of the *chaîne opératoire* (operational sequence), which was first defined by A. Leroi-Gourhan, was gradually refined by his successors, and was then applied to archaeology.[1] The idea is that a close study of the different elements that characterize the operational sequence of a workshop, including materials, tools, gesture, knowledge, energy, and actors, combined with an analysis of their interaction, leads to further understanding of social and economic issues, particularly if one tries to take a more systemic point of view aimed at understanding the *système technique* or the *complexe techno-économique*.[2]

In order to test how this approach works in practice, this chapter presents a case study of the bakeries of Pompeii: although they are described in every book on Pompeii, previous studies have always portrayed them as an unsatisfactorily random assemblage of equipment. Early descriptions, written by Sir William Gell and François Mazois, include precious observations and interpretations of the bakeries but remain far too general to be completely useful.[3] August Mau's

---

[1] Leroi-Gourhan (1964: 26–64); Balfet (1991); Creswell (2003); Pernot (2006).

[2] First defined by Gille (1978: 19), as 'l'ensemble [en équilibre] de[s] cohérences [techniques] aux différents niveaux de toutes les structures de tous les ensembles de toutes les filières', the *système technique* was then questioned by Lemonnier (1983). Garçon (1997: 24–5) defined the *complexe techno-économique* on a smaller scale.

[3] Gell and Gandy (1817–19: 189–91, pl. XXXVII); Mazois (1824: 56–61, pls XVI–XVII).

description of bakeries does follow the operational sequence from milling to baking, but lacks precision, owing to his high degree of generalization.[4] Betty Jo Mayeske failed to go much further than presenting a mere update of these data based on the excavation reports published since Mau's time.[5] Since then, Pompeian bakeries have appeared only as a starting point—even if often implicitly—for larger syntheses about ancient food technology.[6]

Consequently, there is still much to be learned from Pompeian bakeries, by studying their equipment closely and trying to interconnect the individual installations through an analysis of their spatial disposition. It is the aim of this chapter to discuss the different sets of equipment found in Pompeian bakeries in order to reconstruct the operational sequence and then evaluate the rationalization of their organization. Two preliminary points need to be made. First of all, as far as the number of bakeries within the city walls is concerned, some forty-one bread ovens have been recognized to date (Fig. 7.1). These include those with a baking chamber with an internal diameter of 1 metre or more, regardless of the destination of the bread—commercial or otherwise.[7] The second point is that not all the thirty-nine identified bakeries were in operation in AD 79: some were partially or totally inactive, either because of damage that occurred shortly before the eruption, during the 'ongoing seismic activity' in the region, or due to some cessation of activity.[8]

RECONSTRUCTING THE OPERATIONAL SEQUENCE: FROM GRAIN TO BREAD

The main outlines of bread-making have not changed radically since the Neolithic, except for the slow—and even nowadays still incomplete—generalization of leavening: (1) flour, usually obtained by milling grain, is (2) mixed with water—and possibly yeast—in order to obtain dough, which, often after some time of fermentation, has (3) to be baked in a purpose-built

---

[4] Mau (1899: 380–4).   [5] Mayeske (1972).

[6] e.g. Curtis (2001: 341–7, 358–70; 2008: 373–9); Thurmond (2006: 14–72).

[7] Another one could be added (I 8, 15–16), although the oven is only 78 cm wide: situated in the back room of a food outlet (*caupona*), this oven is embedded in a smoking shed most probably associated with cheese production. The presence of a human-driven mill and the whole commercial character of this installation make bread a minor but real production in this food workshop and retail shop. In the present chapter, this one will be ignored, as none of the other ovens studied is smaller than 1.25 metres in diameter.

[8] For 'ongoing seismic activity', see Allison (1995). The bakery installed in VII 1, 25.46–7 was partially dismantled in AD 79, as shown by the removal of the three mills, whose surrounding pavement has been partly covered by a wall—constructed and painted during the first years of the AD 70s; cf. Esposito (2009: 57, 77–80). During the last years of Pompeii, though the oven seems to have been functioning.

Fig. 7.1. Location of the bakeries in Pompeii. Map: Nicolas Monteix.

oven. What has changed from one culture to another are the tools used to perform these broad operations and their subtle subdivisions.

Milling

In the Roman world, as far as we actually know from archaeological remains, milling was performed independently of baking only in cases where hydraulic energy was used, despite the etymology of the Latin term for baker—*pistor* comes from *pinsere*, pounding. In Italy outside Rome, contrary to what Pliny suggests, known water-mills are relatively few, and all are later than the destruction of Pompeii and Herculaneum.[9] Around Pompeii, no water-mill has been identified, and we have to assume, until further discovery, that the grain was milled in villas and urban bakeries. Yet the primary preparation of grain—threshing and winnowing—was completed before its arrival in the bakery, as is suggested by the lack of any traces of chaff, not even phytoliths, in excavated contexts in some recently studied workshops.[10] That the grain arrived clean does not mean that the first operation was the milling: preparation might have occurred beforehand. According to Pliny, tempering the grain in salt water before milling would have given whiter flour.[11] It is not clear why salt should be added to water, but soaking the grain, as is still done nowadays, enables better separation between the bran—which has gained elasticity—and the kernel, and thus produces, after milling and sifting, flour that has a whiter colour than that produced with a non-tempered grain which contains many small bran fragments.

Until now, only three or four examples of tempering facilities have been identified in Pompeian bakeries (Fig. 7.2). The first one, initially interpreted in this way by Fiorelli, is located in bakery IX 3, 19–20, where recent cleaning has improved the understanding of its functioning.[12] In room 5, where the pavement sloped slightly towards a cistern, a symmetrical structure was built: two containers—a reused millstone set upside down and a *dolium*—were placed in the south-west and north-west corners. Both have a hole for emptying. Corresponding to each of these basins, a row of tiles was inserted obliquely into the pavement, most probably to support some wooden element. A connection to the piped water network shows that at least the reused millstone was filled up with

---

[9] Plin., *HN* 18.97. On the few examples of known water-mills in Italy, cf. Brun (2007); on water-mills in general, see Wikander (2008).

[10] The carpological study has been conducted by M. Derreumaux (Centre de recherches archéologiques de la vallée de l'Oise) and V. Matterne (CNRS – UMR 7209 Muséum National d'Histoire Naturelle). Phytolith analysis was conducted by C. Hamon (CNRS – UMR 7041 ArScAn).

[11] Plin., *HN* 18.87: *Nam quae sicca moluntur, plus farinae reddunt, quae salsa aqua sparsa, candidiorem medullam, uerum plus retinent in furfure.*

[12] Fiorelli (1873: 53–4).

0 1 2 3 4 5 6 7 8 9 10m

—— Water distribution network --- Restored water distribution network

Fig. 7.2. Tempering structure in bakery IX 3, 19–20. Image: Nicolas Monteix.

water continuously. In bakery V 3, 8, low walls were built on the edge of the *impluvium*, which itself was divided into two parts with a wall that could let water pass through, either to the cistern mouth or to a channel that discharged into the street in front of the building. A similar construction might have occurred in bakery VII 1, 36–7, albeit without a dividing wall in the *impluvium*. A small basin, seen in the *impluvium* of bakery VII 2, 3.6–7, might have been used for the same purpose. Although the water supply was different in volume, both structures allowed grain to be tempered for a few hours before the next step, milling.

Some information about the operational sequence might be derived from the basalt pavement that was generally set around the mills in order to prevent the floor being worn by the repeated circular movement of the working animals. This pavement does not appear in all cases: one bakery in Pompeii (I 12, 1–2) has a mill without a basalt pavement, as did both bakeries in Herculaneum. The absence of this pavement, especially in Herculaneum, is difficult to explain. However, observations made in several bakeries give an indication of the construction of this pavement. In some cases, a masonry base is set in a shallow cylindrical foundation. The basalt blocks, whose thickness might vary greatly, from 15 to 30 centimetres, are placed around it, in a pit whose lower part is filled with plaster fragments, most probably in order to facilitate the setting of the blocks. If a bakery was extended with further mills, strikingly, the paving blocks already installed—which might be in common with the new ones—were partly dismantled in a way that allowed the new mill to have a new pavement laid completely around it (Fig. 7.3). Once the paving had been installed, the *meta*—the bed stone—was either just laid directly on it or inserted in the circular pit. A small wall was then built around it and was

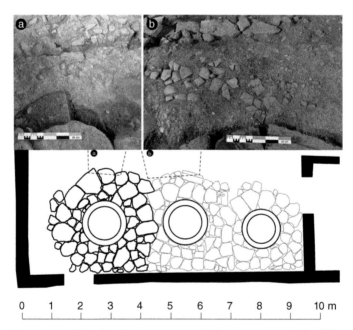

Fig. 7.3. Extension of the basalt pavement in bakery I 12, 1-2. The filling for the second pavement, seen under excavation (a), cuts the one used for the first pavement (b) that abutted the blocks. As the plan shows, the first pavement has been partly dismantled to install the second. Image: Nicolas Monteix.

most likely rebuilt each time the *meta* was replaced when it had become too worn to be used. Once the *catillus*—the running stone—had also been set up, a lead sheet was placed at the joint between the *meta* and the small wall around it to facilitate flour recovery.

It is not necessary to discuss here, at length, the general functioning of the most typical tool—at least if one looks at ancient representations—used in mill-bakeries, the animal-driven 'Pompeian' mill.[13] Yet, as has already been mentioned in the introduction to this chapter, it has always been assumed that all bakeries and thus their components were functioning in AD 79. A careful study of the state of wear of the mill elements shows a different picture.[14] In the thirty-nine bakeries, ninety-one animal-driven mill pedestals have been identified: only twenty-eight (31 per cent) of these were functional at the moment of the eruption, of which only three were almost new, not worn.[15] Only further research could indicate—and not without difficulty—whether this disrupted image is to be linked with ongoing earthquakes or if it indicates some other changes.

Once the grain had been ground, the result had to be cleaned, in order to separate the flour from the undesired parts it contained—mostly bran and germ. The use of bolters is attested by both literary and iconographic sources.[16] According to Pliny, three successive siftings, corresponding to three qualities of flour, would have helped to increase grain output.[17] Although none of these tools has been observed or preserved, some recurring structures in Pompeian bakeries can be linked with this operation: in some bakeries, there are L-shaped walls about 80 centimetres high; these are often in the milling-room and have generally been built against a load-bearing wall. As such a structure seems unfit for storage, it is likely that they were used for sifting, and were once covered by some wooden installation.[18]

---

[13] For a general account, see Moritz (1958: 74–90) and now D. Peacock (2013: 77–97). The provenience of mills has been studied by D. P. S. Peacock (1989), with updates in Buffone et al. (1999).

[14] The study of the mills has been conducted by S. Longepierre (Post-doc. CNRS – UMR 5140).

[15] These statistics have been partly revised to include information from the unpublished and published excavation reports: a few mills appear non-functional nowadays owing to their progressive destruction since their unearthing; in some cases, the reports mention that mills suffered damage during the eruption and in post-eruptive disruption. For instance, one of the *catilli* from bakery I 12, 1–2 was discovered 2.5 m above the ancient ground level. Cf. *Giornale degli Scavi di Pompei*, 13–19 February 1961.

[16] Cat., *Agr.* 76.3; Plin., *HN* 18.108. Bolters are carved either on the Bologna relief, on P. Nonius Zethus's urn holder, or on a fragmented relief from Ostia. Cf. Zimmer (1982: 114). Only on the latter might it be a sieve rather than a pre-grinding bolter.

[17] Plin., *HN* 18.89–90.

[18] The excavation of this structure in bakery I 12, 1–2 did not show any beaten soil inside the double L-shape. Only the central part, which permitted access to it, seemed to reveal signs of a prolonged stay; hence some planks might have prevented bakers from treading on it.

Kneading and Forming Loaves

The next step is technically the first in bread-making—what happens prior to this can be seen as 'milling', and could potentially have been separated from bread-making, occurring in a different workshop. The procedure is to mix flour with water, and also yeast if the bread is to leaven, which, according to carbonized material remains of loaves, was mostly the case in first-century AD Pompeii.[19] Traditionally—and until most recent times—kneading was per-formed by hand, in a wooden chest.[20] But from at least the very late Republic, as the frieze on the tomb of M. Vergilius Eurysaces shows, an alternative to hand kneading had been developed.[21] This alternative, already identified by August Mau, was a kneading machine, consisting of a hollowed cylindrical stone fixed firmly in the pavement. Generally basalt was used, but occasionally travertine was used as well. At Pompeii, most kneading machines were made of local basalt, and not all of them were originally made as kneading machines: three were reused *metae*. The main active part was a vertical shaft, fixed to the stone through an iron pivot hole at the bottom of the vat and kept in a vertical position thanks to its insertion in a horizontal beam that was fixed in the surrounding walls (Fig. 7.4).[22] At the lower end of the shaft, just above the pivot, an iron blade, turned slightly upwards at its extremities, was fixed to it. Further, on the inner side of the vat, two to six holes were carved; they allowed wooden sticks to be inserted inside the vat at various heights. A horizontal arm higher up the shaft made it possible for it to be turned around; the rotary movement made the blade rotate and mix all the ingredients that were partly blocked by the wooden sticks and thus better kneaded together.[23] From the lack of basalt pavement around the kneading machines, we might deduce that in Pompeii they functioned with human energy, although, as discussed in the section on milling, this argument has to be employed with caution.[24] Throughout

---

[19] None of the loaves discovered in Pompeii or Herculaneum has the flat shape of unleavened bread; cf. Borgongino (2006: cat. nos 457–83). Most of the Pompeian loaves that were preserved come from bakery VII 1, 36–7.

[20] For hand-kneading in Roman times, see Wilson and Schörle (2009). This implement is now attested in Pompeii in bakery VII 2, 3.6–7; see Monteix et al. (2014: 20–1). Such chests are still depicted in Diderot and D'Alembert's *Encyclopédie*. Kneading machines began to replace them again at the beginning of the twentieth century.

[21] See Ciancio Rossetto (1973); Wilson (2008a: 358).

[22] In his first study of the feature, Mau (1886: 46) clearly mentions the horizontal beam, while in his second less accurate description (Mau 1899: 384, fig. 214 p. 383), which is more often used as a reference, he does not.

[23] Contrary to what has been written by Mau (1899: 384) and his followers, nothing permits the restoration of arms projecting from the vertical shaft, notably because the sockets fixed into the side of the vat would have forbidden their rotation, as careful and exhaustive measurements have demonstrated. Cf. e.g. Mayeske (1972: 22); Strocka (1991: 61); Thurmond (2006: 66).

[24] Not only does the frieze on the tomb of M. Vergilius Eurysaces show a kneading machine functioning with a donkey or a horse, but also bakeries in Ostia have a basalt pavement around the kneading machines. See Bakker (1999).

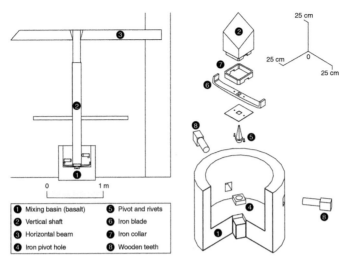

❶ Mixing basin (basalt)	❺ Pivot and rivets
❷ Vertical shaft	❻ Iron blade
❸ Horizontal beam	❼ Iron collar
❹ Iron pivot hole	❽ Wooden teeth

Fig. 7.4. Cross-section and exploded isometric view of the kneading machine in the House of the Chaste Lovers (IX 12, 6). Image: Nicolas Monteix.

the city, some twenty-three stone tubs once used as kneading machines have been identified.[25] However, in AD 79, only twenty bakeries might have had such a tool, and in two of these, the only evidence found consists of holes in the walls used to insert the horizontal beam that fixed the shaft.[26]

As soon as the different ingredients have been mixed and kneaded to form a dough, the rising begins.[27] The importance of this phase is inversely proportional to the evidence related to it: there is no mention of it in ancient literature, no detailed iconographic representation has been found, and it is only very briefly alluded to in modern studies. This absence can be explained by the numerous details given in ancient texts about yeast or by the difficulty in representing—on stone or in painting—a rising loaf with enough details in order to distinguish it from a baked one. Nevertheless, some features of Pompeian bakeries must be linked with this phase. In seven bakeries terracotta tubs have been found that are characterized by their wide opening (Fig. 7.5). Depending on their size, those tubs are either embedded in masonry or fixed on a reused *catillus*. Mostly, they are situated in the immediate vicinity of the kneading machine or the oven. Two striking features need to be emphasized.

---

[25] Two of them are to be found reused in bakeries as hydraulic implements, two others outside and not necessarily in the vicinity of any bakery as kerb- or stepping-stones. Even noting that 'such basins are easily broken or removed', Mayeske (1972: 169) counted only eight of them.

[26] Seven bakeries still have their kneading machine in the place where it was used. In eleven it has been moved either within the room or in other rooms.

[27] In fact, there are two phenomena occurring at the same time: modification of the gluten structure and carbon dioxide production. For detailed explanation of these changes, see Cauvain (2007: 21–5).

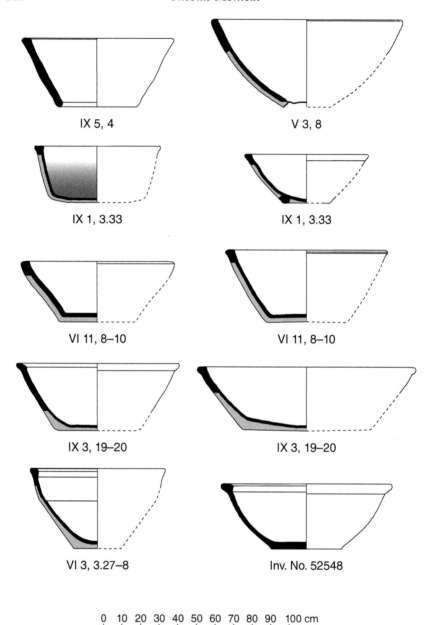

Fig. 7.5. Vessels used for the first rising of the dough. The two on the first row had a lead sheet as a bottom (scale: 1/10). Image: Nicolas Monteix.

First, they are to be found only in bakeries that are provided with a kneading machine, though not all of these have these rising tubs. Secondly, these recipients withstand any typological grouping: they do not seem to have been produced for this specific purpose. Furthermore, two examples, one being set in a disused *catillus* (Fig. 7.6), are in fact *dolia* truncated before firing and hence exhibit a lead sheet as a bottom part.[28] All of this suggests do-it-yourself rather than standardized practices. These vessels, combining a wide opening with shallow depth, and installed near the kneading machine, can be understood to serve for the first rising of the whole batch of dough, which was then remixed—by 'punching it down' or 'folding it' in modern bakery terms.[29]

It is after this first rising—when and if it has occurred—that loaves are formed. In a rare correspondence with iconographic representations, this operation was performed on tables whose feet are generally preserved in

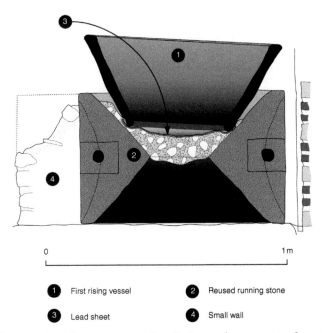

1 First rising vessel   2 Reused running stone

3 Lead sheet   4 Small wall

Fig. 7.6. Cross section of a runner stone (*catillus*) reused to support a first rising vessel in bakery IX 5, 4. The fitting vessel was preserved on site in the same room. Image: Nicolas Monteix.

---

[28] The second example lies in bakery V 3, 8, embedded in a masonry structure in a small space between the kneading machine room and the oven. During the cleaning of this room, the imprint of a second tub was seen (Monteix et al. 2013: §7, fig. 3).

[29] The main problem with this modern terminology is that it assigns a gesture to the process, while even now both techniques coexist. The effect of this first rising followed by a remixing is to restart yeast development.

Pompeian bakeries. Though their dimensions differ from one bakery to another, their general shape is always the same: they are rectangular and have
usually been built in masonry—though some blocks of local limestone might
have been used. They are 60–70 centimetres high and were most likely covered
by wooden planks. Typically placed in the centre of the room, they allowed
workers to form loaves on both sides of the table. The dough had to be divided
into lumps; either these would have been weighed, or their weight estimated by
eye. The forming in itself must be inferred from the result: fourteen loaves,
partially or completely preserved, have been found in Pompeii and Herculaneum and can still be studied.[30] They are all pre-divided into six or eight parts
on the upper face, and into two parts on their sides. Such a result could have
been obtained by scoring the loaves either with a knife, after a time of fermentation, just before baking them in the oven, or—hypothetically—with a string
that was left around the loaf while it was leavening. In any case, none of the
Pompeian—or Herculanean—loaves of bread preserved after the eruption
shows any sign of moulding.[31] Once the loaves had been shaped, with or
without the subdivision, the dough had to finish its leavening: the loaves were
left on shelves, which are almost always visible in the preparation room when
the wall preservation is sufficient. At least one example, known in a domestic
context (house VIII 2, 34), attests that loaves might have been covered by many
pieces of cloth—more than fifty in this case—in order to preserve humidity
while rising.[32] That this use of textile covers was also practised in commercial
productive space remains conjectural. Nevertheless, it should be emphasized
that rising works better in a relatively high ambient temperature (35–40°C).

Baking

Once loaves have leavened sufficiently, the last step in bread-making is baking.
Although until now we have only considered leavened bread, the consumption
of a second type—called *clibanus*—is at least attested by an electoral notice.[33]
If this Latin term used in Pompeii has the same significance as in literary
sources, it should refer to flat bread, pancake-baked after slapping it onto the
internal side of a terracotta or metal oven in which a fire burns.[34] Yet, while

---

[30] Of eighty-one loaves discovered in VII 1, 36–7, only six are still preserved. The other eight
come from Herculaneum. Cf. Borgongino (2006: 140–5).

[31] The alleged moulds supposedly found in bakery Or. II, 8 in Herculaneum, which have
always been used since then as an example to demonstrate that bread was moulded, were
discovered not in this workshop but in the flat above it, which lacks any connection with
productive spaces. See Monteix (2010: 151–2); *contra* Maiuri (1958: 457–8).

[32] Médard, Borgard, and Moulhérat (2011: 84–6).

[33] CIL 4.677: *Trebium aed(ilium) o(ro) u(os) f(aciatis) | clibanari rog(ant).*

[34] André (1981: 67); Thurmond (2006: 64–5).

such earthenware has been found in southern France, it has not been discovered in the AD 79 levels of Pompeii or Herculaneum, nor has any unleavened bread been preserved.[35] Hence, this chapter will consider only the
'traditional' bread oven built in masonry.

The principal parts of an oven consist of its base, which is generally square
and 70–80 centimetres high, and its baking chamber, which, besides some rare
exceptions, always has a domed shape (Fig. 7.7). The base is always deeper
than the chamber in order to create a shelf for the oven at the front. The way in
which those minimal though essential elements are built helps in understanding
how such ovens worked. The dome is built directly on the base. The oven floor,
where loaves are laid to be baked, is made of tiles—or much more rarely of square
bricks. These are set on a layer of sand, 10–40 centimetres thick, which covers the
masonry base of the oven.[36] In Pompeii and Herculaneum, the first row of the
floor is always made of lava stones, the function of which has long been
questioned. While Luigi Fulvio believed that this material was chosen in order
to protect the oven against damage from the bread shovel, its actual purpose
might have been related to the characteristics of the lava: basalt has high thermal
effusivity, owing to both its high conductivity and its high volumetric heat
capacity.[37] Thus, it can stock a huge amount of heat internally and then release
it slowly, either by radiative or by convective heat transfer. The sand underneath
it, on the contrary, particularly when dry, has low heat conductivity. Its presence
under the tiles or bricks thus avoids heat loss through the base and prevents heat
from being concentrated under the loaves.

Besides these general characteristics, which are common to all Pompeian
ovens, some optional features might have been added. A diaphragm wall,
which is characterized by an arch in its front part, might be built against the
shelf, thus creating a space 30–40 centimetres wide before the oven mouth. In
the upper part of this, a chimney might be inserted, designed with various
techniques, from reused amphorae to built-in masonry flue. This would allow
smoke to be vented out of the workshop.[38] Within the space created, mostly

[35] Barberan et al. (2006). The vessels found there differ extensively from Italian examples such
as those published by Cubberley, Lloyd, and Roberts (1988). Given the similarity between these
ovens and *dolia* when fragmented, they may yet still be found in Italy. A Latin label being needed,
I would use *clibanus* for *tabouna*-like ovens, while I would keep *testa* for baking pans. *Clibani*
would have been in use in Pompeii, as suggested by *CIL* 4.677; see also Monteix et al. (2015 §3g).

[36] 10 cm is the height of this sand layer as reconstructed in ovens that have lost their tiled floor
or in those where it has been possible to measure where it was preserved. A thickness of 40
centimetres was observed in Herculaneum, in Or. II, 1a, according to the excavation reports
(*Giornale degli Scavi di Ercolano*, 11 July 1935: '11 luglio. Un ambiente non ancora numerato
perché in corso di sterro, tiene il pavimento di grosse tegole di terracotta che poggiano sopra uno
spessore di metri 0.40 di sabbia marina . . .').

[37] Fulvio (1879: 285).

[38] The height of these flues probably helped post-eruption looters to locate bakeries in order
to salvage items—mostly metallic ones, notably lead-boilers, but also mills. See n. 15.

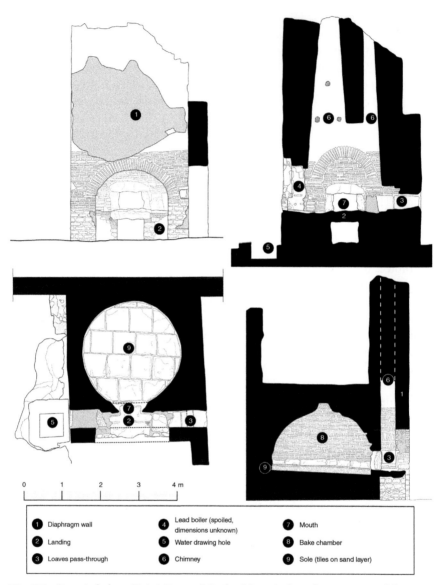

Fig. 7.7. Oven in bakery V 4, 1. Image: Nicolas Monteix, based on survey and drawing by François Fouriaux and Sandrine Mencarelli.

available on the two sides of the mouth, two implements might be added. First is the lead-boiler, embedded between the diaphragm wall and the oven, slightly above the landing, so that fuel could be inserted under it (Fig. 7.8). Of the twenty-four ovens that had a diaphragm wall (or where one might be reconstructed), twenty-two had a boiler, of which only two are still

Fig. 7.8. Lead boiler embedded in the oven of bakery VII 12, 11 and its heating surface. Image: Nicolas Monteix.

preserved.[39] While their volume shows considerable variation, their functioning remains identical: one lead pipe fills the boiler, while a second drains it; both are inserted into one of the sides and pass through the diaphragm wall. It cannot be ascertained that these boilers were connected directly to the water distribution network. Yet on the side or the front of the diaphragm wall, there is always an inlet that received water and let it go to a drain.[40] As for the use of this warmed water, one should think of kneading: water that was warm, but not too hot, could be of use in dough preparation.[41] The second feature generally linked to the diaphragm wall, first defined by August Mau, is a pass-through. This is a window-like opening through which loaves could be passed directly from the preparation room to the oven shelf.[42] Twenty-three of these pass-

---

[39] In I 12, 1–2 (volume: 109 L) and VII 12, 11 (volume: 26 L).

[40] An intermediate vat might be used to stock warm water, as in I 12, 1–2. Most boilers seem to empty directly in those vats that are directly linked to a sewer. Warm—if not hot—water passed through, as limited calcareous deposits indicate in IX 12, 6. The form of these vats differs greatly from one bakery to another reused Dressel 20 being quite frequent.

[41] On temperatures in modern bakeries, see Cauvain (2007: 42). Thurmond (2006: 71) also suggests that sprinkling water on loaves would have helped them rising while baking. If so, it would not be the main purpose of this feature. Such a practice would have been counter-productive though: opening the oven would generate a loss of temperature.

[42] Mau (1899: 383).

throughs have been observed in Pompeii, some also in bakeries that do not have a diaphragm. In these cases, it is an opening in the dividing wall between the *panificium* and the oven. It is unlikely that these pass-throughs were also used to bring baked bread back into the preparation room.

With or without the diaphragm wall, the functioning of the oven remains the same: it is first heated, while its mouth remains opened in order for both the basalt ring and the sand layer to reach the right temperature, which should be slightly above 250°C. Once this has been done, all the fuel is removed (and possibly stocked—for instance, in basalt recipient—or moved under a boiler), and the loaves are placed on the oven floor. The iron door is shut, and the baking starts. While this reconstruction is mainly based on an analysis of oven architecture, it is confirmed by the situation in bakery VII 1, 36–7: when this building was unearthed in 1862, eighty-one loaves were discovered in the oven. Their dimensions—they had a diameter of 19–23 centimetres, about 20 centimetres on average—exclude the possibility that there was any remnant fuel in the oven during the baking itself.[43]

Excavations especially in bakery I 12, 1–2 and IX 3, 19–20 in Pompeii led to the discovery of one component of the fuel used for baking: some 99 per cent of vegetal macro-remains found in these workshops consist of olive stones, while beech is predominant among identified wood species (58 per cent).[44] The choice of olive pits might be explained by their calorific power, which is 12 per cent higher than the wood species more commonly used in first-century AD Pompeii.[45] It must be emphasized that, even if the proportions of different fuels used at the same time will never be quantified, the over-representation of olive stones does represent a technical choice that must be linked with the baking process: published domestic contexts show a total lack of such remains.[46] It remains quite difficult to estimate the length of the pre-heating

---

[43] About this bakery, and the loaves discovered in it, see *Giornale degli Scavi di Pompei*, 9 August 1862; Fiorelli (1873: 16–17; 1875: 171–2).

[44] The carpological identification was conducted by M. Derreumaux and V. Matterne (see n. 10). Charcoal analysis and determination were run by S. Coubray (Institut National d'Archéologie Préventive). For complementary details on these results, see Coubray, Matterne, and Monteix (forthcoming).

[45] According to the sample from the Casa delle Vestali, beech (47%), *Corylaceae* (23%), and oak (10%) are the most predominant species used in this domestic context in the first century AD; see Veal and Thompson (2008). They have a higher heating value (HHV) respectively of 5.14 kWh/kg, 4.97 kWh/kg, and 5.04 kWh/kg (data <http://www.onf.fr> (accessed 10 July 2015)), while the HHV for olive stones has been estimated recently as 5.69 kWh/kg (20,500 J/kg) (data <http://www.afidoltek.org/index.php/Valorisation_énergétique_des_grignons> (accessed 10 July 2015)).

[46] No olive stone has been found in the six samples studied in the Casa delle Vestali; see Veal and Thompson (2008: 294). Olive stones, complete and fragmentary, discovered in several bakeries contradict the explanation used by the two authors to justify their lack in domestic context: 'if used as kindling, olive would have been the most likely to burn completely due to its oily character' (2008: 294).

phase and of the baking procedure, given the multiple factors that might have interfered, notably the quantity of fuel and the size of the oven.[47]

After baking, the loaves were ready to be sold. This final operation could either take place in front of the bakery, if it had a shop—as nineteen bakeries did—or through an intermediate retailer.

THE OPERATIONAL SEQUENCE IN ITS TECHNICAL, SPATIAL, AND ECONOMICAL CONTEXT

Before I move on to discuss the spatial arrangement of Pompeian bakeries, a few points concerning the operational sequence have to be discussed. The three main steps described—grinding, kneading, and forming loaves, baking—and their various subdivisions do reflect the technological knowledge in bread-making used in the Pompeian bakeries. Furthermore, those observations remain fully valid only for the third quarter of the first century AD; changes in practice, greater or smaller, might have occurred before and after this period.

Nevertheless, I must emphasize that this reconstruction is a *theoretical* synthesis: of the thirty-nine bakeries included in this study, not one presented *all* the features discussed above; not one produced bread using all of the possible steps mentioned. For instance, bakery IX 3, 19–20 contained the main three structures used during grinding—a water system for soaking, four mills, and the L-shaped small wall for sieving—and most of those necessary to knead and form loaves—including a kneading machine, a boiler to warm water, embedded terracotta vessels for the first rising, and a table with two masonry feet.[48] However, there are no clear traces of shelves, neither in the room where the kneading machine and vessels were situated, nor in the space where the table on which loaves were formed stood. In this particular bakery, the lack of shelves could be due to preservation factors: although shelves identified by holes in walls are the most common type of feature used for rising loaves in bakeries, they might not be the only one. Indeed, as all known loaves found in Pompeii were leavened, allowing the dough to rise would have been a crucial step in the operational sequence; without it, loaves would have remained flat. Conversely, the practice of leavening is attested in IX 3, 19–20, thanks to the two large terracotta vessels situated in the kneading room. Thus, we need to consider in this case that, despite the lack of

---

[47] Experiments conducted in the Saalburg, after the reconstruction of ovens found in a fort occupied by the second Rhaetian cohort, led to a pre-heating phase that lasted twelve hours. Cf. Knierriem and Löhnig (1997).

[48] As it was not discovered during the excavation, the reconstruction of the boiler has had to be based on the shape of the oven.

evidence in the standing remains, some space had been devoted to rising loaves, most probably in the room where they had been formed just before.

Bakery I 12, 1–2, on the other hand, lacks two features that can be found in IX 3, 19–20: no hydraulic system that would have enabled the grain to be soaked before milling has been identified, nor was there any vessel that could have been used for the first rising. The absence of these features does not seem to have restrained production capacity, even over the long term if one accepts the reconstructed evolution of this bakery, which will be discussed in more detail in a later section. Thus, these two features, which are observed in only a few bakeries, seem related to non-crucial steps whose presence is more significant than their absence. Adding them to the operational sequence could have represented a substantial initial cost, especially when the grain-tempering installation had a connection to the water distribution network, as was the case in IX 3, 19–20. All these non-crucial steps also imply the need for more manpower. An interpretation of the textual evidence could lead one to assume that facilities were added to enable a production process that, at least according to Roman taste, put more emphasis on quality than on quantity. Tempering and sifting are both used to whiten flour, which would have resulted in lower productivity, because of loss of both flour and time, but at the same time would have produced a bread that would have been greatly appreciated.[49] But not all non-crucial steps served to improve quality: the use of warm water while kneading would have permitted a productivity increase, by shortening the time needed for kneading and rising.

Finally, a last technical point has to be made, despite its triviality: even at Pompeii, only production phases that can be traced through material remains can be reconstructed. Many, sometimes even crucial, operations cannot be studied owing to lack of physical evidence. For instance, after the first rising—if it occurred—the difference between 'punching down' or 'folding' the dough has crucial repercussions for the general leavening of the loaf, but we cannot reconstruct this for any ancient bakery. Some missing operations could perhaps be restored from textual or iconographic evidence, but such evidence should be treated cautiously in order to avoid over-interpretation. For example, although the way in which the baker's assistants have been carved on the Bologna relief seems very 'realistic'—notably, the hands forming the loaves sink into the dough—it is highly improbable that one person ever formed two loaves with both hands at the same time. In this manner, however precise our reconstruction of the operational sequence may be, it will necessarily always remain incomplete, although this does not invalidate it as a heuristic tool for further analysis.

---

[49] On the preference for white bread, see Thurmond (2006: 52–3).

SPATIAL INSERTION AND PATH STANDARDIZATION

Almost all previous literature has failed to go further than providing a synthetically designed description of the main features of bakeries; the first step beyond this would be to insert each operation into the space of the workshop. This should lead to an understanding of how technical challenges have been solved—or not—within a peculiar spatial layout. Bakeries are not necessarily rationally organized or closely built up. Of the three main stages, milling might be completely separated from kneading and baking: eleven of the thirty-nine bakeries had no milling space in AD 79.[50] If one discards the traditional interpretation of these bakeries as *pistrina dulciaria*, this statement has two implications.[51] First, some of the milling complexes, which as far as is known in Pompeii and surroundings were always linked with baking structures, had flour outputs beyond their baking capacities, allowing the development of bakeries without mills.[52] Secondly, this possible technical separation has consequences for the spatial layout of the workshops: when installing a bakery, it is not necessary to completely reshape the plan of the pre-existing building in order to nucleate all the rooms linked with production. In particular, milling space does not need to be directly adjacent to other production facilities. However, probably because of their own building history, only two bakeries present that kind of layout.[53]

On the other hand, the two last stages are always arranged in close proximity. That is to say, most rooms dedicated to the forming and final rising of loaves were deliberately sited directly adjacent to the oven. Two factors played a role in this choice. In the first place, it would have facilitated the heating of the room, which would have made rising easier. Moreover, the proximity limited the distance between the rising spot and the oven, so that risen loaves were less likely to be dropped or damaged during the transfer. For the same reason, the kneading machine and the potential first rising vessels also needed to be placed as close to the preparation tables as possible, though a longer path would have had less consequence on bread quality, since the loaves still needed to be formed at this step. Hence, even if clustering all structures linked to the second and third stages would have shortened work paths and thus enhanced

---

[50] A *catillus*, discarded and reused as a puteal, has been observed in VII 12, 11. As Fiorelli (1873: 18) noticed, it might be a place where milling had ceased before the eruption. No sign of milling has been revealed by a partial cleaning; see Monteix et (2015: 40–8).

[51] Mayeske (1972: 171–2), but see Monteix (2010: 162–4).

[52] Once chronological data for all bakeries have been obtained, it would be worth analysing whether the simple bakeries were constructed after the mill-bakeries or after their progressive enlargement. If the two phenomena do not appear to be linked, then milling complexes would need to be looked for elsewhere—other places in the town, in villas, or even in water-mills.

[53] Those two bakeries are situated in I 12, 1–2 and VI 5, 15.

productivity, there was no technical problem in setting kneading and/or first rising apart from the forming of loaves.

As an example, bakery V 3, 8 illustrates such issues (Fig. 7.9). The first stages are arranged around the atrium, in whose slightly transformed *compluvium* the grain was soaked and then ground with the three mills disposed around it. The ingredients were kneaded in the room south-east of the oven, where the four feet of a table were also fixed in the ground. Once made, the dough was left for a first rising in the small room between the oven mouth and the preparation room, where it finally went back to be formed into loaves.

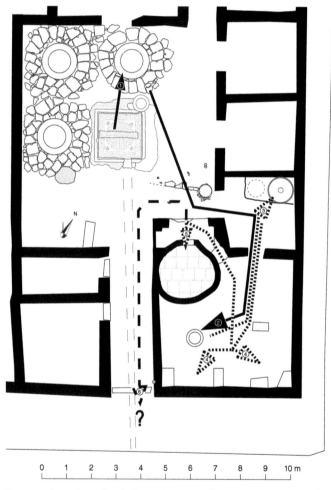

Fig. 7.9. From grain to bread in bakery V 3, 8. 1. from tempering to milling; 2. from milling to kneading; 3. from kneading to first rising; 4. from first rising to loaves forming; 5. from loaves forming to bakery; 6. from baking to selling. Image: Nicolas Monteix.

In the bakery of the *Casa dei casti amanti*, the path is more rationalized. All the productive structures were divided between two rooms, around the oven. Four mills are clustered in the north-western part. South-east of those, in front of the oven, are the kneading machine, close to the warm water, and two reused *catilli*, transformed into the base of vessels for the first rising of the dough. Once the dough had risen, it was brought to the room immediately south of the oven, where there were three stone blocks supporting the bread-shaping table. After the second rising, the loaves were transported to the oven, thanks to the pass-through on its left. In this bakery, from grain to bread, the product took a 'circular' clockwise path.

These two examples clearly exemplify how the apparent uniformity of bakery structures is in fact misleading. There are no two identical bakeries: the whole spatial structure depended both on the features used but also, and more importantly, on the evolution of the workshop, and whether or not its owner was able and or willing completely to restructure the existing layout of the building.[54]

ECONOMIC INVESTMENT

Studying the spatial organization of bakeries in this way also brings up the issue of investment, and the scale on which this took place. In Pompeii, no house was built around a bakery: there is no trace of any workshop built completely from scratch to incorporate the various rooms needed for the technical processes of bread-making. Any installation thus had—at least to some extent—to be adapted to a pre-existing general spatial layout. Thus there was a tension between the technical requirements of the bakery and the transformation works required to fit it into the pre-existing house. The solution to this tension never seems to have favoured either a perfectly rationalized bakery with a strictly linear or circular organization, or an un-structured workshop thoroughly determined by the pre-existing building. Varying degrees of spatial rationality emerge. The question is to determine the point beyond which the spatial organization of a bakery *had* to be rationalized in order to be functional, not to say profitable. Two examples illustrate this issue.

Bakery I 12, 1–2 was inserted into a pre-existing house built on a narrow strip plot (Fig. 7.10). The previous building on this site had a south/north drain with a row of narrow rooms on its east side; the back part would have

---

[54] This changing degree of rationalization in Pompeii can be compared with that observed in Ostia, particularly in the *Casseggiato dei Molini*. See Bakker (1999) and Wilson (2008b: 406–8).

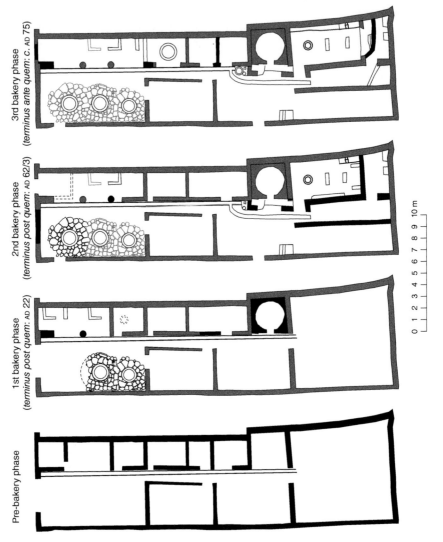

Fig. 7.10. The historical evolution of bakery I 12, 1–2. Image: Nicolas Monteix.

been used as a garden. Only minimal changes were undertaken in the building of the initial bakery, which had only two animal-driven mills. In the front part, the shop that opened on Via dell'Abbondanza was retained. A room was connected to the mill room in order to install two L-shaped walls for sieving. Just south of this, in another room that retained its original plan, a kneading machine might have been installed.[55] In the southern part of the house, a first oven was built, which lacked the diaphragm wall. According to the excavations conducted in this workshop, the first phase of the bakery has a *terminus post quem* of AD 22.[56] The second phase, which can be linked with the AD 62/63 earthquake, incorporated an extension to the bakery: a third mill was put in place, with the surrounding pavement, the shop opening was closed, and the mill room was unified by knocking down two dividing walls. The L-shaped structure was transformed. Yet the most drastic changes took place in the southern part of the house. By abolishing the garden, space was freed to install a preparation room furnished with a kneading machine, two tables, and some shelves. As part of this extension, a diaphragm wall was added to the oven, allowing the insertion of a pass-through and a boiler. Because of these transformations, the drain was slightly diverted. In the latest phase, dated to the AD 70s, only a few changes occurred.[57] Both the milling room and the preparation room were extended south, at the expense of other spaces. Thus, a fourth mill was added and the bread-shaping table was rotated, allowing more people to form loaves.

In this bakery, a more rationalized production path emerged during the second phase, when a third mill was installed. At this point, together with the increase in production capacity, substantial building works were performed to change the spatial layout. From this moment on, milling was strictly separated from kneading, forming, and baking. A second point that emerges is a correlation between the number of mills—the flour production capacity—and the number of people theoretically involved in forming loaves.

Despite the lack of absolute dating, bakery IX 5, 4 offers a similar pattern of expansion. From the investigation of its building history, it seems that the creation of the bakery involved the knocking-down of half the plot. In the first phase, three mills were installed in what was already a somewhat rationalized plant: south of the milling room, a vast space was created for the kneading and forming stages. The oven made the most of a pre-existing arched space. It is

---

[55] The installation pit for this feature was observed during excavations. Amphorae fragments had been used to wedge the kneading machine in place.

[56] A Tiberian as (*RIC* I²: no. 81, p. 99) has been discovered in the backfill used to complete the installation of the first basalt pavement.

[57] A door, leading to a staircase and an upper-floor apartment, was opened in the north-east part of the facade after the damages linked with the AD 62/63 earthquake had been repaired. This door could have been closed and the staircase dismantled after the construction of the fourth mill. After that, the apartment would have been accessible from the mill room.

possible that in this phase a pass-through already connected it with the preparation room. The growth of the bakery in the next phase did not alter the general layout: a fourth mill was added, and a first rising structure was installed near the kneading machine. The main transformation linked with these changes is the closing-off of the preparation room. During the last phase, which most probably was unfinished in AD 79, the bakery seems to have been dismantled, as would seem to be indicated by the raising of the floor level in front of the oven by 20–30 centimetres.

This second case also suggests that three mills could be considered as the point beyond which the spatial organization of the workshop had to be rationalized, so that it followed the operational sequence as far as possible. This spatial layout might be obtained either through substantial investment during the initial construction of the workshop if it involved three or more mills, or by subsequent changes if the original bakery had two or fewer mills.[58]

CONCLUSIONS

As far as can be reconstructed from archaeological remains, the bread-making process in Pompeii was divided into three work clusters. The first one, grinding, had three steps: tempering, milling, and sifting, the first and the last being in some way optional: building a structure devoted to those steps was not compulsory. The second stage, dedicated to kneading and bread-shaping, shows fewer optional steps: it was possible to use warm water to knead the dough, or to leave out the first rising. The third and last stage seems, from a material point of view, to have been quite uniform throughout the city: all thirty-nine bread ovens were broadly built in the same way and most probably functioned similarly. Only minor differences can be observed, but these relate to the presence of certain optional features and are not directly linked with baking itself.

Focusing on the materialization of some technical clusters—such as the eventual separation of milling from other operations, and the strong link between rising and baking—helps in understanding the spatial layout of the Pompeian bakeries. No one bakery is exactly identical to any of the others, owing to the necessity of using pre-existing spaces to install or develop these workshops: the spatial organization seems to have been a compromise between technical needs and investment capacity. As they become bigger, Pompeian bakeries tended to be laid out less in a do-it-yourself way, and to gain in rationalization. Finally, besides shedding light on the bakeries of

---

[58] In a forthcoming monograph on Pompeian bakeries, the author will test this hypothesis and then connect it to a broader interpretative framework that discusses workshops as an economic investment.

Pompeii, the approach presented in this chapter also suggests that analysing the *chaîne opératoire* must be seen as a useful heuristic tool for a better understanding of Roman urban crafts, even beyond technical matters.

ACKNOWLEDGEMENTS

This chapter would have been impossible to write without the kind permission of the Soprintendenza Archeologica di Napoli e Pompei to study all Pompeian bakeries, or, in the case of bakery IX 3, 19–20, without the opportunity to engage in collaboration with the *Expeditio Pompeiana Universitatis Helsingiensis* (EPUH—University of Helsinki). The majority of the research presented here is derived from the ongoing project '*Pistrina*—Recherches sur les boulangeries de l'Italie romaine', funded by the École française de Rome and the French foreign office through the Centre Jean-Bérard (Naples). Additional funding was also provided by the Institut Européen d'Histoire et des Cultures de l'Alimentation (IEHCA, Tours). All my thanks go to the team who have been involved in the project since 2008, particularly to S. Aho, A. Coutelas, M. Derreumaux, L. Garnier, C. Hartz, É. Letellier, S. Longepierre, V. Matterne, and S. Zanella. J. Andrews and F. Trifilò kindly read and commented on this contribution, trying to enhance its English. Any remaining mistakes are my own.

REFERENCES

Allison, P. M. (1995). 'On-Going Seismic Activity and its Effects on the Living Conditions in Pompeii in the Last Decades', in T. Fröhlich and L. Jacobelli (eds), *Archäologie und Seismologie: La regione vesuviana dal 62 al 79 DC : Problemi archeologici e sismologici.* Munich, 183–90.

André, J. (1981). *L'Alimentation et la cuisine à Rome* (Collection d'études anciennes). Paris.

Bakker, J. T. (1999). *The Mills-Bakeries of Ostia: Description and Interpretation* (Dutch Monographs on Ancient History and Archaeology, 21). Amsterdam.

Balfet, H. (ed.) (1991). *Observer l'action technique: Des chaînes opératoires, pour quoi faire?* Paris.

Barberan, S., Piquès, G., Raux, S., and Sanchez, C. (2006). 'Un dispositif de cuisson original en Languedoc dans l'antiquité: Les Fours à pain à cloche mobile en céramique', in *SFECAG—Actes du Congrès de Pézenas.* Marseilles, 257–71.

Borgongino, M. (2006). *Archeobotanica: Reperti vegetali da Pompei e dal territorio vesuviano* (Studi della Soprintendenza archeologica di Pompei, 16). Rome.

Brun, J.-P. (2007). 'Les Moulins hydrauliques en Italie romaine', in J.-P. Brun and J.-L. Fiches (eds), *Énergie hydraulique et machines élévatrices d'eau dans l'Antiquité* (Collection du Centre Jean Bérard, 27). Naples, 201–14.

Buffone, L., Lorenzoni, S., Pallara, M., and Zantin, E. (1999). 'Le macine rotatorie in rocce vulcaniche di Pompei', *RSP* 10: 117–30.

Cauvain, S. P. (2007). 'Breadmaking Processes', in S. P. Cauvain and L. S. Young (eds), *Technology of Breadmaking*. New York, 21–49.

Ciancio Rossetto, P. (1973). *Il sepolcro del fornaio Marco Virgilio Eurisace a Porta Maggiore* (I Monumenti romani, 5). Rome.

Coubray, S., Matterne, V., and Monteix, N. (forthcoming). 'Of olives and wood: Baking Bread in Pompeii', in R. Veal and V. Leitch (eds), *Fuel and Fire in the Ancient Roman World: Towards an Integrated Economic Approach* (McDonald Institute Monographs). Cambridge.

Cresswell, R. (2003). 'Geste technique, fait social total: Le Technique est-il dans le social ou face à lui?', *Techniques & Culture* 40: 125–51.

Cubberley, A. L., Lloyd, J. A., and Roberts, P. C. (1988). '*Testa* and *Clibani*: The Baking Covers of Classical Italy', *PBSR*, 56: 98–119.

Curtis, R. I. (2001). *Ancient Food Technology* (Technology and Change in History, 5). Leiden and Boston.

Curtis, R. I. (2008). 'Food Processing and Preparation', in J. P. Oleson (ed.), *The Oxford Handbook of Engineering and Technology in the Classical World*. Oxford and New York, 369–92.

Esposito, D. (2009). *Le officine pittoriche di IV stile a Pompei dinamiche produttive ed economico-sociali* (Studi della Soprintendenza archeologica di Pompei, 28). Rome.

Fiorelli, G. (1873). *Gli scavi di Pompei dal 1861 al 1872*. Naples.

Fiorelli, G. (1875). *Descrizione di Pompei*. Naples.

Fulvio, L. (1879). 'Delle fornaci e dei forni pompeiani', in *Pompei e la regione sotterrata dal Vesuvio nell' anno 79 Memorie e notizie publicate dall' Ufficio tecnico degli scavi delle province meridionali*. Naples, 273–91.

Garçon, A.-F. (1997). 'L'Innovation au regard du complexe technique minéro-métallurgique armoricain', *Annales de Bretagne et des Pays de l'Ouest* 104/3: 23–38.

Gell, W., and Gandy, J. P. (1817). *Pompeiana: The Topography, Edifices, and Ornaments of Pompeii*. London.

Gille, B. (1978). 'Prolégomènes à une histoire des techniques', in B. Gille (ed.), *Histoire des techniques : Technique et civilisations, technique et sciences* (Encyclopédie de la Pléiade, 41). Paris, 1–118.

Knierriem, P., and Löhnig, E. (1997). '*Panificium* im experiment : Ein Erfahrungsbericht aus dem Saalburgkastell', in M. Junkelmann (ed.), *Panis militaris : Die Ernährung des römischen Soldaten oder der Grundstoff der Macht* (Kulturgeschichte der antiken Welt, 75). Mainz, 134–6.

Lemonnier, P. (1983). 'L'Etude des systèmes techniques, une urgence en technologie culturelle', *Techniques & Culture* 1: 11–34.

Leroi-Gourhan, A. (1965). *Le Geste et la parole* (Sciences d'aujourd'hui). Paris.

Maiuri, A. (1958). *Ercolano. I nuovi scavi, 1927–1958*. Rome.

Mau, A. (1899). *Pompeii: Its Life and Art*. London.

Mayeske, B. J. (1972). 'Bakeries, Bakers and Bread at Pompeii: A Study in Social and Economic History', Ph.D. thesis, University of Maryland.

Mazois, F. (1824). *Les Ruines de Pompéi: Seconde partie*. Paris.

Médard, F., Borgard, P., and Moulhérat, C. (2011). 'Le Travail du textile à Pompéi : Ateliers et restes de tissus', in C. Alfaro Giner, J.-P. Brun, and P. Borgard (eds), *Purpureae vestes III: Textiles y tintes en la ciudad antigua* (Collection du Centre Jean Bérard, 36). València and Naples, 83–90.

Monteix, N. (2010). *Les Lieux de métier: Boutiques et ateliers d'Herculanum* (BEFAR 344). Rome.

Monteix, N., Zanella, S., Aho, S., Macario, R., and Proudfoot, E. (2013). 'Pompéi, Pistrina', *Chronique des activités archéologiques de l'École française de Rome* <http://cefr.revues.org/954> (accessed 30 September 2014).

Monteix, N., Aho, S., Coutelas, A., and Zanella, S. (2014). 'Pompéi, Pistrina', *Chronique des activités archéologiques de l'École française de Rome* <http://cefr.revues.org/1242> (accessed 30 September 2014).

Monteix, N., Aho, S., Delvigne-Ryrko, A., and Watel, A. (2015). 'Pompéi, *Pistriana*', *Chronique des activités de l'école française de Rome* <http://cefr.revues.org/1380> (accessed 6 July 2015).

Moritz, L. A. (1958). *Grain-Mills and Flour in Classical Antiquity*. Oxford.

Oleson, J. P. (ed.) (2008). *The Oxford Handbook of Engineering and Technology in the Classical World*. Oxford and New York.

Peacock, D. P. S. (1989). 'The Mills of Pompeii', *Antiquity* 73: 205–14.

Peacock, D. (2013). *The Stone of Life: Querns, Mills and Flour Production in Europe up to c.500 AD* (Southampton Monographs in Archaeology, NS 1). Southampton.

Pernot, M. (2006). 'La Place de la technique dans les sociétés anciennes', *Cahiers d'Épistémé* 1: 7–25.

Strocka, V. M. (1991). *Casa del Labirinto (VI 11, 8–10)* (Häuser in Pompeji, 4). Munich

Thurmond, D. L. (2006). *A Handbook of Food Processing in Classical Rome: For her bounty no Winter* (Technology and Change in History, 9). Leiden.

Veal, R., and Thompson, G. (2008). 'Fuel Supplies for Pompeii: Pre-Roman and Roman Charcoals of the Casa delle Vestali', in G. Fiorentino and D. Magri (eds), *Charcoals from the Past: Cultural and Palaeoenvironmental Implications* (BAR International series, 1807). Oxford, 287–97.

Wikander, Ö. (2008). 'Sources of Energy and Exploitation of Power', in Oleson (2008), 136–57.

Wilson, A. I. (2008a). 'Machines in Greek and Roman Technology', in Oleson (2008), 337–66.

Wilson, A. I. (2008b). 'Large-Scale Manufacturing, Standardization, and Trade', in Oleson (2008), 393–417.

Wilson, A. I., and Schörle, K. (2009). 'A Baker's Funerary Relief from Rome', *PBSR* 77: 101–23.

Zimmer, G. (1982). *Römische Berufsdarstellungen* (Archäologische Forschungen, 12). Berlin.

III

People

8

Disciplina, patrocinium, nomen: The Benefits of Apprenticeship in the Roman World

Christel Freu

Professional training in the ancient world has long been thought primitive, as it was not formally practised in schools but depended only on the personal relationship between the master and the apprentice.[1] However, the absence of schools does not necessarily mean that society did not consider ways to institutionalize and regulate apprenticeship. Although informal training continued to play its role in the Roman Empire, we also have signs of the formalization of technical training: when a family wanted to send a child away to some friend or to some renowned master and expected good training, the teaching could be an object of contract.

Because of the benefits it offered for masters as well as for their pupils, formalized technical training was a much sought-after activity. Most scholarship on the issue has focused on master craftsmen, who had reached the top of their craft and were often also teachers, deriving authority and wealth from their teaching, and taking advantage of a cheap labour force that over the years acquired better skills, thus contributing to the good reputation of their workshop.[2] Yet, for their pupils too, benefits were considerable. There is no doubt

---

[1] Marrou (1948: 286–7); cf. Schulz-Falkenthal (1972: 194): 'sich . . . die berufliche Ausbildung im Handwerkerstand für unsere modernen Begriffe noch weitgehend unsystematisch, unorganisiert, mehr spontan als geregelt vollzog.' It is true that the choice of a master was certainly not regulated; but the attention of the imperial cities towards their apprentices was not completely non-existent, at least with regard to the taxes they raised. For Egypt, see Freu (2011: 28–35).

[2] See Schulz-Falkenthal (1972: 196–8); Tran (2010; 2011: 128–30; 2013: 147-85) for *magistri* and *didaskaloi* seen as honoured craftsmen in Greek and Latin inscriptions. Tran highlighted well the existence of craftsmen specialized in training. I use the English term 'craftsman' to qualify a professional involved, in one way or another, in the production process. See Monteix (2011) for a reflection and better definition of the craftsmanship concept. He prefers not to employ the French terms *artisanat* and *artisan*. But I have not found an English word to replace 'craftsman'.

that a qualified person earned more than a manual worker. As shown by Stanislas Mrozek and Richard Duncan-Jones, qualified slaves were more expensive than basic unskilled workers. These costs undoubtedly reflect their scarcity but also the level of income that could be earned in the labour market.[3] This fact was stressed by Cicero in his defence of the actor Roscius, when he claimed that educating a slave as an artist would increase his basic value a hundredfold.[4] This plea, the *Pro Roscio Comoedo*, incomplete and difficult to date, deals with a conflict between a slave-owner and his associate Fannius, who, as it seems, was granted half the ownership of the slave, Panurgus. When the slave died, Cicero defended Roscius' rights of ownership and also the fact that he owed nothing to his former associate, Fannius. Not being fully able to show that the slave was really shared by both, Cicero mostly underlined how much the teaching itself could account for the fact that part of the increased value should go to the teacher who had trained him.

Disciplina, patrocinium, nomen, which can be translated as 'the teaching of skills, patronage, and fame', were, for Cicero, the rewards that an apprentice in art or craftsmanship could expect to get.[5] Although the topic of his discourse is only artistic training, which is specific, because artists can be much sought after and very rich, the text can be regarded as paradigmatic. To different degrees, the craftsmen who had succeeded all seem to agree that apprenticeship had brought much to them: on their funeral stones, they recall their professional skills, their master's reputation, and their integration in his social networks, thus imitating the way of life and social ideals of the elite. They are, for us, the best examples of the middle classes' rise in the empire.

To explore this social practice, I will focus mostly on sources from the eastern part of the Roman Empire: Egyptian contracts of apprenticeship, *didaskalikai*, which have already been much studied, some literary texts, and some inscriptions—obtained with the help of the Packard Humanities Institute database, although some had already been collected by Louis Robert.[6] In this corpus, we find dedications from pupils to their teachers, and also from teachers to their pupils, some signatures of *mathètai* who liked to recall the name of their teacher, and, finally, epitaphs, which provide interesting details

---

[3] Duncan-Jones (1974: 348–50; app. 10); Mrozek (1975: 45–8); Tran (2011: 122).

[4] Cic., *Q. Rosc.* 28, ed. J. Axer, Leipzig: this edition of the text, published in 1975, is based on the only manuscript of the text, rediscovered some time previously. The figures used by Cicero are more coherent than in other modern editions: *Panurgum tu, Saturi, proprium Fanni dicis fuisse, at ego totum Rosci fuisse contendo. Quid erat enim Fanni? Corpus. Quid Rosci? Disciplina. . . . Ex qua parte erat Fanni, non erat HS 6,000, ex qua parte erat Rosci, amplius erat HS 600,000* ('Satyrus, you say that Panurgus was the property of Fannius. And I contend that he belonged entirely to Roscius. What belongs to Fannius? His body. What belongs to Roscius? His teaching. . . . Fannius' part did not make him worth 6,000 sesterces; Roscius' part made him worth more than 600,000 sesterces'). See also Tran (2013: 164–77) for other examples showing how important the training was to increase the value of slaves (*Dig.* 6, 1, 27, 5; 6, 1, 28; 13, 7, 25).

[5] Cic., *Q. Rosc.* 30.   [6] Robert (1936: 56–7).

about training and success in the craft. Compared with the numerous inscriptions referring to professionals of *artes liberales*, rhetoricians, sophists, physicians, or grammarians, detailed tombstones of craftsmen are rather rare.[7] There may be several reasons for that. In the first place, there is the relative modesty of the craftsmen's background: although their names often appear on stones, little additional information is given; fortunately for us, there are some exceptions.[8] Secondly, when the training took place inside the family circle, which seemed to have still been regular practice in some milieux, pupils did not have an incentive to specify the name of their master.

In order to examine the benefits of apprenticeship, I shall begin with the content of the training, the *disciplina*; then, I shall show how the apprentices, as Cicero said, wanted to claim legitimacy from the name and fame (*nomen*) of their masters and from the social networks (*patrocinium*) they built during the time of the training. To conclude, I will examine some clear-cut cases of upward mobility resulting from apprenticeship.

DISCIPLINA

Informal apprenticeship undoubtedly existed in Greece and Rome: Plato tells us about it in his *Protagoras*.[9] The details of this training appear in our sources

---

[7] Some epitaphs of physicians or *rhetores* are discussed later in the chapter. It must be noted that the Greeks had the same world, *technè*, to qualify the activity of an artist, a physician, or a craftsman. Therefore, the differences between them are of degree, not of nature. Cf. Frasca (1994: 6). Even though the Roman elites differentiated *artes liberales* and craftsmanship (e.g. *Dig.* 50, 13, 1), the same term, *ars*, applies to these occupations, and excellence of professional know-how was claimed similarly by intellectuals and craftsmen. For that matter, the middle classes did not have the same point of view as the elite. In Petronius, *Satyricon* 46, *artes liberales* were seen by a rich *centonarius*, Euchion, as a profession like any other: *quod si resilierit, destinaui illum artificii docere, aut tonstreinum aut praeconem aut certe causidicum ... Litterae thesaurum est, et artificium nunquam moritur* ('if he gives it up [*sc.* his juristic studies], I decided to have him learn a craft: either hairdresser, or herald, or pleader ... Education is a treasure, and the science of a craft never starves'). See Mayer (2012: 22–60); Monteix (2011: 13); Tran (2011: 122): 'en réalité l'apologie de la *doctrina* et du travailleur *doctus* était commune à l'artisanat et à d'autres activités que les modernes classent parmi les métiers intellectuels.'

[8] For the 'silence' of workers in antiquity, see Joshel (1992: 8–15), who wished to 'give voice to the silent Roman'; see also Salvaterra (2006: 19; 22).

[9] Pl., *Prt.* 328 a: οὐδέ γ᾽ ἄν, οἶμαι, εἰ ζητοῖς τίς ἂν ἡμῖν διδάξειεν τοὺς τῶν χειροτεχνῶν υἱεῖς αὐτὴν τὴν τέχνην ἣν δὴ παρὰ τοῦ πατρὸς μεμαθήκασιν, καθ᾽ ὅσον οἶός τ᾽ ἦν ὁ πατὴρ καὶ οἱ τοῦ πατρὸς φίλοι ὄντες ὁμότεχνοι ('it won't be easy, I think, if you try to find out who could teach our craftsmen's sons the same craft as their father, which they learnt from their father himself, as much as the father is able to do, or his friends, who share the same craft'). Feyel (2006: 457–63) believed that the text attests apprenticeship inside the family circle. However, in reality, Plato is more subtle: even if he underlines the secret that surrounds the apprenticeship (*Prt.* 327 b), he says here that the friends of the craftsman can also teach the young men. For informal apprenticeship in Rome, see Tran (2010: 198; 2013: 161–70), who thinks that this type of apprenticeship was the most common in the Roman world.

only rarely, as apprenticeship was practised inside the craftsmen's home and was fully integrated into family labour and parental education.[10] Yet even in classical or Hellenistic times, this informal training was not the only scenario, and the mobility of apprentices looking for well-known masters all over the Greek world is widely attested.[11] During the late Roman Republic, where the *gentes* were still a leading element in society, we know about apprenticeship in the circle of the *gens*, with *liberti* who learned the craft chosen by the *dominus*. Yet the texts do not say where the training took place and under whose guidance.[12]

As for imperial provinces, the Egyptian *didaskalikai* of the Roman period show, for their part, that many craftsmen families wanted to place their children outside the family, be it at friends' homes, or in the households of close or even distant relatives, as if moving to another home was already part of the training. Plato certainly thought that the friends of fathers were like the family. Nevertheless, they brought a distinct *savoir faire* and an authoritarian distance. It is not surprising that Lucian of Samosata left his position as an apprentice at his uncle's, and ran back to his mother's arms, after being beaten on the very first day: we see here a clear difference between the two worlds.[13] *Disciplina*, far from being secret, was thus shared by professional circles of friends, which could contribute to improving techniques.[14] Yet in the imperial period, at least in Egypt, an interesting evolution may be observed: even though, in the beginning of the imperial era, apprenticeship was still often entrusted to friends, longer training entrusted to more remote craftsmen seems to have become increasingly frequent.[15]

Undoubtedly, apprenticeship was provided not in a school but in the master's workshop or in his house. In most cases, the child was thus placed in a subordinate position to an external authority and had to comply with discipline imposed by a relative stranger, which was all new for him.[16] We do

---

[10] Nevertheless Greek sculptors were in the habit of including the name of their master or father in their signatures. Examples can be found in the work of Marcadé (1953); e.g. Charmolas and Menodotos, Rhodian, sons of Artemidoros and active *c*.100–80 BC (I.17–20); Cephisodotos II and Timarchos of Athenes, sons of Praxiteles and grandsons of the sculptor Cephisodotos I, active at the end of the fourth century BC (I.53–6). See also I.65, and I.110–11. For more complete information, see now Muller-Dufeu (2002).

[11] In his *Periegesis* Pausanias gives examples of apprentice sculptors travelling for their training, from the archaic to the imperial period. Pausanias' sources were either the sculptors' signatures, or the local guides (*exegetai*). e.g. *Periegesis* 5, 17.1, 3-4, 20.2; 6, 1.3; 3.4–6, on Cantharos from Sicyon, active in the fourth century BC; 6, 3.11, and 4.4 on Pythagoras from Rhegion, active in the fifth century BC. For a complete survey of ancient sources mentioning Greek sculptors, see Muller-Dufeu (2002).

[12] Donderer (1996: 58), giving the example of the *gens* Cossutia, who specialized in marble production and whose freedmen were famous temple architects.

[13] Lucian, *Somn.* 4.   [14] Freu (2011: 30–1).   [15] Bergamasco (1995: 150–61).

[16] See Cribiore (1996: 6) for the writing schools, and Frasca (1999) for a comparison between apprenticeship in literary *ludus* and in *taberna* (sp. 151: 'la bottega artigiana si sostituisce alla casa, il *magister* si assume *in toto* le prerogative del *pater*, e con analoga autorità dispone di loro'). Whatever the place used for the teaching was, the important thing was that it was away from home.

not know much about the content of the teaching. Most testimonies alluding to this issue are quite vague, merely mentioning that the master will teach all he knows. The *didaskalikai* say: ὥστε μαθεῖν ... τέχνην πᾶσ[αν αὐτὸ]ν ὡ[ς καὶ αὐτὸς ἐπίσταται ('so that he learns all the art, as [the teacher] himself knows about it').[17] Indeed, contracts insisted mostly on the personal and individual character of the professional *technè* taught by the master. Only the teaching contract—the *Lehrvertrag*, which differs from the *Lehrlingsvertrag* and is much rarer—shows the different steps: in the two or three years of the training, the child must learn precise techniques, in a predefined order.[18]

It has already been pointed out by Heinz Schulz-Falkenthal that professional training did not only provide technical instruction; it also introduced the young apprentice into social networks that would be useful for his career.[19] First of all, it brought a *nomen*—that is, a reputation, even fame.

NOMEN

Nowadays, in the crafts and in the liberal arts, the name and fame of the master still reflect upon his pupils. No matter what the personal quality of the apprentice, being able to highlight the name of one's master, especially a renowned one, is an immediate benefit. When a craftsman's skills were transmitted inside the family, the reputation of the family was transmitted from generation to generation, and spread locally or over larger areas; father and son, uncle and nephew, grandfather and grandson, could work together and the youngest could benefit from the name and reputation of his ancestors: in Greece, temple archives show collaborations of this type between fathers and sons.[20] In imperial times, the obvious example of Lucian's life reminds us of this fact; in Roman Egypt, the papyri tell the same story.[21]

When the master was not a relative, but a renowned skilled worker, his name was all that the pupil inherited from him, and thus was all the more important. Artistic and intellectual groups took good advantage of this: they inscribed themselves in the lineage in which fictive and symbolic affiliations

---

[17] *P. Wisc.* 4 (Oxyrhynchos, AD 53). See also *P. Tebt.* 385 (Tebtunis, AD 117); *P. Fouad* I.37 (Oxyrhynchos, AD 48); *P. Oxy.* II.322 (AD 26); *P. Oxy.* XL.2971 (AD 66); *PSI* 1,132 (Talei, AD 61), with lacunas.

[18] We possess only three of these contracts, two about the shorthand apprenticeship and the third about an apprenticeship of playing music. Cf. Bergamasco (1995: 100–1).

[19] Schulz-Falkenthal (1972: 196).

[20] Feyel (2006: 457–8). For painters, see Plin. *NH* 35.53–148, where apprenticeship appears to have been a family practice for some classical Greek painters (*NH* 35.54; 35.60; 35.108–11).

[21] Lucian was apprenticed to his uncle, whose father was already a sculptor. Lucian, *Somn.* 1–2; see Jones (1986: 9–10).

enabled one to claim the transmission of professional art. This phenomenon is known for artists and sophists.[22] For the Greek sophists of imperial times, the bonds between pupils and master were so tight that they were compared with family ties: the ζηλωταί or ἑταῖροι were brothers, son of their masters; in late antiquity, Athenian philosophers used to claim that their families went back to Plutarch or Philostratus.[23]

For that reason, placing emphasis on the master's name was crucial. Cicero highlights precisely this point:

> What hope and expectation Panurgus aroused, what interest and favour he brought to the stage for the reason he was the pupil of Roscius! Those who loved Roscius favoured his pupil, those who admired Roscius, approved his pupil, those, in short, who heard Roscius' name pronounced, felt that his pupil was well and perfectly trained. Such is the crowd: many of its judgements are inspired by fame, a few by truth.[24]

What is true for artistic training also holds for a craftsman's apprenticeship. Thus, a detailed funeral *carmen* found in Tarragona, written on an altar by a *discipulus*, begins by underlining the importance of the master craftsman's name and renown: *Iulius hic fuerat nomine summo artificioque Statutus* ('This was Julius Statutus, very great by his name and art').[25]

Another way for a *mathètès* to emphasize his master's name was to sign his product with his name set side by side with the name of the *didaskalos* or the *magister*. We thus find in Rome beautiful statues signed by sculptors who liked to draw their glory from their famous master: a statue representing Orestes and Electra, dating from the Augustan or Tiberian era and belonging to the Ludovisi collection, is signed by Menelaos, *mathètès*, 'pupil', of Stephanos;[26] another statue representing an athlete and dating from the second half of the first century BC is signed by Stephanos, *mathètès* of Pasiteles, who, according to art specialists, was a famous sculptor from the middle of the first century, known for imitating classical models.[27] The signature mentions the name of the master in the same position as a patronymic, thus showing an interesting parallel between biological and intellectual affiliation. In the same way, apprentices of workers in mosaics could mention proudly the name of their

---

[22] For Greek painters, see Plin. *NH* 35.75–77; 25.110–14.

[23] Goulet-Cazé (1982: 255–6) underlines the existence of idealized kinship ties between the philosopher's pupils and the master; see also Puech (2012).

[24] Cic., *Q. Rosc.* 29: 'Quam enim spem et expectationem, quod studium et quem fauorem secum in scaenam attulit Panurgus quod Rosci fuit discipulus! Qui diligebant hunc, illi fauebant, qui admirabantur hunc, illum probabant, qui denique huius nomen audierant, illum eruditum et perfectum existimabant. Sic est uolgus; ex ueritate pauca, ex opinione multa aestimat.'

[25] *RIT* 447 = *AE* 2000, 802.

[26] *IGUR* 4.1575: Μενέλαος Στεφάνου μαθητὴς ἐπόει ('Menelaos, pupil of Stephanos, made [it]').

[27] *IGUR* 4.1584: Στέφανος Πασιτέλους μαθητὴς ἐπόει ('Stephanos, pupil of Pasiteles, made [it]').

master, as an example in Michael Donderer's corpus of mosaic inscriptions shows: a Gallic mosaic-worker in Lillebonne signed side-by-side with his master from Puteoli, as his *discipulus*.[28] Their names, within the *tabulae ansatae*, were put clearly in parallel.

PATROCINIUM

The master did not only transmit his skills and his fame; like a father to his son, he bequeathed also his social networks, friends, and customers. In Cicero's speech, the master left to his pupil his *patrocinium*: raised, nourished, and educated during the time of his training, the apprentice belongs to his master's 'house', like his friends or his children.[29]

As is well known, the large houses of the elite became, in the late republic and during the empire, hives of economic activity where slaves, freedmen, salaried persons, and apprentices lived and worked.[30] Working there was the best way to get acquainted with customers and friends of the master. The better off the master was, the more important was the number of the *threptoi*, or persons living in.

Craftsmen, generally, did not possess the means of the Roman elite. Their workshops seem, on average, to have been rather small, especially in small towns or villages.[31] At best, they had a couple of pupils. Nevertheless, they claimed to model themselves on the masters of the big households, where *amicitia* and *philia* ruled the relationships between free persons.[32] In Egypt, too, apprentices lived with their master from dawn to dusk and even slept at their master's home when their families were far away.[33] Gravestones that

---

[28] The mosaist's signature at Lillebonne is in *CIL* 13.3225 (=*AE* 1978, 500): *T(itus) Sen(nius) c (iuis) Puteolanus fec(it)* || *et Amor, ciuis Kaletus, discipulus.* ('Titus Sennius, citizen of Puteoli, and Amor, citizen of *Cales*, his pupil, did [it].'). See Donderer (1989:108–11 (no. A86)).

[29] Cic., *Q. Rosc.* 30–1.

[30] For social relationships within the Roman house, see Wallace-Hadrill (1994).

[31] For Asian trades, see Drexhage (2007: 182–6), and, for more general views, see Kehoe (2007: 559–66), who nevertheless recognizes the existence of big workshops in great cities. Hawkins (2012) emphasizes that Roman craftsmen during the Roman Empire, when labour costs increased, preferred to 'accommodate an increasingly specialized workforce in subcontracting networks rather than in integrated firms'. But his best examples come mostly from the building industry, which is specific because of the irregular employment of workers on building sites (as we see also in Egyptian papyri). We also have evidence for permanent workshops and service industry on a greater scale in big cities or on large estates. For example, as Flohr (2011: esp. 91–3; 2013), showed, Italian fulling workshops in big cities such as Rome or Ostia can be of significant size. On this issue, see also the important and nuanced remarks of Wilson (2008).

[32] e.g. Lucian, Περὶ τῶν ἐπὶ μισθῷ συνόντων, 1 (= *On salaried posts*), where *philia* appears as a bond claimed hypocritically between the house's master and his employees.

[33] For references, see Bergamasco (1995: 127–8); see also Laes (2011: 192).

commemorate teachers and pupils, whatever their crafts were, corroborate this picture. We see apprentices, alone or as part of a group, paying for the gravestone of their master.[34] Pupils participated with family members in their homage to the deceased. Conversely, masters paid tribute to their deceased pupils.[35] Most significant gravestones placed *mathetai* after the children: in one inscription from Saittai in Lydia, a city that has revealed a great number of craftsmen's epitaphs, the *mathètès* of an unknown trade was recalled as a relative outsider, after the children and the *threptoi*—the young slaves born in the house or exposed children raised by the family—but he clearly belonged to the home that took him in: 'The 211th year, in the sixth day of Xandikos month, Ioulios and Loukios honoured their mother Eirene and so did her daughter-in-law Ammia, the *threptoi* Eirenaios and Peia, and Gaius the apprentice.'[36]

Similarly on a stone from Rome, of the Severan era, a man from Smyrna who was perhaps a doctor or a *rhetor* set up a funerary monument for himself and the members of his big household:

> To the Manes. Caius Septimius Heracleitos made [this monument] for himself and his companion Aufidia Capitolinè, for their freedmen and their descendants, for his heirs and their descendants, for Satorninos Claudianos son of Abascantos from Smyrna and his descendants, for Loucios Catilios Chryserôs, his pupil, and Marcos Gabios Dios and their descendants. As for the rest, Heracleitos, rejoice without envy, for you have to die one day, claimed by the Fates.[37]

---

[34] A sophist who taught his art in Ephesos is thus honoured by a monument voted by the local senate with a donation of his pupils: *IEph.* 1548, l. 4–5= *SEG* 13.506: κ[ατ’ ἐπίδοσιν] | τῶν μαθ[ητῶν]. Puech (2002: 455) reads κ[αὶ στησάντων?] | τῶν μαθ[ητῶν] ([statue] erected by his pupils).

[35] *IG* 10.2.1, 879. This inscription, from second-century AD Thessaloniki, shows a certain Dioscorides honouring the memory of his pupil Iulianos: Διοσκουρίδης | Ἰουλιανῷ τῷ | μαθητῇ | ἐκκ τῶν ἐκίν- | ου μνείας χάριν. See also Laes (2011: 193–4) for two other examples from Cordoba (*CIL* 11.2243) and Rome (*CIL* 6.10013).

[36] *SEG* 31, 1006 (second century AD): ἔτους σια′, | μη(νὸς) Ξανδικοῦ | ϛ′. Ἰούλιος καὶ Λούκιος | Εἰρήνην τὴν μητέ- | ρα, Ἀμμια νύμφη, Εἰρη- | ναῖος, Πεία οἱ θρεπτοὶ | καὶ Γάϊος ὁ μαθητὴς | ἐτείμησαν (I do not know how to interpret the link between the honoured woman and the apprentice. Was she his mistress or his master's wife?). For the *threptoi* in the family, see Nani (1943–4). See also Frasca (1999: 151–3), who speaks of a 'coinvolgimento affettivo implicito in questo singolare tipo di rapporto docente-discente'. A literary but important testimony of the middle of the nineteenth century, referring to a particular context of pre-industrial type of trade, seems to illustrate perfectly what we read in our Roman sources. H. de Balzac describes the familial integration of young apprentices in a Parisian shop: 'Les maîtres adoptaient leurs apprentis. Le linge d'un jeune homme était soigné, réparé, quelque fois renouvelé par la maîtresse de maison. Un commis tombait-il malade, il devenait l'objet de soins vraiment maternels. En cas de danger, le patron prodiguait son argent pour appeler les plus célèbres docteurs ; car il ne répondait pas seulement des mœurs et du savoir de ces gens à leurs parents. Si l'un d'eux … éprouvait quelque désastre, ces vieux négociants savaient apprécier l'intelligence qu'ils avaient développée, et n'hésitaient pas à confier le bonheur de leur fille à celui auquel ils avaient pendant longtemps confié la fortune' (H. de Balzac, *La Maison du chat-qui-pelote* (Paris, 1842)).

[37] *IGUR* 2.936: Θεοῖς Καταχτονίοις {Καταχθονίοις} Γ(άιος) Σεπτίμιος Ἡράκλειτος ἐποίη- | σεν ἑαυτῷ καὶ Αὐφιδίᾳ Καπετωλίνῃ | συμβίῳ καὶ | ἀπελευθέροις καὶ τοῖς | μετ’ αὐτοὺς ἐσομένοις καὶ κληρο- | νόμοις ἑαυτοῦ καὶ τοῖς ἐξ αὐτῶν | ἐσομένοις καὶ Σατορνίνῳ Ἀβα- | σκάντου Κλαυδιανῷ

These cases are, of course, rare; moreover, the inscriptions underline that some pupils were beloved and more integrated into the family. One pupil stood out from the group of his companions, because of his skills or his social origins, or because he had gained the special affection of his master: in a stone from Thessalonike, dating from the second century AD, the master *dedicator* said that the *mathètès* for whom he carved the inscription was one of his pupils (ἐκκ τῶν (μαθητῶν)).[38] On the altar from Tarragona, the beloved pupil says: *scripsi haec unus ego ex discipulis prior omnibus illis* ('I, the one and first of all pupils, wrote this').[39] He was the one who profited most from his master's relations and friends.

For the master also bequeathed to his pupils his *patrocinium*—that is, in this context, his trade and customers. This is how we should understand their insistence in recalling how much their master was cherished and popular. The altar of Tarragona emphasizes: *non uno contentus erat, pluribus gaudebat amicis . . . Reliquit suboles suae posteros stationis futuros,* | *per quos ut statio Statutiq(ue) nomen habebit,* | *tres paene aetate pares artificio ministros* ('He did not content himself with one friend, but he enjoyed many . . . He left as offspring, heirs of his workshop, through whom the workshop and the name of Statutus will remain, three servants almost equal in age and skill').

Σμυρναίῳ | καὶ τοῖς ἐξ αὐτοῦ ἐσομένοις καὶ | Λουκίῳ Κατιλίῳ Χρυσέρωτι μα- | θητῇ καὶ Μ(άρκῳ) Γαβίῳ Δίῳ καὶ τοῖς | [ἐ]ξ αὐτῶν ἐσομένοις τὰ δὲ | [λοι]πά Ἡράκλειτε εὔφραινε | [σαυτ]ὸν ἀφθόνως τὸ γάρ ποτε | [δεῖ]ν σε θανεῖν Μοίραις | μ ἐμέληται.

[38] *IG* 10.2.1, 879.

[39] *RIT* 447 = *AE* 2000, 802. I quote the reference *in integro*, for its particular interest: *Iulius hic fuerat nomine summo artificioque Statutus/tractabatque uiris aurum, mulieribus atque puellis. Plenus omni ope moribus, uita, disciplina beatus, non uno contentus erat, pluribus gaudebat amicis.* | *H(a)ec illi semper uita fuit: mane et sexta lauari.* | *Reliquit suboles suae posteros stationis futuros,* | *per quos ut statio Statutiq(ue) nomen habebit,* | *tres paene aetate pares artificio ministros.* | *Scripsi haec unus ego ex discipulis prior omnibus illis,* | *Secundinius Felicissimus ego, set nomine tantum.* | *Hoc quot potui, magister: tibi contraria munera fo[ui]?* | *Addo scriptura tuis tumulis sensus, siue exter ubique serues utque tuos amicos meque cum illis;* | *ut quotienscumque tibi annalia uota dicamus,* | *ut et uoce pia dicamus : Carnunti sit tibi terra leuis* ('This was Julius Statutus, very great by his name and art. He worked gold for men, women and young girls. Full of every kind of wealth, happy with his lifestyle, life, and profession. He did not content himself with one friend, but he enjoyed many. This was always his life: to bathe in the morning and at six. He left as offspring, heirs of his workshop, three servants almost equal in age and skill, through whom the workshop and the name of Statutus will remain; I, Secundinius Felicissimus ["very happy"], but only by name, the one and first of all apprentices, wrote this. Master, I did what I could: and I promoted gifts converse to those given by you. I bestow to your grave, by these words, ideas and feelings, in order that, everywhere, whatever stanger you may be, you could keep your friends and I among them; in order that, whenever we pronounce birthday vows for you and that we say with a pious voice: may the earth of Carnuntum rest lightly on you'). For commentary, see Gomez Pallarès (2000: 417–28), and for the interpretation of the last line see *AE* 2000, 802: Carnuntum may be the *signum* of Statutus or the place of his death, which is the interpretation I retain because of the lines 12–13 (*siue exter ubique serues utque tuos amicos*).

A Bithynian epitaph from the imperial period illustrates how an apprentice, thanks to his master, acquired many friends:

> In fond memory of you, master, I engraved this stele and set it on your grave, I Euphras, who love Vestalis, even though he lies dead, for when one has received some good, he does not forget it; he taught me his art with the greatest devotion possible; he gave me the means to live and eat, by making me a craftsman tailor dear to all my friends; after raising and teaching me his art, in the hope that he would get back from me as much gratefulness, he did not get it but died at the age of thirty-five.[40]

These lines evoke very clearly the reciprocity of favours, typical of the exchange between *amici* or *philoi*.[41] This *amicitia* motif is a privileged theme of funerary inscriptions of the *plebs media*, because it emphasizes the sociability of the deceased as well as his ties of friendship with the dedicator. There was surely a desire to imitate the sociability of the elite and to reinforce the dignity of the craftsman by depicting him as surrounded by many friends. We must dwell on this point for a while: it has been said that middle-class members, among whom we have to rank the craftsmen who celebrate, with a 'modest pride', their memory on stone, cultivated a 'class wisdom' through which they could differentiate themselves from the *infima plebs*, on the one hand, and from the civic elite, on the other.[42] To be sure, they valued their work and skills with a specific and proper emphasis, but this did not prevent them from imitating the elite to some extent: the focus on *amicitia* must be seen in that light.[43] But does this mean that there really was a specific class wisdom? I doubt it. To explain the claim of these epitaphs, it makes more sense to use the model of 'cultural revolution'—the upward mobility of popular classes and the desire to imitate the elite's culture now spread throughout the empire.[44]

---

[40] *TAM* 4, 132 = Labarre and Le Dinahet (1996: no. 76: 6). Gravestone from the area around Nicomedia, imperial period (Bithynia): μνήμης χάριν γλυκίας σῆς, ἐπιστάτα, | στήλην ἔγρ<α>ψα τήνδε κὲ ἐθέμην τάφῳ | Εὐφρᾶς ποθῶν Βεσταλιν, κὲ ἂν κεῖτε νέκυς· | ὁ γὰρ καλῶς παθών τις λήθην οὐκ ἔχει· | τέχνην διδάξας τῆς πάσης μετ' [ε]ὐνοίας | ἔδωκεν ἀφορμὴν τῆς [ζ]ωῆς κὲ τῆς τροφῆς | ράπτην τεχνείτην παρὰ πᾶσιν φίλοις φίλον· | ὅτα<ν> ἐξέθρεψε κὲ ἐδιδάξατο τέχνην, | ἐλπίζων παρ' ἐμοῦ χάριτας [—] τὰς αὐτὰς ἀμοιβὰ[ς] λαβεῖν, | οὐκ ἔτυχεν, ἀλλ' ἔ[θ]ανε πέντε κὲ τρειάντα ἐτῶν.

[41] Was there a difference between Roman *amicitia* and Greek *philia*? It depended on the cases, of course, but we may consider that the two terms were roughly equivalent: the definition of *philia* by Greek philosophers helped to theorize Latin *amicitia*. And, in practice, *amicitia* and *philia* were equally an essential social tie in imperial times, supporting exchanges of goods and services in Latin West as well as in the Greek world. On this topic, see Verboven (2011).

[42] Veyne (2005: 131–61), also insists on the *amicitia* motife. e.g. the excellent *faber tignuarius* from Arles, Q. Candidus Benignus, was also remembered by his wife and daughter as a good friend: 'he knew how to entertain his friends' (*CIL* 12.722: *'nosset qui pascere amicos'*).

[43] Veyne (2005: 137–40) underlines this elite's imitation ('ces épitaphes s'inspirent de la tradition indigène de l'éloge funèbre des grands personnages: à son heure dernière, la classe moyenne imite l'aristocratie'), which seems to me somewhat contradictory to the assumption of a specific 'class wisdom'.

[44] For discussion of this model, see Wallace-Hadrill (2008: 28–37, 435–54); Mayer (2012: 100–65) contests the model, by emphasizing the specificities of middle-class culture. I think that, even if there are some cultural peculiarities in the craftsmen's self-representation, forms of

After becoming masters of their craft, thanks to an apprenticeship, skilled 'craftsmen' belonged to the same world as the Roman elite.[45]

However, their imitation of the elite did not prevent craftsmen from appropriating in their own way other cultural models: for the Greek author of the Bithynian poem, this kind of friendship made it easier to become richer by practising the craft ('he gave me the means to live and to eat, by making me a tailor dear to all my friends'). The reciprocity of favours is here expressed in terms of economic benefits. We know indeed how *amicitia* served as a framework for economic exchanges in Roman society, allowing friends to justify and to structure deposits and guarantees, money loans, legacies, and donations.[46] In the context of crafts, these *philoi* or *amici* would include, in my opinion, both befriended craftsmen who might help the craftsman in his work and also regular customers, those who brought prosperity to his shop by their orders. In the Bithynian epitaph already quoted, the master expected his pupil to share his new 'friends'. Apprenticeship would thus be a means for the adults to control the youth's work, by demanding from them a return on investment.[47]

APPRENTICESHIP AND SOCIAL ADVANCEMENT

As we have seen, the few existing testimonies show that some craftsmen, rather than develop their own ethics, were eager to integrate into the prevailing social order, appropriating the values and moral codes of the elite, and placing public emphasis on their reputation, their life of ease, and their many friends.

Clearly, depending on circumstances, on the reputation of the teacher, and on the fortune the child owned previously, the benefits of apprenticeship could be more or less important and fast. It is not, therefore, surprising that manual crafts had attracted some members of the notability. While gravestones do not say much about the social origins of the young apprentices, Egyptian papyri remind us that, although craftsmen's children were predominant in some branches, professional training was also attractive for middle-class children, and sons of veterans or of privileged town residents. One could object that statutory origins do not always reflect levels of wealth and that these

---

imitation (in portrait sculpture or in values publicized in inscriptions) are evident. On imitation processes, see especially Tarde (1979: 205–64); see also Elias (1973).

[45] For the pride of craftsmen and their search for social recognition, see Morel (1992: 290–3); Ferdière (2001: 8).

[46] Verboven (2002; 2011: 415–18). See also Veyne (2005: 142–8).

[47] Bradley (1991: 116–18); Dixon (1999: 222); Tran (2013: 184–5).

honourable families who placed their offspring within a craftsman's house had become impoverished and expected benefits from the work of their children. However, we do not have any proof for such a scenario, while, on the contrary, we know that at least one of these middle-class families was well off.[48]

The fact that apprenticeship could attract children of a good family, not acquainted with craftsmanship, implies that economic benefits could be expected from that training. Some gravestones evoke the accomplishments of men who, having gained their skills in apprenticeship, have succeeded in reaching the top of their urban or rural community. A beautiful piece of marble, probably a statue base, inscribed on three sides and found in a large village of Pisidia, honouring a master ironsmith, very fond of his art, who executed various difficult works in iron, recalls his training, in the imperial period, in one of the most famous cities of the eastern Empire, Alexandria:

> but he [the son] behaves well and has erected a very precious monument; because of which his father, the craftsman that much loved his work and, thanks to Hephaistos's fire, worked hard to make various objects, a beloved man, is talked about by the whole of this city, and that of Alexandria, where he learned perfectly the great laborious art of working iron . . .[49]

This text shows that initiatory journeys were not reserved for the sons of important people who became artists, sophists, or physicians; the middle classes too, in this peaceful *imperium Romanum*, had the ambition to send their offspring to the best teachers of *technai*. At the end of the training the new *technitès* had the choice of remaining in the big city or returning to his native home, where he could become one of the local masters. Craftsmen do not seem to have preferred one option over the other: perhaps the choice between moving for professional reasons and settling in their local town may have been influenced by local traditions. Moreover, the fame of one's business could be local, regional, or more distant.

In his biographical dream, where a contest between Sculpture (Ἑρμο-γλυφικὴ τέχνη) and Liberal Education (Παιδεία) takes place, the Syrian Lucian of Samosate presents the benefits of apprenticeship of a *technè*: Paideia considers the sculptor's *technè* to be a synonym for *penia*—that is, poverty and anonymity—and thinks that it does not promote a man.[50] *Technè*, on the contrary, estimates that she will bring a certain comfort and social reputation to the sculptor:

---

[48] Bergamasco (1995: 112–13). The question arises about the professional future of these apprentices of good families. On this issue, see Ferdière (2001: 9) and Freu (2011: 30, 36–40).

[49] SEG 31.1284: l. 2–7 (Konana, Pisidia; imperial period): ἀλλὰ καλῶς ποιεῖ μνήμην στήσας πολύτειμον, | ἐξ ἧς τὸν γονέα, τὸν φιλότεχνον ὅλον | καὶ πυρὶ ἐργοπόνον πολυποίκιλον Ἡφαίστοιο | τεχνείτην, ἐρατὸν πᾶσα πόλις λαλέει | ἥδε κἀλεξάνδρεια, [τῇ] ἐν τέχνην πολύεργον | ἐξέμαθεν μεγάλην τήν γε σιδηρόδετον. For text and translation, see Merkelbach and Stauber (2001).

[50] Lucian, *Somn.* 11: ὁ νῦν πένης ὁ τοῦ δεῖνος ('you are a poor man now, son of no one').

If you want . . . to follow me and live with me, first you'll be generously fed and you will have strong shoulders and you will be a total stranger to envy. Moreover you will never have to go abroad, after leaving your country and your relatives, and it will not be for mere words, either, that everyone will praise you.[51]

Although the speech is only a school and literary exercise, the opposition between Paideia and Technè is not without relevance.[52] Whereas sculptors and builders were sometimes itinerant craftsmen, exporting their abilities, they might also be local craftsmen integrated in powerful associations and part of local civic life.[53] In Lucian's speech, Sculpture offers to her followers the comfort of notability. This is not so surprising: we find in fact, in the same geographical context, a parallel in a Syrian epitaph dating from the beginnings of the fourth century AD. It comes from the rich region of Apamene, which in this period was thriving. The inscription is written upon a beautiful grave with a *dromos*: the man, looking back on his career, underlines how much professional training in an unnamed trade made him prosperous, so that he could buy some lands and stay in the village, near his local deity:

This is what Abedrapsas says, giving thanks (to the God): when I was young, my ancestral god, god of Arkesilaos, having clearly appeared to me, bestowed upon me many benefits. For at the age of twenty-five, I was committed to learn the craft, and after a short period, I acquired this craft, and thanks to his foresight, I bought myself a small estate, without anybody knowing. And I freed myself from going down to town. And I was right and I was rightly led.[54]

He explains his enrichment by the benefits given to him by the local deity. However, one should be more inclined to think that the *mathèsis*, mentioned first, was the real reason for the success of his enterprise. It is very interesting to see Syrians seeking in the craft an insurance of social

---

[51] Lucian, *Somn.* 7: εἰ δ᾽ἐθέλεις . . . ἕπεσθαι δὲ καὶ συνοικεῖν ἐμοί, πρῶτα μὲν θρέψῃ γεννικῶς καὶ τοὺς ὤμους ἕξεις καρτερούς, φθόνου δὲ παντὸς ἀλλότριος ἔσῃ. Καὶ οὔποτε ἄπει ἐπὶ τὴν ἀλλοδαπήν, τὴν πατρίδα καὶ τοὺς οἰκείους καταλιπών, οὐδὲ ἐπὶ λόγοις . . . ἐπαινέσονται σε πάντες.

[52] Jones (1986: 8–10).

[53] For the integration of professional associations in public life of the Roman East, see the now classic Van Nijf (1997), to which add the more recent article by Drexhage (2007: 168–82, 189–95). Robert (1960: 30–9) sketches Lucian's first steps in the sculptor's career and the craft of marble sculptors in the Roman Empire. The craftsmen from Nicomedia or from Prokonnesos were famous all over the empire and travelled to export their skills: some had been buried in Asia Minor, Macedonia, Tripolitana, and Rome; others were involved in local guilds and stayed home (e.g. *IGBulg.* 2.674, ὑ]πὲ[ρ] τῆς συνόδου Νει- | κομηδέων λιθο- | ξόων).

[54] *IGL Syr* 4. 1410 (*Frikya* in Apamene; AD 325): ταῦτα εὐχαριστῶν λέ<γι> | Ἀβεδράψας· ἐμοῦ ἐφ᾽ ἡλικίας | ὄντος, ὁ πατρῷός μου θεὸς | Ἀρκεσιλάου, δήλως μοι φ[ε]νό- | μενος, ἐν πολλοῖς με εὐέ|ργησεν. ὡς ἐτῶν γὰρ κὲ παρεδό- | θην εἰς μάθησιν τέχνη|ς, καὶ διὰ ὀλίγου χρόνου παρέλα- | {λα}βον {παρέλαβον} τὴν αὐτὴν τέχνην, | καὶ ἔτι διὰ τῆς αὐτοῦ προνοίας | ἐπριάμην αὐτῷ χωρίον, μηδένος γνόντος, | καὶ ἐλευθέρωσα αὐτὸν μὴ καταβένιν αὐτὸν εἰ<ς> | τὴν πόλιν· κὲ ἐ<γ>ὼ δίκεος ἤμην, κὲ δικέως ὁδηγήθην.

stability: Lucian offers the same ideal in his work.[55] But, in this regard, things were complex: other regions of the empire were lands of departure for skilled migrants.[56]

CONCLUSION

Apprenticeship, when it was formally guaranteed by a contract, was thought to be an essential element of qualification and social promotion inside the hierarchy of a craft. In increasing the value of the skilled worker trained by renowned masters, outside the family, it was not really that archaic and even played a role in the functioning of the labour market. The best pupils acquired chances to improve their condition and enter the local notability by gaining friends and customers from their previous master. Even if forms of apprenticeship could vary a lot in history, the social and economic benefits of technical formation seem to be a permanent historical fact.[57]

My arguments are based on scarce evidence, that is certain. Yet I think that, as the workshops were similar everywhere, there were similar models of sociability in the Roman world, especially as the empire carried on. The small number of mentions of the kind of success that was due to the apprenticeship does not allow us, of course, to evaluate this phenomenon. Of all the pupils of a master, how many were to climb the social ladder and improve their social condition? It is difficult to tell, but it does seem that there existed some 'beloved pupils'. This becomes clear in cases where one of the apprentices was charged to write the epitaph or was mentioned among the members of the family. Moreover, evidence for the hierarchy of shop employees and workshops indicates clearly that former apprentices had different fates. In Egypt, as elsewhere, papyri show the existence of at least three groups of workers in a shop: the head, who was the most specialized of all and supervised

---

[55] See also Lucian, Πατρίδος ἐγκώμιον.

[56] e.g. Asia Minor, and especially the provinces of Pontus and Bithynia and Asia. See Pliny, *Ep.* 10, 37–42 and 61–2; in letters 37 and 39, Pliny asks Trajan, as a *legatus pro praetore* of Pontus and Bithynia, to send him skilful architects in order to help build the Nicomedian aqueduct, the theatre of Nicea, and the *balineum* at Claudianopolis. The emperor's answer (letter 40) is very interesting: '*Architecti tibi deesse non possunt. Nulla prouincia non et peritos et ingeniosos homines habet; modo ne existimes breuius esse ab urbe mitti, cum ex Graecia etiam ad nos uenire soliti sint*' ('You cannot lack architects. There is no province where there are no such skilful and inventive men; unless you think it quicker to have one sent from Rome, whereas they usually come to us from Greece'). See also Robert (1960: 30–9); Drexhage (2007: 181); Ruffing (2008).

[57] As was suggested by one of the anonymous reviewers, the Roman period was not an isolated case for the search of good masters: in the early modern period, for instance, well-reputed masters often charged premiums from apprentices who wished to learn from them.

the labour; specialized employees, who were former apprentices and earned different types of wages; and unskilled workforce.[58] Interestingly, the craftsmen who recalled their apprenticeship in their inscriptions called themselves *technitai*, skilled workers and possessors of the craft: apprenticeship was obviously very helpful to promote oneself.[59]

Thus, whatever the apprentice's former condition was, and regardless of whether he worked for himself or became a specialized employee, his earnings increased.[60] At the same time, apprenticeship also had important benefits for the economy as a whole because of the transmission and even the improvement of technical skills.[61]

ACKNOWLEDGEMENTS

This chapter has benefited from the useful remarks of Ilias Arnaoutoglou and Patrice Hamon on Greek inscriptions, and of A. Cristofori and A. Ripoll for the whole. The anonymous reviewers and the editors, Miko Flohr and Andrew Wilson, also improved it with their readings, for which I am very grateful to them. Errors remain the sole responsibility of the author.

REFERENCES

Bergamasco, M. (1995). 'Le διδασκαλικαί nella ricerca attuale', *Aegyptus* 75: 95–167.
Bradley, K. R. (1991). 'Child Labour in the Roman World', in K. R. Bradley (ed.), *Discovering the Roman Family: Studies in Roman Social History*. Oxford, 103–24.
Cribiore, R. (1996). *Writing, Teachers and Students in Graeco-Roman Egypt*. Atlanta.
Dixon, S. (1999). 'The Circulation of Children in Roman Society', in M. Corbier (ed.), *Adoption et fosterage*. Paris, 217–30.
Donderer, M. (1989). *Die Mosaizisten der Antike und ihre wirtschaftliche und soziale Stellung*. Erlangen.
Donderer, M. (1996). *Die Architekten der späten römischen Republik und der Kaiserzeit: epigraphische Zeugnisse*. Erlangen.
Drexhage, H.-W. (2007). *Wirtschaftspolitik und Wirtschaft in der römischen Provinz Asia in der Zeit von Augustus bis zum Regierungsantritt Diokletians*. Berlin.

---

[58] Freu (2011); Tran (2013).

[59] It is the case in the stele from Bithynia (*TAM* 4, 132) and in the Pisidian text (*SEG* 31, 1284).

[60] Morel (1992: 280–2), has a phrase that seems to me a good concluding word: 'un spécialiste vaut de l'or'.

[61] Tran (2013: 175–85).

Duncan-Jones, R. (1974). *The Economy of the Roman Empire: Quantitative Studies*. Cambridge.

Elias, N. (1973). *La Civilisation des mœurs*. Paris.

Ferdière, A. (2001). 'La "Distance critique": Artisans et artisanat dans l'Antiquité romaine et en particulier en Gaule', *Les Petits Cahiers d'Anatole* 1: 2–31.

Feyel, C. (2006). *Les Artisans dans les sanctuaires grecs aux époques classique et hellénistique à travers la documentation financière en Grèce* (BEFAR, 318). Paris.

Flohr, M. (2011). 'Exploring the Limits of Skilled Craftsmanship: The *fullonicae* of Roman Italy', in N. Tran and N. Monteix (eds), *Les Savoirs professionnels des hommes de métier romains*. Naples, 87–100.

Flohr, M. (2013). *The World of the* Fullo: *Work, Economy, and Society in Roman Italy*. (Oxford Studies on Roman Economy). Oxford.

Frasca, R. (1994). *Mestieri e professioni a Roma: Una storia dell'educazione*. Florence.

Frasca, R. (1999). 'Il profilo sociale e professioniale del maestro di scuola e del maestro d'arte tra repubblica e alto impero', in G. Firpo and G. Zecchini (eds), Magister: *Aspetti culturali e istituzionali*. Turin, 129–58.

Freu, C. (2011). 'Apprendre et exercer un métier dans l'Égypte romaine (Ier–VIe siècles ap. J.-C.)', in N. Tran and N. Monteix (eds), *Les Savoirs professionnels des hommes de métier romains*. Naples, 27–40.

Gomez Pallarès, J. (2000). 'Nueva lectura, con commentario, del epitafio métrico de Julio Estatuto (*R.I.T.*, 447)', in G. Paci (ed.), Ἐπιγραφαί: *Miscellanea epigrafica in onore di Lidio Gasperini*. Rome, 417–28.

Goulet-Cazé, M.-O. (1982). 'L'Arrière-plan scolaire de la *Vie de Plotin*', in L. Brisson et al. (eds), *Porphyre, 'La Vie de Plotin'*, I. *Travaux préliminaires et index grec complet*. Paris, 231–327.

Hawkins, C. (2012). 'Manufacturing', in W. Scheidel (ed.), *The Cambridge Companion to the Roman Economy*. Cambridge: 175–94.

Jones, C. P. (1986). *Culture and Society in Lucian*. London.

Joshel, S. R. (1992). *Work, Identity, and Legal Status at Rome: A Study of the Occupational Inscriptions*. Norman, OK, and London.

Kehoe, D. P. (2007). 'The Early Empire: Production', in W. Scheidel, I. Morris, and R. Saller (eds), *The Cambridge Economic History of the Greco-Roman World*. Cambridge, 543–69.

Labarre, G. and Le Dinahet, M.-Th. (1996). 'Les Métiers du textile en Asie Mineure de l'époque hellénistique à l'époque impériale', in *Aspects de l'artisanat du textile dans le monde méditerranéen (Égypte, Grèce, monde romain)*. Lyons, 49–115.

Lattimore, R. (1962). *Themes in Greek and Latin Epitaphs*. Urbana.

Marcadé, J. (1953). *Recueil des signatures de sculpteurs grecs*. Paris.

Marrou, H.-I. (1948). *Histoire de l'éducation dans l'Antiquité*, i. *Le Monde grec*. Paris.

Mayer, E. (2012). *The Ancient Middle Classes: Urban Life and Aesthetics in the Roman Empire*. Cambridge, MA, and London.

Merkelbach, R., and Stauber, J. (2001). *Steinepigramme aus dem griechischen Osten*, III. Leipzig.

Monteix, N. (2011). 'De "l'artisanat" aux métiers', in N. Tran and N. Monteix (eds), *Les Savoirs professionnels des hommes de métier romains*. Naples, 7–26.

Morel, J.-P. (1992). 'L'Artisan', in A. Giardina (ed.), *L'Homme romain*. Paris, 267–302.

Mrozek, S. (1975). *Prix et rémunération dans l'Occident romain (31 av. n.è.–250 de n.è.)*. Gdansk.

Muller-Dufeu, M. (2002). *La Sculpture grecque: Sources littéraires et épigraphiques*. Paris.

Nani, T. G. (1943–4). 'ΘΡΕΠΤΟΙ', *Epigraphica* V–VI: 45–84.

Puech, B. (2002). *Orateurs et sophistes grecs dans les inscriptions d'époque impériale*. Paris.

Puech, B. (2012). 'Transmission de pouvoir et transmission de valeurs: Les Dynasties d'intellectuels en Orient du IIIe au Ve siècle', in Chr. Badel et Chr. Settipani (eds), *Les Stratégies familiales dans l'Antiquité tardive (IIIe–VIe siècle)*. Paris, 301–20.

Robert, L. (1936). *Collection Froehner: Inscriptions grecques I*. Paris.

Robert, L. (1960). 'Épitaphes et acclamations byzantines à Corinthe', *Hellenica* 11–12: 21–39.

Ruffing, K. (2008). *Die berufliche Spezialisierung in Handel und Handwerk: Untersuchungen zu ihrer Entwicklung und zur ihren Bedingungen in der römischen Kaiserzeit im östlichen Mittelmeerraum auf der Grundlage griechischer Inschriften und Papyri*. 2 vols. Rahden.

Salvaterra, C. (2006). 'Labour and Identity in the Roman World: Italian Historiography during the Last Two Decades', in B. Waaldijk (ed.), *Professions and Social Identity. New European Historical Research on Work, Gender and Society*. Pisa, 15–38.

Schulz-Falkenthal, H. (1972). 'Zur Lehrlingsausbildung in der römischen Antike—*discipuli* und *discentes*', *Klio* 54: 193–212.

Tarde, G. de (1979). *Les Lois de l'imitation: Étude sociologique*. Paris and Geneva.

Tran, N. (2010). 'L'Apprentissage et le statut de travail des artisans en Gaule romaine', in *Aspects de l'artisanat en milieu urbain: Gaule et Occident romain*, Revue archéologique de l'Est, 28e supplément. Dijon, 195–200.

Tran, N. (2011). 'Les Gens de métier romains: Savoirs professionnels et supériorités plébéiennes', in N. Tran and N. Monteix (eds), *Les Savoirs professionnels des hommes de métier romains*. Naples, 119–33.

Tran, N. (2013). Dominus tabernae: *Le Statut de travail des artisans et des commerçants de l'Occident romain* (BEFAR, 360). Rome.

Van Nijf, O. M. (1997). *The Civic World of Professional Associations in the Roman East*. Amsterdam.

Verboven, K. (2002). *The Economy of Friends: Economic Aspects of 'Amicitia' and Patronage in the Late Republic*. Brussels.

Verboven, K. (2011). 'Friendship among the Romans', in M. Peachin (ed.), *The Oxford Handbook of Social Relations in the Roman World*. Oxford, 404–21.

Veyne, P. (2005). 'La Ville de Rome et la "plèbe moyenne"', in P. Veyne, *L'Empire gréco-romain*. Paris, 117–61.

Wallace-Hadrill, A. (1994). *Houses and Society in Pompeii and Herculaneum*. Princeton.

Wallace-Hadrill, A. (2008). *Rome's Cultural Revolution*. Cambridge.

Wilson, A. I. (2008). 'Large-Scale Manufacturing, Standardization, and Trade', in J. P. Oleson (ed.), *The Oxford Handbook of Engineering and Technology in the Classical World*. Oxford, 393–418.

9

Women, Trade, and Production in Urban Centres of Roman Italy

Lena Larsson Lovén

This chapter discusses the involvement of women in production and trade in urban centres of Roman Italy and the possibilities of identifying women's economic and professional roles in manufacturing and retail. For modern scholars, working women belong to the most invisible groups in the Roman world: literary texts do not offer detailed information about female workers and working lives and neither does archaeology. While there is epigraphic and iconographic evidence for female working lives, earlier studies have demonstrated very clearly that there is an extensive gap between the documentation of male work, on the one hand, and that of female work, on the other. The marginalization of women is obvious in any category of evidence for work and occupations in the Roman world. The scarcity of evidence has meant that female working lives were long understudied. Largely neglected by modern scholars, working women appear to us as a marginal group.[1]

The present chapter will focus primarily on how female occupations and professional identities were represented in funerary epigraphy, and discusses what this evidence can tell about female economic roles and gender structures in Roman society. The majority of the texts that will be discussed in this chapter come from the *Corpus Inscriptionum Latinarum*, and there is a certain emphasis on the city of Rome, but evidence from some other Italian cities will be discussed as well. The intention here is not to discuss an extensive list of female jobs (as has been done by some in the past), but rather to analyse how female professional identities have been documented and represented, and how socio-economic roles of women can be interpreted in relation to overarching Roman gender hierarchies.

---

[1] For an overview of previous research on work and gender issues, from the last decades of the twentieth century and the early twenty-first century, see Salvaterra (2006); see Knapp (2011) for a recent study of marginal or invisible groups in the Roman world.

APPROACHING THE WORKING LIVES OF WOMEN

Epigraphy has been used unevenly in studies on aspects of Roman economy and more rarely with the specific purpose of discussing the economic roles of women.[2] Ground-breaking work was done by Susan Treggiari in the 1970s, when she published two articles focusing on female occupations.[3] Both are based on epigraphic evidence from the city of Rome in the imperial period. Treggiari's work can be seen as part of the 1970s trend towards greater interest in women's history in general.[4] She discussed an extensive number of female jobs in the imperial household and in the domestic staff of wealthy families in the city of Rome as well as among non-domestic craftspeople and traders. These studies showed how women's work was represented in epigraphy, but they also made the gender imbalance in the documentation of male and female work in the epigraphic record very obvious: not surprisingly, the inscriptions commemorating men's work comprised a much wider range of job titles than those commemorating female work. Treggiari made several important conclusions about male and female jobs, and her work was an eye-opener to many, but it did not engage in a wider discussion of the economic and social parameters of women's work. However, Treggiari's work is still a point of departure for further studies of the occupational roles of Roman women.

After the 1970s, the history of women was gradually and partly replaced by gender studies; in the search of women or 'the female' in history, new methodologies developed. These entailed new ways of reading ancient sources and started from the notion that gaps and silences are as significant as what is actually in the sources. For instance, Sandra Joshel, in her 1992 study on work, identity, and legal status in the city of Rome, raised the issue of 'listening to silence' right at the beginning of her argument.[5] Suzanne Dixon made a similar point in her paper on the epigraphy of textile production aptly called 'How do you count them if they're not there?' Dixon argued that, in addition to what is in the sources, it is also vital to look for what is *not* there.[6] This methodological approach starts from the issue of exclusion.[7] The exclusion of information, such as on women's work, Dixon says, can be either deliberate or casual, but in both cases it is likely to have some significance.[8] Recent work by

---

[2] Edmondson (2015: 671–3).   [3] Treggiari (1975, 1976).

[4] Treggiari's paper on jobs in the household of Livia was published within a year of Sarah Pomeroy's *Goddesses, Whores, Wives and Slaves: Women in Classical Antiquity*.

[5] Joshel (1992: 3–23). 'Listening to silence' is again the argument in Amy Richlin's recent monograph on women in the Roman world (*Arguments with Silence*). Richlin (2014: esp. 1–35).

[6] Dixon (2000–1).   [7] Dixon (2000–1: 10).

[8] In her 2001 study on *Reading Roman Women*, Dixon presented a wider methodological discussion of how to read ancient genres in general, not only epigraphic sources, and discussed how male and especially female social identities were constructed through work. Dixon (2001: 16–25, 113–33).

Roth, Groen-Vallinga, and Holleran builds further upon these observations, also emphasizing the gap between the picture suggested by the evidence and historical reality.[9] In short, recent scholarship has emphasized the need for a deepened rereading of various genres and types of evidence, and for alertness to gaps, silences, and absent information. In this way, it becomes possible to reach not only a reliable, but also a more complex and nuanced, picture of female working lives, and to give women their due place in debates about craftsmen and traders in the Roman world.

JOB COMMEMORATION IN THE IMPERIAL HOUSEHOLD

In her paper on jobs in the household of Livia (1975), Treggiari used funerary inscriptions from the *Monumentum Liviae*, a *columbarium* on the Via Appia, as the basis for a discussion of jobs in the imperial household.[10] The men and women buried here were slaves and freedmen and freedwomen of the early imperial city household; more than 1,100 persons are estimated to have been buried in this complex between the later part of the reign of Augustus and shortly after the deification of Livia in AD 41. It is named after Livia, who appeared most frequently as the owner of slaves in the inscriptions from this sepulchral complex. Some of the slaves and freed persons were commemorated with a job title, and this information reveals part of the structure of this extensive household in terms of job specializations and work hierarchies. It also gives an indication of the distribution of male and female jobs. Not all jobs that could be expected to occur in this type of household are represented in the inscriptions from the *Monumentum Liviae*, but the dissimilarities in the frequency of male and female jobs are still clear.[11]

The epigraphic evidence from the *Monumentum Liviae* showed a variety of professional specialists divided over several occupational sectors, including administrators, an extensive domestic staff, and craftsmen. Among the craftsmen of the imperial household was a shoemaker and a few occupations involved in dealing with luxury goods such as some goldsmiths (*aurifices*), a silversmith (*argentarius*), a *margaritarius* (a dealer or trader in pearls), and,

---

[9] Roth (2007: 1–24); Groen-Vallinga (2013: 309); Holleran (2013: 328).

[10] The *Monumentum Liviae* no longer exists but was excavated in the early eighteenth century: Treggiari (1975: 48–9).

[11] It is important to take into consideration that the inscriptions do not give a full picture but may be reflecting only part of the staff and that they do not record the entire staff at one moment. Cf. Treggiari (1975: 57). See also Joshel (1992: 100–5) for a discussion of slaves, freedmen/ freedwomen, and occupational titles in the *Monumentum Liviae*.

possibly, a gilder (*inauratur*) who belonged to one of Livia's freedmen.[12] One inscription documents a *lanipendus*, who would be responsible for weighing the wool for the spinners—who were normally women.[13] The occurrence of a *lanipendus* may point to textile manufacturing, but, as there is only one single inscription, this does not in itself mean that textiles were produced in the imperial household: such a conclusion would require the presence of other occupational categories as well, such as spinners and weavers, who represent the central stages in the production chain. Yet no inscriptions mentioning these occupations are known from this *columbarium*.

In most job categories from the *Monumentum Liviae*, women are not attested, but some female workers appear in a group of inscriptions linked to textile work, as clothes-menders (*sarcinatrices*).[14] Only a fifth of the women from the *Monumentum Liviae* are commemorated with a job title. Treggiari noted that, on the whole, 'one striking factor in the job structure is the low proportion of women'.[15] Thus, the *sarcinatrix* appears as one of the few female jobs documented by several texts from the household of Livia Some other attestations of *sarcinatrices* are known from Rome, but they come from outside the imperial household.[16] A few examples come from other cities elsewhere in central and northern Italy.[17] Some of the *sarcinatrices* from *Monumentum Liviae* had been manumitted, but the majority of the women commemorated with this job title were slaves.[18]

WOMEN IN THE PRODUCTION AND TRADE OF LUXURY GOODS

Luxury products, such as jewellery, silk clothes, gems, pearls, gold, purple, perfumes, and more, were available in many Roman cities, and a number of occupational titles exist that reflect their manufacturing and retail. Some of

---

[12] Shoemaker: *CIL* 6.3939; Treggiari (1975: 54); *aurifices*: *CIL* 6.3927, 3945, 3949; *argentarius*: *CIL* 6.8727; *margaritarius*: *CIL* 5.3981; gilder: *CIL* 6.3928.

[13] *CIL* 6.3976.

[14] *CIL* 6.3988, 4029–31, 5357, 8903, 9038. There is also a possible male mender (*sarcinator*): *CIL* 6.4028. In Rome, evidence for *sarcinatrices* is found outside the imperial household too (Treggiari 1976: 85). The majority of the *sarcinatrices* are female slaves.

[15] Treggiari (1975: 58). The total number of women in *Monumentum Liviae* will, however, be higher, as many were commemorated after being freed and married, with no mention of a job. See also Treggiari (1976: 94).

[16] See Treggiari (1976: 85) for inscriptions of *sarcinatrices* from Rome, from the household of Livia, other imperial women, and from the Statilii family. According to Eichenauer, the total number of inscriptions of *sarcinatrices* is 26; cf. Eichenauer (1988: 94).

[17] *CIL* 5.2542 (Este), 5.2881 (Padua), and 11.5437 (Assisi); Eichenauer (1988: 96).

[18] Eichenaurer (1988: 94, n. 4).

these appear in the inscriptions from the *Monumentum Liviae*, generally
referring to male workers. In general, epigraphically attested dealers of luxury
products are men, but women have been documented in this branch of the
urban economy as well. Female perfume-sellers, *unguentariae*, have been
attested both in Rome and in Puteoli.[19] In Rome, luxury products were sold
along the Via Sacra, as is attested by several inscriptions, including the
combination of occupational titles and the name of the street.[20] An example
is an inscription listing a group of five persons who were jewellers (*gemmarii*).
The first of these is a woman named Babbia Asia, while the others are male.[21]

Other inscriptions from the neighbourhood of the Via Sacra attest traders in
purple, which was a symbol of status throughout antiquity.[22] The most
frequently recurring job title in epigraphy linked to purple products is the
purpurarius, variously interpreted as either 'producer or dealer of purple
dyestuff' or 'producer or dealer of purple products'.[23] Whatever its actual
meaning, the term has a wide distribution in urban centres in Italy from the
south to the northern regions. In addition to the evidence from Rome,
purpurarii have been found in urban centres such as Puteoli, Capua, Parma,
Chiusi, Sarsina, and Aquileia. Numerically, there is a male dominance.[24]

The most direct evidence that women were involved in purple trade and
production is an inscription from Rome that documents a group of freedwomen
who may all have been in the trade of purple products.[25] In addition to this,
there are several inscriptions from Rome mentioning *purpurarii*.[26] In some of
them, both men and women appear, but the occupational title is primarily
linked to men. These inscriptions can be used to highlight the difficulties in
reading the evidence concerning female involvement in Roman trade, production, and the Roman labour market in general.[27] One example commemorates a
couple from the Veturii family, well known for its involvement in the textile
trade. The couple is a man named D. Veturius Atticus, described as *purpurarius
de Vico Iugario*, and a woman Veturia Tryphea (Fig. 9.1).[28] The inscription does

---

[19] *CIL* 6.10006 refers to a woman in Rome commemorated by her husband after thirty years
of marriage; *CIL* 10.1965 refers to a woman from Puteoli who died at the age of 71; Treggiari
(1979a: 71).

[20] For a more detailed discussion of the commercial activities in the Forum district, see Papi
(2002); for shopping in Rome in general, see Holleran (2012).

[21] *CIL* 6.9435. All five persons were ex-slaves and two of them were manumitted by a woman,
see Treggiari (1979a: 67); Papi (2002: 58); Holleran (2013: 314).

[22] For a detailed discussion of purple as a long-lasting symbol in antiquity, see Reinhold (1970).

[23] For a discussion and various interpretations of *purpurarius* see von Petrikovits (1981: 100);
Gregori (1994: 742); Pelletier (1996: 133). See also Hughes on the discussion of *purpurarii* as
producers/dealers of purple products other than textiles: Hughes (2007: 89–91).

[24] *CIL* 5.1044 (Aquileia); 10.1952 (Puteoli); 10.3973 (Capua); 11.1069a (Parma); 11.2136
(Chiusi); 11.6604 (Sarsina).

[25] *CIL* 6.9846, *purpurar(ii)*.   [26] Gardner (1986: 238–9).

[27] Joshel (1992: esp. ch. 1); Dixon (2000–1).

[28] *NSA* 1922, 144 = *AE* 1923, 59; from the Via Praenestina; cf. Dixon (2001: 118–19).

Fig. 9.1. Purple-dealers from the Vicus Iugarius (*AE* 1923, 59). Photo: Miko Flohr.

not specify whether the woman also worked in the purple trade, but it is possible that both the man and the woman worked in a shop in the *Vicus Iugarius* trading purple products. The same can be said about an inscription of three freed people, one man—another *purpurarius*, L. Plutius Eros, who worked in the *Vicus Tuscus*—and two women, named Plutia Auge and Veturia Attica.[29] The man and one of the women are from the family of the Plutii, while the other woman is from the Veturii family. One of the women, Plutia Auge, commissioned the monument for all three of them, but the relationships between these individuals and between the two families are not altogether clear.[30] In this case, too, the occupation of the women is not specified, but both women may have been involved in the trade of purple products.[31] The inscriptions of *purpurarii* may serve as examples of how 'reading the silence' can work. When an occupational group of mixed sex occurs in an inscription with a job title in the masculine form, it is obvious that it refers to male work, but it does not exclude that women were involved in the business as well. If, in analysing the inscriptions with such job titles, women are more regularly considered, this still does not constitute direct evidence for female work, but it does offer a better understanding of women's occupational possibilities and of their roles in urban economies and the labour market.

More luxury textiles were cloth and clothes made of silk, which was imported from the east. In the early imperial period, silk clothes became highly fashionable in Rome, not just for women but also for men, which probably caused an increasing demand for silk products.[32] Most known

---

[29] *CIL* 14.2433.   [30] Gardner (1986: 238).   [31] Eichenauer (1988: 98).
[32] See Hildebrandt (2013) for a recent chapter on silk clothing in Rome.

Latin inscriptions referring to people involved in the silk trade come from the city of Rome or urban centres in its vicinity.[33] Again, most of these inscriptions document men, *sericarii*, but there is evidence for at least one female silkworker, a woman named Thymele, who was commemorated as a *sericaria*.[34]

Further specialists in luxury production are attested by two funerary inscriptions from Rome. Dating to the fourth century AD, both commemorate women who appear to have been involved in highly specialized jobs related to the textile economy. One epitaph documents a girl who was an *aurinetrix*, a spinner of gold thread; the other records an *aurivestrix*.[35] These are very specific job titles reflecting a high degree of specialization in the manufacturing economy of the Roman metropolis. However, as both are attested only once, it is hard to tell how common such jobs may have been, though it is significant that they come from the city of Rome, where demand for luxury products is likely to have been exceptionally high.[36] Sellia Epyre, the *aurivestrix* from the Via Sacra, was possibly a specialist in gold embroidery; her case is another example of the trade of luxury products in the commercial district in and around the Via Sacra (Fig. 9.2). For the *aurinetrix*, the spinner of gold thread, there is no indication in the inscription of where her work took place, but it is worth noting that the inscription is an epitaph to the memory of a girl named Viccentia, *dulcissima filia*, who died at the age of only 9 years and 9 months.[37] The girl was commemorated by her parents; while the occupation of these people is not mentioned in the text, it is possible that the girl worked in a family business where she was trained by her parents from an early age.[38]

As demonstrated by the examples discussed so far, inscriptions documenting the trade of luxury goods are found in cities throughout Roman Italy, but the lion's share of the evidence is concentrated in the Roman metropolis and its vicinity. The variation in job titles related to luxury trades reflects the

---

[33] Cf. two epigraphic instances from Tivoli commemorating the same man, M. Nummius Proculus, who was a *sericarius*; *CIL* 14.3711–12, and two from Gabii of Aulus Plutius Epaphroditus, a *negotiator sericarius*; *CIL* 14.2793 (= *ILS* 5449), *CIL* 14.2812 (= *ILS* 7601). A Greek inscription mentioning a silk specialist comes from Naples (*IG* 14.785). For examples from urban centres outside Italy, cf. also Athens (*IG* 3.3513).

[34] *CIL* 6.9892, Thymele was the slave of a woman named Marcella.

[35] *Aurinetrix*: *CIL* 6.9213. *Aurivestrix*: *CIL* 6.9214. The occupational title *aurivestrix* has also been interpreted as 'dressmaker in gold', see Lefkowitz and Fant (1992: 219, no. 321, n. 21); Gleba (2008: 63); Holleran (2013: 315).

[36] Edmondson (2015: 673).

[37] The age of death of the girl and the occupational title linked to her name raise questions about Roman child labour and at about what age a child might start specialist training for a job, but these are issues beyond the scope of the present chapter. Cf. Bradley (1991); Groen-Vallinga (2013: 305–6).

[38] On the informal training of craftsmen, see Freu, Chapter 8, this volume.

Fig. 9.2. Sellia Epyre, *aurivestrix* from the Via Sacra, Rome (*CIL* 6.9214). Photo: Roger B. Ulrich.

variety of products that were traded and consumed mainly in the capital—the primary market for a conspicuous consumption—and the evidence clearly shows that women played a role in this process as well.

WOMEN IN THE PRODUCTION AND TRADE OF EVERYDAY CONSUMER GOODS: THE CASE OF TEXTILES

If one turns to the evidence for the production and trade of more mundane goods than pearls, perfumes, and silk clothes, the production of everyday textiles may be used as an example. Textile production formed a vital part of the Roman economy, with a large number of people involved as producers, traders, and consumers. Textiles were professionally manufactured and traded, not just in Roman Italy but all over the empire, but the evidence available nowadays is scattered and limited, and has until recently been studied only to a very limited extent.[39] Nevertheless, the economic importance of textile production should not be underestimated. Through information in

---

[39] See Roth (2007: 53–87) for a discussion of evidence for textile production and especially female slave labour.

some literary sources we can get a glimpse of the development and the scale of textile production already in the Republican period. Livy, for instance, reports that towards the end of the Second Punic War, in 204 BC, Tiberius Claudius Nero, who was praetor in Sardinia, had a cargo of 1,200 togas and 12,000 tunics—a huge amount of garments—sent to supply the Roman legions serving in North Africa under Scipio the Elder.[40] Less than four decades later, in 169 BC, an even larger amount of garments, 6,000 togas and 30,000 tunics, was contracted by the urban praetor C. Sulpicius to be sent from Rome for army supply in Macedonia.[41] Cato the Elder advised wealthy estate-owners to buy cheap clothing in Rome for their slaves, as this would be more economical than having clothes for slaves made on the estate.[42] Cato does not specify the scale of the production, but his writings coincide well, chronologically, with the episodes mentioned by Livy and reflect the existence—by that time—of a market for ready-made clothes and possibly other textile products in Rome and other urban centres.

The scale of the textile economy as well as the involvement of female labour has been debated and variously interpreted over the years. In the episodes mentioned above, nothing is said about who produced the textiles contracted for the Roman army or the cheap clothing for slaves. Literary sources give us the names of various textile products, but, again, the best information comes from funerary epigraphy, where a range of occupations related to various stages of textile production and trade. The occupational inscriptions document both men and women in domestic service as well as non-domestic workers. The greatest concentration of textile-related occupations in the city of Rome comes from inscriptions of the families of the Statilii and the Veturii. In the sample of the Statilii family, there is, for example, evidence of a group of spinners, *quasillariae*, who were all women, and a couple of inscriptions of weavers: two male *textores* and one female *textrix*.[43] If we consider that spinning and weaving were two of the central stages in the chain of textile production, the epigraphic evidence of these work moments is very modest. Some more wool-weighers, *lanipendi*, occur, and interestingly there are also some women in this supervisory position as *lanipendae*.[44] As already mentioned, a *lanipendus* or *lanipenda* was primarily responsible for weighing the daily amount of wool to be given to the spinners. Yet this person could probably also have been in charge of the whole sequence of textile manufacturing in households where the entire process was performed.

---

[40] Livy 29.36. Two years later, in 202 BC, the same Tiberius Claudius Nero was elected as Roman consul.

[41] Livy 44.16.   [42] Cato Maior, *De Agr.* 1.135.

[43] Textile-workers from the *Monumentum Statiliorum*: *quasillariae*, CIL 6.6339–46; *textores*, CIL 6.6360–1, and a female weaver, *textrix*, CIL 6.6363.

[44] *Lanipendii*: CIL 3.3976–7, 6300, 8870, 9495, 37755. *Lanipendae*: CIL 6.9496–8, 34273, 37721, AE 1969–70, 49. From outside the city of Rome come CIL 9.3157 (Corfinio) and 4350 (Amiternum).

It is unusual to find a woman in a position as manager or supervisor, and the position as *lanipenda* seems to have been restricted to households outside both the wealthiest families and the imperial circle.[45] More clothes-menders, *sarcinatrices*, appear from wealthy Roman households, and, as in the case of the *Monumentum Liviae*, female workers dominate this occupation.

Occupations related to the stages in production of a finished textile product were the *vestifici* and *vestarii*. Finished cloth could be made into new garments by male and female tailors—*vestifici* and *vestificae*. These people are found among the household staff of private employers.[46] *Vestiarii* were non-domestic traders, and evidence of male *vestiarii* is found in many urban centres of Roman Italy, though the majority comes from Rome.[47] A possible female *vestiaria* appears in an inscription together with a group of men, all *liberti* who seem to have specialized in the business of delicate cloth/clothes: they are described as *vestiarii tenuarii*.[48]

The examples of women's work discussed so far have been defined in epigraphy by a number of job titles, with inscriptions linking women to a job title either on an occupational basis or as part of a group. Most of the epigraphically attested female job titles have parallel titles for men, and, in most occupations, references to men outnumber those to women. One exception appears to be the clothes-menders, the *sarcinatrices*, where the majority consists of women. The only exclusively female group appears to be the spinners, the *quasillariae*, with no obvious equivalent male occupational title.

Outside the textile economy, the same pattern, with more men than women, can be found in most other areas of production as well.[49] Shoe-making may be added as yet another example of an artisan's job pursued by several men and by some women. Most inscriptions referring to *sutores* (cobblers) refer to men. From Milan comes an inscription mentioning a *sutor caligarius*, a specialist in making boots, and from Rome comes the well-known stele of the cobbler Gaius Julius Helius, with an inscription listing his occupation and a portrait showing his professional activities.[50] However, a funerary monument from

---

[45] Treggiari (1976: 83).

[46] *Vestificae*: CIL 6.5206, 9744, 9980. According to Treggiari, there are four *vestifici* in domestic service: CIL 6.7476, 8544, 9979, and 37724; Treggiari (1976: 85).

[47] A sample of inscriptions of *vestiarii* from Roman Italy shows the diffusion from southern urban centres to the north: CIL 4.3130 (Pompeii); 9.1712 (Benevento); 10.3959 (Capua); 1.1216; 6.4044, 4476, 7378, 7379, 9962-6, and 9970-6 (Rome), 11.6839 (Bologna), 11.869, 6962a (Modena), 5.3460 (Verona), 5.774 (Aquileia).

[48] CIL 6.33920. In addition to the women, and men, involved in the production of textiles in wealthy aristocratic households, there were also those who took care of the wardrobe of the master or the mistress, the *vestiplica* (*vestipica*). For *vestipliciae*, see CIL 6.9901, 33393, 33395, 37825. One example of a *vestiplicia* from outside Rome is found in CIL 9.3318, from Castelvecchio Subrego. For the male equivalent, a *vestip(l)icius*, see CIL 6.7301, 8558-60, 9981.

[49] Treggiari (1975, 1975, 1979a); Eichenauer (1988); Groen-Vallinga (2013).

[50] Milan: CIL 5.5919. Rome: CIL 6.33914. Cf. Zimmer (1982: 137-8).

Ostia commemorating a woman named Septimia Stratonice has a partially preserved inscription and an image representing a seated woman, dressed in a simple belted tunic and holding a shoe last in her right hand (Fig. 9.3).[51] The preserved part of the inscription does not provide the job title (*sutrix*), but the image gives a clear but rare indication of a woman in her professional role as shoe-maker.[52]

MALE AND FEMALE JOB TITLES IN THE SAME LINE OF BUSINESS

A majority of those men and women who were commemorated with a job title were slaves and freed persons—people to whom work constituted a central part of their social identity. Sharing work for people in these groups was often a reason for commissioning a shared burial in the form of an epitaph or a memorial. In funerary epigraphy and iconography we meet various

Fig. 9.3. The shoemaker Septimia Stratonice from Ostia (*CIL* 14.4698).

[51] *CIL* 14.4698.
[52] Kampen (1981: 64–9, fig. 47). In the iconography of work the same tendency with fewer women commemorated at work is obvious. Holleran (2013: 218–19).

constellations of people, such as legally married couples, *contubernales*—slave couples that were not legally married—family groups, slaves, and *conliberti*, who refer to their work in words, in iconography, or through both text and image. Artisans' epitaphs including freedmen or freedwomen often indicate a working relation between them.[53] However, only rarely does it occur that male and female workers are attested with the same job title in one inscription. Yet a few examples do exist, among them two from northern Italy.[54] One example is an inscription from Milan that documents a man and a woman involved in the trade of linen textiles and explicitly mentions the occupation of both: *linarius* and *linaria*.[55] While there is more evidence of *linarii*, this particular inscription represents the only known instance of the job title in the feminine form.[56] The inscription was commissioned by the man, the *linarius* Gaius Cassius Sopater, and it commemorates not only the man himself but three freedwomen of his as well, all bearing the name Cassia. One of them, the *linaria* Cassia Domestica, was also his wife. From Turin is an inscription of nailmakers, a female *clavaria* (nail-maker), Cornelia Venusta, and a *clavarius*, a freeborn, P. Aebutius.[57]

Further examples of couples in the same line of business are from Rome. Two texts document producers of gold leaf, each explicitly mentioning a man and a woman as *brattiarius* and *brattiaria*.[58] Both men and one of the women were clearly former slaves, since freed, while the other woman, Fulvia Melema, is of unclear status.[59] A comparable form of closely related male and female work documented in inscriptions concerns men and women doing different jobs but in the same sector of production. An example is an inscription from Rome of a slave couple where both the man and the woman were involved in textile production. The woman, Musa, was a spinner (*quasillaria*), while the man, Cratinus, was a *lanipendus*.[60]

The examples discussed show women in a number of occupational roles among others as producers or traders of jewellery and perfume, dealers in purple, silk, or linens, as spinner, weaver, wool-weigher, clothes-mender, seamstress, tailor, shoe-maker, nail-maker, and more. Women also worked as salespersons of various goods, as is demonstrated by both epigraphy and iconography.[61]

---

[53] Joshel (1992: 138).

[54] Huttunen (1974: 48–9); Treggiari (1976: 98); Dixon (2001: 118).   [55] *CIL* 5.5923.

[56] One inscription from Spain attests a possible *linaria (lintearia)* from Tarragona, Spain: *CIL* 2.4318a.

[57] *CIL* 5.7320; Holleran (2013: 315).   [58] *CIL* 6.9211 and 6939; Treggiari (1979a: 66–7).

[59] In *CIL* 6.9211 the man Gaius Fulcinius Hermeros was clearly a freedman, while there is no clear indication of manumitted status for the woman, Fulvia Melema; Holleran (2013: 315).

[60] *CIL* 6.9495. For more examples of other combinations of male and female occupations in the same inscription, although not always related jobs, see Treggiari (1976: 98).

[61] See Kampen (1982, 1985) for saleswomen in iconography; Holleran (2013: 321–5).

WOMEN'S WORK: READINGS BEYOND
MARGINALITY

Discussing female work through epigraphic evidence where women have been commemorated by an occupational title will give an overview of jobs that were open to and pursued by Roman women. In several of the examples discussed, the link between the women and their work is clear and a combined female and occupational identity have been commemorated through a job title. However, many inscriptions with job titles concern a couple or a whole group of people, often both men and women. In such cases, the name of the job is normally in the masculine plural and often thought to refer to an occupation pursued by the men in the group. Readings of such inscriptions with the grammatical exclusion of women is an example of how women and female work are marginalized and more difficult to identify. Questions of women's occupational roles in such epigraphic contexts have already been touched upon, concerning the evidence of *purpurarii* from Rome. Yet another example—also from Rome—is an inscription commemorating a man named Gaius Cafurnius Antiochus and his wife, Veturia Deuteria (Fig. 9.4).[62] It includes the name of an occupation in connection to the man's name, *lanarius*, but there is no job title linked to the woman's name. Does this mean that the woman did not have a job? Did she perhaps work in the same trade as the husband? Or did she do something completely different? The exact meaning of *lanarius* is not altogether clear, but both 'producer of wool' and 'dealer in wool' have been suggested.[63] Whatever its meaning, the job title has an obvious link with *lana*, wool, and there are more examples of *lanarii* from Rome and from other urban centres in Italy such as Gubbio and Pesaro.[64] As an occupational title in epigraphy, *lanarius* exists only in the masculine. Should this be interpreted as implying that no women were involved in the work done by *lanarii*?

This particular instance, of C. Cafurnius Antiochus and Veturia Deuteria, is, furthermore, one of the few where an inscription with a job title is combined with an image including a possible occupational symbol—a sheep. The sheep is a unique symbol in the iconography of Roman textile production and underlines the close connection of this job to wool. Above the sheep is also depicted a pair of joined hands, one of them a woman's arm with a bracelet. In Roman iconography a man and a woman clasping hands—the gesture of *dextrarum iunctio*—usually symbolizes a married couple.[65] It was of particular

---

[62] *CIL* 6.9489; Zimmer (1982: no. 34), of late Republican date; Larsson Lovén (forthcoming: no. 1.1).

[63] Von Petrikovits (1981: 100); Frayn (1984: 151–2). More recently Suzanne Dixon has suggested it could be a male catch-all comparable to the female *lanifica*; see Dixon (2001: 119).

[64] Rome: *CIL* 6.94990–4, 31898, 33869; *AE* 1971, 49. Gubbio: *CIL* 11.5835. Pesaro: *CIL* 11.6367; this last inscription includes a group of men, among them two *lanarii* and two *vestiarii*.

[65] Larsson Lovén (2010), with further references.

Fig. 9.4. Funerary plaque of the *lanarius* C. Cafurnius Antonchus and his wife Veturia Deuteria, Rome (*CIL* 6.9489). Photo: Lena Larsson-Lovén.

importance for people who had not always had the right of a legal marriage, such as ex-slaves, to demonstrate their acquired rights and new status. In this case, both the man, the *lanarius*, and the woman have clearly attested their status as former slaves, but they come from different households. The woman was an ex-slave from the Veturii family. As Holleran has recently argued, female slaves could learn a trade that could make them more useful to the household.[66] After manumission, such training could become their professional basis and social identity. This may have been the case for a woman like Veturia Deutera. For a female ex-slave of the Veturii—who, as already mentioned, were known for their engagement in textiles and the dyeing trade—it does not seem unlikely that she had been engaged in some form of textile production. If one adds the evidence for marriages between people belonging to different families working in the same branch of the urban economy, it seems plausible that Veturia Deuteria was involved in a family-run textile business, first as a slave and later, in her marriage with the *lanarius*, perhaps together with her husband—but her work was not specified in the commemorative inscription.[67]

Epitaphs commemorating slaves and freed people were more inclined to document work than were those commemorating freeborn. This is particularly true for urban slaves; not all slaves and freed people were equally likely to be commemorated. A work position could influence the way people were remembered, and those with a higher position in the work hierarchy occur

---

[66] Holleran (2013: 315).   [67] For a discussion on this item, see Dixon (2001: 119–21).

more frequently in the epigraphic record than those with a job of a lower status. Thus, a supervisor such as a *lanipenda/-us* stood a better chance of being commemorated than someone who held a low-status position, such as a weaver or a spinner. This situation is clearly reflected in the inscriptions, where only a handful of weavers and spinners are documented, a very meagre body of evidence that does not accurately reflect this type of work, which must have involved an extensive number of workers.

Gender structure is another vital agency directing the modes of commemoration and of how female work was documented in the sources. The public identities of Roman women were usually not defined primarily by their work. However, the reluctance to document women at work, as we can see both in writing and in images, reflects gender roles more than a social reality. The above discussion of textile work can serve as an example of how gender structures affected the commemoration of men's and women's professional roles. Cloth production was considered to be the work of women; in an ideal world it took place in a domestic setting. In spite of the traditional view of a close link between textile production and women's work, male jobs appear much more common in the epigraphic evidence of occupations related to textile production and trade than does the work of women. Instead of information of women's professional and economic roles, the stress in ancient sources is more often on their traditional roles as wives and mothers than on their work.[68]

The absence of explicit information on female work makes the identification of women's professional and economical roles more complex. To make it possible to identify the place and role of women in the Roman labour market beyond simply mapping jobs pursued by women, a reading of the sources needs to be seen in relation to overarching gender structures. This could be done by 'listening to silence' or reading gaps and absences, as discussed at the beginning of this chapter, in order to understand what may have been regularly excluded from the sources. An example of the exclusion of women's work could be what Susan Treggiari has suggested to be a parallel between the absence of women's work in modern evidence and in ancient sources. Treggiari used the signs of shops and businesses that mention a male name in combination with 'and son(s)' or 'and co.' to reinterpret ancient sources where women have been excluded.[69] Does the absence of references to women in modern business signs mean that no women worked in there? From a present-day Western perspective most people would probably not be surprised to find women among the personnel in positions as secretaries, switchboard operators, or cleaning staff, and in other positions as well, in a business called 'NN & son(s)' or 'NN & co.', even without female names appearing in the signs

---

[68] Saller (2007); Groen-Vallinga (2013: 297–9).   [69] Treggiari (1979a: 78–9).

on public display. This forces us to think again about the information of female labour in Roman sources: in contrast to the impression the ancient sources may give, Roman women must have worked extensively in production and trade. They could work as professional partners of their husbands or in family businesses, and were allowed to make profits from their business. However, their contributions were rarely expressed in job titles on inscriptions.

Applying modern theoretical models to ancient sources may give a better understanding of female socio-economic roles, within the family and on the labour market, and by adding information from other types of evidence the picture may be more complex.[70] Ulrike Roth has discussed in-depth methods and the uses of material culture to identify the work of female slaves in agriculture—the most silent and invisible women of all—to identify their work and to discuss their economic significance.[71] Iconography is another source for the working lives of women that can add information, as has already been shown by Natalie Kampen in her pioneering study on images from Ostia of women at work.[72] At Pompeii, the paintings from the facade of what is known as the felt shop of the *vestiarius* M. Vecilius Verecundus provide a key iconographic example of a woman at work.[73] While we know the name and the job title of the man—they are written underneath his portrait on the facade of the workshop—there is no evidence specifying the name or the occupation of the woman who, in one of the paintings on the same facade, stands behind a desk to sell the products of the workshop (Fig. 9.5). The status

Fig. 9.5. Pompeii, facade to the left of shop IX 7, 7: woman selling products in shop. Reproduced from *Notizie degli Scavi di Antichità* (1912: 179).

---

[70] See Groen-Vallinga (2013) for women's work.   [71] Roth (2007).
[72] Kampen (1981); see also Kampen (1982, 1985) for studies of saleswomen in iconography. For an overall study of work in Roman iconography, see Zimmer (1982).
[73] Pompeii, IX 7, 7. *CIL* 4.3130. See also Angelone (1986).

of the woman is ambiguous, but she has been interpreted as the wife of Verecundus because of her prominent place in the iconographic representation of the workshop.[74]

Another example of a man and woman working in the same business is a funerary relief from Rome representing a scene in a butcher's shop (Fig. 9.6). The right half depicts a man at work: dressed in a tunic, he is chopping meat behind a working table. Around him, a variety of meat products and work equipment is displayed. To the left is a woman seated in a high back chair with her feet resting on a stool. She is dressed in a foot-long garment, possibly a tunic, over which she wears a mantle. Her hair is carefully arranged in a style that came into fashion during the reign of Hadrian. She is holding a set of wax tablets that probably symbolize a book of accounts.[75] By dress and pose the woman can be identified as a person of a higher status than the man, and she may actually have been the owner of the shop, the butcher being one of her workers rather than her husband. Women could take over the management of a business after the death of a husband; they could also own property and administer it themselves. They contributed to the commercial culture of Roman urban centres, but only rarely were they commemorated in their professional and economic roles; the woman in the butcher's scene is a rare example.[76] Women's work opportunities were undoubtedly more limited than those for men in Roman society, especially for freeborn women, but still some were commemorated by an occupational or a professional identity and some were obviously financially successful in both smaller and larger businesses in

Fig. 9.6. Funerary relief from Rome depicting a butcher at work and a woman doing accounting. Photo: Dresden, Staatliche Kunstsammlungen.

---

[74] Clarke (2003: 109); Flohr (2013: 282–4, figs 117–18); Holleran (2013: 316–17).
[75] Zimmer (1982: 94–5, n. 2).　　　　[76] Dixon (2004: 65).

various urban centres of Roman Italy. Women from Pompeii such as Euma-chia, Naevoleia Tyche, and Julia Felix are often mentioned as examples of women's successful involvement in business. From Ostia comes the example of a woman named Junia Libertas, who put up a long inscription telling that she left gardens, houses, and shops to her freedman/women. It is not clear what kind of business Junia Libertas was involved in, but she was obviously a wealthy woman who could afford a public legacy to be remembered by.[77] Economically successful women or those from wealthy families could be made more visible in urban centres than women of lower social status. In the imperial period, it was common practice to honour these women with statues, as happened with Eumachia, who got a statue dedicated to her in the role of priestess by the *fullones* of Pompeii. Alternatively, women could pay for statues of themselves or of family members, or could donate *publica munifi-centia* to their city. Emily Hemelrijk has shown in a number of studies how women in cities of Roman Italy and the Latin West demonstrated wealth and social status by paying for public buildings, which were given their (family) name, by erecting lavish funerary monuments, and by becoming visible in the urban landscape by public statuary.[78]

Yet another example of a woman in business is a *liberta* named Trosia Hilaria from Aquileia in the north-east. She identified herself as *lanifica circ(u) latrixs* (= *circulatrix*).[79] The woman had a funerary stele made to herself and to her freed male and female ex-slaves. There is no image on the stele to guide us further about the meaning of the unique job title, but it is quite clear that the expression *lanifica* in this case was used not as the customary praise of an industrious housewife, but rather as a job title. Trosia Hilaria, the *lanifica circulatrix*, may have been a spinner or weaver who worked on a professional basis as a pedlar in different households in the region of Aquileia, but it is also possible that she ran a small-scale business where some of her slaves worked.[80] Trosia Hilaria, and her slaves may have been collecting wool from local households, processing it, and returned it for a fee in a sort of putting-out to cottage industry. The woman had been a slave herself, but at the time of commissioning the funerary stele she was a slave-owner as well, of both male and female slaves. We have no information of how many slaves she had, but at least some of them had been freed and were buried together with the former owner. The fact that she was a slave-owner indicates that Troisa Hilaria had some financial means, but on a more modest scale than, for instance, Naevo-leia Tyche in Pompeii and Junia Libertas in Ostia. Trosia Hilaria was not without professional success or economic means, but commissioning a joint

---

[77] *AE* 1940, 94; Dixon (1992).   [78] Hemelrijk (2012, 2013) with further references.
[79] Museo Archeologico di Aquileia, inv. no. 49941 (= *AE* 2003, 115). The stele is 1.10 m high and 0.59 m wide. The style of the writing points towards a late Republican date.
[80] See Holleran (2013: 322) for a discussion of *circulatrix*.

funerary monument and grave with (some of) her manumitted slaves points more in the direction of shared work and a social identity with slaves and other manumitted persons rather than with the higher echelons in society.

DISCUSSION

Based on epigraphy, the general picture of women's occupational roles is that they were frequent in domestic service jobs, in taking care of small children, in cloth production with partly highly specialized jobs, and in the trade of some goods such as luxury products, while they are completely absent from many other sections.[81] A *prima facie* interpretation of the evidence could lead to the conclusion that this was the occupational realm of women and that most of the labour market was closed to them. Some past scholars have also fallen into this trap. For instance, A. H. M. Jones argued in his influential paper on the cloth industry under the Roman Empire that women's role in the production of textiles appeared to be of no particular significance: their foremost task was spinning, which was done in an 'entirely unorganised' way and in their 'spare time'.[82] Weaving, on the other hand, was, according to Jones, mostly done by men and regularly organized on a large scale.

In all ancient media, we are presented with a stereotyped picture of women and their professional roles, which were more often excluded than included; instead, it was their traditional family roles such as wives and mothers that were regularly stressed. This situation reflects long-standing gender ideologies: for women of various social classes it was not an occupational life, but rather life as a traditional housewife, that remained the ideal. This leads to women being represented as persons who were supposed not to work outside the home but to be dutiful and industrious within the household. In reality, however, both men and women were part of a labour market, but Roman ideologies of work, of masculinity and femininity, had such an impact on the documentation of work that women workers and their economic roles have been strongly marginalized in ancient sources. Thus, the documentation of their professional roles is a result of social conventions and Roman gender ideologies, which encouraged female identities in their family roles rather than their professional roles.

The study of Roman women has developed in many directions since scholars began to address the issue in the 1970s: new theoretical models have been applied to ancient sources, which have led to new readings that have helped us better to understand women's socio-economic roles. Reading

---

[81] Treggiari (1976); see also Holleran (2013).   [82] Jones (1960).

the evidence by trying to see not only what is there but also what is not there opens possibilities to see women as professionally active in more sectors than those that have been documented in epigraphy by a female job title. It is a way of looking beyond marginality and to see a more diversified and less stereo-typed picture of women's professional and economic roles in the labour market in Roman society as well as seeing both male and female craftsmen and traders as vital socio-economic agents in urban Roman communities.

REFERENCES

Angelone R. (1986). *L'officina coactiliaria di M. Vecilio Verecundo a Pompei*. Naples.

Bradley K. R. (1991). *Discovering the Roman Family: Studies in Roman Social History*. Oxford.

Clarke, J. (2003). *Art in the Lives of Ordinary Romans*. Berkeley and Los Angeles.

Dixon, S. (1992). 'A Woman of Substance: Junia Libertas of Ostia', *Helios* 19: 162–74.

Dixon, S. (2000–1). 'How do you count them if they're not there? New Perspectives on Roman Cloth Production', *Opuscula Romana* 25/26: 7–17.

Dixon, S. (2001). *Reading Roman Women: Sources, Genres, and Real Life*. London.

Dixon, S. (2004). 'Exemplary Housewife or Luxurious Slut: Cultural Representations of Women in the Roman Economy', in F. McHardy and E. Marshall (eds), *Women's Influence on Classical Civilization*. London and New York, 56–74.

Edmondson, J. (2015). 'Economic Life in the Roman Empire', in C. Bruun and J. Edmondson (eds), *The Oxford Handbook of Roman Epigraphy*. New York and Oxford, 671–95.

Eichenauer, M. (1988). *Untersuchungen zur Arbeitswelt der Frau in der römsichen Antike*. Frankfurt am Main.

Flohr, M. (2013). *The World of the* Fullo*: Work, Economy, and Society in Roman Italy* (Oxford Studies on the Roman Economy). Oxford.

Frayn, J. (1984). *Sheep-Rearing and the Wool Trade in Italy during the Roman Period*. Liverpool.

Gardner, J. (1986). *Women in Roman Law and Society*. London and Sydney.

Gleba, M. (2008). '*Auratae vestes*: Gold Textiles in the Ancient Mediterranean', in C. Alfaro and L. Karaki (eds), *Purpurare Vestes II. Vestidos, Textiles y Tintes: Estudios sober la produccion de bienes de consumo en la antiguidad*. Valencia, 63–80.

Gregori, G. L. (1994). 'Purpurarii', in *Epigrafia della produzione e della distribuzione: Actes de la VIIe rencontre franco–italienne sur l'épigraphie du monde romaine*. Rome, 740–3.

Groen-Vallinga, M. (2013). 'Female Participation in the Roman Urban Labour Market', in Hemelrijk and Wolf (2013), 295–312.

Hemelrijk, E. (2012). 'Public Roles for Women in Cities of the Latin West', in S. Dillon and S. L. James (eds), *A Companion to Women of the Ancient World*. London, 478–90.

Hemelrijk, E. (2013). 'Female Munificence in the Cities of the Latin West', in Hemelrijk and Wolf (2013), 65–84.

Hemelrijk, E., and Wolf, G. (eds) (2013). *Women in the Roman City of the Latin West* (Mnemosyne Supplement, 360). Leiden and Boston.

Hildebrandt, B. (2013). 'Seidenkleidung in der römischen Kaiserzeit', in M. Tellenbach, R. Schulz, and A. Wieczorek (eds), *Die Macht der Toga: Dresscode im römischen Weltreich*. Mannheim, 58–61.

Holleran, C. (2012). *Shopping in Ancient Rome: The Retail Trade in the Late Republic and the Principate*. Oxford.

Holleran, C. (2013). 'Women and Retail in Roman Italy', in Hemelrijk and Wolf (2013), 313–30.

Huttunen, P. (1974). *The Social Strata in the Imperial City of Rome: A Quantitative Study of the Social Representations in the Epitaphs Published in the CIL VI*. Oulu.

Jones, A. H. M. (1960). 'The Cloth Industry under the Roman Empire', *Economic History Review* 13/2: 183–92.

Joshel, S. R. (1992). *Work, Identity, and Legal Status at Rome: A Study of the Occupational Inscriptions*. Norman, OK, and London.

Kampen, N. (1981). *Image and Status: Roman Working Women in Ostia*. Berlin.

Kampen, N. (1982). 'Social Status and Gender in Roman Art: The Case of the Saleswoman', in N. Broude and M. D. Garrard (eds), *Feminism and Art History: Questioning the Litany*. New York, 63–71.

Kampen, N. (1985). 'Römische Strassenhändlerinnen: Geschlechte und Sozialstatus', *Antike Welt* 16/4: 23–42.

Knapp, B. (2011). *Invisible Romans*, Cambridge, MA.

Larsson Lovén, L. (2010). 'Marriage and Marital Ideals on Roman Funerary Monuments', in L. Larsson Lovén and A. Strömberg (eds), *Ancient Marriage in Myth and Reality*. Newcastle upon Tyne, 204–20.

Larsson Lovén, L. (forthcoming). *The Imagery of Textile Making*. Oxford.

Lefkowitz M. R., and Fant, M. B. (1992). *Women's Lives in Greece and Rome: A Source Book in Translation*. London.

Le Gall, J. (1970). 'Métiers de femmes au Corpus Inscriptionum Latinarum', *REL* 47bis: 123–30 (= *Mélanges M. Durry*).

Papi, E. (2002). 'La turba inpia: Artigiani e commercianti del Foro Romano e dintorni (I. sec. a.C.–64 d.C.)', *JRA* 15/1: 43–62.

Pelletier, A. (1996). 'Les Métiers du textile en Gaule d'après les inscriptions', in *Aspects de l'artisanat du textile dans le monde méditerranéen (Egypte, Grèce, monde romain)*. Paris, 133–6.

Petrikovits, H. von (1981). 'Die Spezialisierung des römischen Handwerks', in H. Jankuhn, W. Janssen, R. Schmidt-Wiegand, and H. Tiefenback (eds), *Das Handwerk in vor- und frühgeschichtlicher Zeit*. Göttingen, 63–131.

Pomeroy, S. (1976). *Goddesses, Whores, Wives, and Slaves: Women in Classical Antiquity*. New York.

Reinhold, M. (1970). *History of Purple as a Status Symbol in Antiquity*. Brussels.

Richlin, A. (2014). *Arguments with Silence: Writing the History of Roman Women*. Ann Arbor.

Roth, U. (2007). *Thinking Tools: Agricultural Slavery between Evidence and Models*. London.

Saller, R. P. (2007). 'Household and Gender', in W. Scheidel, I. Morris, and R. P. Saller (eds), *The Cambridge Economic History of the Greco-Roman World*. Cambridge, 87–112.

Salvaterra, C. (2006). 'Labour and Identity in the Roman World: Italian Historiography during the Last Two Decades', in B. Walldijk (ed.), *Professions and Social Identity: New European Historical Research on Work, Gender and Society*. Pisa, 15–38.

Treggiari S. (1975). 'Jobs in the Household of Livia', *PBSR* 30: 48–72.

Treggiari S. (1976). 'Jobs for Women', *American Journal of Ancient History* 1: 76–104.

Treggiari S. (1979a). 'Lower Class Women in the Roman Economy', *Florilegium* 1: 65–83.

Treggiari S. (1979b). 'Questions on Women Domestics in the Roman West', in M. Capozza (ed.), *Schiavitù, manomissione e classi dipendenti nel mondo antico: Atti del Colloquio internazionale (Bressanone, 25–27 novembre 1976)* (Pubblicazioni dell'Istituto di storia antica, 13). Rome, 186–201.

Zimmer, G. (1982). *Römische Berufsdarstellungen* (Archäologische Forschungen, 12). Berlin.

10

Freedmen and Agency in Roman Business

Wim Broekaert

When analysing the division of a society's workforce according to status, economic historians of the medieval or modern periods usually present tables, figures, and graphs, for statistical evidence neatly illustrates which status group conducted a specific trade and offers an explanation for the dominance or absence of particular status classes in the professional world. Yet, when trying to analyse the relationship between status and work division for the Roman world, this kind of evidence is generally lacking. The reasons are all too well known. First, archival records in which a person's profession and status were explicitly cited are virtually absent, with the obvious exception of Egypt. Secondly, serial analysis of occupational inscriptions has turned out to be a less than ideal alternative. Limitations include the inevitable loss of thousands of texts and the so-called epigraphic habit, which forces us to reconsider the actual value and representativeness of the surviving inscriptions.[1] We need to take into consideration that some social groups were far more likely to be commemorated in an inscription than others, and that many reasons may determine whether or not to include a profession and status marker. Regional differences in the epigraphic habit also blur the overall picture of the Roman workforce. Particularly striking is, for example, the fact that the epigraphy of the Spanish and African provinces so far has yielded only a handful of inscriptions mentioning traders, even though one would expect several traces of the activity of merchants and shippers, as both regions are rich in epigraphic remains and played a crucial role in Rome's food supply. Yet it seems that merchants originating from these provinces mentioned their trade only when erecting an inscription in an area where citing one's profession was part of the local epigraphic habit. Most telling are the inscriptions of the oil merchant L. Marius Phoebus. His name, without any additional information, features among the initiators of a monument located in Cordoba, presumably his

---

[1] MacMullen (1982); Mouritsen (2001, 2005).

native town, but only his epitaph in Rome mentions his profession.[2] In this particular case, one might argue that the nature of the inscriptions (dedicatory versus funerary) determined whether or not to include a profession. This is not an isolated instance, for it is probably no coincidence either that African shippers and merchants decorated their offices on the Piazzale delle Corporazioni in Ostia with mosaics identifying their profession and cities of origin, but that so far none of these cities has yielded a contemporary inscription of a *negotiator* or *navicularius*.[3]

Still, despite these difficulties, the importance of status easily features among the most contested topics of Roman trade and, in a wider sense, the Roman economy. No ancient historian will deny that a major part of commerce was conducted by slaves and freedmen, but the consequences of having trade run by legally dependent and semi-dependent businessmen have been hotly debated. This chapter therefore aims to discuss the importance of status and dependency in the organization of Roman trading.

The outline of the text is as follows. First, I will briefly sketch out the role attributed to status and dependency in earlier discussions of Roman trade and the apparent evolution in assessing both features. The second section will discuss the relationship between principals and agents and rely on several case studies to illustrate how agency by freed businessmen was organized. The third section focuses on the ratio of economic dependence and independence among freedmen. A final section will offer some concluding remarks.

STATUS, DEPENDENCY, AND AGENCY IN HISTORICAL RESEARCH

Since the 1970s, economic historians have tried various ways to incorporate the notion of status in the analysis of the Roman economy. For some, the status of people engaged in trade determined the very nature of the economy and proved to be a crucial part in assessing the economic performance of the Roman business world. For others, status mattered only in describing the economic relationship between patrons and freedmen and the analysis of aristocratic portfolios. This section offers a quick overview of the dominant views.[4]

Every discussion of status and dependency in the Roman trading world obviously starts with Finley's *The Ancient Economy*. Finley and the adherents of the substantivist view argued that status is a crucial trait of Roman business, which therefore clearly separates the Roman economy from contemporary economies. They claim that the way of organizing a business enterprise and

---

[2] Cordoba: *AE* 2000, 734. Rome: *CIL* 6.1935. See also Remesal Rodríguez (2000).
[3] *CIL* 14.4549.10–14, 17–19, 21–2, 34–6, 38–9.   [4] Schleich (1983); Andreau (1995).

spending profits was heavily influenced by the status of the people involved: economic behaviour is completely determined and even predictable by the place one occupies along the 'spectrum of statuses'.[5] The substantivist model thus centres around a proposed bipolar structure of the Roman economy. At one end of the economic spectrum, we find people of freeborn status and social prominence concentrating on agriculture and recoiling from the risks of financing trade and industry, so that these last two sectors of the economy remained deprived of major capital investments. The other end consists of people of low and freed status who did not have sufficient means to run their own estate and were thus forced into a profession in trade and industry. Being freedmen and foreigners, they could rely on only a small starting capital and limited means of investment. Small-scale trade and commercial failure was the evident consequence.

This model thus relies on two interrelated premises. First, the economic world of the aristocracy, specializing in agriculture, is virtually separated from that of the lower social strata, which engaged in trade and industry. Agency by slaves and freedmen or silent partnerships were only a marginal phenomenon in the economic decision-making of the Roman aristocracy.[6] This economic dichotomy can easily be recognized in Finley's description of the business community in Gaul, clearly separating the freed and foreign merchants from the local aristocracy.[7] Castrén offered a similar description of the Pompeian society, in which he stressed the differences between freedmen dominating urban production and commerce, and the landed aristocracy.[8] Secondly, as soon as a businessman becomes wealthy and powerful, he immediately turns away from commerce to live as a landed aristocrat. Money made in trade and industry never returned to the business world to start a new enterprise, but was used to invest in land and to enhance the merchant's social prominence by ostentatious display of wealth and benefactions.

With a landed elite shunning investments in commerce, the Roman business world was apparently doomed to failure, inefficiency, and small-scale transactions. Yet, despite his categorical conclusion, Finley duly recognized that his model relied mainly on literary evidence and that scrutinizing the epigraphic evidence might adjust, even alter, the picture of the Roman trading world. Only recently has this call been answered by a few researchers who have ventured on a systematic analysis of Greek and Roman occupational inscriptions.[9]

The substantivist model met severe criticism, most notably in the work of John D'Arms, who claimed that Finley's sociological model could indeed work for a few members of the imperial upper class, but did not accommodate the

---

[5] Finley (1973: 68, 87).   [6] Finley (1965: 37; 1973: 57–9).   [7] Finley (1973: 59–60).
[8] Castrén (1975: 121).
[9] Ruffing (2008); Broekaert (2011, 2012a, b). Joshel (1992) offers an interesting sociological insight into the occupational world of Rome, but is disappointing for economic historians.

economic portfolios of the majority of the senators, knights, and members of the local urban aristocracies.[10] He convincingly argued that the imperial and municipal aristocracy did invest in trade and industry, but only indirectly, by relying intensively on their slaves and freedmen. Nevertheless, his model provided for major capital injections in business by the Roman aristocracy. Hence, with the presumed bipolarity of the economy adjusted, the importance of status in the organization of Roman trade evidently dwindled and status lost its meaning as a variable in the assessment of the performance of the Roman economy. Nonetheless status did not disappear completely. In D'Arms's model, members of all status groups apparently engaged in commerce, but assumed different roles: high-status groups only invested in trade, while dependent, lower-status groups were responsible for the actual day-to-day business deals and voyages. The Finleyan gap between high and low status was bridged, but it did not disappear.

In 2007, a new analysis of the interrelation of dependency and agency was put forward in the *Cambridge Economic History of the Greco-Roman World*, in which the rich contributions of the New Institutional Economics were applied to the ancient business world.[11] This modern analytical framework describes how law and institutions influence and shape a society's economy and try to find solutions to inherent constraints. One of the topics most relevant for this chapter concerns agency. It is well known that agency always suffers from a major inhibitory problem—namely, the risk of assigning an untrustworthy agent. One always has to reckon with the problem of information asymmetry, for the agent usually has far more information and immediate control of the economic activities than his principal, so the latter may be unable to closely supervise and assess his agent's decisions. Hence, the agent may be tempted to neglect his principal's interests or to capture part of the investments and profits. To prevent this, the principal must either offer sufficient incentives to his agent, or be able to have recourse to additional control mechanisms. This is where the real value of working with dependent managers becomes apparent, for legal and social dependency can be crucial assets in monitoring the actions of an agent. Freedmen, for instance, could be obliged by their patron to perform well-defined *operae* or services. Ulpian asserted that a freedman is under a natural obligation to perform services for his patron.[12] If a patron stipulated that managing his affairs belonged to his freedman's *operae*, then neglect, theft, and any other kind of fraud would be interpreted as a refusal to perform legally compulsory services and would hence be liable to punishment. Patrons were well aware of the potential benefits this *operae*-system had to offer, for one of the categories comprised *operae fabriles* or professional services, with very few restrictions as to the nature or setting of

---

[10] D'Arms (1977, 1981). [11] Frier and Kehoe (2007: 122–34). [12] *Dig.* 12.6.26.12.

the services.[13] Additionally, the deliberately vague duty of *obsequium* or compliance, which every freedman was obliged to follow and which included gratitude, obedience, and respect to one's patron, may also have eased agency. Paul, for instance, states that 'a freedman is ungrateful when he does not show proper respect for his patron, or refuses to administer his property, or undertake the guardianship of his children'.[14] Thus, freedmen who operated as managers and deceived or robbed their patron clearly violated the *obsequium*. In theory, this legal obligation was thus supposed to stimulate freedmen to behave as trustworthy and honest business agents.

This short overview has stressed the changes in assessing the role of status and dependency in the Roman business world. From an apparent structural weakness hampering the growth of the economy at large in the substantivist model, status and dependency have become important features easing agency and stimulating large-scale business ventures.

So far, however, the analysis of Roman agency has predominantly relied on legal sources, and for obvious reasons: business management by slaves is meticulously analysed in the various *actiones adiecticiae qualitatis*, and agency by freedmen is regularly hinted at when the patron's rights are discussed.[15] This chapter, on the other hand, intends to adduce mainly inscriptional evidence to clarify the interaction between dependency and agency by freedmen and assess whether inscriptional evidence fits the model of freedmen as managers par excellence. The discussion will focus on three main topics.

First, all three models accept that aristocratic patrons did not engage in trade personally. Apparently, in this respect status continues to matter for the organization of the Roman business world. But was it actually true that high-status investors never took an active part in the decision-making and merely provided financial back-up and infrastructure to their freedmen in exchange for a share in the net return?

Secondly, when agency by freedmen provided a solution to the dangers of information asymmetry, how did principals actually employ their agents? Is inscriptional evidence able to offer some insights in the actual structure of agency and the tasks assigned to freedmen?

Thirdly, if agency by freedmen proved to be a successful tool in organizing business, why would patrons ever forgo the opportunity of using their former slaves as agents? Do inscriptions allow us to detect economically independent freedmen?

---

[13] *Dig.* 38.1.16–19 and 38.1.26 pr.; Waldstein (1986).
[14] *Dig.* 37.14.19. Cf. also *Dig.* 1.12.1.10, 1.16.9.3 and Joshel (1992: 33–4).
[15] Kirschenbaum (1987); Wacke (1994); Földi (1996); Stelzenberger (2008); Gamauf (2009). Aubert (1994) also includes inscriptional evidence, but focuses mainly on production and shop management.

TRADE AND THE ROMAN ARISTOCRACY: TRACING THE INVISIBLE

The Roman aristocracy apparently attached high value to two attitudes towards the sources of wealth on which the family fortune was based: highlighting the virtues of the socially respectable gentlemanly absentee landownership, and creating as much distance as possible between personal engagement and investments in commerce. Yet surely some members of the aristocracy had a keen eye for business and may have preferred closely to monitor their agents' activities or even to organize part of the enterprise themselves. The lack of archives and the loss of correspondence between investors and managers prevent a straightforward substantiation of this assertion, yet inscriptions mentioning merchants may provide some telling hints.

The most famous example is that of Sex. Fadius Secundus Musa.[16] In AD 149, Musa was honoured as a rich and generous magistrate in his native city of Narbonne.[17] His name also occurs on twenty-five *tituli picti* on Spanish oil amphorae, all discovered on Monte Testaccio in Rome.[18] These *tituli* identify the merchant distributing the vessel's contents, so there can be no doubt that Musa, a municipal aristocrat, was personally engaged in commerce. Yet, one could argue that perhaps Musa was shipping oil only before joining the local upper class and that his rise in the Gallic society started only when he had retired from trade, so no deprecation would hinder his political career. Luckily, however, the *tituli picti* are carefully dated. The monumental inscription from AD 149 remarked that, by then, Musa had attained every single function in the local *cursus honorum*. Moreover, the family's social mobility did not end there, for the text also stresses that his grandson Iucundus had joined the *ordo senatorius*. Apparently, one of Musa's children married a member of the senatorial aristocracy. Surely one would expect that the Gallic Fadii by then had started imitating the lifestyle of the rich and famous and shunned away from trade. Yet, the *tituli* mentioning Musa's name prove otherwise. His engagement in the oil business ranges from AD 146 to 161, so we can safely conclude that, both during his political career as well as after having reached the highest functions and married one of his children to a member of the imperial aristocracy, Musa continued shipping Spanish oil to Rome. *Tituli* also attest to the presence in the oil trade during the same period of other members of the Sexti Fadii, whose freedman status is indicated by their Greek *cognomina* and who most likely belonged to Musa's *familia*.[19] We thus encounter a socially prominent patron, a wealthy member of the Gallic aristocracy who personally engaged in trade and launched

---

[16] Héron de Villefosse (1915).   [17] *CIL* 12.4393.

[18] *CIL* 15.3863–73a–p.

[19] *CIL* 15.3855–61a–d (Anicetus); Rodríguez Almeida (1972: no. 16 [Antiochus]) and *CIL* 15.3862 (Paon).

several of his freedmen in the same business. Musa was responsible for the decision-making and organization of the oil trade and had at least the opportunity of closely monitoring his freedmen. He may even have cooperated with them in a commercial partnership, for seven *tituli* document a *societas* of Fadii.[20] Sadly, these *tituli* never cite *cognomina*, so we cannot know for sure whether Musa had concluded a partnership with his freedmen or the latter were cooperating without their patron's personal involvement. The rich dossier of the Sexti Fadii indeed neatly illustrates how prominent patrons could move across the boundaries of status and work in the same economic environment as their freedmen.

For the next example illustrating the simultaneous presence of aristocratic merchants and their freedmen in trade, we turn to the Ostian grain market. Given the importance of Rome's port in organizing the imperial supply system, Ostia must have housed a large association of grain merchants. One of its most prominent members seems to have been P. Aufidius Fortis, who was doing business during the second quarter of the second century AD. He originated from the African city of Hippo Regius, where he was elected a *duovir*. Yet he appears to have left his native city and settled permanently in Ostia to organize his trade. There he again quickly rose to the ranks of the local elite, for an honorary inscription initiated by the *mercatores frumentarii* mentions that he attained the functions of *decurio*, *duovir*, and *quaestor aerarii Ostiensium*.[21] Wealth and prestige made Fortis one of the most influential Ostian businessmen, with extensive connections in the local professional associations. The *fabri* granted him the honorary title of *praefectus*, the grain-measurers and divers elected him a patron, and his own association of grain merchants honoured him as *quinquennalis* for life. In AD 146, Fortis eventually became patron of the city, a distinction he celebrated by donating two silver statues and organizing games for three days.[22] Fortis was not the only Aufidius who engaged in the grain trade. Around the middle of the second century, the Ostian grain merchants dedicated a statue to Q. Calpurnius Modestus, a *procurator ad annonam*. The inscription on the pedestal mentions several of the association's magistrates, among them P. Aufidius Faustianus, a *quinquennalis*, and P. Aufidius Epictetus, a *quaestor*.[23] These grain merchants, whose *cognomina* suggest a freed status, obviously belonged to the same family as Aufidius Fortis. Another Ostian inscription clarifies the exact relationship, for both Faustianus and Epictetus, together with their *coliberti* Euphrosynus and Ianuarius, feature among the initiators of a statue, dedicated to their former master Fortis.[24] The same four freedmen also financed the erection of yet another statue, this time in honour of P. Aufidius

---

[20] *CIL* 15.3874; Rodríguez Almeida (1991: no. 3) and Blázquez Martínez and Remesal Rodríguez (2003: nos 61–6).
[21] *CIL* 14.303 and 14.4621.   [22] *AE* 1946, 204.   [23] *CIL* 14.161.
[24] *CIL* 14.4621.

Fortis *iunior*, the homonymous son of their patron.[25] We can thus follow the continuation of the family's interests in the grain trade. Are we to assume that Fortis was still monitoring his freedmen's actions? It seems at least very likely that Fortis's personal engagement did not end with his rise in Ostian society. When his colleagues in the grain trade honoured Fortis as *quinquennalis perpetuus*, he was already a member of the city council and had been elected *quaestor aerarii* four times. Moreover, the fact that both Epictetus and Faustianus managed to rise in the ranks of the *mercatores* and hold magistracies in the association when their former master still held the highest magistracy can hardly be a coincidence. Being freedmen of Aufidius Fortis apparently guaranteed them a favourable starting position, protection, and success in the grain trade. This again suggests that Fortis, as a lifetime member and magistrate of the association actively supported his agents. We can imagine he shared his experience and commercial network and provided financial back-up.

These two case studies suggest that at least some local aristocrats with commercial interests did far more than merely financing their freed agents' business. Some, like Fadius Secundus, may have continued trading, even after having introduced several freedmen into the same business, and perhaps cooperated with them in partnerships. Others, like Aufidius Fortis, used their privileged position in professional associations to support not only their agents' business, but also their rise within these associations. These aristocratic businessmen can hardly be styled absentee investors, but seem to have actively monitored and sustained their agents' transactions. How exceptional or commonplace this kind of cooperation really was is still difficult to tell, for more detailed prosopographical analysis of local aristocracies, their freedmen, and sources of wealth is called for. With the current state of knowledge, however, this kind of personal engagement in business by local elites apparently did occur, but still seems to be rather uncommon.

MODELLING ROMAN AGENCY:
A FREEDMAN IN EVERY PORT

When discussing the nature of agency in the Roman business world, the focus often turns to agency by slaves, and for good reasons. Legal sources succinctly analyse the *actiones adiecticiae qualitatis*, determining the liability of each partner and documenting the presence of slaves in shops, land transport, and maritime trade. Literary texts, too, frequently hint at slaves active in business.[26]

---

[25] *CIL* 14.4622.   [26] Lucian, *Nav.* 13; Plut. *De lib.* 7; Libanius, *Ep.* 177.1.

The information on freed agents, however, is not systematically discussed by the Roman jurists, for, theoretically, there was no need for a distinctive body of laws structuring the cooperation between a patron and his freedman. From a legal point of view, both were citizens with the right to enter into a standard labour contract, which legalized the agreement, so no additional clauses concerning liability were necessary. The consequence is that only mere glimpses of agency relations between patrons and former slaves survive. Still, legal and literary sources suggest that management by freed agents was very similar to the way in which slaves were running their masters' business. Paul, for instance, depicts the difficulties of agency in commercial enterprises beyond the sea and makes no distinction between slaves and freedmen.[27] Papinianus describes how a master had a slave working as a manager in banking, and the same business was carried on by his freedman after he had been given his freedom.[28] Cicero notes that freedmen were used to administer business in distant provinces, in the same way as slaves did.[29] These sources suggest a continuity between management by slaves and freedmen. Not surprisingly, for freedmen often performed the same professions already entrusted to them when they were still slaves. Manumission hardly ever entailed a rupture with the patron's family and previous labour experience, because freedmen often continued to live in the patron's house and kept close relations.[30] The location of workshops, shops, and *tabernae* directly linked to large residential houses presumably belonging to the urban elite can in fact reflect this extended cooperation.[31] Continuing relationships indeed made perfect sense, for a prolonged cooperation offered benefits to both the patron and the freedman. The former had invested time and money in teaching his slaves a trade; he had had the opportunity to assess their character, aptitude for business, and honesty, most likely based on previous experience when his slaves were still managing their *peculium*; he would now be able to rely on a well-known and trusted pool of skilled labour, instead of having to train new and potentially unreliable slaves; and he could expect favourable terms of cooperation. The latter continued to benefit from their patron's investments, business connections, and the infrastructure necessary to conduct their trade; they were able to exploit previous experience and networks; and were not forced to seek either another profession and new training or initial capital to continue their trade independently.

If freedmen indeed continued to cooperate with their former master, and agency by slaves or freedmen was very similar from an organizational point of view, one may wonder why manumission was at all necessary. The answer is

---

[27] *Dig.* 40.9.10.   [28] *Dig.* 14.3.19.1. See also *Dig.* 26.7.58.pr.   [29] Cic. *Fam.* 13.33.
[30] Plin. *Ep.* 2.17.9; *Dig.* 7.8.2.1 and 7.8.6; Fabre (1981: 131–40); Kirschenbaum (1987: 135–8); López Barja de Quiroga (1991: 163–4).
[31] Wallace-Hadrill (1994).

provided by the legal background to agency. As long as the agent remained under the *potestas* of his master, agency was regulated by the *actiones adiecticiae qualitatis*, which made the master liable for the business transactions of his slave agent. Business partners of his agent could therefore bring the master to court to claim damages. Once, however, the agent had been manumitted, he became a person *sui iuris*. As a freedman, he could represent his patron in court, join commercial partnerships with his patron, and cover all legal aspects of agency. He was now completely liable for his business deals. A patron investing in trade by relying on a freedman was thus never responsible for any of the damages a partner of his agent incurred. No wonder, then, that Ulpian mentions that slaves were manumitted in order to become agents or that Gaius notes manumission before the age of 30 was allowed in cases where a patron wished his former slave to become an agent.[32] This regulation was indeed very advantageous to patrons, but not to the agent (for he continued to be liable) or the agent's business partners (for they were never able to recover the damage from the principal). By the end of the second century AD Roman law recognized this discrepancy in responsibility and decided to protect agent and partners with the introduction of the *actio quasi institoria*. Now the principles of agency for agents *in potestate* also applied to free persons (freed or freeborn), and the principal was liable for all transactions conducted by his representatives.[33] However, long before the introduction of this *actio*, several other agency regulations, which made representation by free persons (including freedmen) easier, were provided for by Roman law, such as *mandatum*, *negotiorum gestio*, and *procuratio*.[34] Their applicability for agency by freedmen would repay detailed analysis, but cannot concern us here, for none of them left any trace in the epigraphy of the Roman business world. Suffice it to say that Roman law duly recognized that indirect agency by free persons was an essential part of the Roman trading world and required separate legislation.

In short, many slaves working in the service of their master must eventually have been manumitted to become, as Fronto calls them, *liberti fideles ac laboriosi*.[35]

When trying to model management by freedmen, we need to account for a large variety of agency relationships. On one side of the model, we have a patron who is monitoring every single phase of the enterprise, who insists on making the important decisions and assigns only small tasks to his freedmen with little or no independence. On the other, we have a patron who is merely financing or enabling business ventures, who completely relies on his freedmen for the practical organization, and expects only a rent or share in the profits. To capture these differences, we need to reckon with three main variables.

---

[32] *Dig.* 40.2.13; Gai. *Inst.* 1.19.
[33] *Dig.* 3.5.30, 14.3.19, 19.1.13.25. Kirschenbaum (1987: 142–3); Aubert (1994: 91–5).
[34] Aubert (1994: 105–12); Verboven (2002: 227–51).   [35] Fronto, *Ep.* 2.7.2.

First, the social status of the patron. The higher he ranks among the local aristocracies and the closer his involvement in politics or other magistracies, the less likely he will be personally engaged in business. The previous section, however, made clear that there are exceptions to this rule. The patron's wealth and place in society also determine the magnitude of his household and thus the amount of freedmen he will be able to rely on. The number of potential agents is again crucial to the scale of business and the possibility of constructing networks of agents.

Secondly, the geographical range of the enterprise. A freedman working in or close to the city where his patron lived could easily be monitored by the patron himself, his family, or friends. On the other hand, when a freedman was doing business in distant places, control was far more difficult. The patron could then either put his trust in the agent's honesty and aptitude for business but run the risk of being cheated, or try to create 'check points' by placing other freedmen in ports along the route his freedman was frequenting, thus creating a network of agents. As a few case studies will indicate, this strategy proved to be particularly efficient in long-distance trading.

Thirdly, the nature of the merchandise. When an agent was managing high-value merchandise, a patron may have wished to try and protect his investment by monitoring his freedman's actions by either interfering personally or relying on his network of freedmen. When, on the other hand, small or low-value cargoes were marketed, the loss of which would cause only minor damage to the patron's portfolio, strict control may not have been worth the effort.

With these variables in mind, we can now construct a typology of agency by freedmen in Roman trade and try to fit in the dispersed data epigraphy has to offer. Six basic levels of agency can be distinguished.

Freedmen sell the merchandise they receive from their patron

This category unites all freedmen marketing agricultural surpluses from their patron's estates or other merchandise produced or supplied by the patron. They either run a shop, often situated close to the patron's workshop, travel around to distribute merchandise, or even settle in distant markets. This organizational scheme must have structured a major part of agency relations, yet is rather difficult to trace in epigraphy. Nonetheless, the following case studies may reflect this particular business organization.

We first focus on the wine trade. During the first quarter of the second century, a certain Caedicia M.f. Victrix was producing Dressel 2–4 wine amphorae in the vicinity of Sinuessa, a city located slightly to the north of Naples.[36] It seems likely she was a descendant of L. Caedicius, a *duovir* in the same city mentioned in an

---

[36] Manacorda (1985: 143–4) and Tchernia (1996: 209).

epitaph of the late first century BC, and thus belonged to the local aristocracy of Sinuessa, and possessed estates in the vicinity of the city.[37] The amphorae produced in her workshop may have been used to transport wine grown on the family's estates. During the same period, the freedman A. Caedicius Successus occurs in two inscriptions from Ostia, where he was a magistrate of both the *seviri augustales* and the *navicularii maris Hadriatici*.[38] This association of shippers seems to have specialized in the distribution of wine, for two colleagues of Successus, L. Scribonius Ianuarius and Cn. Sentius Felix, were also engaged in the wine trade.[39] Consequently, the *gens* Caedicia may very well have been producing wine on their estates, making amphorae in workshops, and relying on freedmen such as Successus to ship the wine to the capital and provincial markets. Moreover, Festus notes that several *Caediciae tabernae* were sited along the Via Appia.[40] Perhaps the Caedicii were also involved in organizing local distribution and had other freedmen and slaves running various inns.

A second case-study centres on modes of business organization in the second-century Spanish oil trade. Several *tituli picti* on Dr. 20 oil amphorae identify merchants belonging to the *gens* Aemilia. It seems, however, that two different branches of the Spanish Aemilii had interests in the oil trade, the MM. Aemilii and the LL. Aemilii. When the status of the merchants belonging to these families is compared, a remarkable difference can be traced. The MM. Aemilii all have Latin *cognomina*, none of which clearly points to a freed status.[41] The LL. Aemilii, on the other hand, are represented by a freedman, Onesimus, and another merchant, whose *cognomen* is now illegible.[42] An explanation for this striking difference may be offered by Baetica's monumental epigraphy. MM. Aemilii frequently occur in the epigraphy of cities bordering the Guadalquivir, where most of the Spanish oil was produced, or in Cadiz, from where the oil was exported.[43] Yet not a single inscription explicitly linked the MM. Aemilii to the local aristocracies. So far, it seems this family was part of the wealthier levels of the *plebs media*, but never advanced to the ranks of the elite. The LL. Aemilii, on the other hand, belonged in several Baetican cities to the ruling classes and were seated in the city council of Carmona, Montemayor, Arjona, and Villanueva del Rio.[44] They no doubt possessed several oil-producing estates in the vicinity of these cities and were marketing

---

[37] *AE* 1986, 153.   [38] *AE* 1959, 149 and *AE* 1987, 191.

[39] *CIL* 6.9682 and 14.409. De Salvo (1992: 433).   [40] Festus, *Verb. Sign.* 39L.

[41] Rodríguez Almeida (1972: no. 3: Cutianus); *CIL* 15.4084a–b: Pastor; Rodríguez Almeida (1979: no. 20: Rusticus).

[42] Rodríguez Almeida (1994: no. 5: Onesimus). *CIL* 15.3695a–b (Alt[—]).

[43] *AE* 1974, 380 (El Rubio); *AE* 1982, 559 (Jerez de la Frontera); *CIL* 2.1350 (Ronda); 2.1487 (Ecija); 2.1752–3 (Cadiz); 2.5539 (Peñaflor); 2.7.81 (Arjona); 2.7.812a (Fuente Obejuna); 2.7. 949 (Cabeza del Buey); *ILS* 6920 (Montellano).

[44] *CIL* 2.1378; 2.1535; 2.2106 and *AE* 1972, 265 respectively. See also *CIL* 2.2150, a funerary inscription of C. Pomponius Marullus, a *duovir* in Bujalance, dedicated by his relatives L. Aemilius Avitus and C. Pomponius Lupus.

surpluses, for which they relied on the family's freedmen. The MM. Aemilii apparently did not belong to this upper class and organized the distribution of oil themselves. This way each family's background may account for the differences in organizing trade.

A final case study introduces the freedman M. Volcius Herma, an ivory merchant who was running a shop in Capena, a city located slightly to the north of Rome.[45] His tombstone was decorated with a relief, depicting Venus, Amor, and a large elephant, symbolizing his trade. When the *gens* Volcia is traced in monumental epigraphy, it appears that, apart from a few inscriptions in Italy, the Volcii were living mainly in Africa Proconsularis.[46] We can imagine that Herma's family was somehow involved in the export of ivory to Italy and that this freedman had settled in Capena to organize local distribution.

Freedmen produce or supply merchandise, which will be sold by their patron

In this category, we find freedmen working in their patron's workshop, while the patron sells the merchandise in a shop, often adjacent to the workplace; freedmen scouting the newly arrived ships in the port, in search of goods that their patron can later resell; and freedmen shipping merchandise to their patron's stores.

These types of division of labour, though undoubtedly omnipresent in the Roman business world, again leave few traces in the epigraphic record, for occupational inscriptions usually do not distinguish between the level of production or supply and that of resale. Inscriptions of a patron and his freedmen jointly running a shop cite only one occupation, irrespective of the actual contribution of each partner. In Rome, for instance, the freedwoman Cameria Iarine dedicated a tomb to her fellow-freedman and husband Onesimus, their patron Thraso, and their patron's patron Alexander.[47] All of them had been working in the same shop as tailors of fine clothing on the vicus Tuscus (*vestiarii tenuarii de vico Tusco*). Are we to assume that the senior artisan Alexander still engaged in tailoring or did he perhaps concentrate on selling the clothing the other freedmen were producing? A hint at the latter division of labour between patron and freedman can be found in the epitaph of the engraver M. Canuleius Zosimus.[48] The tomb was dedicated by his patron, who explicitly added that Zosimus had done nothing contrary to his wishes and never committed any fraud, even though he had always had much gold and silver in his possession. The phrasing suggests that the patron was supplying Zosimus with raw material and making a profit from selling the finished products. Nevertheless, we cannot

---

[45] *CIL* 11.3948.   [46] *ILAfr.* 479, 59; *AE* 1955, 126; *CIL* 8.1262, 1321.
[47] *CIL* 6.37826.   [48] *CIL* 6.9222.

completely rule out the possibility that Zosimus was marketing his produce in the shop and giving his patron a share in the profits.

Merchants are also likely to have used their freedmen to import foreign merchandise to their home market. This practice may be reflected in a legal note by Paul, in which he discusses the case of a patron sending his freedman into Asia for the purpose of buying purple.[49] The text is silent about the patron's occupation or the destination of the merchandise, but nonetheless confirms that this kind of task was entrusted to freedmen. An epigraphic trace of this business organization might be found in the votive altar that P. Arisenius Marius dedicated to the goddess Nehalennia, after having successfully crossed the North Sea.[50] Marius certainly was engaged in business, for he thanks the goddess for having protected his merchandise (*merces bene conservatas*) during the voyage. It is remarkable, however, that he fails to mention his own occupation, while explicitly stating that he was a freedman of P. Arisenius V[-]hus, a *negotiator Britannicianus*. The *gentilicium* Arisenius seems to be unique but apparently points to a Germanic origin, for the name may be derived from the *cognomen* Arusenus, attested in a third-century inscription from Bonn.[51] Apparently Marius considered himself to be not a true merchant, but merely a shipper working for a merchant—namely, his patron. It is possible that Marius' patron was specializing in commerce with Britain but was running his business from the German mainland and asked his freedman to undertake the actual voyages to distant markets.

Freedmen and patron work closely together in every single business stage

Here, freedmen remain closely tied to the patron and other *coliberti*, for they constantly cooperate in a specific trade. They either worked together in a single workshop, ran several workshops simultaneously, or jointly organized business voyages. Each of these organizational schemes can be discovered in occupational inscriptions.

First, the cooperation of a patron and one or several of his freedmen working in the same shop must have been the key organization of many small-scale urban enterprises, although, as mentioned before, no further division of labour can be inferred from the inscriptions. For instance, D. Veturius Diogenes and his former slaves Nicepor and Flora were all working together as *purpurarii* in a shop on the Esquiline in Rome.[52]

Secondly, patrons deciding to organize business on a larger scale had their freedmen running separate workshops with a modest degree of independence.

---

[49] *Dig.* 34.2.4.   [50] *AE* 1983, 721.   [51] *CIL* 13.8066.
[52] *CIL* 6.37820.

Constant monitoring was impossible, as the patron was still engaged in business himself, but regular visits and checking profits and expenses may have been sufficient. The family business of A. Umbricius Scaurus, who together with his slaves and freedmen dominated the Pompeian fish-sauce industry, is a case in point: *tituli picti* on Pompeian amphorae indicate that Scaurus and at least two of his freedmen, Agathopus and Abascanthus, were each running an *officina*.[53]

Thirdly, the business organization in which patron and freedman travel together to distant markets is reflected in the epitaph of Q. Dellius Optatus, a merchant from Ravenna, who was doing business in southern Italy together with his freedman Priscus.[54] Optatus died in Venosa and was buried there by Priscus. This kind of close cooperation is even reflected in Roman law, for, according to Callistratus, the *operae* a patron was entitled to request from his freedman included travelling together and transacting business.[55]

Freedmen are each separately responsible for all business stages with their patron merely providing infrastructure and finance

Freedmen belonging to this category organized their trade without constant cooperation and supervision by the patron. They were each responsible for purchasing or producing merchandise and marketing the goods. This, however, does not exclude mutual assistance and cooperation by freedmen from the same family. They obviously were best acquainted with their *coliberti* and knew about their character and trustworthiness, so joining forces in the business world may have been an attractive and efficient strategy. Nevertheless, the freedmen had to answer separately to their patron.

In starting up a trade, they received some kind of support from their patron. He may have provided capital investment or the necessary equipment and infrastructure, such as a ship, a workshop, or a shop. These he could either lease for a fixed sum or supply in exchange for part of the profits.

Contrary to business organizations in which the patron personally cooperated with his freedmen and hence engaged in the same trade, here the patron could either decide to focus on a single trade or diversify his investments.

The first option implies specialization and has several advantages to offer. For instance, specific information and experience can be shared with all family members, thereby consolidating their position in the business community. Information on the best routes, trustworthy and cheap suppliers, stable markets, or reliable customers could quickly be dispersed within the family network. In

---

[53] *CIL* 4.2574a, 7110, 5689. Curtis (1984) and Étienne and Mayet (1991).
[54] *CIL* 9.469.   [55] *Dig.* 38.1.38.1.

this way, members theoretically would be able to optimize and accelerate commercial decision-making. We might trace this kind of agency organization in two small Roman inscriptions, mentioning two cloak-dealers, the *coliberti* L. Arlenus Demetrius and L. Arlenus Artemidorus.[56] They originated from Cilicia and Paphlagonia respectively and had both been sold to L. Arlenus Philogenus. The latter's epitaph, dedicated by his freedmen, fails to mention a profession, so we do not know whether Philogenus had been active in the textile trade or not. Nevertheless, his two freedmen both specialized in the same trade, apparently prompted to this profession by their patron. More telling, however, is the information on freedmen's involvement in the oil trade. Several merchant families, such as the DD. Aticii, the LL. Memmii, and the LL. Segolatii, appear to have relied almost completely on freedmen to ship Baetican oil to Rome.[57] Within a time span of a mere ten years, these families stimulated a number of freedmen to engage in the same trade, so it seems plausible that at least some of them were *coliberti* backed by a patron with a major interest in the oil trade. So far, none of their patrons has been identified as a businessman actively participating in commerce, so this business organization fits the typology quite well.

The second option allowed patrons to diversify their business interests. The major advantages of this agency organization include the ability of allocating each freedman to the profession he was best at and the possibility of spreading risks over several trades. This strategy was in practice reserved for larger households with major assets to manage and many freedmen to rely on. Although we can safely assume that this kind of agency was part of aristocratic economic policies in Roman business, evidence is scarce owing to the absence of accounts describing aristocratic portfolios and the various investments made by patrons through their freedmen. Literary sources, however, sometimes offer an insight in the management of large fortunes by freedmen. Cicero's letters, for instance, illustrate how single tasks were entrusted to different freedmen. Hilarus, for instance, was staying in Macedonia to collect debts made by Antonius, while another freedman, Eros, recovered the rents of Cicero's urban property. Many of his estate bailiffs presumably were freedmen too.[58] Even though this example mainly concerns financial and agricultural management, one can easily imagine how the administration of commercial investments was organized along similar lines. The famous passage in Plutarch's biography of Cato the Elder, describing how Cato was represented by his freedman Quintio in a commercial partnership, may be a case in point, as one can assume that Cato had more freedmen working in the many investments cited by Plutarch.[59] Epigraphy, on the other hand, rarely allows us to identify several

---

[56] *CIL* 6.9675, 12331.
[57] DD. Aticii: *CIL* 15.3735–40, 4057; Rodríguez Almeida (1972: no. 10; 1979: no. 29; 1983: no. 2) and Ehmig (2007: no. 128). LL. Memmii: *CIL* 15, 3962–70; Rodríguez Almeida (1972: no. 24–5, 66). LL. Segolatii: *CIL* 15.3993–9.
[58] Shatzman (1975: 421–2).   [59] Plut. *Cat. Mai.* 21.6.

freed agents working for one and the same patron in different trades. Moreover, inscriptions usually reflect more small-scale and specialized enterprises and can hence contribute little to understanding this specific kind of business organization.

Different business stages are entrusted to different freedmen, with the patron providing merchandise or cooperating in one or more stages

Patrons with an active interest in business may have wished to reduce risk and uncertainty and enhance efficiency by exerting control over different stages of an enterprise. Instead of using their freedmen to monitor a single stage, such as production or distribution of merchandise, they assigned different tasks to different freedmen, thus creating a network of agents, with each manager being responsible for a single part of the business enterprise. Ideally, every single stage (production or purchase of merchandise; transport; distribution) would be supervised by either the patron or one of his freedmen. The benefit of this business organization is evident: agents can now concentrate on a single business stage, gather specific experience, and become specialized managers. In this construction, freedmen often settled for longer periods of time or even permanently in towns that were of particular importance for the enterprise. One can imagine that some were living close to the spot where merchandise was produced or could easily be purchased, while others settled in cities where demand was particularly high in order to organize local distribution. This way, agents would be able to gather relevant information for a long time, gain a better insight into the organization of local markets, supplies, and demands, and create long-standing business relationships. Especially on shuttle routes between two ports or regions, these networks of freedmen were able to maximize knowledge about markets, goods, routes, buyers, and sellers.

This occupational specialization and the creation of networks offered several advantages and must have resulted in a more efficient enterprise. First, permanent agents in distant cities had the opportunity to take over the merchandise imported by their patron or fellow-freedmen immediately and have a return cargo ready. Family members responsible for transport would thus be less dependent on current market conditions and lose no time waiting in the port searching for customers and suppliers. The period during which capital outlays were tied up could hence be reduced. This particular advantage of working with fixed agents has frequently been analysed as a major time-saving technique and prerequisite for an increase of scale, in particular in the study of eighteenth-century transatlantic trade.[60] Secondly,

---

[60] Walton (1967); North (1968); Price and Clemens (1987). See also French (1987) for a comparable study of the Atlantic shipping industry.

permanent agents were able to stock merchandise and wait for favourable market conditions to achieve larger profits. Thirdly, they were firmly rooted in local business communities and became acquainted with native producers, entrepreneurs, and bankers. These connections may again ease transactions for the whole family, as finding suppliers, customers, and investors was organized by local agents. Itinerant businessmen, on the other hand, would find it far more difficult to create this kind of network. Fourthly, these intra-family networks may have stimulated the dissemination of reliable business information. Members were more likely to receive trustworthy information from other members than from businessmen they were not connected to. Fifthly, dense networks of freedmen may discourage free-riding. A merchant doing business with colleagues he had never met before and would perhaps not encounter again in the near future was far more vulnerable to cheating than an agent transacting with *coliberti* who were all linked to the same family. Frequent communication and the fact that each was responsible for a different stage made fraud easier to detect.

The commercial benefits of this agency model are thus self-evident. Epigraphy now allows us to detect traces of this kind of business organization in the Roman trading world.

First, we return to the Gallic merchant family of the Sexti Fadii. We have already mentioned in the previous section that several *tituli picti* indicated that Fadius Secundus Musa and at least three of his freedmen were shipping Baetican olive oil to Rome. These *tituli*, however, offer very little information on the actual organization of the oil trade or the identity of trading partners. Yet the distribution of inscriptions mentioning other Sexti Fadii can be revealing, for members of the *gens* Fadia only rarely adopt the *praenomen* Sextus, and it is therefore very likely that the few Sexti Fadii who do feature in inscriptions were somehow related.[61] When we map the presence of Sexti Fadii in monumental epigraphy, the geographical distribution clearly suggests that these businessmen were able to rely on a large network of family members, and freedmen in particular, who had settled in specific ports to assist in managing the export and distribution of olive oil. Apart from two isolated occurrences in Venosa and Verona, Sexti Fadii appear only in the epigraphy of cities closely linked to the family's origin or their involvement in the oil trade.[62] A first cluster of inscriptions can be found in Narbonne, the family's home city.[63] Secondly, the Fadii also occur in Baetica, for in Astigi the epitaph of Sex. Fadius Lamyrus, obviously a freedman, has been discovered.[64] This town was a major fiscal control centre for the oil trade, where oil, originally stored in skins, was poured into amphorae. Many *tituli picti* document this stage, as they invariably start with the phrase 'checked in Astigi'.[65] The monument is dated

---

[61] Di Stefano Manzella (1989).   [62] Venosa: *CIL* 9.422. Verona: *CIL* 5.3607.
[63] *CIL* 12.4393, 4486, 4802, 4804.   [64] *CIL* 2.1495.   [65] Aguilera Martín (2000).

to the first decades of the third century, but, as Lamyrus apparently had died at the age of 50, he may very well have been involved in the oil trade organized by the Fadii during the 160s and beyond. Perhaps he was responsible for the purchase and packaging of the oil in Astigi and the onward transport to one of Baetica's ports, where his family members would collect the merchandise. The third cluster is located in Ostia and Rome, the final destination of the oil transport.[66] The Sexti Fadii mentioned in these inscriptions and their relatives may have assisted the family business by accepting, storing, and distributing the merchandise and purchasing return cargoes. This geographical distribution of inscriptions thus reflects the business interests of the Fadii and at least suggests how the family was relying on freedmen, settled in distant ports, to organize trade.

The second case study focuses on another merchant family we have already encountered, the Publii Aufidii. We previously described how, around the middle of the second century, P. Aufidius Fortis, a member of the aristocracy of both Hippo Regius and Ostia, was selling grain in Ostia and introduced at least two of his freedmen to the same trade. Yet it seems that the Aufidii were using their family members to monitor an additional stage of the grain trade. In AD 173, an honorary inscription was dedicated at Ostia to the grain merchant M. Iunius Faustus by the African and Sardinian shipowners.[67] Among the initiators was a certain P. Aufidius [—]us, who no doubt belonged to the same family as Fortis. It seems at least plausible that this shipper was one of Fortis' freedmen, who was entrusted with a different task from that of the grain merchants in Ostia. He may have been responsible for shipping the merchandise, which was then handed over to Fortis and his freedmen and distributed in the port. The Aufidii may even have controlled yet another stage. As Fortis was a member of the city council in Hippo Regius, he must have possessed some estates in the vicinity of this town, which most likely were used to grow grain. One can thus imagine that part of the grain that the Aufidii were shipping to Ostia had been produced on their own lands. This way, the Aufidii apparently managed to monitor every single stage in the grain trade, from the production in Africa and the shipment to Italy to the final distribution in Ostia. Fortis and his family hence created a perfect vertically integrated business, which had many benefits to offer.[68] Their involvement in production provided them with information on expected yields, so shippers would know how much additional grain they had to purchase to fill the hold and the agents in Ostia could perhaps make an educated guess on the future availability of grain. The Aufidii possessed their own ships, so there was no need to rely on the services of strangers to have the grain shipped across the Mediterranean. Once arrived in Ostia, the merchandise could immediately be handed over to

---

[66] Ostia: *CIL* 14.995–6, 4563.5. Rome: *AE* 1989, 97; *CIL* 6.17651, 26537.
[67] *CIL* 14.4142.   [68] Broekaert (2012b).

Fortis and his freedmen. Like the Fadii, the Aufidii appear to have installed managers in the area of production, the shipping industry, and the port of destination.

These two case studies illustrate the possibilities of employing freedmen as business agents and the potential advantages of simultaneously monitoring different stages. One may argue that the increase in business efficiency these two merchant families successfully introduced may very well have engendered the families' wealth and display of benefactions. Nevertheless, this kind of business organization, depending on the widespread use of freedmen as managers, obviously demanded a major initial investment: only families who were able to purchase and manumit sufficient quantities of slaves to manage every single stage could hope to initiate this agency mechanism successfully. It comes as no surprise then that the businessmen who controlled this system, P. Aufidius Fortis and Sex. Fadius Secundus Musa, each belonged to the local aristocracy of their native town.

Different business stages are entrusted to different freedmen, without the patron being personally engaged in business

This commercial organization obviously also requires a large household, for the more freedmen a patron could engage in trade, the more business stages could be monitored. The advantages of this strategy combine those of the two previous typologies. First, the patron can allocate each agent to the profession he excels in and use this division of labour to corner as many business stages as possible. Secondly, he has the additional benefit of eliminating personal engagement and completely relying on his network of freedmen. He interferes only to provide finance or infrastructure.

As already noted, this kind of complex business organization, in which several freedmen from the same patron operated simultaneously in a specific trade and in which the patron remained anonymous, is difficult to trace in epigraphy. We can hope only for inscriptions mentioning freedmen who most likely belonged to the same family and followed different trades that may have coincided with the various stages of a business enterprise. This obviously implies that, even though a few inscriptions hint at this agency organization, they will hardly ever provide clear-cut evidence.

The first case study will analyse the local business interests of the *gens* Caedicia in the city of Rome. During the last decades of the republic or the first of the empire, two former slaves of this family, M. Caedicius Eros and M. Caedicius Iucundus, were working as goldsmiths in the Via Sacra.[69]

---

[69] *AE* 1971, 41 and *CIL* 6.9207.

Another freedman, M. Caedicius Faustus, operated as a merchant in the same street.[70] Nothing is known of their patron(s), but we can imagine that the MM. Caedicii were running one or several workshops in the Via Sacra, maybe belonging to their patron(s), with Eros and Iucundus apparently producing gold jewellery and Faustus selling the finished objects.

The second example shows the application of a similar strategy in the long-distance trade. The famous dossier of the Puteolean aristocratic *gens* Annia illustrates how agency by freedmen, each responsible for a single business stage, can even be traced in the organization of Roman trade with Arabia and beyond.[71] The central node in this commercial network is P. Annius Plocamus, who, during the reign of Claudius, had contracted to farm the customs dues in the Red Sea. During the same period, he must have used his freedmen to invest in the import of eastern luxuries, for Pliny notes that one of them had accidentally discovered Sri Lanka while sailing to Arabia.[72] Moreover, two graffiti of AD 6, discovered in the Egyptian Wadi Menih near Coptus, mention a certain Lysas, slave of Annius Plocamus.[73] The site was located close to the ancient caravan route connecting Coptus and Berenice on the Red Sea coast and used to transport Indian and Arabian merchandise to the Nile. The early date of the graffiti may suggest that Plocamus' network of slaves and freedmen was already active in the first decade of the present era. The final chain in the network—the distribution of the goods in the Mediterranean and Italy in particular—may be represented by the presence of another freedman of Annius Plocamus in Puteoli, P. Annius Eros.[74] Each of these freedmen and slaves monitored a single aspect of the import of eastern merchandise, but, together, the family's agents cornered every stage in this trade. Plocamus must have financed their transactions, but may also have used his connections in the eastern tax system to assist and protect his agents. This kind of long-distance trade had to rely on a dense family network of agents and could thus be conducted only by a large and wealthy household. Moreover, wealth was also a prerequisite to invest in the eastern trade, for huge sums were involved in the import of luxuries. This way, prosperous families like the Annii could combine both their fortune and their freedmen to build and finance a commercial network stretching from the Mediterranean to the Indian Ocean. Furthermore, onomastic research on Roman citizens in Egypt during the second century AD has shown that the network of the Annii had survived the first century and that the family probably continued to engage in trade with Arabia and India.

These six models of agency aptly illustrate the wide application of the system and the variety of assignments entrusted to freedmen. The success of this strategy is self-evident. Freedmen enabled their patrons to organize business far more efficiently than working with hired personnel could ever have done. Patron

---

[70] *CIL* 6.9662.   [71] Camodeca (1979); Rathbone (2003: 221–2).
[72] Plin. *NH* 6.84.   [73] *SEG* 13, 614.   [74] *CIL* 10.2389.

and freedmen had long been acquainted with each other, so they were never trading with complete strangers whose trustworthiness could not be taken for granted. The ready availability of possible agents thus saved the patron time seeking and evaluating representatives. Large households that could rely on the services of several freedmen were able either to diversify business interests as Cato did; to intensify their engagement in a single trade, such as the Spanish merchant families did in the oil trade; or to expand the geographical range of their investments by creating a widespread network of local agents, as the Puteolean Annii did.

THE FREQUENCY OF AGENCY: IN SEARCH OF THE SELF-MADE BUSINESSMAN

If agency by freedmen was such a convenient tool to organize trade, was there any reason for patrons not to continue business relations with their former slaves? Or, slightly rephrased, assuming that the patron was still alive, do we even need to search for independent freedmen in Roman business at all?

This question is closely related to another, well-known debate.[75] How frequently did the imperial and municipal aristocracy rely on slaves and freedmen to invest in business? Are we to assume that investments in trade and industry commonly occurred in the aristocratic portfolios, or did only a minority diversify its assets? Again, for obvious reasons, we cannot hope for decisive statistical evidence listing the various properties and investments of aristocratic families.[76] Nonetheless, this subject has major implications for the specific role of dependent and semi-dependent status groups—slaves and freedmen—in business. The higher the proportion of aristocrats investing in business with their freedmen operating as middlemen, the more likely it is that the freed businessmen we encounter in inscriptions were working as agents. In that case, legal independency must very often have coincided with economic dependency. This is obviously not to say that behind every freedman in business lurked a patron reaping the benefits of his managers' successes, but the occurrence of economically dependent freedmen or managers should have increased according to the rate of aristocrats financing business enterprises.

Although historians nowadays accept that Roman elites were involved in financing business enterprises, so far, however, no consensus on the ratio of

---

[75] See now, also Mouritsen (2011) whose argument goes in a similar direction as the one presented here.

[76] See, however, Shatzman (1975) and Mratschek-Halfmann (1993). These prosopographical studies, however, focus on literary sources, which offer information on senatorial and equestrian wealth only. We still lack a detailed analysis of the fortunes of municipal aristocracies. Moreover, valuable insights could also have been gained by confronting the literary evidence with archaeological data, to identify the involvement of aristocratic families in the production of amphorae, tiles, etc. So far, this kind of detailed analysis is available only for Baetica and Campania. For Baetica, see Haley (2003); for Campania, see Los (2000).

agriculture and business in aristocratic portfolios has been achieved.[77] Some, focusing on the rich evidence of Pompeii, claim that the local aristocracy commonly engaged in commerce and that the category of economically independent freedmen was only marginal.[78] In this view, agency was 'the normal form of employment of freedmen in sea-trade: the freedmen were agents and employees of the patron'.[79] Others, however stress the difficulties in linking freedmen in business to local aristocracies. Garnsey, for instance, claimed that one could only 'conclude that a sizeable number of freedmen attained a position of independence or relative independence and wealth'.[80] Yet the criteria suggested to identify these independent freedmen are vague and hardly applicable to the surviving evidence. Garnsey suggested wealth and positions of responsibility as the two main candidates.[81]

The first criterion seems a rather odd choice, for which businessman would have the best chances for success: the completely independent freedman, forced to start up, organize, and finance his enterprise all by himself, or the freedman-agent, who was able to rely on investments and contacts provided by his patron? Why, indeed, would dependency and wealth be mutually exclusive? Agents working on commission or for a fixed wage were probably better protected against business failure than independent entrepreneurs. Moreover, economic dependency does not automatically imply that the patron was deciding on the limits of enrichment. A patron who had entrusted some money to his freedman to invest in seaborne trade created the possibility for his agent to take aboard a small sample of merchandise and to trade on his own account. The patron was actually financing the 'infrastructure', thus allowing the agent to make a small profit on the side. This kind of incentive must have been very common in maritime trade and was even institutional-ized in the organization of the early modern Indian trade. The agents of the India Companies who were directing the ships' voyages, the so-called super-cargoes, were officially allowed to take aboard their own merchandise, often amounting to no less than 5 per cent of the cargo.[82] Furthermore, Garnsey added that possible indicators of this wealth of independent freedmen in-cluded membership of a professional association or the erection of inscriptions. If this were true, then the clear majority of freedmen in business should be styled independent, for inscriptions are the only traces they have left for us. The case studies previously discussed are sufficient proof that neither membership of a *collegium* nor the ability to finance an inscription can be used as circumstantial evidence to identify independent merchants. The freedmen of the *gens* Aufidia, who had all joined a shippers' or trade association and erected inscriptions but

---

[77] López Barja de Quiroga (1991: 165–6).   [78] Andreau (1973); Mouritsen (2001).
[79] Treggiari (1969: 103).
[80] Finley (1973: 64, 78). Garnsey (1981: quotation from p. 369).
[81] Garnsey (1981: 368).   [82] Morse (1921); Lee-Whitman (1982).

clearly operated as agents, may be a case in point. The rise of two freed Aufidii in the association of grain merchants can even be attributed to the lobbying of their patron, who had been elected *quinquennalis perpetuus* of the same *collegium*. Yet it is only when analysing these occupational inscriptions as different parts of a larger business organization that a family network of dependent agents appears. Take, for instance, the large and beautifully decorated inscription of the oil merchant D. Caecilius Onesimus, who was trading in Rome during the Antonine age and attained the office of *viator*, one of the most respected functions held by the *apparitores*.[83] According to Garnsey's criteria, he may have been a successful independent merchant, as both his career and the costs of erecting the stone indicate at least a moderate level of wealth. However, when *tituli picti* of the same period identify several oil traders all belonging to the same family and all former slaves, one may conclude that it seems far more likely that Onesimus was but one of the many agents in a family network of oil merchants.[84]

The second criterion, positions of responsibility, is equally problematic. Garnsey has in mind 'the ownership or management of or partnership in a business, preferably a sizeable one or one that can be seen to be profitable'.[85] Owning production facilities or commercial infrastructure (shops and ships) may indeed point to independent freedmen, but does not necessarily exclude cooperation with the patron and his family. The latter may still rely on the marketing and transport services offered by his freedmen, as he was undoubtedly entitled to preferential treatment or profitable business deals. Partnership is an equally dubious indicator. For instance, several members of the previously cited merchant family of the DD. Caecilii entered into a *societas* with their own freedmen.[86] In Capua, an epitaph dedicated to P. Octavius A.l. Philomusus had been erected by Philargurus, his *libertus et socius*.[87] Partnerships with freedmen were also mentioned by Cicero.[88] The final part in Garnsey's definition, sizeable and profitable businesses, again discords with the analysis of wealth as a possible indicator: the size and success of a business would be increased by a patron's financial backing and could, therefore, rather be used as markers for dependency.

Apparently, identifying independent freedmen proves to be as difficult as recognizing traces of dependent freedmen. Maybe Garnsey himself recognized

---

[83] *AE* 1980, 98.

[84] DD. Caecilii of the Antonine age, who were certainly freedmen: *CIL* 15.3751–3 (Calliphytus); 15.3754–5 (Chrysogonus); 15.3756, 3758–61 (a *societas* of Daphnus and Euelpistus); Rodríguez Almeida (1994: no. 7: Nicephorus); *CIL* 15.3784 (Papia).

[85] Garnsey (1981: 368).

[86] *CIL* 15.3788–90 (*Caeciliorum et lib(ertorum)*). It is true that the reading *lib(erorum)* is equally possible, but this seems less likely: *tituli* recording a cooperation between a father and his children always use the words *filius* and *filia*. Cf., e.g. Blázquez Martínez and Remesal Rodríguez (2003: no. 89). For the structure and rationale of commercial partnerships, see Broekaert (2011).

[87] *ILLRP* 938.   [88] Cic. *Parad.* 46.

the problems in applying his model to inscriptional evidence, for his discussion lacks a concrete test of his two criteria. Nevertheless, D'Arms did try to apply Garnsey's model to Ostian epigraphy and the association of *augustales* in particular, the freedman elite parallel to the municipal aristocracy and mainly consisting of wealthy freedmen who operated in trade and industry.[89] He argued that their level of wealth, membership in professional associations, the frequency of marriages outside the own *familia*, and the fact that none of their patrons was explicitly mentioned indicated that these freedmen 'clearly operated independently'.[90] But did they really? For the majority of the *augustales* we can neither prove that they were doing business in their own interests nor that they operated as agents. Some case studies, however, may be indicative. For instance, we have already noted that the Gallic Fadii specialized in the Spanish oil trade and had managers in Spain and Ostia. When Sex. Fadius Rufus, who clearly belonged to this network, became a member of the Ostian *augustales*, this promotion should be seen in connection to the wealth he had accumulated as local manager of his family's business interests.[91] A recently discovered inscription from Pesaro can corroborate this kind of network analysis. The fragmentary text mentions a T. Ancharius T.l. G—], *sevir augustalis* and *negotiator s[—]*, who erected the stone for his late wife, Gavellia L.l. Ma[—].[92] A wealthy freedman who married someone from a different family and did not mention his patron seems, according to D'Arms's model, a plausible candidate for an independent businessman. Yet when the occurrence of the TT. Ancharii is mapped, doubts arise. A first inscription was also discovered in Pesaro and indicates that the freedman probably belonged to the family of T. Ancharius T.f. Priscus and his son T. Ancharius T.f. Priscianus, two members of the municipal elite and wealthy benefactors.[93] A certain Ancharius Abascanthianus, who erected an epitaph for his late wife in the same city, may also be linked to this family. It is interesting to note that, outside Pesaro, epigraphy yields only a few texts mentioning TT. Ancharii: apart from single attestations in Dacia and Africa Proconsularis, several Ancharii were living in Salona, a commercial hub located more or less opposite Pesaro on the other shore of the Adriatic.[94] One of them, T. Ancharius Anthus, was a member of the local *seviri augustales*. It does not seem too far-fetched to assume that these two wealthy freedmen were local managers in a commercial network stretching from Italy to the Balkans and beyond, especially because Salona was one of the major ports connecting Italy to the Danube regions.[95]

Very similar problems are encountered when applying D'Arms's criteria to freedmen who held the office of *sevir*. This word may be a mere abbreviation

[89] Duthoy (1974).   [90] D'Arms (1981: 144–6; quotation from p. 144).
[91] *CIL* 14.4563.5.   [92] *AE* 2005, 484.   [93] *CIL* 11.6357.
[94] Dacia: *AE* 1914, 116. Africa Proconsularis: *ILTun* 580a. Salona: *CIL* 3.2092, 2169, 2291, 2595, 9131.
[95] For the importance of trade between Italy and Salona, see Tassaux (2004) and Glicksman (2005).

for *sevir augustalis*, but can also denote membership of another prestigious association not connected to the imperial cult.[96] Whether or not the *seviri* belonged to the same social milieu as the Ostian *liberti* is thus difficult to find out. Nevertheless, the fact that they managed to attain this office clearly identifies them as belonging to an urban elite, which at least justifies a comparison with the *augustales*. Two case studies may suffice. In Bologna, an epitaph was erected for two *coliberti*, M. Papuleius M.l. Pudens and M. Papuleius M.l. Primus, who were both members of the association of *seviri* and iron merchants.[97] They appear to have belonged to the same family as M. Papuleius Latro, who held the quaestorship in the same city, for the rare *gentilicium* is otherwise unknown.[98] Whether these freedmen operated independently or as agents cannot be discerned, but at least their business organization fits one of the typologies discussed earlier, in which an aristocratic patron stimulates his freedmen to work in the same trade and thus increases the scale of his business interests. A very similar analysis can be made for an epitaph from Cordoba, dedicated to the *sevir* L. Vibius Polyanthus by his wife Fabia Helpis and dated to the final quarter of the second century.[99] Polyanthus' name also occurs in a *titulus pictus* on a Spanish oil amphora, discovered in Rome and precisely dated to AD 147.[100] It seems this oil merchant meets the criteria laid down by D'Arms rather well. However, several *tituli* from the middle of the second century indicate that Polyanthus was but one of the freedmen of the LL. Vibii engaged in the oil trade, so again we may assume that he was operating as one of the family's agents.[101]

We can hence safely conclude that, even for the freedman elites of the *augustales* and *seviri*, the criteria for identifying independent entrepreneurs hardly seem applicable to the inscriptional evidence. D'Arms's statement, that the majority of these elites were independent freedmen 'in a position . . . where success depended upon his own capacities, contacts and initiative', still remains to be proven.[102]

Perhaps we should then rely on circumstantial evidence, such as the continuity or discontinuity of powerful families who controlled the means of production and distribution.[103] It has been argued that, if freedmen were indeed mainly employed as agents, one would expect the domination of a

---

[96] For more details, see Duthoy (1978).   [97] *AE* 1922, 82.   [98] *CIL* 11.697.
[99] *CIL* 2.7.329.   [100] *CIL* 15.4045.

[101] Other LL. Vibii in the second-century oil trade: Blázquez Martínez and Remesal Rodríguez (2003: nos 128, 162: Vibius [—]); *CIL* 15.3949; 3951–5, 3957–9 (a *societas* of Restitutus and Viator). The LL. Vibii seem to have relied on the services of their freedmen since the beginning of the first century, for an early Dr. 20 amphora discovered in Castra Praetoria already records the name of an oil merchant L. Vibius Hermes (*CIL* 15.3668).

[102] D'Arms (1981: 146). On the same page, the author calls the parallels between these freedmen and Trimalchio 'obvious and close', but one should note that at the time Trimalchio started to invest in business his former master was already deceased and had left him a fortune!

[103] Meiggs (1960: 209); D'Arms (1981: 140–1); López Barja de Quiroga (1991: 168–9).

handful of families in the urban economy to continue for several generations. If, on the other hand, freedmen were allowed to operate more independently, regular changes in the composition of the governing classes and sons of wealthy freedmen entering the local aristocracy would be expected. We may, however, wonder whether the dichotomy between 'closed' and 'open' elites really matters in discussing freedmen's (in)dependence. First, we have already noted that, from an economic point of view, agency by freedmen is expected to have benefited both parties. In this scenario, dependent freedmen would only consolidate their patrons' economic dominance, while independent freedmen would hardly ever be able to capitalize on the best business opportunities, would fail to accumulate wealth, and thus would never have gained access to the governing class. In both cases, the outcome would be a rather closed urban elite, as indeed applies to the majority of the Roman cities. Secondly, when alterations in the composition of the local elites do appear, they should not necessarily be attributed to independent freedmen and their families pervading the urban social structure. The openness of the municipal elites to sons of freedmen, a phenomenon well attested in major commercial centres such as Ostia and Puteoli, never distinguishes between descendants of dependent or independent freedmen.[104] Yet, because many merchant families from all over the Mediterranean, such as the Gallic Fadii or the Spanish Caecilii, settled their freed agents in Italian port cities and because from an economic point of view these agents were most likely to accumulate personal wealth and enable social mobility for their children, the chances are that newcomers in the municipal elites of commercial hubs were rather descendants of dependent than of independent freedmen.

One may thus conclude that, in cities such as Ostia and Puteoli, wealth could buy you a ticket to the council, irrespective of the money's origin or the economic background of the families who had earned it. Yet, given the cosmopolitan character of the population and the presence of freed managers belonging to provincial business families, regular changes in the governing classes may be attributed to agency rather than to the economic success of independent freedmen.

This outcome, based primarily on dispersed inscriptional evidence, corresponds quite well to the conclusion of similar research by Mouritsen, restricted to the city of Pompeii, and to the institutional analysis of agency recently put forward by Frier and Kehoe in the *Cambridge Economic History if the Greco-Roman World*:

> This method of managing businesses through friends or social dependants had significant implications for the organization of the Roman economy. For one, it tended to reinforce the strict social hierarchy that helped to preserve the economic

---

[104] Gordon (1931).

and social privileges of the landowning elite: there was little capacity for developing a class of artisans let alone entrepreneurs who were fully independent of elite patronage or control. Successful freedmen who gained wealth as artisans or business managers were ultimately dependent on a master or patron for an initial investment in skills and capital, and they often remained socially bound at least to some degree to their patron.[105]

CONCLUSION

Will we ever be able to guesstimate the ratio of dependent and independent freedmen and assess the true relevance of status and dependency? Probably not. What we can do, however, is to try and determine the economic rationale of both options. From this point of view, continuing economic relationships had far more benefits to offer to both the patron and his freedmen than immediately ending their cooperation upon manumission. Why indeed would someone cede control and access to a ready labour force or allow potential competitors onto the economic scene? From an entrepreneurial point of view, manumission makes sense only when the patron would have the opportunity to continue the cooperation with his former slaves. This clearly does not imply that all or even the majority of freedmen in business were dependent. Some, like the illustrious Trimalchio, would have been freed by testamentary manumission and would never have known a patron. Others may not have had the opportunity to continue the relationship with their patron, whatever the reason may be. The patron may have terminated his investments and no longer needed agents, or he may have found more qualified agents. We can only conclude that, for patrons eager to invest in business, relying on freedmen was the first and most rational option. Assuming they opted for the easiest and quickest way to find agents—and there is no reason why they would have failed to do so—agency by freedmen offered the best solution, or a decent one at least. Relying on freedmen to manage business interests provided an answer to the problem of information asymmetry and the difficulties of finding honest agents, but never excluded the possibility that, in the end, it might become clear that the patron had mistakenly entrusted them with his money. Trimalchio himself relates how one of his guests, C. Iulius Proculus, used to possess more than one million sesterces, but had lost his fortune to his cursed freedmen, who had squeezed him dry. Nevertheless, in the same account Trimalchio also makes clear that his own business interests were still managed by freedmen.[106] The advantages of having familiar agents ready at hand

[105] Mouritsen (2001); Frier and Kehoe (2007; quotation from p. 134).
[106] Petron. *Sat.* 43, 76.

apparently outweighed the risks, which at any rate would still be much smaller than working with complete strangers. The outcome must hence be that, logically, as long as patrons were still alive and continued to invest in business, in these families dependent freedmen would be expected to be far more numerous than independent ones. This business organization, however, did not necessarily result in ruthless economic exploitation of freedmen. The majority of the freedmen-agents may actually have gained from the agency relationship and worked in their own and their patron's interests. If the prospect of manumission was the incentive for a slave to work in his master's interests, then the potential benefits of a prolonged cooperation may have urged freedmen to operate as agents. Perhaps the many success stories of prosperous freedmen and the stock character of the wealthy but uncivilized *libertus* as a *nouveau riche* in Roman satire mirror this continued relationship.

REFERENCES

Aguilera Martín, A. (2000). 'Los tituli picti delta del convento astigitano en el primer tercio del s.III d.C.', in *Actas del Congreso Internacional Ex Baetica Amphorae. Conservas, aceite y vino de la Bética en el Imperio Romano (Écija y Sevilla, 17 al 20 de Diciembre de 1998).* Écija, 1231–40.

Andreau, J. (1973). 'Remarques sur la société pompéienne (à propos des tablettes de L. Caecilius Jucundus)', *Dialoghi di Archeologia* 7: 213–54.

Andreau, J. (1995). 'Présentation: Vingt ans après L'Économie antique de Moses I. Finley', *Annales ESC* 50: 947–60.

Aubert, J.-J. (1994). *Business Managers in Ancient Rome: A Social and Economic Study of Institores, 200 B.C.–A.D. 250.* Leiden.

Blázquez Martínez, J. M., and Remesal Rodríguez, J. (2003). *Estudios sobre el Monte Testaccio (Roma) III.* Barcelona.

Blázquez Martínez, J. M., and Remesal Rodríguez, J. (2007). *Estudios sobre el Monte Testaccio (Roma) IV.* Barcelona.

Bonsangue, M. L. (2001). 'Les Relations commerciales entre Pouzzoles et l'Égypte au IIᵉ siècle ap.J.-C.', *CCG* 12: 199–212.

Broekaert, W. (2011). 'Partners in Business: Roman Merchants and the Potential Advantages of being a *collegiatus*', *AncSoc* 41: 221–56.

Broekaert, W. (2012a). 'Joining Forces: Commercial Partnerships or *societates* in the Early Roman Empire', *Historia* 61/2: 221–53.

Broekaert, W. (2012b). 'Vertical Integration in the Roman Economy: A Response to Morris Silver', *AncSoc* 42: 109–25.

Camodeca, G. (1979). 'La gens Annia puteolana in età giulio-claudia; Potere politico e interessi commerciali', *Puteoli* 3: 17–34.

Castrén, P. (1975). *Ordo Populusque Pompeianus: Polity and Society in Roman Pompeii.* Rome.

Curtis, R. I. (1984). 'A Personalized Floor Mosaic from Pompeii', *AJA* 88/4: 557–66.

D'Arms, J. H. (1977). 'M. I. Rostovtzeff and M. I. Finley: The Status of Traders in the Roman World', in J. H. D'Arms and J. W. Eadie (eds), *Ancient and Modern: Essays in Honour of Gerald F. Else*. Ann Arbor, 159–79.

D'Arms, J. H. (1981). *Commerce and Social Standing in Ancient Rome*. Cambridge.

De Salvo, L. (1992). *Economia privata e pubblici servizi nell' impero romano: I corpora naviculariorum*. Messina.

di Stefano Manzella, I. (1989). 'Nuova iscrizione sepolcrale con doppia datazione consolare', *ZPE* 76: 262–6.

Duthoy, R. (1974). 'La Fonction sociale de l'augustalité', *Epigraphica* 36: 134–54.

Duthoy, R. (1978). 'Les Augustales', *Aufstieg und Niedergang der römischen Welt II* 16/2: 1254–1309.

Ehmig, U. (2007). 'Tituli picti auf Amphoren in Köln', *KJ* 40: 215–322.

Étienne, R., and Mayet, F. (1991). 'Le Garum à la mode de Scaurus', in J. M. J. M. Blázquez and S. Montero (eds), *Alimenta: Estudios en homenaje al dr. Michel Ponsich*. Madrid, 187–94.

Fabre, G. (1981). *Libertus: Recherches sur les rapports patron-affranchi à la fin de la République Romaine*. Rome.

Finley, M. I. (1965). 'Technical Innovation and Economic Progress in the Ancient World', *Economic History Review* 18: 29–45.

Finley, M. I. (1973). *The Ancient Economy*. Berkeley and Los Angeles.

Földi, A. (1996). 'Remarks on the Legal Structure of Enterprises in Roman Law', *RIDA* 43: 179–211.

French, C. J. (1987). 'Productivity in the Atlantic Shipping Industry: A Quantitative Study', *Journal of Interdisciplinary History* 17: 613–38.

Frier, B. W., and Kehoe, D. P. (2007). 'Law and Economic Institutions', in W. Scheidel, I. Morris, and R. Saller (eds), *The Cambridge Economic History of the Greco-Roman world*. Cambridge, 113–43.

Gamauf, R. (2009). 'Slaves Doing Business: The Role of Roman Law in the Economy of a Roman Household', *European Review of History* 16: 331–346.

Garnsey, P. (1981). 'Independent Freedmen and the Economy of Roman Italy under the Principate', *Klio* 63: 359–71.

Glicksman, K. (2005). 'Internal and External Trade in the Roman Province of Dalmatia', *Opuscula Archaeologica* 29: 189–230.

Gordon, M. L. (1931). 'The Freedman's Son in Municipal Life', *JRS* 21: 65–77.

Haley, E. W. (2003). *Baetica Felix: People and Prosperity in Southern Spain from Caesar to Septimius Severus*. Austin, TX.

Héron de Villefosse, A. (1915). 'Deux armateurs narbonnais: Sex. Fadius Secundus et P. Olitius Apollonius', *BSAF* 74: 153–80.

Joshel, S. R. (1992). *Work, Identity and Legal Status at Rome: A Study of the Occupational Inscriptions*. Oklahoma.

Kirschenbaum, A. (1987). *Sons, Slaves and Freedmen in Roman Commerce*. Jerusalem and Washington.

Lee-Whitman, L. (1982). 'The Silk Trade: Chinese Silks and the British East India Company', *Winterthur Portfolio* 17: 21–41.

López Barja de Quiroga, P. (1991). 'La dependencia económica de los libertos en el Alto Imperio Romano', *Gerión* 9: 163–74.

Los, A. (2000). 'Les Affaires "industrielles" des élites des villes campaniennes sous les Julio-Claudiens et les Flaviens', *MEFRA* 112: 243–77.

MacMullen, R. (1982). 'The Epigraphic Habit in the Roman Empire', *AJPh* 103: 233–46.

Manacorda, D. (1985). 'Schiavo "manager" e anfore romane: A proposito dei rapporti tra archeologia e storia del diritto', *Opus* 4: 141–151.

Meiggs, R. (1960). *Roman Ostia*. Oxford.

Morse, H. B. (1921). 'The Supercargo in the China Trade about the Year 1700', *English Historical Review* 36: 199–209.

Mouritsen, H. (2001). 'Roman Freedmen and the Urban Economy: Pompeii in the First Century AD', in F. Senatore (ed.), *Pompei tra Sorrento e Sarno: Atti del terzo e quarto ciclo di conferenze di geologia, storia e archeologia, Pompei, gennaio 1999–maggio 2000*. Naples, 1–27.

Mouritsen, H. (2005). 'Freedmen and Decurions: Epitaphs and Social History in Imperial Italy', *JRS* 95: 38–63.

Mouritsen, H. (2011). *The Freedman in the Roman World*. Oxford.

Mratschek-Halfmann, S. (1993). *Divites et Praepotentes: Reichtum und Soziale Stellung in der Literatur der Prinzipatszeit*. Stuttgart.

North, D. C. (1968). 'Sources of Productivity Change in Ocean Shipping, 1600–1850', *Journal of Political Economy* 76: 953–70.

Price, J., and Clemens, P. G. E. (1987). 'A Revolution of Scale in Overseas Trade: British Firms in the Chesapeake Trade, 1675–1775', *Journal of Economic History* 47: 1–43.

Rathbone, D. (2003). 'The Financing of Maritime Commerce in the Roman Empire, I–II AD', in E. Lo Cascio (ed.), *Credito e moneta nel mondo romano: Atti degli incontri capresi di storia dell'economia antica (Capri 12–14 ottobre 2000)*. Bari, 197–229.

Remesal Rodríguez, J. (2000). 'L. Marius Phoebus, mercator olei hispani ex provincia Baetica: Consideraciones en torno a los términos mercator, negotiator y diffusor olearius ex Baetica', in G. Paci (ed.) *Epigraphai. Miscellanea Epigrafica in onore di Lidio Gasperini*. Rome, 781–97.

Rodríguez Almeida, E. (1972). 'Novedades de epigrafía anforaria del Monte Testaccio', in P. Baldacci, J. Kapitän, and N. Lamboglia (eds), *Recherches sur les amphores romaines*. Rome, 107–242.

Rodríguez Almeida, E. (1979). 'Monte Testaccio: I mercatores dell'olio della Betica', *MEFRA* 91: 873–975.

Rodríguez Almeida, E. (1983). 'Altri mercatores dell'olio betico', *Dialoghi di Archeologia* 1: 79–86.

Rodríguez Almeida, E. (1991). 'Ánforas olearias béticas: Cuestiones varias', in J. M. Blázquez and S. Montero (eds), *Alimenta: Estudios en homenaje al dr. Michel Ponsich*. Madrid, 243–61.

Rodríguez Almeida, E. (1994). 'Scavi sul Monte Testaccio, novità dai tituli picti', in *Epigrafia della produzione e della distribuzione: Actes de la VIe Rencontre franco-italienne sur l'épigraphie du monde romain*. Rome, 111–31.

Ruffing, K. (2008). *Die berufliche Spezialisierung in Handel und Handwerk: Untersu-chungen zu ihrer Entwicklung und zu ihren Bedingungen in der römischen Kaiserzeit im östlichen Mittelmeerraum auf der Grundlage der griechischen Inschriften und Papyri*. St Katharinen.

Schleich, T. (1983). 'Überlegungen zum Problem senatorischer Handelsaktivitäten, T. I: Senatorische Wirtschaftsmentalität in moderner und antiker Deutung', *MBAH* 2/2: 65–90.

Shatzman, I. (1975). *Senatorial Wealth and Roman Politics*. Brussels.

Stelzenberger, B. (2008). *Kapitalmanagement und Kapitaltransfer im Westen des römischen Reiches*. St Katharinen.

Tassaux, F. (2004). 'Les Importations de l'Adriatique et de l'Italie du Nord vers les provinces danubiennes de César aux Sévères', in *Dall'Adriatico al Danubio, L'Illirico nell'età greca e romana, Convegno internazionale (Cividale 2003)*. Cividale, 167–205.

Tchernia, A. (1996). 'Maesianus Celsus et Caedicia Victrix sur des amphores de Campanie', in *Les Élites municipales de l'Italie péninsulaire des gracques a Néron: Actes de la table ronde de Clermont-Ferrand (28–30 novembre 1991)*. Naples and Rome, 207–11.

Treggiari, S. (1969). *Roman Freedmen during the Late Republic*. Oxford.

Verboven, K. (2002). *The Economy of Friends: Economic Aspects of* amicitia *and Patronage in the Late Republic*. Brussels.

Wacke, A. (1994). 'Die adjektizischen Klagen im Überblick, I: Von der Reeder- und der Betriebsleiterklage zur direkten Stellvertretung', *ZRG* 111: 280–362.

Waldstein, W. (1986). *Operae libertorum: Untersuchungen zur Dienstpflicht freigelassener Sklaven*. Stuttgart.

Wallace-Hadrill, A. (1994). *Houses and Society in Pompeii and Herculaneum*. Princeton.

Walton, G. M. (1967). 'Sources of Productivity Change in American Colonial Shipping, 1675–1775', *Economic History Review* 20: 67–78.

11

The Social Organization of Commerce and Crafts in Ancient Arles: Heterogeneity, Hierarchy, and Patronage

Nicolas Tran

In an article published in 1985 and entitled 'Economic Modernity and Status of Businessmen', Jean Andreau discussed the social and legal position of economic agents in the Roman world. In the historiographical context of the revival of the Bücher–Meyer controversy, he commenced by exposing the opposition between the two schools of thought that one traditionally refers to as 'primitivist' and 'modernist'. For Moses Finley and his followers, the world of 'work' was populated with small people.[1] The majority were slaves or freedmen, despised by the elite. Their social inferiority was symptomatic of the marginal place of crafts and commerce in the ancient economy. Conversely, scholars inspired by Mikhail Rostovtzeff, particularly John D'Arms, defended the idea that Roman commerce fostered the emergence of a category of businessmen of a significant calibre, symbolized by the rich, independent freedman.[2]

Yet Andreau did not limit himself to noting and describing the controversy: he pointed out the contradictions inherent to both positions, thus showing the urgent need to escape from their opposition:

> In this regard, the conclusions of Finley and D'Arms, while they contradict each other, are also contradictory in themselves. Finley, who wants to insist on the social humility of financiers, but also on the limitations imposed on the economy by the existence of ties of dependence, describes freedmen as very dependent on their patron, but he tends to minimize the financial interests of that same patron, without noting that this means that decision-making processes become incomprehensible, and that one can no longer see who benefits from the profits. Conversely, D'Arms, who wants to reduce

---

[1] Finley (1985: 60–1).
[2] Rostovtzeff (1957: pp. xiv, 142–79); D'Arms (1981: 146–8). On the notion of the independent freedman, see Garnsey (1981). Cf. Garnsey (1998) with an updated bibliography.

the importance of juridical and social differences, but hesitates to show that the elites were involved in commerce and financing, does not stop emphasizing the autonomy of freedmen and the role of patrons in financing them. However, if, in the end, all freedmen were independent (legally and financially), what role would be left for the patrons to play? One has to escape from the opposition of these two models . . . [3]

If we phrase this differently, the strong roots of craftsmen and traders in the servile population suppose the involvement of masters and higher-ranking patrons in artisanal and commercial activities, while independence is at odds with the status of freedman. This argues against the emergence of a class of business people made up of freedman parvenus. If the two leading models are so unsatisfactory, how are we to escape from their opposition? First of all, the question of the wealth or humble status of people involved in crafts and trade can be understood only through detailed prosopographical analysis. In reality, the world of work was diverse: like the urban *plebs* and the servile population in general, it was finely stratified. Slaves and freedmen did not make up the totality of the world of crafts and trade, nor did they form a homogeneous whole. Still, they all had in common the fact that they had a master or a patron. One thus has to explain the vertical relations that tied artisans and traders to their master or patron and their impact on the economy and on social hierarchies.[4]

It is impossible to address all these issues in this short chapter, but the problem posed by the shortcomings of both primitivist and modernist ideas about craftsmen and traders will form its background. The primary focus will be on the professional associations of Arles, in the second and third centuries AD. To enable us better to understand this port society, the *seviri Augustales corporati* will also be included in the analysis. The *corpora* fostered the social and civic integration of their members, and preserved them from the marginality to which their individual economic and legal condition could have consigned them.

HIERARCHICAL COMMUNITIES: THE MELTING POT OF A PLEBEIAN ELITE

The epigraphic record of Arles attests a fair number of professional associations, which is a characteristic feature of large places of commerce in the western part of the Roman Empire.[5] The texts of these inscriptions are given at

---

[3] Andreau (1985: 389).

[4] This theme is developed in H. Mouritsen's chapter on the place of Roman freedmen in economic life (Mouritsen 2011: 206–43). This book was not yet available in France when I planned this chapter (during summer 2011) and, as a result, I integrated it later into my research. Its conclusions, especially its criticism of the model of the rich and independent freedman (pp. 228–34), and mine are very similar.

[5] Waltzing (1895–1900) is still essential.

the end of this chapter. In the colony of Arles, we know of *corpora* of seafarers (nos 1–8), carpenters (9–14), *utricularii* (15–18), ship-builders (19–21), *centonarii* (19), and *lenuncularii* (22–3). To these should be added an association of *lapidarii Almanticenses* (24), whose provenance is unknown, and the shippers of the Durance (7, 16, 25), of whom we know two examples and one patron in relation to Arles. The *partiarii*, who appear on an altar dedicated to the *Manes* of a slave (no. 26; Fig. 11.1), are enigmatic. Because the monument was decorated with the representation of a ship, and because *partiarius* derives from *pars*, which alludes to the act of dividing and thus to distributing, Marc Heijmans has thought of *partiarii* as dockers.[6] Yet this is only one hypothesis among others. It is possible that the *partiarii* shared their burial grounds and thus formed a purely funerary association, instead of a professional one.[7] In any case the list of *collegia* from Arles may grow longer in the future through new discoveries: the two inscriptions of the *corpus lenunculariorum* were taken

Fig. 11.1. Funerary altar of Hermias (inscription 26). Musée de l'Arles antique. Photo: Nicolas Tran.

[6] Heijmans (2003).   [7] Christol (2010b: 413–14); Laubry (2012: 111–12).

out of the Rhône only in 2007.[8] This *corpus* is known through an altar dedicated to its Genius and through the pedestal of a statue of Neptune, which was donated by a certain Publius Petronius Asclepiades. This person does not highlight any collegial title, so it makes sense to consider him an external benefactor of the *corpus*. No *lenuncularius* has thus been attested—nor do we know of an individual *centonarius*. In fact, only the patronage of Gaius Paquius Pardalas of the *corpus centonariorum* attests the existence of this community. On the other hand, the names of fifteen *corporati* have been inscribed on epitaphs, which make up a small prosopographical series.[9]

One of the typical features of the evidence concerns the prominent representation of the dignitaries of the *corpora*. On his epitaph, Marcus Iunius Messianus mentions that the *utricularii* had made him *magister* four times (no. 17). Among the six known *fabri tignuarii*, Lucius Aventius (or Aventinius) Avitianus, Quintus Candidius Benignus, and Caius Publicius Bellicus report the same title (nos 9–10, 14). For their part, an anonymous from Saint-Gilles, Caius Iulius Pomp[—] and Marcus Frontonius Euporus were *curatores* of their *corpus*: the first of that of the *utricularii* (no. 18), the second of the *fabri navales* (no. 20), the third of the *navicularii marini* (no. 7). Such magistracies brought with them certain costs *ob honorem*, and, in general, their award reflected the social position of the benefactors, singling out the individuals and families that were seen as the most respectable.[10] Further, among the simple *corporati*, Lucius Iulius Secundus was at once *utricularius* at Arles and shipper of the Durance (no. 16). This combination can be explained in different ways. Secundus could have exercised both occupations successively. It is also possible that he practised only one of them but maintained business relations with other *corporati*, who, as such, accepted him as a member of their association. Finally, Secundus may have been shipper and *utricularius* at the same time. The second profession is very enigmatic. Given the places where the inscriptions mentioning them have been discovered, one has to accept, at the very minimum, that the activity of *utricularii* was related to the transport of merchandise and to transhipment points between river transport and land transport. Some historians have gone so far as to define *utricularii* as muleteers; others prefer to consider them, still, as river transporters.[11] I have not solved this enigma, but I would just emphasize that the occupations of shippers and *utricularii* were two different things, and beyond that leave it at the level of hypothesis. So, Lucius Iulius Secundus could have been involved in the transport of merchandise—wine, for example, if one thinks about the relief of Cabrières d'Aygues—relying on several modes of transport.[12] He should, in any

---

[8] Christol and Fruyt (2009).

[9] *ILGN* 116, of which the reading is very uncertain, has been excluded from the study.

[10] On the relation between collegial *honores* and social rank, see Tran (2006: 164–74).

[11] On this complex issue, see Verdin (2005), who gives earlier bibliography.

[12] For the relief of Cabrières d'Aygues, see Espérandieu (1907–66: ix. 6699).

case, be seen not as a simple muleteer or a modest boatman, but as a freight specialist, capable of organizing commercial relations on a regional scale.[13] Only then is the relative wealth suggested by his epitaph comprehensible: Secundus left 200 *denarii* to the *utricularii* to sacrifice at his tomb each year. The sum of this foundation is limited, but it nonetheless suggests that Secundus did not belong to the most humble workers of the port.

The *corporati* known from epigraphy were no marginal, poor people, neither at Arles nor elsewhere. On the contrary, the position that many of them occupied in their association seems to reflect their success in their respective economic activities. Of course, this does not mean that there were only a few poor workers in the port of Arles. Epigraphy simply fails to shed light on these milieux, as it concentrates on the upper strata of society, and on the upper strata of the *plebs* itself. This, at least, is the norm that seems to apply to the epigraphy of professional associations, as Michel Christol has emphasized for *Gallia Narbonensis*.[14] Above all, no association can be considered purely on its own terms: besides the internal hierarchy of each community, there were big differences between organizations.

A HIERARCHY OF *CORPORA* AND OF ECONOMIC ACTIVITIES

The harbour society of Arles was no homogeneous ensemble, and the occupations and associations that emerged from it were unequal in dignity and prestige.[15] As one might expect, the *navicularii* occupied the top of the pyramid. All epigraphic indications point in the direction of regarding maritime shipowners as the exception rather than the norm. The inevitable consequence of this observation is that it is impossible to base an understanding of the occupational structure of Arles on the *navicularii*.

As far as the social composition of the *corpora* of Arles is concerned, the *corpus* of the *navicularii marini* is the only known association that counted *seviri Augustales* among its members. In this quality, Lucius Secundius Eleuther and Marcus Frontonius Euporus advanced to a level of prestige close to that of the colonial elite (nos 4 and 7). The latter was elevated to the same dignity by the cities of Arles and Aix-en-Provence. As their Greek *cognomina* suggest, the role of these two persons as *seviri* had to compensate for the fact that—as freedmen— they were ineligible for municipal magistracies.[16] These former slaves, however,

---

[13] An anonymous individual from Saint-Gilles (no. 18) probably had the same professional status: he was a *curator* of the *utricularii Arelatentes* and of the *nautae* shipping on the rivers Ouvèze and Archèche. On this character, see Burnand (1971); Provost (1999: 625).
[14] Christol (2010a: 536–46).   [15] Christol and Tran (2014).   [16] Duthoy (1974).

were rich: access to the function of *sevir* supposed, effectively, the payment of a *summa honoraria* of several thousands of sesterces, and, on top of that, the undertaking of acts of generosity.[17] Besides, the shippers of the Durance and the *utricularii* of *Ernaginum* must have expected the generosity of their patron.[18] As protector of these two communities, Marcus Frontonius Euporus reversed the patronage relationship that tied him to his former master—and compensated for it. Yet whose dependant was he? Michel Christol has discussed this question in an article that, forty years after it was published, still remains fundamental.[19] Secundius and Frontonius correspond to two *gentilicia* of patronymical origin, created in Gaul from the *cognomina* Secundus and Fronto, which were very popular amongst the Celtic population. In fact, these *nomina* were common among notables in the eastern part of the territory of Nîmes. Simultaneously, it is possible that the ties of Euporus with Aix-en-Provence stemmed from the origin of the *familia* where he was born. From these observations, Christol built a convincing hypothesis according to which Lucius Secundius Eleuther and Marcus Frontonius Euporus must be regarded as representatives of a harbour elite with ties to the powerful families of the hinterland. Through such individuals, the landowners of the countryside invested part of their wealth in the harbour economy of Arles. As patrons, they probably granted loans to their freedmen, as happened in the imaginary case of Trimalchio, or formed a joint venture with them.[20] Some will have profited abundantly. However, the marine shippers of Arles collectively do not fit into this picture. Quintus Capitonius Probatus was probably one of them, even if his epitaph from Lyons refers to him as a *navicularius marinus* without referring to Arles (no. 8).[21] Originally from Rome, he was *sevir* at Lugdunum and at Puteoli. In fact, the links that Capitonius Probatus constructed between his native Italy and the Rhône valley necessarily passed through Arles, where the *naviculari* are the only ones known as *marini*. As a *sevir* in more than one city, like Euporus, Probatus was a rich businessman.

The social origins and the wealth of the marine *navicularii* seem to have had a profound influence on the organization of their *corpus*. As far as we know, the *navicularii* were the only *corporati* that were epigraphically visible in public space. At an unspecified date in the first or second century, they erected a statue for Cnaeus Cornelius Optatus, *duumvir* and a priest of the colony, on the *forum adiectum* of the city (no. 2). Subsequently, probably around the turn of the second and third centuries, they honoured an *eques* in charge of the *annona* for the province of *Gallia Narbonensis* and Liguria: Cominius Bo[- - -]

---

[17] Duncan-Jones (1974: 152–4, 215–17); Duthoy (1981: 1267, 1279).

[18] Tran (2006: 450–9).   [19] Christol (1971).

[20] On the credit, see Petronius, *Sat.* 76.9. On joint ventures, see the attitude of Crassus in Cic. *Par.* 6.46.

[21] According to Rougé (1965), Probatus exercised his occupation from Lyons, which is improbable.

Agricola Aurelius Aper (no. 1).[22] The base was installed in the harbour quarter of Trinquetaille. In this way, because of the status of their occupation and the fact that they signed contracts with the state, the *navicularii* formed the only known professional association from Arles that developed patronage ties outside the world of labour.[23] The shippers of the Durance and the *utricularii* of *Ernaginum* had to make do with a patron who was distinguished, but who was no member of the leading class (no. 7). Likewise, the *lenunculari* benefited from the generosity of a probable freedman, Publius Petronius Asclepiades, who must have belonged to the harbour society rather than to the local elite (no. 22). By contrast, the *navicularii* were in a position to extend their relations to networks outside their milieu. Their *corpus* was wealthy: it seems to have possessed a *statio* where an *apparitor* (no. 5) operated as well as some slaves: Quintus Navicularius Victorinus could have been their freedman (no. 6): the official right to use the *ius manumittendi* was granted to a minority of privileged colleges by Marcus Aurelius.[24]

The wealth and prestige of the *navicularii* resulted most notably from the services they performed for the *annona*. This is attested by two, probably contemporary, documents: the honorific base dedicated to Cominius Bo[- - -] ius Agricola Aurelius Aper and a famous inscription from Beirut, preserved on the back of a small, chiselled slab (nos 1, 3). Between 198 and 203, the *navicularii* complained before the prefect of the *annona* Claudius Iulianus about fraud, of which they claimed to have become victims.[25] Part of the fiscal grain that they transported to the capital was returned. Threatening to break their contracts, and following the example of other professionals serving the *annona*, they obtained an agreement from the prefect that public authorities would regain control over the organization of Rome's supply. Firm orders were given to a procurator placed under command of the prefect. It is precisely in the light of the relations with the *annona*, at the turn of the second and third centuries, that the shippers from Arles were described as the *navicularii marini Arelatenses quinque corporum*. On his epitaph, engraved during the second century, Marcus Frontonius Euporus was described as the curator of a single *corpus* (no. 7). Starting from this, two hypotheses are possible. Either the *corpus* was divided later, according to the model of the five *corpora* of *lenuncularii* of Ostia.[26] However, it is difficult to know the logic behind this division. The alternative is that, at the turn of the second and third centuries, the *corpus* of Arles and four other *corpora*, having their seat elsewhere in the empire, were treated as a joint unit by the Roman state. I would favour the

----

[22] The date is discussed by Christol and Demougin (1984) and Alföldy (1986). I follow the opinion of the former.

[23] On the diverse background of patrons of professional associations, see Clemente (1972).

[24] Dig. 40.3.1 (Ulpian, *ad Sab.* 5).   [25] Virlouvet (2004); Corbier (2006: 233–56).

[26] This is, for example, the hypothesis of Salvo (1992: 409), based on *CIL* 14.352 and 4144.

second possibility, following Michel Christol, and would add an argument in support of his position. A problem is posed by the eastern origin of the slab. As Catherine Virlouvet has shown, it is likely that the plaque, from which the slab comes, was set up in an eastern Mediterranean port.[27] Beirut appears too small; Tyre would be more suitable; Alexandria still more so. The transport of a decorative object from Egypt to Lebanon, during the early modern era, is not at all implausible. Indeed, if they had formed one of the five *corpora* that stood in direct contact with the state, the *navicularii* of Alexandria would have had an interest in putting up the decisions of Claudius Iulianus publicly: the problems raised by the *navicularii* of Arles ended in a general resolution that the five *corpora* could claim.[28] This reconstruction allows us to make the best of a hypothesis that, though it cannot be excluded, is still fragile: there is no indication that ports in the Greek-speaking East were frequented by ships from Arles. The radius of action of the *navicularii* was probably not as large as some historians have supposed, but the Roman state had placed the shippers from Arles on an equal footing with those of four other ports or regions of the empire that were essential to the supply of Rome.

Because of their modest character, the other professional associations of Arles were far from getting the attention of imperial authorities. For example, the *lapidarii Almanticenses* were, in the social hierarchy of the colony, undoubtedly in a very different position from the *corpus naviculariorum* (no. 24). Probably originating from a still unknown place called *Almanticum* or *Almantica*, the stone-cutters paid the final honour to Sextus Iulius Valentinus. The amount of money from the dues paid by their colleague permitted the purchase of a sarcophagus. The *lapidarii Almanticenses* thus formed a funerary association based on a professional network. Yet, 300 kilometres away, at Cimiez, they dedicated an altar to Hercules.[29] This mobility allows us to discuss the way in which *lapidarii* conducted their work, and the nature of the group that they formed. Were they itinerant workers, travelling from building site to building site? This seems possible.[30] In that case, they would have formed a group of limited size that played a marginal role within the society of Arles. By contrast, the *navicularii*, the *utricularii*, and the *fabri tignuarii* often made sure that they described themselves as *corpora colonia Iulia Paterna Arelate*. This description was not insignificant: it served to emphasize not only the roots, but also the official existence and the legal

---

[27] Virlouvet (2004: 356–7, particularly n. 82 on a possible provenance from Alexandria).

[28] The prefect alludes to an enlargement of the conflict (*cum eadem querella latius procedat, ceteris etiam implorantibus auxilium aequitatis*) and takes measures valid for the *homines qui annonae deserviunt*, in general: the *ceteri* mentioned could correspond to four other *corpora*. A large part of the text is lost, and the reason for which the plaque was put up in the eastern part of the empire will forever remain unknown to us.

[29] *CIL* 5.7869.

[30] The *opifices lapidarii*, known at Vaison through one simple epitaph, could have worked in a similar way (*CIL* 12.1384).

recognition of the *corpora* in the city.[31] Possibly, the *lapidarii Almanticenses* and the *partiarii* (no. 26; Fig. 11.1) did not belong to the same juridical category. In any case, they give the impression that they place themselves in the lowest echelon of the hierarchy of associations at Arles. It is that humble image that the *lenuncularii* must have wanted to get rid of when they decorated a gathering place with all possible care and made it into a matter of *honor* (nos 22–3).[32] Through social activities, these boatmen, who maintained the contacts between Arles and its pre-ports, as well as the crossing of the Rhône, tried to show and confirm their respectability. Socially, however, they placed themselves clearly below the seafarers and traders.

ABOVE AND BEYOND THE ASSOCIATIONS: THE HIGHEST LEVELS OF HARBOUR SOCIETY

A curiosity of the epigraphic record of Arles has to do with the absence of traders and merchants of the highest level, usually referred to as *negotiatores* and *mercatores*. The only exception confirms the rule. As *negotiator familiae gladiatoriae*, Marcus Iulius Olympus was the impresario of a group of gladiators, not a professional involved in long-distance trade.[33] In this respect, Arles contrasts with Lyon and Ostia. The harbour society of Ostia was dominated by *mercatores* and *negotiatores*, united in various associations— examples are the *mercatores frumentarii* and the *negotiatores olearii ex Baetica*.[34] At Lyon, the *negotiatores vinarii* formed the most prestigious *collegium*.[35] Other specialized *negotiatores* stood alongside them.[36] Parallels from the abundant documentation of Narbonne are less numerous, but still, one *negotiator* and two *mercatores* are known; two people whose occupation has partially been erased could perhaps be added.[37] How then are we to explain the silence of the epigraphy at Arles? One could, legitimately, explain it from the coincidental nature of archaeological finds or from the loss of inscriptions; texts mentioning the occupations in question may perhaps be found at Arles in the future. However, about 800 inscriptions have already been discovered.

---

[31] In Lyons, the *Omnia corpora licite coeuntium* formed an official category that without doubt did not include all associations (*CIL* 13.1921 and 1974).

[32] Christol and Tran (2014).

[33] *CIL* 12.727.

[34] *Mercatores frumentarii*: *CIL* 14.161, 4142, 4620. *Negotiatores olearii ex Baetica*: *CIL* 14.4458.

[35] *CIL* 13.1911, 1921, 1954, 11179; *ILGN* 423.

[36] *AE* 1982, 702, 709; *CIL* 13.1906, 1948, 1966, 1972, 1996, 2018, 2023, 2025, 2029, 2030, 2033, 2035.

[37] *CIL* 12.4496, 4492; *ILGN* 586. The two uncertain cases correspond to *CIL* 12.5971, 5973.

The absence of these professionals from the epigraphic record is thus strange, since it is beyond doubt that *mercatores* and *negotiatores* operated at Arles. A fragment from the *Digesta* refers to a slave *merci oleariae praepositus Arelate*: anyone would associate him with a *mercator*.[38]

The hypothesis that can be proposed is that, besides the three known *navicularii*, major businessmen are already present in the epigraphy from Arles, but remain unnoticed because they did not make their involvement explicit. Why? Because they had a more valuable aspect of their identity to put forward. The group of the *seviri Augustales corporati* from Arles consists of individuals that, based on their name, seem to be freedmen; their wealth is sometimes palpable. For example, in the course of the first century, Caius Fabius Hermes was able to have a vast mausoleum built for himself, his family, his patron, and the brother of his patron (no. 27). It is, of course, likely that the wealth of these freedmen *seviri* came from their involvement in the harbour economy. This is, for example, the case with a certain Lucius Pacullius Ephoebicus with a remarkable Greek *cognomen* (no. 28). In short, among the people from Arles who, on their tombstone, referred to themselves as only *seviri Augustales*, there were, in all probability, *negotiatores*, *mercatores*, *navicularii*, and other professionals.

Several texts make it possible to corroborate this hypothesis. Gaius Paquius Pardalas was described by his freedman Epigonus as patron not only of the *corpus* of the *seviri Augustales* (of which he was a member), but also of the shipbuilders, the *utricularii*, and the *centonarii* (no. 19; Fig. 11.2).[39] These three professional associations had turned to the rich freedman to find support and protection, probably because, after the success of his activities in the port, they considered him a distinguished person in the city. Similarly, as donor of a statue of Neptune, Publius Petronius Asclepiades was without doubt socially superior to the *lenunculari* that profited from his generosity (no. 22). He probably did not belong to their *corpus*, because he did not refer to it on the inscription recording the donation. However, he must have been close to the *lenuncularii* in his professional activities—if he did not do business with them.

While they remained silent about their occupation and the provenance of their wealth, certain *seviri Augustales* did emphasize that they had multiple geographical ties. Indeed, mobility was one of the characteristic features of the lives of Roman businessman: the itineraries of Marcus Frontonius Euporus and Quintus Capitonius Probatus have already suggested this. Like Euporus, Publius Sextius Florus was *sevir Augustalis* at Aix-en-Provence and Arles (no. 29). Marcus Silenius Symphorus obtained the same title at Lyons, at Arles, and at Riez (no. 30). The tomb of the *sevir Augustalis* L. Subrius La[- - -] and his wife, from Arles, stood in Cartagena, where the couple had probably installed themselves for business reasons (no. 31). Thus, the *corpus* of the *seviri*

---

[38] *Dig.* 14.13 pr. (Ulp. *Ad Edict.* 28).
[39] The combination recalls the case of Cnaeus Sentius Felix at Ostia (*CIL* 14.409).

Fig. 11.2. Funerary altar of G. Paquius Pardalas (inscription 19). Musée de l'Arles antique. Photo: Nicolas Tran.

Augustales of Arles welcomed individuals whose social and, probably, professional horizon surpassed that of the city.[40] At least some of them must have organized long-distance transport.

This type of trade was sometimes so lucrative that it made it possible for people to escape from their condition and advance in society. Cicero refers to this practice: '[trade] even seems to deserve the highest respect, if those who are engaged in it, satiated, or rather, I should say, satisfied with the fortunes they have made, make their way from the port to a country estate, as they have often made it from the sea into port.'[41]

Seen from the top of the social hierarchy, the *mercatura* was not really honourable until a *mercator* had stopped being one, and reinvested his profit

---

[40] In 2007, an epitaph of a *sevir Augustalis* of Lyons, V[er]ecun[dius - - -] and one other city was extracted from the Rhône. If one accepts that the letters PA were part of the title of the *colonia Iulia Paterna Arelate*, this was Arles (no. 32).

[41] Cic. *De off.* 1.151.

in landed property. This was probably the route of Aebutius Agatho in the second half of the second century: his epitaph should not be read as a picture of his social identity, but as a *curriculum vitae* (no. 33). Agatho died aged 70 in a city inland, where the function of *curator peculi rei publicae* was entrusted to him. The *Glanici* had recognized in him the expertise of a businessman that he had built up as shipper on the Saone.[42] This occupation of river transporter, which he exercised at Lyon, perhaps with financial support from a patron from that city, should have led him to nurture ties with the colonies of Arles and Apt, where he obtained the title of *sevir*.[43] Finally, he installed himself in *Glanum*, maybe to enjoy his retirement from business. It is possible that Quintus Cornelius Zosimus did the same, installing himself in a village in the eastern part of the territory of Arles—the *pagus Lucretius* (no. 34).[44] There, in the reign of Antoninus Pius, he used his wealth and network to defend the interests of the inhabitants with the imperial authorities: the *pagani* considered themselves wronged, because they were denied free access to the public baths, contrary to the rights that their status of inhabitants of Arles gave them. One cannot, however, be certain that Zosimus fits within the model of Trimalchio's retirement from business: his presence in the *pagus Lucretius* could equally well be explained through the fact that his patron Quintus Cornelius Marcellus possessed land here. He could have been its procurator. Despite all this, the epigraphic silence about the professional activity of Zosimus and the majority of the *seviri augustales* of Arles seems revealing. Their civic status permitted them, if not to live on landed property, at least to detach themselves from their professional identity, while putting up a powerful civic identity.

As a whole, it is plausible to think that the top of the harbour society was dominated by rich freedmen, who were at least partially financed by their patrons and who were judged worthy enough by the civic authorities to be attributed the function of *sevir*.[45] Many owed their financial wealth to occupations in trade and maritime transport, even if very few confirmed this on their epitaph. This idea has an impact on our picture of the harbour society as a whole. That the *seviri augustales* formed more prestigious communities than the professional associations is clear. Indeed, the *sportulae* that some received beyond the public distributions privileged the former.[46] Craftsmen and traders who highlight

---

[42] See also the *quaestura aerarii* entrusted by the colony of Ostia to the *mercatores frumentarii* Publius Aufidius Fortis (*CIL* 14.4620–1) and Marcus Iunius Faustus (*CIL* 14. 4142). Agatho was responsible for the *kalendarium* at *Glanum* (for the account book of the city).

[43] Seneca dedicated his *De Beneficiis ad Aebutium Liberalem*, to a friend from Lyons (*Ep.* 91).

[44] Jacques (1990: 63–4); Gascou (2000); Christol (2008: 133–4).

[45] P. Publicius Eutychus was probably a freedman of the colony.

[46] Van Nijf (1997: 253–4). At Cimiez, the decurions and the *seviri* were invited to a banquet, while the members of the professional *collegia* had to content themselves with a distribution of oil (*CIL* 5.7905). During another distribution, the former received *sportulae* of two *denarii*, the latter received *sportulae* of only one (*CIL* 5.7920).

only their memberships or their responsibilities in professional *corpora* were at an inferior level of the social hierarchy. Indeed, a thorough analysis leaves the feeling that at Arles the two groups had different characteristics, notably regarding onomastics. Excluding Lucius Secundius Eleuther and Marcus Frontonius Euporus, one has to observe that two out of fourteen members of the professional associations had Greek *cognomina* (Table 11.1).[47] Among the *corporati* with a Latin *cognomen*, there is the son of a certain Lucius Iulius Trophimus. However, the list of *seviri Augustales* gives exactly the opposite impression. Seven people of the eleven whose *cognomen* has been preserved had a Greek one.[48] The historian has to make do with fragile hypotheses, since the explicit mention of legal status was no longer the norm in the epigraphy of the second and third centuries, and since onomastic properties give only a very crude indication, and the sample is small. Yet ordinary freeborn people, exercising occupations that were less lucrative than trade—public construction or carpentry, for example—probably occupied a lower rank than did the rich *seviri Augustales*, of whom the majority were freedmen. As it was often related to the self-serving financial support of a patron,

Table 11.1. Names of the *corporati* of Arles known from inscriptions

Members of professional associations	*Seviri Augustales* of Arles
L. Secundius **Eleuther** (no. 4)	
M. Frontonius **Euporus** (no. 7)	
L. Avent. Avitianus (no. 9)	Aebutius **Agatho** (no. 32)
Aur. Septimius **Demetrianus** (no. 24)	Sex. Alfius Vitalis Florens (no. 35)
Caecilius Niger (no. 20)	Q. Cornelius Marcelli lib. **Zosimus** (no. 33)
Q. Capitonius Probatus (no. 8)	C. Fabius C. lib. **Hermes** (no. 26)
Q. Candidius Benignus (no. 10)	C. Iulius Fortunatus (no. 36)
T. Flavius Titus (no. 11)	L. Pacullius **Ephoebicus** (no. 27)
Iulius **Eumenes** (no. 15)	G. Paquius Optati lib. **Pardalas** (no. 18)
C. Iulius Pomp[—] (no. 19)	P. Publicius **Eutychus** (no. 34)
L. Iulius Secundus (no. 16)	P. Sextius Florus (no. 28)
Sex. Iulius Valentinus (no. 23)	M. Silenius **Symphorus** (no. 29)
M. Iunius Messianus (no. 17)	L. Subrius La[—] (no. 30)
L. Iulius Augustalis, son of L. Iulius	
Trophimus (no. 12)	
Pompeius Lucidus (no. 13)	
C. Publicius Bellicus (no. 14)	

Note: Greek *cognomina* are highlighted in bold.

[47] I have excluded from the count the *partiarius* Hermias and Marcus Atinius Saturninus, the *apparitor* of the *statio* of the *navicularii*. One cannot know if he was employed by the *navicularii* or was a member of the *corpus nauiculariorum marinorum*. The names of their wives did not feature any Greek *cognomen*, which reinforces the impression that we are here dealing with a milieu of freeborn plebeians.

[48] Though it did not have a strong social connotation, the *cognomen* Fortunatus was carried by slaves and freedmen (Kajanto 1965: 273); in Gallia Narbonensis: *CIL* 12.752 (Arles); 1370 (Vaison); 1525 (near Sisteron); 3277 (Nîmes); *ILGN* 548 (western territory of Nîmes).

Fig. 11.3. Relief with harbour workers. Musée de l'Arles antique. Photo: Nicolas Tran.

the position of a freedman was thus not always synonymous with marginality and social inferiority—quite the opposite. Though they certainly formed a small minority of the original servile population, freedmen could live in wealth and with prestige, not despite, but because of, their dependence. Hence, this case study of Arles confirms one of the strongest elements in Mouritsen's analysis of the Roman freedman. On the one hand, most of the *liberti* would have considered a break of social and economic ties with their patron as a disadvantage, and not as an asset.[49] On the other hand, when they wanted to invest a part of their wealth in port economies, notables sought the help of reliable persons. Most of the time, they turned to their deserving former slaves, because they had confidence in their loyalty and skills.[50]

To conclude, neither the members and dignitaries of the professional associations, nor the *seviri Augustales* who based their wealth on activities related to the harbour, lived on the margin of the society in Arles in the second and early third centuries. On the contrary, the majority of the people we know seem to have belonged to the highest echelons of the world of work—they

[49] Mouritsen (2011: 228–34).   [50] Mouritsen (2011: 219).

were part of a 'plebeian' elite that was well integrated in the city. However, the identity of these people and the economic activity that supported them cannot be understood in the same vein. In a certain way, the world of work was less marginal than the work itself, in the sense that the civic integration of craftsmen and traders was effected through their participation in more or less prestigious institutions of the city or recognized by the city. Indeed, the primary goal of these institutions was not to organize economic life in the strict sense of the word. It remains to note that epigraphy sheds only very partial light on this milieu. An epitaph like that of Hermias lifts, covertly, the veil from the slaves, who are so rare in the epigraphy of harbours in the Roman west, though their labour force must have been crucial. Free or slaves, the unskilled workers employed as labourers escape the view of the epigrapher, and appear in rare depictions on reliefs or paintings (Fig. 11.3).[51] The epigrapher perceives only the top of the iceberg, and this, in itself, is already enough to illustrate the fundamental heterogeneity of the world of work.

Appendix: Catalogue of Inscriptions

1. Arles: Tribute of the *navicularii marini* to an equestrian procurator

Block of hard limestone, discovered in an 'old wall of the Commanderie', in the quarter of Trinquetaille. *CIL* 12.672.

[.] Cominio [--- f(ilio)] | Claud(ia) Bo[---]io | Agricola[e Aur]elio | Apro, praef(ecto) cohor[t(is)] | tert(iae) Bracaraugustanor(um), | tribun(o) leg(ionis) I Adiut(ricis), procur(atori) | Augustorum ad annonam | prouinciae Narbonensis | et Liguriae, praef(ecto) a[lae] miliariae | in Mauretania Caesariensi, | nauic(ularii) marin(i) Arel(atenses) | corp(orum) quinq(ue) patro[no] | optimo et innocentis | simo.

2. Arles: Tribute of the *navicularii marini* to a local notable

Statue base of marble, with moulded frame. Discovered in 1850 in an excavation conducted in a yard in the Jesuits' college, on the location of the *forum adiectum*. *CIL* 12.692.

Cn(aeo) Cornel(io) | Cn(aei) fil(io) Ter(etina) | Optato, | IIuir(o), pontific(i), | flamini, | nauiculari(i) marin(i) | Arel(atenses) patrono.

---

[51] The only attestation of dockers at Arles is a relief representing two people who are busy packing a bundle depicted on Fig. 11.3. The sculpture comes from a mausoleum, and was thus commissioned by an individual of a higher status than that of the dockers. Cf. Espérandieu (1907–66: i. 164); Rothé and Heimans (2008: 619 (Fig. 890)).

3. Beirut: Letter of the prefect of the *annona* to the *navicularii marini* of Arles

Bronze plaque stemming from the cutting up (in modern times) of an inscribed tablet of the Roman era. *CIL* 3.14165, 8.

[Cl(audius) I]ulianus nauiculariis | [mar]inis Arela[t]ensium quinque | [c]orporum salutem. | [Qui]d lecto decreto uestro scripserim | [[---]] proc(uratori) Augg(ustorum), e(gregio) u(iro), subi|ci iussit. Opto felicissimi bene ualeatis. | E(xemplum) e(pistulae). | Exemplum decreti nauiculariorum ma|rinorum Arelatensium quinque cor|porum, item eorum quae aput me acta|sunt, subieci. Et cum eadem querella la|tius procedat, ceteris etiam imploranti | bus auxilium aequitatis, cum quadam de|nuntiatione cessaturi propediem obsequi | si permaneat iniuria peto, ut tam indemni|tati rationis quam securitati hominum | qui annonae deseruiunt consulatur, | inprimi charactere regulas ferreas et | adplicari prosecutores ex officio tuo iu|beas qui in Vrbe pondus quo susce|perint tradant.

4. Arles: Epitaph of Lucius Secundius Eleuther, *navicularius* from Arles

Marble altar, decorated on the sides with a *patera* and an ewer. Seen in the eighteenth century at Saint-Pierre-de-Galigan. Lost. *CIL* 12.704.

D(is) M(anibus), | L(ucio) Secundio | Eleuthero, | nauicular(io) Arel(atensi), | item IIIIIIuir(o) Aug(ustali) | corpor(ato) c(olonia) I(ulia) P(aterna) A(relate), | Secundia Tatiana{e} fil(ia) | patri pientissim(o).

5. Arles: Epitaph of Marcus Atinius Saturninus, *apparitor* of the *statio* of the *navicularii*

Sarcophagus seen in the second half of the seventeenth century at the Pointe de Trinquetaille. Lost since at least 1766. *CIL* 12.718.

--- | et quieti aeternae | M(arci) Atini Saturnin(i), [ap]|paritor(is) nauicular(iorum) | station[is --].

6. Arles: Epitaph of Quintus Navicularius Victorinus

Sarcophagus seen in 1574 'at the cemetery of the Aliscamps'. Lost. *CIL* 12.853.

Q(uintus) Nauicula|rius Victori|nus, Val(eriae) Seue|rinae, coniugi sanctissimae.

7. Saint-Gabriel: Epitaph of Marcus Frontonius Euporus, *sevir Augustalis* and *navicularius marinus*

Marble altar, discovered in the sixteenth century. Preserved in the chapel. *CIL* 12.982.

[D(is)] M(anibus), || M(arci) Frontoni Eupori, | IIIIIIuir(i) Aug(ustalis) col(onia) Iulia | Aug(usta) Aquis Sextis, nauicular(ii) | mar(itimi) Arel(atensis), curat(oris) eiusd(em) corp(oris), | patrono nautar(um) Druen|ticorum et utric(u)larior(um) | corp(oratorum) Ernaginens(i)um, Iulia Nice, uxor, | coniugi carissimo.

8. Lyon: Epitaph of Quintus Capitonius Probatus, *navicularius marinus*

Altar discovered in 1718 in the river bed of the Rhône. *CIL* 13.1942.

> D(is) M(anibus) | Q(uinti) Capitoni Probati | senioris, domo Rom(a), | IIIIIIuir(i)
> Aug(ustalis) Lugudun(i) | et Puteolis, | nauiculario marino, | Nereus et Palaemon, |
> liberti, patrono | quod sibi uiuus insti|tuit posterisq(ue) suis | et sub ascia
> dedicau(erunt).

9. Arles: Epitaph of Lucius Aventius Avitianus, *magister* of the *fabri tignuarii*

Fragment of a marble sarcophagus, seen in the second half of the seventeenth century, at the Pointe de Trinquetaille. Lost since at least 1766. *CIL* 12.719.

> D(is) M(anibus) || L(ucii) Auent(i *ou* -ini) Auit|iani, fabr(o) ti | gnuar(io) c(olonia) I(ulia)
> P(aterna) Arel(ate), | mag(istro) eiusdem | corp(oris), primo art(ificum), T(itus) Tossiu|s
> Marcus CO|SNA merenti.

10. Arles: Epitaph of Quintus Candidius Benignus, *magister* of the *fabri tignuarii*

Sarcophagus representing on its front side, in the middle of a frame, a metrical inscription that nowadays is illegible. Around the frame are depicted, to the left, an *ascia* and, to the right, a set square with plumb bob. Seen in the seventeenth century by F. de Rebatu, who saw it on the banks of the Rhône 'at La Ponche'. Found around 1725 at the Pointe de Trinquetaille; subsequently brought to mas d'Euminy, in Camargue, and brought back to the Alyscamps in 1844. *CIL* 12.722.

> D(is) M(anibus), || Q(uinti) Candi[di] Benigni, fab(ri) tig(nuarii) c|orp(orati)
> Ar(elate), ars cui summa fuit | fabricae, studium, doctrin(a), | pudorque, quem
> magni | artifices semper dixsere | magistrum, doctior hoc ne|mo fuit, potuit quem
> uinc|ere nemo, organa qui nosse|t facere, aquarum aut duce|re cursum, hic co[n]-
> uiua fui|t dulcis, nosset qui pasce|re amicos, ingenio studio | docilis animoque
> benig|nus, Candidia Quintina, | patri dulcissimo et Val(eria) | Maxsimina, coniugi
> kar(issimo).

11. Arles: Epitaph of Titus Flavius Titus, *faber tignuarius*

Sarcophagus in limestone, seen in 1765 by Gaillard, when he was at the Pointe de Trinquetaille. *CIL* 12.726.

> D(is) M(anibus), || Tit(o) Fl(auio) Tito, corp(oris) | fabror(um) tig|narior(um)
> corp(orato) | Arel(ate), Tit(us) Fl(auius) In|uentus, pa|trono pient(issimo).

12. Arles: Epitaph of Lucius Iulius Augustalis, *faber tignuarius*

Marble altar, found underneath the altar of the Virgin of the monastery of Saint-Césaire. It is probable that a dedication to the *Manes* was inscribed on the *pulvini* of the entablature, which are currently rather damaged. *CIL* 12.728.

> [D(is) M(anibus)] | L(uci) Iuli Augus|talis, fabri | tign(ariorum) corpor(ati) | Arel(ate),
> L(ucius) Iulius Trophimus, | pater infe|licissimus.

13. Arles: Epitaph of Pompeius Lucidus, *faber tignuarius*

Unclear when and by whom it was seen. Provenance unknown. Lost. *CIL* 12.735.

D(is) M(anibus) | Pompei Lucidi, | fabri tignuari | corporati Arelat(e), | e funeraticio eius.

14. Arles: Epitaph of Caius Publicius Bellicus, *magister* of the *fabri tignuarii*

Sarcophagus seen at Pointe de Trinquetaille from 1765 onwards. Decorated on its small sides with an *ascia* and a plumb-line.

D(is) M(anibus), || C(aio) Publ(icio) Bellico, corp(orato) col(oniae) | Iul(iae) Paterne Arel(ate) fabror(um) | tignuarior(um), item magistro, | Venucia Priscilla co(n)iugi | incomparabili item | Venucia Priscilla | uiua sibi fecit.

15. Arles: Epitaph of Julius Eumenus, *utricularius*

Altar of hard limestone, with moulded base and top; on top, two *pulvini* carrying the letters D and M. Between these, a roof shaped like a pediment. On the left, an *ascia*, to the right a plumb-line. Found in 1875 at Trinquetaille. *CIL* 12.729.

D(is) M(anibus), | Iulius Eumenes | uixit ann(os) XXII, | Iulia Agrippina, | patron(a) alumno | et corporato | utriclariorum, | quot tu nobis | debuisti facere, | et mater infelicissimae | posuerunt.

16. Arles: Epitaph of Lucius Iulius Secundus, *utricularius* and shipper of the Durance

Altar found in 1587, under the old church of Saint-Laurent. Broken in eighteenth century, lost since. Underneath the text was an *ascia*. *CIL* 12.731.

L(ucio) Iul(io) Secundo, | utric(u)lario corp(orato) | c(olonia) I(ulia) P(aterna) A(relate), qui legauit | eis testamento suo | (denarios) CC, ut ex usur(is) eor(um) | omnibus annis sacri|ficio ei parentetur, | item naut(ae) Druentic(o) | corpor(ato), Mogituma | Epipodius, filius nat(uralis), | patri pientissimo.

17. Arles: Epitaph of Marcus Iunius Messianus, *magister* of the *utricularii*

Sarcophagus in limestone. The epitaph is on the front side, in a frame held up by two cupids. The two small sides are decorated with a garland. Seen in the sixteenth century 'next to the ruined church of Saint Césaire and near the chapel of Brau'. *CIL* 12.733.

D(is) M(anibus), || M(arco) Iunio Messiano, | utricl(ario) corp(orato) Arelat(e), | eiusd(em) corp(oris) mag(istro) IIII f(acto), | qui uixit ann(os) XXVIII, | m(enses) V, d(ies) X, Iunia Valeria | alumno carissimo.

18. Saint-Gilles: Epitaph (?) of a curator of the *utricularii*, curator of the *nautae* of the Ardèche and of the Ouvèze

Fragment seen in the eighteenth century, reused above the door giving access to the Chapelle Saint-Pierre. *CIL* 12.4107.

> - - - | naut(a) Atr(icae) et Ou(idis), curator | eiusdem corporis, item | utric(u)lar(ius) corp(oratus) Arelat(e), | eiusdemq(ue) corp(oris) curat(or), | - - -

19. Arles: Epitaph of Gaius Paquius Pardalas, *sevir Augustalis*

Marble altar with moulded base and top. Preserved in 1655 underneath the 'high altar' of the church 'of Saint Jean l'Évangeliste of the monastery of Saint-Césaire'. *CIL* 12.700.

> D(is) M(anibus) | G(ai) Paqui Optati | lib(erti) Pardalae, IIIIII(uiri) | Aug(ustalis) col(onia) Iul(ia) Pat(erna) Ar(elate), | patron(i) eiusdem | corpor(is), item patron(i) | fabror(um) naual(ium), utric(u)lar(iorum) | et centonar(iorum), C(aius) Paquius | Epigonus cum liberis suis | patrono optime merito.

20. Arles: Epitaph of Caius Iulius Pom[- - -], curator of the *fabri navales*

Sarcophagus seen after 1739, supposedly preserved in the archbishop's palace, but lost since. *CIL* 12.730.

> C(aius) Iul(ius) Pom[- - -] | collega fab[rum] | naualium c[orp(oris) Arel(ate)], | curator eius[dem] | corporis, et | Seuera uiui s(ibi) | posuerunt et s(ub) [ascia] | dedicauer(unt).

21. Arles: Epitaph of Caecilius Niger, *faber navalis*

Fragment of a marble altar. Discovered in 1886 in the old 'Rue Wauxhall' (now 'Rue Jean-Jaurès'). *CIL* 12.5811; *ILGN* 108.

> [Cae]c[ilio] | Nigro, fa[bro nauali. | Praete]riens quicumque leges h[aec carmina nostra, | qu]ae tibi defuncti nomina uer[a dabunt, | incomptos] elegos ueniam peto ne ue[rearis] | perlegere, et dicas carmen ha[bere bene (?). | C]aecilius Niger est hic ille [sepul]tu[s eundem] | quo cernis titulum sta[re, habet ecce locum]. | Nunc tibi nauales pauci damus ul[tima uota]: | hoc et defuncto corpore munus [habe]. | Ossa tuis urnis optamus dulce quiesc[ant] | sitque leuis membris terra mo[lesta tuis]. | Arti[f]ic[i] artifices Nigro damus ista s[odali] | carmina, quae claudit iam res[oluta salus].

22. Arles: Dedication to the Numina of the emperors and to the honour of the association of *lenuncularii*

Inscription on the socle of a statue of Neptune found in the Rhône in 2007. Christol and Fruyt (2009: 104–9); *AE* 2009, 822.

Numinibus Auggg(ustorum) nnn(ostrorum), | honori corporis renunclariorum, P(ublius) Pe|tronius Asclepiades donum dedit.

23. Arles: Dedication to the Genius of the association of *lenuncularii*

Fragmentarily preserved altar, found in the Rhône in 2007. Christol and Fruyt (2009: 104–9); *AE* 2009, 823.

[Neptuno?, | Genio cor|po]ris, len|[u]nclari | sacrum.

24. Arles: Epitaph of Sextus Iulius Valentinus, dedicated by the *lapidarii Almanticenses*

Sarcophagus seen after 1588 near Saint-Honorat, now lost. *CIL* 12.732.

D(is) M(anibus) || Sex(ti) Iul(i) Valen|tini, lapida|ri(i) Almanti|censes ex fu|nere eius et || Pomp(eiae) Gra | tiniae co(n)iugi | inconpara | bili posuer(unt).

25. Arles: Epitaph of Aurelius Septimius Demetrianus, shipper of the Durance

Sarcophagus seen in 1739, discovered 'close to Trinquetaille'. *CIL* 12.721.

Aur(elius) Septimius Demetrianus, | nauta Druenticus, uiuus | sibi posuit.

26. Arles: Epitaph of Hermias

Marble altar with moulded socle and top. Discovered in 2001 in the Rhône, near Trinquetaille. Underneath the inscription a ship has been depicted, a plumb-line, and an *ascia*. *AE* 2003, 1079.

D(is) M(anibus) | Ermie | partiari | college | posuerunt.

27. Arles: Epitaph of Caius Fabius Hermes, *sevir Augustalis*

Limestone plaque with moulded frame, probably intended to decorate a mausoleum. Discovered in 1763 'in the quarter of Molleirez'. *CIL* 12.694.

C(aius) Fabius C(ai) lib(ertus) Hermes, | IIIIIIuir Aug(ustalis) c(olonia) I(ulia) P(aterna) Arel(ate), | uiuos fecit sibi et suis et | C(aio) Fabio L(uci) f(ilio) Secundo, patron(o), | et L(ucio) Fabio L(uci) f(ilio) Primo, fratri | eius. | H(oc) m(onumentum) h(eredem) m(eum) n(on) s(equetur).

28. Arles: Epitaph of Lucius Pacullius Ephoebicus, *sevir Augustalis*

Altar seen in 1783 'in the middle of a small garden at Mas des Passerons', in Camargue. *CIL* 12.699.

D(is) M(anibus), | IIIIIIuir(o) Aug(ustali) | Arelate | L(ucio) Pacullio Ephoe|bico, Aurelia | Eutychia uxor.

29. Arles: Epitaph of Publius Sextius Florus, *sevir Augustalis*

Marble tablet, discovered in 1543 'near the church of Saint-Antoine'. Comes from the necropolis of Trébon. Lost. *CIL* 12.705.

P(ublius) Sextius Florus, IIIIIuir Aug(ustalis) | col(onia) Iul(ia) Aquis et col(onia) Iul(ia) P(aterna) Arel(ate), | Valeriae Spuri f(iliae) Lassinae, | uxori pientissimae, | Sex(to) Valerio Proculino et suis.

30. Lyons: Epitaph of Marcus Silenius Symphorus, *sevir Augustalis*

Altar discovered, in the Chemin de la Favorite; decorated with an *ascia* and a plumb-line. *ILTG* 241; *AE* 1935, 17.

D(is) M(anibus) | M(arci) Sileni Symphori, | IIIIIIuir(i) Aug(ustalis) | Lug(duni), Arelate, Reis, | Silenia Latina, | liberta idemque uxor, | patrono et marito | erga se optimo | et sibi uiua posuit.

31. Cartagena: Epitaph of Lucius Subrius La[---], *sevir Augustalis*

Marble plaque discovered in 1975, in a necropolis in the north-west part of the city. *AE* 1975, 523.

L(ucius) Subrius La[---], | IIIIIIuir Au[g(ustalis) ---] | c(olonia) I(ulia) P(aterna) Arela[te], | et Subria L(uci) l(iberta) [---] | DA.

32. Arles: Epitaph of Verecundius [---], *sevir Augustalis*

Altar found in the Rhône in 2007. Heijmans (2009: 340, n. 1); *AE* 2009, 816.

--- ? | V[er]cun[dio] | C[.]V[.]TO[..] IIII[IIuiro Aug(ustali)] | co[rp(orato)] col(oniae) C[laud(ia) | L]u[gud(uni)] item [--- | ---] PA [--- | ---] AV[--- | --- | --- | ---] XX F [--- | ---] dulci[ssimo].

33. Saint-Rémy-de-Provence. Epitaph of Aebutius Agatho, *sevir Augustalis*

Altar, discovered in 1740 in the ruins of the chapel of Sainte-Trophime. *CIL* 12.1005.

[D(is) M(anibus) et | me]mori(a)e aeterna[e] | Aebuti Agathon[is], | [IIIIII]uiro Aug(ustali) corp(orato) [col(oniae) Iul(iae) | Pat]er(nae) Arel(ate), curat(ori) eius|[de]m corp(oris) bis, item IIII[II|ui]ro col(oniae) Iul(iae) Aptae, nau|[t]ae Ararico, curator[i] | peculi r(ei) p(ublicae) Glanico(rum), qui | uixit annos LXX, | Aebutia Eutychia patro|no erga se pientissimo.

34. Géménos: Tribute of the *pagani* of the Pagus Lucretius to Quintus Cornelius Zosimus, *sevir Augustalis*

Moulded marble table, seen for the first time in the seventeenth century. It served as altar table in the chapelle Notre-Dame. *CIL* 12.594; *AE* 2000, 883; *AE* 2006, 783.

[P]agani pagi Lucreti qui sunt fini|bus Arelatensium, loco Gargario, Q(uinto) Cor(nelio) | Marcelli lib(erto) Zosimo, IIIIIIuir(o) Aug(ustali) col(onia) Iul(ia) | Paterna Arelate, ob honorem eius. Qui notum fecit | iniuriam nostram omnium saec[ulor]um sacra|tissimo principi T(ito) Aelio Antonino [Aug(usto) Pio te]r Romae | misit per multos annos ad praesides pr[ouinci]ae perse|cutus est iniuriam nostram suis in[pensis e]t ob hoc | donauit nobis inpendia quae fecit ut omnium saecu|lorum sacratissimi principis Imp(eratoris) Caes(aris) Antonini Aug(usti) Pii | beneficia durarent permanerentque, quibus frueremur | [aquis] et balineo gratuito quod ablatum erat paganis, | quod usi fuerant amplius annis XXXX.

35. Arles: Epitaph of Publius Publicius Eutychus, *sevir Augustalis*

Moulded marble tablet, perhaps from the Alyscamps (?). *CIL* 12.702.

D(is) M(anibus), | P(ublio) Publicio | Eutycho, | IIIIIIuir(o) Aug(ustali) | c(olonia) I(ulia) P(aterna) Arel(ate).

36. Arles: Epitaph of Sextus Alfius Vitalis Florens

Sarcophagus discovered in 1809 in the ancient circle of Vauxhall. *CIL* 12.689.

D(is) M(anibus), || Sex(tus) Alfius Vitalis Forens, | IIIIIIuir Aug(ustalis) corp(oratus) c(olonia) I(ulia) P(aterna) Arel(ate), et | Alfiae Epauxesi, lib(ertae) uxoriq(ue) | suae, quae uixit ann(os) XL, m(enses) II, | d(ies) XXVII, sibi posterisquae | suis uiuus fecit.

37. Arles: Epitaph of Veria Filtata and of Caius Iulius Fortunatus, *sevir Augustalis*

Marble altar decorated with foliage; seen in the eighteenth century at Saint-Honorat-des-Alyscamps. *CIL* 12.709.

[D(is)] M(anibus), | Veriae Filtate, | amica dolens | posuit in honorem | C(ai) Iuli For|tunati, IIIIIIuir(i) | Augustalis, | uxori.

REFERENCES

Alföldy, G. (1986). 'Zur Nomenklatur und Laufbahn eines römischen Ritters aus Concordia', *ZPE* 63: 173–80.

Andreau, J. (1985). 'Modernité économique et statut des manieurs d'argent', *MEFRA* 97/1: 373–410.

Burnand, Y. (1971). 'Un aspect de la géographie des transports dans la Narbonnaise rhodanienne: Les Nautes de l'Ardèche et de l'Ouvèze', *RAN* 4: 149–58.

Clemente, G. (1972). 'Il patronato nei collegia dell'impero romano', *SCO* 21: 142–229.

Christol, M. (1971). 'Remarques sur les naviculaires d'Arles', *Latomus* 30: 643–63.

Christol, M. (2008). 'Colonie de vétérans et communautés indigènes', in J.-M. Rouquette (ed.), *Arles: Histoire, territoires et cultures*. Arles, 125–34.

Christol, M. (2010a). *Une histoire provinciale: La Gaule narbonnaise de la fin du IIe siècle av. J.-C. au IIIe siècle ap. J.-C.* Paris.

Christol, M. (2010b). 'Formes de la vie économique et formes de la vie sociale à Arles au IIe et au IIIe siècle: Sources et travaux récents', in M. Silvestrini (ed.), *Le Tribù romane: Atti della XVIe Rencontre sur l'épigraphie.* Bari, 405–16.

Christol, M., and Demougin, S. (1984). 'Notes de prosopographie équestre', *ZPE* 57: 163–78.

Christol, M. and Fruyt, M. (2009). 'Neptune: Étude épigraphique', in L. Long and P. Picard (eds), *César: Le Rhône pour mémoire.* Arles, 104–9.

Christol, M., and Tran, N. (2014). '*Tituli et signa collegiorum* en Gaule méridionale et ailleurs: Réflexions sur le décor des sièges de collèges à partir du cas arlésien', *École antique de Nîmes* 31: 15–31.

Clemente, G. (1972). 'Il patronato nei collegia dell'impero romano', *SCO* 21: 142–229.

Corbier, M. (2006). *Donner à voir, donner à lire: Mémoire et communication dans la Rome ancienne.* Paris.

D'Arms, J. H. (1981). *Commerce and Social Standing in Ancient Rome.* Cambridge and London.

Duncan-Jones, R. P. (1974). *The Economy of the Roman Empire: Quantitative Studies.* Cambridge.

Duthoy, R. (1974). 'La Fonction sociale de l'augustalité', *Epigraphica* 31: 134–54.

Duthoy, R. (1981). 'Les **Augustales*', in *ANRW* II 16/2: 1254–309.

Espérandieu, E. (1907–66). *Recueil général des bas-reliefs, statues et bustes de la Gaule romaine.* Paris.

Finley, M. I. (1985). *The Ancient Economy.* 2nd edn. Berkeley and Los Angeles.

Garnsey, P. (1981). 'Independent Freedmen and the Economy of Roman Italy under the Principate', *Klio* 63: 359–71; repr. in Garnsey (1998), 28–44.

Garnsey, P. (1998). *Cities, Peasants and Food in Classical Antiquity: Essays in Social and Economic History.* Cambridge.

Gascou, J. (2000). 'L'Inscription de Saint-Jean-de-Garguier en l'honneur du sévir augustal Q. Cornelius Zosimus', *MEFRA* 112/1: 279–95.

Heijmans, M. (2003). 'Récentes découvertes épigraphiques dans le Rhône à Arles (Bouches-du-Rhône)', *RAN* 36: 377–81.

Heijmans, M. (2009). 'Les Inscriptions lapidaires et diverses', in L. Long and P. Picard (eds), *César: Le Rhône pour mémoire.* Arles, 340–3.

Jacques, F. (1990). *Les Cités de l'Occident romain.* Paris.

Kajanto, I. (1965). *The Latin Cognomina.* Helsinki.

Laubry, N. (2012). '*Ob sepulturam*: Associations et funérailles en Narbonnaise et dans les Trois Gaules sous le Haut-Empire', in M. Dondin-Payre and N. Tran (eds), *Collegia: Le Phénomène associatif dans l'Occident romain.* Bordeaux, 103–33.

Mouritsen, H. (2011). *The Freedman in the Roman World.* Cambridge.

Nijf, O. M. van (1997). *The Civic World of Professional Associations in the Roman East.* Amsterdam.

Provost, M. (1999). *Carte archéologique de la Gaule. Le Gard. 30/3.* Paris.

Rostovtzeff, M. I. (1957). *Social and Economic History of the Roman Empire.* 2nd edn. Oxford.

Rothé, M. P., and Heijmans, M. (2008). *Carte archéologique de la Gaule. Arles, Crau, Camargue. 13/5.* Paris.

Rougé, J. (1965). 'Les Relations de Lyon et de la mer: À propos de *CIL* XIII, 1942', in *Actes du 89ᵉ Congrès des Sociétés savantes (Lyon 1964)*. Paris, 137–52.

Salvo, L. de (1992). *Economia privata e pubblici servizi nell'impero romano. I corpora naviculariorum*. Messina.

Tran, N. (2006). *Les Membres des associations romaines: Le Rang social des* collegiati *en Italie et en Gaule sous le Haut-Empire*. Rome.

Verdin, F. (2005). 'Encore les utriculaires . . .', in A. Bouet and F. Verdin (eds), *Territoires et paysages de l'âge du Fer au Moyen Age: Mélanges offerts à Philippe Leveau*. Bordeaux, 275–82.

Virlouvet, C. (2004). 'Les Naviculaires d'Arles: À propos de l'inscription de Beyrouth', *MEFRA* 116/1: 327–70.

Waltzing, J.-P. (1895–1900). *Étude historique sur les corporations professionnelles chez les Romains*. Louvain.

12

Hierapolis and its Professional Associations: A Comparative Analysis

Ilias Arnaoutoglou

Since the middle of the 1990s, there has been a clear shift in the way associations are treated by scholars. In sharp contrast to the holistic approach of late-nineteenth-century scholarship, there is a growing body of literature examining associations in their geographical and historical context.[1] I have attempted a similar approach, underlining the duality in the associative experience in Roman Lydia through the examination of the relevant epigraphic *testimonia* from Thyateira and Saittai.[2] The aim of this chapter is to enlarge the frame and add the nearby Phrygian city of Hierapolis to the picture.[3] Hierapolis provides an interesting comparison, not so much because of its geographic proximity, but rather because, as is the case in Thyateira and Saittai, its epigraphic record provides an above-average concentration of evidence for professional associations.[4] After some introductory remarks on

---

[1] Earlier scholarship: Ziebarth (1896); Poland (1909); Waltzing (1895–1900). More recently: Ritti (1995); Labarre and Le Dinahet (1996); Dittmann-Schöne (2000); Zimmermann (2002); Sommer (2006). On the historiography of Roman associations, see Perry (2006) and Dissen (2009).

[2] Arnaoutoglou (2011).

[3] Ancient Hierapolis, near modern Denizli in Turkey, has become a tourist destination thanks to the impressive travertine cascades, i.e. deposits formed as a result of the flow of water from thermal springs (35° C). Reduction of pressure results in loss of carbon dioxide and deposits of calcium carbonate in a thin layer at a rate of 3 cm/annum. For the excavations and the restoration on the site, see the report of D'Andria (2006).

[4] The unique nature of the Hierapolitan record becomes apparent when it is compared with associations attested in the nearby towns of Colossae and Laodikeia on the Lykos. For Colossae, see *MAMA* 6.47 (= *BE* (1939: 392); second/third century AD): honorary inscription for Glykon referring to οἱ ἑταίροι; *MAMA* 6.48 (= Ritti 2007, 73; *BE* (1939: 392); second/third century AD): dedication to Tatianos Bartos referring to συνγενικὸν νεώτερον. For Laodikeia on the Lykos, see *IK* 49.32, 33 (= *BE* (1997: 585); imperial period): seats in theatre mentioning an [ἐ]ργασίας κλ—. Cf. Dittmann-Schöne (2001: 232); *IK* 49.50 (= *IGR* 4.863, *BE* (1938: 447); third century AD): fragment of an honorary decree mentioning [ἡ ἐργασία] τῶν γναφέ[ων καὶ] ἁπλουργῶν, cf. Waltzing (1895–1900: 3, no. 129), Labarre and Le Dinahet (1996: no. 55), Dittmann-Schöne (2001: 232), Zimmerman (2002: 191), Ramsay

the history of Hierapolis, the comparison with the *fenomeno associativo* in Lydia will develop around five questions.[5] First, who were forming associations? Second, how did craftsmen name their groups? Then, what was the social positioning of professional associations and what was their social composition? This leads to the question of what was the image of an association of craftsmen in society. Finally, the analysis will focus on the issue of memory management, and the role of professional associations in it.

INTRODUCING HIERAPOLIS

Hierapolis lies in the south-west corner of Phrygia, close to Colossae and Laodikeia on the Lykos, on a plateau looking out over the valley of the river Lykos, which is a tributary of the Maeander. Because of its location, Hierapolis controlled the route into Lydia from the south-east, as well as the routes connecting inner Anatolia to the coastal towns of Ephesos and Miletos and to north-west Caria.

Herodotus refers to a Phrygian border town called Kydrara, which was situated in the area of Hierapolis.[6] Yet Hierapolis itself was founded only sometime in the third century BC, most probably by the Seleucids.[7] The area was the centre of a local cult of Cybele, but, in the Greek *polis*, the cult of Apollo *Archegetes* was dominant.[8] After the peace of Apameia in 188 BC, Hierapolis became part of the Attalid kingdom and followed the latter's destiny when it passed under Roman control in 133 BC. Roman merchants were probably well established in the city: two inscriptions attest the existence of an association (*conventus*) of Romans.[9] From the second century BC to the

(1890: i. 74, 8), Poland Z70; *MAMA* 6.11 (= *IGR* 6, 858; *BE* (1939: 393); second/third century AD): honorary inscription mentioning a [ἡ θ]ρεμματι[κή ἐργασία?]; *MAMA* 6.24 (= *BE* (1939: 393); second/third century AD). Tombstone of Meltine referring to τὸ συγγενικὸν; *Olba* 19 (2011), 186 (= Simsek 2013: 237; imperial period): seats in the northern theatre mentioning a ἐργασία ὀρθοκουρων?; Thonemann (2011: 188; imperial period): inscription found in forum of Laodikeia mentioning a τόπος βαφέων.

[5] See already Labarre and Le Dinahet (1996: 67), who note the differences between the testimonies on professional associations from Lydia and Hierapolis. Sanidas (2011) compares textile production in mainland Greece and Asia Minor.

[6] Hdt. 7.30 describes how the army of Xerxes leaves Colossae and proceeds through the border region between Phrygia and Lydia in the direction of Sardis: 'ἐκ δὲ Κολοσσέων ὁ στρατὸς ὁρμώμενος ἐπὶ τοὺς οὔρους τῶν Φρυγῶν καὶ Λυδῶν ἀπίκετο ἐς Κύδαρα πόλιν, ἔνθα στήλη καταπεπηγυῖα, σταθεῖσα δὲ ὑπὸ Κροίσου, καταμηνύει διὰ γραμμάτων τοὺς οὔρους.'

[7] Kolb (1974) and Debord (1997).

[8] On cults in Hierapolis, see Ramsay (1895-7: i. 85-90); Cichorius (1898: 42-3). On the sanctuary at Hierapolis: Ritti (1989-90). On evidence for the cult of Apollon *archegetes*: Judeich (1898: 4); *SEG* 56.1500. For the oracle, see Pugliese Carratelli (1963-4); Ruffing (2008: 260-1). In the 1960s Italian excavators identified a cavity to the right side of the temple of Apollo with what was interpreted as the *Ploutoneion* (cf. Strabo, *Geogr.* 13.4.14).

[9] See Judeich (1898: 32, 15-17): κονβεντᾳ [ρ]/χήσαντα τῶν Ῥωμᾳ [ί]/ων, and *SEG* 53.1464 (*AE* 2007: 1696; *SEG* 58.1510), Ῥωμαίων κωουέντarχον, with Hatzfeld (1919: 165).

first century AD there is a clear development of manufacturing activities, particularly wool-working and dyeing of textiles.[10] Strabo refers to the hot springs in the city, emphasizing the property of fixing colours in woollen textiles; the plant used, madder root (*robia tinctorum*), produced a red dye, similar to purple but a lot cheaper: 'The water at Hierapolis is remarkably adapted also to the dyeing of wool, so that wool dyed with roots rivals that dyed with the coccus or with the marine purple. And the supply of water is so abundant that the city is full of natural baths.'[11]

In AD 60, an earthquake destroyed the city as well as the neighbouring cities of Colossae and Laodikeia.[12] Reconstruction started under Domitian (AD 81–96).[13] The city prospered under Hadrian, Antoninus Pius, Marcus Aurelius, and Septimius Severus. At some point between AD 218 and 222, Hierapolis was granted the title *neokoros*.[14]

Most of the epigraphic *testimonia* of the Hierapolitan associations can be dated on the basis of letter style to the period between the mid-second and mid-third century AD.[15] Despite the lack of an up-to-date epigraphic corpus,[16] two salient features emerge. First, we are short of information about their internal structure and life. Secondly, associations were involved in the management of the memory of the deceased: several inscriptions mentioning associations are in fact part of funerary monuments, and they specify that fines for the violation of a tomb or endowments are to be paid to a particular professional group.[17]

---

[10] Ritti (1995: 71–2) and D'Andria (2001). The rapid development of Hierapolis as an urban centre after AD 60 may be reflected in the prosperity of craftsmen in the period between the mid-second and mid-third century, as suggested for towns in the western part of the empire by Patterson (2006).

[11] Strabo, *Geogr.* 13.4.14: ἔστι δὲ καὶ πρὸς βαφὴν ἐρίων θαυμαστῶς σύμμετρον τὸ κατὰ τὴν Ἱερὰν πόλιν ὕδωρ, ὥστε τὰ ἐκ τῶν ῥιζῶν βαπτόμενα ἐνάμιλλα εἶναι τοῖς ἐκ τῆς κόκκου καὶ τοῖς ἁλουργέσιν· οὕτω δ' ἐστὶν ἄφθονον τὸ πλῆθος τοῦ ὕδατος ὥστε ἡ πόλις μεστὴ τῶν αὐτομάτων βαλανείων ἐστί, trans. H. L. Jones. Cf. Ritti (1995: 67). On the plants producing the natural dye in the area, see now Huttner (2009) and Ruffing (2009).

[12] See Ritti (1997: 346–8).

[13] See, e.g. the bilingual inscription *AE* 1969/1970, 593, AD 86/87): [Αὐτοκράτορι [Δομιτιανῷ] Καίσαρι Σεβασ]τῷ Γερμανικῷ, ἀρχιερεῖ με[γίσ]τῳ, δημαρ[χι]/[κ]ῆς ἐ[ξουσίας τὸ ζ΄, αὐτοκράτορι τὸ ιδ΄, ὑπάτῳ τὸ ιβ΄, πα]τρὶ πατρίδος, τὴν πύλην καὶ τοὺς πύ[ργους ἐποίη]σεν Σέξτος ['Ι]ούλιος Φρον[τῖνος ἀνθύπατος — — —].

[14] See Ritti (2003) and Burrell (2004: 135–41), and the two letters of Hadrian to Hierapolis sent in AD 117 (*SEG* 55.1415) and AD 130 (*SEG* 55.1416).

[15] See Ritti (1995: 66, 70), and, more generally, Dittmann-Schöne (2000: 13).

[16] Judeich (1898) and more recently Ritti (1995, 2004). See also the overview of epigraphic research in Ritti, Miranda De Martino, and Guizzi (2007).

[17] The question of the origin of these associations cannot be dealt with in this chapter. On this topic, see Debord (1982) and Ritti (1995). According to Debord (1982: 15, 305), these associations continue the pre-Hellenistic (i.e. Achaemenid) tradition of guild organization and activities. Ritti (1995: 68–9) claims that the use of hot water from the sacred water springs, controlled by the priesthood, for dyeing the wool reinforces the link between the priesthood and the craftsmen, the latter perhaps being descendants of earlier sacred slaves working in the sanctuaries.

In Lydia, the epigraphic evidence for professional associations peaks at roughly the same time, but it spans a period from the first to the end of the third century AD. The existence of a corpus for Thyateira and Saittai facilitates analysis. As in Hierapolis, we are badly informed about the internal structure of professional associations; while in Thyateira they do not seem to have been involved in funerary activities, associations in Saittai are attested only in funerary contexts, but not in the same way as in Hierapolis, as it will become clear below.[18] The funerary monuments themselves are also different: in Hierapolis, funerary inscriptions can be found on a variety of monuments; they frequently appear on sarcophagi placed upon a base, sometimes upon a building with a room and funerary beds, or upon a mortuary chapel with a gabled roof.[19] By contrast, in Saittai, funerary inscriptions are rather formulaic, inscribed on simply decorated *stelae*. In Thyateira, most epigraphic evidence is found on statue bases.

WHO WERE FORMING PROFESSIONAL ASSOCIATIONS?

Of the thirty-three testimonies of associations in Hierapolis, twelve concern religious associations or associations of a different kind; the remaining twenty-one inscriptions mention professional associations of craftsmen. Together, these texts contain twenty-eight references to craftsmen groups, of which seven are to πορφυραβάφοι (purple-dyers),[20] three to βαφεῖς (dyers) and ἐριοπλύται (wool-washers), two to ἐργαστηριάρχαι (manufacturers), θρεμματική (cattle-breeders),[21] κηπουροί (gardeners), and χαλκεῖς (coppersmiths), and one each to ἀκαιροδαπισταί (carpet-weavers), ἡλοκόποι (nail-makers), κοπιδερμοί (cutlers), λινωταί (linen-weavers?), ἀρτοποιοί (bread-makers), and ὑδραλέται (water-mill operators).[22]

---

[18] On the importance of the funerary evidence for questions of status and social influence, see van Nijf (2010: 165–71).

[19] See the discussion of monumental tombs and their overall environment in Roman Asia Minor by Cormack (2004).

[20] For an overview of the evidence for this profession, see Drexhage (1998).

[21] Suggested already by Cichorius (1898: 48). Judeich (1898: 143), followed by van Nijf (1997: 82 n. 152), disagrees. Ramsay (1895–7: i. 119) suggested the far-fetched explanation that it was an organization for looking after foundlings (from *threptoi*).

[22] Ritti (1995: 72–3; 2004: 486–7) refers to unpublished inscriptions mentioning λινουργοί, πιλοποιοί, κοπιδερμοί, ἀρτοποιοί, and a σιλιγνειτοπώλης. Evidence for the various crafts is collected by Ruffing (2008): ἀκαιροδαπιστής (p. 400), βαφεῖς (pp. 453–9), ἐργαστής (pp. 522–3), ἐριοπλύτης (p. 525), ἡλοκόποι (p. 537), κοπιδερμοί (p. 601), λινωταί, λινουργοί (pp. 640–7), πορφυροβάφος (p. 725–7), χαλκεῖς (pp. 814–19). Earlier but still useful is Zimmermann (2002). For κοπιδερμὸς, see also *IK* 36.250, II 21 (Tralleis, third/fourth century AD): τόπος ἐν Παρκάλλοις Ἀλεξάνδρου Κοπιδέρμου ζυ(γὸν) κ(εφάλαιον). Κοπιδέρμου should be understood as a profession; cf. also *MAMA* 3.573 (Korykos, third/fourth century AD) for a κοπιδᾶς. For other professions in Hierapolis,

The prominence of the association of purple-dyers is remarkable: about a third of the inscriptions mentioning professional associations refer to it. In general, associations of craftsmen involved in the clothing industry seem to hold a dominant position: fifteen out of twenty-eight references are related to this branch of the economy.[23]

In Lydia, professional associations also brought together craftsmen involved in textile production—more than half of the inscriptions from Thyateira and the arca of Saiۨtai (thirty-two our of fifty-three) pertain to professional groups in this branch of the economy. There are linen-workers and linen-weavers (λινουργοί, λινύφοι)—linen-workers seem prominent in the area of Saittai (fourteen out of thirty-two references)—wool-workers, wool-sellers (λανάριοι, ἐριουργοί, ἐριοπῶλαι), felt-workers (πιλοποιοί), fullers (γναφεῖς), weavers (ὑφανταί), tow-makers (σιππινάριοι), and dyers (βαφεῖς). Dyers appear particularly active in Thyateira (nine out of twenty-one mentions). Beyond textiles, there are organizations of people involved in leather-processing—tanners (βυρσεῖς) and shoemakers (σκυτεύς, σκυτοτόμοι)—bread-making—bakers (σκυτεύς, ἀρτοποιοί) and 'winter-wheat' sellers (σιλινάριοι)—doll-makers (κοραλλιοπλάσται), coppersmiths (χαλκεῖς, χαλκοτύποι), carpenters (τέκτονες), carpet-cleaners? (ψιλαγνάφοι), potters (κεραμεῖς), gardeners (κηπουροί), musicians (μουσικοί), and people involved in the slave trade (προξενηταὶ σωμάτων, ἐργασταὶ σταταρίου).

HOW DID CRAFTSMEN NAME THEIR GROUPS?

In Hierapolis, craftsmen, in order to denote an association, used two categories of terms. The most widely employed terms underline the craft element behind the organization: ἐργασία (ten inscriptions), συντεχνία (three inscriptions), τέχνη (three inscriptions); less frequently used were more generic terms such as συνέδριον (three inscriptions), and κοινόν. It is important to emphasize that these designations do not reflect any difference in the nature of the organizations; all refer to associations of craftsmen.[24] Take, for example, the 'most

---

see *AAST* 101 (1966–7): 313, no. 37; Judeich (1898: 156): πορφυροπώλης; Judeich (1898: 75): κάπηλος; no. 135: ζωγράφος; no. 222: παστιλλᾶς; no. 262: μυροπώλης (cf. *SEG* 54.1302); no. 274: τεχνίτης; *SEG* 33.1139: ἀνδριαντουργός. Note also *SEG* 57.1385 (Colossae, second/third century AD): διφθεροπὺς for διφθεροποιός.

[23] A similar assessment was made by Ritti (1995: 71–2).

[24] Ritti (1995: 68–9) and Dittmann-Schöne (2000: 25). For remarks on the nomenclature of the professional associations, see Labarre and Le Dinahet (1996: 59). Cf., for Phrygia, Dittmann-Schöne (2000: 18), and, for Lydia, Arnaoutoglou (2011: 263–4). However, such a division does not appear in Hierapolis: Ritti (1995: 66).

revered' (σεμνοτάτη) association of purple-dyers. This association has been described in two different ways, ἡ ἐργασία and ἡ τέχνη τῶν πορφυραβάφων.[25] Similarly the dyers are designated both as ἡ τέχνη and as ἡ ἐργασία τῶν βαφέων. By contrast, the association of wool-washers is called in both instances ἡ ἐργασία τῶν ἐριοπλυτῶν; similarly, gardeners are described as ἡ ἐργασία τῶν κηπουρῶν.

A few words are needed to interpret the terms *proedria* and *synedrion*, which are unusual for associations.[26] The term *synedrion* had a wide range of meanings such as 'gathering' and 'assembly'; by extension, it could also mean the association as such, especially in the context of crafts.[27] More puzzling is the case of the term *proedria*: in an epigraphic context, this term denotes almost without exception the privilege to be seated in the front rows during theatre performances and musical or athletic contests, granted to distinguished citizens and foreigners.[28] However, it is also attested in the nomenclature of the association of purple-dyers of Hierapolis.[29] The term features in three inscriptions; two of these do not shed any light on its meaning. The third, nonetheless, provides some clues; it reads:

εἴ τις δὲ | ἀποκορακώσει ἤ τε κληρονόμος ἤ τι συγγενὴς | θήσει τῇ προεδρίᾳ τῶν πορφυραβάφων ἢ τοῖς | κατὰ ἔτος ἐπειμελη ταῖς προστείμου * υ᾽

If anyone opens [the sarcophagus' lid], either heir or relative, he shall pay to the *proedria* of the purple-dyers or to the annually appointed stewards a fine of 400 *denarii*.[30]

---

[25] Cf. Cichorius (1898: 51): 'Der Name der Zunft ist auf den Inschriften regelmassig ἡ ἐργασία τῶν πορφυροβάφων.'

[26] *Synedrion*: τὸ συνέδριον τῶν ἀκαιροδαπιστῶν in *SEG* 46.1656, τῷ συνεδρίῳ τῶν κοπιδέρμων in Ritti (2004: 544 [ineditum]). Combination of both in Judeich (1898: 227): τὸ συνέδριον τῆς προεδρίας τῶν πορφυραβάφων.

[27] For example, συνέδριον τῆς γερουσίας: Judeich (1898: nos 73, 312); *AAST* 101 (1966–7), 296, no. 4; συνέδριον τῶν νέων: Judeich (1898: 117). Other examples: *IG* 12.8, 388, *IPriene* 246 (συνέδριον τῆς γερουσίας); *IG* 12.7, 271, 14; *TAM* 2.225 (Sidyma, Lycia, imperial) (συνέδριον τῆς βουλῆς); *IPerinthos* 55 (τὸ συνέδριον τῶν φιλαπαμέων); for professional associations see *IMilet* ii 939 (συνέδριον τῶν λινουργῶν), *IK* 13 (Ephesos) 636 (τὸ ἱερὸν συνέδριον τῶν ἀργυροκόπων), *IK* 16 (Ephesos) 2212 (τὸ συνέδριον τῶν ἀργυροκόπων). See Poland (1909: 156–8), who considers the term as highly significant, since it was used by heavyweight groups in the cities, such as the *gerousia*. *Synedrion* can also mean the meeting place, as in *Ath. Agora* 16, 181.39–40 (Athens, 282/1 BC): καὶ στῆσαι ἔμπροσθε τοῦ συνε/δρίου; Petrakos (1999: 10, 11) (248/7 BC): ἀνατέθηκε καὶ συνέδριον πρὸς τῶι στρατηγίωι.

[28] e.g. in Phrygia, *IK* 49.1.22 (Laodikeia on Lykos, 267 BC); 2.17 (third century BC).

[29] Judeich (1898: 227), *SEG* 46.1656, and *SEG* 54.1323. Recently another instance of *proedria*, this time *proedria erioplyton*, appeared in a fragmentary funerary inscription published by Guizzi, Miranda De Martino, and Ritti (2012: 659, no. 15) and dated on the basis of the letter-forms to the second or third century AD; in particular, the *proedria* of the wool-washers is entitled to use the amount of money bequeathed to perform a *stephanotikon*, perhaps for a different association.

[30] *SEG* 54.1323, 5–8.

Here, *proedria* does not designate the association as such but most probably refers to the board of the group.[31] In particular, *proedria* is put on a par with the annually elected stewards (*epimeletai*): the text refers to a fine for tomb violation that will be paid either to the *proedria* of the group or to its *epimeletai*. Therefore, *proedria* and *epimeletai* enjoy some sort of equal status. I think it is unlikely that the clause refers to a payment to the group (that is, *proedria*) distinct from its *epimeletai*. In a sense *proedria* should be understood as something similar to the expression recorded in another inscription from Hierapolis, which refers to 'οἱ τῆς ἐργασίας τῶν ἐριοπλύτων οἱ μετεχόντες τῶν ἐπιμελημένων'—'those partici- pating in the administration of the *ergasia* of wool-washers'.[32] In other words, *proedria* cannot denote something entirely different from *epimeletai*: it should be exercising a similar function. Nevertheless, there was a distinction based on status enjoyed by those included in the *proedria*. Whether *epimeletai* enjoyed the privilege of *proedria ex officio* remains difficult to substantiate. The *proedria* of purple-dyers may originate in the honorary places at the theatre allocated to leading and/or prominent members of the association, such as the seats of *linourgoi* in the theatre of Saittai or those of the undefined *ergasia* in that of neighbouring Laodikeia on the Lykos. In practice, this would imply some sort of hierarchy among purple-dyers. If this interpretation is correct, it gives an interesting view of the administrative structure of this particular association: it means that there were the annually selected stewards and, alongside it, a body of officials—perhaps ex-*epimeletai*—constituting the *proedria*, which could convene perhaps as a separate body.[33] It is, therefore, possible to consider the *proedria* as some sort of executive committee, comprising all ex-magistrates of an association; yet, as far as I know, there is no evidence for a comparable phenom- enon among the other associations in Hierapolis, or in the Greek-speaking Roman East in general. An alternative interpretation would see in the *proedria* a board of senior, prestigious, wealthy, and distinguished members of the group.

In Thyateira and Saittai, the character of professional associations is expressed by a variety of terms, such as θίασος, ὁμότεχνον, πλατεία, πλῆθος, συμβίωσις, συνεργασία, σύνοδος, and φυλή. While there is no clear pattern in the adoption and use of a particular name, two main categories of terms can be distinguished. First, there are the terms borrowed from other areas of

[31] See also Ziebarth (1896: 107); Cichorius (1898: 49); Poland (1909: 126, 415); Labarre and Le Dinahet (1996: 59); Dittmann-Schöne (2000: 35); Zimmermann (2002: 37–9); and Harland (2006a: 237). The term *proedria* appears with a different meaning in *IK* 12.217.3–5 (Ephesos): καὶ νῦν φανερωθῇ ἥ τε ἐξ ἀρχῆς ἔκ τε τῶν νόμων καὶ τῶν θείων | διατάξεων καὶ τῶν δογμάτων τῆς ἱερᾶς συνκλήτου τῇ ὑμετέρᾳ μητροπόλει | προεδρία προσνενεμημένη; 'and in the honorary decree of the council and the people of Attaleia in Lydia for Dionysios, son of Glykon' (*LGPN* vA (490)), *TAM* 5.2.829, 5–7 (AD 211–217?): με|τέχοντα κ(αὶ) τῆς προε|δρίας.

[32] *AAST* 101 (1966–7), 317, no. 45, 5–6: ἀποτείσει|τοῖς τῆς ἐργασίας τῶν ἐριοπλύτων τοῖς μετεχοῦ|σιν τῶν ἐπιμε<με>λημένων * τ': 'he shall pay to those participating in the administration of the *ergasia* of wool-washers 300 *denarii*.'

[33] In this sense, *to synedrion tes proedrias* in inscription: Judeich (1898: 227).

associational activity, such as religious groups (θίασος and συμβίωσις), performance groups (σύνοδος), or from public subdivisions (φυλή); secondly, there are those that seem to be used by artisan groups exclusively. Some emphasize a spatial dimension (πλατεῖα, six cases), or the quantity of people involved (πλῆθος, two cases), but terms stressing craftsmanship (ὁμότεχνον: six cases) or the cooperative aspect of the activity (συνεργασία, eighteen cases) are much more numerous. As far as chronology is concerned, most associations designated as ὁμότεχνον occur around the mid-second century AD; by contrast, the term συνεργασία occurs exclusively in Saittai in the period from the middle of the second century AD to the first decades of the third. Moreover, there are several interesting geographical peculiarities. First, the term φυλή appears almost exclusively in Philadelphia: the only exception is made up by the inscribed seats in the stadion of Saittai. Secondly, at Saittai, the variety of designations is rather limited: there is a substantial predominance of συνεργασία. Finally, at Thyateira, designations are almost completely lacking.

A significant, but usually overlooked, difference between Hierapolis and the Lydian towns of Thyateira and Saittai lies in the agent—the user of the terms designating an association. In Hierapolis few inscriptions reveal the way craftsmen groups were self-designated, while in the Lydian cities there is hardly any document that has not been issued by the association itself. This discrepancy makes comparison a delicate operation, since in Hierapolis the denomination reflects the picture that outsiders had of associations, while in Lydia the denomination is a reflection of how the members themselves defined their own group.

THE SOCIAL POSITIONING OF PROFESSIONAL ASSOCIATIONS

Hierapolitan professional associations display a well-balanced record of social activities in both public and private spheres. They pay the honours due to the local council and local leaders, but also to the procurator of the emperor.[34] In a fragmentary inscription the association of purple-dyers honoured an unnamed ἐπίτροπος τοῦ Σεβαστοῦ (*procurator Augusti*), designated as their benefactor on every occasion or affair (ἐν πᾶσιν).[35] The text suggests that the association had—or rather wished to demonstrate that it had—access to the

---

[34] Procurator: Judeich (1898: 42). Council: *SEG* 41.1201 with Ritti (1989–90: 871 n. 7); Harland (2006b: 40) and Ruffing (2008: 264–5). Local dignitaries: Judeich (1898: 40), with Harland (2006b: 41) and *SEG* 56.1499; his funerary monument probably in Judeich (1898: 46).

[35] Judeich (1898: 42).

Roman authorities and perhaps could exercise some leverage on their decisions.[36] The association of dyers honoured the council of Hierapolis with the erection of a monument on a marble base, and the purple-dyers honoured Tiberios Klaudios Zotikos Boas, a personality with a considerable career, since he had been πρῶτος στρατηγὸς (leading? general),[37] ἀγωνοθέτης, γραμματεὺς of the emperors' temples in the province of Asia, πρεσβευτής, and ἀρχιερεὺς (chief priest).[38] Tiberios Klaudios Zotikos was also honoured by the association of wool-washers with an almost identically worded inscription, the only difference being the committee of three individuals charged with supervising the inscription of the decree on stone.[39] The elevated socio-economic status of the association of purple-dyers in Hierapolis is more clearly revealed in an early third-century AD inscription, which informs us that the association had contributed a substantial amount of money for the decoration of the ceiling of the local theatre:

συνετέλεσεν δὲ καὶ πρὸς τὸν κόσμον τῆς τε πρώτης καὶ τῆς δευτέρας στέγης λίθου
Δοκιμηνοῦ ἀπηρτισμένου [καὶ πρὸς τὴν προ]σάρτησιν παρ' ἑαυτῆς πόδας ἑξακοσ
ίους πεντήκοντα τρεῖς, ἡ τέχνη τῶν πορφυραβάφων.

The association of purple-dyers have contributed towards the ornamentation of the ceiling of both the first and the second storey in worked Dokimeion marble and to that part added to it, for 653 feet.[40]

This shows that the corporation of purple-dyers had access to capital funds that enabled them simultaneously to contribute to the decoration of one of Hierapolis' urban hallmarks, display their attachment to civic ideology, and elevate themselves above the status of the average craftsmen, and alongside the ranks of local benefactors.

The highest number of honorary inscriptions issued by professional associations in Asia Minor comes from Thyateira; among them the association of dyers (9/20 cases) seems to have been particularly active. Associations of craftsmen in Thyateira honoured male Romans, Romanized Greeks, or Greeks.[41] All these people were members of the local elite who had exercised

---

[36] See also the remarks of Cichorius (1898: 49).

[37] For *strategos*, see Ritti (1997: 344) and Dmitriev (2005).   [38] Judeich (1898: 41).

[39] Judeich (1898: 40).

[40] *SEG* 35.1369 (AD 206–9): trans. Ritti (1995: 75). See also Ritti's assessment (1995: 76) that the accumulation of capital by the professional associations involved in the manufacture of luxury goods elevated them to the position of local *euergetai*. Note that the inscription recording the contribution of the purple-dyers follows the dedication of the theatre by Hierapolis to the patron deities and the imperial family. On who paid for the building of theatres, see Sturgeon (2004). For the sculpted reliefs of the Hierapolitan theatre, see Cubak (2008).

[41] With the exception of Kl. Ammion (*LGPN* vA (99)) in *TAM* 5.2.972, all the honoured individuals are men. For office-holding by women, see van Bremen (1996). Roman or Romanized Greeks: *TAM* 5.2.933, 936, 945, 965, 978, 1002, 1019, and *SEG* 49.1669. Greeks: *TAM* 5.2.932, 989, 991.

functions associated with local offices—ranging from the more modest offices like the *agoranomia* to the more significant ones such as the function of secretary of the *boule* and the *demos*, or that of *strategos*.[42] Yet the professional associations of Thyateira could aim at even higher echelons of power: there are at least two texts in which persons of consular rank were honoured.[43] While Saittai provides the largest amount of *testimonia* for professional associations in Lydia and among the most numerous in Roman Asia Minor, the information they supply is limited to a date, the name of the deceased, and that of the association, and does not refer to the role played by these associations in civic life.

As noticed already by Ziebarth in the late nineteenth century, the extent to which professional associations imitated the evolving discourse of the *polis* is striking. This is particularly obvious in the procedures and the language of honouring. In Hierapolis—as no doubt was the case in several other cities as well—the adjective σεμνοτάτη, usually used to qualify the *gerousia*,[44] is also assigned to the purple-dyers.[45] Yet it is not the purple-dyers themselves who employed the adjective in the inscriptions they produced; rather, individuals used this phrase when referring to the association of purple-dyers in the epitaphs on their tombstones. In practical terms, it suggests that the association of purple-dyers was seen as a revered, respectable collective body, (almost) equal in social standing to the *gerousia*. Another example concerns the honorific language used in some texts. In several inscriptions from Hierapolis the term στεφανωτικὸν (*stephanotikon*) appears. This refers to the annual ritual of laying a wreath on the tomb. One text reports a case in which the *stephanotikon* was to be performed by the association of purple-dyers.[46] Its costs were covered by the endowment made to the association. In Saittai a garland is sometimes depicted on the otherwise austere funerary monuments.[47]

---

[42] e.g. *TAM* 5.2.932 (*agoranomos*), *TAM* 5.2.1002 (*agoranomos*, ambassador, legal consultant). Cf. Arnaoutoglou (2011: 266–70).

[43] *TAM* 5.2.935.986.

[44] Judeich (1898: nos 67, 73, 98, 111, 146, 194, 209, 234, 290, 315); *SEG* 33.1123; *AAST* 101 (1966–7), 313, no. 38. The same collocation appears in Lycia (*TAM* 2.210: Sidyma; *TAM* 2.294, 325, *FXanthos* 7, 87: Xanthos), in Myra (Luschan and Petersen (1889: 2.2, 36, no. 57; 45, no. 82)) and in Pamphylia (*IK* 43.26: Side; 54.291: Perge). Σεμνοτάτη βουλὴ is attested in Athens, Rhodes, and Ephesos, while the *fiscus* (ταμεῖον) is most often qualified as ἱερώτατον.

[45] Associations: *IG* 2².1369: Attica, σεμνοτάτην σύνοδον; *IK* 60.63: Kibyra, σεμνοτάτη συνερ-γασία; Judeich (1898: 42); *SEG* 54.1313; 56.1499: σεμνοτάτη ἐργασία; *SEG* 46.1656: σεμνοτάτη προεδρία. See also Poland (1909: 170).

[46] *SEG* 46.1656.

[47] Van Nijf (1997: 63–4) and McLean (2002: 277). This honorary practice had already appeared in the second century BC in Rhodes, when the cult association of *Haliastai–Haliadai* decided to crown the tomb of its head *eranistes* and benefactor, Dionysodoros of Alexandreia. Cf. *IG* 12.1.155, 66–9, with Fraser (1977: 62–8). In second-century BC Kyme in Aeolis (*IK* 5.13 VI. 45–8), in Priene (*IPriene* 99), and in Egypt (e.g. *SEG* 8.529, 42–4 (64 BC); *P. Mich.* 5.243(AD 14–37)). See the explicit reference to *stephanosis* in *SEG* 57.1212 (Saittai, Hellenistic period).

THE SOCIAL COMPOSITION OF PROFESSIONAL ASSOCIATIONS

As far as the social composition of professional associations is concerned, it makes sense to focus on the ethnic background of the individuals involved, and on their socio-economic position with respect to local elites. However, it should first be noted that it is not always straightforward to see, in texts, who actually was a member of a professional association. In particular, there has been some debate about the affiliation of the deceased who made an endowment to a professional association or designated it as the beneficiary of the fine for tomb desecration. While some have believed that the deceased as a rule were members, some scholars, including Ritti and Harland, have recently argued that this is not necessarily the case.[48] In arguing that the situation was not so straightforward, Ritti used an unpublished inscription in which a μολυβδουργός bequeaths property to a θρεμματική association, an equal amount to an association of ἐργαστηριάρχαι and a lesser sum to an association of χαλκεῖς.[49] It is difficult to accept individuals belonging to two different associations, as there was a roughly contemporary imperial edict prohibiting individuals from doing so.[50] This opens up the possibility for other scenarios. The μολυβδουργός in question could have had business links and dealings with the ἐργαστηριάρχαι and χαλκεῖς, while his preference for the θρεμματική association could be interpreted in social terms. Harland is thus probably right that not all individuals referred to in funerary inscriptions mentioning an endowment necessarily belonged to the corporate groups.[51] In the case of Hierapolis, none of the deceased endowing professional associations is otherwise known; thus their relation with these professional associations remains completely unclear, and they should not be included in our analysis of the social composition of professional associations.

As to the ethnic background of the membership of professional associations, the committee of four men elected from among the dyers of Hierapolis to supervise the erection of the statue of the council consisted of two Greeks (Γλυκωνιανός Μένανδρος τοῦ Γλύκωνος, Ἀντίοχος τοῦ Ζωσίμου), one Roman (Γάιος Ἰούλιος Λούκιος Φαβίᾳ Κρήσκεντος), and one Romanized Greek (Γάιος Βαίβιος Γλύκων β'), using their respective onomastic conventions.[52] A similar committee of wool-washers was made up of three Romanized Greeks (Μᾶρ(κον) Αὐρ(ήλιον) Ἀπολλώνιον δὶς Πυλωνᾶ, Μᾶρ(κον) Αὐρ(ήλιον) Ἀμμιανὸν Ἀμμιανοῦ δὶς τοῦ Γλύκωνος, Αὐρηλιανὸν Ἑρμίππου [Ἀρ]ρουντιανόν).[53] It may be premature to draw a conclusion about the social composition of professional associations on the basis of only

---

[48] Cichorius (1898: 49) believed the deceased were generally members.
[49] Ritti (1995: 70–1).   [50] *Dig.* 47.22.1.   [51] Harland (2006a: 234).
[52] *SEG* 41.1201. Ritti (1989–90: 871, no. 7); Labarre and Le Dinahet (1996: no. 56); Dittmann-Schöne (2001: 222); Zimmermann (2002: 196); Guizzi, Miranda De Martino, and Ritti (2012: 648).
[53] *SEG* 56.1499.

two inscriptions, but the evidence at Hierapolis so far suggests a majority of Romanized Greeks. Remarkable is the tombstone of Poplios Aelios Glykon Zeuxianos Ailianos, who endowed the association of purple-dyers and the assembly of carpet-makers with 200 and 150 *denarii* respectively in order to perform celebrations at two Jewish festivals—Passover and Pentecost—and at the Roman festival of the Kalendae.[54] While there is a certain amount of evidence for Jews in Hierapolis, there is no compelling reason to assume that there were exclusively Jewish professional associations of craftsmen: in Roman Asia Minor: professional associations were very rarely constituted along clearly demarcated ethnic lines.[55]

As far as their socio-economic position is concerned, an instructive example of upward social mobility is the case of Μᾶρκος Αὐρήλιος Ἀλέξανδρος Μοσχιανοῦ βουλευτὴς πορφυροπώλης, whose tomb proudly features his profession—he was a purple-seller—but also lists his membership of the local council.[56] In the case of certain craftsmen and traders, their occupation seems to have gained them social prominence.[57]

MEMORY MANAGEMENT, LAW, AND ASSOCIATIONS

What is really unique in the professional associations of Hierapolis are the different ways in which they were involved in the preservation of the memory of the dead.[58] Associations could be designated either as recipients of fines,[59] or as beneficiaries of legacies, or both.[60]

---

[54] *SEG* 46.1656. For the most recent discussion of the complexities of cultural identities attested in the inscription, see Harland (2003a: 207–10; 2006a: 238–9).

[55] See *IJO* II.187–209 and Harland (2006a).

[56] Judeich (1898: 156) and another (anonymous) purple-seller in *AAST* 101 (1966–7), 313, no. 37. See also the case of Titus Flavius Zeuxis in Judeich (1898: 51; with *SEG* 54.1304).

[57] Pleket (1983: 141–2); Ritti (1995: 76); Levick (2004: 190); Ruffing (2004: 96–7). Tombstones of other *bouleutai*: Judeich (1898: 145, 163); *AAST* 101 (1966–7), 298, nos 8–9. See also a wealthy purple-seller in Mysia, *IK* 26.35 (Miletupolis; first/second century AD); a shoemaker carrying the title of *proboulos* in Magnesia on the Meander, *IMM* 111 (first century BC). Discussion: Zuiderhoek (2011: 190–1).

[58] See the excellent discussion in van Nijf (1997: 57–64) about the different facets of professional associations' involvement in memory management. Van Nijf (1997: 59) concludes: 'We can therefore see the inscriptions that mention fines as expressions of how men of middling wealth and status perceived the social hierarchy, and of how they saw the place of *collegia* therein.' The evidence for Hierapolis was collected by Ritti (2004: 562–6). Yannakopoulos (2008: 306–7) confirms that the *gerousia* was receiving endowments from individuals of high social status.

[59] See van Nijf (1997: 57–8); the size of the fines intended for professional *collegia* lower end of the scale. In particular in Hierapolis the *fiscus/tameion* is designated to receive fines ranged between 50 and 10,000 *denarii* (usually 2,500), while *gerousia* is called to collect fines between 100 and 2,500 *denarii* (usually 500).

[60] For a parallel case from imperial Ephesos, see *IK* 16.2446. In neighbouring Laodikeia on the Lykos, professional associations are not designated as administrators of endowments.

The responsibilities of professional associations as recipients of fines for tomb violation and as beneficiaries of endowments are characteristic of the central role they (and especially the association of purple-dyers) played in the society of Roman Hierapolis.[61] In three cases, professional associations were designated as recipients of fines for tomb desecration—together with the *polis*-treasury, in two cases they were to use the fine as the capital of an endowment, while in five cases they were beneficiaries of a legacy.[62] This role not only had profound social effects; it also highlights the way in which associations were legally treated. A decade ago, I argued that Roman authorities followed a hands-off policy with regard to associations in Asia Minor and intervened only when and where public order required it. The evidence from Hierapolis confirms this impression: professional associations performed quasi-juridical duties, since they could be designated as beneficiaries of legacies or appointed as recipients of fines, and consequently, one would imagine, they could appear in the local law courts or before the Roman authorities to denounce a violator or to claim the fine.[63] Professional associations, with their prestige, participated in memory management, which allowed them to build up a social reputation as decent and pious administrators, and therefore as trustworthy partners. To a lesser extent, perhaps with the aid of a bit of creative accounting, it also allowed them to fill the coffers of the group.

The evidence from Hierapolis is unique in one more respect: perhaps because of a lack of capital, the amount of the fine is often added to the legacy. A good example is provided by the inscription on the tomb of Aurelia Pakonia Pauline.[64] The fine for the violation of the tomb—300 *denarii*—is provided to be paid to the association of wool-washers, and it is designated to be used as an endowment to honour the already deceased son of the testator, Tatianos, by laying a wreath on his tomb on a specific date. In this way the association has two reasons to feel compelled to perform the task assigned to it: it was encouraged to protect the tomb, not only to receive the fine but also to be able to perform the ritual every year—thereby enhancing its prestige as a reliable partner. However, what remains unclear is whether the posthumous

---

[61] Out of eighteen inscriptions from Hierapolis mentioning endowments, seven involve professional associations.

[62] Van Nijf (1997: 59–60). For *gerousia*, see now Yannakopoulos (2008: 196–8 (in Hierapolis) and 292–342). See also *IK* 16.3216 in which οἱ ἐν Ἐφέσῳ ἐργάται προπυλεῖται πρὸς τῷ Ποσειδῶνι are endowed with 500 *denarii* ἐπὶ τῷ γείνεσθαι ἀπὸ τοῦ γεινομένου τόκου οἰνοποσίαν καὶ κηριόλους καὶ στεφά(νους) * ιʹ ποιήσουσιν δὲ καὶ τὴν εὐωχίαν μη(νὸς) Ποσ(ιδεῶνος); in case they fail to do so, the measurers of the grain (*prometrai*) of Ephesos shall legally exact the amount of money.

[63] Of course, one may argue that, according to *Digest* 34.5.20, *collegia* were allowed to receive legacies; in this context we have to treat accordingly the surge of related inscriptions in Hierapolis; cf. Waltzing (1895–1900: 2.2.456–62) and Robertis (1970). There is also some similar evidence from Ephesos: *IK* 16.2115; 2446.2 (imperial period). Yet, the practice had already been widespread before the arrival of the Romans, as is shown by the Hellenistic material in Laum (1914) and, recently, by *SEG* 58.1640 (Tlos [Lycia]; second century BC).

[64] *AAST* 101 (1966–7), 317, no. 45.

honours would also have been performed if no one had violated the tomb or when it was not possible to identify who had desecrated it, or even when the desecrator could not (or would not) pay the fine.

Another question concerns the compulsory character of the ritual performance; what would have happened if the association was unable or unwilling to perform the ritual? Five inscriptions show what could happen in such a situation. In the text on the tomb of Aurelios Zotikos Epikrates the testator designates three different associations as recipients of 150 *denarii* to perform the laying of a wreath over his tomb; if the nail-smiths fail, then the copper-smiths will take over, and if they also fail to perform the ritual, the purple-dyers shall get the endowed amount of money.[65] The inscription on the tomb of Markos Aurelios Diodoros Koreskos stated that, if the purple-dyers did not perform the ritual, the association of cattle-breeders would assume the task, and would receive the money to perform it.[66] The epitaph of Markos Aurelios Amianos stated that, if the association of linen-workers failed to perform the *stephanotikon*,[67] they not only had to pass the money to the *philoploi* ('lovers of armed battles') but also had to provide double the amount—as a penalty.[68] Two recently published texts contain a clause stating that, if the association encumbered with the performance of *stephanotikon* fails to comply, a different association will be allowed to exact the bequeathed amount of money.[69] The clause implies that the originally designated association has already received the amount of money for the performance of the ritual.

The question remaining is why we find such a concentration of evidence for this particular practice in Hierapolis. Is this due to the quantity and quality of our sources or can it be ascribed to localized patterns of euergetism? Among the published inscriptions from Hierapolis, there are at least six texts in which an endowment to the council, to the *gerousia* or to a comparable organization is mentioned.[70] The sums provided range between 300 and 2,500 *denarii*.[71] At the same time there are eight endowments to professional associations in which the sums bequeathed range between 150 and 3,000 *denarii*, though in five of these the sum is less than 500 *denarii*.[72] It is likely

---

[65] Judeich (1898: 133).   [66] Judeich (1898: 227).

[67] The same term for the ritual occurs only in neighbouring Laodicea on the Lycus: *IK* 49.84–5 (imperial period); see Yannakopoulos (2008: 314–18).

[68] *SEG* 56.1501.

[69] Guizzi, Miranda De Martino, and Ritti (2012: 659, no. 15): [τοῖς]/ παραγενομένοις καθ' ἔτος ἑκάστῳ τὸ αἱροῦν, εἰ δὲ μὴ δοθῇ τῇ ὡρισμένῃ ἡμέρᾳ,/ πραχθήσεται τούτου ὑπὸ τῆς προεδρίας τῶν ἐριοπλυτῶν; p. 660: τὸν γεινόμενον κατ' ἔτος τόκον δίδοσθαι τοῖς παραγεναμένοις ἐπὶ τὸν τόπον στεφανωτικοῦ ὀνόματει τὸ αἱροῦν, ἅτινα ἐγδώσουσιν οἱ κατ' ἔτος γραμματεῖς μη(νὸς?). δ' ἡ(μέρα?), εἰ δὲ μὴ δοθήσεται πρὸς ἔτος, πραχθήσονται ὑπὸ τῆς ἐργασίας τῶν ἀρτοποιῶν.

[70] Judeich (1898: nos 67, 209, 234, 278, 293, 336).

[71] 300 *denarii*: Judeich (1898: 209, 278, 293); 2,500 *denarii*: Judeich (1898: 234).

[72] Judeich (1898: 133, 153, 195, 227, 342); *AAST* 101 (1966–7), nos 23, 45; *SEG* 56.1501; 150 *denarii*: Judeich (1898: 133); 3,000 *denarii*: Judeich (1898: 227).

Table 12.1. Hierapolis: professional associations and the management of memory

Inscription	Amount	Collectivity	Purpose
SEG 54.1313	1,000 *denarii* 300 *denarii*	Association of gardeners, the denouncer	Fine for violation
AAST 101 (1966–7), 297, no. 7	500 *denarii* 300 *denarii*	The treasury, the association of water-mill operators	Fine for violation
Judeich (1898: 218)	500 *denarii* 300 *denarii*	The treasury, the association of ?gardeners	Fine for violation
SEG 54.1323	400 *denarii*	The association of purple-dyers	Fine for violation, which will serve as an endowment to the association. Interest: 144. Purpose: Feast on the grave
AAST 101 (1966–7), 317, no. 45	300 *denarii*	The association of wool-washers	Fine for violation, which will serve as an endowment to the association. Cost of the ritual, fifteen *denarii* per year. Purpose: *stephanotikon*
Judeich (1898: 227)	3,000 *denarii*	The associations of purple-dyers and *thremmatike* in succession	Endowment; purpose: grave ritual (burning seeds)
SEG 54.1315	1,000 *denarii* per year	The association of dyers	Endowment; purpose: *stephanotikon*
SEG 56.1501	250 *denarii*	The association of linen-workers; if the linen-workers fail to observe the ritual, they shall pay double that amount to the *philoploi* (lovers of armed combat)	Endowment; purpose: *stephanotikon*
SEG 46.1656	200 *denarii* 150 *denarii*	The association of purple-dyers, the association of *akairodapistai*	Endowment; purpose: *stephanotikon*
Guizzi, Miranda De Martino, and Ritti (2012: 659, no. 15)	200 *denarii*	An unknown entity	Endowment?; purpose: *stephanotikon*
Judeich (1898: 133)	150 *denarii*	The association of nailsmiths, coppersmiths, and purple-dyers in succession	Endowment; purpose: *stephanotikon*
Guizzi, Miranda De Martino, and Ritti (2012 : 660)	100 *denarii*	The association of linen clothes makers	Endowment; purpose: *stephanotikon*

that this cluster of evidence for endowments reflects a more widespread diffusion of this particular practice, at least in Hierapolis, if not in Phrygia as a whole. One could interpret it as an expression of middle-class euergetism that parallels similar practices pertaining to the *fiscus* or the city's council or even the local *gerousia*.

Last but not least, two questions need to be addressed. First, why did individuals turn to professional associations to safeguard the integrity of their last residence and, second, what was the relation between the donor and the professional association(s) encumbered with the receipt of the fine or the endowment? It has been argued for a long time that the involvement of associations in funerary rituals is a testimony of weakened family links during the Hellenistic and Imperial period; individuals could not rely on (close or distant) relatives for the performance of the customary honours over their tomb. However, the material from Hierapolis points in another direction. Besides the twelve inscriptions listed in Table 12.1, there are some forty references to the *gerousia* as enforcing the fine for tomb violation or beneficiary of an endowment. Yet, the great majority of funerary inscriptions suggests that people still relied on their immediate family to pay the post-mortem honours.[73] The involvement of *gerousiai* and associations is due to the desire of the owner of the tomb to display his social standing and prestige. There was no need also to be a member of the group: socializing and acquaintance with some of their members provided sufficient ground for including the association among the beneficiaries. It should also be reminded that having a respectable association performing funerary rites did not replace the standard honours paid to the deceased by families but rather supplemented them. Naming a respectable association to perform funerary rites over a tomb can be regarded as a way to secure social distinction and social capital even after death: the individuals who could afford to be buried in the lavish sarcophagi in question were not members of the lower classes. For professional associations, taking care of a tomb or administering an endowment of a distinguished, even middle-class, citizen provided a ready opportunity to boost their respectability within the community.

Professional associations are conspicuously absent from any cult activity in their own right; this is due, perhaps, to the kind of material we have, and it can be argued that fulfilling the wishes of the deceased and performing *stephanotikon* on the grave should be included in the concept of cult activity.[74]

---

[73] See, e.g. *SEG* 57.1212 (Saittai, Hell.); 1148A (Daldis-Charakipolis (Lydia) AD 11/12); 1153 (Daldis area, AD 152/3 or 206/7); 1178 (Iulia Gordos, AD 230/1).

[74] See Ritti (1989–90), Dittmann-Schöne (2002). Cf. Harland (2003b: 23), who argues that 'cultic honours for the imperial gods, which paralleled the sacrifices, mysteries and other rituals directed at traditional deities, were a significant component within numerous associations'. See Rebillard (2003: 53–5) for the priority of the family over the *collegia* in the funerary rituals.

CONCLUSION

The epigraphic evidence for professional associations in Hierapolis is more varied than it is in Saittai or Thyateira. The majority of texts referring to these groups comes from a funerary context, and were inscribed on sarcophagi; in many cases, associations are designated as receivers of fines for tomb violation or beneficiaries of a funerary endowment with ritual duties. This is a remarkable contrast with the situation in Saittai, where professional associations honour people who in all probability were their deceased members. It also contrasts with the situation in Thyateira, where associations appear to have mostly occupied themselves with honouring members of the local and provincial elite.

On a methodological level, the present analysis has highlighted the possibilities of a comparative approach that involves clearly demarcated geographical entities and political units: it has shown that professional associations were not only a defining phenomenon in urban communities—for which hardly any confirmation was needed—but also that specific local circumstances play a crucial role in their formation and development. This also sheds new light on the varying social positions of craftsmen and their associations in the civic constellations of Greco-Roman cities. There was definitely a bias against craftsmen by some members of the elite, but this apparently did not impede professional associations from assuming, in some socio-political settings at least, a prominent place within the urban community, owing to the importance of their trade for the local economy and to the wealth it generated, as was the case with the dyers in Thyateira and the purple-dyers in Hierapolis.[75]

ACKNOWLEDGEMENTS

I wish to thank the organizers for the opportunity to test my approach, the participants for their criticism, and the editors of the volume, Miko Flohr and Andrew Wilson, for their assistance in clarifying various aspects of the argument.

REFERENCES

Arnaoutoglou, I. N. (2002). 'Roman Law and *collegia* in Asia Minor', *RIDA* 49: 27–44.
Arnaoutoglou, I. N. (2005). '*Collegia* in the Province of Egypt in the First Century AD', *AncSoc* 35: 197–216.

[75] For the role of the textile industry in Asia Minor, see Pleket (1998: 122–7) on the export of textiles; Pleket (2003: 87–95) on the development of textile industry independently of urbanization; Poblome (2004); Erdemir (2011), and Thonemann (2011: 186).

Arnaoutoglou, I. N. (2011). 'Professional Associations in Roman Lydia: A Tale of Two Cities?', *AncSoc* 41: 257–90.

Bremen, R. van (1996). *The Limits of Participation: Women and Civic Life in the Greek East in the Hellenistic and Roman Periods*. Amsterdam.

Burrell, B. (2004). *Neokoroi: Greek Cities and Roman Emperors*. Leiden.

Cichorius, C. (1898). 'Geschichte und städtische Verhältnisse', in C. Humann (ed.), *Altertümer von Hierapolis*. Berlin, 18–55.

Cormack, S. (2004). *The Space of Death in Roman Asia Minor*. Vienna.

Cubak, N. (2008). *Hierapolis tiyatro kabartmalari*. Istanbul.

D'Andria, F. (2001). 'Hierapolis of Phrygia: Its Evolution in Hellenistic and Roman Times', in D. Parrish (ed.), *Urbanism in Western Asia Minor: New Studies on Aphrodisias, Ephesus, Hierapolis, Pergamon, Perge and Xanthos*. Portsmouth, RI, 96–115.

D'Andria, F. (2006). 'Hierapolis of Phrygia', in W. Radt (ed.), *Stadtgrabungen und Stadtforschung im westlichen Kleinasien: Geplantes und Erreichtes* (Internationales Symposion, 6/7 August 2004 in Bergama (Türkei)). Istanbul, 113–24.

Debord, P. (1982). *Aspects sociaux et économiques de la vie religieuse dans l'Anatolie gréco-romaine*. Leiden.

Debord, P. (1997). 'Hiérapolis: Du sanctuaire-état à la cité', *REA* 99: 415–26.

Dissen, M. (2009). *Römische Kollegien und deutsche Geschichtewissenschaft im 19. und 20. Jahrhundert*. Stuttgart.

Dittmann-Schöne, I. (2001). *Die Berufsvereine in der Städten des kaiserzeitlichen Kleinasiens*. Regensburg.

Dittmann-Schöne, I. (2002). 'Götterverehrung bei den Berufsvereinen im kaiserzeitlichen Kleinasien', in U. Egelhaaf-Gaiser and S. Schaefer (eds), *Religiöse Vereine in der römischen Antike: Untersuchungen zu Organisation, Ritual und Raumordnung*. Tübingen, 81–96.

Dmitriev, Sv. (2005). *City Government in Hellenistic and Roman Asia Minor*. Oxford.

Drexhage, H.-J. (1998). 'Der Porphyropoles, die Porphyropolis und der Kogchistes in den Papyri und Ostraka', *MBAH* 17: 94–9.

Erdemir, H. (2011). 'Woollen Textiles: An International Trade Good in the Lycus Valley in Antiquity', in A. H. Cadwallader and M. Trainor (eds), *Colossae in Space and Time: Linking to an Ancient City*. Göttingen, 104–29.

Fraser, P. M. (1977). *Rhodian Funerary Monuments*. Oxford.

Guizzi, A., Miranda De Martino, E., and Ritti, T. (2012). 'Acquisizioni epigrafiche: Iscrizioni ritrovate o studiate nel triennio 2004–2006', in F. d'Andria, M. P. Caggia, and T. Ismaelli (eds), *Hierapolis di Frigia V: Le attività delle campagne di scavo e restauro 2004–2006*. Istanbul, 643–78.

Harland, P. A. (2003a). *Associations, Synagogues and Congregations: Claiming a Place in Ancient Mediterranean Society*. Minneapolis.

Harland, P. A. (2003b). 'Imperial Cults within Local Life: Associations in Roman Asia', *AHB* 17: 85–107.

Harland, P. A. (2006a). 'Acculturation and Identity in the Diaspora: A Jewish Family and "Pagan" Guilds at Hierapolis', *Journal of Jewish Studies* 57: 222–44.

Harland, P. A. (2006b). 'The Declining Polis? Religious Rivalries in Ancient Civic Context', in L. E. Vaage (ed.), *Religious Rivalries in the Early Roman Empire and the Rise of Christianity*. Waterloo, 21–49.

Hatzfeld, J. (1919). *Les Trafiquants italiens dans l'Orient hellénique*. Paris.

Huttner, U. (2009). 'Die Färber von Laodikeia und Hierapolis: Eine Nachricht aus dem Corpus der Alchemisten', *MBAH* 26: 139–57.

Judeich, W. (1898). 'Inschriften', in C. Humann (ed.), *Altertümer von Hierapolis*. Berlin, 67–180.

Kolb, Fr. (1974). 'Zur Geschichte der Stadt Hierapolis in Phrygien: Die Phyleninschriften im Theater', *ZPE* 15: 255–70.

Labarre, G., and Le Dinahet, M.-T. (1996). 'Les meticrs du textile en Asie Mineure de l'époque hellénistique à l'époque impériale', in *Aspects de l'artisanat du textile dans le monde méditerranéen (Égypte, Grèce, monde romain)*. Lyon, 49–115.

Laum, B. (1914). *Stiftungen in der griechischen und römischen Antike: Ein Beitrag zur antiken Kulturgeschichte*. Leipzig.

Levick, B. (2004). 'The Roman Economy: Trade in Asia Minor and the Niche Market', *G&R* 51: 180–98.

Liu, J. (2008). 'The Economy of Endowments: The Case of the Roman *collegia*', in K. Verboven, K. Vandorpe, and V. Chankowski-Sable (eds), *'Pistoi dia tēn technēn'. Bankers, Loans and Archives in the Ancient World: Studies in Honour of R. Bogaert*. Leuven, 231–56.

Luschan, F. von, and Petersen, E. A. H. (1889). *Reisen in Lykien, Milyas und Kibyratis*. Vienna.

McLean, B. H. (2002). *An Introduction to Greek Epigraphy of the Hellenistic and Roman Periods from Alexander the Great Down to the Reign of Constantine (323 B.C.–A. D. 337)*. Ann Arbor.

Nijf, O. M. van (1997). *The Civic World of Professional Associations in the Roman East*. Amsterdam.

Nijf, O. M. van (2010). 'Being Termessian: Local Knowledge and Identity Politics in a Pisidian City', in T. Whitmarsh (ed.), *Local Knowledge and Microidentities in the Imperial Greek World*. Cambridge, 163–88.

Patterson, J. R. (2006). *Landscapes and Cities: Rural Settlement and Civic Transformation in Early Imperial Italy*. Oxford.

Perry, J. S. (2006). *The Roman collegia: The Modern Evolution of an Ancient Concept*. Leiden.

Petrakos, V. (1999). *Ho dēmos tou Ramnountos: Synopsē tōn anaskaphōn kai tōn ereunōn (1813–1998), II. Hoi epigraphes*. Athens.

Pleket, H. W. (1983). 'Urban Elites and Business in the Greek Part of the Roman Empire', in P. Garnsey, K. Hopkins, and C. R. Whittaker (eds), *Trade in the Ancient Economy*. Cambridge, 131–44.

Pleket, H. W. (1998). 'Models and Inscriptions: Export of Textiles in the Roman Empire', *Epigraphica Anatolica* 12: 25–37.

Pleket, H. W. (2003). 'Economy and Urbanization: Was there an Impact of Empire in Asia Minor?', in E. Schwertheim and E. Winter (eds), *Stadt und Stadtentwicklung in Kleinasien*. Bonn, 85–95.

Poblome, J. (2004). 'Comparing Ordinary Craft Production: Textile and Pottery Production in Roman Asia Minor', *JESHO* 47: 491–506.

Poland, Fr. (1909). *Geschichte des griechischen Vereinswesens*. Leipzig.

Pugliese Carratelli, G. (1963–4). 'Chresmoi di Apollo Kareios e Apollo Klarios a Hierapolis in Frigia', *ASAA* 25–6: 357–70.

Ramsay, W. M. (1890). *The Historical Geography of Asia Minor*. London.

Ramsay, W. M. (1895–7). *The Cities and Bishoprics of Phrygia: Being an Essay of the Local History of Phrygia from the Earliest Times to the Turkish Conquest*. Oxford.

Rebillard, E. (2003). *Religion et sépulture: L'Église, les vivants et les morts dans l'antiquité tardive*. Paris.

Ritti, T. (1989–90). 'Hierapolis di Frigia: Santuari e dediche votive', *Scienze dell'antichità* 3–4: 861–74.

Ritti, T. (1992–3). 'Nuovi dati su una nota epigrafe sepolcrale con stefanotico da Hierapolis di Frigia', *Scienze dell'antichità* 6–7: 41–68.

Ritti, T. (1995). 'Associazioni di mestiere a Hierapolis di Frigia', in B. M. Giannattasio (ed.), *Viaggi e commerci nell'antichità* (Atti VII giornata archeologica, Genova, 25 November 1994). Genova, 65–84.

Ritti, T. (1997). 'Personaggi di età flavia a Hierapolis', *Miscellanea Greca e Romana* 21: 339–57.

Ritti, T. (2003). 'La neocoria di Hierapolis di Frigia', in *Epigraphica* (Atti delle giornate di studio di Roma e di Atene in memoria di M. Guarducci). Rome, 177–215.

Ritti, T. (2004). 'Iura sepulcrorum a Hierapolis di Frigia nel quadro dell'epigrafia sepolcrale microasiatica: Iscrizione edite e inedite', in *Libitina e dintorni: Libitina e i luci sepolcrali, les leges libitinariae campane, iura sepulcrorum: Vecchie e nuove iscrizioni* (Atti dell' XI rencontre franco-italienne sur l'épigraphie). Rome, 455–625.

Ritti, T. (2006). *An Epigraphic Guide to Hierapolis (Pamukkale)*. Istanbul.

Ritti, T. (2007). *Museo archeologico di Denizli-Hierapolis: Catalogo delle iscrizioni greche e latine*. Naples.

Ritti, T., Miranda, E., and Guizzi, F. (2007). 'La ricerca epigrafica: Risultati dell'ultimo quadrennio e prospettive future', in Fr. d' Andria and M. Piera Gaggia (eds), *Hierapolis di Frigia I: L'attivita delle campagne di scavo e restauro 2000–2003*. Istanbul, 583–618.

Robert, L. (1937). *Études anatoliennes: Recherches sur les inscriptions grecques de l'Asie Mineure*. Paris.

Robert, L. (1960). *Hellenica: Recueil d'épigraphie, de numismatique, et d'antiquités grecques*. xi–xii. Paris.

Robert, L. (1963). *Noms indigènes dans l'Asie Mineure gréco-romaine*. Paris.

Robertis, F. M. de (1970). 'Autonomia statutaria e personificazione giuridica nel regime associativo romano', in *Études J. Macqueron*. Aix-en-Provence, 591–4.

Ruffing, K. (2004). 'Die Selbstdarstellung von Händlern und Handwerkern in den griechischen Inschriften', *MBAH* 23: 85–101.

Ruffing, K. (2007). 'Textilien als Wirtschaftsgut in der römischen Kaiserzeit', in S. Günther, K. Ruffing, and O. Stoll (eds), *Pragmata: Beiträge zur Wirtschaftsgeschichte der Antike im Gedenken an H. Winkel*. Wiesbaden, 41–53.

Ruffing, K. (2008). *Die berufliche Spezialisierung in Handel und Handwerk: Untersuchungen zu ihrer Entwicklung und zu ihren Bedingungen in der römischen Kaiserzeit im östlichen Mittelmeerraum auf der Grundlage griechischer Inschriften und Papyri*. Rahden.

Ruffing, K. (2009). 'Thermalquellen und Kult—das Beispiel Hierapolis', in E. Olshausen and V. Sauer (eds), *Die Landschaft und die Religion* (Stuttgarter Kolloquium zur historischen Geographie des Altertums, 9, 2005). Stuttgart, 287–300.

Sanidas, G. M. (2011). 'Les activités textiles dans les villes grecques aux époques hellénistique et romaine: Questions d'espace et d'économie', in C. Alfaro, J.-P. Brun, Ph. Borgard, and R. Pierobon Benoit (eds), *Tissus et teintures dans la cité antique* (Actas del III Symposium international sobre textiles y tintes del Mediterraneo en el mundo antiguo, Naples, 13–15 November 2008). Valencia and Naples, 31–40.

Simsek, C. (2013). *Laodikeia [Laodicea ad Lycum]*. Istanbul.

Sommer, St (2006). *Rom und die Vereinigungen im südwestlichen Kleinasien* (133 v. Chr.–284 n. Chr.). Hennef.

Sturgeon, M. C. (2004). 'Dedications of Roman Theaters', in A. P. Chapin (ed.), *Charis: Essays in Honor of Sara A. Immerwahr*. Princeton, 411–30.

Thonemann, P. (2011). *The Maeander Valley: A Historical Geography from Antiquity to Byzantium*. Cambridge.

Waltzing, J.-P. (1895–1900). *Étude historique sur les corporations professionelles chez les Romains*. Louvain.

Yannakopoulos, N. (2008). *O thesmos tēs gerousias tōn ellēnikōn poleōn kata tous rōmaikous chronous: Organōssē kai leitourgies*. Thessalonike.

Ziebarth, E. (1896). *Das griechische Vereinswesen*. Leipzig.

Ziebarth, E. (1903). 'Beiträge zum griechischen Recht: I. Die Stiftung nach griechischen Recht', *Zeitschrift für vergleichende Rechtswissenschaft* 16: 249–315.

Zimmermann, C. (2002). *Handwerkereine im griechischen Osten des Imperium Romanum*. Darmstadt.

Zuiderhoek, A. (2011). 'Oligarchs and Benefactors: Elite Democracy and Euergetism in the Greek East of the Roman Empire', in O. M. van Nijf and R. Alston (eds), *Political Culture in the Greek City after the Classical Age*. Leuven, 185–95.

IV

Space

13

Working Together: Clusters of Artisans in the Roman City

Penelope Goodman

In the fields of economics and geography, spatial clusters made up of similar, interconnected firms are widely recognized. They were originally discussed by Alfred Marshall in the nineteenth century, and the last two decades have seen the development of an extensive literature concerned with questions such as what constitutes a cluster, how and why they form, and what advantages they offer.[1] This literature already has a historical element, because clusters often develop slowly and function over long periods.[2] Historical enquiry has been important, for example, in understanding industrial clusters in northern Italy, while some researchers are now examining historically attested clusters in the context of their own time.[3] As yet, though, these enquiries have not extended into the ancient world. Individual clusters from the Roman era have been identified, but an overview of the phenomenon has not been attempted, nor have the known examples been set in dialogue with the literature on their modern equivalents.

This chapter addresses that omission. In doing so, it has two main aims: to broaden the range of cultures in which economic clustering has been explicitly recognized, and to extend our understanding of Roman clusters through comparison with more recent examples. Some comment is first needed on the legitimacy of this exercise. Is it meaningful to compare Roman economic clusters with those of the modern world, given the very different social, technological, and economic conditions in which they must have evolved? In terms of the polarizing debates of the 1950s and 1960s,

---

[1] Marshall (1890: 267–77; 1919: 283–8, 599–608). Key recent publications include Porter (1990, 1998); Pyke, Beccatini, and Sengenberger (1990); Krugman (1991); Enright (1998); Beccatini et al. (2003); Asheim, Cooke, and Martin (2006); Cumbers and MacKinnon (2006).

[2] Krugman (1991: 59–63); van der Linde (2003: 139–40).

[3] Wilson and Popp (2003b); Akoorie (2011); Lesger (2011). On industrial clusters in northern Italy, see Capecchi (1990); Beccatini (2003).

committed formalists would claim that the same basic economic factors were active in both contexts, while substantivists would counter that ancient society was too different from the post-industrial world for the comparison to be useful.[4] But the extreme stances of both positions have largely been left behind, and it is now possible to acknowledge that ancient individuals could pursue profit maximization while also recognizing that all economic activity—ancient and modern—is socially embedded.[5]

Indeed, economic clustering is already recognized across a wide range of cultures, both contemporary and historical. Contemporary examples have been identified in neo-liberal Western economies, developing countries, and social corporatist states such as China or Taiwan.[6] Research into historical examples has focused largely on post-industrial Europe, but Akoorie argues that clustering was already common in medieval industry, where it was connected with the social networks provided by the guilds.[7] Each individual cluster of course responds uniquely to its particular historical, social, and geographical context.[8] But researchers who have taken a broad perspective on the phenomenon have been able to identify comparable factors at work across a wide range of individual cases.[9] Thus, for example, while post-industrial clusters are no longer associated with medieval-style guilds, social networks remain consistently important to their success.[10] Economic clustering appears to be a widespread characteristic of complex human societies, akin to institutions such as households or cities that can similarly be recognized across a range of different cultures. We should not be too surprised if we can also identify it in the Roman Empire.

Meanwhile, research into modern economic clusters can cast valuable light on their Roman equivalents. Clearly, we should not expect individual Roman clusters to have developed or operated identically with those from any other society: or indeed other Roman examples, given the cultural diversity of the empire. But we may at least ask whether the broad-brush economic, social, and political factors at work in better-documented modern clusters are plausible in a Roman context. Such comparisons may also enhance our understanding of the effects of elite control or regulation on the spatial distribution of economic activity in Roman cities. Debate surrounding this issue has long been shaped by a belief that the locations of some forms of economic activity were influenced by elite concerns about literal or moral pollution.[11] But these ideas are starting

---

    [4] Morley (2004: 43–5).
    [5] Rathbone (1991); Silver (1995: 172–5); Morley (2004: 48–50).
    [6] Western economies: Enright (1998); van der Linde (2003: 135–6); developing countries: Schmitz and Nadvi (1999); van der Linde (2003: 135–6); social corporatist states: Kim (2005); Feldman and Francis (2006: 128–9).
    [7] Akoorie (2011).   [8] Krugman (1991: 59–63); van der Linde (2003: 145–8).
    [9] e.g. Enright (1998); Porter (1998).
    [10] Beccatini (1990); Wilson and Popp (2003a: 11–15); Kim (2005).
    [11] Wallace-Hadrill (1995); Béal (2002); Robinson (2005); Laurence (2007: 82–101).

to be questioned in the context of work that instead explores the contribution of free-market factors in determining the same patterns.[12] A systematic investigation into a form of economic activity with a distinctly spatial aspect—the cluster—offers the opportunity to contribute further to this debate.

CONTEMPORARY CLUSTERS

I will begin by reviewing the main factors behind the development and operation of contemporary clusters, as identified in the academic literature. This will include both industrial and retail clusters, on the grounds that these two sectors were not sharply distinguished in the Roman world. Goods were often made in and sold from the same premises,[13] while descriptive terms for artisans, such as *unguentarius*, could equally well refer to manufacturers or retailers.[14] Roman economic clusters may thus have formed in response to a combination of the factors now identified separately for modern industrial and retail clusters. To clarify the practicalities of cluster operation, I will use two real examples: Birmingham's Jewellery Quarter and London's Bond Street. Both are located in built-up urban environments, and occupy no more than 1 square kilometre, so that they operate on a scale that is not reliant on modern transport. Indeed, both developed in the eighteenth century, well before this was available. But this is not to say that clusters cannot also form on a larger scale, or in a non-urban environment. Many such clusters do exist today, and they are also recognized in the context of the Roman pottery industry in particular.[15] I have chosen to focus on urban examples in order to explore the specific issue of elite control or regulation in this context.

Industrial Clusters

Industrial clusters generally develop in response to local attractors such as cheap land, suitable raw materials, skilled workers, or consumers.[16] In Birmingham (Fig. 13.1), a major prompt for the development of jewellery-making in the late eighteenth century was a decline in the local buckle-making industry.[17] Such conditions encourage entrepreneurialism, as unemployed workers seek new sources of income.[18] In Birmingham, it was relatively easy for former

---

[12] Ellis (2004); McGinn (2004); DeFelice (2007); Monteix (2010).
[13] Mac Mahon (2005); Pirson (2007).   [14] See also Ruffing, Chapter 5, this volume.
[15] Modern examples: van der Linde (2003: 135–6); ancient examples: Peacock (1982: 99–113); Peña (2007: 32–3); Goodman (2013).
[16] Porter (1998: 253–6).   [17] Mason (1998: 31–2); Carnevali (2003: 192).
[18] Feldman and Francis (2006: 117–18).

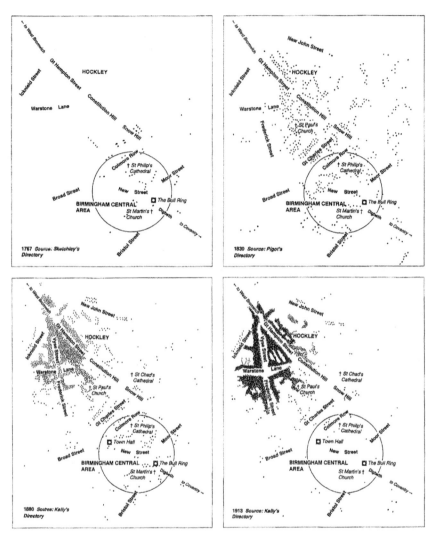

Fig. 13.1. Progressive clustering in the Birmingham jewellery industry between 1767 and 1913. Reproduced from Mason (1998: 10–11, fig. 5a–d).

buckle-makers to set up new businesses, since the equipment required was modest and there were no guilds to control entry into the trades.[19] Meanwhile, the Colmore estate on the north-western edge of the town was being sold off for property development.[20] This was attractive to small-scale artisans, because much of the land was packaged up into small plots available for a low rent,

<hr />

[19] Smith (1989: 97); Carnevali (2003: 192–3).   [20] Mason (1998: 34–6).

while an absence of restrictive leases allowed workshops to be installed in attics and backyards.[21] Furthermore, the development of Birmingham's canal and railway networks between the 1780s and 1840s offered good transport facilities for raw materials and finished products.[22]

Once an industrial cluster has taken hold, it becomes an economic attraction in itself. This is because it allows individual firms to achieve agglomeration economies: efficiencies arising from cooperation and collaboration, similar to economies of scale in large single firms.[23] Examples of agglomeration economies include drawing on the same supplies of raw materials.[24] Suppliers' travel costs are reduced by the geographical concentration of their customers, so they can offer better deals. Similarly, firms within a cluster can interact efficiently with one another by specializing in one stage of production, subcontracting or outsourcing work, or sharing capital such as machinery or furnaces.[25] In the Jewellery Quarter, a range of specialized firms had developed by the mid-nineteenth century, and items of jewellery regularly passed through several workshops before completion.[26] Subcontracting also began early on, with larger firms giving out weekly orders to smaller firms and home workers.[27]

In a cluster, transaction costs are reduced, partly because firms are close together, but also because their personnel usually know one another, and much can be done on trust.[28] Firms also draw from the same pool of labour and expertise, meaning that workers can transfer between firms without their skills being lost, and that information and innovations can spread quickly.[29] Thus in late eighteenth- and early nineteenth-century Birmingham, the jewellery industry helped to generate a rate of patent applications second only to London.[30] Finally, goods can be promoted collectively or passed to salespeople on favourable trading terms, since their travel costs are again reduced.[31] Examples from the Jewellery Quarter include trade publications, shows, and an official website.[32] The importance of spatial proximity to achieving agglomeration economies is clear from research into 102 Jewellery Quarter firms that moved 1–2 miles out of the cluster between 1946 and 1971.[33] These experienced a 77 per cent failure rate, apparently because their

---

[21] On the small size of plots and low rent levels, see Smith (1989: 97); Mason (1998: 9). On the absence of restrictive leases, see Smith (1989: 103); Carnevali (2003: 194).

[22] De Propris and Lazzeretti (2007: 1304).

[23] Krugman (1991: 36–38); Enright (1998).

[24] Krugman (1991: 49–52); Enright (1998: 324–5); Porter (1998: 230–2).

[25] Marshall (1919: 233–4); Lazerson (1990); Enright (1998: 326).

[26] De Propris and Lazzeretti (2007: 1309–13, 1321–5).

[27] Smith (1989: 96–9); Mason (1998: 10).   [28] Dei Ottati (2003); Carnevali (2003: 195).

[29] Porter (1998: 232–3, 236–9); Krugman (1991: 38–49, 52–4).

[30] De Propris and Lazzeretti (2007: 1316–17).

[31] Porter (1998: 233–4); Enright (1998: 324–5).

[32] Mason (1998: 127–31); Jewellery Quarter Marketing Initiative (2011).

[33] Smith (1989: 101–2).

reduced access to agglomeration economies was not sufficiently compensated for by a reduction in rents.

A cluster may develop its own institutions.[34] One crucial example for the Jewellery Quarter was the Birmingham Assay Office.[35] Before this was founded, Birmingham jewellery had to be hallmarked in Chester, which incurred expense and sometimes damage during the journey. Birmingham's Assay Office was founded in 1773, initially in the town centre, but it moved into the Jewellery Quarter itself in 1877.[36] In 1890, a School of Jewellery was also founded, ensuring an ongoing supply of skilled labour.[37] At the same time, the jewellers began to form professional associations: in particular, the Birmingham Jewellers and Silversmiths Association in 1887.[38] This sought to promote the industry, develop overseas markets, train new workers, engage with parliament, deal with rogue traders, and detect and punish wrongdoing. A Trade Enquiry and Debt Collection scheme also developed in 1898, with the aim of protecting its members against fraudulent transactions and helping to collect unpaid debts.[39]

Bodies of this type can enhance the profitability of an industry by allowing conscious decisions about how the cluster is governed—in particular, striking a mutually beneficial balance between cooperation and competition.[40] They also enhance social connections within the cluster, facilitating business transactions and the sharing of expertise. But far less formal social institutions can serve the same purpose.[41] In the Jewellery Quarter, family networks helped to bind workers together, as did shared social spaces like St Paul's Church or the Jeweller's Arms pub.[42] Meanwhile, at any stage, the actions of powerful individuals from within the industry can help to develop a cluster. Jewellery Quarter examples include Matthew Boulton, a leading industrialist who secured the opening of the Birmingham Assay Office, and Jacob Jacobs and Charles Green, jewellery manufacturers and local councillors who drove the establishment of the professional associations.[43]

The Jewellery Quarter today enjoys support from Birmingham City Council.[44] Indeed, policy-makers worldwide regularly encourage the formation or development of clusters, in the hope of fostering economic growth and social regeneration.[45] But Van der Linde, and Feldman and Francis, have found that such initiatives are not usually effective on their own.[46] Feldman and Francis

[34] Porter (1998: 234–5).   [35] Mason (1998: 26–8).   [36] Mason (1998: 70–1).
[37] Mason (1998: 82–4).   [38] Mason (1998: 79–81); Carnevali (2003: 196–206).
[39] Carnevali (2003: 204–5).   [40] Enright (1998: 326–7); Porter (1998: 274–6).
[41] Porter (1998: 241–3); Wilson and Popp (2003a: 11–15).
[42] Family networks: Mason (1998: 73–5, 133–4). Shared social spaces: Haddleton (1987: 25–6); Mason (1998: 35, 54); De Propris and Lazzeretti (2007: 1313–16).
[43] On Boulton, see Carnevali (2003: 193). On Jacobs and Green, see Mason (1998: 82–4); Carnevali (2003: 196–201).
[44] Smith (1989); Jewellery Quarter Marketing Initiative (2011).
[45] Brusco and Pezzini (1990); Enright (1996); Porter (1998: 261–71).
[46] Van der Linde (2003: 147–8); Feldman and Francis (2006).

maintain that cluster success depends chiefly on entrepreneurs, who can best determine what they need to help their businesses grow.[47] Meanwhile, Duranton argues that policy-makers' interventions are often ineffective or actively harmful because of a poor understanding of the problems that they are trying to correct, a mistaken belief that larger clusters are always more efficient, or a preference for pleasing key supporters over achieving real economic growth.[48] Indeed, the Jewellery Quarter has seen its own aborted regeneration initiative. After decline caused by the Second World War, the Birmingham Jewellers and Silversmiths Association, together with the city council, proposed the regeneration of the quarter by replacing its small Victorian workshops with large factory blocks.[49] In the event, only one was built, and firms proved reluctant to move into it.[50] The quarter's ongoing success relates more to the development of direct retail to the public, the updating of the School of Jewellery, and its promotion as a tourist attraction.[51]

Retail Clusters

Bond Street in central London has been an up-market shopping street since the eighteenth century.[52] This is no surprise, since it is easily accessible from a number of wealthy residential areas, and close to other attractions such as parks, theatres, and the political centres of Westminster and Whitehall. During the late nineteenth and early twentieth centuries, the street was increasingly populated by art dealers and antique shops, and also became the home of the Fine Art Society and Sotheby's the auctioneers.[53] The smaller shops acquired goods and expertise from these institutions while retailing to the general public, until many of them were forced to close in the recession of the late 1980s.[54] A small cluster persists around Sotheby's and the Fine Art Society, but Bond Street is now dominated by the designer fashion industry (Fig. 13.2).[55]

The fashion outlets of Bond Street lack a clear industry hub such as Sotheby's and the Fine Art Society provided for the art and antique shops. But they can still benefit from clustering together. This is because customers who buy high-value items like designer clothing (or art and antiques) generally prefer to shop around and compare the goods on offer before making their purchases. For this reason, such items are often described as 'shopping goods' or 'comparison goods': and research into this form of retail shows that customers will spend more if they

---

[47] Feldman and Francis (2006: 129–31). See also Enright (1996) and Porter (1998: 240–1).
[48] Duranton (2011).   [49] Smith (1989: 104–5); Mason (1998: 138–40).
[50] Mason (1998: 150–4).   [51] Smith (1989); Mason (1998: 156–7, 160–70).
[52] Glennie (1998: 937); Rappaport (2000: 10).
[53] Scott (1970: 29); Hermann (1980: 135–7, 153–7).
[54] Hermann (1980: 298); Wrigley and Lowe (2002: 192).
[55] Wrigley and Lowe (2002: 192–6).

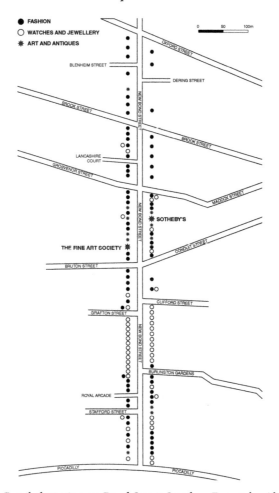

Fig. 13.2. Retail clustering on Bond Street, London. Drawn by Alex Santos.

can make their comparisons easily, without incurring extensive travel costs.[56] Thus, although the individual shops on Bond Street compete with one another for custom, each still attracts more customers than it would alone—another form of agglomeration economy. Clustering allows their customers to make comparisons easily, while competition occurs on price and quality, rather than location.[57]

This forms a sharp contrast with low-value 'convenience goods'—that is, daily purchases such as bread and milk.[58] Shops selling these goods compete on location rather than price, since customers are generally unwilling to travel

[56] Scott (1970: 26–7); Jones and Simmons (1990: 119).
[57] Jones and Simmons (1990: 41).
[58] Scott (1970: 96); Jones and Simmons (1990: 38–45).

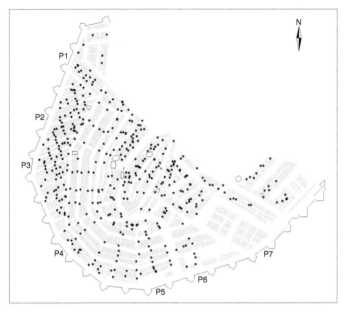

Fig. 13.3. The distribution of bakeries in Amsterdam, 1742. Reproduced from Lesger (2011: 32, fig. 2).

long distances in order to save a few pence on a low-value purchase. As a result, they are usually fairly evenly distributed across a city. In eighteenth-century Amsterdam, Lesger has observed clear differences in the distribution of convenience and comparison retailers.[59] Contemporary tax registers show that bakeries were distributed evenly through most parts of the city, while retailers of high-value goods such as books and fine fabrics were located in the city centre: sometimes in distinct clusters (Fig. 13.3). Lesger emphasized that, although eighteenth-century Amsterdam possessed extensive civic regulations, these included no restrictions on the distribution of shops.[60] Thus, the retail patterns observed were shaped primarily by market forces rather than legislation.

Once a retail cluster has developed, it too becomes self-replicating. Bond Street now has an international reputation as a centre of fashion, making it essential for any firm wishing to position itself as a designer retailer to open a shop there.[61] Its businesses also promote themselves collectively, like those in the Jewellery Quarter—for example, through an official website.[62] Retail clusters may also develop into social hubs. This is certainly true for Bond Street, which has become a place to 'be seen' for fashionable celebrities and professionals, complete with bars and restaurants where they can congregate. These constitute another attractor to the area, and enhance social connections between both customers and workers.

---

[59] Lesger (2011).   [60] Lesger (2011: 44–6).   [61] Fernie et al. (1997).
[62] Bond Street Association (2011).

CLUSTERING IN ROMAN URBANISM

We can now look at Roman economic clusters in the light of their modern equivalents. The focus here is again on urban examples, so that the potential impact of elite regulation or control in this context can be explored. Competition for space is also usually more intensive in the centre of a city than on its periphery or in the countryside. This means that economic clusters in urban centres should be the result of stronger imperatives towards cluster formation, because competition from other activities is also stronger.

Clusters Attested in the Archaeological Record

Clear examples of urban economic clustering are preserved at Pompeii in Italy, Timgad in North Africa, and Silchester in Britain. These sites are unusual in two respects. First, occupation at all three ceased during or at the end of antiquity, meaning that their Roman-period remains were not obscured by later buildings. Secondly, they have undergone large-scale clearance excavations that uncovered all or most of the built-up urban area. This is important for the identification of clustering, since we need to be able to compare the distribution of workshops across a city in order to determine whether a particular type occurs with above-average frequency in one area. But rapid clearance excavations are often achieved at the expense of collecting proper dating evidence and recording the work in detail. This can make it difficult to be certain whether all of the workshops within an apparent cluster were in use simultaneously. Clearance excavations are also much better at identifying workshops with fixed installations than those used by artisans working with lighter equipment: for example, shoe-makers, basket-weavers, or indeed jewellers. Such industries are therefore likely to be under-represented in the archaeological record, while the clusters that we can see represent industries that required significant capital investment for each new workshop. Once formed, such clusters must have been relatively inert, but other industries may have clustered and dispersed more flexibly.

Pompeii

In the 1960s, Walter Moeller identified workshop types in Pompeii that he believed were involved in textile production.[63] Most occurred throughout the city, but one group formed a distinct cluster, particularly in regio VII, insulae

---

[63] Moeller (1966, 1976).

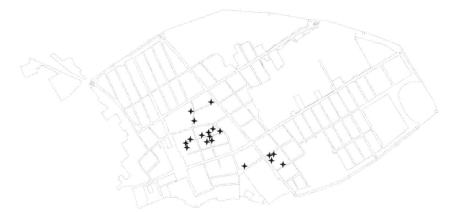

Fig. 13.4. *Officinae lanifricariae* at Pompeii. Map: Miko Flohr.

Fig. 13.5. An example of an *officina lanifricaria*, Pompeii VII 2, 17. Photo: Miko Flohr.

9–12, just east of the city's forum (Fig. 13.4). These workshops contained long masonry tables, small vats, and lead-lined pans with furnaces underneath (Fig. 13.5). On the basis of a graffito on the street front close to one reading *lanifricari dormis* ('wool-scrubber, you sleep'), Moeller dubbed them *officinae lanifricariae*.[64] He suggested that the tables were used for beating the dirt out of raw wool fleeces, the vats for soaking the wool, and the pans for heating and scouring it. Moeller argued that the *lanifricarii* must have been organized into

---

[64] *CIL* 4.1190; Moeller (1966; 1976: 12–13).

a *collegium*, but that there was no evidence for such a group because it operated as part of the *collegium* of the fullers.[65]

Moeller's interpretation of these workshops was heavily criticized by Willem Jongman.[66] Jongman questioned the relevance of the *lanifricari dormis* graffito, which actually comes from the wall of an inn two doors away from one of the workshops, and suggested that the establishments may instead have served hot food.[67] Certainly, large quantities of bones were discovered in at least some of the workshops, indicating some form of animal processing.[68] He further pointed out that Moeller's identification of I 4, 26 as an *officina lanifricaria*, based on an 1875 excavation report, was not supported by any surviving remains.[69] But even Jongman agreed that the remainder of workshops formed an 'archaeological type'—that is, they all shared the same distinct characteristics.[70] This is enough to identify the group as an economic cluster, since the workshops clearly all performed the same function. Meanwhile, Pompeii's destruction by Vesuvius means that these workshops represent the last usage of the plots that they occupy before AD 79. This does not prove that they were all active at that time, but it does mean that they all existed simultaneously, and strongly suggests that most were active during the mid-first century.

Without being sure what went on in these workshops, it is difficult to say why they were clustered in this area of Pompeii. Moeller argued that the people operating them bought their raw materials from the nearby *macellum* or Eumachia building.[71] This is perfectly likely, even if the materials were not wool fleeces, while either building could equally have been used to sell their finished products. Both had back entrances leading directly into the quarter, and this would have allowed access even after the eastern edge of the forum had been sealed off by a line of monumental public buildings.[72] But this monumentalization project itself must have affected the streets east of the forum. Dobbins dates its final phase to the post-62 earthquake restoration period, but adds that the eastern streets may already have been blocked in the Augustan era.[73] After this, pedestrians could reach the *macellum* and Eumachia building from the east, but steps or narrow passages would have barred animals and carts, while of course the buildings' back entrances may not always have been open. The district thus became one of the least accessible in the city. Kaiser has shown that, whether the streets here were approached

---

[65] Moeller (1976: 74–5).   [66] Jongman (1991).   [67] Jongman (1991: 166–9).

[68] Flohr (2013: 59) argues for animal bone finds in at least two, perhaps three, of these workshops. Monteix (2013: 81–4) believes that contemporary excavation journals confirm the existence of only one.

[69] Jongman (1991: 168). The same could be said about VII 3, 24 and VII 4, 39–40. Cf. Moeller (1976: 31–2). However, even if all three are discounted, the cluster in insulae VII 9–12 remains unaffected.

[70] Jongman (1991: 167). Cf. Monteix (2013).   [71] Moeller (1976: 68–71).

[72] Dobbins (1994).   [73] Dobbins (1994: 689–91).

from the city gates or the forum, an above-average number of junctions needed to be negotiated by comparison with other Pompeian streets in order to reach them.[74]

Various activities considered immoral or illegal by the elite, including gambling and prostitution, were also concentrated in this area.[75] Wallace-Hadrill and Laurence see this as a deliberate choice on the part of the urban elite, though they place different emphasis on the question of whether it was achieved through direct regulation or other methods such as social coercion and property ownership.[76] But McGinn has questioned whether this aspect of the quarter's character was really so sharply different from the rest of Pompeii.[77] In any case, the reasons behind it are difficult to assess without knowing when the streets leading east from the forum were blocked, since some uses of space here may be relics of an earlier period before this happened. We can say only that, once it did happen, it should have had an economic impact. Ellis, Laurence, and Kaiser have all shown that plots with entrances on accessible main streets were favoured for most other private land use in Pompeii: commerce, other forms of production, and elite housing.[78] Once blocked, the back streets east of the forum would have become unattractive for these activities. Rents in the area may have fallen, and have represented a particular bargain for those whose activities did not depend on access to busy streets and passing traffic. This might plausibly include workshops that traded via the *macellum* or Eumachia buildings, but did not sell directly to the general public.

The distinction between convenience goods and comparison goods may cast further light on the operation of these workshops, and particularly Jongman's suggestion that they produced hot food. A relatively low-value purchase such as a meal for immediate consumption is a convenience good rather than a comparison good, making customers unlikely to travel long distances to buy it. We should expect to find hot food shops spread relatively evenly throughout the city, and indeed do see this for other convenience goods in Pompeii— for example, bars that *are* known to have sold hot food and bakeries with attached shops.[79] In this context, Jongman's theory appears weak. But the focus of the cluster in a quarter with low accessibility would make comparison shopping equally unlikely. Its position matches better with what we would expect for an industrial cluster with little emphasis on retail. This is supported by Flohr's investigation of these workshops, which found that they were

---

[74] Kaiser (2011: 120). [75] Wallace-Hadrill (1995: 51–5); Laurence (2007: 87–8, 95–6).
[76] Wallace-Hadrill (1995); Laurence (2007: 83, 99).
[77] McGinn (2004: 78–84, 240–1).
[78] Ellis (2004: 378–80); Laurence (2007: 116); Kaiser (2011: 125–9).
[79] Ellis (2004); Monteix (2010)—though Monteix notes that bakeries with shops gravitate towards the centre of Pompeii. This is itself explicable as an attempt to capture the greatest market share. Cf. Jones and Simmons (1990: 44).

around half as likely to include a recognizable shop front as the bakeries, fulleries, dyeries, or tanneries of Pompeii.[80]

Many of the workshops were also neighbours, occupying units directly adjacent to or opposite one another.[81] Much as in Birmingham's Jewellery Quarter, their occupants could hardly have avoided knowing one another, and this would have put them in a good position to cooperate and achieve agglomeration economies if they had chosen to do so. Indeed, while Moeller may have been overstretching the evidence when he identified them as *lanifricarii* operating under the oversight of a fullers' guild, the extensive evidence for trade associations in Pompeii means that it would be surprising if these artisans had no association of their own. A social structure of this type would have brought them together, offering opportunities to strike formal or informal business agreements. There is also considerable variation in the size of the installations, from the single-room workshop at VII 9, 41 to the complex at VII 12, 22–3, which was over ten times the size.[82] Flohr found that, out of fourteen identifiable *officinae lanifricariae*, almost half had four rooms or fewer, while only three had fifteen or more.[83] This suggests an industry consisting mainly of small firms, but with a few larger enterprises. If so, this may have encouraged outsourcing from larger to smaller firms of the kind attested in the Jewellery Quarter: though, of course, there is no direct evidence for this.

Timgad

Working from late-nineteenth- and early twentieth-century excavation reports, Andrew Wilson identified at least twenty-two workshops in Timgad equipped with similar rectangular vats, circular tubs, and wells (Fig. 13.6).[84] Wilson believes that these workshops were probably fulleries, with the circular tubs used for treading cloth, but he adds they could also have been used for cold-water dyeing.[85] The poor quality of the excavation reports meant Wilson was unable to locate all the workshops precisely within the urban plan. However, eighteen workshops *could* be traced to one or more rooms within an insula block, while the rest could be located to the level of the block as a whole. This is quite enough to be sure that the workshops formed a distinct cluster in the north-east corner of the city (Fig. 13.7), where seventeen of the twenty-two were located.[86] Moreover, Wilson suggests that the sheer number of workshops points towards more than local service fulling. He envisions the

[80] Flohr (2007: 133–4).
[81] Adjacent: VII 11, 2–3 and 4–5; VII 12, 22–3 and VII 12, 24. Opposite: VII 11, 2–3 and VII 10, 13.
[82] Moeller (1966: 496; 1976: 31–5).   [83] Flohr (2007: 132–3).
[84] Wilson (2000; 2002: 237–41).   [85] Wilson (2000: 273–5).
[86] Wilson (2000: 278).

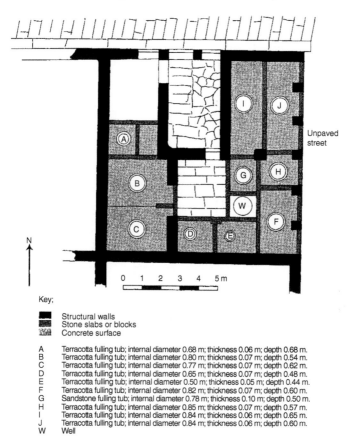

Key;

■	Structural walls
▨	Stone slabs or blocks
▨	Concrete surface

A   Terracotta fulling tub; internal diameter 0.68 m; thickness 0.06 m; depth 0.68 m.
B   Terracotta fulling tub; internal diameter 0.80 m; thickness 0.07 m; depth 0.54 m.
C   Terracotta fulling tub; internal diameter 0.77 m; thickness 0.07 m; depth 0.62 m.
D   Terracotta fulling tub; internal diameter 0.65 m; thickness 0.07 m; depth 0.48 m.
E   Terracotta fulling tub; internal diameter 0.50 m; thickness 0.05 m; depth 0.44 m.
F   Terracotta fulling tub; internal diameter 0.82 m; thickness 0.07 m; depth 0.60 m.
G   Sandstone fulling tub; internal diameter 0.78 m; thickness 0.10 m; depth 0.50 m.
H   Terracotta fulling tub; internal diameter 0.85 m; thickness 0.07 m; depth 0.57 m.
I   Terracotta fulling tub; internal diameter 0.84 m; thickness 0.06 m; depth 0.65 m.
J   Terracotta fulling tub; internal diameter 0.84 m; thickness 0.06 m; depth 0.60 m.
W   Well

Fig. 13.6. An example of a probable fullers' workshop at Timgad. Reproduced from Wilson (2000: 274, fig. 12.01).

large-scale finishing of cloth, probably linked with the presence of at least two textile markets in the city.[87]

No dating evidence is available for these workshops. They simply represent the last recognizable structures on the plots that they occupied before the city was abandoned in late antiquity. Nonetheless, the similar characteristics of the workshops suggest that they were set up around the same time, following a common template. Indeed, this may represent a simple version of the dissemination of innovations widely recognized in modern industrial clusters. Wilson further points out that the circular tubs were generally found unbroken, making it unlikely that some were dismantled or allowed to fall into disrepair while others remained in operation.[88] As at Pompeii, the individual workshops vary considerably in scale. Some contain up to ten circular tubs

[87] Wilson (2000: 281–7).   [88] Wilson (2000: 280).

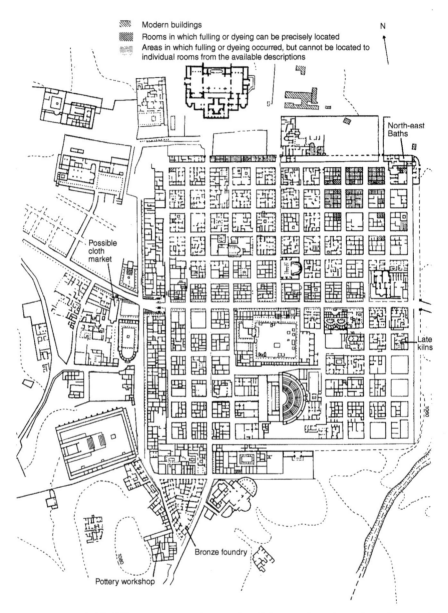

Modern buildings
Rooms in which fulling or dyeing can be precisely located
Areas in which fulling or dyeing occurred, but cannot be located to individual rooms from the available descriptions

N

North-east Baths

Possible cloth market

Late kilns

1060

Bronze foundry

Pottery workshop

1060

Fig. 13.7. Probable fulleries at Timgad. Reproduced from Wilson (2000: 279, fig. 12.08).

and occupy a quarter of an insula, while others have only one or two within a single room.[89] Again, the right conditions for outsourcing are in place, but there is no direct evidence for it.

[89] Wilson (2000: 274–8).

Between the uncertainty over the function of these workshops and an absence of written evidence to illuminate their economic or social context, it is difficult to be certain why they are clustered in one area of the city. But the cluster's relationship with its surroundings offers some grounds for speculation. It is noticeable that no workshops are located along the main roads leading towards the forum at the centre of the city. In fact, all are situated at least three blocks away from these routes. Two possible scenarios could explain this. One is that the landowning elite in Timgad used formal legislation or informal agreements to keep workshops away from the main roads. The other is that the workshops were simply priced out of this area by other competing forms of land use. As at Pompeii, this could include shops or workshops that sold goods directly to passing customers, or wealthy householders who wished to live at prominent locations within the urban network.

It is certainly quite likely that land values, and thus also rental prices, were comparatively low in the north-eastern quarter, especially away from the main thoroughfares. By the end of the second century AD, the south-western part of Timgad had become a prime focus of development. The west gate had been rebuilt as a monumental arch with a temple and market outside it; houses, including two atrium-peristyle *domus*, had been constructed along a demolished stretch of the city wall; and the city's Capitolium had been built at the south-western corner of the city.[90] Elite expenditure was clearly focused on this area, and this is likely to have been associated with higher land values. By contrast, the north-eastern quarter lacked a piped water supply, and its housing occurs in small units with little architectural decoration.[91] It seems to have been comparatively unattractive to developers or tenants, suggesting that rents were lower, and thus perhaps favouring the use of the area for artisanal activity. If so, this would bear some similarity with the development of the Jewellery Quarter on the north-western edge of Birmingham.

The workshops also gravitate around two infrastructural features: a small north-eastern gateway and the northern 'intra-pomerial' road running along the interior of the city's walled circuit. This circuit in itself seems to have become obsolete in the latter half of the second century. Parts of it were demolished, and new arches were built 200–300 metres out along the major approaches to the city, probably reflecting an extension of the urban boundaries.[92] But much of its course was preserved by structures built against it or over its remains. In the north-eastern quarter, this meant that the gateway and road remained important channels of movement. It is thus probably significant that the north-eastern gateway opens directly onto an insula more than half taken up by four workshops, while the majority of the rest lie within a

---

[90] West gate quarter: Lezine (1966–7); Tourrenc (1968). City wall development: Lassus (1966). Capitolium: Ballu (1903: 193–206).

[91] Lohmann (1979: 179); Wilson (2000: 286–7).

[92] Demolition: Lassus (1966). New east and west arches: Ballu (1903: 111; 1911: 10–13).

radius of 100 metres. Similarly, at least seven workshops line the intra-pomerial road, including three that are otherwise displaced in relation to the main cluster. It is tempting to suggest that the gateway and road were important to the activity of these workshops, perhaps for transporting their raw materials or finished products. It is also worth noting that the north-eastern gateway was one of only two purpose-built openings cut through Timgad's walled circuit after its construction.[93] Without proper dating evidence, we cannot be certain, but it is possible that this modification related directly to the needs of the adjacent cluster.

Silchester

Finally, at least thirty-one distinctive circular furnaces were identified by the Victorian excavators of Silchester (Fig. 13.8).[94] These were built from terracotta tiles, although no more than three courses of any are preserved. All were around 2.5 to 3 feet wide, with a short flue about a foot wide and evidence of

George E. Fox del., 1894.

Fig. 13.8. Circular furnace discovered in Insula XI, Block III, Silchester. Reproduced from Fox (1895: fig. 2).

[93] Ballu (1903: 11–13).
[94] Main discussion: Fox (1895). Other references: Fox (1893: 560); Fox and St John Hope (1896: 217 and 246); St John Hope (1897: 411); St John Hope and Fox (1898: 104; 1899: 239; 1900: 93); Fox and St John Hope (1901: 237 and 240–1); St John Hope (1902: 18, 29; 1905: 335–7; 1906: 154).

heat damage on the furnace floors and the ground in front. Most were apparently built outside, but some were inside buildings, and others could have stood in wooden structures missed by the excavators.[95] The furnaces do not resemble pottery kilns, and no diagnostic waste products were found with them. Fox suggested that they were dyeing boilers on the basis of comparisons with similar furnaces at Pompeii, but others have since suggested beer-making or baking.[96] No dating evidence was collected from the furnaces, so we cannot say when they were active or how they relate to one another chronologically. But their similar dimensions and materials suggest that most were built and used around the same time.

The Silchester furnaces occur throughout the city, including close to the forum and the basilica. But they are particularly prominent in the north-western quadrant of the city. Fourteen occur in insulae X, XI, XIII, and XIV near to the west gate, while at least four are in insula XXIII, mainly in its north-western corner (Fig. 13.9).[97] Again, it is difficult to say why this might

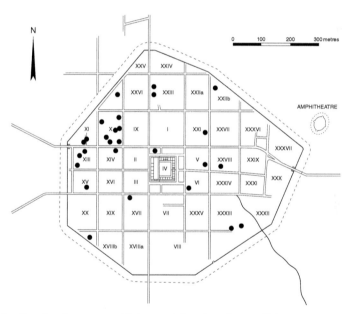

Fig. 13.9. Circular furnaces at Silchester. The plan shows all furnaces mentioned in Fox and St John Hope's excavation reports that can be securely associated with a precise location on the city plan. Drawn by Alex Santos.

[95] Clarke and Fulford (2002). Fox (1895: 463) acknowledges this possibility.

[96] Fox (1895: 459–67); Boon (1974: 286–9); Wacher (1995: 287).

[97] Fox and St John Hope (1901: 237) actually reports remains of at least eight furnaces in insula XXIII, but only four are shown on their plans. It appears that only fairly well-preserved remains were drawn onto the excavation plans, so that there were probably more furnaces in the city than can now be located accurately.

be. But fifteen of the furnaces are within 50 metres of the main routes into the city from the west or north gates. This is rather different from the workshops at Pompeii and Timgad, which were situated away from busy main roads. Here, we must assume that the local elite were perfectly happy for furnaces to cluster along these routes, since their political and economic power would have enabled them to displace the industry if not. The pattern may also suggest that direct retail was more important for this industry than for the workshops previously discussed. Certainly, the rectangular strip-buildings along the route in from the west gate suggest that this was a busy thoroughfare with plenty of passing trade, since these represent a way of maximizing access to an economically attractive street frontage.[98] Meanwhile, proximity to the gates would facilitate the delivery of raw materials, as well as the collection of any finished products not sold directly from the workshops.

Clusters Attested in Texts

Written evidence also hints at the presence of clusters in some cities where they are not attested archaeologically. Rome is particularly well documented in this respect, and yields a number of toponyms likely to reflect artisanal clustering (Table 13.1).[99]

Table 13.1. Toponyms from Rome that suggest artisanal clustering

Toponym	Product or service	Reference
clivus argentarius	Banking	*LTUR* 1.280
clivus capsarius	Bathing supplies?	*LTUR* 1.281
scalae anulariae	Rings	*LTUR* 4.238–9
sigillaria	Gifts	*LTUR* 4, 310
vicus caprarius	Goats	*LTUR* 5.156
vicus cornicularius	Horn	*LTUR* 5.160
vicus frumentarius	Corn	*LTUR* 5.166
vicus lorarius	Harnesses	*LTUR* 5.175
vicus materiarius	Carpentry/timber?	*CIL* 6.975
vicus mundiciei	Luxury objects/toilet articles?	*LTUR* 5.181
vicus sandaliarius	Shoes	*LTUR* 5.189
vicus t(h)urarius	Incense	*LTUR* 5.194–6
vicus unguentarius	Perfume	*LTUR* 5.197–8
vicus vitrarius	Glass	*LTUR* 5.200

[98] Perring (2002: 55–60).

[99] References are given where possible to entries in the *LTUR* (Steinby 1993–2000), which provide full details of the primary sources. See also MacMullen (1974: 130), Morel (1987), and Holleran (2012: 51–60).

Though toponyms alone are not conclusive evidence for the presence of clusters, an analogy used by Augustine shows that the two could go together:

> We laugh, indeed, when we see them [*the gods*] distributed by the fiction of human imagination into their separate roles, like those who farm small portions of the public revenue, or like workmen in the *vicus argentarius*, where one vessel, in order that it may go out perfect, is passed between many craftsmen . . .[100]

Augustine seems to be thinking of a *vicus argentarius* in Carthage, rather than Rome,[101] but he wrote for a cosmopolitan audience, suggesting that the scenario would be widely recognized. He also reveals that the artisans in this particular *vicus*[102] specialized and collaborated, much like the workers in Birmingham's Jewellery Quarter. Back in Rome, references to the *vicus sandaliarius* also show that clusters might form and disperse while toponyms remained unchanged. Though the name suggests a cluster of shoe-makers, Aulus Gellius and Galen in the second century describe it as lined with booksellers.[103] Rome also shows that clusters could exist without generating toponyms. In late republican and early imperial literature, the Via Sacra appears as a focus for jewellers, and the *vicus tuscus* for fine clothes traders, while work by Monteix on the workplaces recorded on artisans' tombstones reflects these same concentrations.[104] Some texts also use the formulae *in . . .* or *inter. . .* to locate activities or places 'among the' practitioners of a particular trade.[105] Arguably, these are more persuasive evidence for economic clustering than straightforward toponyms, since they show that at the time of writing these districts really were recognizably dominated by a particular trade.

Not all of these examples can be located within Rome, but several of those that can occur around the forum (Fig. 13.10). It is striking that these relate to high-value items such as jewellery, books, or luxury fabrics: in other words, comparison goods. They thus match up well with eighteenth-century Amsterdam and modern Bond Street, where similar clusters were also located close to the accessible hearts of the cities. Indeed, in a world without telephone directories or the Internet, the impetus towards retail clustering may have been even stronger, since it would help customers to find the goods they wanted. Meanwhile, Gellius' and Galen's comments about the *vicus sandaliarius* recall Bond Street's role as a social hub. Both report encountering intellectual disputes there: one about the meaning of certain words in Sallust, and

---

[100] August., *De civ. D.* 7.4.　　　[101] Rougé (1966: 323–4); Wilson (2002: 259).

[102] The etymologists define an urban *vicus* as a 'district' or 'quarter' (Varro, *Ling.* 5.145, 160; Isid., *Etym.* 15.2.22), but the word was often also applied to its main street (e.g. Livy 1.48.6–7).

[103] Gell., *NA* 18.4.1; Gal., *Libr. Propr.* Kühn 19.8.

[104] Morel (1987: 145); Holleran (2012: 55–7); Monteix (2012).

[105] *in figlinis* (potteries: *LTUR* 2.252–3), *inter aerarios* (bronze-workers: *CIL* 6.9186), *inter falcarios* (scythe-makers: Cic. *in Cat.* 1.8 and *pro Sulla* 52), *inter figulos* (potteries: *LTUR* 2.253), *inter lignarios* (carpenters: Livy 35.41.10), *inter olivarios* (olive-sellers: *CIL* 6.37043 (= 1².809)), *inter vitores* (basket-makers: *LTUR* 5.207).

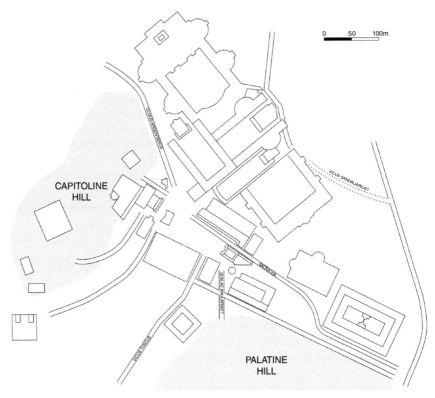

Fig. 13.10. Streets characterized by retail clusters in the Forum area, Rome. Drawn by Alex Santos.

the other about the authorship of a work attributed to Galen.[106] The *vicus* thus seems to have functioned as a place to discuss as well as buy books. Rome also boasted numerous *atria, basilicae, fora, horrea, macella,* and *portici* named after particular goods or trades.[107] These are purpose-built structures, and as such represent the outcomes of conscious decisions to devote space to a particular economic activity. Nonetheless, they would have allowed artisans or traders to achieve agglomeration economies or attract comparison shoppers in the same way as clusters of many individual shops or workshops.

Elsewhere, papyri, inscriptions, and literary references suggest the presence of similar clusters in streets, districts, porticoes, or marketplaces across the empire. Stöckle collected twenty-three such examples from Egyptian papyri, now supplemented by Krüger for Oxyrhynchus, while MacMullen identified

---

[106] Gell., *NA* 18.4; Gal. *Libr. Propr.* Kühn 19.8–9.
[107] MacMullen (1974: 132); Morel (1987: 137–40, 148–54).

another fourteen in Italy, Greece, Asia Minor, and Judaea.[108] This evidence is clearly affected by the embeddedness of the epigraphic habit and the survival of papyrus, and thus bypasses the north-western provinces. Most examples are also only brief mentions, which do not prove the existence of economic clusters. But some use the formula ἐν τοῖς..., the Greek equivalent of *in*... or *inter*..., which does point towards genuine concentrations of artisans.[109] The textual corpus also covers a wider range of activities than the archaeological examples, including trade in perishable goods or service provision, which would be all but undetectable through excavation.[110] It also ranges over a considerable period, from Cicero's scythe-makers in the late first century BC to Augustine's *vicus argentarius* in the fifth century AD.

Broadening the Picture

The examples presented above confirm that economic clustering was a real phenomenon in the Roman world. It is probably under-represented in the surviving evidence, since we can expect to see it only in places that have undergone large-scale clearance excavations or left an unusually rich textual record. Few sites meet these criteria, but where they do, clusters can be detected: albeit in limited detail. The known cases range widely across the empire and through time. They also vary in character, involving many different trades and industries, and ranging from back-street industrial clusters, as at Pompeii and Timgad, to those geared more towards direct retail, as in Rome. The local circumstances that gave rise to them must have varied, as must the details of how they operated. But such variation is already allowed for within the literature on contemporary clustering, and does not prevent the ancient examples from being recognized as part of the same phenomenon.

Meanwhile, by going beyond the urban examples introduced above, we can speculate further about the possible mechanisms under which they operated. Non-urban clusters provide more concrete evidence for economic co-operation, and this is especially true of the *terra sigillata* industry, thanks to the information provided by name-stamps and close dating techniques. Here, decorative schemes and stamp designs tended to evolve quickly, especially during periods of peak production (for example, between 15 BC and AD 30 at Arezzo)—a phenomenon that is comparable with the rapid spread of

---

[108] Stöckle (1911: 149–52); MacMullen (1974: 133); Krüger (1990: 82–8). See also Droß-Krüpe, Chapter 14, this volume.

[109] Arsinoë: *BGU* 1087 5, 7.8 (bakers) and 4, 13 (garland-makers). Thebaïs: *P. Grenf.* 1, 21 (potters) and *P. Grenf.* 1, 42 (gooseherds).

[110] e.g. wool-traders in Jerusalem (Joseph. *BJ* 5.8.1.331) or barbers in Velitrae, Italy (*CIL* 15.7172).

innovations in modern clusters.[111] The shared use of fixed capital such as kilns is also demonstrated by surviving firing lists, while Dannell has argued for the use of outsourcing at la Graufesenque.[112] Specialization is also attested in *terra sigillata* production centres, with some individuals, for example, concentrating on the production of moulds that were then used in more than one workshop.[113] Such conditions did not apply in all *sigillata* production centres, but they do demonstrate that these methods of working, all of which are familiar from modern clusters, could also develop in a Roman context. In fact, Ruffing argues that specialization in particular may have been more common across all types of Roman industry than is usually recognized, and regularly occurs in conjunction with spatial clustering.[114]

Roman social structures could also have provided support for economic clusters, as is attested in other periods and cultures. Trade associations existed throughout the empire, in spite of restrictions sometimes imposed by the emperors.[115] Interpretations of their character have ranged from religiously oriented social clubs to organized economic interest groups: and of course we should not assume a universal model.[116] But, even if their functions were primarily social, such groups could support spatial clustering by enhancing personal connections within the trade. Indeed, Hawkins argues that they lowered transaction costs between small firms by creating networks of trust, thus reducing the incentives to form larger, but less flexible, integrated firms, and leaving the very clusters of small workshops under investigation here.[117] Although none of the archaeologically attested clusters discussed is known to have had a related trade association, a link does emerge in the context of toponyms. In Lydia, the Greek word *plateia* (broad street) was used to describe some trade associations, strongly suggesting that they formed a spatial cluster as well as a social network.[118] Family networks could similarly strengthen social connections, and plenty of trades were certainly family-dominated. For example, pottery stamps and inscriptions reveal that the production of mortaria in a group of kilns at Aoste in Gaul was led by the local *Atisii* for over a hundred years.[119] Apprenticeships also provided access to professional social networks, and could have encouraged spatial concentration—as suggested by the case of an Egyptian boy apprenticed to a coppersmith in the same street as his father.[120] Again, there is no direct evidence for the influence of family

---

[111] Kenrick (2004: 256).   [112] Polak (1998); Dannell (2002).   [113] Mees (1994).

[114] Ruffing (2008; Chapter 5, this volume).

[115] Cotter (1996); van Nijf (1997); Aubert (1999); Diosono (2007).   [116] Perry (2006).

[117] Hawkins (2012: 186–93).

[118] *TAM* 5.1 79–81, 146; Arnaoutoglou, Chapter 12, this volume.

[119] Rémy and Jospin (1998).

[120] *PSI* 871 in Johnson (1936: 391–2). On apprenticeship in general, see Freu, Chapter 8, this volume.

networks or apprenticeship schemes in the urban clusters discussed, but such institutions were part of their wider social context.

ELITE REGULATION AND CONTROL

We can now return to the relationship between the spatial distribution of Roman economic activity and conscious control or regulation by the urban elite. Local elites were certainly in a good position to control the economic topography of Roman cities. The wealth inequalities of the ancient world would lead us to expect that most shops and workshops were owned by the wealthy elite and staffed by their dependants or rented to artisans (directly or through business managers), and this is supported by the evidence of rental notices and property development patterns in Pompeii.[121] Where workshops included fixed equipment, Egyptian papyrus contracts show that it was typically provided and maintained by the owner, and some Italian evidence points towards the same practices.[122] The urban elite could thus determine the locations and functions of shops or workshops, either via direct legislation or as property-owners.

The case for legislation is weak. Wallace-Hadrill argued that the locations of brothels and gambling dens in Pompeii were restricted by rulings enforced by the aediles.[123] But he could present no direct evidence for legal restrictions on the spatial distribution, as opposed to the conduct, of economic activity, while his concept of moral zoning has since been criticized.[124] The closest fit among the ancient evidence is the Urso charter, which forbids the construction of 'tile-kilns with a capacity of more than three hundred tiles or tile-like objects in the *oppidum* [i.e. urban centre] of the colony'.[125] But, if this restriction was breached, the kiln was simply forfeited to the civic authorities—not demolished or put out of action. Large tile kilns *could* exist in the centre of Urso, then, so long as they were not privately owned, while smaller kilns and other workshops were apparently unrestricted.[126] This leaves us with no credible evidence for the use of civic legislation to control the economic topography of Roman cities.

As large-scale property-owners or benefactors, the elite clearly did exercise control over urban space. But this does not mean that they used it consistently to

---

[121] Pirson (1997, 1999); Robinson (2005).
[122] For Egypt, see, e.g. *BGU* 1067 (mill), *BGU* 1117 (bakeshop), *BGU* 1127 (goldsmith's), *P. Teb.* 342 (pottery). See further Cockle (1981). For Italy, see *CIL* 10.2226 (wool workshops), *CIL* 4.1136 (baths), *CIL* 4.3340.142 (fullery).
[123] Wallace-Hadrill (1995).   [124] McGinn (2004); DeFelice (2007).
[125] *Lex Coloniae Genetivae Iuliae* 76.24–8; Crawford (1996: 393–454).
[126] Goodman (2007: 106–8).

prioritize moral and aesthetic values over the maximization of profits, as some
have implied. Dio Chrysostom's speeches about the construction of a colonnade
in Prusa, Bithynia, which entailed the displacement of some workshops, are a
case in point.[127] Béal sees these texts as revealing an elite belief that artisanal
activity compromised the dignity of a city, and should not be the basis of its
wealth.[128] But Dio's plans were opposed by other members of the local elite, who
specifically defended the workshops.[129] No doubt the argument was a proxy for
wider rivalries, but the case does show that elite consent to the removal of
workshops from urban centres was not automatic. Meanwhile, Dio built new
workshops in two other locations.[130] This would have given him control over
how the workshops were used: perhaps rather like the third-century benefactor,
Marcus Nikephoros, who awarded places between the columns of a portico along
the 'Marble Street' in Ephesus.[131] These spaces were shared between at least
seven different trade associations, but, where a single individual controlled a
comparable block of commercial space, it is perfectly plausible that they might
offer units first to one particular trade group, especially if they served as its
patron. Indeed, Nikephoros donated at least four places to the *taurinadoi*
(probably shoemakers)—just over 20 per cent of the eighteen surviving alloca-
tions.[132] This may not be representative of their original share, but within a
colonnade around 180 metres long, even four *taurinadoi* would seem like
something of a cluster.

Private property-ownership might have a comparable effect. The Insula
Arriana Polliana and the Praedia Julia Felix in Pompeii are examples of
concentrated property holdings: complete blocks owned by single individuals,
within which smaller units were available for rent.[133] Something similar may
have existed in the south-western corner of Timgad, where a strip of land was
developed for housing after the demolition of the city wall.[134] Lassus pointed
out that the decision not to build any new roadways through this development
is characteristic of a profit-driven private entrepreneur—probably the Sertius
who owned a large *domus* at the southern end of the development and
financed a public market alongside its northern end. Property-owners in this
position could rent on the open market like the Pompeian landlords, who
would presumably let to whomever offered the highest price. But again they
might plausibly privilege a particular group of artisans by offering places to
them privately and/or on favourable terms, thus helping to create a cluster.
Such behaviour would have to be socially motivated, since it would reduce the
owner's rental income, but enhanced status and influence as a patron might

---

[127] Dio Chrys., *Or.* 40.6–10, 45.12–16, 47.   [128] Béal (2002: 5–7).
[129] Dio Chrys., *Or.* 40.8–9, 47.11; Bekker-Nielsen (2008: 125–7, 130–1).
[130] Dio Chrys., *Or.* 40.9, 46.9.   [131] Knibbe (1985); van Nijf (1997: 83–5).
[132] *IK* 16.2080, 2081.
[133] Insula Arriana Polliana: *CIL* 4.138; Pirson (1997). Praedia Julia Felix: *CIL* 4.1136.
[134] Lassus (1966); Wilson (2002: 261).

compensate for this.[135] Equally, those who controlled continuous blocks of property could have chosen *not* to rent them out to the practitioners of a given trade, thus pushing them out of one area of the city and encouraging them to cluster in another. Again, the motive would have to be social, and here moral and aesthetic preferences are the only available explanation. Thus, for example, Sertius could have encouraged the concentration of fullers' workshops in the north-eastern quarter of Timgad because he preferred not to rent out suitable units in the property that he controlled in the south-west.

But work on contemporary clustering suggests that the consistent application of such moral or aesthetic preferences is more likely to have impeded the creation of clusters. Economists and geographers emphasize the action of the free market, and particularly individual entrepreneurs, in their accounts of modern cluster development.[136] If Roman property-owners consistently prioritized moral considerations when equipping and renting shops and workshops, this should have distorted whatever profit motivations were being expressed by artisans or traders. In modern terms, it would dampen the input of entrepreneurs, acting as a barrier to the formation and development of clusters. Yet clusters did form. This should suggest that some property-owners were willing to listen to the views of artisans concerning the most profitable uses of particular economic units. In doing so, the property-owners might be motivated by a combination of 'pure' economic and social factors: a desire to maximize both their profits as landlords and their social standing as patrons. Indeed, the social role of the elite as trade patrons may actively have encouraged clustering, though it is unlikely that this was a conscious aim, as it is for modern policymakers. The formation of economic clusters in Roman cities, then, can be explained with reference to both social and economic motivations on the part of the urban elite. The two are not always easily separable, and it needs remembering that social factors are important in modern clustering too—for example, through the influence of social networks. But the findings of research into modern clustering weigh against explaining the distribution of Roman urban workshops in terms of the moral preferences of the urban elite. Where economic clustering can be identified, it is more likely that this particular social factor was not at work.

ACKNOWLEDGEMENTS

I would like to thank Andrew Wilson and Miko Flohr for inviting me to participate in the ESF workshop, my fellow participants for their responses, Andy Evans and Dan Olner for comments on a written draft, and Charlotte Trémouilhe for proof-reading.

---

[135] Pirson (2007: 470).
[136] Enright (1996); van der Linde (2003: 147–8); Feldman and Francis (2006).

REFERENCES

Akoorie, M. (2011). 'A Challenge to Marshallian Orthodoxy on Industrial Clustering', *Journal of Management History* 17/4: 451–70.

Asheim, B., Cooke, P., and Martin, R. (2006). *Clusters and Regional Development: Critical Reflections and Explanations*. London and New York.

Aubert, J. (1999). 'La Gestion des collegia: Aspects juridiques, économiques et sociaux', *CCG* 10: 49–69.

Ballu, A. (1903). *Les ruines de Timgad (antique Thamugadi): Nouvelles découvertes*. Paris.

Ballu, A. (1911). *Les ruines de Timgad (antique Thamugadi): Sept années de découvertes 1903–1910*. Paris.

Béal, J.-C. (2002). 'L'artisanat et la ville: Relecture de quelques textes', in J.-C. Béal and J.-C. Goyon (eds), *Les artisans dans la ville antique*. Lyons and Paris, 5–14.

Beccatini, G. (1990). 'The Marshallian Industrial District as a Socio-Economic Notion', in F. Pyke, G. Beccatini, and W. Sengenberger (eds), *Industrial Districts and Inter-Firm Cooperation in Italy*. Geneva, 37–51.

Beccatini, G. (2003). 'Industrial Districts in the Development of Tuscany', in Beccatini et al. (2003), 11–28.

Beccatini, G., Bellandi, M., Dei Ottati, G., and Sforzi, F. (2003). *From Industrial Districts to Local Development: An Itinerary of Research*. Cheltenham and Northampton, MA.

Bekker-Nielsen, T. (2008). *Urban Life and Local Politics in Roman Bithynia: The Small World of Dion Chrysostomos*. Aarhus.

Bond Street Association (2011). 'Bond Street Luxury Shopping London' <http://www.bondstreet.co.uk/> (accessed 15 October 2011).

Boon, G. C. (1974). *Silchester: The Roman town of Calleva*. London.

Brusco, S., and Pezzini, M. (1990). 'Small-Scale Enterprise in the Ideology of the Italian Left', in Pyke, Beccatini, and Sengenberger, (1990), 142–59.

Capecchi, C. (1990). 'A History of Flexible Specialisation and Industrial Districts in Emilia-Romagna', in Pyke, Beccatini, and Sengenberger (1990), 20–36.

Carnevali, F. (2003). '"Malefactors and Honourable Men": The Making of Commercial Honesty in Nineteenth-Century Birmingham', in Wilson and Popp (2003b), 192–207.

Clarke, A., and Fulford, M. (2002). 'The Excavation of Insula IX, Silchester: The First Five Years of the "Town Life" Project, 1997–2001', *Britannia* 33: 129–66.

Cockle, H. (1981). 'Pottery Manufacture in Roman Egypt: A New Papyrus', *JRS* 71: 87–97.

Cotter, W. (1996). 'The *collegia* and Roman Law: State Restrictions on Voluntary Associations, 64 BCE–200 CE', in J. S. Kloppenborg and S. G. Wilson (eds), *Voluntary Associations in the Graeco-Roman World*. London and New York, 74–89.

Crawford, M. H. (1996). *Roman Statutes*, i. London.

Cumbers, A., and MacKinnon, D. (2006). *Clusters in Urban and Regional Development*. London and New York.

Dannell, G. B. (2002). 'Law and Practice: Further Thoughts on the Organization of the Potteries at la Graufesenque', in M. Genin and A. Vernhet (eds), *Céramiques de la Graufesenque et autres productions d'époque romaine: Nouvelles recherches. Hommages à Bettina Hoffmann*. Montagnac, 211–42.

Dei Ottati, G. (2003). 'Trust, Interlinking Transactions and Credit in the Industrial District', in Beccatini et al. (2003), 108–30.

DeFelice, J. (2007). 'Inns and Taverns', in J. J. Dobbins and P. W. Foss (eds), *The World of Pompeii*. London and New York, 474–86.

De Propris, L., and Lazzeretti, L. (2007). 'The Birmingham Jewellery Quarter: A Marshallian Industrial District', in *European Planning Studies*, 15/10: 1295–1325.

Diosono, F. (2007). *Collegia: Le associazioni professionali nel mondo romano*. Rome.

Dobbins, J. (1994). 'Problems of Chronology, Decoration, and Urban Design in the Forum at Pompeii', *AJA* 98/4: 629–94.

Duranton, G. (2011). 'California Dreamin': The Feeble Case for Cluster Policies', *Review of Economic Analysis* 3: 3–45.

Ellis, S. (2004). 'The Distribution of Bars at Pompeii: Archaeological, Spatial and Viewshed Analyses', *JRA* 17: 371–84.

Enright M. J. (1996). 'Regional Clusters and Economic Development: A Research Agenda', in U. Staber, N. V. Schaefer, and B. Sharma (eds), *Business Networks: Prospects for Regional Development*. New York, 190–214.

Enright, M. J. (1998). 'Regional Clusters and Firm Strategy', in A.D. Chandler, P. Hagström, and Ö. Sölvell (eds), *The Dynamic Firm: The Role of Technology, Strategy, Organization and Regions*. Oxford, 315–42.

Feldman, M., and Francis, J. L. (2006). 'Entrepreneurs as Agents in the Formation of Industrial Clusters', in B. Asheim, P. Cooke, and R. Martin (eds), *Clusters and Regional Development: Critical Reflections and Explanations*. London and New York, 115–136.

Fernie, J., Moore, C., Lawrie, A., and Hallsworth, A. (1997). 'The Internationalization of the High Fashion Brand: The Case of Central London', *Journal of Product and Brand Management* 6/3: 151–62.

Flohr, M. (2007). '*Nec quicquam ingenuum habere potest officina?* Spatial Contexts of Urban Production at Pompeii, AD 79', *BABesch* 82: 129–48.

Flohr, M. (2013). 'The Textile Economy of Pompeii', *JRA* 26/1: 53-78.

Fox, G. E. (1895). 'Excavations on the Site of the Roman City at Silchester, Hants, in 1894', *Archaeologia* 54: 439–72.

Fox, G. E., and St John Hope, W. H. (1893). 'Excavations on the Site of the Roman City at Silchester, Hants, in 1892', *Archaeologia* 53: 539–73.

Fox, G. E., and St John Hope, W. H. (1901). 'Excavations on the Site of the Roman City at Silchester, Hants, in 1900', *Archaeologia* 57: 229–56.

Glennie, P. (1998). 'Consumption, Consumerism and Urban Form: Historical Perspectives', *Urban Studies* 35: 927–51.

Goodman, P. J. (2007). *The Roman City and its Periphery: From Rome to Gaul*. London and New York.

Goodman, P. J. (2013). 'The Production Centres: Settlement Hierarchies and Spatial Distribution', in M. Fulford and E. Durham (eds), *Seeing Red: New Economic and Social Perspectives on terra sigillata*. London, 121–36.

Haddleton, M. E. (1987). *The Jewellery Quarter: History and Guide*. Birmingham.

Hawkins, C. (2012). 'Manufacturing', in W. Scheidel (ed.), *The Cambridge Companion to the Roman Economy*. Cambridge, 175–94.

Hermann, F. (1980). *Sotheby's: Portrait of an Auction House*. London.

Heichelheim, F. (1938). 'Roman Syria', in T. Frank (ed.), *An Economic Survey of Ancient Rome*, iv. Baltimore, 121–257.

Holleran, C. (2012). *Shopping in Ancient Rome: The Retail Trade in the Late Republic and the Principate*. Oxford.

Jewellery Quarter Marketing Initiative (2011). 'Official Website of Birmingham's Jewellery Quarter' <http://www.jewelleryquarter.net/> (accessed 15 October 2011).

Johnson, A. C. (1936). *Roman Egypt to the Reign of Diocletian* (= T. Frank (ed.), *An Economic Survey of Ancient Rome*, ii). Baltimore.

Jongman, W. (1991). *The Economy and Society of Pompeii*. Amsterdam.

Jones, K., and Simmons, J. (1990). *The Retail Environment*. London.

Kaiser, A. (2011). 'What was a *via*? An Integrated Archaeological and Textual Approach', in E. Poehler, M. Flohr, and K. Cole (eds), *Pompeii: Art, Industry, and Infrastructure*. Oxford, 115–30.

Kenrick, P. (2004). 'Signatures on Italian sigillata: A New Perspective', in J. Poblome, P. Talloen, R. Brulet, and M. Waelkens (eds), *Early Italian Sigillata: The Chronological Framework and Trade Patterns*. Leuven, 253–62.

Kim, J. Y. (2005). 'The Formation of Clustering of Direct Foreign Investment and its Role of Inter-Firm Networks in China: Case Study of Qingdao Development Zones', in C. Karlsson, B. Johansson, and R. Stough (eds) *Industrial Clusters and Inter-Firm Networks*. Cheltenham and Northampton, MA.

Knibbe, D. (1985). 'Der Asiarch M. Fulvius Publicianus Nikephoros, die ephesischen Handwerkszünfte und die Stoa des Servilius', *JÖAI* 56: 71–7.

Krüger, J. (1990). *Oxyrhynchos in der Kaiserzeit: Studien zur Topographie und Literaturrezeption*. Frankfurt.

Krugman, P. (1991). *Geography and Trade*. Belgium and Cambridge, MA.

Lassus, J. (1966). 'Une opération immobilière à Timgad', in R. Chevallier (ed.), *Mélanges d'archéologie et d'histoire offerts à André Piganiol*. Paris, 1221–31.

Laurence, R. (2007). *Roman Pompeii: Space and Society*. London and New York.

Lazerson, M. H. (1990). 'Subcontracting in the Modena Knitwear Industry', in Pyke, Beccatini, and Sengenberger (1990), 108–33.

Lesger, C. (2011). 'Patterns of Retail Location and Urban Form in Amsterdam in the Mid-Eighteenth Century', *Urban History* 38/1: 24–47.

Lezine, A. (1966–7). 'Note sur l'arc dit de Trajan à Timgad', *Bulletin d'Archéologie Algérienne* 2: 123–7.

Linde, C. van der (2003). 'The Demography of Clusters: Findings from the Cluster Meta-Study', in J. Bröcker, D. Dohse, and R. Soltwedel (eds), *Innovation Clusters and Interregional Competition*. Berlin, 130–49.

Lohmann, H. (1979). 'Beobachtungen zum Stadtplan von Timgad', in *Diskussionen zur Archäologischen Bauforschung*, 3. Berlin, 167–87.

Mac Mahon, A. (2005). 'The Shops and Workshops of Roman Britain', in A. Mac Mahon and J. Price (eds), *Roman Working Lives and Urban Living*. Oxford, 48–69.

McCallum, M. (2011). 'Pottery Production in Pompeii: An Overview', in E. Poehler, M. Flohr, and K. Cole (eds), *Pompeii: Art, Industry, and Infrastructure*. Oxford, 103–14.

McGinn, T. (2004). *The Economy of Prostitution in the Roman World: A Study of Social History and the Brothel*. Ann Arbor.

MacMullen, R. (1974). *Roman Social Relations, 50 BC to AD 284.* New Haven and London.

Marshall, A. (1890). *Principles of Economics.* London.

Marshall, A. (1919). *Industry and Trade: A Study of Industrial Technique and Business Organization, and of their Influences on the Conditions of Various Classes and Nations.* London.

Mason, S. (1998). *Jewellery Making in Birmingham 1750–1995.* Chichester.

Mees, A. (1994). 'Potiers et moulistes: Observations sur la chronologie, les structures et la commercialisation des ateliers de terre sigillée décorée', in *SFECAG: Actes du Congrès de Millau.* Marseilles, 19–41.

Moeller, W. O. (1966). 'The *lanifricarius* and the *officinae lanifricariae* at Pompeii', *Technology and Culture* 7: 493–96.

Moeller, W. O. (1976). *The Wool Trade of Ancient Pompeii.* Leiden.

Monteix, N. (2010). 'La localisation des métiers dans l'espace urbain: quelques exemples pompéiens', in P. Chardron-Picault (ed.), *Aspects de l'artisanat en milieu urbain: Gaule et Occident romain.* Dijon, 147–60.

Monteix, N. (2012). '"Caius Lucretius . . . marchand de couleurs de la rue du fabricant de courroies": Réflexions critiques sur les concentrations de métiers à Rome', in G. Sanidas and A. Esposito (eds), *Quartiers artisanaux en Grèce ancienne: Une perspective méditerranéenne.* Villeneuve d'Ascq, 333–52.

Monteix, N. (2013). 'The Apple of Discord: Fleece-Washing in Pompeii's Textile Economy', *JRA* 26/1: 79–87.

Morel, J.-P. (1987). 'La topographie de l'artisanat et du commerce dans la Rome antique', in École française de Rome (ed.), *L'Urbs: Espace urbain et histoire.* Rome, 127–55.

Morley, N. (2004). *Theories, Models and Concepts in Ancient History.* London and New York.

Nijf, O. van (1997). *The Civic World of Professional Associations in the Roman East.* Amsterdam.

Peacock, D. P. S. (1982). *Pottery in the Roman World: An Ethnoarchaeological Approach.* London.

Peña, J. T. (2007). *Roman Pottery in the Archaeological Record.* Cambridge and New York.

Perring, D. (2002). *The Roman House in Britain.* London.

Perry, J. (2006). *The Roman Collegia: The Modern Evolution of an Ancient Concept.* Leiden.

Pirson, F. (1997). 'Rented Accommodation at Pompeii: The Insula Arriana Polliana', in R. Lawrence and A. Wallace-Hadrill (eds), *Domestic Space in the Roman World: Pompeii and Beyond.* Portsmouth, RI, 165–81.

Pirson, F. (1999). *Mietwohnungen in Pompeji und Herculaneum.* Munich.

Pirson, F. (2007). 'Shops and Industries', in J. J. Dobbins and P. W. Foss (eds), *The World of Pompeii.* London and New York, 457–73.

Polak, M. (1998). 'Old Wine in New Bottles: Reflections on the Organization of the Production of *terra sigillata* at la Graufesenque', in J. Bird (ed.), *Form and Fabric: Studies in Rome's Material Past in Honour of B. R. Hartley.* Oxford, 115–21.

Porter, M. (1990). *The Competitive Advantage of Nations.* Basingstoke.

Porter, M. (1998). 'Clusters and Competition', in M. Porter (ed.), *On Competition*. Boston, 213–303.

Pyke, F., Beccatini, G., and Sengenberger, W. (1990). *Industrial Districts and Inter-Firm Cooperation in Italy*. Geneva.

Rappaport, E. (2000). *Shopping for Pleasure: Women in the Making of London's West End*. Princeton and Oxford.

Rathbone, D. (1991). *Economic Rationalism and Rural Society in Third-Century AD Egypt: The Heroninos Archive and the Appianus Estate*. Cambridge.

Rémy, B., and Jospin, J.-P. (1998). 'Recherches sur la société d'une agglomération de la cité de Vienne: Aoste (Isère)', *Revue archéologique de Narbonnaise* 31: 73–89.

Robinson, D. (2005). 'Re-Thinking the Social Organisation of Trade and Industry in First Century AD Pompeii', in A. Mac Mahon and J. Price (eds), *Roman Working Lives and Urban Living*. Oxford, 88–105.

Rougé, J. (1966). *Expositio totius mundi et gentium: Introduction, texte critique, traduction, notes et commentaire*. Paris.

Ruffing, K. (2008). *Die berufliche Spezialisierung in Handel und Handwerk: Untersuchungen zu ihrer Entwicklung und zu ihren Bedingungen in der römischen Kaiserzeit im östlichen Mittelmeerraum auf der Grundlage griechischer Inschriften und Papyri*. Rahden.

Schmitz, H., and Nadvi, K. (1999). 'Clustering and Industrialization: Introduction', *World Development* 27/9: 1503–14.

Scott, P. (1970). *Geography and Retailing*. London.

Silver, M. (1995). *Economic Structures of Antiquity*. London.

Smith, B. (1989). 'The Birmingham Jewellery Quarter: A Civic Problem that has Become an Opportunity in the 1980s', in B. Tilson (ed.), *Made in Birmingham: Design and Industry 1889–1989*. Studley, 96–112.

St John Hope, W. H. (1897). 'Excavations on the Site of the Roman City at Silchester, Hants, in 1896', *Archaeologia* 55: 409–30.

St John Hope, W. H. (1902). 'Excavations on the Site of the Roman City at Silchester, Hants, in 1901', *Archaeologia* 58: 17–36.

St John Hope, W. H. (1905). 'Excavations on the Site of the Roman City at Silchester, Hants in 1903 and 1904', *Archaeologia* 59: 333–70.

St John Hope, W. H. (1906). 'Excavations on the Site of the Roman City at Silchester, Hants, in 1905', *Archaeologia* 60: 149–68.

St John Hope, W. H., and Fox, G. E. (1896). 'Excavations on the Site of the Roman City at Silchester, Hants, in 1895', *Archaeologia* 55: 215–56.

St John Hope, W. H., and Fox, G. E. (1898). 'Excavations on the Site of the Roman City at Silchester, Hants, in 1897', *Archaeologia* 56: 103–26.

St John Hope, W. H., and Fox, G. E. (1899). 'Excavations on the Site of the Roman City at Silchester, Hants, in 1898', *Archaeologia* 56: 229–50.

St John Hope, W. H., and Fox, G. E. (1900). 'Excavations on the Site of the Roman City at Silchester, Hants, in 1899', *Archaeologia* 57: 87–112.

Steinby, E. M. (1993–2000). *Lexicon Topographicum Urbis Romae*. Rome.

Stöckle, A. (1911). *Spätrömische und byzantinische Zünfte*. Leipzig.

Tourrenc, S. (1968). 'La Dedicace du Temple du Genie de la colonie à Timgad', *AntAfr* 2: 197–220.

Wacher, J. (1995). *The Towns of Roman Britain*. London.

Wallace-Hadrill, A. (1995). 'Public Honour and Private Shame: The Urban Texture of Pompeii', in T. J. Cornell and K. Lomas (eds), *Urban Society in Roman Italy*. London, 39–62.

Wilson, A. (2000). 'Timgad and Textile Production', in D. J. Mattingly and J. Salmon (eds), *Economies beyond Agriculture in the Classical World*. London, 271–96.

Wilson, A. (2002). 'Urban Production in the Roman World: The View from North Africa', *PBSR* 70: 231–73.

Wilson, J. F., and Popp, A. (2003a). 'Districts, Networks and Clusters in England: An Introduction', in Wilson and Popp (2003b), 1–18.

Wilson, J. F. and Popp, A. (eds) (2003b). *Industrial Clusters and Regional Business Networks in England, 1750–1970*. Aldershot.

Wrigley, N., and Lowe, M. (2002). *Reading Retail: A Geographical Perspective on Retailing and Consumption Spaces*. London.

14

Spatial Concentration and Dispersal
of Roman Textile Crafts

Kerstin Droß-Krüpe

Certain toponyms of ancient Rome such as *vicus materiarius, vicus frumentarius,* or *scalae anulariae* suggest the presence of distinct quarters of urban craftsmen.[1] These toponyms—or perhaps better hodonyms and prodonyms—raise the question of whether they point to the location of specialized traders' and workers' quarters in ancient towns.[2] A close look at Egyptian documentary papyri enables us to investigate the distribution of crafts within Roman cities. Using textile crafts—dyeing and fulling in particular—as a case study, this chapter will discuss the spatial distribution of textile workshops within settlements in the province of Egypt in the Roman imperial period. First, a close look will be taken at the sources that shed light on the location of these crafts. As a second step, modern clustering theory will be used to explain the presence or absence of textile craft quarters.

URBAN TOPOGRAPHIES OF TEXTILE CRAFTS

Three large trade tax registers dating back to AD 276 survive from Ptolemais Euergetis, the capital of the Arsinoite nome in Egypt.[3] These accounts of various trade taxes paid by individuals, grouped by occupations, allow decent insight not only into the amount of tax paid but also into the geographical distribution of certain crafts within the city: for the overwhelming majority of the craftsmen listed, the tax records specify the town quarter in which they

---

[1] *Vicus materiarius* and *vicus frumentarius*: *CIL* 6.975 (= *ILS* 6073). *Scalae anulariae*: Suet. *Aug.* 72.1. Cf. Goodman, Chapter 13, this volume.

[2] As stated, e.g. by Kolb (1995: 496). On hodonyms and prodonyms, see Koß (1995: 458–63).

[3] *BGU* I.9, *BGU* IV.1087, and *BGU* XII.2280.

lived. In interpreting these documents, one has among the other peculiarities of these registers to bear in mind their fragmentary character. This means, among other things, that the data preserved indicate a minimum number of persons exercising the stated profession: they cannot be used to reconstruct the actual number of people performing a certain craft. Nevertheless, assuming that workspace and living space overlapped, they reveal a vivid impression of the topography of crafts in Ptolemais Euergetis.

The tax registers show an extensive number of craftsmen of different occupations. There are γρυτοπῶλαι (presumably traders of junk or trinkets), μυροπῶλαι (traders of ointments), βάφοι (dyers), στιβεῖς (fullers), ἀρτυματᾶτες (traders of spices), ζυτοπῶλαι (traders of beer), ἀρτοκόποι (bread-makers/bakers), κορσασᾶτες (barbers), and κασσιτερᾶτες (pewterers). In total, the three documents list 121 different people practising at least 11 different occupations. The trade tax these people had to pay varied according to what they did. Dyers, for example, had to pay 24 drachmas a month, whereas traders of junk were supposed to pay 8 or 12 drachmas; traders of ointment even had to pay 60 drachmas.

The dyers form one of the largest professional groups in each of the three fragments: up to twelve are attested; their distribution over the registers is shown in Table 14.1. The number of dyers, and the amount of tax they pay, suggest that they were an important group in the local economy. Some people appear in more than one tax register, while each fragment also gives names of dyers not mentioned in the other two. Taking a closer look at the dyers, a profession appearing in all three tax registers of that very year, shows a surprisingly fixed number of dyers within the nome capital. Only in one case (*BGU* I.9) is the list of dyers complete, consisting of twelve people, several of whom appear in one or both of the other tax registers. In *BGU* XII.2280 seven dyers are mentioned by name. The total recorded amount of payments by this group of craftsmen indicates that an additional four monthly payments had to be made, thus suggesting that the number of members of the dyeing craft was eleven. The third register (*BGU* IV.1087) lists seven dyers, including one name not appearing in the other lists. Only one dyer, Εὐδέμων, appears on all three lists. All in all, within the short time span of a few months, fifteen different dyers are identifiable.

Together, these three lists from the same year provide important information about the society of this nome capital and its craftsmen, and they allow us to assess the spatial position of the textile craftsmen. As we know the town quarter of almost all craftsmen, we can discuss how they were distributed across the town: the fifteen dyers mentioned lived in at least thirteen different town quarters. As Table 14.2 shows, the same is true for the other professions listed.

Craftsmen performing the same craft were spread over the whole town (Tables 14.2, 14.3). This is all the more surprising for the craft of dyeing, since the process of dyeing with its chemical procedures and the related material were bound to produce considerable smells: such factors have often led scholars to

Table 14.1. Dyers in Ptolemais Euergetis according to papyrological evidence

Name of dyer	*BGU* I.9	*BGU* IV.1087	*BGU* XIII.2280
Διοκωρος ουπουπα παρὰ Ἀλύπιν	x	—	x
Παῦλος ἐν τῇ Μύρι	x	—	x
Εὐδέμων ἐν τῇ Συριακῇ	x	x	x
Σαβῖνος ἐν τῷ Καπίτωνος	x	—	x
Κόννυμος ἐν τῷ Νυμ[.]σίου	x	—	—
Σαραπιὰς ἐν τῇ Παληᾷ Παραπωλης	x	x	—
Μέλας ἐν τῷ Σεβήρου	x	—	—
Ἡρακεδης ἐν τῇ Ἀθηνᾷ	x	x	—
Κουτᾶς ἐν τῇ Μύρι	x	—	x
Μωρίων ἐν τῷ Καπίτωνος	x	x	—
Κύριλος ἐν τῷ Λαγίῳ	x	x	—
Εὐπωρίων ἐν τῷ Φρέμι	x	x	—
Εὐπωρίων	—	x	—
Μέλας ἐν τῷ Παλαστίῳ	—	—	x
Κούκωμος ἐν τῷ Γυμασίῳ	—	—	x

Table 14.2. Spatial distribution of craftsmen in Ptolemais Euergetis

Profession	Craftsmen	Town quarters
γρυτοπῶλαι	3	3
μυροπῶλαι	4	4
βάφοι	15	13 or 14
στιβεῖς	7	7
ἀρτυματᾶτες	4	3 or 4
ζυτοπῶλαι	7	5 to 7
ἀρτοκόποι	9	7 to 9
κορσασᾶτες	4	2 to 4
κασσιτερᾶτες	4	4

assume that those kinds of workshops were found on the peripheries of settlements. The situation with fullers is similar: the seven fullers listed in *BGU* IV.1087 all lived in different parts of the town, although their use of urine and other chemical substances was bound to produce unpleasant odours.[4]

Analysing also the other professions listed in these three tax registers shows that spatial concentration in the sense of explicitly allocated craft quarters cannot be detected at Ptolemais Euergetis. Dyers and fullers are not an exception, but follow the usual local pattern of craftsmen in Ptolemais Euergetis, even though their work—unlike other crafts—produced 'unsavoury fragrances' for the neighbours.

In total, ninety-six craftsmen from forty-five town quarters can be identified. Most of the town quarters host one (22) or two craftsmen (10); the

---

[4] A different view is presented by Flohr (2003: 448); cf. Droß-Krüpe (2011: 45 with n. 117) and Flohr and Wilson (2011).

Table 14.3. Spatial distribution of dyers in Ptolemais Euergetis

Town quarter/geographical specification	Number of dyers
παρὰ Ἀλύπιν	1
ἐν τῇ Μύρι	2
ἐν τῇ Συριακῇ	1
ἐν τῷ Καπίτωνος	1
ἐν τῷ Νυμ[.]σίου	1
ἐν τῇ Παληᾷ Παραπωλης	1
ἐν τῷ Σεβήρου	1
ἐν τῇ Ἀθηνᾷ	1
ἐν τῷ Καπίτωνος	1
ἐν τῷ Λαγίῳ	1
ἐν τῷ Φρέμι	1
ἐν τῷ Παλαστίῳ	1
ἐν τῷ Γυμασίῳ	1
Quarter lost	1

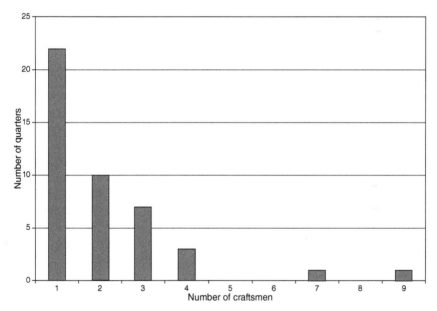

Fig. 14.1. Number of town quarters in Ptolemais Euergetis hosting 1 to 9 craftsmen. Image: Kerstin Droß-Krüpe.

highest number of craftsmen living in the same part of the town is nine (Fig. 14.1). Thus, specific working quarters cannot be detected, and it seems that craftsmen did not live separated from townspeople who had different occupations or belonged to different social strata. The question arises whether this situation was particular to Ptolemais Euergetis, or whether dyers and fullers lived and worked right among their fellow craftsmen in other towns and villages as well. From the late second century AD we learn from a papyrus—probably from Antinoopolis—that Aurelia Claudia Leontarion (alias Amonilla) leased properties for commercial purposes to different craftsmen.[5] These properties were located in two different streets: the ἐργαστήια ἐπὶ τῆς πλατείας comprised not only of a ὀθονιοπώλιον and an χρυϲοχοεῖον, but also of several ἱματιοπώλης, a κιστοπλόκιορ, a ὑδραγώγιον, and an ἐνδικοπλύτιον. Those ἐπὶ τῆς ῥύμης ἐργαστηρίων hosted a παλαιοράφιον and a πλοκόπιον. Again, very different workshops could be found in close proximity to each other.

A remarkable document from Oxyrhynchos dating to the late third century provides an insight into workshops in another nome capital. *P.Oxy.* XLVI.3300, written in AD 271–2, depicts the ownership of properties that had to be registered with the town council. Listed are the names of owners and occupiers of properties, and sometimes their occupations are also added. It shows a random pattern of very diverse professions working and living side-by-side, as shown in Fig. 14.2. The dyer Aniketos lives and works directly next to Aphynchios, who is an embroiderer, and near the fisherman Pasois, and Harpokr[—], a builder. Obviously this city did not require a spatial grouping of individual craftspeople.

Panopolis, another nome capital, provides a similar but much longer and much more detailed document: a real estate register, first published in 1975 and—after undergoing substantial corrections—later presented as *SB* XXIV.16000.[6] This is an exceptional document that sheds light on the occupational and economic structure of this town, which played a significant economic role in the Panopolites nome. Dating to the early fourth century AD, the document lists properties arranged by their geographical position within the town, mentioning not only the name of the owner of each property but in a third of all cases also his profession. Again, people performing the same occupation appear distributed randomly over the urban area, and there is no evidence for people in the same occupation living in adjacent houses. In total, thirty-three different professions are verifiable. Textile crafts are also well represented; listed are λινόϋφος (four times), λινεψός (twice), λινέμπορος (twice), γέρδιος (twice), γναφεύς (three times), and ἱματιοπώλης (once). They are spread over the whole town of Panopolis.

That textile professions and textile crafts in Egyptian towns were not spatially concentrated is also clear from the situation at Kellis. This village in the Dakleh Oasis was occupied from the late Ptolemaic Period until the end of the fourth century AD and was known for its textile production. Implements used for spinning and weaving alike were found in almost every household, including spindles, spindle whorls, loom weights, shuttles, combs, and unspun

---

[5] *SB* XIV.11978.   [6] Borkowski (1975: 160). *SB* VIII. 9902 with BL 6, 160.

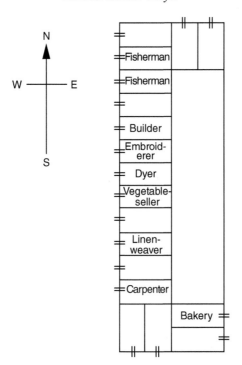

Fig. 14.2. Craftsmen in a neighbouring residential area according to *P.Oxy.* 46/3300. Image: Kerstin Droß-Krüpe.

yarns.[7] In one complex, inhabited from the mid-third until the end of the fourth century AD, the excavators found many loom weights fallen in position, together with the remains of loom beams. The discovery of large quantities of loom weights all over the settlement indicates that many villagers were involved in the production of cloth. While it is possible that the textiles they produced were meant to cater for family needs, the evidence also suggests that the craft of weaving was highly professionalized and did not only serve to satisfy internal domestic demand of households: many textiles were produced to be sent to other settlements or to be sold. Papyrological evidence further corroborates this picture: two papyri from the middle of the fourth century AD refer to (small-scale?) textile production at Kellis. One indicates that textiles were sent to the Nile valley.[8] Several Coptic papyri, originating from the housing complex mentioned above, show a weaving and tailoring business conducted under the direction of a woman, Tehat, with the help of a male relative.[9] Yet there is no evidence that textile crafts at Kellis were spatially concentrated.

---

[7] Carroll (1988: 23–5) and Bowen (2001: 18–28); see also *P.Kellis* I.71.   [8] *P.Kellis* I.51.
[9] *P. Kellis Copt.* XVII. 44, 46, 48. Cf. Gardner, Alcock, and Funk (1999) and Nevett (2011: 19–24).

But what was the situation elsewhere in the Empire? From the city of Ephesos inscriptions show a mixture of different crafts: in the third century AD, M. Fulvius Publicianus Nicephorus refurbished a *stoa* linking the theatre and the stadium of the city. Epigraphic evidence shows that he gave away the *intercolumnia* of this *stoa* to at least eighteen different groups of craftsmen (or professional associations) that were offering their products in close proximity to each other.[10]

Well-known cities such as Ostia and Pompeii can serve as further comparative examples. When it comes to detecting workshops of textile craftsmen especially, those crafts needing specific technical equipment can be identified with the help of archaeology. In Ostia, six fulling workshops (*fullonicae*) have been identified.[11] One *fullonica* was situated on the other side of the Tiber, while the other five are lying within the city walls. These five *fullonicae* are spread over the whole town, covering four of the *regiones* into which modern scholars divide the town.[12] Bakeries show a similar pattern. We can thus argue that, also in Ostia, identifiable workshops were not clustered in one or several town quarters.

A similar picture emerges in Pompeii. The six dyeing workshops and the twelve fulleries identified can be found in several districts, including the town centre (Figs 14.3–4).[13] Other crafts do not seem to be spatially concentrated either.[14] Regardless of the degree of nuisance for the neighbouring people and buildings, it is evident that not only the workshops of dyers but also those of bakers and fullers were distributed throughout the whole area of the town. Only one occupation could perhaps form an exception: the so-called *officinae lanifricariae* are remarkably concentrated within *regio* VII.[15] As the traditional interpretation of these workshops as wool-washing facilities was based on a graffito found adjacent to one of these workshops, the function of these workshops is still puzzling researchers.[16] It is however interesting to see that Dionysius, a freedman of Lucius Popidius Secundus, who probably worked in an *officina lanifricaria*—his name appears in several graffiti near the doorway

---

[10] *IK* 12.444–5, 549; *IK* 16.2076–82. Cf. Ruffing (2008: 378).

[11] These include *fullonica* I xiii 3 along the cardo, the two *fullonicae* in the *caseggiato della fullonica* (II xi 1 and 2), the *fullonica* behind the Temple of the *Fabri Navales* (III ii 2), and the *fullonica* in the *Via degli Augustali* (V vii 3). The sixth workshop, across the Tiber, has not been published yet. Cf. De Ruyt (2002).

[12] Cf. De Ruyt (2002: 51): 'On ne constate pas pour elles [i.e. *fullonicae*] de concentration en quartier. Au contraire, leur implantation est très dispersée et évite la zone des quartiers centraux autour de la place publique.' The same observation occurred to her when analysing the spatial distribution of bakeries.

[13] *fullonicae*: I 10, 6; I 4, 7; I 6, 7; V 1, 2; VI 3, 6; VI 8, 20–21.2; VI 14, 21–22; VI 15, 3; VI 16, 3–4; VI 16, 6; VII 2, 41, and IX 6, a.1; cf. Flohr (2007, 2008, 2011); dyeing workshops: I 8, 19; V 1, 4; V 1, 5; VII 2, 11; VII 14, 5.17–18, and IX 3, 1–2.

[14] Cf. Flohr (2007: 148).   [15] Moeller (1966); Goodman, Chapter 13, this volume.

[16] *CIL* 4.1190. See now Flohr (2013: 57–60); Monteix (2013).

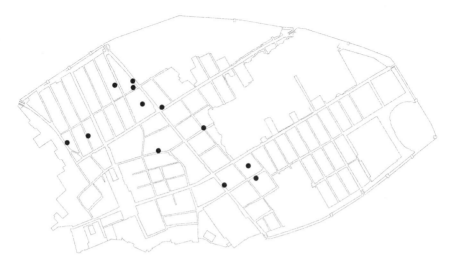

Fig. 14.3. Fulleries in Pompeii. Map: Miko Flohr.

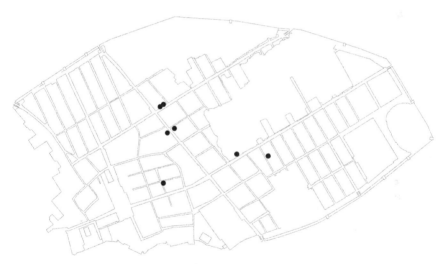

Fig. 14.4. Dyeing workshops in Pompeii. Map: Miko Flohr.

of one of these workshops—designated himself as *fullo*.[17] Given the debate about the function of *lanifricariae*, further research on their productive facilities would be essential to understand their spatial pattern.

Despite the situation with the so-called *officinae lanifricariae* at Pompeii, it is still true that textile workshops do not usually show a clear spatial concentration and are not locally clustered in particular parts of cities and towns.

[17] *CIL* 4.2966.

They are distributed across the entire urban area. In this respect, the picture from the nome capitals of Egypt is similar to the well-excavated Italian cities.[18]

While the evidence suggests the same spatial peculiarities occurred in different parts of the Roman world, it also indicates a fundamental difference with some later pre-industrial economies—in medieval Europe, the clustering of crafts in special quarters or streets is widely attested. This all raises several issues: on the one hand, the question arises of what factors lead to a localized concentration of certain crafts; on the other hand, the question remains of how to understand ancient toponyms suggesting artisanal clustering. Furthermore, one has to make sense of the differences in spatial distribution between antiquity and the Middle Ages.

CLUSTERING IN THEORY AND PRACTICE

The phenomena of clustering, (industrial) concentration, and regional specialization have been the subject of growing interest in economic research. In particular, the main advantages of forming clusters attracted attention. As early as 1890, Alfred Marshall published the first volume of his *Principles of Economics* in which he developed his theory about industrial districts—the foundation of modern cluster research.[19] Marshall dealt with the phenomenon of the localization of industry, focusing on the concentration of specialized industries of the secondary sector (manufacturing) in particular localities, which he called 'industrial districts'.[20] According to Marshall, the main advantages of a clustered industry—both regionally and within one settlement—were (1) an environment that promotes innovation and (2) the development of a local labour market for highly specialized workers.[21] One hundred years later, Michael Porter's influential *The Competitive Advantages of Nations* led to the breakthrough of modern cluster theory.[22] In this book, Porter argued that the geographical concentration of industries and crafts increases productivity, as it gives entrepreneurs access to specialized skills. Moreover, it fosters innovation: competition between adjacent firms or workshops raises the incentive to innovate. Though Porter focused on regional and national clusters, his considerations may be applied to intra-urban situations as well. Modern cluster research has shown that the tendency of economic activity to cluster in particular locations is driven mainly by efficiency advantages (such as lowered transaction costs), flexibility advantages (such as high mobility of labour), and innovation

---

[18] This observation once more challenges the old paradigm that Egypt was a place where circumstances were different from those in all other regions of the Roman Empire.
[19] Marshall (1890).   [20] Marshall (1890: 268–84).   [21] Marshall (1890: 328–33).
[22] Porter (1990).

advantages.[23] When it comes to the establishment of clusters, external forces such as the historical and cultural background of a region or city, its geographical and infrastructural characteristics, and existing institutions and organizations are, however, crucial as well. Infrastructural prerequisites, such as access to waterways and other transport connections, play an especially decisive role.[24] Favourable local circumstances, such as the vicinity to a junction of several major roads or an advantageous ground water level, can encourage clustering.

Yet in Roman cities, none of these factors seems to have had any influence in the location choice of textile crafts. In cities, access to fresh water, a *condicio sine qua non* for fulleries and dye-works alike, was generally unproblematic— even in Egypt: *P.Lond.* III.1177, an extensive part of a set of accounts of the urban water supply in Ptolemais Euergetis dating to the reign of Trajan, shows that the water supply of the nome capital of the Arsinoites was extremely well organized and that several quarters of the town were connected to the water supply system.[25] A brewery even had a direct connection to the piped system. While no other workshops are explicitly mentioned in the document, this papyrus clearly attests the existence of a widely accessible and well-organized water infrastructure. The implication is that spatial concentration of water-intensive businesses was unnecessary: water was available everywhere across town without great difficulty, and therefore did not prompt a concentration of fulling or dyeing workshops in a particular part of town.[26]

While infrastructural conditions did not foster clustering, neither did textile workers to have benefited from economies of scale. On the contrary, compared to the cluster benefits already discussed, it seems to have been more advanta-geous and more convenient for craftsmen to have an even distribution of weavers, fullers, and dyers (and thus of qualified craftsmen) over the area of a town or city. To some extent, this might be explained from the fact that the innovative nature of the techniques used in these crafts was rather poor—the most important innovations being the invention of the spinning-wheel and treadle loom during the High Middle Ages. Though several apprenticeship contracts for weavers from Roman times are known, next to nothing is known about the education of fullers and dyers at that time.[27] It seems that highly

---

[23] Porter (1990: 33); cf. Goodman, Chapter 13, this volume.

[24] Sölvell (2009: 24–5).   [25] Habermann (2000).

[26] If we extend our geographical horizon, we may also include an inscription from Antioch on the Orontes, dating to the reign of the emperor Vespasian. This inscription seems especially interesting with regard to the integration of fulleries into an existing water supply network. In it, the construction of a 'fullers' canal' 2.5 kilometres long and 3.5 square metres in cross-section is mentioned, leading the water from the river Orontes into the city. Cf. Feissel (1985); *SEG* 35.1483.

[27] Hoernes (2011) was able to detect sixty-two references to apprentices for different crafts and arts from Roman times. Up to now only two references from the Hellenistic period are known. From the middle of the third century BC one tax register mentions apprentices of fullers (*SB* X.10447 from the Herakleopolites). From the Delphian manumission reports from the

specialized workers were not needed, or needed only to a small extent—at least when it comes to fulling and dyeing. In summary, for these crafts no efficiency advantages emerged, nor were there flexibility advantages or innovation advantages.

Yet not only was it true that clustering would not have brought advantages for textile craftsmen; it is also possible that they would have benefited from being more-or-less evenly distributed across a settlement. This does not mean that there was an active spread policy or that ancient textile workers reasoned along the lines of modern economists—but, even if their workshops did not follow any planned pattern, it is wrong to think that they were unaware of good locations and competitive pressure.[28] The crucial thing is that, even though dyed fabrics can, to a certain extent, be regarded as better-quality products, most textiles and garments predominantly serve basic human needs. Therefore, they should be considered convenience goods.[29] Producers and retailers of convenience goods face strong competition compared to those dealing with luxury goods or niche products. This makes it extremely important for them to keep their customers loyal and satisfied.[30] As both demand for and supply of textiles is omnipresent, textile craftsmen are under constant pressure to secure the loyalty of their customers: the convenience goods they produce are not very specific. Moreover, textiles are also 'search goods': their quality can be checked before they are purchased and used.[31] If these craftsmen were clustered, very similar products and services would be on display directly next to each other. A conglomerate of textile workshops would make comparing qualities and prices much easier for the customers. Quality and price advantages would carry more weight, especially because the loyalty of customers of convenience goods is comparatively small anyway. Conversely, if textile workshops were spread over the settlement, comparability would be reduced because search costs—and thus transaction costs—for the consumers would increase. In the case of fulling and dyeing, an equal distribution of workshops throughout the city would increase customer loyalty. In such a situation, it would be more likely that customers would return to a fuller or a dyer that was either situated in their neighbourhood or with whom they maintained intense social relations—provided that price differences were not too dramatic.

second century BC we learn that a certain Sosas obtained his liberty and was required to learn the craft of fulling with Artemidoros. After finishing his apprenticeship, he was supposed to work for his former master Dromokleidas (*SGDI* II.1904). Later sources are lacking.

[28] e.g. *Tab.Vindol.* II.343: Octavius reports that a *contubernalis* of his friend Frontius had come to him and asked for hides, but did not turn up again, because he already gathered them elsewhere. Cf. Grønlund Evers (2011: 15–18). For considerations about dealing with competition in ancient times, see Kudlien (1994).

[29] Holton (1958).   [30] Cf. Bufe (1981: esp. 21–43).   [31] Nelson (1970: 318 ff.).

TOPONYMS

To sum up, local city administrations or governmental institutions did not regulate or promote the spatial concentration of individual business sectors, and infrastructural factors, such as access to fresh water, nor did they foster clustering. External factors or obligations, therefore, did not lead to spatial concentrations of textile artisans. Moreover, producers of convenience goods like everyday textiles had few advantages to expect from clustering: from their point of view, it seems to be much more reasonable to foster an equal spread of production and retail across the whole settlement. The logical consequence, however, is that clustering might have been advantageous for producers and retailers of shopping or luxury goods. This brings us back to the toponyms discussed at the start of this chapter.

Ancient toponyms connected to crafts are actually rather scarce—and almost all of them come from the city of Rome.[32] As can be seen from Table 14.4, craft toponyms cover a wide timeframe. Strikingly, all *vici* whose name refers to an occupation are mentioned only once; the late antique descriptions of the Roman regions list several toponyms, but not one is known from earlier sources. One suspects that the earlier designations were no longer used during the fourth century.

Some of the crafts mentioned in Table 14.4 indeed deal with luxury items or shopping goods. These people, who include perfume-sellers, ring-makers, and glassworkers, may have found it attractive to form clusters because their products were subjected to different market rules.[33] The precious raw materials they process or the products they trade find their way to their workshops by means of only a few tradesmen or retailers: they are not offered by a great quantity of providers; clustering may improve the position of these craftsmen by strengthening their bargaining power vis-à-vis the traders. Furthermore, a spatial concentration of these craftsmen would automatically lead to a spatial concentration of the demand for their products. Again, this does not mean any active cluster policy existed; a formation of clusters of luxury products may have followed practical reasons or the trial-and-error method. The clustering of *materiarii* and *frumentarii* may be explained by a peculiarity that connects these two occupations: both are related to goods that not only had to be brought in from rather far away, but also were relatively expensive to transport, given their small margins of profit. Thus they were to a much bigger extent than textile workers depending on imported products, transported over land or sea from outside. If we take this into consideration, these craftspeople might actively have chosen to build their workshops next to the warehouse districts.

---

[32] Some older publications list the *vicus mundiciei* among the craft toponyms, but, according to Richardson (1992: 426), the name is related to the well-attested *gens Mundicia*.

[33] Rogers (1965); Porter (1990).

Table 14.4. Toponyms from Rome referring to crafts

Toponym	Source	Date	Location
forum vinarium	*CIL* 6.9181–2 = *ILS* 7502	Unknown	Unknown
portus vinarius	*CIL* 6.9189 = *ILS* 7929; *CIL* 6.9090; *CIL* 6.37807 = *ILS* 9429	Unknown	Unknown
vicus lorari	*CIL* 6.9796	Unknown	Unknown
inter lignarios	Livy 35.41.10	192 BC	Outside the Porta Trigemium
inter figulos	Varro, *LL* 5.154	first century BC	Unknown
inter falcarios	Cic. *Catil.* 1.8.4; *Sull.* 52	63/62 BC	Unknown
scalae anulariae	Suet. *Aug.* 72,1	Augustan	Near Forum Romanum?
vicus sandaliarius	*CIL* 6.761	AD 12	Regio IV, probaby north-east of the Templum Pacis
basilica argentaria	*Not. Reg.*	fourth century AD; building identified as Trajanic	Forum Nervae
vicus materiarius	*CIL* 6.975 = *ILS* 6073 (Capitoline base)	AD 136	Regio XIII, warehouse district between the Aventine and the Tiber
vicus frumentarius	*CIL* 6.975 = *ILS* 6073 (Capitoline base)	AD 136	Regio XIII, warehouse district between the Aventine and the Tiber
vicus vitrarius	*Cur. Urb. Rom.*	fourth century AD	Regio I
vicus unguentarius	*Not. Reg.*	fourth century AD	Regio VIII
aream carruces	*Not. Reg.*	fourth century AD	Regio I, between Porta Appia and the temple of Mars?
porticus margaritaria	*Not. Reg.*	fourth century AD	Regio VIII
campus lanatarius	*Not. Reg.*	fourth century AD	Regio XII
porticus fabaria	*Not. Reg.*	fourth century AD	Regio XIII, between the warehouses of the lower Aventin?
forum pistorum	*Not. Reg.*	fourth century AD	Regio XIII, near the *horrea* at the southern Aventine?

Some other towns offer similar toponyms, but the evidence is scarce. Quite often leatherworks are mentioned as ἡ σκυτικὴ in Apamea, ἡ πλατεία τῶν σκυτοτόμων in Saittai, and ἡ πλατεία σκυτέων in Hermoupolis Magna.[34] From some eastern regions we also know of ἄμφοδα boring the name of crafts or

---

[34] Apamea: *IGR* 4.788 ff.; Saittai: *TAM* 5.79 ff. (AD 153), *TAM* 5.146 (AD 166–7), and *TAM* 5.81 (AD 173–4); Hermoupolis Magna: *P. Brem.* 23 (AD 116).

trade: τὸ ἄμφοδον λινυφείων in Ptolemais Euergeteis, Soknopaiou Nesos, and Theadelpheia, τὸ ἄμφοδον ποιμενικόν and τὸ ἄμφοδον χηνοβοσκῶν in Oxyrhynchos, and, finally, τὸ ἄμφοδον σειτικόν in Skythopolis.[35] If we recall the tax registers from Ptolemais Euergetis, it can be shown that craft toponyms are hardly reliable as witnesses of spatial distribution. As indicated, these registers mention several bakers (ἀρτοκόποι), while, at the same time, they refer to a street as ἐν τοῖς ἀρτοκόποις.[36] Though there are indeed two bakers living in this street (Πλούταρχος and Σαβεῖνος), six others practise their profession in different parts of the nome capital. Thus, a toponym deriving from a craft or trade does not necessarily refer to a spatial concentration of these particular economic activites.

ANTIQUITY AND MEDIEVAL EUROPE

One final point concerns the difference between antiquity and the Middle Ages: the picture from the Roman world contrasts sharply with that from medieval Europe. Especially for later medieval Europe, the concentration of crafts in specific parts of the town is well known. Smithies, tanneries, glassmaking workshops, and fulleries—workshops either bearing a high fire risk or causing strong olfactory nuisance—were often located in the periphery of towns in somewhat less popu-lated areas. The existence of manufacturing quarters in medieval London has been identified by archaeological excavations.[37] The establishment of such craft quarters was often controlled by town officials. For example, bakers, potters, and bell-founders were banned from the city of Basel by a decision of the town council after the city fire of 1427. In Siegen, in 1561, tanners and butchers were forced to live and work in one particular street because of the bad smell of their workshops, while blacksmiths and locksmiths were brought together in another street because of the noise their crafts produced.[38] Some textile crafts were spatially concentrated as well. For example, wool-weaving workshops in medieval Göttingen were concen-trated in one town quarter—even though it was a fairly innocuous craft.[39]

The origin of these differences between antiquity and the Middle Ages may lie in the different roles—and therefore different power—of both town officials and professional associations. Where medieval guilds were in control, they shaped labour, production, and trade within their town and their craft.[40] Guilds con-trolled and restricted economic interaction and market activity by creating

---

[35] *SEG* 8.43 (first century AD). Ruffing (2008: 379) remains sceptical about the diagnostic value of these toponyms and considers it 'fraglich, inwieweit die Toponyme auf eine tatsächliche Konzen-tration der jeweiligen Gewerbe in dem betreffenden Viertel oder an der betreffenden Straße deuten'.
[36] *BGU* IV.1087.   [37] Schofield and Vince (2003: 144).
[38] Cramer (1981: 75 with nn. 283, 284).   [39] Steenweg (1990: 300).
[40] Cf. Kluge (2007) and Epstein and Prak (2008).

oligopolies or monopolies. Guild coercion could also lead to a forced amal-gamation of all craftsmen performing the same craft: concentrating craftsmen in certain streets or town quarters made it easier to check whether members complied with the rules and regulations established by the guilds. Thus, one advantage of spatial clustering was that it reduced enforcement costs for guilds. For town councils, clustering made it easier to reach all people performing one craft. Apart from that, concentrating crafts causing unpleasant smells, environ-mental pollution, or noise in marginal town quarters was a way of banning them from the sight of the upper classes: in many medieval towns not only safety aspects but also pride of place led to the establishment of craft quarters.

CONCLUSION

To sum up: for ancient textile production hardly any concentration of workshops in special parts of towns can be identified.[41] Concentrating their workshops in certain streets or squares was no reasonable strategy for textile craftsmen. In contrast to later times, no state-controlled restrictions can be found that would have led to an organized settlement of any specialized craft in determined zones of a settlement. Indications for clustered craftsmen deriving from craft toponyms mainly come from Rome itself. Maybe the size of this city encouraged the use of toponyms of all kinds to ensure guidance; craft toponyms may date from a certain agglomeration of craftsmen in a street or town quarter, but evidence shows that they neither mean that all these craftsmen were to be found in these areas nor indicate that the location of craft shops remained unchanged over the years. Thus, researchers have to resist the temptation to see any craft toponym that occurs as an indicator of clustering, and should investigate each individual case carefully.

ACKNOWLEDGEMENTS

Special thanks are due to Markus Diedrich (Marburg) for his comments on the English version of this chapter. I would like to thank Ramona Grieb (Frankfurt) for her useful comments on the theoretical approach and my colleagues at Philipps-Universität Marburg and Kassel University for discussing the available sources and their interpretation with me.

---

[41] One notable exception is Timgad, where workshops associated with fulling or dyeing were concentrated in the north-eastern part of the town. Cf. Lohmann (1979), Wilson (2000), and Droß-Krüpe (2011: 126–7, 134). See also Goodman, Chapter 13, this volume.

REFERENCES

Beltrán de Heredia Bercero, J. (2000). 'Los restos arqueológicos de una fullonica y de una tinctoria en la colonia romana de Barcino (Barcelona)', *Complutum* 11: 253–9.

Beltrán de Heredia Bercero, J., and Jordi y Tresserras, J. (2000). 'Nuevas aportaciones para el estudio de las fullonicae y tinctoriae en el mundo romano: Resultados de las instalaciones de la colonia de Barcino (Barcelona, España)', in D. Cardon and M. Feugère (eds), *Archéologie des textiles des origins au Ve siècle: Actes du colloque de Lattes*. Montagnac, 241–6.

Borkowski, Z. (1975). *Une description topographique des immeubles à Panopolis*. Warschau.

Bowen, G. E. (2001). 'Texts and Textiles: A Study of the Textile Industry at Ancient Kellis', *Artefact* 24: 18–28.

Bradley, M. (2002). '"It all comes out in the wash": Looking Harder at the Roman Fullonica', *JRA* 15: 20–44.

Bufe, R. H. (1981). *Güterbeschaffung des täglichen Bedarfs: Ein Betrag zur Ressourcen-allokation privater Haushalte unter dem Einfluß der Einkaufsstättengestaltung* (Betriebswirtschaftliche Schriften, 108). Berlin.

Carroll, D. L. (1988). *Looms and Textiles of the Copts: First Millennium Egyptian Textiles in the Carl Austin Reitz Collection of the California Academy of Science*. Seattle and London.

Cramer, J. (1981). *Gerberhaus und Gerberviertel in der mittelalterlichen Stadt* (Studien zur Bauforschung, 12). Bonn.

De Ruyt, C. (1995). 'Ricerche archeologiche nel tempio dei Fabri Navales a Ostia', *Archeologia Laziale* 12: 401–6.

De Ruyt, C. (2001). 'Les Foulons, artisans des textiles et blanchisseurs', in J.-P. Descoedres (ed.), *Ostia : Port et porte de la Rome antique*. Geneva, 186–91.

De Ruyt, C. (2002). 'Boulangers et foulons d'Ostie à l'époque impérial: Quelque réflexions sur l'implantation de leurs ateliers et sur leurs fonctions précises dans la ville portuaire', in J.-C. Béal and J.-C. Guoyon (eds), *Les Artisans dans la ville antique* (Collection archéologie et histoire de l'antiquité Université Lumière Lyon, 2, 6). Paris, 49–53.

Droß-Krüpe, K. (2011). *Wolle–Weber–Wirtschaft: Die Textilproduktion der römischen Kaiserzeit im Spiegel der papyrologischen Überlieferung* (Philippika, 46). Wiesbaden.

Epstein, R. S., and Prak, M. (eds) (2008). *Guilds, Innovation, and the European Economy, 1400–1800*. Cambridge.

Feissel, D. (1985). 'Deux listes de quartiers d'Antioche astreints au creusement d'un canal (73–74 après J.-C.)', *Syria* 62: 77–103.

Flohr, M. (2003). 'Fullones and Roman Society: A Reconsideration', *JRA* 16/2: 447–50.

Flohr, M. (2007). 'Nec quicquam ingenuum habere potest officina? Spatial Contexts of Urban Production at Pompeii, AD 79', *BABesch* 82: 129–48.

Flohr, M. (2008). 'Cleaning the Laundries II: Report of the 2007 Campaign', *Fasti Online Documents & Research* 111 <www.fastionline.org/docs/FOLDER-it-2008-111.pdf> (accessed 1 March 2015).

Flohr, M. (2011). 'Cleaning the Laundries III: Report of the 2008 Campaign', *Fasti Online Documents & Research* 214 <http://www.fastionline.org/docs/FOLDER-it-2011-214.pdf> (accessed 1 March 2015).

Flohr, M. (2013). 'The Textile Economy of Pompeii', *JRA* 26/1: 53–78.

Flohr, M., and Wilson, A. I. (2011). 'The Economy of Ordure', in A. O. Koloski-Ostrow, G. C. M. Jansen, and E. M. Moormann (eds), *Roman Toilets: Their Archaeology and Cultural History* (BABesch, Supplement 19). Leiden, 147–56.

Gardner, I., Alcock, A., and Funk, W.-P. (1999). *Coptic Documentary Texts from Kellis I*. Oxford.

Grønlund Evers, K. (2011). *The Vindolanda Tablets and the Ancient Economy* (BAR British Series, 544). Oxford.

Habermann, W. (2000). *Zur Wasserversorgung einer Metropole im kaiserzeitlichen Ägypten. Neuedition von P. Lond. III 1177. Text–Übersetzung–Kommentar* (Vestigia, 53). München.

Hoernes, M. (2011). '". . . er wird dem Lehrling das Handwerk gänzlich beibringen, wie er es selbst versteht": Zur römischen Lehrlingsausbildung in Handwerksberufen', *historia.scribere* 3: 37–79.

Holton, R. (1958). 'The Distinction between Convenience Goods, Shopping Goods and Speciality Goods', *Journal of Marketing* 23/1: 53–6.

Kluge, A. (2007). *Die Zünfte*. Stuttgart.

Kolb, F. (1995). *Rom. die Geschichte der Stadt in der Antike*. Munich.

Koß, G. (1995). 'Die Bedeutung der Eigennamen: Wortbedeutung/Namensbedeutung', in E. Eichler, G. Hilty, H. Löffler, H. Steger, and L. Zgusta (eds), *Name Studies: An International Handbook of Onomastics/Les Noms propres: Manuel international d'onomastique/Namenforschung: Ein internationales Handbuch zur Onomastik* (Handbücher zur Sprach- und Kommunikationswissenschaft, 11). Berlin and New York, 458–63.

Kudlien, F. (1994). 'Die Rolle der Konkurrenz im antiken Geschäftsleben', *MBAH* 13/1: 1–39.

Lawrence, R. (1992). *A New Topographical Dictionary of Ancient Rome*. London.

Lohmann, H. (1979). 'Beobachtungen zum Stadtplan von Timgad', in *Wohnungsbau im Altertum* (Diskussionen zur archäologischen Bauforschung, 3). Berlin, 167–87.

MacMullen, R. (1974). *Roman Social Relations 50 BC to AD 284*. New Haven and London.

Marshall, A. (1890). *Principles of Economics*. London.

Moeller, W. O. (1966). 'The "Lanifricarius" and the "Officinae Lanifricariae" at Pompeii', *Technology and Culture* 7/4 (Autumn), 493–6.

Monteix, N. (2013). 'The Apple Of Discord: Fleece-Washing in Pompeii's Textile Economy: A Response to M. Flohr', *JRA* 26/1: 79–87.

Nelson, P. (1970). 'Information and Consumer Behavior', *Journal of Political Economy* 78: 311–29.

Nevett, L. (2011). 'Family and Household, Ancient History and Archaeology: A Case Study from Roman Egypt', in B. Rawson (ed.), *A Companion to Families in the Greek and Roman World*. Oxford, 15–31.

Pietrogrande, A. L. (1976). *Le Fulloniche* (Scavi di Ostia, 8). Rome.

Porter, M. E. (1990). *The Competitive Advantages of Nations*. New York.

Richardson, L., Jr (1992). *A New Topographical Dictionary of Rome*. Baltimore.

Rogers, A. (1965). 'A Stochastic Analysis of the Spatial Clustering of Retail Establishments', *American Statistical Association Journal* 60: 1094–1103.

Ruffing, K. (2008). *Die berufliche Spezialisierung in Handel und Handwerk: Untersuchungen zu ihrer Entwicklung und zu ihren Bedingungen in der römischen Kaiserzeit im östlichen Mittelmeerraum auf der Grundlage griechischer Inschriften und Papyri* (Pharos, 24). Rahden.

Schofield, J., and Vince, A. (2003). *Medieval Towns: The Archaeology of British Towns*. 2nd edn. Leicester.

Sölvell, Ö. (2009). *Clusters: Balancing Evolutionary and Constructive Forces*, 2nd edn. Stockholm.

Steenweg, H. (1990). *Göttingen um 1400*. Göttingen.

Taylor, C. (2005). 'The Disposal of Human Waste. A Comparison between Ancient Rome and Medieval London', *Past Imperfect* 11: 53–72.

Thüry, G. E. (1995). *Die Wurzeln unserer Umweltkrise und die griechisch-römische Antike*. Salzburg.

Wilson, A. I. (2000). 'Timgad and Textile Production', in D. J. Mattingly and J. Salmon (eds), *Economies beyond Agriculture*. London, 271–96.

15

Industry and Commerce in the City of Aquincum

Orsolya Láng

In over 120 years of archaeological excavations in the city of Aquincum, several shops, workshops, and even town quarters dedicated to industrial and commercial activities have been identified. This evidence was usually connected to the heyday of the town in the second and third centuries AD and draws a suggestive picture of traditional trade routes in the area and of the inhabitants of Aquincum. However, thus far the discussion has mainly been based on the results of early excavations, whose methodology does not meet modern criteria. This chapter will start with a brief overview of the history of the civilian settlement of Aquincum and a brief description of the economic aspects of the urban topography of Aquincum as it was reconstructed in earlier scholarship; it will then present a case study focusing on recent control excavations carried out in the north-eastern zone of the civilian settlement. These shed new light on the topographic position and importance of this town quarter, its functions, and the phases in its development. Of particular interest is the probably quite malodorous glue-, hide-, and horn-making workshop that is the first fully excavated workshop of its kind in the town. It appears that such smelly, dirty, and even flammable activities were not prohibited from the urban centre, but indeed welcomed. This chapter will discuss some of the reasons for this attitude.

THE HISTORY OF THE CIVILIAN SETTLEMENT OF AQUINCUM

The civilian settlement of Aquincum is part of the tripartite settlement complex of Aquincum that was established on the left bank of the Danube, in the area of modern Budapest (Fig. 15.1). The first military forts were built

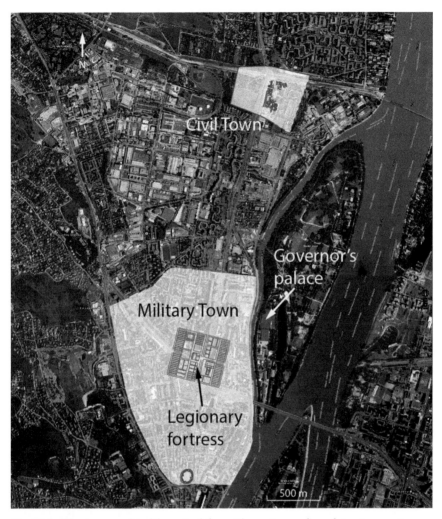

Fig. 15.1. The topographical layout of the settlement complex of Aquincum. Image: Orsolya Láng.

between the middle and the last third of the first century AD.[1] During the reign of Domitian a permanent legionary fortress or *castra* was established at one of the main crossing points of the river.[2] A military town (*canabae*) grew around the *castra*, and by the late first century a forerunner of the later civilian settlement was developed some 5 kilometres to the north. This town started out most probably as a roadside settlement dominated by dwellings in the

---

[1] H. Kérdő (2003: 81).   [2] Németh (2003: 87).

form of sunken-floored housing.[3] Among the settlers there were veterans and their families, merchants and native Celts.[4]

When in AD 106 the province of Pannonia was divided into two parts, Aquincum became the capital of the province of Pannonia Inferior.[5] This new role may have provided a strong impetus for the development of the town. Structures with adobe walls appeared, and within a short time buildings with stone foundations were erected. The aqueducts, which primarily served the fort, but also supplied water to the civilian settlement, may have been completed during the reign of the emperor Trajan. This may also have been the moment in which the city's first street network was laid out. It was adapted to the existing main roads and the aqueduct.

A milestone in the life of the town was the year AD 124, when the settlement was raised to the rank of *municipium* and acquired an independent town council. Around this time, Aquincum began to develop a genuinely urban character: in connection with the aqueducts, a sewer system was completed, the construction of the town walls began, and, to the north, outside the walls, the civilian amphitheatre may have been built. In this period, urban development within the already established system of *insulae* was still rather spotty: plots were not yet entirely built up. Yet the buildings were made primarily of stone, and the majority of the public buildings known today were completed, including the so-called Great Public Baths and a small open-air shrine to Fortuna Augusta. A podium temple devoted to the Capitoline Triad already stood in the middle of the *forum*. The main north–south road, the *cardo*, was still several metres wider than what is now visible; it was bordered by a row of shops or workshops on the western side and an arcade with rows of columns on the east. Strip buildings appeared on the north side of the *decumanus*. Their shorter sides opened onto the road with shops and workshops, while living quarters were towards the back. A small pottery workshop was built south of the Great Public Baths. To the east the so-called Double Baths also had a second-century phase.

Yet the golden age of the city came with the economic boom following the Marcomannic Wars and, especially, with its promotion to the rank of *colonia* in AD 194, which led to an increase in population (Figs 15.2. and 15.3). The physical appearance of the prosperous city changed: the urban landscape became much more densely built up, with structures using every bit of space available, separated only by narrow alleyways. Existing buildings were expanded where this was possible, and the city ventured out beyond the city walls. Public buildings, such as the Great Public Baths, took on their most

---

[3] For the earlier research, see Nagy (1971b: 59–81). The earliest history of the town, and particularly of its north-eastern zone, is discussed in Láng (2012).

[4] Nagy (1973: 132).

[5] For the history of the civilian settlement, see Zsidi (2004: 188–99).

Fig. 15.2. Plan of the civilian settlement in the third century AD. Map: K. Kolozsvári.

Fig. 15.3. Aerial photo of the civilian settlement. Photo: G. Rákóczi.

elaborate forms, and the podium temple of the *forum* received a new function: it became a shrine to the cult of the emperor. An elite district developed with luxurious residences—such as the House of the Dirce Mosaic—and the merging of several buildings created the most magnificent complex of the city—the so-called Great Mansion, with its peristyle courtyard, its richly decorated dining room, and its own bath wing. Additionally, strip buildings were constructed along the southern edge of the town. At this time a broader class of merchants joined the population, which thus far had consisted mainly of native inhabitants and retired soldiers and their families from the western provinces. These merchants included many people of eastern origins: the epigraphic and archaeological record suggests that people from North Africa and the Middle East appeared in Aquincum.[6] Many soldiers from these areas also ended up here.[7]

This golden age may have lasted until about the middle of the third century, when life in the city appears to have deteriorated owing to frequent barbarian raids, the unstable political situation in the empire, and economic decline. Except for a few larger construction projects—such as the *macellum*—only minor repairs were performed on the buildings, and, judging from the material finds, the civilian settlement went through a difficult period. Unfortunately, this is all that can be said about this period on the basis of the archaeological finds. This is related partially to fluvial erosion, and partially to quarrying in the Middle Ages, though the primitive techniques of the first excavations have also played a role. In the eastern half of the civilian settlement, early excavations destroyed the later strata mostly without a trace, and without proper recording. As a consequence, we know essentially nothing about the city from the end of the third century onwards—with the possible exception of the zone around the *cardo*, where traffic must have continued. After the year 307 we no longer know the names of the city officials. From the eastern half of the urban area, remains from the fourth century are almost entirely lacking. Instead, scattered burials were discovered here: during this period the population may have moved away from the banks of the Danube, which were increasingly dangerous owing to the uncertain military situation.

THE PROBLEM OF IDENTIFYING WORKSHOPS

Though the civilian settlement of Aquincum, and particularly its eastern part, has been the subject of constant archaeological investigations since the 1880s,

---

[6] Recently: Póczy (2002: 184–5); Topál (2003: 278).   [7] Póczy (1996: 144–7).

surprisingly little is known about its economic life.[8] This might be due partly to the fact that during the most extensive excavations of the late nineteenth and early twentieth centuries only the latest construction phases of buildings were brought to light, and partly to the problem that attention was paid chiefly to tracing their ground plans. Even during the large-scale conservation programme that took place between 1959 and 1973, only a few deeper trenches were opened. These were mainly in the zone of the *forum*, and in buildings along the *cardo*.[9] Nowadays, as the eastern half of the town is functioning as an archaeological park, the possibility of such control excavations is even more limited. Besides the problematic situation of the excavated areas, it should not be forgotten that the western part of the settlement is basically unknown: only scattered data are available on its street system and its buildings.[10]

In spite of these problems, some workshops and shops were identified in the course of the nineteenth and twentieth centuries. These identifications, however, were mainly based on ground plans, persisting misinterpretations, and speculation. The evidence is very thin. For example, Tibor Nagy identified a soaking pit of a late-first-century tannery in the north-eastern section of the town on the basis of sediments observed on the walls of the structure.[11] The so-called House of the Merchant of the second and third centuries was identified based on the sole fact that there are large rooms in the building.[12] The House of the Butcher—possibly dating to the third century—owed its name and its identification to the large amounts of animal bones found there, and to its proximity to the *macellum*. However, there is no information on the character of the bones, and it is unclear whether they were household or workshop refuse.[13] A 'wine or oil pressing workshop'—dated to the second and third centuries—was located in one of the strip buildings in the north-eastern zone of the settlement, and got its name from a large press slab and three barrels filled with limelike material that were found in one of the rooms. A *fullonica* was located in Building ix in the south-eastern zone of the settlement, and its identification was based on a cross-shaped, stone-paved construction that could instead have been a heating channel.[14] Stories about these workshops still live on, and they cannot be proven wrong, either because

---

[8] For the history of research of the civilian settlement, see Zsidi (2006: 11–18).

[9] For a summary of the programme until 1967, see Póczy (1970: 177–94).

[10] Only small-scale, mainly rescue excavations were carried out here: Zsidi (2003a: 143; 2003b: 151); Láng (2009b: 18–19). However, a geophysical survey carried out with the Österreichisches Archäologisches Institut in 2011 will, it is hoped, shed some new light on the structure of this part of the town.

[11] Nagy (1964a: 16). However, according to a re-evaluation of the excavation documentation, the pit turned out to be a drainage ditch, and the same type of sediments were observed during a control excavation in the neighbourhood: these are mainly precipitations of iron and other minerals as a result of the steeping-sinking ground water: Láng (2012).

[12] Recently: Zsidi (2006: 97).   [13] Zsidi (2006: 95–6).

[14] Heating channel: Kuzsinzsky (1899: 27); *fullonica*: Zsidi (2006: 89) with earlier bibliography.

the layers, finds, and structures related to the room or building in question are already destroyed or because there is no possibility for a control excavation.

However, there are a few examples of workshops with more promising evidence as well. Beneath the *macellum*, a small pottery workshop dating to the beginning or middle of the third century was discovered. Finds confirming its identification included a small kiln, moulds for oil lamps, fragments of firing waste and even a clay rod to hold the vessels in the kiln, and a thick, burnt, layer of debris.[15] Further, while the *fullonica* probably never existed, the presence in its environment of houses with large backyards, wells, and mill-stones does point towards a quarter with a strongly economic character in the southern zone of the town, and it has been thought of as an artisanal quarter.[16]

Besides the archaeological data, epigraphic evidence also attests the presence of a number of commercial or industrial activities in the city. Commemorative inscriptions from the necropoleis around the city attest the presence of different *collegia* from the period of the *municipium* onwards. The most frequently mentioned was the *collegium fabrum et centonariorum*, which started off as a combined *collegium* but was later divided into two separate ones.[17] Its best-known *praefectus* was Caius Iulius Viatorinus, who famously donated a water organ to the *collegium* in AD 228.[18] Inscriptions mentioning a *collegium negotiantium*, a *collegium dendrophorum*, and a *nummularius* attest other occupations that were performed in the civilian settlement of Aquincum.[19]

THE ECONOMIC HISTORY OF AQUINCUM

It is clear that our understanding of the economic history of Roman Aquincum is compromised by the quality of the evidence. Besides the difficulties already mentioned of identifying specific economic processes, another problem that plays a role is that of periodization and dating. In what follows, only the workshops and shops that are identifiable in the archaeological record will be discussed, and there will be an emphasis on their chronological development. This may help us to discuss whether there are broader historical tendencies in the economic life of the civilian town of Aquincum (Fig. 15.4).

In the very first phase of the settlement, in the late first century, the roadside sunken-floored houses of the *vicus*-like settlement and other structures were

---

[15] Recently, on the dating of this workshop: Láng (2003: 167, 172–3).

[16] For a summary on this quarter, see Zsidi (2006: 77–89).

[17] Sometime around the middle of the second century: Nagy (1973: 136); Zsidi (2002a: 112); Liu (2008: 66).

[18] Nagy (1934).

[19] *Collegium negotiantium*: CIL 3.10430; *dendrophorum*: see Nagy (1973: 137); Póczy and Zsidi (2003: 198); *nummularius*: CIL 3.3500 (of unknown provenance); Ürögdi (1964: 239–45).

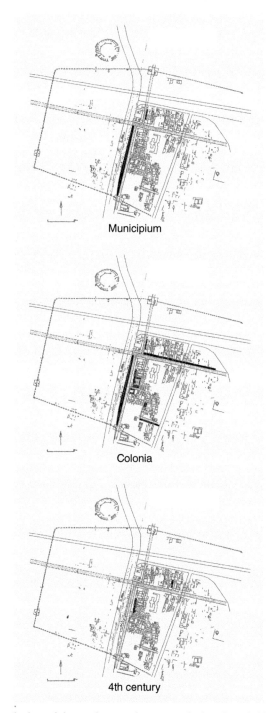

Fig. 15.4. Ground-plan of the civilian settlement with the identifiable workshops and shops of different periods. Map: K. Kolozsvári.

concentrated along the *decumanus* running down to the Danube. Thus, the first workshops must also have been located here. Metal-working could have been one of the most important activities; a smelting oven was identified during a deep probe below the northern part of the so called Basilica (Building i).[20]

The early decades of the second century, when Aquincum became a proper town, still saw the existence of industrial activity in the area of the former *vicus*: here, north–south-oriented strip buildings were constructed with large rooms opening on the *decumanus*.[21] Their northern parts were perhaps used as dwellings, while the southern parts facing the road could have been used for economic purposes.[22]

This is also the time when the emphasis was shifted to the main north–south road (*cardo*) coming from the legionary fortress: the road was lined with a wooden portico on the east side of the *cardo*; the first phase of the row of shops along the western side is also datable to this period, or slightly earlier.[23] The small pottery workshop along the main north–south road was also established in this period. From stylistic analyses of gravestones, it is thought that two stone-carving workshops were active in second-century Aquincum, but the locations of these workshops are uncertain.[24]

Most of the ruins that are presently visible date from the most flourishing period of the town's life—the *colonia* period of the third century—and information on the town's economic life in this period is more abundant. The shops along the west side of the *cardo* were reconstructed at this time (Fig. 15.5).[25] Guidebooks to the site usually specify the function of these shops:[26] allegedly, the retail of local pottery, statuettes, oil-lamps, and Samian Ware is attested, and one shop is even thought to have accommodated a money-changer.[27] Yet, because of the lack of finds and proper excavation records, the purposes for which the shops were used are actually completely unknown.[28] Moreover, the situation of these rooms seems to have been more complex: the western part of the rooms remains hidden underneath the modern road. Rescue excavations connected to a reconstruction of the road in the 1970s revealed ample remains of this part of the complex, including the remains of doors and window at the rear below the arches of the aqueduct and a staircase leading to an upper floor.[29] The rooms, 6 metres wide, measured 15–20 metres from east to west. Their relatively large size, the discovery of underground storage rooms during the rescue excavation, combined with the fact that large amounts of fresco fragments were discovered in one of these and the additional evidence for

[20] Nagy (1971b: 64).   [21] Láng (2012: 215).

[22] This is mainly based on the periodization of Building xxix. See Láng (2012: 216).

[23] Németh and Hajnóczi (1976: 423).   [24] Nagy (1973: 158).

[25] Nagy (1964b: 302).

[26] Recently, with earlier bibliography: Póczy (2003: 148–9); Zsidi (2002a: 167; 2006: 74–6).

[27] Juhász (1936: 33–48); Zsidi (2002a: 67).

[28] The rooms were excavated in the nineteenth century, and only two of them were checked by later excavations. None of these later excavations produced finds enabling the function of the rooms to be identified: Nagy (1964b: 302); Pető (1976b: 423).

[29] Póczy (1984: 21).

Fig. 15.5. Row of workshops or/and shops along the western side of the *cardo* of the settlement. Photo: P. Komjáthy.

upper storeys, suggest that we are dealing with a large-scale building that included workshops, shops, and houses. However, further research would be needed to determine the exact details of the complex.

Elsewhere along the *cardo*, the small second-century pottery workshop was, by the middle of the third century, replaced by a tholos-type *macellum* built after North African models.[30] Further, the craftsmen's houses in the southern zone of the town are also dated to this period, while the strip houses of the north-eastern zone received their present form. Change in the industrial activities can also be observed here: the metal-working gave way to a glue-manufacturing workshop (Building XXIX). This is the period when most of these buildings must have had some industrial or commercial functions. Outside the city centre, raw materials as well as semi-finished and finished products indicated the presence of a stone-carving workshop next to the amphitheatre just outside the town wall.[31]

Evidence for manufacturing and retail is very limited for the period after AD 250. The row of workshops/shops along the cardo was rebuilt and retained its commercial function.[32] The *macellum* was heavily rebuilt around AD 270, but its role afterwards is still uncertain; the west part of the building, which

---

[30] Láng (2003: 165–204; 2007a: 817–30).
[31] Póczy and Zsidi (2003: 201); Nagy (1973: 159).
[32] Németh and Hajnóczi (1976: 423).

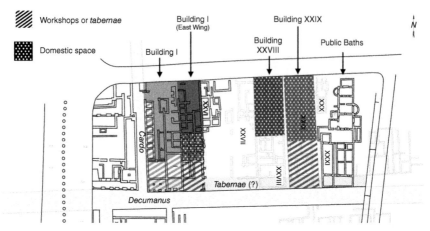

Fig. 15.6. Plan of the industrial-commercial quarter in the north-east zone of the civilian settlement. Image: K. Kolozsvári and Orsolya Láng.

faced the road, was divided into smaller units, possibly shops. Further rebuilding seems to have taken place in the fourth century.[33] In the north-eastern zone, the glue-manufacturing workshop was still functioning, and a small, late bronze-casting workshop was excavated in one of the strip buildings.[34]

To conclude, there are not many securely identifiable workshops and shops in Aquincum. Still, some general remarks can be made. Unsurprisingly, it seems that the location of workshops and shops depended on the position of the most important roads in the city.[35] In the early phase of the settlement the *decumanus* was the dominant route, which meant that the first workshops of Aquincum concentrated along this road. However, from the first decades of the second century onwards, the *cardo*, which connected the city to the legionary fortress, became more important. Workshops and shops were built along this road to take advantage of the busy traffic. At the same time, the still important *decumanus* became the focus of a row of strip buildings with commercial functions. The *colonia* period brought the spread of workshops and shops all over the town, though still with a concentration along the *cardo* and the *decumanus*. The situation in the last period is less well known, but some commercial buildings must have retained their function, while some new ones were also established.[36]

---

[33] Láng (2003: 173–4).

[34] The workshop was located in the eastern wing of Building I. Small bronze statuettes, a casting ladle, and pan were discovered on the floor of one of the rooms: Póczy and Hajnóczi (1973: 34) and excavation documentation (*BTM RA* inv. no. 19–73)

[35] Again, we must bear in mind that here only the eastern part of the town is dealt with, so the conclusions pertain only to this area.

[36] A similar shift of emphasis of areas can be observed in case of cemeteries and large pottery workshops outside the town: Zsidi (2002b: 135–9).

A CASE STUDY: BUILDING xxix IN THE
NORTH-EASTERN ZONE

New excavations carried out in Building xxix in the north-eastern zone of the settlement and the re-evaluation of some old excavation records and materials of some of the strip buildings here seem to confirm the presence of a commercial quarter in this part of the town.[37]

History of Research

The first excavations were carried out in 1890 and 1891 by Bálint Kuzsinszky, who discovered an *atrium*-like room with a floor covered by stone slabs together with column bases (Fig. 15.7).[38] Some of the rooms opening from the *atrium* were equipped with a hypocaust system (rooms 6, 9, and 10). An altar dedicated to Diana and Silvanus Silvestris by M. Aurelius Pompeius was probably discovered during Kuzsinszky's work, together with a small marble bust of Minerva and another female portrait in marble (Fig. 15.8).[39]

The excavation was extended to the southern part of the building by János Szilágyi shortly after the Second World War.[40] He identified some of the rooms as a pottery- or lime-manufacturing workshop, based on the discovery of three pits lined with barrel staves and filled with lime. At the same time, a carved limestone slab, probably a press, found in the eastern part of the building led him to the conclusion that the building also contained an oil- or wine-pressing workshop. The coins discovered here (minted by Commodus, Septimius Severus, and Severus Alexander) permitted Szilágyi to date this phase to a period after the Marcomannic wars.[41] The most recent excavations were carried out between 2004 and 2007 by the present author.[42] They served to define the construction phases of the building, but it also proved possible to identify some of the activities that took place in this building complex in certain periods in the material record. Using small finds and stratigraphic data, it was possible to identify six major construction phases in the building dating

---

[37] Láng (2012).

[38] Kuzsinszky (1891: 134–40). Kuzsinszky excavated rooms 6–11, and rooms B and D. For a more detailed history of research, see Láng (2009a: 273–4).

[39] Altar of Diana and Silvanus. The description of the excavation is not clear. According to the museum register, the findspot of the altar was in Building xxix, inv. no.: 64.10.96. Bust of Minerva: inv. no.: 64.11.177. Recently: Zsidi (1993: 186). Female portrait: inv. no.: 64.11.85. Recently: Zsidi (2006: 57).

[40] Szilágyi (1950: 312–17). Szilágyi excavated rooms 16–18 and 58–64.

[41] Szilágyi (1950: 317).

[42] Láng (2005: 68–80; 2007b: 117–28; 2008a: 71–80; 2008b: 271–84).

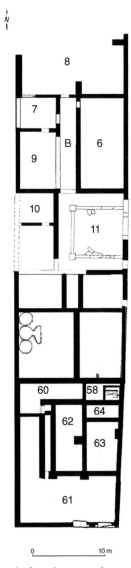

Fig. 15.7. Plan of Building xxix before the control excavations. Plan: K. Kolozsvári.

from the end of the first to the end of the third century AD (Fig. 15.9).[43] Each phase was dated based on the finds that came from it, although phases from other previously excavated buildings in the civilian settlement were also taken into consideration.[44]

[43] Láng (2012).
[44] Most recently with earlier bibliography: Láng (2009a: 276–7; 2012).

Fig. 15.8. Finds from B. Kuzsinszky's excavation: an altar stone and two marble statues. Image reproduced from *BudRég* 3 (1891: 138, fig. 10).

Fig. 15.9. Construction phases in Building XXIX. Image: K. Kolozsvári.

Industrial Activities

Traces of industrial activities could be observed in the southern part of the building from the second phase onwards. Some kind of metal-working was practised here in the second and third phases of the building; work installations were concentrated on the side of the *decumanus*—probably not by accident. Large amounts of metal slag were discovered from the layers in the southern part of the house; vessels filled with slag were also found (room 62); a row of three ovens was built along the southern end wall of the building. The workshop was probably oriented towards the busy *decumanus*. Similar arrangements have been found elsewhere in the empire, as at Sapperton (Britain), where the ovens of a metal workshop were also placed in the street-front rooms of one of the buildings.[45] A row of small melting ovens built of stone was found close to the street in strip buildings in Bad Wimpfen (Germany).[46]

However, from the fourth phase onwards the picture changed: a large amount of horns, horn-cores, metapodia, crushed knuckle bones of animals, and the archaeological features related to this phase (plastered working benches, press slab, fireplace, vats lined with barrel staves) indicate a kind of industrial activity different from metal-working. Archaeozoological research has determined that these bones were mainly of cattle (60–80 per cent), though sheep, goats, and even dogs were also present.[47] Most of the bones from the excavated rooms were workshop waste, but food residue, particularly pig, was also discovered.[48] Interestingly, while workshop waste mainly comes from the southern, commercial area, food residue dominates in the northern, domestic zone (Fig. 15.10).

Elsewhere in the Roman world, similar situations have primarily been associated with tanning or accompanying activities, such as glue-boiling and horn-working.[49] In our case the character of the archaeozoological material makes glue-manufacturing the most likely interpretation, as the evidence suggests that marrow was being extracted from the crushed bones.[50] This by-product of meat-processing had a high significance in Roman times: it was used as glue for furniture, military equipment, and a range of other objects and as fuel in oil lamps.[51]

---

[45] MacMahon (2005: 62).   [46] Filgis (2001: 21–2, figs 4, 6).

[47] The proportion changed from room to room: nos 18, 58, 60–4: 60%; nos.10–10a, 11: 80%. Lyublyanovics (2005: 4; 2007: 1); Daróczi-Szabó (2009: 1).

[48] More than half of the bones were found as workshop waste in rooms 17, 18, 61, 62, 64. Lyublyanovics (2005: 9–14).

[49] Regarding the problem of the identification of tanneries, see van Driel-Murray (2011: 69–72). From a methodological point of view, Building XXIX meets the criteria of this workshop type, because of the presence of special installations and raw material waste: Csippán (2010: 32).

[50] Serjeantson (1989: 139–41); Lees and Woodger (1990: 32); Láng (2005: 76–9; 2007b: 124–5).

[51] Van Driel-Murray (2011: 78).

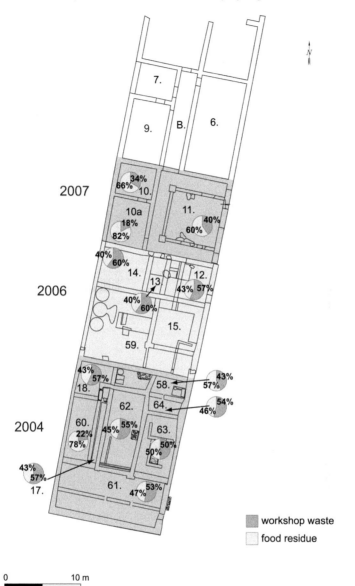

Fig. 15.10. Proportion of workshop refuse and food residue in Building xxix. Image: K. Kolozsvári.

The features discovered in the building can all be associated with this activity: benches could have been used for cutting the bones, and the fireplace was used for boiling the glue.[52] Even the press slab, which was previously

---

[52] The case is similar in Augusta Raurica: Deschler-Erb, Schibler, and Plogmann (2002: 170, fig. 171). Similar working benches are depicted on an eighteenth-century woodcut, along with

Fig. 15.11. Press slab from Building XXIX. Photo: O. Láng.

thought to be used as a grape or oil press, can be reinterpreted (Fig. 15.11): it may have been used for horn-pressing.[53] This is suggested by the presence of so many horns and horn cores: after the appropriate treatment and pressing, they could be turned into a range of objects, such as furniture inlays, vessels, and combs.[54] Some of the loose finds dated to this period also may be related to bone-working: a bone-pricker was found in room 64, and a knife handle of antler came to light in room 62.

Interesting are the three circular vats lined with barrel staves. Elsewhere, such vats have been seen as obvious indicators of tanneries.[55] This is true in Vitudurum, where excavators found circular wooden-lined vats, at Pompeii, where the tannery has circular vats of *opus signinum* technique, and at Saepinum, where tanning was done in conical vats made of bricks.[56] At

tanning pits filled with lime: Petényi and Bartosiewicz (2010: 232, fig. 3). It is less likely that they were used for slaughtering, as this was normally done outside the town: Choyke (2003: 217) and van Driel-Murray (2011: 70).

[53] The press slab had been considered to be for a wine or oil press, from its discovery until the control excavations in 2004: Pető (1976a: 116); Zsidi (2002a: 77–8).

[54] Van Driel-Murray (2011: 77–8). For an ethnographical analogy from York in the nineteenth century, see Wenham (1965: 11, 14–16).

[55] Serjeantson (1989: 135); van Driel-Murray (2001: 60; 2011: 72).

[56] Vitudurum: Hedinger and Leuzinger (2003: 52–3); Pompeii: Adam (1998: 351–2) and Leguilloux (2002: 277); Saepinum: Leguilloux (2004: 50). Other tanneries have been identified in the UK: Alchester: Wilson and Wright (1965: 208–9; 1966: 206); Burnham and Wacher (1990:

Fig. 15.12. One of the vats during its second recovery. Photo: O. Láng.

Carnuntum, eight large, circular late Roman constructions made of clay bricks and stone have recently been interpreted as tanning pits.[57] Pannonian examples are rare, though Nagy identified 'soaking pits' in the *vicus* of the fortress of Alberfalva and in the northern zone of the Aquincum *canabae*.[58] A soaking vat and other installations were also reported from the vicinity of the fortress in Intercisa.[59]

While no channel related to the vats was discovered, the Aquincum features were in fact connected to each other, and they might not be placed incidentally next to the western end wall of the building, where a channel ran outside the building. The first excavator of the site noticed some 'white material' in the filling of the vats, but the nature of this material is not clear (Fig. 15.12).[60] As we do not know the exact filling of the vats, we cannot exclude the possibility

95); Calleva: MacMahon (2005: 63); Hope (1907: 448); Boon (1974: 290–1); Durobrivae: Burnham and Wacher (1990: 75); Londinium: Hall (2005: 135–6); Lakin et al. (2002: 22–3); Salinae: Wilson and Wright (1969: 210–11); Burnham and Wacher (1990: 46); Viroconium: Burnham and Wacher (1990: 46); MacMahon (2005: 63).

[57] Gugl (2009: 1405–19). Van Driel-Murray (2011: 74) argues against this identification.

[58] *Alberfalva*: Nagy (1971b: 62 n. 5); *Aquincum*, III. Raktár str. 8: Nagy (1971a: 25).

[59] Visy (1977: 28–9).

[60] Unfortunately, no remains of this material survives; however, some materials other than lime can also be considered, like ash. Even though lime was used for tanning in medieval times,

that tanning took place in Building xxix, although, based on the data given, horn-soaking/rotting seems more plausible.[61] The closest analogies to the Aquincum glue-manufacturing and horn-pressing workshop can be found in Liberchies, Augusta Raurica, and Venta Silurum.[62]

Where did the Bones Come from and who were the Customers?

The large amount of animal bones found in Building xxix could have reached this workshop after professional cutting and sorting. The location of the workshop is relevant in this respect. As mentioned earlier, raw material must have been transported via the *decumanus*, which led down to the harbour.[63] It is possible that large-scale butcheries were clustered outside the settlement, in the zone of the harbour, because water was easily available here, and because there was an important crossing point to the Barbaricum.[64] It cannot be ruled out that most of livestock transports arrived here from the other bank of the river.[65] Indeed, it is suggested by Cassius Dio that livestock was imported from the Barbaricum, and it seems highly probable that this was the case here at Aquincum as well.[66] Given the lack of detailed archaeometrical research, it is hard to decide what proportion of the bones found in Building xxix came from beyond the border.[67] In any case, the roadside location of the workshop close to the river was also convenient for getting rid of the refuse.[68]

The *decumanus* was important not only from the point of view of the raw materials and waste management, but also from the point of view of the customers. The glue manufactured here—and possibly the hides as well—was used for a variety of purposes and was also purchased by civilian customers. However, it

there is no evidence for the same process in the Roman period: Sőregi (1939: 34), Írásné Melis (1996: 226); van Driel-Murray (2001: 60; pers. comm.).

[61] Van Driel-Murray (2011: 78). Even in the eighteenth century, this was the process for preparing horn for pressing: Csippán (2010: 33).

[62] Liberchies: Leguilloux (2004: 51–2) and van Driel-Murray (2011: 70); Augusta Raurica: Schibler and Furger (1988: 76, 80, 94–5; more tanneries are predicted: see pp. 39, 42, 60–1, 90, 99–100, 109–10, 120, 124–5); Venta Silurum: Brewer (1993: 58).

[63] The end of the road is still unknown: it is still traceable under the neighbouring housing estate, but becomes uncertain in the area of the large Roman pottery workshop, where some thirty wells were discovered in 1911–12: Kuzsinszky (1932: 71–5). The same problem occurs with the location of the harbour which is still unknown: Tóth (2006: 212–13).

[64] Zsidi (2007: 67).

[65] Recently: Láng (2009a: 281). A similar example is known from Alchester (Britain): here tanneries processed the hides of cattle regularly transported over the river Avon. Burnham and Wacher (1990: 47).

[66] Cassius Dio LXXI, 11.2 and Gabler (1990: 204).

[67] Isotopic analyses would be the most useful method in this case, but, as barbarian herds possibly also drank Danube water, barbarian and Roman herds could not be distinguished.

[68] In case of the fortress at Velsen, refuse (including leather off-cuts and animal bones) was thrown into the water, between the piers of the harbour: van Driel-Murray (1985: 50–1 and fig.4).

might not be an accident that this workshop started to work sometime around the middle of the second century: examples from the Western provinces show that, while in the first century the Roman army was self-supplying with leather products or had them produced centrally, this changed from the first half of the second century. Certain leather products—such as shoes—began to be produced by civilian craftsmen, which boosted the business of local workshops.[69] Thus, we cannot exclude the possibility that this workshop not only supplied civilians but also worked for the legionary fortress of Aquincum.

TOPOGRAPHICAL AND SOCIO-ECONOMIC CHARACTERISTICS OF THE NORTH-EAST ZONE

Building XXIX is in the north-eastern zone of the civilian settlement of Aquincum. The topographical position and characteristic buildings of this part of the town raise interesting questions—especially from the second half of the second century onwards. The type of houses that dominates the quarter—the strip building or *Streifenhaus*—is often considered as a characteristic building in *vici* and other roadside settlements of Gallo-Roman origin as well as in towns in the north-west provinces.[70] These buildings are often thought of as inhabited by merchants and craftsmen. They have been found facing the main roads of settlements such as Corstopitum (Corbridge), Londinium, Alchester, Venta Silurum (Caerwent), Bliesbruch, and Bad Wimpfen.[71] This central position in the urban topography is obviously due to their function: merchants and craftsmen who used the houses partly as dwellings and partly as workshops tried to locate their business in the busiest parts of town. In the case of the Aquincum example, this was along the *decumanus*.

CONCLUSION

If we review the research history of the civilian settlement, it is clear that the identification of workshops and shops of the settlement in nearly all periods is problematic. This is partly due to the old, mainly inadequate, excavation techniques, which brought only the latest phases to light, and concentrated on

---

[69] Van Driel-Murray (1985: 55–62, 65–6) and Kocsis (2010: 171).

[70] Oelman (1923: 82–8); Lohner (1999: 31); Schalles (2000: 104–6); Hales (2003: 180). Some would trace its origins back to the days of the oppida (e.g. Bibracte in France): Ellis (2000: 87).

[71] Corbridge: Burnham and Wacher (1990: 18, 46, 60); London: Milne and Wardle (1993: 34); Alchester: Burnham and Wacher (1990: 102); Caerwent: Oelman (1923: 91); Bliesbruch: Schaub, Petit, and Brunella (1992: 110); Bad Wimpfen: Filgis and Pietsch (1990: 455–8).

complete ground plans, while little work was done in later periods to check what had been found before. This is partly due to the fact that the function of most establishments was identified according to their plans and to the misinterpretation of artefacts discovered in them. Before we are able to discuss the socioeconomic history of the settlement, the commonplaces of the past century of scholarship need to be deconstructed. At this point, it is very hard to place the economic situation of the civilian town of Aquincum into a broader context and compare it with other provincial settlements. However, on the basis of more recent archaeological observations, and making extensive use of comparisons with evidence from elsewhere, a few shops and workshops could be more securely identified. These include the row of shops and workshops along the western side of the *cardo*, the *macellum* along the same road, a small metal workshop, and a glazed pottery workshop in the north-eastern zone of the town where strip buildings were built from the first half of the second century onwards. A bronze-casting workshop can be identified in the same area.

Recent fieldwork revealed the traces of different industrial activities in building XXIX in the same zone: while from the beginning to the middle of the second century there was a small metal workshop in the southern part of the house, close to the *decumanus*, the character of the industrial activity changed from the last third of the second century. A glue-manufacturing and possibly also a horn-pressing workshop were established here. The latter is the first workshop in Aquincum to be identified securely, on the basis of its finds record (the workshop refuse of animal bones), of features related to this industry (soaking vats, a press slab, a small fireplace, and working benches), and of analogies with comparable remains elsewhere in the Roman world.

Based on what has been discussed in this chapter, the north-eastern zone of the civilian settlement of Aquincum, with its strip buildings opening to the *decumanus*, should be considered one of the key industrial and commercial quarters of the town. A closer look at its topographical setting and its parallels also revealed that this zone developed because of the proximity of the busy *decumanus* leading to the harbour. Yet, even though the north-eastern quarter of the civilian town has already revealed some promising examples, there is still a long way to go before the economic landscape of the settlement is fully understood. Further fieldwork and revaluations of old documentations are needed critically to reassess extant hypotheses and to fill in critical gaps in our knowledge.

REFERENCES

Adam, J. A. (1998). *Arte di costruire presso i Romani*. Milan.
Boon, G. C. (1974). *Silchester: The Roman Town of Calleva*. London.
Brewer, R. J. (1993). 'Venta Silurum: A Civitas–Capital', in B. C. Burnham and J. L. Davies (eds), *Conquest, Co-existence and Change: Recent Work in Roman Wales*. Lampeter, 56–65.

Burnham, B. C., and Wacher J. C. (1990). *Small Towns of Roman Britain*. London.

Choyke, A. (2003). 'Animals and Roman Lifeways in Aquincum', in Zsidi (2003c), 210–30.

Csippán, P. (2010). 'Az állati nyersanyagokat feldolgozó műhelyek azonosítási lehetőségei', in J. Gömöri and A. Kőrösi (eds) *Csont és bőr: Az állati eredetű nyersanyagok feldolgozásának története, régészete és néprajza*. Budapest, 31–7.

Daróczi-Szabó, M. (2009). 'Jelentés a Peristyl–ház 2007-es ásatásának állatcsontanyagáról'. Unpublished archaeozoological report. Budapest.

Deschler-Erb, S., Schibler, J., and Hüster Plogmann, H. (2002). 'Viehzucht, Jagd und Fischfang', in L. Flutsch, U. Niffeler, and F. Rossi (eds), *Die Schweiz vom Paläolithikum bis zum frühen Mittelalter 5–SPM V. Die Römerzeit in der Schweiz*. Basle, 165–71.

Driel-Murray, C. van (1985). 'The Production and Supply of Military Leatherwork in the First and Second Centuries AD: A Review of the Archaeological Evidence', in M. C. Bishop (ed.), *The Production and Distribution of Roman Military Equipment* (BAR International Series, 275). Oxford, 43–81.

Driel-Murray, C. van (2001). 'Technology Transfer: The Introduction and Loss of Tanning Technology during the Roman Period', in M. Polfer (ed.), *L'Artisanat romain: Évolutions, continuités et ruptures (Italie et provinces occidentales)* (Monographies Instrumentum, 20). Montagnac, 55–68.

Driel-Murray, C. van (2011). 'Are we Missing Something? The Elusive Tanneries of the Roman Period', in R. Thomson and Q. Mould (eds), *Leather Tanneries: The Archaeological Evidence*. London, 69–83.

Ellis, S. P. (2000). *Roman Housing*. London.

Filgis, M. N. (2001). 'Ausgewählte Baubefunde des Handwerks und Gewerbes in römische *Vicus* von Wimpfen', in S. Altekamp and A. Schäfer (eds), *The Impact of Rome on Settlements in the North Western and Danube Provinces* (BAR International Series, 921). Oxford, 19–37.

Filgis, M. N., and Pietsch, M. (1990). 'Das römische Bad Wimpfen am Neckar–Odenwaldlimes–Ergebnisse neuerrer Ausgrabungen', in H. Vetters and M. Kandler (eds), *Akten des 14. Internationalen Limeskongresses 1986 in Carnuntum*. Vienna, 455–62.

Gugl, C. (2009). '*Carnuntensis scutaria (Not.Dign.Occ. IX, 20)*. Archäologische Evidenz für spätantike Ledererzeugung im Legionslager Carnuntum?', in A. Morillo, N. Hanel, and E. Martín (eds), *LIMES XX: Estudios sobre la Frontera Romana. Vol III*. Madrid, 1405–17.

Hales, S. (2003). *The Roman House and Social Identity*. Cambridge.

Hall, J. (2005). 'The Shopkeepers and Craft-Workers of Roman London', in A. MacMahon and J. Price (eds), *Roman Working Lives and Urban Living*. Oxford, 125–44.

Hedinger, B., and Leuzinger, V. (2003). *Tabula rasa—Les Helvètes et l' artisanat du bois*. Avenches.

H. Kérdő, K. (2003). 'Das Alenlager und Vicus der Víziváros', in Zsidi (2003c), 81–4.

Hope, St J. (1907). 'Excavations on the Site of the Roman City at Silchester, Hants, in 1906', *Archaeologia* 60/2: 431–50.

Írásné Melis, K. (1996). 'Középkori lakóházak és egy XV. sz-i vargaműhely', *ComArcHung* 211–39.

Juhász, Gy. (1936). 'A lezouxi terrasigillata gyárak aquincumi lerakata', *Arch. Érsito* 49: 33–48.

Kocsis, L. (2010). 'Mire használta a római hadsereg az állati eredetű nyersanyagot a Kr.u. évszázadokban?', in J. Gömöri and A. Kőrösi (eds), *Csont és bőr: Az állati eredetű nyersanyagok feldolgozásának története, régészete és néprajza.* Budapest, 165–74.

Kuzsinszky, B. (1891). 'Az aquincumi amphiteatrum: Függelékül: Két lakóház. Az 1890 és részben a 1891-i papföldi ásatások', *Budapest Régiségei* 3: 81–139.

Kuzsinszky, B. (1899). 'A papföldi ásatások 1897–98 években', *Budapest Régiségei* 6: 19–36.

Kuzsinszky, B. (1932). 'A gázgyári római fazekastelep Aquincumban', *Budapest Régiségei* 11: 3–423.

Lakin, D., Seeley, F., Bird, J., Reilly, K., and Ainsley, C. (2002). *The Roman Tower at Shadwell, London: A Reappraisal.* London.

Láng, O. (2003). 'Reconsidering the Aquincum Macellum: Analogies and Origins', *Acta ArchHung* 54: 165–204.

Láng, O. (2005). 'The Peristyle House: Authenticating Excavation in the Northeast Part of the Aquincum Civil Town', *AqFüz* 11: 68–80.

Láng, O. (2007a). 'Did the Cosinii Build Macella? The Possible Builder of the *macellum* in Aquincum', in M. Mayer, O. G. Baratta, and A. G. Almagro (eds), *Acta XII: Congressus Epigraphiae Graecae et Latinae 2002.* Barcelona, 817–30.

Láng, O. (2007b). '"Strip House with an Atrium Residence Wing": Authenticating Excavation in the Northeastern Part of the Aquincum Civil Town II', *AqFüz* 13: 117–28.

Láng, O. (2008a). '"Strip House with an Atrium Residence Wing": Authenticating Excavation in the Northeastern Part of the Aquincum Civil Town III', *AqFüz* 14: 71–80.

Láng, O. (2008b). 'Functions and Phases: The "Peristyle-House" in the Civil Town of Aquincum', in P. Scherrer (ed.), *DOMUS: Das Haus in den Städten der römischen Donauprovinzen. Akten des 3. Internationalen Symposiums über römische Städte in Noricum und Pannonien.* Vienna, 271–84.

Láng, O. (2009a). '"Unpleasant to Live in, yet it Makes the City Rich": Functions of Strip-Buildings in the Aquincum Civil Town, in the Light of New Discoveries', in Sz. Bíró (ed.), *Ex officina: Studia in honorem Dénes Gabler.* Győr, 271–86.

Láng, O. (2009b). 'Richly Decorated Building in the Western Part of the Civil Town of Aquincum', *AqFüz* 15: 18–29.

Láng, O. (2012). 'Urbanistic Problems in the Aquincum Civil Town: The So Called NE Zone'. Unpublished Ph.D. dissertation, Universtity Eötvös Lorand, Faculty of Arts, Doctoral School of History, Archaeology, Budapest.

Lees, D., and Woodger, A. (1990). *The Archaeology and History of Sixty London Wall, London EC 2.* London.

Leguilloux, M. (2002). 'Techniques et équipments de la tannerie romaine: L'Exemple de l'officina coriaria de Pompéi', in F. Audoin-Rouzeau and S. Beyries (eds), *Le Travail du cuir de la préhistoire á nos jours. XXIIe rencontre internationale d'archéologie et d'histoire d'Antibes.* Antibes, 267–82.

Leguilloux, M. (2004). *Le Cuir et la pelleterie à l'époque romaine.* Paris.

Liu, J. (2008). 'Pompeii and *collegia*: A New Appraisal of the Evidence', *AHB* 22/1–4: 53–69.

Lohner, U. (1999). 'Zivile Vici im Umfeld von Flavia Solva', in N. C. Hazel and C. Schucany (eds), *Colonia–Municipium–Vicus: Struktur und Entwicklung städtischer Siedlungen in Noricum, Räetien und Obergermanien* (BAR International Series, 783). Oxford, 29–41.

Lyublyanovics, K. V. (2005). 'Jelentés az, Aquincum–polgárváros, Peristyl-ház' lelőhely állatmaradványainak vizsgálatáról'. Unpublished archaeozoological report, Budapest.

Lyublyanovics, K. V. (2007). 'Jelentés a Peristyl-házban 2006-ban végzett ásatásállatmaradványainak vizsgálatáról'. Unpublished archaeozoological report, Budapest.

MacMahon, A. (2005). 'The Shops and Workshops of Roman Britain', in A. MacMahon and J. Price (eds), *Roman Working Lives and Urban Living*. Oxford, 48–69.

Milne, G., and Wardle, A. (1993). 'Early Roman Development at Leadenhall Court, London and Related Research', *Transactions of the London and Middlesex Archaeological Society* 44: 23–170.

Nagy, L. (1934). *Az aquincumi orgona*. Budapest.

Nagy, T. (1964a). 'Perióduskutatások az aquincumi polgárváros területén', *Budapest Régiségei* 21: 9–54.

Nagy, T. (1964b). 'A Budapesti Történeti Múzeum leletmentései és ásatásai 1960–1961-ben', *Budapest Régiségei* 21: 295–336.

Nagy, T. (1971a). 'n. 34', *Régészeti Füzetek* 171: 25–6.

Nagy, T. (1971b). 'Der Vicus und das Municipium von Aquincum', *Acta ArchHung* 23: 59–81.

Nagy, T. (1973). *Budapest története I*, ed. L.Gerevich. Budapest.

Németh, M., and Hajnóczi, G. (1976). 'The Works of Rescue and Planned Excavations Conducted by the Historical Museum of Budapest in the Years 1971–1975.– Szentendrei út 139', *Budapest Régiségei* 24: 423.

Németh, M. (2003). 'Die Militäranlagen von Óbuda', in Zsidi (2003c), 85–92.

Oelman, F. (1923). 'Gallo-Römische Strassensiedlungen und Kleinhausbauten', *Bonner Jahrbücher* 128: 77–97.

Petényi, S., and Bartosiewicz, L. (2010). 'Tímárkodással kapcsolatos adatok a Baj-Öregkovács-hegyi koraújkori nemesi udvarház területén', in J. Gömöri and A. Kőrösi (eds), *Csont és bőr: Az állati eredetű nyersanyagok feldolgozásának története, régészete és néprajza*. Budapest, 229–42.

Pető, M. (1976a). 'Feltárások a II.–III: Századi aquincumi legiostábor retenturájában', *Budapest Régiségei* 24: 113–19.

Pető, M. (1976b). 'A Budapesti Történeti Múzeum ásatásai és leletmentései 1971 és 1975 között', *Budapest Régiségei* 24: 391–444.

Póczy, K. (1970). 'Anwendung neuerer Ausgarbungergebnisse bei der Ruinenkonservierung in der Bürgerstadt Aquincum', *ATASH* 67: 177–94.

Póczy, K. (1984). 'Aquincum—Castra, Canabae, Colonia', *Budapest Régiségei*, 25: 15–29.

Póczy, K (1996). 'Der afrikanische Saturnus in Aquincum an der Donau', in G. Bauchhenß (ed.), *Akten des 3. internationalen Kolloquiums über Probleme des provinzialrömischen Kunstschaffens*. Cologne, 141–7.

Póczy, K. (2002). 'Aquincum als Provinzhauptstadt zur zeit der Severer', in K. Kuzmová, K. Pieta, and J. Rajtár (eds), *Zwischen Rom und dem Barbaricum: Festschrift für T. Kolník zum 70. Geburtstag*. Nitra, 183–92.

Póczy, K. (2003). 'Wasserver- und entsorgung, Gebäude des Stadtzentrums', in Zsidi (2003c), 144–9.

Póczy, K., and Hajnóczi, G. (1973). 'Nr. 63', *Régészeti Füzetek* 26: 34–5.

Póczy, K., and Zsidi, P. (2003). 'Lokales Gewerbe und Handel', in Zsidi (2003c), 185–206.

Schalles, V. H.-J. (2000). 'Städte im Rheinland: Das Beispiel Xanten', in L. Wamser (ed.), *Römer zwischen Alpen und Nordmeer: Zivilisatorisches Erbe einer europäischen Militärmaacht: Katalog zur Landesausstellung des Freisraates Bayern, Rosenheim 2000.* Mainz, 104–7.

Schaub, J., Petit, J.-P., and Brunella, P. (1992). 'Bliesbruch', *Gallia Informations* 2: 108–11.

Schibler, J., and Furger, R. A. (1988). 'Die Tierknochenfunde aus Augusta Raurica: Grabungen 1955–74', *Forschungen in Augst* 9.

Serjeantson, D. (1989). 'Animal Remains and the Tanning Trade', in D. Serjeantson and T. Waldron (eds), *Diet and Crafts in Towns: The Evidence of Animal Remains from the Roman to Post-Medieval Periods* (BAR British Series, 199). Oxford, 129–46.

Sőregi, J. (1939). 'Jelentés a Déri Múzeum 1939: Évi működéséről és állapotáról', *DDMÉ* 5–70.

Szilágyi, J. (1950). 'Jelentés a Fővárosi Ókortörténeti (Aquincumi) Múzeum kutatásairól és szerzeményeiről az 1945–1948: Évek folyamán', *Budapest Régiségei* 15: 305–21.

Topál, J. (2003). 'Ägyptische und orientalische Götter und Kulte', in Zsidi (2003c), 274–83.

Tóth, J.-A. (2006). 'Budapest III: The Bed of the Danube and the Aquincum Bridge', *AqFüz* 12: 212–14.

Ürögdi, G. (1964). 'A banküzlet nyomai Aquincumban', *Budapest Régiségei*, 21: 239–45.

Visy, Z. (1977). *Intercisa.* Budapest.

Wenham, L. P. (1965). 'Hornpot Lane and the Horners of York', *Annual Report of the Council of the Yorkshire Philosophical Society* 2–19.

Wilson, D. R., and Wright, R. P. (1965). 'Roman Britain in 1964', *JRS* 55: 199–228.

Wilson, D. R., and Wright, R. P. (1966). 'Roman Britain in 1965', *JRS* 56: 196–225.

Wilson, D. R., and Wright, R. P. (1969). 'Roman Britain in 1968', *JRS* 59: 198–246.

Zsidi, P. (1993). 'Zur Verehrung der Minerva in Aquincum', *Budapest Régiségei* 30: 185–208.

Zsidi, P. (2002a). *Aquincum polgárvárosa.* Budapest.

Zsidi, P. (2002b). 'Transformation of the Town Structure in the Civil Town of Aquincum during the Severi (AD 193–235)', *Acta ArchHung* 53: 132–49.

Zsidi, P. (2003a). 'Verkehrsverbindungen, Wehranlagen, Straßennetz', in Zsidi (2003c), 137–43.

Zsidi, P. (2003b). 'Öffentliche Gebäude und Wohnhäuser außerhalb des Stadtzentrums', in Zsidi (2003c), 150–5.

Zsidi, P. (2003c) (ed.). *Forschungen in Aquincum 1969–2002.* Budapest.

Zsidi, P. (2004). 'Aquincum topográfiája', *Specimina Nova* 18: 167–226.

Zsidi, P. (2006). *Az aquincumi polgárváros: Vezető az aquincumi múzeum romkertjében* (Aquincumi Zsebkönyvek, 1). Budapest.

Zsidi, P. (2007). 'A Duna szerepe Aquincum topográfiájában', *Budapest Régiségei* 41: 45–84.

16

The Potters of Ancient Sagalassos Revisited

Jeroen Poblome

In 1987, during the initial exploratory survey campaigns at the archaeological site of Sagalassos (Pisidia, south-west Turkey), which mostly focused on epigraphic recording, and urban and monumental architectural reconnaissance studies, considerable amounts of pottery production waste were found concentrated in a large area to the east of the theatre (Fig. 16.1). The perceived importance of the discovery was translated into the designation of this area as the Potters' Quarter of Sagalassos. Sigillata, red gloss or red slipped tableware, was considered to be its main product.[1] Nobody in the community of Roman archaeology or ceramology, let alone in the Sagalassos Archaeological Research Project, had anticipated this discovery.

This chapter goes back to basics and (re)builds step by step the world of the potters of ancient Sagalassos. The natural and environmental setting of the site is presented, as well as aspects of path dependency in the development of the local potter's craft. Shifts in scale of production are discussed, along with the economy of the raw clay materials, the production process and its organization, policies of investment and ownership, and the workings of *familia* and *collegia*. I switch between general observations and testing on the ground so as to give as complete a picture as possible.

Sagalassos is located in the west part of the Turkish Taurus Mountains. This system of mountain ranges separates the Mediterranean coast of Turkey from the central Anatolian plateau. The complex Mesozoic–Tertiary genesis of the research area resulted in a particular triangular-shaped formation, the so-called Isparta Angle. Sagalassos is located on the west limb of this formation, as part of the Lycean Nappe Complex, fronting the autochthonous carbonate Bey Dağları Platform. The Lycean nappe is mainly composed of an ophiolitic mélange, volcanic rocks and allochthonous carbonate platforms. During the Tertiary

---

[1] Mitchell and Waelkens (1988: 60).

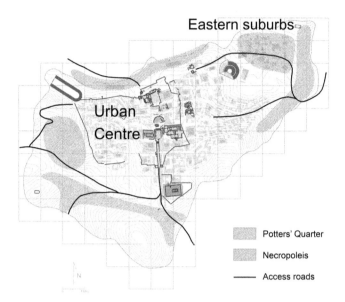

Fig. 16.1. The eastern suburbs of Sagalassos featuring the local Potters' Quarter. Map: Sagalassos Archaeological Research Project.

nappe emplacement, flysch deposits were formed. Another late Tertiary landscape element worth mentioning is the volcanic Lake Gölçük and the associated lava and tuff deposits, about 5 kilometres to the north-west of the site.[2]

The ancient town is tucked away in a large bend of the Ağlasun Dağı range (*c.*1,800 metres above sea level) (Fig. 16.2), forming the spectacular crest to the north of the site, with the Akdağ (2,271 m.a.s.l.) dominating the north-east end of the range. From its position at the top of a V-shaped valley cut into the mountains, the ancient town (1,490–1,600 m.a.s.l.) overlooked the lower areas to the east and south. The valley acts as a permanent creek, draining several springs where permeable limestone formations end on more impermeable ophiolite and flysch deposits. These springs feed the middle course of the Ağlasun Çayı, a permanent stream in the valley south of Sagalassos and a tributary of the ancient river Kestros, part of which formed the east border of the territory of Roman imperial Sagalassos.[3]

As far as connectivity is concerned, the site can be reached from the Ağlasun Valley from its south and east sides. To the north-west of Sagalassos, the mountain ridge is interrupted by a pass at an altitude of *c.*1,730 metres, leading into the Isparta Plain.[4] The Ağlasun Çayı and Valley provided a corridor towards the east, reaching the valley of the ancient river Kestros after some 20 kilometres.

[2] Degryse et al. (2008a); Muchez et al. (2008).   [3] Paulissen et al. (1993: 229–31).
[4] Paulissen et al. (1993: 230).

Fig. 16.2. View from the Akdağ towards ancient Sagalassos. The town was laid out on the plateaux in the centre of the image. Photo: Sagalassos Archaeological Research Project.

To the west, this valley connected into the Çanaklı Plain. Most of the research area is actually a series of interconnected mountain basins. The Burdur Plain represents the largest tract of flat, fertile lands within the territory of Sagalassos, about 30 kilometres from the town. Natural corridors from the Bay of Fethiye and Antalya reach the plain, connecting into the Isparta Plain. The Augustan *via Sebaste* followed the east corridor, representing, together with the Kestros Valley, the major lines of communication from the south coast to the interior.[5]

Pronounced winter precipitation and summer dryness characterize the climate in the vicinity of Sagalassos as Mediterranean, with a shorter dry season and lower temperatures in all seasons compared to coastal zones and significantly colder winters with a high number of frost–thaw cycles.[6]

The area of the site formed part of an Oromediterranean vegetation belt, with deciduous oak forests found below needle-leaved forests. Two palynological profiles were reconstructed from core-drillings in the central depression of the Potters' Quarter of Sagalassos. In their lower parts, a period of *Artemisia* pollen dominance was defined, possibly indicating large-scale disturbance of the soil in the depression in the course of the Hellenistic period. Various light-demanding herbaceous taxa indicate the absence of forest vegetation in the same period. Re-afforestation is reconstructed from late Hellenistic times on the slopes north and east of the site, resulting in a cedar forest, possibly mixed with some pine and *Abies cilicica* as a minor constituent throughout the Roman imperial and early

---

[5] Mitchell (1993: 70–9).   [6] Paulissen et al. (1993: 231–3); Vermoere (2004: 8).

Byzantine periods. In the same periods, patches of deciduous oak woodland were growing on the hills below Sagalassos, as were walnut trees. Grapes were cultivated not far from the Potters' Quarter, possibly on the slopes south of it. Olive trees, on the other hand, were not grown at or near Sagalassos. In general, the continuity of the pollen signal hints at rational exploitation schemes of the forests and cultivated tree species at least until early Byzantine times.[7]

In the evaluation of how nature–society interactions sustained or limited the initiation and organization of the local potter's craft, a variety of quality raw clay materials was found to be available at and around the site, as were sufficient quantities of water as well as fuel sources. Sensible management schemes would have needed to be developed optimally to exploit these natural resources, and to avoid scheduling conflicts with other primary economic activities, as well as to keep the balance between the different social parties involved in artisanal production. Transport of the produce would have needed to be organized, but would not have been a greater obstacle than for other resources and goods transported to and from the site. The main drawback that nature would have forced upon the production cycle was the winter months, when potting, as much as any other professional activity for that matter, was simply impossible.[8] In considering these mostly processual aspects, however, we need to avoid assuming that pottery production at Sagalassos was a natural thing to happen in Roman imperial times.

Apart from integrating an interdisciplinary research strategy into the project's archaeological research programme, right from the stage of applying for funds, no specific theoretical or conceptual disciplinary framework was put forward to study and 'explain' the pots and potters of ancient Sagalassos. The intention was to keep an intuitive, broad orientation within the discipline and to consider primarily how patterns in the archaeology of the pots and potters of Roman Sagalassos could fit with ideas and concepts of social complexity and its region-ally specific evolution in the long term. This bottom-up approach, grounded in the detailed study of the artefacts and the archaeological record, was preferred, building consciously on the conviction that archaeology, as a discipline, harbours the unique potential to explore societal development by combining the dimen-sions of materiality and cognition with time and space.[9]

THE ORIGINS OF SCALE

To be sure, Sagalassos and *a fortiori* Roman imperial Sagalassos red slip ware did not always exist. The exact circumstances of the genesis of Sagalassos as a

---

[7] Vermoere et al. (2003); Vermoere (2004: 171–90).

[8] For feedback mechanisms affecting pottery production, see Arnold (1985).

[9] More inspiration in, e.g. Bintliff (2011) and Lucas (2012).

community are still somewhat shrouded in the mist.[10] During recent excavation seasons, a construction fill behind a terracing wall was excavated in the north part of the Potters' Quarter, as well as some material retrieved from below the pavement slabs of the Upper Agora.[11] The pottery finds from these contexts represent the oldest material found at Sagalassos so far and are datable to the (later) fifth to the (early) third centuries BC. No contemporary potting activities are attested in the Potters' Quarter, although the macroscopical fabric characteristics are in line with clay resources at and around the site. The actual slope gradient of the excavated area in this part of the Potters' Quarter is about 30 per cent, so for any organized activity to take place over time the laying-out of terraces would have been beneficial. Although it remains unclear where and how civic life was organized in Late Classical and Early Hellenistic Sagalassos, the use of this steep terrain and the construction of terraces would have required some sort of communal initiative at organization.

From the fifth century BC onwards, another, larger community had settled on the nearby plateau of Düzen Tepe, only 1.8 kilometres south from Sagalassos.[12] We need not dwell on this socially complex community in this context, apart from mentioning that the remains of a Classical/Hellenistic (fifth–second centuries BC) potter's workshop were excavated there.[13] The wares in question were of variable quality and are best considered to reflect contemporary Pisidian styles and functions.[14]

Against the background of Sagalassos and Düzen Tepe coexisting at least partially, and in the context of this chapter, it is important to consider which raw clay materials were selected from the environment. First, potters of both settlements processed clays that were available locally. In the case of Sagalassos, the quarrying of ophiolitic clays has been proven by core-drilling and deep-soil tomography in the central depression of the Potters' Quarter. A palaeosol developed on top of the quarried surfaces, the formation of which was C^{14}-dated to between 370/360 BC and 50/40 BC, providing a *terminus ante quem* for the clay-quarrying activities.[15] Such activities could also be reconstructed on the east slope of the quarter, generally pre-dating the installation of an early Roman imperial potter's workshop in this zone, while parts of a clay-quarrying pit were excavated in the south-east area, which was backfilled with material datable to the first half of the second century AD.[16] The nature of the geophysical anomalies

---

[10] Poblome et al. (2013a).

[11] Excavations at Site F 2011 and 2012 were supervised by Johan Claeys (unpublished). The 2014 and 2015 excavations on the Upper Agora were coordinated by Peter Talloen. See Talloen et al. (2015).

[12] Vanhaverbeke et al. (2010).

[13] Excavations at Tepe Düzen 2008 and 2011 were supervised by respectively Hannelore Vanhaverbeke and Kim Vyncke. The workshop remains unpublished.

[14] Poblome et al. (2013a).   [15] Six (2004).

[16] On the east slope, cf. Degryse et al. (2003). Excavations at Site PQ3 2012 were supervised by Elizabeth Murphy. Unpublished.

in the south-east part of the quarter is indicative of more clay-quarrying activities, while it is possible that the specific herbaceous vegetation in Hellenistic times already mentioned hints at the period during which most of these activities took place.[17] At Düzen Tepe, archaeometric analysis of clays and sherds has indicated that the clays mostly selected by potters came from an ophiolitic provenance.[18]

Secondly, additional raw clay materials were quarried in the environment of both sites. Although difficulties remain in discriminating provenances of comparable clay bodies in great detail in the terrain, clays with similar properties are available in the wider Ağlasun Valley, located at the foot of both sites.[19] Other than that, archaeometric analysis at the Leuven Centre for Archaeological Sciences has associated the earliest use of the so-called north-west Çanaklı-clays with Classical/ Hellenistic pottery. Whereas the Ağlasun Valley clays were available within a 1–3 kilometre radius, the distance to the north-west Çanaklı-clays was somewhat larger, representing, as the crow flies, about 4–5 kilometres from Düzen Tepe and about 7–8 kilometres from Sagalassos (Fig. 16.3). The greenish grey clays, which had originally accumulated as part of a sequence of lake deposits in the north-west section of the Çanaklı Valley, were confirmed as having a consistent and

Fig. 16.3. General view of the north-west part of the Çanaklı Valley. Ancient Sagalassos was located on the mountain slopes at the back of the image, on the left. Photo: Sagalassos Archaeological Research Project.

---

[17] Personal communication by Branko Mušič.
[18] Braekmans et al. (2011); Neyt et al. (2012).   [19] Neyt et al. (2012).

analytically definable geochemical signature in comparison to other clays from the same valley or elsewhere in the study region.[20] This particular clay resource was found in clay preparation pits in excavated Roman imperial workshops in the Potters' Quarter of Sagalassos and was archaeometrically confirmed as the main component of contemporary Sagalassos red slip ware.[21] Its exploitation had already been confirmed in Hellenistic times and recently archaeometrical analysis has indicated that a line of black glazed vessels was made from these clays too.[22] The latter ware was found during excavations at both Sagalassos and Düzen Tepe, albeit only in secondary deposits, which has prevented the establishment of a stratigraphically anchored chronology. Typological features suggest a fourth–third-century BC bracket for the ware. Although black glazed pottery was never common at both sites, it did represent the higher end of the contemporary tableware market. In this respect, the link between the qualities of the ware and the selection of a specific clay source is important. When, in contrast to more conservative Düzen Tepe, the potters of Sagalassos initiated the local production of a Hellenistic form repertoire around 200 BC, the same link between the quality clays of north-west Çanaklı and the better tableware was maintained.[23] Although clays were available at and around Sagalassos and Düzen Tepe and tableware was made with these, they mainly served the production of cooking ware and other utilitarian vessels. The extra effort to cover the distance towards the north-west part of the Çanaklı Valley was clearly made to achive better-quality end products, mainly tableware.

One way or another, (coexisting) Sagalassos and Düzen Tepe were dependent on largely the same catchment area. Whether this condition resulted in tension between both communities is not revealed by the current archaeological record, but it must have had consequences for ownership patterns of land as well as for marketing options for produce. Similar mechanisms must have played a role in owning and accessing lands where clays could be quarried. In this context, control over the clays of north-west Çanaklı should be considered. These were apparently exploited by both sites though not by other Classical/Hellenistic communities. Whereas in its original, Classical, phase, Düzen Tepe seems to have been the larger settlement of the two, possibly commanding more materials and produce, around 200 BC Sagalassos seems to have taken over the lead in the area. The launching at Sagalassos of the production of only quality Hellenistic tableware, implying full, if not unique, access to the clay beds of north-west Çanaklı, seems to confirm the process of increasing control of land and resources by Sagalassos. Unfortunately, the details of contemporary landownership patterns cannot be reconstructed. Unlike the wares of Düzen Tepe, however, the Hellenistic pottery of Sagalassos was distributed to other sites within the wider

---

[20] Neyt (2012: 109–23).
[21] Poblome et al. (2001: 159–64); Degryse and Poblome (2008).
[22] Poblome et al. (2002a); Braekmans et al. (2011).   [23] Poblome et al. (2013a).

study area, which possibly indicates a widening radius of action.[24] Düzen Tepe dwindled from the second century BC onwards, whereas Sagalassos continued to develop. When Sagalassos red slip ware was launched in Augustan times, Sagalassos was not only in control but also had extensive experience with the quality raw clay materials of north-west Çanaklı, while its pottery was also established in a wider zone of distribution.

As a result, when we approach the pots and potters of Roman imperial Sagalassos, it is important to consider their long-term historical background. Pottery production can be considered to have been endemic in the area, possibly from the early days of the formation of the community in the Late Classical period onwards. This implies that knowledge and skill had reached a developed stage as factors of production when Sagalassos red slip ware was launched. This condition could also imply tradition, in the sense that both potters and customers reacted in particular ways to patterns of change and continuity in the market. The continued importance of mastoid drinking cups in the Sagalassos tableware repertoire from mid-Hellenistic times into early Roman imperial times can serve as an example.[25] When, in Augustan times, Sagalassos red slip ware was initiated with a programme of investment in the local Potters' Quarter, more or less the entire Roman world was following the apparent typological attractions of Italian *terra sigillata*.[26] The introduction of a comparable set of tableware in the local Potters' Quarter should have been an option, especially considering new market conditions created by the recent influx of thousands of veterans and their families into the region as a result of Augustus' policy of creating veteran *coloniae* in the wider Pisidian region.[27] In its initial stages, however, Sagalassos red slip ware continued to follow Hellenistic morphological traditions, exemplified by the popularity of the mastoid drinking cups. In other words, existing local processes of ontogenesis and tradition seem to have played a role at Sagalassos, as they did with other types of eastern sigillata.[28] Possibly, such conditions could also have had an effect on aspects such as production organization and market policies, when not everything was done *à la romaine* from day one, if at all.

Apart from aspects of continuity, such as knowledge, skill, and tradition in making pottery, the long-term trajectory also points at shifts. When comparing Düzen Tepe and Sagalassos, or Classical with Roman imperial times, it should be clear that the scale of production as well as the choice of products can be seen to reflect a community's ambitions and potential, and to some extent also its identity. At Düzen Tepe, the partially excavated Classical/Hellenistic potter's

---

[24] Poblome et al. (2013b).
[25] Poblome, Bes, and Lauwers (2007); Poblome et al. (2013b).
[26] Poblome et al. (2002b); Poblome and Zelle (2002); Wallace-Hadrill (2008: 407–21).
[27] Mitchell (1993: 73–9).
[28] For Cypriot Sigillata, see Lund (2002); for Eastern Sigillata B, see Ladstätter (2007).

workshop is so far one of a kind and does not seem to have formed part of a dedicated artisanal neighbourhood. The presence of other workshops should not be ruled out, but there are no indications, archaeological, geophysical, or otherwise, for the presence of such installations in the immediate vicinity. At Sagalassos, a badly damaged mid-Hellenistic potter's kiln was discovered underneath the remains of the Roman imperial odeon. Geophysical analysis provides hints at the presence of five more kiln structures immediately to the east of the excavated example.[29] The evidence is not yet strong enough to be considered as direct proof, but it provides at least fairly substantial indications for the identification of the Hellenistic potters' quarter of Sagalassos. If its location is established by future excavations, the Hellenistic potters' quarter would be located in the (intra-mural) eastern part of the contemporary urban community. Taken together with the incorporation of Hellenistic techniques of production as well as design trends by the potters of Sagalassos, the presence of an area dedicated to mostly potting activities indicates differences of scale from Düzen Tepe. Moreover, these indications imply a relocation of the potters of Sagalassos in early Roman imperial times. The expansion of the contemporary townscape, together with the investment made in the local potter's craft with the launching of Sagalassos red slip ware, presumably resulted in the abandonment of the Hellenistic location and the reorganization of part of the eastern necropolis into an artisanal quarter, which from now on formed part of the eastern suburbs (Fig. 16.4). Some degree of involvement and planning on behalf of the local community must be considered in these operations, especially if we take the afore-mentioned efforts at reforestation of the area into account. In sum, the long-term pattern implies a build-up in importance of the potter's craft for the local communities, from a potter at Classical/Hellenistic Düzen Tepe mostly providing for his own community, resulting in a marginal income to sustain his family, to the Potters' Quarter of Roman imperial Sagalassos, working for markets beyond its own community, representing an asset in a regional investment portfolio.

THE ROMAN IMPERIAL POTTERS' QUARTER OF SAGALASSOS

So, how did things work in the Roman imperial Potters' Quarter of Sagalassos? An initial attempt at reconstructing the local production organization noted the absence of potters' stamps on Sagalassos red slip ware.[30] Such is still the case, preventing the identification of individual potters, their output, or the distribution

---

[29] Poblome et al. (2013b).   [30] Poblome (1996).

Fig. 16.4. Aerial view of the eastern suburbs. The town centre is located in the top part of the image. Photo: Sagalassos Archaeological Research Project.

of their wares, which is, to some degree, possible with other specific types of sigillata, produced mostly in Roman Italy or Gaul.[31] A collection of stamped roof tiles found at Sagalassos was published in the meantime.[32] Of these, one Claudius Alexandros could have been a tile workshop owner, and a member or a freedman of one of the frequently occurring Tiberii Claudii families, holding Roman citizenship. Other stamped personal names included Makedonikos and Demeas. Both could have been tile workshop owners, workmen, or even slaves of an unknown owner. If the stamp *ΠΟΛ* is shorthand for πολέως, then a municipal tile workshop may have existed too. Apart from some smaller categories, so-called *ΕΛΑΙΟΥ* stamps form an important category, possibly referring to a toponym of an olive-oil (and tile-)producing estate. An unpublished study by Philip Mills noted the variety and complexity of signatures and stamps on Sagalassos tiles in comparison to those of other sites studied in the eastern or central Mediterranean. The presence of stamps as well as signatures on a number of pieces suggested that not only tile-makers were represented. Possibly tenant farmers paid for (part of) their rent with the production of tiles, with additional identification of landholdings or landlords. Although tiles represent a different medium from tableware, the attested variety in tile production agents is interesting. This being said, no such

---

[31] Oxé, Comfort, and Kenrick (2000); Hartley and Dickinson (2008–12).
[32] Loots et al. (2000).

evidence at the personal level is available for the reconstruction of the organization of the production of Sagalassos sigillata.[33]

Since 1996, a targeted interdisciplinary research programme has resulted in the excavation of some workshops.[34] In general terms, the workshops of the Potters' Quarter are concentrated in the central zone of the eastern suburbs, totalling 3.5–4 hectares of the latter suburban area. The excavations confirmed the initial laying-out of workshop infrastructure from Augustan times onwards, while the potters moved away from this specialized production environment in the course of the second half of the sixth century AD. At all periods, other activities too, such as burying the dead, were organized in the eastern suburban quarter, which covered 7.5 hectares. Typically, the potters of this neighbourhood made Sagalassos red slip ware, and no other type of ceramic product.[35] Other products and fabrics were established as part of the Sagalassos pottery production repertoire, but these fabrics are linked with clays and possibly places of production in the rural vicinity, adding to the impact and scale of the pottery-producing enterprise.[36] The excavations of complete workshops (Fig. 16.5) as well as the interpretation of large-scale geophysical work in the Potters' Quarter indicated that the traditional

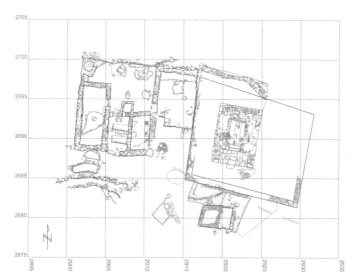

Fig. 16.5. The East Slope Workshops. The original workshop is datable between Augustan times and the first half of the second century AD, and the late Roman phase between the fourth and the sixth centuries AD. Plan: Sagalassos Archaeological Research Project.

[33] Cf. Fülle (1997).
[34] Poblome et al. (2001); Poblome (2006); Murphy and Poblome (2011).
[35] Poblome (1999).   [36] Degryse and Poblome 2008; Neyt et al. 2012.

infrastructural scale of production units is small. However, if we consider their shared use of the raw clay material resource in the north-west part of the Çanaklı Valley for the fabric of Sagalassos red slip ware and the weathered ophiolitic clays found locally or in the Ağlasun Valley for the slip layer, the common concept of design of the Sagalassos tableware vessels, as well as the same markets these workshops were targeting, the concept of production is perhaps best compared to that of nucleated workshops.[37] Even though rows of potters in a single (manu)factory were absent from Sagalassos, I did once propose to the world of Roman ceramic studies the idea that the production of Sagalassos red slip ware constituted a manufactory, based mainly on the collective impact on the urban framework of Sagalassos and the scale of the gross output of the quarter.[38] Thus, depending on the classification criteria, the potters of Sagalassos red slip ware were active in either workshops, nucleated ateliers, or a manufactory. Perhaps this says more about the *rigueur* of the classification exercise and methodology than about the varied life experience of the potters in antiquity.[39] The reality of the local archaeological record is such that there is no easy link between the excavated structural remains of workshops and the mode and scale of the production organization that took place within the attested infrastructure.

Production encompasses all types of activities generating goods and services that are made available to consumers at the appropriate time and place. In essence, production processes are cyclical, in the sense that input in the process generates output, affording the continued investment in input. On the input side, the raw materials that are transformed in the production process are defined as flowing inputs (clays, water, and fuel). Factors of production such as labour (time and ability) and capital (tools, infrastructure, knowledge) are also considered as input. As part of the production process, factors of production add value to the flowing inputs, resulting in the output. Selling the output should generate at least sufficient income to cover the renewal of the flowing inputs as well as sustain the factors of production. Additional income is surplus. The mode of production represents both the scale of input and output, as well as the proportional balance between these. The concept of the 'firm' as developed in New Institutional Economics provides a useful insight into aspects of efficient investment in physical and human capital, governance and incentives for employees.[40] Even in a pre-industrial context, there was a sufficient legal and practical framework to facilitate the economic activity of ancient 'firms'. To be sure, economic activity is more than just production in this respect; distribution, trade, exchange, and

---

[37] On the ophiolitic clays, see Degryse et al. (2008b). On nucleated workshops, see Peacock (1982: 9).

[38] Poblome, Malfitana, and Lund (2001).   [39] Murphy and Poblome (2011).

[40] Frier and Kehoe (2007: 126–34).

consumption are the other side of the coin. Although there is nothing wrong with studying distribution and consumption patterns of wares, I would like to argue that such research needs to be linked to production studies to achieve a more integrated and complete understanding of the operationability of 'firms' in antiquity. Distribution studies in Roman ceramology in particular tend to favour the 'bigger' wares. These are important in many ways, but the evidence is mounting that the local level of pottery production was more than just a niche. In a pre-industrial context, most goods and services consumed by communities were typically produced in a local or regional setting. More or less organized production units came and went in a constant but unsystematic way. The longevity and sustainability of the production process interplay with the mode of production.

The region of south-west Anatolia forms a good example in this respect. In 2012, evidence was presented for seven pottery production centres, at or within the territories of Balboura (Middle Hellenistic and Late Roman), Kibyra (Late(?) Hellenistic to Early Byzantine), Patara (Late Roman to Early Byzantine), Xanthos (Late Roman to Early Byzantine), Araxa (Roman imperial), Pednelissos (Late Roman to Early Byzantine) and Sagalassos.[41] No doubt, more production units are still out there to be discovered, but what there is should be illustrative of the importance of the local/regional level of production, and its variation in time, space, and output, as well as how the 'bigger' wares form only part of the ceramological picture of this region—in a lot of cases even a relatively small part. More work needs to be done on aspects of production, distribution, and consumption of these local/regional south-west Anatolian wares, integrating hard-core ceramology with archaeometry and conceptual archaeological approaches.

One of the factors that can help explain the impact of these different types of local/regional pottery is investment.[42] The latter mechanism can be added to each segment of the production process, from exploiting more clays to employing more potters or developing technologies. Potters can make investments themselves, using generated surplus, but the higher modes of production can also attract third-party investment.

The open question is whether the production of Sagalassos red slip ware was entirely in the hands of potters or whether (other) investors were involved as well. I have argued in the past for a third-party investment model, partly based on the nature of the raw clay materials.[43] My null hypothesis was double: if each potter at Sagalassos was running his own workshop, variety in raw clay materials, fabrics, and slips of Sagalassos red slip ware should be expected, and, if archaeometric evidence proved uniform clay, fabric, and slip compositions, the total amount of clays quarried from such unique locations should suggest

[41] Armstrong (2012: 35–8).   [42] Poblome, Malfitana, and Lund (2011).
[43] Poblome (1996, 2006).

large-scale landownership beyond the traditionally expected means and social position of 'simple' potters. The provenance and the diachronic unchanging nature of the raw clay materials are sufficiently established in the case of Sagalassos red slip ware.[44] What is more, different, but technically viable clay resources were identified in the north part of the Çanaklı Valley, located closer to Sagalassos, which were apparently not used for Sagalassos tableware.[45] The non-selection of the latter clays was interpreted as being linked with land property rights, where the owner(s) of the lands in the north part of the valley could or would not consider converting agricultural land to a clay quarry. The owner(s) of land in the north-west part of the valley, on the other hand, were considered to have used access to their clay beds as an asset in their ownership and investment portfolio, but also, taking the scale of the enterprise into account, to have been in a position to discriminate against other landowners, such as the ones in the north part of the Çanaklı Valley.

Knowing now that the north-west Çanaklı clays were exploited from Classical/Hellenistic times into the seventh century AD I no longer consider it plausible to presume such a static, limited, and high-profile pattern of landownership over a millennium or so. The attested variety in Sagalassos tile production agents can be seen as an indication to allow more flexibility as far as landownership and clay exploitation rights are concerned. Tradition of use as well as proven qualities of the raw materials directed attention mostly to the north-west Çanaklı clays. This aspect of path dependency can be combined with more varied and evolving patterns of landownership and estate management, allowing more parties to be a stakeholder in the Sagalassos tableware production process. Estates could have been of variable size, and their owner had the choice whether and to what extent to exploit the raw clay materials on the property. This scenario also gives the potters more breathing space, in the sense that they could choose from which landowner to acquire clays, for how much, and for how long. Both parties had to come to an agreement, but both had options. Possibly, as suggested in the case of tile production, landownership and the leasing of rights to produce pottery need not have been only private. Rents from the leasing of public lands are known to have represented additional sources of income for the cities of Asia Minor, at times managed by a specific public official.[46]

In cases where historical information is available on the ownership of clays or lands on which clays were quarried, the evidence indicates private ownership of the raw materials by the landlord. Raw clay materials were made available to potters as part of work or lease contracts.[47] In the same way, juridical sources

---

[44] Degryse and Poblome (2008); Degryse et al. (2008b).

[45] Degryse et al. (2003).

[46] Macro (1980: 684). For Laodikeia on the Lykos, see Corsten (1997: 97–9); for Colossae: *IGR* 4.870.

[47] Mees (2002: 253).

indicate that the matrix for usufruct of clays is leasing agreements on private landownership.[48] In his study of the relationship between Roman private law and the rural economy Dennis Kehoe highlights the imperial policies of privileging management systems based on small-scale landholding and tenancy on imperial estates, instead of promoting the social and economic interests of the landowning elite. Also on private land, state policy promoted the security of land tenure as a form of stable and long-term management, while striking a careful balance with protecting the property rights of landowners. Although this was not at all intended to preclude large-scale landowning by members of the social elite, the latter mostly put management systems in place based on small-scale tenants cultivating the estates. In Kehoe's view, the produce of small-scale farming represented the core of the Roman economy.[49] Therefore, the general pattern of expectancy, also in the case of the north-west section of the Çanaklı Valley, seems to be that tenancy played a role in exploiting rural properties and the raw clay materials these contained and that there was a variety of players in the field. In this way, our idea of the degree to which the Sagalassos elite were involved in Sagalassos red slip ware becomes dependent on more general issues of our reconstruction of the Roman economy.

The Çanaklı Valley has not yet been intensively surveyed. Geo-archaeological fieldwork located the clay source area in its north-west zone and determined an extent of 62.5 hectares within which clays were quarried in antiquity and a wider area of 288.86 hectares within which clays could have been quarried. The fact that modern brick factories have been extracting substantial amounts of clays especially in the north-west part of the valley could have destroyed the archaeological record to some extent, including traces of the presumed farming estates. The presence of a small, Roman imperial rock-cut necropolis at the edge of that part of the valley where the clays were quarried, which was originally associated with the clay-quarrying activities, is perhaps better inter-preted as the final resting place of the farmers who lived and worked nearby.[50] Indeed, the clay-quarrying activities were seasonal at best and did not need to result in permanent occupation of the area, as the destination of the raw material was Sagalassos. The farmers, on the other hand, may have considered the community necropolis as the translation of their permanent link with these lands. The fact that, although a new Potters' Quarter was laid out with the early Roman imperial initiation of Sagalassos red slip ware and that this ware uniquely used north-west Çanaklı clays for its fabric, there was no intention to locate the potting infrastructure in this valley, is a further indication that the potters considered themselves part of the urban community of Sagalassos: they are likely to have been buried there and not in the north-west Çanaklı necropolis.

---

[48] Wieling (2000: 10-b, 17-b).   [49] Kehoe (2007a).
[50] For the original interpretation, see Waelkens et al. (2000: 199).

WHERE ARE ALL THE PEOPLE?

It is very difficult to establish the social status of the individuals involved in pottery production. Moreover, status may have differed between owners and tenants of land and facilities, workshop managers and craftsmen, while, depending on scale, these roles could have been combined in one person. In so far as the evidence of stamps on Italian sigillata is relevant, variation in the practice and meaning of stamping varied widely between different workshops, combining slaves, freedmen, and freeborn.[51] What is perhaps more important is how these different social backgrounds were typically combined within *familia* or extended households as basic training, production, business, and juridical units, allowing a fairly flexible, mutually dependent, and to some extent sustainable management strategy.[52] Along with the local/regional scale of production, the *familia* as typical operational matrix represented the hallmarks of the artisanate in Roman antiquity. To be sure, management policies based on social dependency were restrictive in the sense that genuine social advancement for the not already privileged was very limited, but this embedded condition was buffered by the fact that investment and initiative could be shouldered by a socially diverse, yet networked unit, granting relative operational independence.

The scale at which pottery workshops operated was in balance with this social context. Throughout the empire, successful tableware brands were produced by clusters of fairly autonomous workshops, generally quite modest in their layout. As attested in the case of the transition from the Hellenistic to the Roman imperial Potters' Quarter at Sagalassos, some growth was possible, but this was generally less dependent on direct investment by upper classes in production infrastructure—they kept their fortunes mostly tied to the land— and more on how the elite created favourable conditions in the urban economy in order to market the surplus from their landed estates, as well as the level of income in the hands of small landholders and tenants, creating opportunities for enterprising, economically independent (but possibly socially tied) craftsmen.[53]

Successful types of tableware did not generate economies of scale or manufactories; rather the basic and economically independent production unit of the workshop was multiplied. When opportunity arose, loosely integrated networks of artisans and workshops were created based on subcontracting arrangements, possibly formulated in terms of *locatio-conductio*.[54] Third parties, such as

---

[51] Oxé, Comfort, and Kenrick (2000: 15–24).

[52] Frier and Kehoe (2007: 133). For the juridical framework of work in *familia* context, see Drexhage, Konen, and Ruffing (2002: 105–7).

[53] Kehoe (2007b: 559–66).

[54] Drexhage, Konen, and Ruffing (2002: 107–12); Wieling (2000).

members of the social elite, could also issue contracts in these terms, possibly in conjunction with providing access for tenants to raw materials and workshop infrastructure.

In case sufficient critical mass in craft production was reached, *collegia* could be founded. These voluntary associations of professionals traditionally offered opportunities for sociability and conviviality, communal religious celebrations, a degree of social competition, and visibility in the local community.[55] In New Institutional Economics terms, *collegia* could also represent a so-called private-order enforcement network, representing an alternative organizational form next to the market and the firm. The entrepreneurial members preferred to close contracts for goods and services within such networks, not because this was necessarily cheaper—on the contrary, network membership will have represented some additional cost—but mainly because the concerns for maintaining individual professional reputation and mutual respect proved a guarantee for the execution of the contract, in accordance with the clauses of good faith typical for *locatio-conductio* type of agreements.[56] Whether *collegia* worked exactly according to the logic of private-order enforcement networks is impossible to prove, but professional associations have sufficient social functions, allowing a good level of acquaintance between their members.

HOW DID THIS WORK ON THE GROUND?

Research into the Potters' Quarter of Sagalassos is a testimony to the research history of the Sagalassos Archaeological Research Project, as well as, in some respects, to the evolution of archaeological fieldwork on classical Mediterranean sites in general. While excavations were intermittent, each time in answer to a different set of research questions forming part of the wider interdisciplinary research agenda of the project, the introduction of large-scale geophysical research around the turn of the millennium laid the foundations for a more complete understanding of the area.[57] By 2013 the excavations had covered about 3 per cent of the study area. Geophysical prospecting extended over almost the entire area (Fig. 16.6). Between the first and the sixth centuries AD, the plateau to the east of the local theatre can be defined as the eastern suburbs of Sagalassos, referring to how, besides the making of pottery tablewares, other activities also made it into a busy place.[58] The second most commonly documented features were the burial grounds, gardens, and monuments of the east necropolis, located mainly in the north and

---

[55] Van Nijf (1997); Zimmermann (2002).   [56] Hawkins (2012).
[57] Martens et al. (2012).
[58] Excavation and Ph.D. research results by Johan Claeys, University of Leuven.

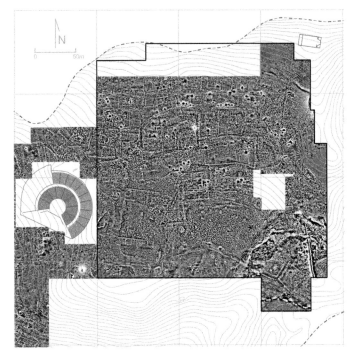

Fig. 16.6. The results of geophysical prospection in the eastern suburbs. Image: Sagalassos Archaeological Research Project.

east zones of the quarter.[59] These slopes were the most visible to those entering the eastern suburbs from the east access road into town. The church that was discovered in the north-east section possibly continued the funerary and communal functions into Early Byzantine times.[60] A street network accessed the various suburban parts, often combined with water infrastructure. Aqueducts provided fresh water to the centre of Sagalassos and smaller channels and pipelines serviced the suburbs. In the south-east area a couple of small-scale limestone quarries were located, and, as mentioned, near the south-east opening of the so-called central depression of the eastern suburbs ophiolithic clays were extracted.[61] The latter activity stopped in the course of the first century AD, after which the quarry pits were backfilled and the terrain re-purposed as part of the necropolis. A core-drilling programme provided indications for (communal?) waste-dumping practices in the central depression.[62] The general excavation and survey programme at Sagalassos has provided indications of other craft activities, such as fulling, metal-working, glass-making, and bone-cutting.[63]

---

[59] Köse (2005).   [60] Fieldwork coordinated by Femke Martens in 2007. Unpublished.
[61] Degryse et al. (2008c).   [62] Degryse et al. (2003).
[63] De Cupere, van Neer, and Lentacker (1993); Lauwers et al. (2005).

Although some of these are presumed to have been located in the eastern suburbs, by 2013 no actual traces had been discovered here.

From the geophysical overview, twenty-five workshop areas can be defined and eighty-nine kilns. After the excavations, another nine workshops and eighteen kilns could be added to these totals, with attested average life spans of about two centuries. These are conservative estimates. The more northerly reaches of the quarter have not yet been systematically covered by the geophysics team, mainly because of the nature of the terrain, which is partly covered in mountain screes. At Site F in 2011, however, in a location beyond the geophysical overview, new workshop remains were located, including a badly preserved kiln.[64] It will always remain difficult to present a final complete picture of the quarter, as excavations have also indicated that kiln remains and walls of workshops can be blurred for geophysics if they lie deeper in the stratigraphy or are badly preserved or partly overbuilt by later structures. Moreover, the geophysical results are non-chronological, revealing no aspects of chronological allocation or evolution through time. Furthermore, by workshop areas I mean something different from workshops *pur sang*. The latter can be fully established only upon excavation. 'Workshop area' represents a more general site definition, encompassing walls and kilns, within which one or more workshops could have been operational. The workshop area of the so-called Coroplast Workshops (Fig. 16.7), for example, revealed the existence of at least six workshop units upon excavation, while the East Slope Workshops (see Fig. 16.5) are actually two consecutive ateliers.[65] Although no indications have yet been found, it also cannot be excluded that some craft activities other than tableware production were being organized in these workshop areas. Be that as it may be, the workshop areas seem to make up their own clustered neighbourhood on the centrally located, middle terraces of the eastern suburbs. The question arises as to how far the move away from the Hellenistic workshops and the dedicated function of the artisanal part of the eastern suburbs reflected planning and management coordinated by the city council. Indeed, an artisanal cluster of between 3.5 and 4 hectares can hardly have grown spontaneously. Lack of relevant comparative material makes it difficult to judge just how important the quarter could have been in the urban landscape, society, and economy. The estimation of the Potters' Quarter compares to the 25.2 hectares reconstructed for residential purposes, the 37.5 hectares for the urbanized area of Sagalassos, and the *c.*90 hectares that included the necropolis and suburban functions. Based on these figures, the local population has been estimated at less than 10,000—possibly between 2,500 and 3,750 inhabitants.[66]

Although the early imperial relocation of the tableware craft away from its Hellenistic quarter and into this new neighbourhood has already been attested in two excavated workshops and associated pottery waste dumps, it does not

---

[64] Excavations at Site F 2011 were supervised by Johan Claeys. Unpublished.
[65] Murphy and Poblome (2011).   [66] Willet (2012: 182–3).

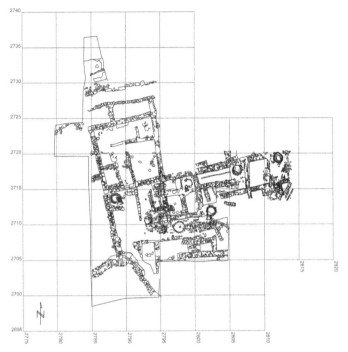

Fig. 16.7. The so-called Coroplast workshops, fourth to sixth centuries AD. Plan: Sagalassos Archaeological Research Project.

seem to be the case that the new Potters' Quarter was packed into all its corners at once, but that the scenario was one of gradual yet steady growth. As excavating all the workshops is impossible and unnecessary, the evolution in production can best be approached from output curves of Sagalassos red slip ware. In a previous paper, output data were reconstructed based on the urban survey results and a range of selected excavated deposits from the wider urban excavation programme.[67] Output and presumed amount of workshops peaked between Flavian and Severan times and again between the Leonid dynasty and the reign of Justinian. Although the estimated output is lower in the intervening period, there are no typo-chronological indications that production of Sagalassos red slip ware was interrupted in late Roman times. That being the case, the local weather conditions, especially in winter, need to be taken into account, as these made year-round craft production impossible. These conditions must have affected general patterns in demand for goods and services too, with life running in different cycles in winter. The climate conditions, together with the social context of production already discussed, imply that large-scale, vertically integrated manufactories with permanently employed

[67] Poblome et al. (2013c).

staff were not a feasible management scenario, and that small-sized, flexible solutions were favoured instead.

This is also the type of workshop that has been documented in the excavations. The ateliers typically contain one or two kilns each, and a couple of rooms and spaces with specific functions in the production process (Fig. 16.8). The attestation of sometimes three potter's wheel installations in one workshop and the finding of sets of tools with engraved names within another workshop setting indicate that, generally, a couple of craftsmen were involved in each separate workshop.[68] On the ground floor, no signs that the potters were also living in these ateliers have been found, and none of the workshops studied seems to have had an upper floor, all of which implies that the craftsmen rented or owned a small house somewhere else in town. Private workshop ownership within the *familia* as a typical operational nucleus seems plausible.[69] As with anything in the real world, things will have been more complicated in this respect too. The fact that architectural changes in layout and function of the different workshops involved in making Early Byzantine mould-made products seem to be happening more or less simultaneously could possibly hint at a third-party stakeholder in the production process. Workshops also seem to specialize and restrict their output to

Fig. 16.8. 2013 aerial view of the so-called Coroplast workshops, fourth to sixth centuries AD. Photo: Sagalassos Archaeological Research Project.

---

[68] Murphy and Poblome (2012).
[69] This depends on more general patterns of reconstruction of the ancient economy and how much non-elite members of society were allowed to breathe. Cf. Scheidel and Friesen (2009).

a specific set of types of the general typology of Sagalassos red slip ware, creating options for collaboration on orders or contracts.[70]

So far, no *collegium* of potters has been attested at Sagalassos, epigraphically or otherwise. The dedication *IGR* 3.360 was set up in the later second–third centuries AD in the area of the south Gate into Sagalassos by ἡ συντεχνία τῶν βαφέων to support the statue of its local patron and imperial high priest Aelius Quintus Claudius Philippianus Varus in honour of his funding gladiatorial games. This is the only local reference to a craftsmen association, but at least it indicates the phenomenon was not unknown at Sagalassos.[71] It is, however, possible that, if there was a role for public and/or sacred landownership in the section of the Çanaklı Valley where the clays for the local tableware industry were dug, a religious association emerged, instead of an association of potters.[72]

The preliminary interpretation of an unpublished structure excavated since 2011 at the west edge of the artisanal zone within the eastern suburbs could provide further indications for *il fenomeno associativo* (Fig. 16.9).[73] The

Fig. 16.9. Aerial view of the presumed early Roman imperial *Vereinshaus*. Photo: Sagalassos Archaeological Research Project.

---

[70] Excavation and Ph.D. research results by Elizabeth Murphy, Brown University.

[71] See Brandt (1992: 137–9) for other craftsmen and professional associations attested in the ancient regions of Pamphylia and Pisidia, with potters epigraphically represented at Baris.

[72] On sacred landownership, see Dignas (2005) and Zuiderhoek (2009: 37–52).

[73] Excavations at Site PQ2 2011, 2012, 2013, and 2014 were supervised by Johan Claeys, Sven Van Haelst, and Peter Talloen. See also <http://journal.antiquity.ac.uk/projgall/poblome342> (accessed 8 July 2015).

original phase of the building was erected around the middle of the first century AD. It was rectangular in ground plan (10.4 × 9 m), with its entrance from the street on the north side. Against the inside of the back wall a water feature was built (1.7 × 2.8 m). Around 100 AD, the building was extended on its south side (10.2 × 12.3 m) and a new entrance created in the south wall. After a while, three smaller rooms were created in the north part of the building, the water feature levelled, and the floor level raised. No direct evidence related to the function of the building was found, yet its location at the interface between the town and the artisanal quarter, its simple rectangular plan forming one (articulated) space inside, the width and finish of its entrances, the quality of part of its wall construction using ashlars, the presence of the water feature, and the absence of functional indicators make it stand out in the building corpus of the area. Moreover, during the second half of the second century AD, a dump accumulated against the outer east wall with concentrations of discarded sets of tableware mixed with particular parts of some goats/sheep, pigs, and mainly cattle, which would have provided low-quality meat. The waste is indicative of a soup kitchen, and its association with the building under excavation hints at practices of communal dining and sociability. That the building was designed to receive groups of people became clear in 2014, when in three of these rooms enormous quantities of archaeological material were found, as though they were left only yesterday; in fact, they date to around AD 270. The finds include objects made of materials such as metal and carved bone, as well as glass flasks and drinking cups, oil lamps, and large quantities of ceramic tableware. Many of the latter, especially bowls and dishes, were preserved intact and discovered upside down, containing original food remains. These finds seem to relate to ancient communal dining practices involving dozens of participants. The tableware and food remains were not tidied away, but rather thrown along the walls of the building and left behind; this was a one-off event, not resulting from accumulation and seemingly associated with the end of the building as such. Although the excavation needs to be completed and preferably an inscription found, at this stage I should like to propose, as a working hypothesis, that the group of people that made use of this building could have been an association, albeit of an unidentified nature.[74]

The final identification of this building should be helpful, but, in the meantime, the collected evidence on the potters of Sagalassos is already enough to further sustain recognition of and research into the ancient middle classes.[75] Social and economic historians are warming to the idea not only that the main sector of the Roman economy, agriculture, could not depend solely on elite

---

[74] Published parallels from Asia Minor are unknown to me. In so far as the situation in contemporary Italy is helpful, see Bollmann (1998).

[75] Mayer (2012).

landowners, requiring the crucial involvement of small-scale farmers and tenants to develop successfully, but also that towns, that other playground of elite investment in representative projects, could not come to life without the participation of proficient craftsmen, merchants, professionals, and entrepreneurs. The archaeology of Sagalassos will, it is hoped, further develop in this respect. In the meantime, this community should most of all be considered as one of many other such provincial towns in the Roman Empire, fostering active groups of artisans contributing to all aspects of urban life in antiquity.

ACKNOWLEDGEMENTS

The research for this paper was supported by the Belgian Programme on Interuniversity Poles of Attraction (IAP 07/09), the Research Fund of the University of Leuven (GOA 13/04), and Projects G.0562.11 and G. 0637.15 of the Research Foundation Flanders (FWO). The archaeometric analyses were carried out at the Leuven Centre for Archaeological Sciences. I wish to acknowledge the most excellent excavation qualities of Elizabeth Murphy, Johan Claeys, Sven Van Haelst, and Peter Talloen, who shared the adventure of working in the eastern suburbs. Arjan Zuiderhoek most kindly commented on the early stages of this chapter's composition.

REFERENCES

Armstrong, P. (2012). 'The Survey Pottery: Hellenistic and Later', in J. J. Coulton (ed.), *The Balboura Survey and Settlement in Highland Southwest Anatolia*, 2. *The Balboura Survey: Detailed Studies and Catalogues* (British Institute at Ankara Monograph, 43). London, 31–82.

Arnold, D. E. (1985). *Ceramic Theory and Cultural Process*. Cambridge.

Bintliff, J. (2011). 'The Death Of Archaeological Theory?', in J. Bintliff and M. Pearce (eds), *The Death of Archaeological Theory?* Oxford, 7–22.

Bollmann, B. (1998). *Römische Vereinshäuser: Untersuchungen zu den Scholae der römischen Berufs-, Kult-, und Augustalen-Kollegien in Italien*. Mainz.

Braekmans, D., Degryse, P., Poblome, J., Neyt, B., Vyncke, K., and Waelkens, M. (2011). 'Understanding Ceramic Variability: An Archaeometrical Interpretation of the Classical and Hellenistic Ceramics at Düzen Tepe and Sagalassos (Southwest Turkey)', *Journal of Archaeological Science* 38: 2101–15.

Brandt, H. (1992). *Gesellschaft und Wirtschaft Pamphyliens und Pisidiens im Altertum* (Asia Minor Studien, 7). Bonn.

Corsten, T. (ed.) (1997). *Die Inschriften von Laodikeia am Lykos* (Inschriften Griechischer Städte aus Kleinasien, 49). Bonn.

De Cupere, B., van Neer, W., and Lentacker, A. (1993). 'Some Aspects of the Bone-Working Industry in Roman Sagalassos', in Waelkens and Poblome (1993), 269–78.

Degryse, P., and Poblome, J. (2008). 'Clays for Mass Production of Table and Common Ware, Amphorae and Architectural Ceramics at Sagalassos', in Degryse and Waelkens (2008), 231–54.

Degryse, P., and Waelkens, M. (eds) (2008). *Geo- and Bio-Archaeology at Sagalassos and in its Territory* (Sagalassos, 6). Leuven.

Degryse, P., Poblome, J., Donners, K., Deckers, J., and Waelkens, M. (2003). 'Geoarchaeological Investigations of the "Potters' Quarter" at Sagalassos, Southwest Turkey', *Geoarchaeology* 18: 255–81.

Degryse, P., Muchez, P., Sintubin, M., Clijsters, A., Viaene, W., Dederen, M., Schrooten, P., and Waelkens, M. (2008a). 'The Geology of the Area around the Ancient City of Sagalassos', in Degryse and Waelkens (2008), 17–24.

Degryse, P., Poblome, J., Viaene, W., Kucha, H., Ottenburgs, R., Waelkens, M., and Naud, J. (2008b). 'Provenancing the Slip of Sagalassos Red Slip Ware', in Degryse and Waelkens (2008), 255–60.

Degryse, P., Heldal, T., Bloxam, E., Storemyr, P., Waelkens, M., and Muchez, P. (2008c). 'The Sagalassos Quarry Landscape: Bringing Quarries in Context', in Degryse and Waelkens (2008), 261–90.

Dignas, B. (2002). *Economy of the Sacred in Hellenistic and Roman Asia Minor.* Oxford.

Dignas, B. (2005). 'Sacred Revenues in Roman Hands: The Economic Dimension of Sanctuaries in Western Asia Minor', in S. Mitchell and C. Katsari (eds), *Patterns in the Economy of Roman Asia Minor.* Swansea, 207–24.

Drexhage, H.-J., Konen, H., and Ruffing, K. (2002). *Die Wirtschaft des Römischen Reiches (1.-3. Jahrhundert): Eine Einführung.* Berlin.

Frier, B. W., and Kehoe, D. P. (2007). 'Law and Economic Institutions', in Scheidel et al. (2007), 113–43.

Fülle, G. (1997). 'The Internal Organization of the Arretine Terra Sigillata Industry: Problems of Evidence and Interpretation', *JRS* 87: 111–55.

Hartley, B. R., and Dickinson, B. M. (2008–12). *Names on Terra Sigillata: An Index of Makers' Stamps and Signatures on Gallo-Roman Terra Sigillata (Samian Ware)*, vols 1–8. London.

Hawkins, C. (2012). 'Manufacturing', in W. Scheidel (ed.), *The Cambridge Companion to the Roman Economy.* Cambridge, 175–94.

Jones, A. H. M. (1940). *The Greek City from Alexander to Justinian.* Oxford.

Kehoe, D. P. (2007a). *Law and the Rural Economy in the Roman Empire.* Ann Arbor, MI.

Kehoe, D. P. (2007b). 'The Early Roman Empire: Production', in Scheidel, Morris, and Saller (2007), 543–69.

Köse, V. (2005). *Nekropolen und Grabdenkmäler von Sagalassos in Pisidien in hellenistischer und römischer Zeit* (Studies in Eastern Mediterranean Archaeology, 7). Turnhout.

Ladstätter, S. (2007). 'Mode oder politisches Manifest? Überlegungen zur Übernahme römischen Formenguts in die frühkaiserzeitliche Keramik von Ephesos', in Meyer (2007), 203–20.

Lauwers, V., Degryse, P., Poblome, J., and Waelkens, M. (2005). 'Le Verre de Sagalassos: De nouvelles preuves d'une production locale de verre', *Bulletin de l'association française pour l'archéologie du verre* 26–9.

Loots, L., Waelkens, M., Clarysse, W., Poblome, J., and Hübner, G. (2000). 'A Catalogue of the Tile Stamps found at Sagalassos', in Waelkens and Loots (2000), 685–96.

Lucas, G. (2012). *Understanding the Archaeological Record*. Cambridge.

Lund, J. (2002). 'The Ontogenesis of Cypriot Sigillata', in A. Rathje, M. Nielsen, and B. Bundgaard Rasmussen (eds), *Pots for the Living: Pots for the Dead* (Acta Hyperborea, 9). Copenhagen, 185–223.

Macro, A. D. (1980). 'The Cities of Asia Minor under the Roman Imperium', in H. Temporini and W. Haase (eds), *Aufstieg und Niedergang der Römischen Welt II*, 7.2. Berlin, 658–97.

Martens, F., Mušič, B., Poblome, J., and Waelkens, M. (2012). 'The Integrated Urban Survey at Sagalassos', in F. Vermeulen, G.-J. Burgers, S. Keay, and C. Corsi (eds), *Urban Landscape Survey in Italy and the Mediterranean*. Oxford, 84–93.

Mayer, E. (2012). *The Ancient Middle Classes: Urban Life in the Roman Empire 100 BC–250 AD*. Cambridge, MA.

Mees, A. W. (2002). *Organisationsformen römischer Töpfer-Manufakturen am Beispiel von Arezzo und Rheinzabern unter Berücksichtigung von Papyri, Inschriften und Rechtsquellen* (Römisch-Germanisches Zentralmuseum. Forschungsinstitut für Vor- und Frühgeschichte Monographien, 52). Mainz.

Meyer, M. (ed.) (2007). *Neue Zeiten–neue Sitten: Zu Rezeption und Integration römischen und italischen Kulturguts in Kleinasien* (Wiener Forschungen zur Archäologie, 12). Vienna.

Mitchell, S. (1993). *Anatolia. Land, Men, and Gods in Asia Minor, 1. The Celts and the Impact of Roman Rule*. Oxford.

Mitchell, S., and Waelkens, M. (1988). 'Cremna and Sagalassus 1987', *Anatolian Studies* 38: 53–64.

Muchez, P., Lens, S., Degryse, P., Callebaut, K., Dederen, M., Hertogen, J., Joachimski, M., Keppens, E., Ottenburgs, R., Schroyen, K., and Waelkens, M. (2008). 'Petrography, Mineralogy and Geochemistry of the Rocks in the Area of the Archaeological Site of Sagalassos', in Degryse and Waelkens (2008), 25–52.

Murphy, E. and Poblome, J. (2011). 'Producing Pottery *vs* Producing Models: Interpreting Workshop Organization at the Potters' Quarter of Sagalassos', in M. L. Lawall and J. Lund (eds), *Pottery in the Archaeological Record: A View from the Greek World* (Gösta Enbom Monographs, 1). Aarhus, 30–6.

Murphy, E., and Poblome, J. (2012). 'Technical and Social Considerations of Tools from Roman-Period Ceramic Workshops at Sagalassos (Southwest Turkey): Not Just Tools of the Trade?', *Journal of Mediterranean Archaeology* 25: 69–89.

Neyt, B. (2012). 'Mineralogical Resources for Ceramic Production in the Territory of Sagalassos: A Geochemical, Mineralogical And Petrographical Study'. Unpublished Ph.D. thesis, University of Leuven.

Neyt, B., Braekmans, D., Poblome, J., Elsen, J., Waelkens, M., and Degryse, P. (2012). 'Long-term Clay Raw Material Selection and Use in the Region of Classical/Hellenistic to Early Byzantine Sagalassos (South-West Turkey)', *Journal of Archaeological Science* 39: 1296–305.

Nijf, O. M. van (1997). *The Civic World of Professional Associations in the Roman East* (Dutch Monographs on Ancient History and Archaeology, 17). Amsterdam.

Oxé, A., Comfort, H., and Kenrick, P. (2000). *Corpus vasorum arretinorum: A Catalogue of the Signatures, Shapes and Chronology of Italian Aigillata* (Abhandlungen zur Vor- und Frühgeschichte, zur Klassischen und Provinzial-Römischen Archäologie und zur Geschichte des Altertums, 41). Bonn.

Paulissen, E., Poesen, J., Govers, G., and De Ploey, J. (1993). 'The Physical Environment at Sagalassos (Western Taurus, Turkey): A Reconnaissance Survey', in Waelkens and Poblome (1993), 229–47.

Peacock, D. P. S. (1982). *Pottery in the Roman World: An Ethnoarchaeological Approach.* London.

Poblome, J. (1996). 'Production and Distribution of Sagalassos Red Slip Ware: A Dialogue with the Roman Economy', in M. Herfort-Koch, U. Mandel, and U. Schädler (eds), *Hellenistische und kaiserzeitliche Keramik des östlichen Mittelmeergebietes.* Frankfurt am Main, 75–103.

Poblome, J. (1999). *Sagalassos Red Slip Ware: Typology and Chronology* (Studies in Eastern Mediterranean Archaeology, 2). Turnhout.

Poblome, J. (2006). 'Made in Sagalassos: Modelling Regional Potential and Constraints', in S. Menchelli and M. Paquinucci (eds), *Territorio e produzioni ceramiche: Paesaggi, economia e società in età romana* (Instrumenta, 2). Pisa, 355–63.

Poblome, J., and Zelle, M. (2002). 'The Tableware Boom. A Socio-Economic Perspective from Western Asia Minor', in C. Berns, H. Van Hesberg, L. Vandeput, and M. Waelkens (eds), *Patris und Imperium: Kulturelle und politische Identität in den Städten der römischen Provinzen Kleinasiens in der frühen Kaiserzeit.* Leuven, 275–87.

Poblome, J., Bes, P., and Lauwers, V. (2007). 'Winning Hearts, Minds and Stomachs? Artefactual or Artificial Evidence for Romanization', in Meyer (2007), 221–32.

Poblome, J., Malfitana, D., and Lund, J. (2011). 'Investing in Roman Antiquity. Modelling Moderate Growth', *FACTA: A Journal of Roman Material Culture Studies* 5: 9–13.

Poblome, J., Bounegru, O., Degryse, P., Viaene, W., Waelkens, M., and Erdemgil, S. (2001). 'The Sigillata Manufactories of Pergamon and Sagalassos', *JRA* 14: 143–65.

Poblome, J., Degryse, P., Viaene, W., Ottenburgs, R., Waelkens, M., Degeest, R., and Naud, J. (2002a). 'The Concept of a Pottery Production Centre: An Archaeometrical Contribution from Ancient Sagalassos', *Journal of Archaeological Science* 29: 873–82.

Poblome, J., Degryse, P., Viaene, W., and Waelkens, M. (2002b). 'An Augustan Pottery Workshop at Sagalassos', in V. Kilikoglou, A. Hein, and Y. Maniatis (eds), *Modern Trends in Scientific Studies on Ancient Ceramics* (BAR International Series, 1011). Oxford, 335–41.

Poblome, J., Braekmans, D., Waelkens, M., Fırat, N., Vanhaverbeke, H., Kaptijn, E., Martens, F., Vyncke, K., Willet, R., and Degryse, P. (2013a). 'How did Sagalassos Come to be? A Ceramological Survey', in M. Tekocak (ed.), *Studies in Honour of K. Levent Zoroğlu.* Antalya, 527–40.

Poblome, J., Braekmans, D., Mušič, B., Van Der Enden, M., Neyt, B., De Graeve, B., and Degryse, P. (2013b). 'A Pottery Kiln underneath the Odeon of Ancient Sagalassos, South-West Turkey: The Excavation Results, the Table Wares and their Archaeometrical Analysis', in N. Fenn and C. Römer-Strehl (eds), *Networks in the*

Hellenistic World according to the Pottery in the Eastern Mediterranean and Beyond. (BAR International Series, 2539). Oxford, 193–204.

Poblome, J., Willet, R., Fırat, N., Martens, F., and Bes, P. (2013c). 'Tinkering with Urban Survey Data: How Many Sagalassos-es do we Have?', in P. Johnson and M. Millett (eds), *Archaeological Survey and the City* (University of Cambridge Museum of Classical Archaeology Monograph, 2). Oxford, 146–74.

Scheidel, W., and Friesen, S. J. (2009). 'The Size of the Economy and the Distribution of Income in the Roman Empire', *JRS* 99: 61–91.

Scheidel, W., Morris I., and Saller, R. (eds) (2007). *The Cambridge Economic History of the Greco-Roman World.* Cambridge.

Six, S. (2004). 'Holocene Geomorphological Evolution of the Territory of Sagalassos. Contribution to the Palaeo-Environmental Reconstruction of Southwest Turkey'. Unpublished Ph.D. thesis, University of Leuven.

Talloen, P., Daems, D., Beaujean, B., and Poblome, J. (2015). 'The 2014 control excavations on the Upper Agora of Sagalassos', *ANMtD. News of Archaeology from Anatolia's Mediterranean Areas* 13: 99–107.

Vanhaverbeke, H., Waelkens, M., Vyncke, K., De Laet, V., Aydal, S., Mušič, B., De Cupere, B., Poblome, J., Braekmans, D., Degryse, P., Marinova, E., Verstraeten, G., van Neer, W., Šlapšak, B., Medarič, I., Ekinci, H. A., and Erbay, M. O. (2010). 'Pisidian Culture? The Classical–Hellenistic Site at Düzen Tepe near Sagalassus (Southwest Turkey)', *Anatolian Studies* 60: 105–28.

Vermoere, M. (2004). *Holocene Vegetation History in the Territory of Sagalassos (Southwest Turkey): A Palynological Approach* (Studies in Eastern Mediterranean Archaeology, 6). Turnhout.

Vermoere, M., Six, S., Poblome, J., Degryse, P., Paulissen, E., Waelkens, M., and Smets, E. (2003). 'Pollen Sequences from the City of Sagalassos (Pisidia, southwest Turkey)', *Anatolian Studies* 53: 161–73.

Waelkens, M., and Loots, L. (eds) (2000). *Report on the Survey and Excavation Campaigns of 1996 and 1997* (Sagalassos, 5). Leuven.

Waelkens, M., and Poblome, J. (eds) (1993). *Report on the Third Excavation Campaign of 1992* (Sagalassos, 2). Leuven.

Waelkens, M., Vanhaverbeke, H., Paulissen, E., Poblome, J., Reyniers, J., Viaene, W., Deckers, J., De Cupere, B., van Neer, W., Ekinci, H. A., and Erbay, M. O. (2000). 'The 1996 and 1997 Survey Seasons at Sagalassos', in Waelkens and Loots (2000), 17–216.

Wallace-Hadrill, A. (2008). *Rome's Cultural Revolution.* Cambridge.

Wieling, H. (2000). 'Vertragsgestaltung der römischen Keramikproduktion', in K. Strobel (ed.), *Forschungen zur römischen Keramikindustrie: Produktions-, Rechts- und Distributionsstrukturen* (Trierer Historische Forschungen, 42). Mainz, 9–22.

Willet, R. (2012). 'Red Slipped Complexity: The Socio-Cultural Context of the Concept and Use of Tableware in the Roman East'. Unpublished Ph.D. thesis, University of Leuven.

Zimmermann, C. (2002). *Handwerkvereine im griechischen Osten des Imperium Romanum* (Römisch-Germanisches Zentralmuseum: Forschungsinstitut für Vor- und Frühgeschichte Monographien, 57). Mainz.

Zuiderhoek, A. (2009). *The Politics of Munificence in the Roman Empire: Citizens, Elites and Benefactors in Asia Minor.* Cambridge.

Index